Manchester Medieval Sources Series

series advisers Rosemary Horrox and Simon MacLean

This series aims to meet a growing need amongst students and teachers of medieval history for translations of key sources that are directly usable in students' own work. It provides texts central to medieval studies courses and focuses upon the diverse cultural and social as well as political conditions that affected the functioning of all levels of medieval society. The basic premise of the new series is that translations must be accompanied by sufficient introductory and explanatory material and each volume therefore includes a comprehensive guide to the sources' interpretation, including discussion of critical linguistic problems and an assessment of the most recent research on the topics being covered.

also available in the series

Andrew Brown and Graeme Small *Court and civic society in the Burgundian Low Countries c. 1420–1520*

Martin Heale *Monasticism in late medieval England, c.1300–1535*

David Jones *Friars' Tales: Thirteenth-century exempla from the British Isles*

Graham Loud *Roger II and the making of the Kingdom of Sicily*

T.J.H. McCarthy *Chronicles of the Investiture Contest: Frutolf of Michelsberg and his continuators*

A.K. McHardy *The reign of Richard II*

Simon MacLean *History and politics in late Carolingian and Ottonian Europe: The Chronicle of Regino of Prüm and Adalbert of Magdeburg*

Anthony Musson and Edward Powell *Crime, law and society in the later middle ages*

Andrew Rabin *The political writings of Archbishop Wulfstan of York*

I. S. Robinson *Eleventh-century Germany: The Swabian Chronicles*

Craig Taylor *Joan of Arc: La Pucelle*

Diana Webb *Saints and cities in medieval Italy*

for a full list of titles available in this series, please see www.manchesteruniversitypress.com

HERESY AND INQUISITION IN FRANCE, 1200–1300

Manchester University Press

Medieval Sources*online*

Complementing the printed editions of the Medieval Sources series, Manchester University Press has developed a web-based learning resource which is now available on a yearly subscription basis.

Medieval Sources*online* brings quality history source material to the desktops of students and teachers and allows them open and unrestricted access throughout the entire college or university campus. Designed to be fully integrated with academic courses, this is a one-stop answer for many medieval history students, academics and researchers keeping thousands of pages of source material 'in print' over the Internet for research and teaching.

titles available now at Medieval Sourcesonline include

Trevor Dean *The towns of Italy in the later Middle Ages*

John Edwards *The Jews in Western Europe, 1400–1600*

Paul Fouracre and Richard A. Gerberding *Late Merovingian France: History and hagiography 640–720*

Chris Given-Wilson *Chronicles of the Revolution 1397–1400: The reign of Richard II*

P. J. P. Goldberg *Women in England, c. 1275–1525*

Janet Hamilton and Bernard Hamilton *Christian dualist heresies in the Byzantine world, c. 650–c. 1450*

Rosemary Horrox *The Black Death*

David Jones *Friars' Tales: Thirteenth-century exempla from the British Isles*

Graham A. Loud and Thomas Wiedemann *The history of the tyrants of Sicily by 'Hugo Falcandus', 1153–69*

A. K. McHardy *The reign of Richard II: From minority to tyranny 1377-97*

Simon MacLean *History and politics in late Carolingian and Ottonian Europe: The* Chronicle *of Regino of Prüm and Adalbert of Magdeburg*

Anthony Musson and Edward Powell *Crime, law and society in the later Middle Ages*

Janet L. Nelson *The Annals of St-Bertin: Ninth-century histories, volume I*

Timothy Reuter *The Annals of Fulda: Ninth-century histories, volume II*

R. N. Swanson *Catholic England: Faith, religion and observance before the Reformation*

Elisabeth van Houts *The Normans in Europe*

Jennifer Ward *Women of the English nobility and gentry 1066–1500*

Visit the site at www.medievalsources.co.uk for further information and subscription prices.

HERESY AND INQUISITION IN FRANCE, 1200–1300

selected sources translated and annotated

by John H. Arnold and Peter Biller

Manchester University Press

Published by Manchester University Press
Altrincham Street, Manchester M1 7JA
www.manchesteruniversitypress.co.uk

British Library Cataloguing-in-Publication Data
A catalogue record for this book is available from the British Library

Library of Congress Cataloging-in-Publication Data applied for

ISBN 978 0 7190 8131 6 hardback
ISBN 978 0 7190 8132 3 paperback

First published 2016

Typeset in Monotype Bell
by Servis Filmsetting Ltd, Stockport, Cheshire
Printed in Great Britain
by Bell & Bain Ltd, Glasgow

CONTENTS

Acknowledgements *page* viii
Editorial approach and conventions ix
Abbreviations xi

Introduction 1

The translations:

I: Heretics' texts 11
Introduction to Part I 13
1. Heretical Council of St-Félix 16
2. Durand of Huesca, *The Book against the Manichees* 20

II: Chronicles 29
Introduction to Part II 31
3. Robert of Auxerre on northern France 33
4. *Deeds of the Bishops of Auxerre* 36
5. Peter of Les Vaux-de-Cernay 39
   – Appendix A: Bernard of Simorre and the King of Aragon, 1203 51
   – Appendix B: Abjuration of Stephen of Servian, 1219 52
6. Aubri of Trois-Fontaines on the Inquisitor Robert Lepetit 53
7. Robert Lepetit's magic charter 57
8. Matthew Paris 59
9. Bernard Gui, *On the Foundations and Priors of the Preachers' Convents in the Provinces of Toulouse and Provence* 64

III: Treatises 85
Introduction to Part III 87
10. Gerald of Wales 89
11. The Albi *Summa Auctoritatum* 92
12. William of Auxerre and theology 98
13. Roland of Cremona on heretics' endurance 102
14. Lucas of Tuy, *On the Other Life* (*De Altera Vita*) 104
15. Rainerio Sacconi OP, *Summa about the Cathars and Poor of Lyon* 111

IV: Sermons 113
Introduction to Part IV 115
16. A sermon from c. 1200 117
17. Stephen of Bourbon: tales about heresy 120
18. Humbert of Romans on inquisition and heresy 134
19. A sermon from Italy 143

V: Letters and papal bulls 147
Introduction to Part V 149
20. Innocent III, bulls concerning La Charité-sur-Loire 151
A. Letter 35/6 from Innocent's fifth pontifical year, 1202/3 151
B. Letter 206 from Innocent III's tenth pontifical year, 1207/8 154
21. Conrad of Porto's letter on Bartholomew of Carcassonne 157
22. Gregory IX and the Inquisitor Robert Lepetit 159
A. *Gaudemus* ('We rejoice') (19 April 1233) 159
B. To the prior and Brother Robert of the Order of Preachers, of Paris (23 November 1234) 162
C. To Brother Robert, of the Order of Preachers (23 August 1235) 162
D. To the Bishop of Orléans and others (10 April 1236) 163
23. Urban IV, regarding Robert Lepetit and La Charité in 1234/5 (bull of 25 October 1263) 165
24. Urban IV, regarding Franciscan inquisitors in Provence (bull of 25 November 1263) 168
25. Royal letters concerning inquisition 170
A. Louis IX, 14 October 1258 170
B. Royal commissioners, March 1261 171
26. Two letters of Alphonse of Poitiers 172
A. To James Dubois, 13 January 1268 172
B. To the inquisitors Pons of Pouget and Stephen of Gâtine, 13 January 1268 173
27. John Galand OP, Inquisitor 1282–93 174
A. Galand's prison instructions, 1282 174
B. The complaints of Carcassonne against John Galand, 1285 175
28. Clement V's Commission to investigate inquisition, 1306 182

VI: Councils and statutes 185
Introduction to Part VI 187
29. Council of Toulouse, 1229 190
30. Edict of Count Raymond VII of Toulouse, 1233 198
31. Council of Béziers, 1246 202
32. Acts of the provincial chapters of the Dominican Order 208

VII: Legal consultations and inquisitors' manuals 211
Introduction to Part VII 213
33. A legal consultation, 1235 215
34. Council of Tarragona, 1242 218
35. The *Consilium* of Guy Foulques 230
36. Council of Narbonne, 1243/4 236
37. Consultation of Béziers, 1246 250
38. Formulae from a later inquisitor's handbook 262
39. An inquisitorial manual: *Instruction about the Way in which One should Proceed against Heretics* 270

40. Bernard Gui on *perfecti* 289
A. From *On the Authority and Form of Inquisition* 289
B. From Gui, *Treatise on Practice* 289

VIII: Inquisition trials 291
Introduction to Part VIII 293
41. Raymond Jean of Albi, 1238: the Council of Pieusse and bishops 298
42. Selections from the penances of Peter Seila, 1241–2 310
43. Marquesa, the spy, 1243 332
44. Helis of Mazerolles, 1243 337
45. William Donadeu of *Elves*, 1244 351
– Appendix: Sentence on William of *Elves* 357
46. Imbert of Salles, 1244: Montségur and the massacre of the inquisitors at Avignonet 359
47. Peter William d'Arvigna, 1246 375
48. Depositions before Bernard of Caux and John of St-Pierre, 1245–6 380
– Appendix: Sentence on Esclarmonda Bret 440
49. Inquisition in Carcassonne, 1250–9 442
– Register of the notary of the inquisition of Carcassonne, Part I 443
– Register of the notary of the inquisition of Carcassonne, Part II 451
50. The two confessions of Jordan of Saissac, 1279 (and 1244) 458
51. The plot against inquisitorial archives, Carcassonne, 1284 463
52. Bartholomew Vesian, regarding the Carcassonne appeal against the Inquisitor John Galand, 1291 467
53. Anonymous tract, *On the Way and Life … of the Poor of Lyon*, c. 1300 (?) 469
54. Peter of Gaillac of Tarascon, notary, 1308 476
55. Guilt of the Sicre family, 1308–12 490
A. Guilt of William Sicre the younger, 1312 490
B. Guilt of Raymond Sicre, 1308 491
C. Guilt of Peter Sicre, 1308 492
D. Guilt of William Sicre the elder, 1308 493
56. A renegade priest and Waldensians in Gascony, 1319 497
57. Opposition to inquisition in the early fourteenth century 501
A. Charges against Bernard Délicieux, 1319 501
B. A witness to events in Carcassonne, 1319 506

Index 509

ACKNOWLEDGEMENTS

We are grateful to the Bibliothèque muncipale de Lyon for permission to reproduce the image from MS P.A. 36 on the cover of this book. We are extremely grateful firstly to the series editors and publisher for their patience with what turned into a very lengthy project. John D. Green, Catherine Léglu and Ruth Harvey all very kindly provided invaluable assistance in deciphering small irruptions of southern French vernacular within the predominantly Latin records. We are grateful to the production staff at Manchester University Press for their courtesy and efficiency, and to Gerard Hill of Much Better Text for his superlative copy-editing of the whole book. We are particularly indebted to Shelagh Sneddon for her careful checking of a large number of translations; and we are also very grateful to Joe Canning, Zoë Arnold, Victoria Howell and Miggy Biller for additional assistance in checking the translation of particular documents.

John H. Arnold
Peter Biller

EDITORIAL APPROACH AND CONVENTIONS

Our translations attempt to follow the medieval Latin closely, providing editorial glosses within the text or footnotes where this may help to clarify. Additions within pointed brackets – < > – indicate conjectural expansions of the texts. Additions within square brackets indicate editorial glosses and clarifications: those italicised are editorial comments, those unitalicised are alternative translations, biblical references or a citation of the original Latin of the document. Any text in rounded brackets is part of the original document itself (though the brackets themselves are not).

We have annotated some, but by no means all, named individuals in the documents; given the vast numbers of people named in the deposition records, the reader is better served by the index, where we have listed prominent figures and those who appear in several different texts. The modern equivalents for the Latin place-names in the inquisition records of Languedoc have been found with the help of the lists in *Saisimentum Comitatus Tholosani*, ed. Y. Dossat (Paris, 1966) and M. François, Ch.-E. Perrin and J. de Font-Réaulx, eds, *Pouillés des Provinces d'Auch, de Narbonne et de Toulouse*, 2 vols (Paris, 1972), and the locations in the Institut Geographique National's CD-ROM *Dictionnaire des Toponymes de France* and 1:2500 maps. We warn the reader that there is sometimes uncertainty in these identifications, that the same place-name is often used for several places, and that some famous regional place-names (for example, Aragon and Paris) are also the names of places in southern France.

Biblical translations are taken from the Douay–Rheims translation of the Bible, following its recommendation by Beryl Smalley, who knew medieval readership of the Bible better than any other modern scholar.[1] We have used the following additional conventions:

- Italics are used to pick out quotation or allusion in texts and for unidentified place-names.

1 See also *The Practice of the Bible in the Middle Ages: Production, Reception and Performance in Western Christianity* (New York, 2011), p. 5: 'it preserves in English the sense that would have been known to most medieval readers of the Latin Bible'. The Bible text is accessible at www.drbo.org.

- Italics are also used in Part VII (Docs 33–40) to pick out terms describing types of heretic and suspect, which are discussed or defined in those texts.
- We have left *castrum/castra* in italics, in Latin, rather than translating as 'castle/s', because *castrum* in southern France usually indicated a fortified town or village.
- For translations from manuscript documents (and some lengthier edited documents) in the 'Depositions' section, we have included folio numbers (fol., fols) – like this: /261r/ – to allow the reader to cross-refer to other modern scholarship on these materials, indicating the front and back of each folio with 'r' (for *recto*) and 'v' (for *verso*).
- We have presented female first names as they appear in documents, but translated male first names into English where possible.[2]
- Titles – bishop, lord, count, inquisitor etc. – are capitalised when applied to a specific person.
- We have not followed the technical abbreviations used by specialists on canon law,[3] but have specified 'Case, question, chapter' when referencing Gratian's *Decretum.*

2 See the discussions of female and male first names in J. H. Mundy, *Men and Women at Toulouse in the Age of the Cathars* (Toronto, 1990), pp. 39–40, and *Inquisitors and Heretics*, pp. 124–7.

3 For which, see J. Brundage, *Medieval Canon Law* (Harlow, 1995), pp. 190–205.

ABBREVIATIONS

Arnold, *Inquisition and Power*	J. H. Arnold, *Inquisition and Power: Catharism and the Confessing Subject in Medieval Languedoc* (Philadelphia, 2001)
BnF	Bibliothèque nationale de France
Borst, *Cathares*	A. Borst, *Les Cathares* (Paris, 1974)
Borst, *Katharer*	A. Borst, *Die Katharer*, Schriften der Monumenta Germaniae Historica 12 (Stuttgart, 1953)
CdF	*Cahiers de Fanjeaux* (1966–)
Doat	Paris, Bibliothèque nationale de France, Collection Doat
Doc., Docs	the numbered documents in this book
Dossat, *Crises*	Y. Dossat, *Les Crises de l'Inquisition toulousaine au XIIIe siècle (1233–1273)* (Bordeaux, 1959)
Douais, *Documents*	C. Douais, ed., *Documents pour servir à l'Histoire de l'Inquisition dans le Languedoc*, 2 vols (Paris, 1900)
dpt	*département* (administrative district)
Feuchter, *Ketzer*	J. Feuchter, *Ketzer, Konsuln und Büßer: die städtischen Eliten von Montauban vor dem Inquisitor Petrus Cellani (1236/1241)* (Tübingen, 2007)
Friedberg	E. Friedberg, ed., *Corpus Iuris Canonici*, 2 vols (Leipzig, 1879–81)
Friedlander, *Hammer*	A. Friedlander, *The Hammer of the Inquisitors: Brother Bernard Délicieux and the Struggle against the Inquisition in Fourteenth-Century France* (Leiden, 2000)
HGL	C. de Vic and J. J. Vaissète, *Histoire Générale de Languedoc, avec des notes et les pièces justificatives*, 3rd

	edn, ed. A. Molinier et al., 16 vols (Toulouse, 1872–1905)
Inquisitors and Heretics	P. Biller, C. Bruschi and S. Sneddon, eds, *Inquisitors and Heretics in Thirteenth-Century Languedoc: Edition and Translation of Toulouse Inquisition Depositions, 1273–1282* (Leiden, 2011)
Léglu, Rist and Taylor, *Cathars*	C. Léglu, R. Rist and C. Taylor, eds, *The Cathars and the Albigensian Crusade: A Sourcebook* (London, 2014)
Maisonneuve, *Études*	H. Maisonneuve, *Études sur les Origines de l'Inquisition* (Paris, 1960)
Mansi, *Sacra concilia*	G. D. Mansi, *Sacrorum Conciliorum nova et amplissima Collectio*, 56 vols (Venice 1759–98)
MGH	Monumenta Germaniae Historica
Peters, *Heresy and Authority*	E. Peters, ed., *Heresy and Authority in Medieval Europe* (Philadelphia, 1980)
Sackville, *Heresy*	L. Sackville, *Heresy and Heretics in the Thirteenth Century: The Textual Representations* (York, 2011)
Sibly, *William of Puylaurens*	*The Chronicle of William of Puylaurens: The Albigensian Crusade and its Aftermath*, trans. W. A. Sibly and M. D. Sibly (Woodbridge, 2003)
Tanner, *Ecumenical Councils*	*Decrees of the Ecumenical Councils*, ed. N. P. Tanner, 2 vols (London and Washington, 1990)
Wakefield, *Heresy*	W. L. Wakefield, *Heresy, Crusade and Inquisition in southern France, 1100–1250* (London, 1974)
WE	W. L. Wakefield and A. P. Evans, eds, *Heresies of the High Middle Ages* (New York, 1969; reprint 1991)

INTRODUCTION

The editors of this book first met at the University of York, when one was a junior lecturer teaching a special subject on 'Heresy in the Middle Ages' and the other was a student on that course. Our first intellectual engagements were entwined with study of the textual sources for medieval heresy, at that point drawn from the just-reprinted and wonderful collection of material edited by Walter L. Wakefield and Austin P. Evans,[1] and from a large pile of photocopied transcriptions of inquisition trials produced by the tutor (Pete), the latter texts scrappy and riddled with typos. The friendship has continued, as has our delight in teaching students about heresy and inquisition (for John at the University of East Anglia, and then at Birkbeck, University of London; for Pete, still at York). Heresy is a topic that exerts almost universal fascination, but the particular excitement of teaching it is to work with students in getting beyond the initial frisson of perceived transgression, to excavate and analyse the complex relations between belief, power and human lives; and to do so from the abundant surviving documents.

This book arises from such teaching experience. It focuses on France in the thirteenth century, particularly southern France, where the surviving sources are richest, but also includes some largely neglected evidence for northern France.[2] There are various other parts of medieval Europe to which one could turn to find heretics and inquisitors – most obviously those in the Italian peninsula, also to some extent in Iberia, and in various German-speaking kingdoms – but the geographic and rough temporal limits provide a way of keeping the collection manageable. Readers should be aware however that the documents translated here nonetheless represent only a small portion of the surviving evidence. Various factors have guided our selections. One is to ignore

1 W. L. Wakefield and A. P. Evans, eds, *Heresies of the High Middle Ages* (1969; repr. New York, 1991).

2 One exception to the neglect of northern France is the fundamental study by J. Bird, 'The wheat and the tares: Peter the Chanter's circle and the *fama*-based inquest against heresy and criminal sins, c.1198–c.1235', *Proceedings of the Twelfth International Congress of Medieval Canon Law*, ed. U.-R. Blumenthal, K. Pennington and A. A. Larson (Vatican City, 2008), pp. 763–856.

heresy in intellectual settings – condemnations at the University of Paris for example – and to ignore also wider aspects of unorthodox or heterodox behaviour, such as non-attendance at mass, magic-working or variant lay beliefs found in episcopal visitation. Our focus thus mainly falls upon those heretics often called 'Cathars' and – to a lesser extent – those called 'Waldensians', two groups that demonstrably held some wider appeal in medieval society.[3]

The existence and availability of other sets of translations have also guided us over what to include. Thus we have mostly left the Albigensian crusade alone,[4] and have been particularly conscious of providing an alternative and complement to the wealth of material edited by Wakefield and Evans.[5] Their compilation ranges broadly in time and space, and has a marked preference for narrative or descriptive sources. It includes material of considerable importance, such as the main texts produced *by* medieval dualist heretics and those portions of inquisitorial handbooks and anti-heresy treatises that describe in detail heretical sects and their beliefs. Nonetheless, there are lacunae. Wakefield and Evans focus particularly on heresy, largely ignoring the practical and legal aspects of its repression, unlike the selections in Peters, whereas Moore – who also focused on heresy – helpfully included more texts from earlier periods than either this present collection or Wakefield and Evans.[6] The latter give very useful commentary on each source, informed among other things by the importance of recognising different 'genres' of primary source; but the approach to these is essentially confined to the empiricist ambition of identifying what was more or less 'trustworthy' in the substantive information it contained.

One of the most interesting aspects of the academic study of heresy is the importance and inescapability of thinking critically about the sources. The foundational work in the early twentieth century of Herbert Grundmann – identifying the recurrent *topoi* or literary stereotypes used to depict heretics, and the gap between these and

3 Since we are dealing with individuals and groups that were labelled by the Church, readers are advised to supply mental quotation marks around the key terms: 'heresy', 'heretic' and sect names.

4 See Léglu, Rist and Taylor, *Cathars.*

5 Also important are the documents translated in the appendices to Wakefield, *Heresy,* which include more material focused on persecution.

6 Peters, *Heresy and Authority*; R. I. Moore, ed., *The Birth of Popular Heresy* (London, 1975).

reality – has since been joined by a host of other works.[7] Historians have focused particularly on critical approaches to inquisition records, seeing them as containing 'filters' or framing elements that distort the picture they provide, but arguing nonetheless for their multivocal character: the voice of the witness is never truly erased.[8] Careful study of the contours of different genres of source has been very fruitful, identifying contrasting elements in orthodox discourse against heresy, and unpacking the manuscript history and intellectual contexts for materials such as inquisitors' manuals and anti-heresy treatises.[9]

Overlapping with source criticism has been recurrent argument over the reality or 'inventedness' of heresy, an approach founded particularly on R. I. Moore's influential *Formation of a Persecuting Society* (1985), reinvigorated by a wave of revisionist work begun in France in the late 1990s,[10] and by Mark Gregory Pegg and Moore himself in the early twenty-first century.[11] In this century, work has focused particularly on whether there was any reality to a 'Cathar Church'

7 H. Grundmann, 'Der Typus des Ketzers in mittelalticher Anschauung', in *Kultur- und Universalgeschichte: Festschrift für W. Goetz* (Leipzig, 1927); repr. in H. Grundmann, *Ausgewählte Aufsätze*, 3 vols, MGH Schriften 25, I, 313–27.

8 See further the Introduction to Part VIII, below.

9 See Sackville, *Heresy*, and introductions to parts I–VIII below. See also Borst, *Katharer*, sections i–v; H. Grundmann, 'Ketzerverhöre des Spätmittelalters als quellenkritisches Problem', *Deutsches Archiv für Erforschung des Mittelalters* 21 (1965), 519–75 (repr. in Grundmann, *Ausgewählte Aufsätze*, I, 364–416); D. Iogna-Prat, *Order and Exclusion: Cluny and the Church Face Heresy, Judaism and Islam (1000–1150)*, trans. G. R. Edwards (Ithaca, 2002); I. Bueno, *Defining Heresy. Inquisition, Theology, and Papal Policy in the Time of Jacques Fournier* (Leiden, 2015). For an interesting analysis of the visual 'genre', see A. Trivellone, *L'hérétique imaginé: Hétérodoxie et iconographie dans l'Occident médiéval, de l'époque carolingienne à l'inquisition* (Turnhout, 2009).

10 See particularly M. Zerner, ed., *Inventer l'hérésie? Discours polémique et pouvoirs avant l'inquisition* (Nice, 1998); U. Brunn, *Des Contestataires aux 'Cathares': Discours de réforme et propagande antihérétique dans les pays du Rhin et de la Meuse avant l'inquisition* (Paris, 2006).

11 M. G. Pegg, *The Corruption of Angels: The Great Inquisition of 1245–1246* (Princeton, 2001); M. G. Pegg, *A Most Holy War: The Albigensian Crusade and the Battle for Christendom* (Oxford, 2008); R. I. Moore, *The War on Heresy: Faith and Power in Medieval Europe* (London, 2012). For opposing views, see C. Taylor, *Heresy, Crusade and Inquisition in Medieval Quercy*, Heresy and Inquisition in the Middle Ages 2 (York, 2012); C. Taylor, 'Evidence for dualism in inquisitorial registers of the 1240s: a contribution to a debate', *History* 98 (2013), 319–45; Sackville, *Heresy*; C. Sparks, *Heresy, Inquisition and Life-cycle in Medieval Languedoc*, Heresy and Inquisition in the Middle Ages 3 (York, 2014); A. Brenon and C. Dieulafait, eds, *Les Cathares devant l'histoire: Mélanges offerts à Jean Duvernoy* (Cahors, 2005). A key collection of debates is forthcoming in A. Sennis, ed., *Cathars in Question* (York, 2016).

that connected southern France, northern Italy and the Balkans, and espoused a dualist heretical faith ('dualist' here meaning belief in two Gods, one good and one bad, the latter creating corporeal matter). There has also been argument about the coherence and organisational extent of Waldensianism.[12]

In part linked to these debates is discussion over the extent of orthodox repression of heresy, and the nature of inquisition in particular. The foundational modern historiography was strongly marked by confessional allegiances: Protestant historians such as Henry Charles Lea emphasised the unprecedented and cruel power of 'the inquisition', whereas Catholic historians sought to rebut this depiction, arguing that heresy was deeply threatening to medieval society and that inquisition had to be seen in the context of its period (and, as a legal process, as more 'just' and careful than contemporary secular law). More recent historiography has explored the nature of inquisitiorial power. In 1995, Richard Kieckhefer argued forcefully that historians were too quick to see an institution – 'the Inquisition' – when what was in fact brought into existence in the thirteenth century was the application of a legal mechanism (*inquisitio heretice pravitatis* – 'inquisition into heretical wickedness'), which specific people were appointed to carry out in a particular place for a set period of time. In the late 1990s, Jim Given presented a study of inquisition as a form of early 'state' power and governance, and Christine Caldwell Ames has emphasised the religious foundations to inquisition and the extent to which it was entwined with wider aspects of the spiritual programmes of the mendicant orders.[13] In the 1990s the Catholic Church supplied another impetus: a policy initiated by John Paul II (but not continued by his successor) called upon the Catholic Church to confront its past and apologise for its faults. This produced reflection on the history of the inquisition at a symposium held in the pope's presence in the Vatican in 1998 and remarkable fundamental papers on its medieval form by Grado Merlo, Jean-Louis Biget and Lorenzo Paolini, and also a conference held by

12 See P. Biller, 'Goodbye to Waldensianism?', *Past and Present* 192 (2006), 3–33.

13 R. Kieckhefer, 'The office of inquisition and medieval history: the transition from personal to institutional jurisdiction', *Journal of Ecclesiastical History* 46 (1995), 36–61; J. B. Given, *Inquisition and Medieval Society* (Ithaca, 1998); C. Caldwell Ames, *Righteous Persecution: Inquisition, Dominicans and Christianity in the Middle Ages* (Cornell, 2008). See also Dyan Elliott, *Proving Woman: Female Spirituality and Inquisitional Culture in the Later Middle Ages* (Princeton, 2004); Damian J. Smith, *Crusade, Heresy and Inquisition in the Lands of the Crown of Aragon, c. 1167–1276* (Leiden, 2010).

the Dominicans for the same purpose, to confront the history of their own order's involvement.[14] It is notable that these historians did not embrace Kieckhefer's push away from an 'institutional' interpretation; and there is explicit resistance to that interpretation from Jacques Chiffoleau, the author of one of the two most important recent studies of inquisition in medieval France.[15]

These contexts of debate have informed our selection and presentation of materials. We have mostly not translated material available elsewhere, with a couple of important exceptions: the Cathar council of St-Félix charter (much debated with regard to the reality of Catharism) and some key passages from the chronicle of Peter of Les Vaux-de-Cernay (Docs 1 and 5). To balance the focus of Wakefield and Evans's *Heresies*, we have included a large amount of inquisitorial material, ranging from legal consultations and conciliar decisions on its operation, to an extensive section of depositions and sentences.[16] Thus this collection seeks to illustrate both heresy and the processes used against heresy; in line with much recent historiography, we would argue that the two cannot be analysed very securely unless brought together. The volume of inquisitorial material will, we hope, provide the reader with an opportunity to research issues of reality and constructedness for themselves, in sources that are rather different from the more lurid and rhetorical anti-heresy polemics. We have sought to present materials by genre, rather than chronologically, although in some cases – particularly in regard to the legislation produced around inquisition – it should be noted that where to place a particular source is a slightly arbitrary choice. In doing this, we are not suggesting that each kind of text operated in isolation from others; in fact, it is clear that, for instance, those writing 'how to' advice for the practice of inquisition might also be involved in the collation or indeed oral delivery of preaching stories that used tales of heresy as moral examples.

14 *L'inquisizione. Atti del Simposio internazionale, Città del Vaticano, 29–31 ottobre 1998*, ed. A. Borromeo (Rome, 2003); *Praedicatores Inquisitores – I: The Dominicans and the Medieval Inquisition. Acts of the 1st International Seminar on the Dominicans and the Inquisition, Rome, 23–25 February 2002* (Rome, 2004). Acts of the 4th Dominican seminar (2009) were not published; the series ground to a halt.

15 See J. Chiffoleau, 'L'Inquisition franciscaine en Provence et dans l'ancien Royaume d'Arles (vers 1260 – vers 1330)', *Frati minori e inquisizione* (Spoleto, 2006), pp. 153–284, at p. 157 n.7: 'Je me sépare radicalement de la position de R. Kieckhefer'. The other fundamental recent study is the magisterial account in Feuchter, *Ketzer*, of inquisition and heresy in Montauban.

16 The publication in 2011 of *Inquisitors and Heretics* has led us to bypass all but one of the records of interrogations held in Toulouse between 1273 and 1282.

Nonetheless, differences in purpose, structure, rhetoric, style and audience become more readily apparent when particular kinds of document are grouped together, and we include some discussion of these in the introductions to parts I–VIII in this book. We have also tried – wherever practical – to include entire documents, or at least to sketch their relevant structure. In some cases, such as extracts from much larger chronicles, this is simply not possible, but for most things we have indicated how the whole documentary record worked, even if we are unable to reproduce it fully in the space available.

As noted, the most pressing current debates concern the reality of Catharism and the nature of inquisition, and readers will find much here that speaks to both topics. But we would also note some other aspects of particular interest. One is evidence for inquisitorial and episcopal activity against heresy beyond the most well-known periods and places. Thus we have included evidence for the activities of Robert Lepetit (or 'Robert le Bougre'), the papally-commissioned inquisitor in northern France in the 1230s (see Docs 6–8, 22–3), and evidence demonstrating the activity of inquisitors in Provence, where no trial records have survived (see Docs 24, 25, 53). Also interesting is the development of detailed discussions in the mid- to late-thirteenth century on how to conduct inquisition, for which we provide translations of considerable legislative activity and legal consultation in southern France (Docs 29–32, 34–7) and two 'guides for inquisitors' (Docs 38, 39), where among other things the degree of overlap between legislation and inquisitorial manual becomes apparent. In terms of the material then produced by inquisitors, for reasons of space we have left certain areas aside and have allowed ourselves to stray only slightly beyond 1300. We have regretfully thus ignored the very rich records of inquisition carried out by Bishop Jacques Fournier in 1318–25 (the basis for Emmanuel Le Roy Ladurie's famous *Montaillou*), though we have included brief examples from the slightly earlier inquisition by Geoffrey of Ablis and two sets of inquisition documents from Bernard Gui. Our focus has been, rather, on the riches of the thirteenth century, including one of the earliest depositions to survive (Doc. 41), and extensive selections from the lengthy sets of sentences given by the inquisitor Peter Seila (Doc. 42) and from the vast set of interrogations carried out by Bernard of Caux and John of St-Pierre (Doc. 48). The introductions to each document aim to set it in context and indicate some features which may be of particular interest. Across the materials presented here, we have sought to achieve a balance between what is representative (in the sense that one could provide many more examples) and what is unusual and intriguing. Much of the surviving documentary record reminds us of the power of the Church, and its determination to crush what it saw as a subversive heretical threat. But there was resistance, and that too is part of the history that can be told.

Further reading

As noted above, part of what has informed our selection is knowledge of what exists elsewhere in translation. We list here additional translations into English and French to assist the reader.[17]

J. Berlioz, '*Tuez-les tous, Dieu reconnaîtra les siens*'. *La Croisade contre les Albigeois vue par Césaire de Heisterbach* (Portet-sur-Garonne, 1994), pp. 12–20 (translation of Caesarius)

P. Biller, C. Bruschi and S. Sneddon, eds, *Inquisitors and Heretics in Thirteenth-Century Languedoc: Edition and Translation of Toulouse Inquisition Depositions, 1273–1282* (Leiden, 2011)

J. Bird, E. Peters and J. M. Powell, eds, *Crusade and Christendom: Annotated Documents in Translation from Innocent III to the Fall of Acre, 1187–1291* (Philadelphia, 2013), Part 1, section 7 (the Albigensian Crusade)

P. Bonnassie and G. Pradalié, *La Capitulation de Raymond VII et la fondation de l'université de Toulouse, 1229–1979: Un Anniversaire en question* (Toulouse, 1979), pp. 43–51 (Council of Toulouse, 1229)

E. Bozóky, ed., *Le Livre secret des Cathares.* Interrogatio Iohannis, *apocryphe d'origine bogomile* (Paris, 1980)

R. B. Brooke, *The Coming of the Friars*, Historical Problems: Studies and Documents 24 (London, 1975)

Caesarius of Heisterbach, *The Dialogue on Miracles*, ed. H. von E. Scott and C. C. Swinton Bland, 2 vols (London, 1929), I, pp. 148–50, 338–53, 489–90; II, pp. 118, 156–7, 212, 279

J. Duvernoy, ed., *Guillaume de Puylaurens, Chronique, 1203–1275* (Paris, 1976)

J. Duvernoy, ed., *Le Registre d'inquisition de Jacques Fournier*, 3 vols (Paris, 1978)

J. Duvernoy, ed., *Registre de Bernard de Caux, Pamiers 1246–1247* (St-Girons, 1990)

17 There are also further records from the Fournier register, translated into English by Nancy P. Stork from Duvernoy's French translations, at www.sjsu.edu/people/nancy.stork/jacquesfournier/ (accessed 11 December 2014). Note that, following Duvernoy, these alter the texts from the third to the first person.

J. Duvernoy, ed., *Guillaume Pelhisson, Chronique (1229–1244)* (Paris, 1994)

J. Duvernoy, ed., *Le Dossier de Montségur* (Toulouse, 1998)

J. Duvernoy, ed., *L'Inquisition en Quercy: Le Registre des pénitences de Pierre Cellan, 1241–1242* (Paris, 2001)

J. Duvernoy, ed., *Le Procès de Bernard Délicieux, 1319* (Toulouse, 2001)

P. Geary, ed., *Readings in Medieval History*, 4th edn (Toronto, 2010), pp. 482–501 (selections from Fournier inquisition trials)

P. Guébin and H. Maisonneuve, eds, *Pierre des Vaux-de-Cernay, Histoire albigeoise* (Paris, 1951)

J. Hamilton and B. Hamilton, eds, *Christian Dualist Heresies in the Byzantine World, c. 650–c. 1405* (Manchester, 1998)

Jacobus de Voragine [James of Varazze], *The Golden Legend*, ed. V. G. Ryan, 2 vols (Princeton, 1993), I, pp. 254–66 (Peter Martyr); II, pp. 44–58 (Dominic)

Jordan of Saxony, *On the Beginnings of the Order of Preachers*, ed. S. Tugwell (Dublin, 1982)

C. Léglu, R. Rist and C. Taylor, eds, *The Cathars and the Albigensian Crusade: A Sourcebook* (London, 2014)

F. C. Lehner, *Saint Dominic: Biographical Documents* (Washington, 1964)

[Gerard of Frachet], *Lives of the Brethren of the Order of Preachers*, ed. P. Conway (London, 1955)

S. R. Maitland, *Facts and Documents Illustrative of the History, Doctrines and Rites of the Ancient Albigenses* (London, 1832), section 10 (translation of Bernard Gui sentences)

E. Martin-Chabot, ed., *La Chanson de la croisade albigeoise*, 3 vols (Paris, 1957–61)

A. Pales-Gobilliard, ed., *L'Inquisiteur Geoffroi d'Ablis et les Cathares du comté du Foix (1308–1309)* (Paris, 1984)

A. Pales-Gobilliard, ed., *Le Livre des sentences de l'inquisiteur Bernard Gui (1308–1323)*, 2 vols (Paris, 2002)

Peter of Les Vaux-de-Cernay, *The History of the Albigensian Crusade*, trans. W. A. Sibly and M. D. Sibly (Woodbridge, 1998)

E. Peters, ed., *Heresy and Authority in Medieval Europe* (Philadelphia, 1980)

S. Shahar, *Women in a Medieval Heretical Sect: Agnes and Huguette the Waldensians* (Woodbridge, 2001), appendix, pp. 131–56 (interrogations from Fournier register of two women supporters of Waldensians)

J. Shinners, ed., *Medieval Popular Religion*, 2nd edn (Toronto, 2006)

J. Shirley, ed., *The Song of the Cathar Wars* (Aldershot, 1996)

N. P. Tanner, *Decrees of the Ecumenical Councils*, 2 vols (London and Georgetown, 1990), pp. 230–5 (4th Lateran Council), 282–3 (1st Council of Lyon, heresy of Frederick II), 380–3 (Vienne, reform of inquisition)

J. Théry, ed., *Le Livre des sentences de l'inquisiteur Bernard Gui* (Paris, 2010)

Thomas de Cantimpré, *Les Exemples du* Livre des abeilles, ed. H. Platelle (Turnhout, 1997), nos. 10, 153, 238

C. Thouzellier, ed., *Une Somme anti-Cathare. Le* Liber contra Manicheos *de Durand de Huesca* (Louvain, 1964), pp. 67–85 (Prologue)

C. Thouzellier, ed., *Rituel Cathare*, Sources Chrétiennes 236 (Paris, 1977)

W. L. Wakefield, *Heresy, Crusade and Inquisition in southern France, 1100–1250* (London, 1974), appendices 1–6

W. L. Wakefield and A. P. Evans, eds, *Heresies of the High Middle Ages*, 2nd edn (New York, 1991)

William of Puylaurens, *The Chronicle of William of Puylaurens: The Albigensian Crusade and its Aftermath*, trans. W. A. Sibly and M. D. Sibly (Woodbridge, 2003)

PART I: HERETICS' TEXTS

INTRODUCTION TO PART I

Both Waldensian and Cathar heretics made considerable use of texts. Some of these related to theology – books and apocrypha of the Bible, theological treatises,[1] tracts drawn up for use in debate[2] – and some contained prayers.[3] The dualist heretics also had books which set out the liturgical performance of their rituals.[4] Heretics could display scholarly concern with the precise wording of a text,[5] and some of their texts were used and read not only by the heretical elite but also by the literate among their followers.[6] In common with wider practices in the society around them, there were also letters relating to administration,[7] charters recording agreements (see Doc. 1, following a Cathar council to reform church boundaries) and documents relating to finance such as accounts and bequests in wills.[8] Some of these were everyday texts: the Waldensians used to consider an annual account (*ratio*) of income and expenditure at their general chapters.[9]

Only a small proportion of these heretics' writings survive.[10] Consequently, historians have strained to make accessible what little there is. Wakefield and Evans devoted a quarter of their large anthology to heretics' texts, and their focus, as in scholarship elsewhere,

1 *Un traité cathare inédit du début du XIIIe siècle d'après le* Liber contra Manicheos *de Durand de Huesca*, ed. C. Thouzellier (Louvain, 1961), and *Livre des deux principes*, ed. C. Thouzellier, Sources Chrétiennes 198 (Paris, 1973), translated in WE, nos. 58–9, are two surviving treatises. Among lost works, see the references to a *Secret* in Doc. 5 §11 and *Ladder of Sciences* in Doc. 14.

2 See a conversation about the loss of one of these in *Chronicle of William of Puylaurens*, pp. 26–7.

3 The 'Our Father' appears frequently in the 'Cathar Ritual'; a dualist commentary on it is translated in WE no. 60.

4 See n.13 below.

5 Doc. 2, ch. 1.

6 Doc. 42, fols 201r, 234v, 274r.

7 Doc. 42, fols 187v, 303v; Doc. 46, fols 171v–172r, 178r.

8 Doc. 42, fol. 206r; Doc. 49, fol. 94v.

9 WE, p. 393; compare Doc. 53, fourth part.

10 See the essays in *Heresy and Literacy*, ed. Biller and Hudson, and P. Biller, 'Editions of trials and lost texts', *Valdesi medievali*, ed. M. Benedetti (Milan, 2009), pp. 23–36.

tends to privilege the heretics' theological voice (though the latter has become less marked in recent scholarship where the concern is to diminish the reality of heresies).[11] This largely reflects what does remain: more theology, less ordinary stuff. Inquisitors were interested in books that contained 'erroneous' doctrine. Thus the fact that the archive of the Dominicans in Carcassonne contained a dualist text – originating in Bulgaria and transmitted via Italian heretics – reflected what an inquisitor was once interested in obtaining from heretics and preserving.[12] An inquisitor was less likely to be interested in texts that were prosaic or everyday, tools in the sects' organisational activities. The subsequent loss of heretics' administrative records has added to the difficulty felt by historians in imagining them as past entities and organisations: the opposite of 'reality effect'.

In the case of southern France, there are three important textual survivals. The first is an early fourteenth-century manuscript in the Occitan vernacular (following a vernacular translation of the New Testament) that specifies the words and prayers to be uttered in Cathar rituals – a sort of equivalent of the orders of service contained in the Catholic Church's liturgical books. An illuminated initial from it is reproduced on the cover of this book, but we have not tried to replace the complete and very fully annotated translation in Wakefield and Evans.[13] The second is a copy and its authentication, made by Cathars in the 1220s, of a charter relating to their 'Council' of St-Félix in 1167. Controversy has led to new discoveries about this material, and we have therefore

11 WE, nos. 46, 56–60.

12 The *Questions of John*, trans. *WE*, pp. 458–65, under the title *Secret Supper*. For its listing in the Carcassonne archive, where it was copied in 1669, see Dossat, *Crises*, p. 50 n.130; the modern edition is *Le Livre secret des Cathares.* Interrogatio Iohannis, *apocryphe d'origine bogomile*, ed. E. Bozóky (Paris, 1980).

13 Latin and Occitan versions are translated in WE, no. 57, A and B. The Latin version used by dualist heretics in Italy is edited in *Rituel cathare*, ed. C. Thouzellier, Sources Chrétiennes 236 (Paris, 1977); the Occitan version is available as 'Cathar ritual', ed. M. R. Harris, at www.rialto.unina.it/prorel/CatharRitual/CathRit.htm – it will appear in the *Concordance of Medieval Occitan.* See on this M. R. Harris, 'The Occitan New Testament in Ms. Bibl. Mun. de Lyon, PA 36: A Cathar or Waldensian translation', *Heresis* 44–5 (2006), 167–86, and Jean Duvernoy's introduction to his online edition (http://jean.duvernoy.free.fr/text/pdf/cledat_intro.pdf). The Occitan version is essentially in the language spoken in the Toulousain–Carcassès–Foix triangle in the thirteenth century, and was clearly something that had been drawn up during this period for the dualist heretics of Languedoc, whose rituals, as attested in depositions, are clearly performances of what is prescribed in this normative liturgical text. This manuscript seems to be a late witness to the text, since it contains one or two Piedmontese texts, suggesting that it was produced for those Cathars who fled from Languedoc to Piedmont, especially to Cuneo and the surrounding area.

made a new translation from a new edition (Doc. 1). The third is a Cathar theological tract, sizeable extracts from which survive in its refutation in a treatise by the former Waldensian, Durand of Huesca. The reader should consult the fine and extensively annotated translation by Wakefield and Evans; they, however, translated only the heretics' text. We have provided, therefore, some samples illustrating how much is gained when the heretics' text is read together with the surrounding commentary and the attack on it written by Durand of Huesca.

1. HERETICAL COUNCIL OF ST-FÉLIX

From at least 1223 until his execution in 1226 Peter Isarn was bishop of the heretics of the church of Carcassonne.[14] In his first year in this office he instructed Peter Pollan (himself later bishop of the same church, 1238–67) to draw up a copy of one or several earlier documents, relating to a Council held in 1167. This copy shows the existence in the 1220s of an archive among the Cathars, their historical memory and the continuing importance among them of formal organisation and documentation. In particular it shows them engaging in the conventional documentary practice of a *vidimus*, 'we have seen': formally authenticating a copy of an older act. This action may relate to Isarn's accession to the bishopric and uncertainties brought about by disagreements among Cathar churches in this decade.

The account of the Council of St-Félix and the commission on church boundaries should be compared to the extensive account of the Council of Pieusse (see Doc. 41), and descriptions of other Cathar Councils in depositions (e.g. Doc. 47, fol. 240v–241r; Doc. 48, fol. 214r). Peter Pollan [*or* Polhan *or* Pola] appears in inquisition records from the 1240s; see for example, Doc. 44 (fol. 175r), Doc. 48 (fol. 125r), Doc. 49 (part 2, no. 32). The authenticity of the St-Félix text, which survives only through an edition of 1660 by Guillaume Besse and two copies in Besse's hand, has been much contested, but it was definitively established at a conference devoted entirely to this question, held in 2001.[15] French specialists on medieval documents analysed its language and format exhaustively, concluding that it conformed exactly with other documents of the period, while Monique Zerner's discovery of copies of the text hand-written by Besse brought to light slight variations which removed what had earlier been seen as a chronological problem.

Translated from D. Zbiral, 'Édition critique de la Charte de Niquinta selon les trois versions connues', in *1209–2009, Cathares: une histoire à pacifier*, ed. A. Brenon (Portet-sur-Garonne, 2010), pp. 47–52. We have inserted the section numbers in square brackets.

14 Noted as bishop in Doat 23, fols 80r, 85r.

15 M. Zerner, ed., *L'Histoire du Catharisme en discussion: Le 'Concile' de Saint-Félix, 1167* (Nice, 2001), pp. 135–201. For a broader account of the Council, Niquinta/Nicetas and Bogomil influence, see B. Hamilton, 'Introduction', in B., J. and S. Hamilton, *Hugo Eteriano,* Contra Patarenos (Leiden, 2004), pp. 1–102 (at 73–89).

[1] The year 1167 of the Lord's Incarnation, in the month of May. *In those days* [Luke 2.1 and *passim*] the church of Toulouse brought Papa[16] Niquinta into the *castrum* of St-Félix, and a great multitude of men and women of the church of Toulouse and of other neighbouring churches gathered themselves there in order to receive the *consolamentum*.[17] And the lord Papa Niquinta began to consolate. And afterwards Robert of Épernon,[18] Bishop of the church of the French,[19] arrived with his council, and similarly Mark of Lombardy came with his council; and Sicard Cellarer, Bishop of the church of Albi, came with his council, and Bernard Catalan came with the council of the church of Carcassonne; and the council of the church of Aran was there.[20] And all <were> thus gathered in countless numbers: the men of the church of Toulouse wanted to have a bishop, and they chose Bernard Raymond. Similarly, moreover, both Bernard Catalan and the council of the church of Carcassonne, asked and mandated by the church of Toulouse and, with the counsel and will and assent of Lord Sicard Cellarer, chose Guiraud Mercier; and the men of Aran chose Raymond of Casals. And afterwards Robert of Épernon received the *consolamentum* and order of bishop from lord Papa Niquinta, so that he should be Bishop of the church of the French. And similarly Sicard Cellarer[21] received the *consolamentum* and order of bishop, that he should be Bishop of the church of Albi. Similarly, moreover, Mark received the *consolamentum* and order of bishop, so that he should be Bishop of the church of Lombardy. Similarly, moreover, Bernard Raymond received the *consolamentum* and order of bishop, so that he should be Bishop of the church of Toulouse. And similarly Guiraud Mercier received the *consolamentum* and order of bishop, so that he should be Bishop of the church of Carcassonne. And similarly Raymond of Casals received the *consolamentum* and order of bishop, so that he should be Bishop of the church of Aran.

[2] *But after these things* [e.g. Tobit 2.1] Papa Niquinta said to the church of Toulouse: 'You have said to me that I should say to you <whether> the customs of the primitive churches are light or heavy. And I say to you:

16 Name given to some of their leaders by the Bogomils.

17 On this ritual, see note 26 to Doc. 41 below.

18 Eure et Loire dpt.

19 Northern French or, more narrowly, those from the Île-de-France

20 Perhaps a mistake for Agen.

21 Mentioned in Doc. 2 below.

the 'seven churches of Asia' [Apocalypse 1.4 and 11] were distinct and marked off from each other, and none of them did anything to the contradiction of another. And the church of *Romania* [= Constantinople] and of Drogometia [= Dragovitsa] and of Melenguia and of Bulgaria and of Dalmatia are divided and marked off, and one of them does not do anything to the contradiction of another, and thus they have peace among themselves.[22] "Do you also in like manner" [Luke 6.31].'

[3] And the church of Toulouse chose Bernard Raymond and William Garsias and Ermengaud of La Forêt and Raymond of Baimiac and Guilabert of Beauville and Bernard Contor and Bernard William of Beauville and Bertrand of Avignonet to be the dividers [*i.e. draw up the boundaries*] of the churches. And the church of Carcassonne chose Guiraud Mercier and Bernard Catalan and Gregory and Peter Chaudes Mains [= Warm Hands] and Raymond Pons and Bertrand of Moulin and Martin of La Salle and Raymond Guibert to be the dividers of the churches.

And congregated there and having taken good counsel, they said that the church of Toulouse and the church of Carcassonne should be defined according to the <boundaries> of the bishoprics <of the Roman Church>.[23] And just as the bishopric of Toulouse is marked off from the archbishopric of Narbonne in two places, and is marked off from the bishopric of Carcassonne – from St-Pons, along the mountains between the *castrum* of Cabaret and the *castrum* of Hautpoul as far as the boundary between the *castrum* of Saissac and the *castrum* of Verdun, and <then> between Montréal and Fanjeaux; and just as the other bishoprics <of the Roman Church> are marked off from each other from the Razès gap right up to Lérida in the direction of Toulouse – so the church of Toulouse is to have <territory bounded in this way> under its authority and administration. And similarly the church of Carcassonne, divided and marked off in this way, is to have under its authority and administration the whole of the bishopric of Carcassonne and the archbishopric of Narbonne and other territory – as has been named and defined – up to Lérida, as it goes to the sea. And

22 On the names of Bogomil churches, see J. and B. Hamilton, eds, *Christian Dualist Heresies in the Byzantine Worlds, c.650–c.1405* (Manchester, 1998), pp. 44–5; index entry 'Bogomil churches', p. 320.

23 There are difficulties in the Latin and geography of this passage on boundaries, and it is worth consulting the discussion and translation provided by B. Hamilton, 'The Cathar Council of Saint-Félix reconsidered', *Archivum Fratrum Praedicatorum* 48 (1978), 40–2.

the churches are divided thus, just as has been said, so that they should have peace and concord among themselves, and rights, <and> so that none of them should do anything to the contradiction of another.

The witnesses and guarantors of this matter are these: <of the church of Toulouse>, Bernard Raymond, and William Garsias, and Ermengaud of La Forêt, and Raymond of Baimiac, and Guilabert of Beauville, and Bernard William Contor, and Bernard William of Beauville, and Bertrand of Avignonet; and, of the church of Carcassonne, Guiraud Mercier, and Bernard Catalan, and Gregory, and Peter Chaudes Mains, and Raymond Pons, and Bertrand of Moulin, and Martin of La Salle, and Raymond Guibert. And all of these mandated and told Ermengaud of La Forêt to do the act and charter for the church of Toulouse. Similarly they mandated and told Peter Bernard to do the act and charter for the church of Carcassonne. And this was done and carried out in this way.

[4] Lord Peter Isarn had this transcript copied, from the old charter that had been made with the authority of those named above, who divided the churches as is written above. On Monday in August, fourteen days from the beginning of the month, in the year 1223[24] of the Lord's Incarnation, Peter Pollan copied all these things, as asked and mandated.

24 Variant reading in one of Besse's ms. copies. The printed text and the other copy give 1232.

2. DURAND OF HUESCA, *THE BOOK AGAINST THE MANICHEES*

Durand (died before 1237) was a Waldensian. But after a debate in Pamiers in 1207 he reverted to the Church, presenting a profession of faith to Innocent III in 1208 and becoming the leader of the Poor Catholics.[25] A theologian of remarkable learning (including some Greek), he used a combination of this and his close personal acquaintance with Cathars and their books in the composition of two polemical treatises against them. His knowledge of heretics' books even extended to textual variants in different copies (ch. 2 below), and he read a copy they used of the *Vision of Isaiah* (chs 16 and 18 below). He wrote and then revised his first treatise, the *Anti-heresy Book* (*Liber antiheresis*) in the years around 1190. Around 1220, it seems likely, a Cathar theological compilation came into his hands, perhaps called by the name that Durand sometimes applies to it, *Contradiction* (*Antifrasis*). Around 1223 he wrote a refutation of it, *The Book against the Manichees* (*Liber contra Manicheos*), each chapter containing a long excerpt from the compilation. When extracted and put together these excerpts provide our only extensive representation of a Cathar treatise from Languedoc in this period. Its translation in WE, pp. 494–510, should be read alongside our translation of selected passages, which is designed to show the advantage of reading together both the heretics' writing and Durand's attacks on it. It is based on *Une Somme Anti-cathare: Le* Liber contra Manicheos *de Durand de Huesca*, ed. C. Thouzellier (Louvain, 1964), pp. 67, 76–9, 82–3, 87–9, 90–1, 104–6, 115–16, 119–21, 135, 138–9, 147, 160, 164, 174, 180, 196, 207, 210–11, 216–17, 226, 235–6, 242–3, 244, 254, 256–7, 272, 286–8, 297, 306, 319.

To the most reverend pillar of the Church of Christ the Lord, Leo,[26] with the title Cardinal-Priest of the Holy Cross in Jerusalem, the Poor Catholics <send> grace in the present and glory in the future.

Here begins the Prologue to the *Book against the Manichees*

... For 'Leviathan' [Isaiah 27.1], that 'winding serpent' [Job 26.13], which 'sleepeth under the shadow in the covert of the reed' [Job 40.16],

25 See D. J. Smith, *Crusade, Heresy and Inquisition in the Lands of the Crown of Aragon (c. 1167–1276)* (Leiden and Boston, 2010), ch. 4; E. Cameron, *Waldenses: Rejections of Holy Church in Medieval Europe* (Oxford, 2000), ch. 2.5 and 4.1.

26 Leo Brancaleone, cardinal 1200–30, protector of the Poor Catholics.

with 'a body molten and shut up close with scales pressing upon one another' [Job 41.6] covered by 'willows of the brook' [Job 40.17], gladdens the minds of prelates that gape at simony, pride, love of money, vainglory, gluttony, concubinage, negligence and other vices – and on of account this the divine mysteries are held in contempt, so that the name of God is enormously blasphemed. And having assembled together the poisons of virtually all heresiarchs and also those that have been found in recent times, and breathing out a most foul and stinking spirit through the mouths of the bishops of wicked heresy, Sicard Cellarer, Gaucelm, Bernard of Simorre and Vigouroux of La Bouconne,[27] and the mouths of their accomplices, it has irremediably stained a very large part of the lands. …

Their compilation, therefore, which I had in my hands, in which they have tried to prove that all things are double, and that the devil made whatever things are visible and that he is a God without beginning: I have decided it is appropriate to insert it chapter by chapter. And then, earnestly and insofar as the wisdom of the Father 'that hath the key of David' [Apocalypse 3.7] deigns to open the aperture for me, I shall blow away their dreadful smoke through it. …

1 Here begins the first chapter in the *Book against the* apostate *Manichees*

… Their depraved compilation, with which they infatuate the unwary and make them abdicate the orthodox faith, begins thus.

From the compilation of the Manichees

> Seeing that some people reproach us badly about <what we believe> about divine works and creatures, we <shall> therefore confess the things we believe on these matters both in <our> words and hearts, so that those who ignorantly impugn us on account of this may, when informed, understand the truth of the matter more clearly.
>
> First of all, then, we utterly defer to the highest and true God, omnipotent Father, through whom were made, we read and believe, 'heaven and earth, the sea and all the things that are in them' [Psalms 145.6], as the testimonies of the prophets confirm and authorities of the New Testament demonstrate

27 Named as Cathar Bishop of Agen in Doat 24 and mentioned in other depositions; e.g. Doc. 42, fol. 186v.

more fully. For the Lord Himself spoke thus through his prophet Isaiah: 'I am the first and I am the last, my hand also hath founded the earth, and my right hand hath measured the heavens' [Isaiah 48.13–14]. And again: 'For behold I create new heavens and a new earth' [Isaiah 65.17]. And the angel in the Apocalypse: 'Fear the Lord and give him honour, because the hour of his judgment is come; and adore ye him, that made heaven and earth, the sea and all the things that are in them' [Apocalypse 14.7]. And again, the twenty-four elders: 'Thou art worthy, O Lord our God, to receive glory, and honour and power: because thou hast created all things; and for thy will they were and have been created' [Apocalypse 4.17].

Item, Paul and Barnabas in the Acts: 'Ye men, why do ye these things? We also are mortals, men like unto you, preaching to you to be converted from these vain things, to the living God, who made the heaven, and the earth, and the sea, and all things that are in them' [Acts 14.14]. Similarly the other apostles in the same Acts: 'Lord, thou art he that didst make heaven and earth, the sea, and all the things that are in them' [Acts 4.24]. Item, Paul in the same: 'God, who made the earth, and all things therein; he, being Lord of heaven and earth, dwelleth not in temples made with hands' [Acts 17.24]. And David: 'Blessed be you of the Lord, who made heaven and earth' [Psalms 113.15]. And in the Apocalypse: 'And to the angel of the church of Laodicaea write: These things saith the Amen, the faithful and true witness, who is the beginning of the creation of God' [Apocalypse 3.14].

With these testimonies, therefore, and many others, we believe that the omnipotent God made and also created heaven, earth, sea, the world and all the things that are in them. Etc. – Thus far.

In this first chapter of their compilation, the Manichees cover up their apostasy, but in the following ones they reveal it openly

In this, however, we should use all our strength imitating the Son of God, who judges the intention of the heart rather than words, as is often clearly read in the Gospels.

Referring to the aforesaid testimonies both in heart and word, we shall confine ourselves to resisting their perverse meaning. For the authorities <themselves> are good and true, expressed by the Spirit through the mouths of saints. But I know certainly that the Cathars who have placed the aforesaid authorities at the beginning of their treatise do not believe or understand the aforesaid witnesses as having said anything about our visible creatures that we see in this world. But in their conventicles they indoctrinate their hereticules [heresiotas] and urge that whatever can be seen in this world was made by the devil. …

Item, we say boldly that all the other authorities written above, with which they say God made all things, were not said to apply only to invisible things, according to the understanding of the Manichees, but also to visible creatures: which will be shown sufficiently in the following, with God originating my argument. To this – that in fact they say that the apostle said, 'God, who made the world' – we say that they have subtracted from that sentence the demonstrative pronoun 'this'. For in properly corrected books it goes like this: God, it is, who made *this* world and all the things that are in it, which we read in libraries at Rome and in many other churches, written at the beginning. And it is always in our books, and we have also seen the same 'this' written in some of the heretics' books. But because it is much against their depraved understanding, when they have heard it brought up as an objection, they have erased it [*the word 'this'*] from their manuscripts. …

2 On the beginning of disclosure, and their interpretation

… We know, in truth, that they call the orthodox faith of the apostles and prophets and the other saints, that the Roman Church, the Jerusalem Church, the Byzantine, the Antiochan, <and> the Alexandrian profess, 'error', and they believe that all those zealous for this faith are 'infidel heretics', and they make their suporters refer to them as 'the Good Men' or 'the Christians'. …

3 The opinion of the Cathars about the two worlds [seculis], and afterwards the reply against them

…

4 On the two world [mundis]

From the compilation of the Manichees

> James speaks thus in his Epistle about the present evil world and evil and 'of the whole seated in wickedness' [1 John 5.19]: 'Adulterers, know you not that the friendship of this world is the enemy of God? Whosoever therefore will be a friend of this world, becometh an enemy of God' [James 4.4]. And Paul: 'For the fashion of this world passeth away' [1 Cor. 7.31]. And John: 'Love not the world nor the things which are in the world. For all that is in the world, is the concupiscence of the flesh' [1 John 2.15, 16], etc. …[28]

28 See WE, pp. 498–9, for the rest of this passage.

… Item, 'Do not love the world'. … If the heretics understand this as <applying> to the present world, that is, to visible creatures, and that it ought to be understood in this way, we boldly say that they deliberately act against this. For, as we have seen and heard in some parts of the provinces of Gothia[29] and Aquitaine, and as has become known to virtually all the inhabitants of the dioceses in which <the heretics> lived: they had fields, vineyards and their own houses, workshops, oxen, asses, mules and horses, gold and silver and many of the earthly possessions of this world, and they were at work day and night, they were very great businessmen in the acquisition of earthly money.[30] If the aforesaid testimonies are to be understood as <applying> to this visible world, as they dogmatise, they themselves deliberately act against the apostle who said, 'Love not the world nor the things which are in the world', for they love land and possessions and the fruits which come forth from them. …

5 The opinion of the Cathars about the two kingdoms, and the invalidation of this

… Item, if the kingdom of the world, that is, the Roman Church, is not the kingdom of God, because many in it are corrupt and ingrained with evil deeds, their kingdom, that is the 'church' that is called <the assembly> 'of the malignant' [Psalms 25.5] is not the kingdom of Christ. For we know that it has had many corruptions and is also divided into three parts and each part judges the other and condemns it. For some of them obey Greek heretics, others however Bulgarians, and others Dragovitsans [Drogovetis].

6 The opinion of the Manichees about the new heaven and earth, and the quashing of this

…

29 See *Une Somme Anti-cathare*, ed. Thouzellier, pp. 119–20 n.15 on Durand's use of this obsolete term to denote a large part of Languedoc ruled by the counts of Toulouse.

30 See A. Roach, 'The Cathar economy', *Reading Medieval Studies* 12 (1986), 51–74, the theme of avarice in Doc. 10, and passing references to work and money in inquisition records in Part VIII below.

7 The opinion of the Cathars about *his own, unto* which the Word of the Father *came* [John 1.11]: and against it

…

8 The opinion of the wicked about the sowing of the field, that is to say, the cockle and the weed

…

9 The opinion of the Manichees about good and evil days, and afterwards the reply to it

…

10 The opinion of the Manichees about good and evil works, and the reply to it

…

11 The opinion of the Manichees about the double creation

…

12 The evasion of the heretics about this word 'all', which they say is understood in two ways

… On this point, however, that the Cathars write, that there is the greatest discord in virtually all that exists in these lands, and in this way they aim to prove that the Lord did not make them, we say <this>. If this is an argument demonstrating that God [*or* the God] who is good did not make these temporal things that are seen, because there is discord in some of them, by the same argument it is demonstrated that the benign God did not make the souls of the Cathars. For they disagree among themselves and on each side they condemn each other, as we and the majority of the people, both clergy and lay have seen and heard clearly being done by them in the dioceses of Carcassonne, and Toulouse, and Albi. Further, the Greek Manichees dissent from the Bulgars, and the Dragovitsans [Drogvethi] are out of tune with both.

13 The opinion of the perfidious about this word 'nothing'

... Some – such as the Manichees, that is to say the modern Cathars who live in the dioceses of Albi and Toulouse and Carcassonne, and their accomplices – regard this word 'nothing' as signifying something, namely some corporeal substance and <some> incorporeal <substance> and all visible creatures, as they have written in their *Contradiction* compilation.

14 The opinion of the Cathars on the good creation, and afterwards against them

... From these words of the apostle [I Tim. 4, 1–5], it is plainly given to be understood that this was prophesied by the Holy Spirit through the apostle, on behalf of foods, granted for human life, and against the heretics, who abhor meat, eggs and cheese. ... the heretics, who live in the dioceses of Carcassonne, Toulouse and Albi.

... For the same Cathars call those who profess the orthodox faith 'heretics' and 'demented', because they do not reject the faith of Christ they received at baptism and go over to their accursed error, <do not exchange> light for darkness, truth for lies, and sweet things for bitter ones. ...

... In their words and deeds, equally, all the holy prophets and apostles and all their successors have condemned the faith – if it is right to call it 'faith' – of the heretics, who have themselves called 'the Good Men' by their supporters.

15 The opinion of the Manichees on the new earth, and the reply against it

...

16 On the same, that is, the opinion of the Cathars on the new earth, and its falsification

… They understand that there is materially another earth above the firmament of the sky, according to what we have heard from them; and not just one but even seven, as is contained in a certain secret book of theirs [in quodam libro secreto suo], which we have seen and read, which they frivolously entitle under the name of the prophet Isaiah.[31]

17 The opinion of the Manichees on the new heavens, and the quashing of this

…

18 The opinion of the heretics about the sheep of the house of Israel, and against it

What the heresiarchs secretly read to their believers about the seven lands, which they falsely pretend Isaiah said, is not true nor verisimilar. Nor did the holy Isaiah think such lies. Rather it was fabricated by the evil spirit in the mind of some heresiarch, and given a title with the name of Isaiah in order more easily to infatuate the ignorant.

19 The opinion of the Cathars about this word 'render', and afterwards its falsification, the true <opinion> being strengthened by many testimonies

…

31 See also Ch. 18 below. These are the earliest references to use by heretics in Languedoc of the *Vision of Isaiah*, a text which was also read by the Bogomils and Italian Cathars; see B. Hamilton, 'Wisdom from the East: the reception by the Cathars of Eastern dualist texts', in *Heresy and Literacy, 1000–1530*, ed. P. Biller and A. Hudson (Cambridge, 1994), pp. 52–3. It is translated in WE, pp. 449–56.

20 On the creation or origin of souls, both against the Cathars and also all other[32] adversaries of the orthodox faith

...

21 On predestination against modern Manichees and all others who dissent from Catholic truth

...

32 In this chapter Durand allows himself to cite patristic authorities, while noting that the Manichees ⌜Cathars⌝ do not receive them; ibid., p. 312.

PART II: CHRONICLES

INTRODUCTION TO PART II

A large proportion of evidence for heresy in the eleventh and twelfth centuries comes from chronicles,[1] but by the thirteenth century they do not loom quite so large in comparison to other genres (most obviously inquisitorial evidence). Nonetheless, and particularly for the earlier part of the thirteenth century, they provide evidence of events which are otherwise not visible to us. This is particularly the case with the prosecution of heresy in northern France, which has very much shaped our selection here. Were there any inquisition registers or sentences surviving for the activities of the early inquisitor Robert Lepetit (also known as Robert le Bougre), our sense of heresy in this period might be transformed. As it is, the report of Robert's activities, and of the earlier episcopal condemnation of heretics at La Charité, provides a glimpse of major and violent ecclesiastical activity in the north, known to us otherwise only via some papal letters (see Docs 20–3) and mention of La Charité in a sermon of c.1200 (Doc. 16).[2] We include here also a portion of Peter of Les Vaux-de-Cernay's chronicle, focusing not on the Albigensian crusade, but on what he says about the Cathar heresy, which can be compared with other documents in this collection (including the two which we provide as an appendix to our extract from his chronicle).

1 Borst, *Katharer*, pp. 1–10 (*Cathares*, pp. 1–16) provides an overview of the genres of the early texts.

2 On heresy in the north, see É. Chenon, 'L'hérésie à La Charité-sur-Loire et les débuts de l'inquisition monastique dans la France du Nord au XIIIe siècle', *Nouvelle Revue Historique de Droit Français et Étranger* 41 (1917), 299–345; C. H. Haskins, 'Robert Le Bougre and the beginnings of the inquisition in northern France', in C. H. Haskins, *Studies in Medieval Culture* (Cambridge MA, 1929), pp. 193–244; G. Despy, 'Les débuts de l'inquisition dans les anciens Pay-Bas au XIIIe siècle', in G. Cambier, ed., *Problèmes de l'histoire du Christianisme. Hommage à Jean Hadot* (Brussels, 1980), pp. 71–104; P. Biller, 'Northern Cathars and higher learning', in P. Biller and [R.] B. Dobson, eds, *The Medieval Church: Universities, Heresy and the Religious Life. Essays in Honour of Gordon Leff*, Studies in Church History Subsidia 11 (Woodbridge, 1999), pp. 25–53; M. Barber, 'Northern Catharism', in M. Frassetto, ed., *Heresy and the Persecuting Society in the Middle Ages: Essays on the Work of R. I. Moore* (Leiden and Boston, 2006), pp. 115–37; J. Bird, 'The wheat and the tares: Peter the Chanter's circle and the *fama*-based inquest against heresy and criminal sins, c.1198–c.1235', *Proceedings of the Twelfth International Congress of Medieval Canon Law*, ed. U.-R. Blumenthal, K. Pennington and A. A. Larson (Vatican City, 2008), pp. 763–856.

Historians sometimes use the label 'chronicle' as a shorthand term to cover any kind of medieval written account of past events, but in fact there were some different subgenres, with different purposes and assumed audiences, several of which are represented here. Peter of Les Vaux-de-Cernay was writing an account of a specific set of events with heresy at their centre, drawing primarily on first-hand experience; whereas Matthew Paris and Robert of Auxerre, for example, were writing much broader works, often making use of news and documents brought to them by others, and thus the extracts presented here are but moments within much broader works. The 'Deeds of bishops' were another popular subgenre, focused of course on a particular diocese and its sequence of incumbents. In other words, the various possible reasons why accounts of heresy may enter a written history may include the particular purposes and contexts of each different source. We have included here also extracts from another kind of history-writing, the work which the Inquisitor Bernard Gui produced on the development of his religious order, the Dominicans, in which his topics were the foundation and spread of Dominican convents in the south of France, and their priors. Our selection concentrates on the many inquisitors that Gui noted and – on occasion – commented upon.

3. ROBERT OF AUXERRE ON NORTHERN FRANCE

Born c. 1156/7, Robert at the age of sixteen entered the monastery of St-Marien in Auxerre, a Premonstratensian house that had been founded c. 1139/40. He was commissioned to write his chronicle by Milo, Abbot of St-Marien (1156–1203), who helped him in the work. Robert continued it until 1211, dying in 1212. For an introduction to its genre in historical writing – that of a universal chronicle, beginning at the creation, with five ages of the world up to Christ, and thereafter a chronological account of Christianity, the Empire and kingdoms – see B. Smalley, *Historians of the Middle Ages* (London, 1974), pp. 95–105; for a comprehensive account, M. Chazan, *L'Empire et l'histoire universelle: de Sigebert de Gembloux à Jean de Saint-Victor (XII*^{e}*–XIV*^{e} *siècle)* (Paris, 1999). Chazan provides a fundamental account of Robert, pp. 332–41, and discusses his writing on heresy, pp. 339–40. On repression of heresy in the diocese of Auxerre, see Bird, 'Wheat and the tares' (cited above), pp. 770–3, 802–16, 844. We have selected the passages on heresy relating to northern France; Robert also wrote vividly about the early stages of the Albigensian crusade. Translated from Robert of Auxerre, *Chronicon*, ed. O. Holder-Egger, MGH Scriptores 26 (Hannover, 1882), pp. 258, 260, 270, 271.

AD 1198. … During that same time a priest from the bishopric of Paris called Fulk, a man of great faith and worthy life, shone out and was famous. With the Lord's inspiration and his bishop's permission he wandered through the neighbouring regions, traversing<northern> France, Flanders and Burgundy, insistently sowing the word of healthy doctrine and truth and harrying in particular the two vices of usuries and lechery. In truth, miracles bore witness to his words, so that through him and with the co-operation of the Lord medicine penetrated not only souls but also bodies. Among the people faith grew warm again. And, as though 'the heavens dropped at the presence of God' and for a time 'the earth was moved' [Psalms 67.9], they were so stirred towards the said man that wherever he went, they both received him with great joy and drank in his words with enormous thirst. The word of God was therefore flowing with great speed, and by his word alone he converted to the Lord many of those women who had sinned publicly and many of those men who had engaged in public profiteering – people who because of their large numbers could not be coerced by ecclesiastical censure. Many, too, returned to the faith from that foulest of all heresies, the Populican [Populicana] heresy,[3] which at that time had spread its poisonous roots widely but secretly. And through their confessions many from this same heresy were revealed. Among them was the heresiarch Thierry [Terricus], the devil's great snare, who had hidden for a long time in an underground cave at Corbigny and had subverted many people. He was brought out of his hiding-places, convicted and burnt. At the town of Nevers the Abbot of St-Martin and the dean of the major church were identified with this most pestilent error. They appeared at a council of bishops that was convoked at Sens, where the abbot was deposed and the dean suspended, and they were sent to the Apostolic See. And very rich men at the town that is called La Charité, who were conspicuous in the aforesaid heresy, absented themselves on the day when they had been summoned to purge themselves from this accusation, and they were cut off from the Church and abandoned to public power. Furthermore, during these days the Jews were harassed with severe pillage and affliction.

AD 1201 The knight Évrard, whom Count Hervé of Nevers had put in charge of his land, was a man well versed in the ways of the world and quite an oppressor of lesser people. In front of a legate he was accused of what they call 'the heresy of the Bulgars',[4] and a day was arranged for him to purge himself publicly of the alleged heresy. The legate convoked a council at Paris, archbishops and bishops of the kingdom and Paris masters sat alongside the legate, and Évrard was made to appear. Much evidence and many witnesses against him were produced. In the face, above all, of the urgent insistence of Hugh, Bishop of Auxerre, he was convicted of heresy, and after the pronouncement of the judgment he was handed over to the <secular> power to be punished. He was handed over in the interim to the Count of Nevers, to render account of his management. Thence he was taken to Nevers and he was consumed

3 From Publicani, Latin version of Greek name for Paulician heretics, and a term probably crossing wires with the name of the notorious sinners of the Bible, 'publicans' (publicani); references gathered in Borst, *Katharer*, p. 247 (*Cathares*, pp. 209–10).

4 The widespread use of the words *Bulgari* and *Burgari* (in French, *Bougres*) to denote heretics in France has been taken to be rooted in broad awareness of their sect's indebtedness to the Bogomil heretics of Bulgaria and the eastern Roman Empire; see Borst, *Katharer*, pp. 249–50 (*Cathares*, pp. 210–11). See thus Stephen of Bourbon (Doc. 17, xii), and note Anselm of Alessandria: 'Because the French were originally led astray in Constantinople by Bulgars, throughout France these persons are called Bulgarian heretics' (WE, pp. 168–9). We have noted variants of the name in the texts we present.

in the flames, in the sight of everyone to whom he had made himself hateful through the burdens he had imposed.

AD 1206 Hugh, Bishop of Auxerre, travelled to Rome and died there. … He applied himself strenuously to hunting down the heretics they call 'Burgars' [Burgarii], and his determination brought it about that many were stripped of their goods, others expelled and others burnt.

AD 1207. During this same time the execrable heresy of the Bulgars, the lowest scum of all error, gained ground in many places, all the more harmfully the more secretly it did this. But it had grown to greatest strength in the land of the Count of Toulouse and of neighbouring princes.

4. *DEEDS OF THE BISHOPS OF AUXERRE*

The *Deeds* were compiled over a long time by many authors, all clerics of Auxerre. There is no very detailed discussion of 'deeds of bishops' as a genre for this period, but they were a not uncommon form of historical writing, focused on the succession of bishops in one diocese, sometimes edging towards hagiography.[5] The author in question here, the biographer of Hugh of Noyers, also wrote the account of his successor, William of Seignelay, Bishop of Auxerre (1206–20) and then Bishop of Paris, drawing up these accounts shortly after the latter's death in 1223. Translated from *Les gestes des évêques d'Auxerre*, ed. G. Lobrichon and M. Sot, 3 vols (Paris, 2002–9), vol. 2, pp. 140, 146, 177, 179.

About Hugh of Noyers, the length of his episcopacy

Hugh of Noyers presided over his diocese for about 24 years. Raised from the treasury to become bishop AD 1183, on the feast of the Purification of the Blessed Virgin [2 February 1184], he was a man remarkable for the nobility of his blood and even more for the splendour of his spirit.

With what fervour he fought for the Catholic faith against the heretics of La Charité

He was also a magnificent promoter of the Catholic faith. He burnt with such fervent regard for it that he strove with great vigilance to capture 'the little foxes that destroy the vine of the Lord' [Song of Songs 2.15] and try through heretical dogmas to make it degenerate into wild vines [*see* Isaiah 5.2, 4]. At a noble place in his diocese, La Charité, the ardour with which he armed himself was even more than the ardour with which he knew the error of heretics was flourishing there. And he persecuted heretics there with such constancy of spirit that in various dioceses some of the heretics returned to the bosom of our mother Church for the sake of their salvation, abjuring heresy and doing public penance. Others – to the detriment of their

5 See M. Sot, *Gesta episcoporum, gesta abbatorum* (Turnhout, 1981).

salvation – were more obstinate, fleeing to Italy or to the Albigenses, to accomplices of their error, and becoming exiles from the land of their birth, their kin and their heritage. And the bishop made such progress in this business that he was called, not without reason, the 'hammer of the heretics'.

How he convicted Évrard of heresy

[*Chronicle discusses Peter of Courson, the right-hand man of Peter of Courtenay, Count of Auxerre; and then:*] Évrard of Châteauneuf succeeded him in his office and power. He was not behind him in malevolence or of lesser ingenuity or slacker in his determination to harm people. He was a most ferocious persecutor of the Church, in that, infected with heretical wickedness, he tried to use all his force and daring against those who professed the Church's dogmas. From his crimes we have decided to transmit what follows to the knowledge of posterity. One man who had offended him was harried to death. To escape the imminent danger of death the man took refuge in the church of St-Mary-within-the-Walls, because of the place's immunity. Showing no reverence to God Évrard broke the immunity of the church, and inside the church itself he had the man killed by sword by one of those who were hunting him, atrociously profaning God's sanctuary with this innocent man's blood. But the Lord, a just judge, gave him the right retribution for his merits, as we shall see in the following. Since Count Peter <of Auxerre> had become hostile to him, Évrard left him and took himself off to Hervé, Count of Nevers, to whom the county of Nevers had come through Matilda, the daughter of Count Peter, to whom the county belonged through hereditary right; he had married her, as was said above, with the help of royal favour. Évrard was so well received by this Hervé that he obtained from the Count of Nevers the same position that he had held with Count Peter. The Church suffered many acts of oppression under his rule, as it had done formerly in the county of Auxerre.

The accusation against him of being tainted with heresy was growing, and the bishop, an outstanding zealot for Catholic dogmas and a fervent destroyer of heretical perversity, publicly accused him of heresy at the council convoked at Paris by Octavian, cardinal-priest of the Church of Rome, who was then carrying out the office of legate in France. He did this in the presence of many archbishops, bishops and others present who were of lower ecclesiastical or administrative ranks. He convicted the accused with irrefutable testimonies. Convicted, Évrard received the sentence of condemnation with the approval of the council. Condemned to be burnt by fire, he breathed out his profane soul, receiving the worthy reward for his merits and leaving for his family the fetid mark of his perversity and eternal opprobrium.

5. PETER OF LES VAUX-DE-CERNAY

Peter was a monk at the northern French Cistercian monastery of Les Vaux-de-Cernay. He accompanied the abbot – Guy, his uncle – to southern France in 1212, and, apart from a brief return to the north in 1213, remained there until his death. He began writing possibly as early as 1213, and the last events he describes are in 1218; he presumably died shortly afterwards. Peter knew many of the leading figures of the Albigensian crusade. The picture he presents can be seen as an amalgam of his own direct experience in the south, the views of those noblemen and monks with whom he lived in both northern and southern France, and what he may have derived from Vaux-de-Cernay's library, which was rich in patristic and twelfth-century texts bearing on heresy. He may have had access to a heretical text: see paragraph 11 below. There is an unsurpassed account of Peter and the *History* in Petri Vallium Sarnaii Monachi, *Hystoria Albigensis*, ed. P. Guébin and E. Lyon, 3 vols (Paris, 1926–39), vol. 3, pp. i–xxxix (ii–vi on the abbey's library), and a fine annotated translation by W. A. and M. D. Sibly of Peter of Les Vaux-de-Cernay, *The History of the Albigensian Crusade* (Woodbridge, 1998). We have selected here for re-translation the passages in which Peter discusses heresy in detail.

Translated from *Hystoria Albigensis*, ed. Guébin and Lyon, vol. 1, pp. 6, 10–30. The paragraph numbers introduced by those editors are followed here, to facilitate comparison with this edition and other translations. Note that, for Peter, 'the province of Narbonne' (or, on occasion, just 'the province') indicates the ancient Roman province, which comprised the areas we now call Languedoc and Provence.

[*Prologue, after dedicatory letter to Innocent III*].

…

[3] In the first part of this work I briefly touch upon the sects of heretics, and how those living in the province [*southern France*] have been infected with the leprosy of infidelity for many years past. Then, <in the second part>, I describe how the aforementioned heretics of the province were often admonished and asked by the preachers of the word of God and your Holiness's ministers to return, 'transgressors, to the heart' [Isaiah 46.8]. Then, <in the third part>, I present, in order as far as I can, the coming of the crusaders, the capturing of cities and *castra*, and other things relevant to the course of events of the business of the faith.

[4] One thing readers of the book should know, that in many places in this work the heretics and their defenders from Toulouse and other cities and *castra* are usually called 'Albigensians'. This is because other nations have been accustomed to call the heretics of the province 'Albigensians' …

<First Part: On the Heretics>

…

[10] *On the sects of heretics.* Since the opportunity offers itself, I have decided to cut to the chase with a brief description of the sects and heresies of the heretics.

The first thing to grasp is that the heretics supposed that there are two creators, that is to say, the creator of invisible things, whom they call the 'benign God', and the creator of visible things, whom they named the 'malign God'.

They attributed the New Testament to the benign God, the Old to the malign God, and they rejected the latter entirely, apart from some passages from the Old which are included in the New Testament – through reverence for the New Testament they regarded these as worthy and they received them.

They maintained that the author of the Old Testament was a 'liar', because he said to the first created beings, 'In whatsoever day thou shalt eat of the tree of knowledge of good and evil thou shalt die the death' [Genesis 2.17]. After eating it they did not die, as he said they would – though of course immediately after eating the forbidden fruit they did become subject to the misery of death.

They also called him 'murderer', both because he burnt the people of Sodom and Gomorrah and destroyed the world with the waters of the Flood and also because he submerged Pharaoh and the Egyptians in the sea. They affirmed that all the patriarchs of the Old Testament are damned. They asserted that John the Baptist was one of the greater devils.

[11] They said in their *Secret*[6] that the Christ who was born in terrestrial and visible Bethlehem and was crucified in Jerusalem was 'Evil'

6 Text: in secreto suo. Other modern translators have preferred the non-literal translation 'secret meetings'. *Secret*, *Secretum*, accords with other references to heretics' texts; see L. Paolini, 'Italian Catharism and written culture', in Biller and Hudson, eds, *Heresy and Literacy*, pp. 83–4.

and that Mary Magdalen was his concubine and was that woman who was caught in adultery about whom one reads in the Gospel [John 8.3]. For the 'good' Christ, as they called him, never ate or drank, nor took on true flesh, nor was ever in this world, except spiritually in the body of Paul. This is why we have said, 'in the terrestrial and visible Bethlehem', because the heretics made out that there was another land, new and invisible; and according to some, the 'good' Christ had been born and crucified in that land.

Item, they said that the good God had two wives, Oolla and Ooliba [*see* Ezechiel 23.4], and he procreated from them sons and daughters.

There were other heretics who said that there was one God, but he had two sons, Christ and the devil. These said that <to begin with> all creatures were good, but all were corrupted by the *vials* that are read about in the Apocalypse [16.1].

[12] All of these, members of Antichrist, firstborn of Satan, 'wicked seed, ungracious children' [Isaiah 1.4], 'speaking lies in hypocrisy' [1 Tim. 4.2], 'seducing the hearts of the innocents' [Romans 16.18], had infected virtually the whole of the province of Narbonne with the poison of their perfidy.

They said the Roman Church was 'a den of thieves' [Matt. 21.13], and the whore that is read about in the Apocalypse [17.1–18].

They held the Church's sacraments as nothing, to such a point that they publicly maintained that the water of holy baptism was not remote from river water; that the host of the most holy body of Christ did not differ from ordinary bread; pouring this blasphemy into the ears of the simple that, even if the body of Christ contained within itself the magnitude of the Alps, it would long ago have been consumed and finished by those eating it; they regarded confirmation, extreme unction <and> confession as utterly worthless and empty; they preached that holy marriage was prostitution, nor could anyone be saved generating sons and daughters in it.

Rejecting also the resurrection of the flesh, they made up some unheard-of stories, saying that our souls are those angelic spirits that were thrown out of heaven, because of the apostasy of pride, and who left their glorified bodies in the air. And <they said> that, after successively inhabiting any seven earthly bodies, at long last these spirits return to those bodies that had been left behind, their penance at this point, as it were, having been completed.

[13] Now, it should be known that some among the heretics were called the 'Perfected' or the 'Good Men', others 'Believers' of the heretics.[7]

Those who were called 'Perfected' wore a black habit. They lied that they held to chastity. They utterly detested the eating of meats, eggs, cheese. They wanted to be seen as people who did not lie, though they themselves continually lied, most of all about God. They also say that one ought not ever to take an oath, for whatever reason.

Called 'Believers' of heretics were those who, although living in the world and not reaching towards imitation of the <way of> life of the Perfected, nevertheless hoped to be saved in their faith. Divided, certainly, in their mode of living, they were however one in faith – or rather, in infidelity.

Those who were called 'Believers' were intent on usuries, robberies, murders and pleasures of the flesh, perjuries and all perversities. They sinned with all the more security and lack of restraint, since they believed they would be saved without the restitution of stolen goods, confession and penance, so long as they were able to say the 'Our Father' when at the point of death and receive the imposition of hands from their masters.

[14] From among the 'Perfected' heretics they had officials [magistratus] whom they called 'deacons' and 'bishops', without the laying-on of whose hands none of the believers who was about to die believed he could be saved. In fact their opinion was that if they laid hands on anyone who was dying, however disgraceful, so long as he could say the 'Our Father', he was saved and, according to their vernacular, 'consolated': such that, without any act of satisfaction or any other remedy <to make amends for wrongdoings> he would immediately fly off to heaven.

[15] We have decided to insert here an amusing thing we heard on this point.
Some believer of the heretics received the laying-on of hands or *consolamentum* from his master at the very point of death, but he was not able to say the 'Our Father'; and thus he breathed his last. His consolater did not know what to say about him. Through the laying-on of hands that had been received, he seemed to be saved; because he had

7 Elsewhere, we have usually translated *perfecti* as 'fully-fledged' – see Doc. 40 for our reasoning – but here it seems valid to translate as 'Perfected'.

not said the Lord's prayer, he seemed to be damned. What then? The heretics consulted a certain knight, Bertrand of Saissac, who was a heretic, on how they should adjudicate this. The knight gave this counsel and response: 'Concerning this man, we shall allow and say that he is to be saved. All others, if they have not said the 'Our Father' at the end, we judge to be damned'.

[16] Item, another amusing thing.
At his death some believer of the heretics left the heretics 300 shillings, and he ordered his son to give the heretics this money. When the heretics asked the son for it after the father's death, the son said to them, 'I want you first to tell me, if this is okay, in what state my father is'. 'You should know with complete certainty that he is saved and is now set in place alongside celestial beings'. To this he replied, grinning, 'Thank God, and you! However, since my father is now in glory there is no need for alms for his soul, and I know that you are so kindly that you will not now recall my father from glory. Therefore you should know this – you will not get any money from me!'

[17] We do not think that what some heretics said – that no-one could sin below the navel – should be passed over in silence.

They said that images put into churches are idolatry.

They declared that church bells were 'the devil's wind instruments'.

Item, they said that one did not sin more seriously in sleeping with one's mother or sister than with anyone else.

Among the supreme absurdities of heresies, this also they said, that if one of the perfected sinned mortally – say, through eating the tiniest scrap of meat or cheese or egg or some other thing he was forbidden – all those consolated by him lost the Holy Spirit and they needed to be reconsolated again; and also, because of the consolater's sin, those already saved fell from heaven.

[18] There were, furthermore, other heretics, who were called 'Waldensians' [Valdenses], after some citizen of Lyon called Valdius.[8]

These were bad, but compared to other heretics a lot less perverse. For they agreed with us in many things, dissenting in others. However, to pass over many points in their infidelity, their error consisted

8 Valdio nomine. His real name was Valdesius, a Latin form of Valdes.

principally in four things: in wearing sandals in the manner of the apostles [1], and in this that they said, that one should not take an oath [2] or kill [3], for any reason; in this also that they asserted [4], that in case of necessity anyone of them, so long as he had sandals, and without having received <holy> orders from a bishop, can consecrate the body of Christ.

It is enough that we have briefly selected these things about the heretics' sects.

[19] Mode of conversion, or rather perversion, of the heretics.
When someone surrenders himself to the heretics, the one who is receiving him says to him, 'Friend, if you wish to be one of us, it is necessary for you to renounce the whole of the faith that the Roman Church holds.

He replies, 'I renounce'.

'Therefore receive the Spirit from the good men', and then he breathes seven times into the mouth <of the one being received>.

Again, he says to him, 'Do you renounce that cross that the priest did to you in baptism with oil and chrism on your chest and on your shoulders and on your head?'

'I renounce'.

'Do you believe that that water brings about your salvation?'

He replies, 'I do not believe'.

'Do you renounce that veil the priest put upon your head when you had been baptised?'

He replies, 'I renounce'.

He receives in this way the baptism of the heretics and repudiates the baptism of the Church.

Then all lay their hands on his head, and kiss him, and clothe him in a black habit. And from that hour he is as one of them.

<Second Part: On the preachers>
[20] Here he begins to tell the story of how the preachers came to the Albigensian land.

In the 1206th year of the Word made flesh, the Bishop of Osma, Diego by name, a great man deserving magnificent praise, went to the Roman court, desiring with supreme desire to resign his episcopacy, so as to be able to apply himself more freely to preaching Christ's Gospel to the pagans. The lord Pope Innocent, however, was unwilling to agree with the holy man's desire, in fact he ordered him to return to his own see. It happened that during his return from the curia, when he was at Montpellier, Diego found there the venerable man Arnold, Abbot of Cîteaux, and Brother Peter of Castelnau and Brother Ralph, Cistercian monks: legates of the Apostolic See, through fatigue they wanted to renounce the legateship that had been imposed upon them, since they could make little or no progress through preaching to the heretics. For as often as they wanted to preach to the heretics, the heretics would bring up in opposition the evil way of life of the clergy; and so, if they wanted to correct the way of life of the clergy, they needed to lay off preaching.

[21] The above-mentioned bishop gave healthy counsel to resolve this sort of quandary, urging that they should leave everything else aside and sweat even more ardently in preaching. They should act and teach following the example of the Pious Master, proceeding humbly, and they should go by foot, without gold or silver [*see* Matt. 10.9], in all things imitating the apostolic way of life. Unwilling to take upon themselves all these things – <seeing them>, as it were, as a sort of novelty – the said legates said if someone of authority who was in favour of this wanted them to take the first step, innovating by following this form of life, they would be most willing to follow him. What then? The wholly Godly man offered himself up <as this figure>. He immediately sent on his household and wagons to his city of Osma, and, contenting himself with one companion, he left Montpellier, together with the oft-mentioned monk legates, that is to say Peter of Castelnau and Ralph. The Cistercian abbot journeyed on to Cîteaux, both because the Cistercian chapter general was about to be held and also because after the chapter had been celebrated he wanted to take off with him some abbots of his order, who would help him in carrying out the job of preaching which had been enjoined upon him.

[22] Leaving Montpellier, the Bishop of Osma and the aforesaid monks came to a certain *castrum* called Servian, where they found a certain heresiarch, called Baldwin, and a certain Theodoric, 'a son of perdition' [II Thessalonians 2.3] and kindling for eternal fire. The latter came from Gaul [= *northern France*], what is more he was noble by birth, and he had been a canon of Nevers. Later, however, a certain

knight, who was his uncle and a very bad heretic, was condemned for heresy at a council in Paris, in front of Cardinal Octavian, Legate of the Apostolic See. Seeing that he could not hide any longer <in that region>, Theodoric took himself to the province of Narbonne. There he was regarded by heretics with very great love and veneration, as much because he seemed somewhat cleverer than the others as because they took pride in having as a companion in their belief or a defender of their wickedness someone who came from France [= *Île-de-France*] – where, it is recognised, there is the fountain of knowledge and of Christian religion.[9] Nor should this be passed over, that he had himself called 'William', though earlier he had been called 'Theodoric'.

[23] Having had a debate for eight days with these two, that is to say, Baldwin and Theodoric, our preachers, by their salutary counsels, converted all the people of the said *castrum* to hatred of the oft-mentioned heretics. They would have very willingly driven them out, but the Lord of the *castrum*,[10] infected by the poison of perfidy, had made them his familiars and friends. It would take a long time to recount all the words of this debate, but I have decided it is worth weaving in just this one thing. In the debate, when the venerable bishop had brought the said Theodoric to the last point of the conclusion – 'I know', said Theodoric, 'I know in what spirit you are. You have come "in the spirit of Elias" [Luke 1.17]'. To which the holy man: 'And if I have come "in the spirit of Elias", you have come in the spirit of Antichrist'. When therefore the eight days there had concluded, the venerable men left the *castrum* and the people followed them for almost a league.

[24] Going on then, by a direct route, these men reached the city of Béziers, where, debating and preaching for fourteen days, they strengthened in their faith the few there who were Catholics; and they confounded the heretics. The venerable Bishop of Osma and Brother Ralph advised Brother Peter of Castelnau to leave them for a while. Because the heretics hated him above all others, they feared that Brother Peter might be killed. Accordingly, Brother Peter left the bishop and Brother Ralph for a while. They, however, left Béziers and after an easy walk they arrived at Carcassonne, where they stayed for eight days, and pressed on with preaching and debates.

9 Reference to Paris and its schools.

10 Stephen of Servian; see the translation of his abjuration in Appendix B below.

[25] Miracle
A miracle happened at this time at Carcassonne that ought not to be passed over. Heretics were harvesting their cornfields on the day of the birth of St John the Baptist – for they said he was not a prophet, but very malign. While they were reaping, therefore, one of them, looking at his sheaf, saw that it was bloody. Seeing this, he thought he had cut his hand, but finding that it was unhurt he shouted out to his companions. What then? Looking, each of them, at the sheaves they held, they found they were bloody while their hands remained unharmed. The venerable Abbot of Vaux-de-Cernay, Guy, was in the country at the time, saw the bloody sheaf, and he himself recounted this to me.

[26] Because it would really take a long time to recount in sequence how the apostolic men, that is to say, our preachers, went around castles, evangelising and debating, we pass over things, and alight <only> on the salient ones. All the heresiarchs came together one day at a certain *castrum* in the diocese of Carcassonne that is called Montréal, to debate, united in mind, against the oft-mentioned men. Brother Peter of Castelnau, who as we said a bit earlier had left his companions at Béziers, returned for this debate. Judges <were selected> from the heretics' believers and given to the debaters. The debate extended over fifteen days, and the positions put forward on one side and another were recorded in writing and handed over to the judges, for them to deliver a definitive verdict. These judges, however, seeing that it was utterly obvious that their heretics had been beaten, were unwilling to give a verdict. And they were unwilling to return the writings they had got from our lot, in case they came into the public <domain>; and instead they turned them over to the heretics.

[27] When these things had finished, Brother Peter of Castelnau left and went into Provence and worked to arrange a peace among the nobles of Provence, with this purpose, that with the help of those who had sworn peace he could eliminate heretics from the province of Narbonne. But the Toulousan Count Raymond,[11] an enemy of peace, was unwilling to agree to the said peace, until he was compelled to take the oath of peace, forced to do this as much by the wars the nobles of Provence waged against him – by the design of the man of God – as by the excommunication pronounced by him [*i.e. Peter*] against the same count. But the man who had denied the faith and was worse than

11 Raymond VI, 1156–1222; Count 1194–1214.

an infidel, never deferring to an oath, swore often and perjured often. Out of the great strength of his soul that most holy man Brother Peter used to correct him, fearlessly criticising the tyrant and resisting him to his face, for the count was utterly reprehensible, in fact damnable. The man of great constancy, the man of clear conscience, confounded him, to the point of reproaching him for being fallacious and a perjurer in all things: and he really was like that.

[28–46] [*Here he recounts the unfaithfulness of Count Raymond.*]

[47] Let us now return to the main subject. After the debate at Montréal that was noted earlier had been held, while our preachers were still at Montréal, sowing all around the word of faith and counsels of salvation and begging their bread from door to door, there arrived from the regions of <northern> France the venerable man Arnold, Abbot of Cîteaux, and with him twelve abbots. Men of complete devotion, men of perfect knowledge, men of incomparable holiness, they arrived in accordance with the most holy number of the apostles, the twelve of them together with the father abbot making thirteen, *ready* to provide *reason, for the faith* and hope that was in them, *to everyone* [1 Peter 3.15] who would debate with them. And all of these, together with many monks whom they had brought with them, were going about on foot, adhering to all humility, *according to the pattern that* had been *shown to* them *on the mount* [Exodus 25.40], that is, according to what they had heard from the Bishop of Osma. Immediately the abbots were dispersed individually far and wide by the Abbot of Cîteaux, and to each of them was assigned his own area, within whose borders he was to scurry round, pressing on with preaching, and sweating it out in debates.

[48] The Bishop of Osma wanted to go back to his bishopric, to make dispositions about his house and provide necessities out of his revenues for the preachers of God's word in the Narbonnensian province. While he was on his way back towards Spain, he came to Pamiers in the Toulousan territory. The Toulousan Bishop Fulk and Navarre, the Bishop of Couserans, and many abbots came together with him there. A debate was held with the Waldensians. The Waldensians were clearly defeated and confounded, and for the most part the people of the *castrum*, especially the poor, supported our lot. The man also who had been set up as the judge in the debate, someone who had favoured the Waldensians and was a great man in that *castrum*, renounced heretical wickedness and surrendered himself and his property into the hands

of the Bishop of Osma. And from that day forth, he fought manfully against the followers of heretical superstition. Present at this debate was that worst of traitors, the Count of Foix, that cruellest persecutor of the Church, an enemy of Christ. He had a wife who was an open heretic, of the Waldensians' sect, and two sisters, one of whom professed the sects [*sic*] of the Waldensians, the other the common heresies of other perfidious people. The debate was held in the palace of the count himself. And one day the same count attended to the needs of the Waldensians, the next day that of our preachers. What fake humanity!

[49] After these things the Bishop of Osma travelled on to his bishopric, with the firm intention of returning as soon as possible to carry out the business of faith in the province of Narbonne. In fact, after spending a few days in his bishopric he set out to return; however death prevented him, and in good old age he fell happily asleep.

[50] Before he died, however, the oft-mentioned Brother Ralph, a man of good memory, had yielded to fate in a certain abbey of the Cistercian Order near St-Gilles, called Fourquevaux.

[51] With these two luminaries gone, then, that is to say the Bishop of Osma and Brother Ralph, Guy, the venerable Abbot of Vaux-de-Cernay in the diocese of Paris (later he was made Bishop of Carcassonne), a man noble by birth but nobler by far in learning and virtue, who had come with other abbots for the sake of preaching in the province of Narbonne, was made leader and master of the preachers. For the Abbot of Cîteaux took himself off to other regions, occupied at the time with some affairs of great moment. So, the holy preachers scurried around, manifestly defeating the heretics when debating. However, unable to convert them – because the heretics were obstinate in their malice – they could make little or no progress through preaching or debating, and they returned to the regions of Gaul.

[52] Nor should this be passed over, that the said abbot [*i.e. Guy*] often disputed with the aforesaid Theodoric and a certain other very great heresiarch called Bernard of Simorre, who was held as paramount in the diocese of Carcassonne,[12] and he often overcame them. One day when the aforesaid Theodoric could not produce any other reply, he said to the abbot, 'The whore has held me for a long time, but she will

12 Identified as Cathar Bishop of Carcassonne in 1203 (see Appendix A below).

not hold me any more!' In saying this he was calling the Roman Church 'the whore'.

[53] Nor should there be silence about this, that on another day, when the oft-mentioned Abbot of Vaux-de-Cernay was entering some castle near Carcassonne called Lauran in order to preach, he signed himself with the sign of the cross at the entrance to the castle. When he saw this, some heretic knight who was in the castle said, 'May the sign of the cross never help me!'

[54] A certain miracle.

A certain miracle happened to take place at this time, which we have decided is worth inserting at this point. One day some of our preachers, men of religion, were debating against heretics. One of our lot, called Dominic, a man of total holiness who had been a companion of the Bishop of Osma, put down in writing certain authorities,[13] which he had brought into the open [*i.e. had earlier introduced into debate*]. And he handed the schedule to a certain heretic for him to deliberate on the points brought up in opposition. That night, then, the heretics were gathered in a house, sitting by a fire. The one to whom the man of God had given the schedule brought it out into the open. Then his companions told him to throw it into the midst of the fire. And if that schedule were to be burnt, the heretics' faith – or rather, perfidy! – would be <shown to be> true. If however it remained unburnt, they would confess that the faith we preached was good. What more? All consent to this. The schedule is thrown into the fire. And then, after it had been in the midst of the fire for a little bit, it leapt out of the fire, completely unburnt. One who was harder than the rest said to those who were there, stupefied, 'Let the schedule be thrown into the fire, and then we shall observe the truth more fully'. It was thrown again and again, and leapt out unburnt. Seeing this, the hard one, slow to believe, said, 'Let it be thrown in again, a third time, and then without a doubt we shall know the result of the matter'. It was thrown in a third time: nor did it burn, but it leapt out of the fire whole and unharmed. The heretics however, despite seeing so many signs, were unwilling to convert to the faith. Rather, remaining in their hardness, among themselves they strictly forbade this miracle coming to our knowledge via someone talking. But a certain knight who was with them, who acquiesced a bit

13 Quotations from scripture; possibly also from patristic writings.

in our faith, was unwilling to hide what he had seen, and he told the story to many people. This happened at Montréal, as I heard from the mouth of a most religious man, the one who handed the written schedule to the heretic.

Appendix A: Bernard of Simorre and the King of Aragon, 1203

See Peter of Les Vaux-de-Cernay above, paragraph 52. Translated from C. Compayré, *Études historiques et documents inédits sur l'Albigeois, le Castrais et l'ancien diocèse de Lavaur* (Albi, 1841), Doc. 54, pp. 227–8.

Peter,[14] by grace of God King of Aragon, Count of Barcelona, to all Christ's faithful who will read or hear the present writing, greetings and fidelity in persecuting the enemies of the faith.

You should all know that when I was in the city of Carcassonne, in the month of February AD 1203, since I saw that virtually all of it had lapsed into heresy, I summoned one day the Waldensian heretics on one side and on the other side the Bishop of Carcassonne, and the messengers of the lord pope, Brother Ralph and Peter of Castelnau, in order to get know about the heresy of the Waldensians, and I gave a hearing to <both> parties. After the testimonies of divine law and the decrees of the holy Roman Church had been brought forth during this <hearing>, they were convicted sufficiently of heresy. In fact, after both parties' arguments and allegations had been heard, I recognised and judged them to be heretics. On another day, at the request of the *viguier* [*official with delegated authority*] of the Viscount of Carcassonne, I gave a hearing to other heretics – there were present with me thirteen supporters of heretics and thirteen Catholics – where the heretics' bishop, Bernard of Simorre, and his companions were asked if they believed in one omnipotent God, without beginning and end, creator of all things visible and invisible, and giver of both the Mosaic law and the New Testament. After much evasion and twisting of words, with sacrilegious mouth they publicly confessed that there were three Gods and more, declaring that all visible things were made by a malign God, adding – by way of increasing their blasphemy and damnation – that the giver of the Mosaic law was a malign God.

What is horrible to hear, they also confessed that Jesus Christ had a man as His father, just as He had a woman as His mother. Further,

14 Peter II, 1178–1213.

they completely denied the sacrament of baptism, and of the altar, and the general resurrection of bodies. They also openly claimed that the Blessed Virgin Mary was not born of carnal parents. On all these headings they were sufficiently proved to be heretics by the said messengers of the lord pope, on the basis of authorities from the New Testament. And on the following day, in the presence of the bishop of the said city and many others, I pronounced them heretics.

Appendix B: Abjuration of Stephen of Servian, 1219

See Peter of Les Vaux-de-Cernay above, paragraphs 22–3. Translated from *HGL*, vol. 8, cols 584–5.

In the name of the Father and of the Son and of the Holy Spirit, Amen. In the 1219th year of the incarnation of the Word, in the 13th year of the pontificate of Pope Innocent III, in the month of February, in the town of St-Thibéry.

I, Stephen of Servian, confess that I have gravely erred and have committed a very grave offence against the Catholic faith and against the holy Roman Church. I received in my *castra* heretics and also heresiarchs, that is to say Theodoric, Baldwin, Bernard of Simorre and others who wished to come. I defended them, supported them, and I permitted them to hold schools and to preach publicly and dispute publicly of heresy. For these things I was publicly excommunicated and segregated from the holy Roman Church. Now in truth with compunction in my heart and acknowledging and confessing my sin and desiring to return to the unity and faith of holy mother Church, I abjure every sect and every heresy, by whatever name it may be called. I abjure also all heretics and their believers, receivers, defenders and supporters. I confess the holy Catholic faith …

6. AUBRI OF TROIS-FONTAINES ON THE INQUISITOR ROBERT LEPETIT[15]

Aubri was a monk in Trois-Fontaines, a Cistercian monastery in the diocese of Châlons in Champagne, whose mother-house was the monastery of Clairvaux. His is a universal chronicle (see the introduction to Robert of Auxerre's chronicle above), in which the earlier years are a collage, based on diligent reading and copying of many writings, including manuscripts in the library at Clairvaux. Aubri worked on it between 1227 and 1240, and then again in 1251–2. The topics and author's outlook suggest that Aubri was of German origin. The fundamental modern account is by Chazan in *L'Empire et l'histoire universelle*, pp. 360–9, who suggests Aubri's audience was first of all Cistercian monks, secondly those living in the county of Champagne and then, more broadly, the cultural region of the Rhine and Meuse.[16] Translated from Aubri [Alberic] of Trois-Fontaines, *Chronica Albrichi monachi trium fontium*, ed. P. Scheffer-Boichorst, MGH Scriptores 23, pp. 936, 937, 940, 944–5.

[1234] A certain Master Robert, of the Order of Preachers, who previously was a heretic but has now reverted to the Catholic faith, investigates heretics through <northern> France, and by authority of the pope he dragged them either to conversion, to be absolved, or to judgment, to be burnt.

[1236] Heretics were burnt in the city of Châlons, in the presence of Brother Robert and Master Philip the Chancellor of <the university of> Paris. One of them, the barber Arnolin, who was utterly committed to the demon and extraordinarily loathsome, deceived many in the city. Similarly in Cambrai many were arrested. Among them was a certain little old woman, named Alaydis, who seemed and was believed to be highly religious and an extraordinary almsgiver, but in the end she was accused and arrested. It was said of her that one day she gave money to the man who went around the city calling out, 'Good wine, most excellent wine, precious wine'. And thus she made him go throughout the city, calling out 'Compassionate God, merciful God, good and best

15 Robert also known as 'le Bougre'; see n.2 above, Bird 'Wheat and the tares', pp. 829–32, and Docs 8, 22 and 23 below.

16 See also M. Schmidt-Chazan, 'Aubri de Trois-Fontaines, un historien entre la France et l'empire', *Annales de l'Est*, 5th series, 36 (1984), 163–92.

God', while she followed him, declaring, 'He speaks well, he is saying the truth'. And as became clear later, she did the whole thing for the sake of human praise. She was burnt, therefore, with nearly twenty others, and twenty-one were imprisoned. And in Douai, and parts around there, a good thirty were burnt.

[1237] Brother Robert at this time was burning heretics in Gaul: he <had> apostatised around the time of the great council,[17] for he was a man of great apparent – but not real – religion. And, following a little Manichean woman, he went off to Milan, and made himself one of that most wicked sect for twenty years, such that he was most perfect [*or:* the highest ranking] among them. Coming back to his senses <he returned to the faith>, and on the instructions of the pope he uncovered many heretics. He was arresting them solely on the basis of the heretics' way of speaking and their bearing.

[13 May 1239]. In this year, on the sixth day of the week before Pentecost, there was made a very great *holocaust* and *peace-offering*[18] to the Lord through the burning of Bulgars [Bulgri]. For 183 Bulgars were burnt in the presence of the King of Navarre[19] and the barons of Champagne, at Mont Wimer,[20] which is called of old 'Wedomar's Mountain'. There were present Henry, Archbishop of Rheims; James, Bishop of Soissons; Master Galthier, Bishop of Tournai; Master Guiard, theologian, Bishop of Cambrai; Master Alzo, Bishop of Arras; Peter, Bishop of Thérouanne; Nicolas, Bishop of Noyon; Master Garnier, Bishop of Laon; Master Adam, Bishop of Senlis; Robert, Bishop-elect of Beauvais; Geoffrey, Bishop-elect of Châlons-sur-Marne, uncle of the Count of Grandpré; Master William, Bishop of Orléans; Master Nicolas, Bishop of Troyes; Peter, Bishop of Meaux; Rudolphe of Thourotte, Bishop of Verdun; and his brother, Robert, Bishop of Langres; and many other prelates of the churches, namely abbots, priors and deans.[21]

17 Fourth Lateran Council, 1215.

18 See the language of Leviticus and Numbers, *passim.*

19 Thibaut IV, Count of Champagne (1201–53) and King of Navarre (1234–53). See M. Lower, 'The burning at Mont-Aimé: Thibaut of Champagne's preparation for the Barons' Crusade of 1239', *Journal of Medieval History* 29 (2003): 95–108.

20 Mont-Aimé, hill which had a castle built on it by Thibaud IV's mother; in the canton of Vertus and the *département* of Marne, it is c. 20km WSW of Châlons-sur-Marne.

21 Henry of Dreux, Archbishop of Rheims, 1227–40; James of Bazoches, Bishop of Soissons, 1219–42; Master Galthier Marvisius, Bishop of Tournai, 1219–51; Master Guiard of Laon, theologian, Bishop of Cambrai, 1238–c. 1249 (a theologian of some

Not all of them, however, were present at that burning, but some were coming and others were going during that week when the questioning was taking place. There was present there, moreover, such a a multitude of people, of both sexes, <and of various> estates and conditions, that their number was estimated at 700,000.

And just as in olden times, so it is said, dogs from everywhere came together in one place, fought a battle against each other and tore each other to shreds, in a portent of future things, so these Bulgars – worse than dogs – were exterminated there in one day, to the triumph of the holy Church. Their chief master, who was called the Archbishop of Morains [*or* Murrains],[22] said to them in a loud voice: 'All of you will be saved, absolved by my hands; I alone am damned, because I do not have a superior to absolve me'. They had moreover certain old women, to whom they gave alternative names, so that one would be called 'Holy Mary', another 'Holy Church' or 'The Roman Law', another 'Holy Baptism' or '<Holy> Matrimony' or 'Holy Communion'. And when they said, under interrogation, 'I believe whatever the Holy Church or Roman Law believes', their reference was to that old woman, whom they were calling '<Holy> Church', and similarly with the other women.[23]

---

repute, who spent much of the 1220s and 1230s connected with the university of Paris, briefly acting as its chancellor 1237–8); Master Alzo, Bishop of Arras, 1231–45; Peter (of Doy?), Bishop of Thérouanne, dates uncertain, possibly 1229–51; Nicolas of Roie, Bishop of Noyon, 1228–40; Master Garnier, Bishop of Laon, 1238–49; Master Adam of Chambly, Bishop of Senlis, 1228–58; Robert of Cressonsacq, Bishop-elect (April 1237) of Beauvais (bishop 1237–48); Geoffrey *de Grandiprato*, Bishop-elect of Châlons-sur-Marne (date of election uncertain; bishop 1241–7); Master William of Bussy, Bishop of Orléans, 1238–58; Master Nicolas of Brie, Bishop of Troyes, 1233–69; Peter of Cuisy, Bishop of Meaux, 1223–55; Rudolphe of Thourotte, Bishop of Verdun, 1224–45; Robert of Thourotte, Bishop of Langres, 1232–45.

22 de Moranis: Morains, village in the Marne dpt. The point could be sarcasm about the gap between the grandeur of a title in the sect (here inflated from bishop to archbishop) and the tiny village that was its seat; suggested by J. Duvernoy, *La Religion des Cathares* (Toulouse, 1976; repr. 1989), p. 240 n.85. Since 'morina' meant wool or a fleece taken from a sheep that had died from disease, and came to mean the disease itself, or more broadly cattle disease as in English 'murrain', the title could also mean 'Archbishop of Murrains *or* Dead Sheep Fleeces', combining allusions to heretics as wolves in sheeps' clothing (Matthew 7.15) and to the trope of heresy as disease.

23 'I believe what Holy Church believes' was deceptive but literally true, meaning 'I believe what the woman we have named "Holy Church" believes': an early example of heretics' alleged use of double language, whose classic description is in Bernard Gui's 'Practice of inquisition', translated in WE, pp. 397–402, 408, 437–8.

There was also there a very famous old woman from Provins named Gisla, who was called 'Abbess',[24] whose death was deferred, because she promised Brother Robert she would still be revealing a very large number of the others. Urged on by Brother Robert, some other woman declared how she had been transported all the way to Milan on Good Friday, to serve the Bulgars at table, leaving behind next to her husband a demon transformed into the likeness of the same woman.

It is not now necessary to bring out and display the opinions and assertions of these heretics, who have their origin in the detestable Manichaeus, or what they do in secret, because <their actions> are foul and horrible, and when among other people they stink so much that shrewd people can identify them just from their stench. Brother Robert discovered moreover – and public opinion runs along with this – that the same most evil Manichaean Fortunatus,[25] whom blessed Augustine drove out of Africa, came at that time to these parts of Champagne and found the prince of thieves Wedomar hiding with his men on the same Wedomar's Mountain [Mont Wimer], and he converted him and his companions to his sect. And from that time on there was never a lack of the seed of that most evil Canaan (not that of Judah)[26] in the nearby hamlets around the same mountain.

24 For other documents concerning Gila (rather than Gisla) the Abbess, see Haskins, 'Robert le Bougre', 215–16, n.3.

25 Heretic with whom Augustine disputed in person in 392, and against whom he wrote a treatise.

26 'Cursed be Chanaan' (Genesis 9.25), contrasted with Judah, the fourth and most favoured of Jacob's sons.

7. ROBERT LEPETIT'S MAGIC CHARTER

Richer (c. 1190–1266) frequented schools at Strasbourg and entered the Black Monk [Benedictine] Abbey of Senones, in Lorraine, while it was ruled by Abbot Henry (1202–25). His travels included visits to Würzburg and St-Denis outside Paris, and he was active as a sculptor. Divided into five books, most of his chronicle was written after 1254/5, and it runs up to 1264. In the two chapters preceding the account of Robert, Richer has very hostile passages on the mendicant orders, dealing with the Dominicans in chapter 16 and then the Franciscans in chapter 17, where the concluding words signal a return to and extension of the theme of chapter 16. Chapter 18 is introduced, therefore, as a further contribution to the anti-Dominican dossier. The text is discussed in the introduction to *Texts and the Repression of Medieval Heresy*, ed. C. Bruschi and P. Biller (Woodbridge, 2003), pp. 9–12. Translated from *Chronicon*, iv.17–18, ed. G. Waitz, MGH Scriptores 25, pp. 307–8; Waitz provides an account of Richer and his chronicle, pp. 240–53. Waitz used a smaller font to indicate where Richer was copying an earlier text; he does this with chapter 18, but does not identify a particular source.

[17] ... But because the devil's envy incessantly sows tares in the field of the Lord [Matthew 13.25–40], let us return to those who under the pretext of religion – 'ravening wolves in the clothing of sheep' [Matthew 7.15] – have deceived people in an extraordinary way.

[18] *On Master Robert of Paris of the Order of Preachers, and his deceptions* There was thus in those days a man from Paris, of the highest learning and renowned in eloquence, called Robert, of the Order of Preachers, who had such charm that he was then held second to none. But, as it was reported, he was devoted to worldly glory and lust. By some art he had composed for himself a little charter [cartula], such that, when he placed this little charter on top of anyone's head, whether the person wanted to or not, he would confess whatever he [*Robert*] wished. When preaching one day he spotted a certain shapely woman, and he lusted after her in his heart, and ordered her to speak to him after the sermon. Coming to a certain secret place, she expected he wanted her to confess to him. He speaks to her. And in order to get her to do his will, he presses her with menacing and flattering words. What then? She says no. He urges, threatens. If she does not do this, he may put upon her the charge of heresy and have her burnt by

fire.[27] So, the next day, he made her come to him in the presence of all of the women, and, placing his hand upon her, in a loud voice asks, 'Are you not of the heretics' sect?' She said, 'Truly I am.' 'Do you wish to return to the Catholic faith?' She replied, however, 'No.' He said, 'Would you rather be burnt than deny that sect?' She replied, 'I would.' He said, 'Have you heard the way this woman has confessed her foulness?' They were amazed, in fact – they said they had never heard anything like it from her; and so she was put in custody. This same matron had a clerical son, a good-natured youth. Distressed by his mother's suffering, he went around neighbours and relatives, to get advice from them about whether there was any way to free his mother from the danger of death. Someone who was familiar with this Preacher,[28] sympathising greatly, said to him, 'Go tomorrow to the public consistory, because your mother will be examined again. Then, stand next to her. And when Master Robert has placed his hand on your mother and interrogates her about the faith, you – you are stronger than he is – must take a powerful grip of his hand, and remove the little charter you will find in it, and keep it to yourself; and, with a loud voice, ask Master Robert to question your mother again about the faith.' And that is the way it happened. And when that cleric had taken the said little charter text from that preacher's hand, the matron, questioned as before, swore in front of everyone that she had never heard those words, nor had she ever been interrogated by Robert, nor had she ever made any response to him about anything, nor had she ever heard what heresy was. Then the son showed the little charter to everyone, and that this same preacher was using diabolical art and trapping whoever he wanted with that little charter, and delivering them to death. Hearing this, then, the people tried to kill him; but he was seized by the clergy, put into a stone prison, and shut up for ever. And because he had used this art to have a father and a mother and many other innocents burnt, as though they were guilty, just in order to cast a veil over his own wickedness, God decreed the imposition of a punishment on him in this present life, so that while still alive he might by chance be converted from his wickedness.

27 This blackmail threat is discussed by J. W. Baldwin, *Masters, Princes and Merchants: The Social Views of Peter the Chanter and His Circle*, 2 vols (Princeton NJ, 1970), I, 321–2.

28 *Or* someone who was a member of this Preacher's household.

8. MATTHEW PARIS

In 1217 Matthew Paris (c. 1200–59) became a monk in St Albans, a monastery noted for its tradition of historical writing, and following the death of Roger of Wendover in 1236 he became and remained for the rest of his life its principal historiographer. He produced many works of history and hagiography, and was a cartographer and prolific illustrator. Since he knew, talked to and received documents from a very large number of people – King Henry III, Richard Earl of Cornwall, and countless noblemen, prelates and royal officials – he was part of a very large world of thought and news. He also often put a strong spin on the material he used, but a spin that is not reducible to one particular formula. His outlook included, however, a Benedicine monk's conservative reserve towards such new orders as those of the mendicant friars, which supplies a touch of glee to his account of the Dominican Robert's downfall (compare Richer of Senones, Doc. 7 above).

The letter translated below, addressed to the Archbishop of Bordeaux – potentially important evidence about the schools of Paris and Italian Cathars – needs to be set among the c. 350 documents Paris copied. Paris's occasional abbreviation or interpolation in his use of these texts – done especially where he held passionate views, in letters, for example, concerning pope or emperor, or taxation – mean that we must question this letter. There is, however, no obvious personal engagement in its topic. Its details, such as a papal legate in Bordeaux and the name of an Italian heretical bishop, lend verisimilitude; and the route leading from Bordeaux to St Albans via Southampton and the royal court in Winchester was a channel for much that came to Matthew.[29] See on Matthew, S. Lloyd and R. Reader, 'Paris, Matthew', *Oxford Dictionary of National Biography* (Oxford, 2004; online edition, 2010), S. Lewis, *The Art of Matthew Paris in the* Chronica Majora (Berkeley and Los Angeles, 1987), and B. Weiler 'Matthew Paris and the writing of history', *Journal of Medieval History* 35 (2009), 254–78. Translated from Matthew Paris, *Chronica Majora*, 7 vols, Rolls Series (London, 1876–83), III, 361, 520; IV, 226, 270–1; V, 195.

[1236] *About the heretical wickedness of the Paterines or Bugars*

Around this time, moreover, the heretical perversity of those who are commonly called Paterines and Bugars [Bugares] – of whose errors I would prefer to be silent than to speak – grew strong in the

29 See H.-E. Hilpert, *Kaiser- und Papstbriefe in den Chronica Majora des Matthaeus Paris* (Stuttgart, 1981), pp. 160–1.

transalpine region, to such an extent that they dared to disturb and violate the purity of the faith in the territories of France and Flanders. But through the diligent ministry and indefatigable preaching of the Minors [*Franciscans*] and Preachers [*Dominicans*] and theologians – and especially of Brother Robert of the Order of Preachers (who was surnamed 'Bugre' [*sic*], because converting from them he had donned the habit of the Preachers), who was called 'hammer of the heretics' – their supersition was brought to confusion and their error was detected. Furthermore, he had so many of both sexes, who refused to convert to the faith, burnt by fire that within two or three months he had about fifty burnt or buried alive.

[1238] *About a certain Preacher who was called Robert Bugre*
While the chariots of the days were wheeling on, a certain person of the Order of Preachers, called Robert, surnamed 'Bugre' – a properly literate man and effective and successful in the office of preaching – discovered many people in the kingdom of France stained by heretical depravity, most of all in Flanders, where the inhabitants are wont to be defamed of the sin of usury more than other nations. After diligently questioning all of them about faith, the same Robert had those who were vacillating or deviating condemned to the secular arm and, with the help of the King of France, burnt in the fires. Furthermore he called the same heretics by the name in the vernacular 'Bugars' [Bugaros], whether they were Patarenes or Jovinians,[30] or Albigenses, or stained with other heresies. For in fact this same Robert, before he took on the habit of religion [*of a religious order*] had been a Bugar, on account of which he knew all their accomplices: and he became their accuser, hammer and close enemy. In the end, abusing the power which had been given to him, passing the bounds of propriety and justice, and becoming puffed up, powerful and formidable, he confusedly implicated good people with bad ones, punishing the innocent and the simple. By papal authority, therefore, he was categorically ordered no longer to rage and strike like lightning in that office. And later on, with his guilty acts becoming ever clearer and more manifest – which I think it

30 Followers of Jovinian, late 4th- and early 5th-century heretic. Known through such guides as Isidore's *Etymologies* (bk 8, ch. 5) as maintaining that there was no difference in spiritual value between being married and staying a virgin, and between abstaining from food and eating moderately, 'Jovinian' was a convenient label for those opposed to monastic asceticism.

better to pass over in silence rather than to relate – he was condemned to perpetual imprisonment.[31]

[September 1242] *Financial aid is demanded from the church in France* There was therefore a convocation in Paris of the prelates of the universal Church constituted in the kingdom of France, archbishops, bishops, abbots, priors of the Black Monk, Cistercian and Premonstratensian orders, and procurators of cathedral chapters; from whom the King of France [*Louis IX*] demanded financial aid. And to avoid it seeming reasonable for him to endure a refusal, he presented the grounds, that is, to defeat the Albigensian heretics. For the king imputed to the Count of Toulouse the old slur of heresy, as proof of which he said that recently the count had wickedly slaughtered certain brothers Preacher.[32]

[1243] In these days this letter, sent to the Archbishop of Bordeaux, greatly terrified even the steadiest of men. On many points it confirmed the emperor's letter, that had been sent to many Christian kings, about the ghastly devastation wrought by that inhuman people whom they call Tartars – though in the letter they are named Tattars or Tatars.

To Gerald, by grace of God Archbishop of Bordeaux,[33] Yves, called 'of Narbonne', once the least of his clerics: greetings, and the strength to render account of the talents entrusted to him.[34]

… As you know, I was once accused of heretical wickedness by my rivals, in front of Robert of Courson, then legate of the Roman curia.[35] I declined judgment, not from scruple of conscience but blushing at the shamefulness of the matter, and through this I became more suspect. When therefore I had heard the threats of the man of authority, I fled from the face of the persecutor. Accordingly I was forced to travel around many provinces. To the Paterines who live in the city of Como I complained, and I told the story that sentences had been hurled against me and I was in exile, <saying this was> on account of their faith –

31 On his likely fate, see S. Tugwell, 'The downfall of Robert le Bougre, OP', in W. Hoyer, ed., *Praedicatores Inquisitores I: The Dominicans and the Medieval Inquisition* (Rome, 2004), 753–6.

32 Referring to the killing at Avignonet; see Doc. 46.

33 Gerald of Mallemort, Archbishop 1227–61.

34 See the parable of the talents, Matthew 25.14–30.

35 Robert convoked a council at Bordeaux in June 1214. On him, see J. W. Baldwin, *Masters, Princes and Merchants: The Social Views of Peter the Chanter and His Circle*, 2 vols (Princeton NJ, 1970), 1, 19–25.

though, as God is my witness, I had in fact never learnt or followed their faith! Hearing this they rejoiced and held me as a happy man, for having 'suffered persecution for justice's sake' [Matt. 5.10]. And there I was entertained for three months [splendidly and voluptuously],[36] and I kept quiet while I listened every day to the errors – rather, the horrors – which they asserted against the apostolic faith. Through their kindness to me they bound me to promise them that henceforth I would preach to all Christians with whom I could have deep discussion, persuading them that no-one could be saved in <the apostle> Peter's faith – and I would persist in teaching this doctrine. After I had promised, on my faith, to do this, they began to open up their secrets, revealing that they sent teachable students from almost all the cities in Lombardy and from some in Tuscany to Paris, some to devote themselves to logical sophistries,[37] others to theological discourses, in order to build up their own errors and to refute the profession of the apostolic faith. They also send many merchants to markets with this intent, to pervert rich laymen who are their companions at table and hosts and with whom they have the opportunity to chat informally – thereby engaging in a multiple trade, on the one hand getting the profit for themselves of other people's money, on the other hand gaining souls for Antichrist's treasury. When I sought permission to leave from these degenerate brothers they sent me to Milan, to be hosted by their fellows in faith. And thus I passed through all the cities of Lombardy on the Po, always living with the Paterines, always receiving credentials from them <to present> to the others. I came at last to Gemona, a very famous town in Friuli, where I drank the most noble wines of the Paterines, eating ravioli, *ceratia* [*perhaps seafood*] and other delicacies. I was deceiving the deceivers and professing myself a Paterine, but, as God is my witness, I was continuing to be a Christian, in faith though not in the perfection of my doings. I stayed three days at Gemona, having received permission from the confederates but cursing from a certain bishop of theirs, called Peter Gallus.[38] I was suspected by him. Later, I heard, he was deposed by them for some fornication. Then I journeyed on from there with some lay brother, entering the canals of

36 In margin, therefore perhaps Matthew's addition to the text.

37 This is consonant with what is stated by William of Auxerre writing in northern France (see Doc. 12) and by Moneta of Cremona in Lombardy. Both attribute to Cathars the use of axiomatic logic, of the sort that flourished in Paris, to support their theological propositions.

38 Attested in Italian evidence about Cathars: WE, pp. 167, 698 n.7; Borst, *Katharer*, p. 238 n.29 (Borst, *Cathares*, p. 202 n.10).

Aquileia, and then travelling further we stayed with some brothers in a town called Friesach. The following day I was left on my own by the brother, and I wandered on my own through Carinthia [Kärnten], and from there into a certain town in Austria which is called in German 'Neustadt', that is to say, 'New Town' [Wiener Neustadt], and I was given hospitality by some new religious who are called 'Beguines'. I lay in hiding for some years in the neighbouring city of Vienna and nearby places, mixing, alas, good things and bad things – at the instigation of the devil, living rather unchastely, acting as a harmful enemy to my own soul. However, I did recover many people from the aforesaid <Paterine> error. Because of this <heresy> and many other sins arising among us Christians, God has been angered, becoming a hostile devastator and a frightening avenger. [*The letter then proceeds to a description of Tartar [Mongol] devastations.*]

[1250] At the end of this year, twenty-five fifty year periods have now flowed since the Time of Grace, that is, 1250. It ought to be noted and not lightly passed over, that in none of the other twenty-four fifty-year periods did so many wonderful and extraordinary new things happen as in the last one, the twenty-fifth, the one that has just now finished.

[*There follows a long list of these notable events*]

… The heresies of the Albigensians, Jovinians and many Italians, which had sprouted up, were destroyed.

9. BERNARD GUI, *ON THE FOUNDATIONS AND PRIORS OF THE PREACHERS' CONVENTS IN THE PROVINCES OF TOULOUSE AND PROVENCE*[39]

Bernard Gui (1261/2–1332) entered the Dominican Order in 1280, and had a career of lectureships and priorates before serving as an inquisitor (1307–16 and 1319–23). He was also Dominican Procurator at Avignon (1316–20), and finally Bishop of Tuy (1323–4) and then Lodève. History predominates in his writings, though he preferred to call what he wrote 'chronography' rather than 'history'; see also the introductions to Docs 17 and 32. He began *On the Foundations* between 1294 and 1297, and had produced a first edition by December 1304; he then continued adding and editing until 1316.[40] In 1303, the Dominican convents in southern France were divided into two provinces, that of Toulouse and Provence (previously 'Provence' had covered the entire area). Thus Gui divides his work into two parts, one on each province, each listing convents in the chronological order of foundation. In most cases, a convent's entry contains an account of its foundation, and a list of priors and their dates. Gui was a scholar and researcher, indefatigably looking for sources, whether written (including books in the inquisition archive) or oral (especially early Dominicans). At one level, his work acts as a resource on such topics as the chronology of the spread of Dominican convents in the south, the office of inquisitor, the careers of able Dominican administrators and most of all the popular and violent anti-inquisition movements of the years around 1300 in Albi and Carcassonne. At another level, one can analyse his scholarly methods, for example by comparing his account of events in Toulouse in the 1230s with one of his sources, William of Pelhisson's chronicle.[41] We have selected for translation his accounts of these movements, and his notices of those priors who were also inquisitors. Gui's various comments on these men – ranging from brief hagiography to stony silence in the case of the disgraced inquisitor Fulk of St-Georges (on whom see Doc. 57) – cast light on his own views and how he constructed a view of his order's history. Christine Caldwell Ames, *Righteous Persecution: Inquisition, Dominicans and Christianity in the Middle Ages* (Philadelphia, 2009), pp. 65, 80–1, 88, 90 comments on his hagiography of Bernard of Caux. There is an analysis of his account of troubles in Albi and Carcassonne in Y. Dossat, 'Les priorats

39 The title is modern.

40 See the 'Introduction' to the edn used here, pp. v–xvi.

41 Translated in Wakefield, *Heresy*, pp. 206–36.

de Bernard Gui', *CdF* 16 (1981), pp. 98–103 (the whole of this issue of *CdF* is devoted to Gui). There is a general account of Gui as historian in A.-M. Lamarrigue, *Bernard Gui (1261–1331): Un historien et sa méthode* (Paris, 2000), and of Gui's career overall in B. Guenée, *Between Church and State: The Lives of Four Prelates in the Late Middle Ages*, trans. A. Goldhammer (Chicago and London, 1987), pp. 37–70.

We have inserted numbers for each section, for ease of cross-reference. Translated from Bernard Gui, *De fundatione et prioribus conventuum provinciarum Tolosanae et Provinciae Ordinis Praedicatorum*, ed. Paul Amargier, Monumenta Ordinis Fratrum Praedicatorum Historica 24 (Rome, 1961), pp. 7, 43, 49, 58, 70, 77, 84, 90, 97, 100, 101, 102–5, 109–111, 122, 154, 173, 198–205, 210, 247, 249, 251, 253, 256, 260, 275.

[1] The foundation of the monastery of Prouille

AD 1206 Blessed Dominic … founded a certain monastery that is called Prouille, situated between Fanjeaux and Montréal in the diocese of Toulouse, for the reception of certain noble women. At that time there were many heretics inhabiting these parts and neighbouring places, and by reason of poverty and driven by need, the parents of these girls were handing them over to be brought up and taught by them – or rather, in truth, to be deluded by their errors and destroyed in their souls. Enough can be learnt and gathered about the date and the reason for the foundation from the booklet of the reverend father Jordan of Saxony, Master of the Order, which he produced, entitling it *On the Beginnings of the Order of Preachers*.[42]

[2] … On the foundation of the Toulousan convent

Around the beginning of the time when bishops set off for Rome for the <Fourth> Lateran Council, … two worthy and suitable men of Toulouse offered themselves to St Dominic. One was Brother Peter Seila, later the first Prior of Limoges, the other in fact Brother Thomas, a very charming and articulate man. The first of these was in possession of grand and conspicuous houses in Toulouse around the Château Narbonnais, and he offered and gave these to St Dominic

42 Jordan of Saxony, *On the Beginnings of the Order of Preachers*, trans. S. Tugwell (Oak Park IL, 1982).

and his companions. They first lived together in Toulouse, from this time on, in these houses … Later the inquisitors of heretics inhabited these houses.

[3] … Priors in the Toulousan convent

… Brother Pons of St-Gilles <was prior> twice … He was prior AD 1233, when St Dominic was canonised. Item, he was prior at that time when the brothers Preacher of Toulouse were expelled, by public edict of the prince and the consuls, AD 1235, 5 or 6 November. In the stated year and on 5 November, Peter of Toulouse, the *viguier* of Raymond Count of Toulouse, acting on the command of the count himself, together with the then consuls of Toulouse … threw out of Toulouse Brother William Arnold of the Order of Preachers, by apostolic authority the deputed inquisitor of heretical wickedness.[43] <They did this> because the same <William Arnold> had summoned some believers of heretics <to appear> before him in Toulouse, and because he was exercising the office of inquisition against heretics in Toulouse. Consequently the aforesaid inquisitor, expelled from Toulouse, went off to Carcassonne. And from there he summoned and peremptorily excommunicated all the aforesaid men, as supporters and defenders of heretics, in a sentence delivered on 10 November, as I found more fully contained in a book of inquisition.

In those bad days the inquisitor mentioned above had cited some believers of heretics – through the Prior of St-Stephen, namely, Vital Auriol and William Vaquier, and through parish chaplains – to appear on a certain day in front of him at Carcassonne, to answer about faith. They did not want to appear. And on account of this, the consuls violently ejected all the summoners from the city of Toulouse, threatening that if anyone issued a further summons, he would not be thrown out, but rather he would be killed, whoever he might be. Then the said inquisitor summoned them peremptorily through brothers of the Order of Preachers, namely Raymond of Foix, Gui of Navarre of Limoges, John of St-Michel, <and> William Pelhisson. The said consuls and *viguier* had proclaimed through the town, by herald, that on pain of their goods and bodies no-one should have any trade with the brothers, nor sell nor give them anything. And guards were placed at all the doors

43 Gui bases the following narrative on the chronicle of William Pelhisson.

of the brothers' house, both night and day, for almost three weeks, to prevent any food being carried in, nor did anyone even dare to bring in any water from the Garonne. However, many faithful people who were sorry <about this> and sympathised <with the brothers>, gave them more goods than they were used to, doing this secretly through the garden, throwing loaves and cheeses over the walls, for fear of the heretics' believers. Learning this, the said consuls ejected all the brothers from their house and from the town of Toulouse, dragging them along in public with a great crowd. In truth, amidst the perpetrators of this great insolence, there were a few who showed some restraint. All the brothers confessed, offered themselves as prepared to undergo martyrdom for the faith and obedience of the Roman Church, and were now eagerly awaiting this; and then by the prince's order they were all compelled to leave the city. 'And they went', therefore, from the presence of the council, 'rejoicing that they were worthy to suffer reproach for the faith of Christ' [Acts 5.41]. So they went out in procession, two by two, devoutly singing 'I believe in one God', and then 'Hail holy Queen' [Salve Regina]. This happened, as was stated above, AD 1235, on 5 November, or the following day, that is to say 6 November.

Brother Peter Seila succeeded the aforesaid Brother Pons, AD 1235. Also, as I found in a book of the Toulouse inquisition, 5 June 1237 <is a date when> he was also prior.

Brother William Arnold of Montpellier was prior for a while, but I have not found in what year or for how long. Later on, when an inquisitor, this man became a martyr on the vigil of the Ascension of the Lord, AD 1242.[44]

... Brother William Bernard of Dax, from the <designated> preaching <area> of Bayonne, succeeded Brother Stephen of Salagnac. He was a man of sense and a person worthy of respect. He was in charge for about two years, and then released at the general chapter of Montpellier, AD 1265. He was the Toulouse inquisitor of heretical wickedness. He was Prior of Bordeaux when he died at Bordeaux, AD 1268.

... Brother Peter Rey of Fanjeaux succeeded the aforesaid Brother Danes [1267]. From being Prior of Prouille he became Prior of Toulouse. He was in charge for six years, and was then released at the provincial chapter of Cahors, AD 1273. He was Inquisitor of Carcassonne. Serving God for a long time in good old age, he eventually died at Prouille, 11

44 On the murder of this inquisitor, see further Doc. 46.

August 1299, 55 years after his entry into the order, and he lies there at the entrance to the major church together with his father, who was our brother at his end.

... Brother Hugh Amiel of Castelnaudary succeeded Brother William of Puy [1276]. He was in charge for about two years. From being Prior of Toulouse he became inquisitor, AD 1278. He was a just man, upright and resolute, and much talked about. He was inquisitor and set upon a journey to Rome when he died in the convent at Nice, AD 1281. Later his bones were brought from the Nice convent to the Toulouse convent.

... Brother Arnold of Prat, from the preaching area of Condom, succeeded Brother Bernard of Jusix [1298]. During his priorate that part of the new dormitory was built that sticks out from the south side northwards, that is, one arm of a cross from the scholars' bit. He was in charge for a year, was then released at the provincial chapter of Perpignan, AD 1299. He was the Toulouse lecturer for fourteen years, and in Toulouse and Montpellier and many other convents he acted as lecturer in theology for over thirty years. He was a very good writer and maker-up of songs. He wrote and composed, elegantly, the night and day ecclesiastical Office of King Louis.[45] ... He became Toulouse inquisitor of heretical wickedness, AD 1304, at the beginning of the month of March. While inquisitor and when near Bordeaux – where he was then living at the curia, by reason and cause of the highest pontiff and lord pope, Clement V, who knew him and very much liked him – he died at Cadillac. This was on Friday on the feast of the blessed virgin Euphemia, 16 September AD 1306, fifty-one years from his entry into the order. He was carried from there to Condom and buried in the church of the brothers.

[4] ... Priors in the convent of Limoges

The first prior in the convent of the brothers Preacher at Limoges was the aforesaid Brother Peter Seila, who was, after the blessed Dominic, the first brother of the Order of Preachers, as I found noted by the old man Brother Stephen of Salagnac, who professed there in his hands. On the one hand the blessed Dominic received this Brother Peter Seila

45 The *Ludovicus Decus Regnantium*, rhymed liturgical office for the feast-day of St Louis. See M. C. Gaposchkin, *The Making of Saint Louis* (Ithaca, 2008), particularly pp. 78–9.

into the order as companion and brother, on the other hand Peter gave shelter to the blessed Dominic and all that there was then. In fact, he started the Order of Preachers with himself, in his own house at Toulouse, which is where in the beginning the brothers lived. … This Brother Peter gave the holy habit to many. And he spent his years in the land among the clergy and people like one of the ancient prophets, revered and honoured: most highly esteemed, resolute and straight. He was Prior of Limoges for thirteen years. Towards the end of his days he returned to his place of origin, Toulouse. It was there in 1233 that, together with that most resolute man, Brother William Arnold, he was deputed to carry out the office of inquisition against heretical wickedness in Toulousan parts and throughout the Count of Toulouse's land, as is contained and can be read in the chronicle of Master William of Puylaurens. Eventually and after much good work, he closed his last day in the convent at Toulouse, holy in the Lord – then to receive the fruit of rest and eternal peace from the Lord – on 22 February; from what I have heard, I conjecture the year was 1257.

… I, Brother Bernard Gui, succeeded Brother Stephen Laurel, as nineteenth prior – but the least of all of them – and was confirmed as such on the vigil of blessed Bartholomew the Apostle, at Bordeaux, AD 1305.

At the following Easter, AD 1306, on the feast of blessed George the Martyr, which was a Saturday, the lord pope, Clement V, came to Limoges with eight cardinals, and without deviating came straight to the house of the brothers Preacher to stay there. … The following day, which was a Sunday – dominical letter B[46] – after first visiting the body of St Martial and blessing the people who gathered in St-Gerald Square, the same pope left for Solesmes, wending his way to Bordeaux.

… I was prior for a year and a half. I was released, however, by letter of the Master of the Order, and made Toulouse inquisitor by letter of the prior provincial of France, after receiving letters from both at Limoges on the feast of the blessed Marcellus, pope, 16 January 1307.

[5] … Foundation of the convent of Bayonne

… The convent of the brothers Preacher in Bayonne began to be founded AD 1221 or 1222.

46 Reference to liturgical pattern of the year.

… the aforesaid Brother William Bernard of Dax was prior another time, AD 1257, in the month of May, and then he became inquisitor of heretical wickedness and consequently was absolved from the priorate.

[6] … Foundation of the convent of Cahors, AD 1226

In AD 1244, on the feast of St John the Baptist, Brother Pons was prior and Brother Luke was sub-prior – I found them named thus in a book of the Toulouse inquisition.

[7] … Foundation of the convent of Bordeaux. A little before AD 1230 …

Brother John of St-Pierre of Bordeaux succeeded Brother [*blank in text*]. In AD 1255 he was the Toulouse inquisitor of heretics.[47] He died at Bordeaux.

Brother William Raymond of Peyrecouverte, of Bordeaux, succeeded Brother [*blank in text*] and he was released at the provincial chapter of Toulouse, AD 1254. He was the Toulouse inquisitor of heretics. While Prior of Narbonne he died in the convent at Bordeaux, AD 1261 or 1262.

[8] … Foundation of the convent at Périgueux

As far as I have been able to gather, especially from things heard about the primitive time from one older brother, in AD 1241 or thereabouts brothers Preacher came to the city of Périgueux to receive a place and house to live in.

… Priors in the convent of Périgueux.

…The aforesaid Brother William of Montreveil, prior for a second time, succeeded Brother Raymond Faure. He was prior in 1256. Brother Bernard of Clermont, who recounted the particulars to me, entered under him. He [*William of Montreveil*] was released this time at the provincial chapter of Toulouse, after the general council held in

47 Not the same as the more famous inquisitor of the same name who acted together with Bernard of Caux in the Lauragais, 1245–6.

the same place, AD 1258. He was inquisitor of heretics. He died in the year [*blank in text*].

[9] Foundation of the convent of Carcassonne

In the month of September AD 1247, St Louis, the most pious king of the French, ordered his seneschal in Carcassonne, by royal letter, to assign to the brothers Preacher a plot in the New Bourg of Carcassonne, on which they could build for themselves a suitable residence.

… The first prior in the convent of the brothers Preacher of Carcassonne was Brother Ferrier, by nation a Catalan, who came from Villelongue near Perpignan. He was instituted at the provincial chapter at Montpellier, AD 1252. He was in charge for half a year, and translated thence within the year to the priorate of Béziers. He was an inquisitor and a resolute and magnanimous persecutor of heretics, with an iron rod hammering and beating them together with their supporters and believers, to such an extent that even today his name resonates like a sword in the ears of the hereticals.[48] He died and is at rest in Perpignan, so I have heard it said.

The eighth prior was Brother Hugh Amiel of Castelnaudary. Succeeding Brother Raymond Sicre [1270], he was prior for two years and released at the provincial chapter of Narbonne, AD 1272. He had been Prior of Montauban and Agen, and was later Prior of Toulouse and a famous and good inquisitor of heretics [from 1278]. While inquisitor and travelling to Rome he died in the convent of Nice in Provence, AD 1281, whence his bones were translated to the convent of Toulouse.

The ninth prior was Brother Peter Arsieu, from the castle called 'Malvezie' in the diocese of Toulouse. He succeeded Brother Hugh Amiel, was prior for five years, and was then released from this and made Inquisitor of Toulouse on the Monday after the feast of St James, AD 1277, and he died while inquisitor on the first day of August AD 1278.

The aforesaid [*mentioned earlier as fifth prior*] Brother Peter Rey was prior for a second time, succeeding the aforesaid Brother Peter Arsieu. This time he was prior for ten years, and was released at the provincial

48 *Hereticales* – a word not in common usage as a noun, used in this treatise to indicate people living around 1300 who were not themselves heretics, but deserving in Gui's eyes to be tainted with some degree of heresy through ancestry, sympathy or opposition to inquisition.

chapter of Bergerac, AD 1286. He was Prior of Prouille and Toulouse and inquisitor of heretics at Carcassonne. At last he died in good old age at Prouille, 11 August AD 1299, fifty-five years after his entry into the order.

... For the sake of later people we should note here, in passing, what happened during the priorate of Brother Odon, AD 1295. William Garric and William Brunet, professors of law of Carcassonne, and several others had earlier confessed to and been convicted of heresy. Rising up with their accomplices against the office of inquisition and against the brothers, and with effrontery and defiance, they rebelled against them and stirred up a great sedition among the people. And they brought many evils upon the office of inquisition and the brothers and their friends, and 'evils were multiplied in the earth' [Maccabees 1.10] by them, and many were added to them. It is not easy nor right to write about each of these evils. Their end was confusion and ignominy and the sentence of condemnation to the Wall,[49] as justice demanded.

I, Brother Bernard Gui of the diocese of Limoges – the fifteenth prior by name, though behind all the earlier ones in merit and virtue – succeeded the aforementioned brother and father Odon of Caussens. I was translated from the priorate of Albi, where I was then in my fourth year, to the priorate of Carcassonne, and confirmed on the Sunday after the feast of St Denis, AD 1297, in the monastery of Prouille. I served at Carcassonne for four years, from which pain[50] – if only it were from guilt! – I was released at the provincial chapter of Agen, celebrated on the feast of blessed Mary Magdalene [22 July], the decision being confirmed on the feasts of the saints and martyrs Felix and Adauctus [30 August], AD 1301. I collected and wrote the things stated above.

For the sake of later people we should note here, in passing, that the aforesaid frenzy [rabies] of Carcassonne was still raging savagely, even during my time. The evil things which they were doing and bringing to bear upon the inquisition and the brothers and their friends – I think it better to be reticent about these rather than write them down, one by one, out of respect to the population <of Carcassonne>. This could not be entirely excused, though there were some there who did not consent to the acts of the evildoers against the brothers. These frequently mocked and dishonoured the brothers with words

49 Term used in Languedoc for inquisitors' prison.

50 Penitential language is used here to clothe a commonplace about the burden of office.

and signs, and now and then with blows. And they brought it about that these brothers were outsiders, cut off from communion and participation with them, as though they were excommunicated. It would be shameful to say the other things <they did>. At last, after it was decided in both courts – the court of Rome and the court <of the King> of France – and after the expenditure of a lot of money and treasure, they came to the obedience of the inquisitor Brother Nicholas of Abbeville. On the day assigned for this the community [universitas][51] of Carcassonne was gathered together by public crier in front of the same inquisitor, at a public declaration in the cloister of the brothers Preacher of Carcassonne, in the presence of the seneschal, together with the royal court and landowners. There they admitted their guilt and begged to be absolved and reconciled by the inquisitor. And they obtained this, taking an oath there in public, each of them raising a book of the Gospels in his hands, and they were condemned by the inquisitor to build a chapel in honour of St Louis in the convent of the brothers Preacher of Carcassonne. This was done AD 1299, in the month of October. In fact the chapel was constructed in the following year, 1300, and the town of Carcassonne paid 900 Tours pounds for its building and decoration.

The sixteenth prior, who succeeded me – though he came before me in age, grace and wisdom – was Brother Bertrand of Clermont, of the diocese of Périgueux, from the preaching area of Bergerac. Though he wished for peace and quiet, he was put to labour in the priorate of Carcassonne, confirmed around Michaelmas, AD 1301. He was in charge there for around three years, and while Prior of Carcassonne he was elected Prior Provincial of the province of Toulouse at the provincial chapter of Toulouse, immediately after the general chapter, and was confirmed there by the master of the Order, 26 May 1303. He had been lecturer in many convents for many years, and Prior of Bergerac for many years, and of Narbonne just for a few days, because he was taken from this and made Inquisitor of Toulouse for eight years.

For the sake of later people we should note here, in passing, what happened during his priorate [1301–4] with the frenzy of Carcassonne. As was touched upon above, this had formerly and for a long time raged savagely against the office of inquisition and against the brothers, and now seemed and was believed to be extinct or at least dormant. It was roused up again under John of Picquigny, Vidame of Amiens. The

51 The 'universitas' of a city or town elected its consuls and councillors.

people of Albi and Cordes leagued together in evil with the people of Carcassonne, Brother Bernard Délicieux of the Order of Brothers Minor was the incendiarist of the evils, and Hélie Patrice of Carcassonne – who seemed to be the little king of Carcassonne and a traitor to the true king – was the general and standard-bearer of this evil army that was drawn up against the brothers and the office of inquisition. The pride of these people rose and their wickedness raged to such an extent that the hereticals and their accomplices inflicted many injuries with words and blows on the brothers Preacher, on their persons and things, and harmed them a lot. And out of hatred of the inquisition and the brothers they wrecked and publicly plundered the houses and dwelling places of many men from the Bourg of Carcassonne – up to fifteen of them – who they believed were attached to them. During the day, on the feast of St Lawrence, on Sunday AD 1303, united in a mob they rushed around, shouting 'At the blacked-up [mascaratos] traitors!'.[52] In the long run, with an avenging God, they did not go unpunished.

… To preserve lasting recollection of the affair, we should note here the revelation in AD 1305 of the treachery and the wickedness of traitors from Carcassonne against the King of France. Involved in this, accessory to it and a negotiator in it was Brother Bernard Délicieux of the Order of Friars Minor: also Hélie Patrice, Aimeric Castel and many others from Carcassonne and Limoux. And when machination in treachery had been detected and the truth discovered by the court's inquisition, many traitors were arrested in the midst of their evils, on the vigil of the St Bartholomew the Apostle [23 August]. And the said Hélie Patrice and fourteen other traitors were dragged together through the town and then, facing the sun, as justice required they were hanged from gallows that had been erected recently and with solemnity beside the public thoroughfare, on the vigil of St Michael [28 September], AD 1305. Many other similarly guilty people would have been condemned to a similar penalty had it not been for the clemency and compassion of the lord pope, Clement V, intervening with the king. Taking advantage of flight, Aimeric Castel escaped, but he was caught at Pierre-Buffière in the diocese of Limoges and held for a long time in the king's prison, and was rescued from the punishment of death through the intercession of many people and a lot of money. With the intervention of the pope the pious King Philip spared a multitude of people from death and exile – but not from fines. On this account

52 From *mascarare*, 'to smear black stuff on oneself'.

the community of Carcassonne was deprived of its consulate [= *ruling body*] and condemned to pay an enormous amount of money.[53]

[10] Foundation of the convent of Agen

AD 1252, in the acts of the provincial council of Montpellier, a convent of the brothers of the Order of Preachers was formally sited in Agen and recognised.

… Brother Bernard of Caux, inquisitor and persecutor and hammer of heretics, a holy man and filled with God, was the principal founder and promoter of the convent of Agen during his life, and he dedicated himself to the place in his body. More than twenty-seven years later, when it was raised up from the earth and translated into the church where it now lies, it was found to be entirely intact; by the divine favour of special grace preserved for such a long time. The events and order and time of this translation are more fully contained in the following letter, written by one who was present there and saw each thing in sequence. Its tenor is this:

> To father Brother N., dearest to him in Christ, Brother N. sends a plenitude of sincere love, and greetings. The pious zeal you have for the order and that love which you have had up to now for the convent at Agen and the old, lasting, inviolable and still persisting friendship between us – all these impel me to inform you, as a favour but in brief style, about the translation of the reverend fathers Brother Bernard of Caux, Brother Bertrand of Belcastel and Brother Arnold Belengar. So, on the day after the feast of blessed Mark the evangelist, AD 1281, Brother Raymond Christian and Brother Nicholas of Fiefs, who had now for a long time desired to be present at the august translation, with special devotion gave capable care to exhumation and translation of the holy men. And when they had uncovered the body of Brother Bertrand of Belcastel, they found the whole body consumed, apart only for the bones, and likewise the body of the said Arnold Belengar. However, the body of the reverend and most holy father, Brother Bernard of Caux, which they exhumed last, they found intact, completely without any smell of foulness. And this stupendous fact, this remarkable miracle, we rightly ascribe to divine providence and power …
>
> The face was whole, except that the nose at its tip was very slightly diminished; the forehead, chin, mouth and teeth remained sound. The head was attached via the neck to the body, with no discontinuity. The neck was so thick and the throat under the chin also so prominent, that they did not seem to have suffered any diminution since the day he was buried.

53 On these events, see further below, and see Doc. 57.

Wonderful intactness had preserved the chest, arms, hands, stomach and flanks. In accordance with the position of parts, the skin miraculously and throughout covered all the aforesaid – thus the nails and creases appeared just as distinctly on the skin of his hands as they appeared on him on that very day when he had been handed over to ecclesiastical burial. But what is no less remarkable is that the virile <organs> were entirely intact, according to what was said by those who took a look at these out of curiosity. One foot, however, was found to be apart from the tibia; and this, it seemed, happened because of the shortness of the coffin.

Thus the omnipotent God … has wanted to bring his wonder in his saints, not only in ancient times to extirpate errors from the hearts of the faithful and plant faith in their minds, but also in our times to raise up the hope of those who are making headway, to strengthen the Catholic faith, and to commend evangelical and apostolic doctrine. In this holy man who was wonderful in his life, wonderful in teaching and wonderful in extirpating heretical wickedness, he ordained a wonder to appear after his happy death, in that He so wonderfully and powerfully preserved his body intact, free from the common reduction of bodies to dust.

[11] Foundation and priors of the convent of Montauban

In AD 1251 or 1252, brothers Preacher first came to stay at Montauban, in the diocese of Cahors, and they chose a place for themselves by Tescou, in that part which belongs to the diocese of Toulouse.

[12] Foundation of the convent of Castres[54]

As the eighteenth prior I, Bernard Gui of the diocese of Limoges, succeeded the aforesaid Brother Pons of Quercy, and was confirmed as prior on the morning after the feast of the Assumption of the Blessed Mary ever Virgin, AD 1301. … I served for virtually four years and was released at the provincial chapter of Limoges, celebrated on the feast of blessed Mary Magdalen, AD 1305.

[13] Foundation of the convent of Condom[55]

…

54 Exploration [of the suitability of the location] and formal confirmation, 1258.

55 Exploration 1261, formal confirmation 1263.

[14] Foundation of the convent of Brive[56]

...

[15] Foundation of the convent of Bergerac[57]

The aforesaid Bertrand of Clermont, the third time, succeeded Brother Ermengaud Leutier [1285]. This time he was prior for seven years, and was released at the provincial chapter of Brive, AD 1292, and a little later was elected and confirmed as Prior of Puy, and thence elected and confirmed as Prior of Narbonne, and thence became the Toulouse inquisitor. All these things happened within half a year, that is to say entirely between the feast of the Assumption of the Blessed Mary and the following Lent, in the above-mentioned year, AD 1292. He died in good old age at the convent of Bergerac, 5 November, on a Sunday with the octave of All Saints, AD 1312, fifty-six years in fact after his entry into the order.

[16] Foundation of the convent of Albi[58]

The sixth prior, Brother William Bernard of Gaillac, succeeded Brother Raymond Bletgier [1292]. During the time of his priorate the church of the brothers was founded, AD 1293 ... The reverend father lord Bernard of Castanet, Bishop of Albi ... laid the first stone. ... The bishop did not then offer anything, but later on he gave for the works of the church a part of all the goods that belonged to him, confiscated from two citizens of Albi, who had been sentenced and condemned for the crime of heresy and were now dead, to the value of 1000 Tours pounds, and more.

... I, Brother Bernard Gui of the diocese of Limoges, succeeded the aforesaid Brother William Bernard, the seventh prior and the least of all of them. I was confirmed as prior on the morning after the feast of blessed Mary Magdalen, AD 1294. During this time the great bell of the church was made and the brick wall of the garden <was> partly

56 Exploration 1261, formal confirmation 1262.

57 Exploration around 1260, formal confirmation 1262.

58 Exploration 1275, formal recognition 1276.

ditched. I had been there with the post of lecturer for the two previous years, and was there with the title of prior for three years, and then in the fourth year was translated to the priorate of Carcassonne, confirmed as prior on the Saturday after the feast of St Denis, AD 1297 – I who have gathered together and written the things stated above [*referring to description of dedication of the brothers' church*].

... The tenth prior, Fulk of St-Georges, succeeded Brother Bon Mancip [1299]. ... Many in Albi were condemned by the bishop and the inquisitors for the crime of heresy, up to twenty-five. He was prior for a year and three months, and while prior was made Toulouse inquisitor around Michaelmas, AD 1300. He was released from the priorate of Albi after the following Christmas in Toulouse. He died at Carcassonne on the Wednesday within the octave of Epiphany, 10 January AD 1307. [*see his entry below, under Rodez*]

... As we pass on, we should note here for the sake of people now and later – in order that they might not shrink from bad things – what happened during these years and times. Many hereticals or people of heretical descent from Albi and Cordes rose up, confederated with the people of Carcassonne in evil. They joined together as one body against the office of inquisition, and against inquisitors of heretical wickedness, and also against Bernard of Castanet, lord Bishop of Albi. Their cause and reason was that the inquisitors and the bishop had condemned some people for Albi and Cordes and some other places in the diocese of Albi for the crime of heresy, which they had confessed and for which they had been convicted. They calumniated and impugned in many ways these sentences and their judgment, placing many difficulties and obstacles in the way of further proceedings against some other people from the said places, who remained and were accused and were vehemently suspected of heresy, doing their utmost to taint and defame the processes[59] of the inquisitors and the bishop. And with many false suggestions and slanders they incited the whole country against these inquisitors and the bishop. And through towns and castles they published some false rolls drawn up in the name of the inquisitors and the bishop. An incredible and unheard of number of names of innocent and harmless people, living and dead, was said to be contained in these rolls – <and this was done and said> in order to arouse lots of people's hearts to anger. And they made a great sedition among the people, and under the pretence of piety they

59 Processes: proceedings, or records of proceedings.

strove to rouse up to anger the lord King of France and the Queen and the whole of the King's Council and his court, alleging the wickedness of the inquisitors and the bishops and their processes, in fact justifying those who had been condemned and asserting that they were Catholics. But 'iniquity hath lied to itself' [Psalm 26.12], and in the end truth did not fail.

They brought it about that the Picard knight John of Picquigny – Vidame of Amiens – and the Norman Richard Leneveu – Archdeacon of Auge in the diocese of Lisieux – were sent to these parts by Philip, the lord King of France, with royal power. In their letters they [*i.e. John and Richard*] called themselves 'reformers of the country', and under them 'evils were multiplied in the earth' [Macc. 1.10] against the office of inquisition and inquisitors and the bishop. And many people were added to them and became their support in malice and wickedness. And from this time on they began to raise up their heretical horns and act more savagely and rage even more. And under them the office of inquisition was disrupted and blocked, and some inquisitors' officials were captured at the command of the Vidame, and inquisitors' prisons were invaded by him. In the areas of Albi and Carcassonne, and even Toulouse, all sorts of threats and lots of menaces were directed – and very often – at the inquisitors and their officials and their friends and the Bishop of Albi. They shouted after them, 'At the traitors! At the traitors!' The hereticals brought it about that the temporal goods of the bishop were seized, and his tithes were usurped by some people who called themselves nobles.

And when the aforementioned bishop, who had gone for this reason to Toulouse, was returning to his see of Albi, and was getting near the city, a crowd of men and women came out from the city, united and bound together in evil, and shouted against him, 'Death! Death! Let the traitor die, let him die!' He was set upon by them and drenched with disgraceful words and abuse. Acting in contrast to them and like a good shepherd, he gave them episcopal benediction. Following the example of the Saviour, 'who, when he was reviled, did not revile, when he suffered, threatened not' [1 Peter 2 .23], he patiently and steadily put up with all these things, not looking later on for any revenge or retribution. Rather, pitying them in their error and mercifully feeling compassion in his mind, he was lenient with them, knowing that 'Blessed are they that suffer persecution for justice's sake' [Matt. 5.10]. Earlier he had used very good words to instil the armour of patience in those who were in his company. And he had forbidden them – under pain of loss of his love and anathema – from defending him with the force of arms, in this eventuality, or from retaliation or from bringing force to bear in any way on anyone. Rather when they saw him being killed or slaughtered, they should cry out to God, 'Thee, o God, we praise!', asserting that he was willing to die for the justice of the faith which he had done and held. And he had made all his squires lay down their swords and weapons in front of him before the entrance to the city. On this side joy to see, on this side lamentation. And this took place on 11 February AD 1301.

Among these evils they contrived for the same reason to persecute their enemies and the brothers Preacher everywhere, and to molest them and to assail them with abuse and injuries and to defame them publicly and to block up the word of the Lord in their mouths. This reached such a pitch that brothers Preacher in that city of Albi, who on one Sunday – it was the first in Advent in AD 1302 – had gone to the churches of St-Salvi and Ste-Marciane and elsewhere to preach the word of God, were shamefully and publicly thrown out from the churches and places where they were preparing themselves to put over the word of God, taken off and sent away. One of them – Brother Dominic Leutier – was in the very act of preaching when he was violently dragged and driven and thrown out of a church in the Castelviel. Leaving the order was suggested to his novice companion by evil people, complete strangers to him. But this generated strength of spirit in him. Not only did he not consent to Satan's ministers but in fact he manfully repelled and confounded them; and through this he became more resolute in the order. And there was an outcry after them: 'At the traitors, at the traitors! Let them die, let them die!' Accompanied thus by insults and abuse, they were only just allowed to make their way back to the convent. And from this time on for about five or six years they were not allowed to preach the word of God in the churches, nor did the brothers dare to go about the city, for they would hear cursing and abuse against them. The people of Albi took away all alms from the brothers Preacher, and burials and other benefactions and pious offerings and charitable aids, and they would not come to the brothers' church even to see the body of the Lord.

In addition to these things and making an even greater and more notorious accumulation of madness and for the cause of their perfidy that they were defending, they had destroyed, sacrilegiously, the images and names of St Dominic the Confessor and St Peter Martyr that were beside the image of the crucifix at the gate of the city of Albi that is by <the convent of> the brothers. And there, instead of the saints, they had images of the aforesaid mortal sinners, the Vidame and the Archdeacon, depicted, with their names inscribed above, and two sinful lawyers either side of them, that is to say Peter Pros of Castres and Arnold Garsia of Albi. In this deed they showed their madness to the eyes of all onlookers, rejecting saints of God, approved by the Church, and approving and authenticating stupid and devious sinners. But in the long run truth did not allow false images and writing to remain, for after some years they were removed and rubbed out and the authority and judgment of equity compelled the restoration of the images of the saints whose names are indelibly inscribed in the book of life. They also often attacked the brothers' convent, entering and ruining the gardens, and they brought upon the brothers a lot of distress and damage and afflicted them with abuse, all of which would take a long time to describe item by item: it is recorded more fully elsewhere. But in need as the brothers were, and hemmed in and afflicted, they bore everything in a calm spirit with a great deal of patience – which indeed they needed. Nor did they lack Him who cannot fail, God, 'a helper in due time in tribulation' [Ps. 9.10]: the tribulation which bore down upon them so much.

Among the movers, inciters, co-operators and accomplices in these aforesaid evils, the prominent and larger figures in public were Arnold Garsia, the jurist John Donadieu, Raymond Baudier the younger, citizens of Albi; the jurist and at that time judge of Albi, Galhard Stephen of Cordes; William of Pezens, inhabitant of Montgiscard and *viguier* of Albi; and Peter Nicholay, the sub-*viguier*. These last three could have and should have restrained things, but they inflamed them further; the office of inquisition came under heavy attack from those who were bound by tenure of public office to defend and protect it! The expert lawyer Peter Pros of Castres presented himself everywhere as their defender against the inquisitors and the bishop, unscrupulously engaging in impudent lies against truth and justice. Brother Bernard Délicieux of Montpellier, of the Order of Friars Minor, was the hired mercenary of the people of Carcassonne and Albi and Cordes in this cause and on their behalf. Both publicly and privately he opposed the inquisitors and the Bishop of Albi and their processes, flitting all over the place, throughout the country [= *the south*] and <northern> France, persecuting the inquisitors and the bishop and in many public sermons stirring up the people against them, defending those who had been condemned for heresy and claiming that they had been Catholic and devout. Out of respect for religion I stay silent about many others of the same religion [*religious order*], who were harmful in many things and behaved badly and incited many people against the office of inquisition and agitated the hearts of people.

During the persecution of inquisitors and the disruption of their office, many heretics came together and they began to multiply and heresies began to spring up. They infected many in the dioceses of Pamiers and Carcassonne and Toulouse and within the confines of the Albigeois – as became clear and evident later on, through lawful inquisition and the capture of these heretics and their believers: such seed brought forth such fruit. The aforesaid evils began to appear publicly in AD 1301, and they got worse continuously for the next seven or almost eight years, while this persecution lasted. For the persecutors the end was confusion and ignominy. For on the very same day and one year after the sentence of excommunication was published against him as a notorious obstructor of the office of inquisition, the Vidame of Amiens was struck down by the anathema and died in a foreign land, that is in the Abruzzi in the Kingdom of Sicily, without a cleric and without a priest and without receiving the sacraments of the Church, in the year of our Lord 1304, on the feast of St Michael [29 September]. As for the archdeacon, he later became Bishop of Béziers, was struck with leprosy like Giezi [4 Kings 5:25–27][60] and in this shame died a leper, before Pentecost AD 1309. Brother Bernard Délicieux was later found by inquisition of the royal court at Carcassonne to have been accessory to and participant in treason against the King of France, and he was punished, though not in full measure. As to the rolls mentioned earlier, Raymond Baudier, a monk of the <Cistercian> abbey of Candeil in the diocese of Albi, is said to have forged them. He hanged himself twice with a noose, the last time dying in despair during Easter week like the traitor Judas. In truth, the end and consummation of the afflictions suffered for the defence of the faith of the Lord Jesus Christ: praise and honour and victory with the crown.

60 Thus in the Douay–Rheims Bible; in the King James Bible the name is Gehazi and the book is called 2 Kings.

[17] Foundation of the convent of Rodez[61]

Priors of the convent of Rodez

The fourth prior was Fulk of St-Georges, of Vienne. He succeeded Brother William Bernard, was prior for almost a year – during which he was present in the convent only for a few days – and he was released at the following provincial chapter of Tarascon, AD 1297. Later he was Toulouse inquisitor.[62] He died at Carcassonne, AD 1307, after the Lord's Epiphany.

On the foundation and priors of the convents of the Order of Preachers of the province of Provence

[18] The foundation [and priors] of the convent of Montpellier

… Brother Peter of Monceaux, of the diocese of Limoges, succeeded Brother Ralph, translated from the priorate of Limoges to the priorate of Montpellier. He was prior for pretty well three and a half years, was then released from this and became Toulouse inquisitor a little after Christmas, AD 1289. Later he was prior provincial and while working in the provincialate he died at Montauban on the feast of St Martha, AD 1295. Translated thence, he rests in the chapter house of the brothers of Brive.

The aforesaid Brother John Vigouroux <was four times prior>, the third time, succeeded Brother Peter of Monceaux, when released from the office of the Toulouse inquisition: together and at the same time these two succeeded each other in these two offices. He was released from the priorate by letter of the vicar of the province, that is to say, Brother William Andrew, Prior of Béziers, during the vacancy of the province [= *prior provincial's office*], around the feast of Pentecost, AD 1291.

61 Exploration 1282, formal recognition 1284.

62 Fulk was deposed from his office as inquisitor, 29 June 1302, on the insistence of the French king, Philip the Fair. He had been persuaded by Bernard Délicieux and others of the truth of charges of abuse levelled against Fulk, including the use of unheard-of tortures and imprisoning women in order to have sex with them (see Doc. 57). Gui's silence is notable, on both Fulk's removal from office and Fulk himself.

[19] Foundation [and priors] of the convent of Narbonne

The place of the brothers Preacher in Narbonne was received – I estimate from what I have heard – in AD 1220.

... Brother Bertrand of Clermont, of Bergerac, succeeded the aforesaid Brother John [1292] He was there only a little, because shortly after he arrived at the convent he was made Toulouse inquisitor, before Lent, AD 1292.

[20] Foundation [and priors] of the convent of Perpignan

In AD [*blank in text*] the convent of the brothers Preacher of Perpignan was founded.

Brother Pons of Parnac, from Cahors, a lawyer, succeeded Brother [*blank in text*] and he was prior only a little while, because he became the Toulouse inquisitor, AD 1273.

[21] Foundation [and priors] of the convent of Béziers

The convent of the brothers Preacher in Béziers began to be founded around AD 1247, so I have been able to gather from what I have heard from older brothers of that time.

Brother Ferrier, by nation a Catalan, was translated from the priorate of Carcassonne to the priorate of Béziers almost half a year after the aforesaid provincial chapter of Montpellier, AD 1252, and was released at the provincial chapter of Toulouse, AD 1254. He was an inquisitor and a great persecutor of heretics. He died at Perpignan, I think.

[22] Foundation of the convent of St-Maximin [begun 1295]

...

PART III: TREATISES

INTRODUCTION TO PART III

The materials we translate here do not fit neatly into one genre, but they are all, in different ways, discursive texts in which an author holds forth on a topic, for the benefit of others. We include some brief extracts on the topic of heresy that appear within works which take a much wider overall remit – the edification of the clergy, for example (Doc. 10A), or general theological treatises (Docs 12 and 13). Our choice here is guided by an interest both in orthodox thought regarding heresy (Gerald of Wales, for example, linking heresy to climate) and potential information about heretical doctrine itself, such as heretical use of logical axioms as well as scripture on the topics of dualism and the resurrection (see Doc. 12).

The thirteenth century saw a great upsurge in the writing of theology, both general treatises that contained some material on heresy and polemical treatises specifically directed against heresy, the latter typically listing heretical doctrines, heretics' arguments and authorities in support of these and the Church's opposing arguments and authorities – denouncing and refuting in order to demonstrate the victory of orthodox interpretations of Christian faith over heretical ones. Examples of general treatises are those supplying the extracts translated in Docs 13–14. The writing of anti-heretical treatises flourished during the 1230s and 1240s, principally in Italy, where they seem to have been connected with intellectually high-level, real-life polemical exchanges between Catholics and heretics, in a region where direct inquisitorial repression was not as effective as it was in Languedoc.[1] Southern France has much less to show, after the four-part treatise (including parts against Cathars and Waldensians) written by Alan of Lille, extracts of which are provided in translation by Wakefield and Evans.[2] The *Summa of Authorities* in Doc. 11 provides a textual correlative of

1 On the polemical theological treatise genre, see Sackville, *Heresy*, pp. 18–40; a useful list of polemical tracts is compiled in WE, pp. 633–68. On Italy, see L. Paolini, 'Italian Catharism and written culture', in P. Biller and A. Hudson, eds, *Heresy and Literacy 1000–1530* (Cambridge, 1994), pp. 83–103.

2 WE, pp. 214–20. The evidence connecting Alan with southern France is collected in M.-T. d'Alverny, *Alain de Lille: Textes inédits* (Paris, 1965), pp. 13–14, 16–17, 19 n.48.

the authority-bashing polemics in debates between Catholics, heretics and (sometimes) Waldensians of the late twelfth and early thirteenth centuries.[3] One exception to this rather thin picture is provided by a participant in these debates, the converted former Waldensian Durand of Huesca, whose second polemical treatise we have put in Part I (Doc. 2) because of its copying of a heretical treatise. We have translated extracts from two texts written outside France. One is a somewhat neglected text – Lucas of Tuy's *On the Other Life* – which provides a view on heresy in southern France from the north of Spain. The other is one part of the brief *summa* written by the converted Cathar, turned Dominican friar, Rainerio Sacconi, written in northern Italy but bearing on the Cathar heretics of France.[4]

3 On the 'authorities' genre, see Sackville, *Heresy*, pp. 42–53.

4 We include in Part VIII (below) a short tract against the Waldensians based upon deposition evidence (Doc. 53), but it could alternatively have been placed here as another example of the treatise genre.

10. GERALD OF WALES

Gerald (c.1146–1220/3), of Anglo-Norman and Welsh background, was educated in the schools at Paris, where he also later lectured (1176–9). He spent around twelve years in royal service (from 1184) and was a much-travelled man, visiting Rome three times to pursue his ambition to gain the bishopric of St David's in Wales. He was a prolific writer, who drew widely on other texts, but also on personal experience gained in his travels. The source for the first extract – the *Jewel* – is a compilation on sacraments and morals addressed to the clergy, which Gerald presented in person to Pope Innocent III on his first visit in 1199. The second piece comes from *On the Instruction of the Prince*, which Gerald composed between the early 1190s and c.1216, reflecting (sometimes bitterly) on his experience of the royal court.

On Gerald, see R. Bartlett, *Gerald of Wales 1146–1223* (Oxford, 1982), and its appendix, pp. 213–21, on Gerald's works and their chronology; also Bartlett, 'Gerald of Wales', *Oxford Dictionary of National Biography* (Oxford, 2004; online edn, 2006). Translated from Giraldus Cambrensis, *Opera*, ed. J. S. Brewer, J. F. Dimock and G. F. Warner, 8 vols, Rolls Series 21 (London, 1861–91), vol. 2, pp. 40–1; vol. 8, pp. 68, 70.

(A) *The Jewel of the Church*, Distinction I, ch. 11
On examples that strengthen faith.

I think it fitting therefore to put down here true and outstanding examples that strengthen this faith <in the consecration of the body of Christ>. These are so well known and in so many places and they have been so divinely manifested, not only internally but externally in visible flesh. <They happen> during the utterance of those words <of consecration> over the hosts, sometimes the shape of a lamb <appears> in the hands of <the priest> who is consecrating, sometimes the hosts are turned into a bleeding fragment – and <they are done> in order to make the foundation of faith stronger. So at Rome [*there follows a story about Gregory the Great*] … And so at Ferrara in Italy, in our days, on Easter Sunday the host was turned into a little portion of flesh. After the bishop of this place had been called <to see> this and had delivered a sermon, the citizens of this town, nearly all of whom had been Paterines [Paterini] and held bad opinions about the body of Christ, reverted to the truth. …

In the kingdom of the Franks, to be specific in the town of Arras which is wont to be the capital of Flanders, on a certain Easter Sunday a certain matron placed a consecrated host in a locket, tied at the top of a certain silk head-dress; this had been handed over to her imprudently though the carelessness of a priest, as it were for it to be carried to an ill person. [*A story follows in which the host is forgotten but bleeds, and the miraculous host, part bread, part bleeding flesh, is shown to the people in church*] … When this was heard a great concourse of people gathered not only from that town [*Arras*] but also from neighbouring places, both towns and villages: people who had either doubted or had completely strayed on this article, that is, about the body of Christ. These people saw with their eyes and touched with their hands. Seeing the many special things and signs that God deigned to bring about in that place at that time, they returned to the certainty of the faith and the true path which they had left.

In this way God, who is great in all his works, showed himself especially magnificent, and is rightly to be praised for two things. The first is that He unveiled this <miracle> in those parts of the world where those heretics of our time who are called Patars [Patari][5] or Cathars [Catari] are known to err grievously – and in particular on this article, the confection of the body of Christ – and where they mostly abound, that is to say within the borders of Flanders. The second is that … he showed the light of truth to those who were wandering astray so that they might return to the path of justice … There was therefore great rejoicing in that city. It happened that within the week after this happened I was passing through this place – the city was still praising and to the same degree fervent about the recent miracle.

(ii) *On the instruction of a prince*, i.17

Some say that insofar as they abstain from pork they [*the followers of Mahomet*] Judaise; for Mahomet took certain things from the Jews and certain things from the Christians. In this matter, however – that they abstain from wine on account of the hot regions they inhabit, to avoid danger from excessive heat – they follow their master's medical teaching, etc. [*There follows an account of the rise of Mahomet*] … Note here the amazing cunning and devilish skill that he used, the studied malice

5 Once a name for members of a religious movement in eleventh-century Milan, 'Patarenes' had come by this time to denote Cathar heretics, especially in Italy. See C. Thouzellier, *Hérésies et hérétiques: Vaudois, Cathares, Patarins, Albigeois* (Rome, 1969), ch. 7 'Patarins'.

deployed in all things in order to deceive people. For he set up as law what he knew pleased a man most. Accordingly, knowing that oriental men were lustful, for the heat of the region urges them on and drives them to this, he allowed every man, by point of law, to have as many wives and concubines as he had resources to support.

Likewise the heretics of our time, that is to say the Patars [Patari], are now using the very same skill of the ancient enemy to deceive people. For, in those frigid zones where the cold renders people avaricious, they urge men towards avarice, suggesting and laying down almost as a law that tithes should not be given to people nor offerings made to churches.[6] If they had been of one mind in their error and did not diverge among themselves, splitting into diverse sects of heresies, as we learnt from a certain wise cleric in Italy, there is no doubt that for the most part the Western Church would have been badly damaged in many places, and would have completely gone under, it is believed, within the borders of Provence and Italy.

6 On Gerald's environmental notions here, see Bartlett, *Gerald of Wales*, pp. 166–7.

11. THE ALBI *SUMMA AUCTORITATUM*

Until the Albigensian crusade in 1209, persuasion rather than force dominated in Languedoc: Catholics, heretics and Waldensians met and argued with each other. The habit of debating died slowly; see Doc. 5, nos. 23–4, 26, 47–54, and Doc. 42, e.g. fols 203v, 208v. At some point these debates came to include the composition, presentation and exchange of texts. These texts contained doctrinal propositions and 'authorities' (quotations from scripture) and 'reasons' (arguments) to support or controvert them. The Catholic *Summae* of authorities arose from these. A number of people interrogated in Languedoc in the 1240s – recounting memories that sometimes stretched back into the late twelfth century – said that they knew of heretics' beliefs not from the heretics themselves but from Catholic clergy preaching against them. These preachers might have made use of such *summae* of authorities. Extracts from two of them are provided in WE, pp. 296–300.[7]

The earliest of the several extant *summae* is in a manuscript in Albi, written about 1200, either in Languedoc or Catalonia. Although some doctrines it stated and attacked could be supported by other sects, the compiler was mainly targeting dualist heretics. He addresses the opponent as 'heretic', 'Manichee' and 'Cathar', and makes polemical points out of the heretic calling himself 'Good Man' and heretical imposition of hands – though he does not use the word *consolamentum*. We have selected passages articulating or closely bearing on heretics' doctrines, translating from 'Edizione della Summa auctoritatum contenuta nel MS. 47 della Bibliothèque municipale d'Albi', ed. F. Šanjek, pp. 355–95, which is an appendix to R. Manselli, 'Una "Summa auctoritatum" antiereticale (Ms. 47 della Bibliothèque Municipale di Albi)', *Atti della Accademia Nazionale dei Lincei*, Classe di scienze morali, storiche e filologiche, series 8, vol. 28 (1985), pp. 323–95; see pp. 335–41 for Manselli's situation of this text at a primitive early stage in the development of Catholic polemical texts against heresy.

1. You err greatly, heretic, when you say that a sinful minister cannot consecrate the body of Christ, and in saying this you detract greatly from the word of God. For this consecration comes about not through the merit or virtue of the minister, but through the virtue and power of the word of the living and eternal God. … There are

7 Other *Summae auctoritatum* were edited by C. Douais, *La Somme des autorités à l'usage des prédicateurs méridionaux au XIIIe siècle* (Paris, 1896).

no grounds therefore, heretic, for you to object to ministers, even bad ones. …

2. Authorities against those who sow the word of God indiscriminately, not taking into account the suitability of time or place or thinking about the character of things or persons. …
3. You have listened, Manichee, to what the word of Paul is in faith, listen to what it is in works. …
4. You err greatly, Manichee, when you call yourself 'Good Man'. … You err greatly, Cathar [Catare] … You err greatly, for you compete with the Lord in saying that you are good or righteous or without sin. Similarly, you err greatly because you condemn and judge all men apart from yourself. For you say that all people who are not of your sect are to be damned; you say that all who hold the faith of the Roman Church are to be damned. … …
5. Authorities against the Manichees, who oppose and disdain the Old Testament in the authorisation of the testimonies of the Law and the Prophets. …
6. Authorities against the Manichees, <showing> that the Prophets and the apostles were sent by the same Lord and the same Spirit. …
7. This that the apostle said: 'The God of this world has blinded the minds of unbelievers' [1 Corinthians 4.4]. He blinded thus in many ways. He allowed blinding on account of sins – so the 'Lord hardened Pharaoh' [Exodus 9.12], that is, he allowed him to be hardened, not inflicting the hardness himself but allowing the hardness to get to him. So 'he blinded the unbelievers', not inflicting the hardness, but rather not providing the light of the grace of which their sins made them unworthy. The same with this, 'God gave them up to a reprobate sense or to shameful affections' [Romans 1.28; 1.26]: that is, he allowed them to be given over because of their ungodliness, and he ushered in evils upon them. This that is said, 'The prince of this world cometh, etc.' [John 14.30; *it continues* 'and in me he hath not anything'], and 'the prince of this world is already judged' [John 16.11]. The prince of the world is understood thus: not as the prince of the fabric of the world or of those who are contained within the fabric of the world, but of the world, that is, the prince of the lovers of the world, of the ungodly, of the unbelievers. Similarly this passage of the apostle [Ephesians 6.12], 'against princes and powers of darkness': of darkness – that is, 'of the darkness' of infidels and the ungodly, not 'of darkness' itself, that is, darkness of the air.

Similarly this passage: 'Flesh and blood cannot possess the kingdom of God' [1 Corinthians 15.5]. That is, carnal men, engaged in deeds of the flesh and of blood, which are enmities and unclean things, etc. He does not say this about flesh, that is, about nature and about the substance of this flesh, rather he says it about flesh, that is about carnal men engaged in carnal deeds. …

8. You err, Manichee, because you disdain the author of the Old Testament, in that through himself and his people he exercised justice on the wicked and the impious. For just as it suits God to be merciful so also it suits him to be just; and just as it is impossible for the Lord not to be merciful, so also it is impossible for him not to be just. … You detract as much from God in taking away justice as you would detract from him if taking away mercy.

You err, Manichee, when you do not attribute to the most benign God – apart from whom there is no other God – those middling and short-lived judgments upon the wicked and incorrigible, that occur in the present out of zeal for peace, faith and justice, while at the same time you do attribute to him that most great and eternal judgment by which even the virtues of the heavens are admonished and the ungodly handed over to eternal fire.

You err, Manichee, when you will not attribute to our saving and redeeming God those judgments and retributions of the wicked that are done most mercifully and justly by our most merciful and just Lord. …

9. It has been shown in many ways – and can be shown in many more – that the author of the Old Law is the same as the author of the New, of prophecy and of the Gospel, and that the spirit of the Prophets is the same as the spirit of the apostles, and that the foundation of the earlier and of the later Fathers is the same, that is to say the faith of Our Lord Jesus Christ working through love. …

10. All ancient holy men … In these and in many more ways it can be clearly shown to the perfidious Manichees that ancient righteous men came to <eternal> life, which they do not believe. …

11. <Here are> authorities of the New and the Old Testament, about the unity of the principle, against the Manichees who proclaim the doctrine that there are two principles, one principle of light and the other of darkness, for 'every scribe instructed in the kingdom of heaven is like to a man that is a householder, who bringeth forth out of his treasures new things and old' [Matthew 13.52]: new things about the New Testament, old things about the Old

Testament. The apostle James in his Epistle [2.19], thus: 'Thou believest that there is one God. Thou dost well: the devils also believe and tremble'. In this, therefore, the Manichees are worse than the devils. …

Listen, Manichee: the Lord of the Old Testament is the only Lord, the only God, alone making all things, who was first before all things and created all things, who is the last, who comes at the end of the world to recreate all things; and he is to come to judgment in order to judge. Listen: the principle of light is the same as the principle of darkness. …

And the Lord in the Gospel: 'One is your Father, who is in heaven' [Matthew 23.9]. It has been shown sufficiently by these authorities, against the Manichees, that there is one God, all-powerful, the highest, the only Lord and Father and Creator and redeemer and the judge of all. …

'For of him, and by him, and in him are all things' [Romans 11.36], and in the Epistle to the Hebrews [1.2], 'In these days hath spoken to us by his Son, whom he hath appointed heir of all things, by whom he also made the world'. Listen, Manichee: the world and all things were made by the Son of God, there he is the same 'God born of the virgin[8] and through whom all things were made'.[9]

Isaiah on the same [42.5]: 'Thus saith the Lord God that created the heavens, and stretched them out; that established the earth and the things that spring from it; and that giveth breath to the people upon it and spirit and spirit to them that tread thereon'. Listen, Manichee: the Lord who created heaven and earth and the things that germinate from it is the same as the Lord who made breath and spirit. …

And elsewhere: 'Who makest thy angels spirits, and thy ministers a burning fire' [Psalm 103.4; *see also* Hebrews 1.7]. Listen, Manichee: <the God> who made heaven and earth and the sea and all the things in it is the same as <the God who made> the angels. …

12. Moses on the creation of man: 'God formed man from the slime of the earth, and breathed into him the breath of life' [Genesis 2.7]. Listen, Manichee: he who 'formed man from the slime' is the same as he who 'breathed into him the breath of life'. He does not say

8 See Creed of the first Council of Constantinople, in Tanner, *Ecumenical Councils*, I, 24.

9 Nicene Creed, in Tanner, *Ecumenical Councils*, I, 5.

that one 'formed the body from the slime of the earth', and another <breathed into him> 'the breath of life'; but one and the same 'formed' and 'breathed'. …

Listen, Manichee, that the same Lord, who made the world and all worldly things, gives life and breath to all. Again, David on the aforesaid things: 'the world is mine and the fullness thereof' ⌈Psalm 49.12⌉, 'the world and all that dwell therein' ⌈Psalm 23.1⌉, 'all the beasts of the woods are mine, the cattle on the hills and the oxen' ⌈Psalm 49.10⌉. Behold, it has been sufficiently shown, against the Manichees, that the same Lord and Father made each and every thing: angels, the body and spirit, the four elements, and all their array.

13. You err greatly, heretic, when you say that, unless they are without sin, ministers of the Church cannot consecrate <the body of Christ>, and cannot free or bind, saying that the impure cannot cleanse, that the infirm cannot cleanse, that someone who is bound cannot loose, that a sinner cannot make someone righteous. You err in seeking for a minister without sin, since he cannot be found. For who dares to say to God, 'I am pure and without sin'? We, however, do not say that ministers of the Church make sinners righteous, or cleanse or cure or free the soul from sin, but only the grace of God <does these things> through Jesus Christ. …

17. Authorities against the Manichees, that the Lord and author of the New Testament is the same as the Lord and author of the Old and of the Law and prophecy, the Lord of the Prophets the same as the Lord of the Apostles. …

19. It has been shown sufficiently that all righteousness and salvation derive from the faith of Christ and the turning of the mind towards God and the invocation of his name in the sacraments of the Church, in baptism and penance. And that the merits of ministers take away nothing from nor add anything to the grace of God, which is from faith. … But you, Manichee, when you say, 'The hands of the Good Men are necessary for salvation',[10] you contend with God, but listen to what the Lord says to you and those like you in Job: 'Wilt thou make void my judgment and condemn me, that thou mayst be justified? And canst thou thunder with a voice like him, clothe thyself with beauty and set thyself up on high?' Etc. ⌈Job 40.3–5⌉. When you justify yourself, O Manichee, and

10 We conjecture 'Good Men' as a title here; the phrase could translate simply as 'good men'.

say that you are a just man and glorify yourself as a chaste man, in so doing you compete with God – who is he that shall condemn [Romans 8.34]. When you say that 'No-one is saved except through the hands of the Good Men', you condemn God so as to justify yourself, and you say that you have an arm like God. But, as the Lord says in Job [39.32], 'he that argueth with God ought to answer to him'. Since therefore you argue with and condemn God, justifying yourself and saying that salvation is in the imposition of your hands,[11] answer to God, in holiness and justice: be as good and holy in yourself as He is in himself! …

20. You err greatly, Manichee, when you rebaptise someone who has been baptised in the Church – when you say that the person baptised in the Church has not received the Holy Spirit and has not been reborn by the Holy Spirit. …

Through these authorities, therefore, it is manifest that he who – believing in Christ and the remission of sins that comes about through the faith of Christ in the Holy Spirit – is baptised by a priest in church, or by anyone in necessity, is indued with [puts on] Christ, receives the Holy Spirit and is born again of God. Therefore you do wrong, Manichee, when you say that that person is to be re-indued, reborn, rebaptised in Christ and the Holy Spirit. So someone believing thus and baptised in that way does not need your rebaptising or conversion: even if you were a right believer (though you are a wrong believer) and the priest were a wrong believer.

Item, you err greatly when you say that converted sinners do not receive penance for the remission of sins in the Church. …

11 This is the third of the references in this text to the ritual of the *consolamentum*, all of them without the use of this name.

12. WILLIAM OF AUXERRE AND THEOLOGY

William lived at some point in Auxerre, and also in Paris, where he taught theology. He was among the earliest theologians there to use the works of Aristotle, and he was regarded by his contemporaries as having no peer in debate. He died in 1231. His *Summa aurea*, written between 1215 and 1229, became one of the most widely read of all theological treatises. William incorporated in it views on heresy both from the early Church and from his own time. Where contemporary views are discernible, they are plausibly rooted in William's experience in the diocese of Auxerre and among academic theologians in Paris, among whom there was a trend for the kind of demonstration of theological propositions from axioms that is exemplified below. They are discussed in P. Biller, 'Northern Cathars and higher learning', in P. Biller and [R.] B. Dobson, eds, *The Medieval Church: Universities, Heresy and the Religious Life. Essays in Honour of Gordon Leff*, Studies in Church History Subsidia 11 (Woodbridge, 1999), pp. 25–53. On William, see S. E. Young, *Scholarly Community at the Early University of Paris: Theologians, Education and Society, 1215–1248* (Cambridge, 2014), chapter 3 and pp. 222–3. We have translated from William of Auxerre, *Summa aurea*, ed. J. Ribailler, 4 vols in 7, Spicilegium Bonaventurianum 16–20 (Paris and Grottaferrata, 1980–87), vols 16, pp. 15–16; 17, pp. 168 and 173; 18b, p. 825; 19, pp. 459–60.

Book 1 Prologue

Faith is demonstrated for three reasons. The first is that natural arguments augment and confirm faith among the faithful. …
The second reason is the defence of faith against heretics.
The third is the bringing of the simple to our faith.

Book 2 Treatise 8 On other creatures

Chapter 1 On the first created beings and their principles

At the beginning of Genesis Moses, speaking about the first creatures, said generally and with the guidance of the Holy Spirit, 'In the beginning God created heaven and earth' [Genesis 1.1]. … His saying 'He created heaven' excludes the opinion of the Manichee, who posited two principles of things, that is to say a benign God, principle of incorporeal things and the God of light and of the New Testament, and the other the malign God, whom he calls the God of darkness and the God of the Old Testament. And this one they say is the principle of all visible things, which according to them are evil because they are mutable. They want to prove their opinion by certain maxims, the first of which is 'What has an invariable cause is itself invariable'. Since therefore the benign God is an invariable cause, He is not the cause of variable things. The second is this. 'What is constructive of something is not the same as what is destructive of it'. Since therefore God is the destructive cause of evil men, He is not the constructive cause of the same men. The third is, 'The principles of contraries are contraries'. Since therefore good and evil are contraries, they have contrary principles. Since therefore the Highest Good is the cause of good, the Highest Evil will be the principle of evil.

... Item, they say that although the intellectual soul is from God and made from the substance of God Himself, it can sin. And when it sins it is intruded into the body of something more ignoble, into the body of a dog or something similar. Thus Master Prévostin,[12] who lived a long time among them and was able to bring back <only> a few to the way of truth, used to recount that he heard them saying, when they saw a dog playing with its tail, 'Its soul will soon be purged and freed'.

Book 3 Treatise 43 On the comparison of virtue to vice

Chapter 2 On heretics, who are more prepared to undergo punishment for a fallacious faith than the faithful are for the true faith

In relation to the second heading, an objection is raised about heretics. For the perfect heretic is prepared to suffer everything for his false faith. But the imperfect Christian is not so prepared, as is clear in the case of the blessed Peter. Therefore the infidelity of this heretic is greater than the faith of this Christian. Therefore something evil is more evil than something good is good.

Perhaps one may say that this is on account of stability. But this seems to be false, because less intense whiteness is sometimes

12 Praepositinus of Cremona, Chancellor of Notre-Dame, Paris (1206–9), *The* Summa Contra Haereticos *ascribed to Praepositinus of Cremona*, ed. J. N. Garvin and J. A. Corbett (Notre Dame IN, 1958).

more fixed, however through its fixedness it is not stronger in its effect.

Solution. One should say to this that the imperfect faithful man, because he 'knoweth not whether he be worthy of love or hatred' [Ecclesiastes 9.1], fears incurring eternal punishments. And therefore, although the goodness in him may be greater than the wickedness in the heretic, he is not so prepared to suffer. This happens therefore not because of the slackening of goodness in him but because of what is connected to it – fear.

Book 4 Treatise 18

Chapter 1 On the general resurrection

That bodies will be resurrected is proved by many authorities and arguments. …

Many heretics, however, speak against this, aiming to prove that there is no future resurrection of bodies. And to support this they bring in the authority of the apostle, who says: 'Flesh and blood cannot possess the kingdom of God' [1 Corinthians 15.50]. Therefore there will be no flesh in the kingdom of God.

Item: We 'shall be as the angels of God in heaven' [Matthew 22.30, Mark 12.25]. Therefore without flesh, since the angels are in heaven without flesh; and thus bodies will not rise again.

They try to prove the same thing with arguments. The soul uses a body like an instrument. But nothing is owed to an instrument – for it merits nothing of itself, only the one using the instrument <merits anything>. Therefore since the body merits nothing, nothing is owed it; therefore resurrection is not owed it.

Also, the intellect needs sense for the knowledge of universals and intelligible things. But after it has got to know them it does not need sense any longer – just as someone needs a horse to travel to a certain place where is house is going to be built, but after he has got to that place the horse is not useful to him. Therefore when the soul has arrived at the knowledge of God and other intelligible things, sense will not be useful to it. Therefore there will not be sense, therefore not body. And thus bodies will not rise again.

Item, man was created for this, to have eternal life. But angels, who are without body, have eternal life sufficiently; and therefore souls without body will have eternal life sufficiently. Therefore there is no need for bodies to rise again on account of eternal life.

With these sorts of arguments they deny that there is future resurrection of bodies.

13. ROLAND OF CREMONA ON HERETICS' ENDURANCE

Roland of Cremona (died c.1258) studied arts and medicine at Bologna, entered the Dominican Order in Bologna in 1219, became the first Dominican master of theology in Paris in 1229 and then taught theology in Toulouse until 1233. Vivid glimpses of his preaching and direct action against heretics in Toulouse in 1231 appear in Pelhisson's chronicle.[13] Between 1233 and 1244 he was active as an inquisitor in Lombardy. Though the date is much debated among scholars, the origins of his *Summa* are commonly associated with the years in France, 1229–33. In the passage below he develops William of Auxerre's discussion of heretics' willing endurance, possibly drawing also upon his experience of heretics in Toulouse and Lombardy, and what he may have heard when in Paris. On Roland, see Young, *Scholarly Community at the Early University of Paris*, pp. 220–1, and R. Parmeggiani, 'Rolando da Cremona (✝ 1259) e gli eretici. Il ruolo dei frati Predicatori tra escatologismo e profezia', *Archivum Fratrum Praedicatorum* 79 (2009), 23–84. Translated from *Summae Magistri Rolandi Liber Tercius*, ed. A Cortesi (Bergamo, 1962), book 3, question 377, pp. 1132–3.

How heretics more easily endure torments on behalf of their infidelity than we do on behalf of our faith

Whereas it was shown above that that every virtue is infinitely stronger than a vice, and it follows from this that a <good> man ought to be stronger in good than an evil man in evil, and the greater a sin is the more it injures natural <forces>, and the more injured natural <forces> are the weaker their resistance is, the question is rightly raised from this: how it is that heretics endure atrocious torments more easily on behalf of their infidelity than we do on behalf of our faith.

For they endure them more easily to such an extent that they go rejoicing to the fire, nor do they consider that they are being thrown onto the fire. Thus, therefore, there is here such and such a perfect heretic,[14] and some imperfect faithful man: the former suffers death for

13 Wakefield, *Heresy*, pp. 209–10.

14 On possible meaning of 'perfectus hereticus' as 'fully-fledged heretic', see Doc. 40.

his infidelity, the latter does not for his faith. Therefore that infidelity is stronger than that faith. Therefore not every virtue is stronger than any sin – in relation to which the masters say that charity is strong so that it can resist any temptation.

Perhaps one may say that this is because of the confidence the heretic has – for the man who is imperfect does not have so much confidence. And that heretic is strong from this confidence, not from heresy. Fear, however, enters that man who is imperfect, so that he does not have confidence, and therefore he is not so strong. And this is the solution of William <of Auxerre>.

Against: the heresy in this heretic is the cause of his confidence. But this is the greatest proposition: 'whatever is the cause of a cause is the cause of what is caused' [= *by the second cause*].[15] Therefore – if that confidence is the cause of that courage of the heretic, therefore heresy is the cause of that courage. Therefore the objection that heresy is stronger than faith returns.

Nor can it be said that the heretic is not in his senses, so that he acts like a madman, or like an idiot who kills himself – for the heretic has the benefit of free will.

Solution. We say that there are many causes why the heretic endures such torments. One is the conscience he has, or strength, in his religion. Another because such a wicked soul is not worthy of being in command of a body that Christ formed. Another is because these heretics are accustomed to many vigils and bodily afflictions, and in this way they can more easily endure bodily pain than imperfect delicate men: not more <however> than those who say 'Woe is me, that my sojourning is prolonged!' [Psalm 119.5] and again 'Who shall deliver me from the body' etc? [Romans 7.24]. This is not therefore so – that vice is stronger than virtue. The greatest cause is the fixed direction of the free will, through obstinacy, to the other side.

15 A widespread dictum, found for example in a treatise written by Nicholas of Amiens between 1187 and 1181, *On the Art or Articles of the Catholic Faith*, Patrologia Latina 210.595–6.

14. LUCAS OF TUY, *ON THE OTHER LIFE (DE ALTERA VITA)*

Lucas of Tuy was born in Léon, was a canon of this diocese (1221–39) and later Bishop of Tuy (1239–49). While composing his massive *Miracles of St Isidore* in the 1240s, he interrupted his work to write, in 1234 or 1235, this treatise against heresies. It drew upon patristic writings, Lucas's travels outside northern Spain and his own combatting of heretics in the diocese of Léon, some of whom had come from France. This complex and insufficiently studied work shows the view taken by a northern Spanish churchman of heretics. Its attention to the use of mockery through paintings is unusual. The suggestion of heretics' use of natural philosophers should be compared to William of Auxerre's comments (see Doc. 12).

Lucas uses a rhetorical device combining metonymy and mutation, for example, 'the sword of the double-edged word of God' in place of 'the double-edged sword of the word of God'. On Lucas, see B. Reilly, 'Lucas of Tuy', *Medieval Iberia: An Encyclopaedia* (London and New York, 2003), p. 519; P. Henriet, 'Sanctissima patria, point et thèmes communs aux trois oeuvres de Lucas de Tuy', *Cahiers de Linguistique Hispanique Médiévale* 2001 (24), 249–78. Translated from Lucas of Tuy, *De Altera Vita*, ed. E. Falque Rey, Corpus Christianorum Continuatio Mediaeualis 74A (Turnhout, 2009), pp. 118–20, 190, 191–2, 214–17.

Book 2, ch. 9

… Though they [*heretics*] may *have adverse faces,* disagreeing among themselves, they have however *tails tied together* like Samson's foxes.[16] For, agreeing about falsity in itself, they always try in whatever ways they can to throw the Church of God into confusion and subvert it, such that often they strive to deceive many people through the novelty of false paintings. For they depict the image of the divine Trinity as an old Father, a younger Son, <and> a Holy Spirit in the shape of a dove or smaller than the Son, so that through this simple people, seduced by a depraved interpretation, will be forced to believe that there are three Gods with one will: so that on account of this it may be said, 'One

16 Adapting Lateran IV, can. 3 (Tanner, *Ecumenical Councils,* I, 233–4), based on Judges 15.4–5; see Sackville, *Heresy,* p. 159.

God – though there are three – since they are in agreement in being of one will'.

... Since no-one can form an image of something that cannot be delimited [*i.e. God*], whether it be wholly among all things and wholly outside all things, or because it is not other than itself and other than in itself, let the heretic or painter desist from fabricating an image of blasphemy and venerating an idol of stupidity instead of God. For, as the excellent teacher Augustine said, when regarded in the mind of a just man, Divinity always grows larger. But conversely, I say, in the heart of an evilly presumptuous heretical painter, it continually diminishes, when they endeavour with a sacrilegious painting to demonstrate that there are three Gods or one comprehensible God.

For heretics there is another way of deceiving through paintings, which we have decided not to keep hidden through silence, so that being known by the faithful it can be more carefully avoided. Often they paint misshapen images of saints, so that through looking at them the devotion of the simple Christian people turns into loathing.

In addition, to the derision and opprobrium of Christ's cross, through fixing the image of the Crucified one foot over another with one nail and bringing in various novelties, they strive to empty or bring into doubt faith in the most holy cross and the traditions of the holy fathers. We shall show this more clearly if we bring out into the open what happened within the confines of Gaul at the *castrum* that is called Montcuq,[17] as the story will make plain.

While the heresy of the Manichees was springing up in the regions of Gaul[18] in our times and the virus of error was creeping through various things, some misguided believers in the heretics, urged on by devilish counsel, took the image of the most holy mother of God, rendering it one-eyed and misshapen – to the perdition of their souls, wantonly misrepresenting, as though for the point of view that Our Lord Jesus Christ so humiliated himself that he chose the foulest woman for the salvation of mankind. Blinded with malice they thought up these things and erred, so that they could more easily deceive the simple, and draw their minds and zeal away from devotion to our

17 Monculis. There seem no grounds for the editor's identification with Montségur, Mons Securus. If Lucas intended coarseness – not unlikely – we should read this as Mon Cul, 'My Arse'. Although there is a Moncul, just east of Lyon, the place most probably lurking behind this is Montcuq.

18 From a northern Spanish viewpoint, not excluding southern France.

most glorious Lady, the ever virgin Mary. Further, pretending to be suffering from various illnesses, they brought it about that they appeared to be cured in front of the said image through the working of miracles. The fame spread wide through cities and castles, as though these miracles were true, and many people, led on even by the pity of priests, made similar images and placed them in their churches. Seeing this, the heretics unveiled the deed that they had long kept hidden, and they mocked the swarms of people which were converging on the said image out of piety. At the time the heretics made a cross with only three arms, on which the image was with one foot above another and fixture with three nails to a cross lacking the top arm [*i.e. shaped like a T*]. Coming to <this cross>, people adored it, in the place of Christ's cross, with great devotion. Revealing the net that they had spread out, the enemies of truth wickedly caught the souls of the simple, and they also argued against the ministers of God, saying, 'If the things you formerly believed about the cross are true, what you now adore is not true. And if what you now believe is true, the things you taught earlier are false. If Christ was fixed to the cross with four nails and the same cross had four arms, as you taught in the past, this – which now you adore and teach – is not the similitude of the Christ's cross. Look at how you wobble, look at how doubtful you are and take uncultivated people with you through ambiguous things and into error. Your authority is nothing, and in fact tradition is self-contradictory'. Blaspheming these and many other things against Catholics, the heretics have snared many of the simple in the traps of their errors, and up to now they are not laying off spreading further the wicked dissension they have started.

Book 3, ch. 1

It was stated earlier how the heretics try in all ways to subvert the Catholic faith, in their books adulterating the teaching of the holy fathers, adding false things or cutting out true things, and also through novelty in pictures changing the traditions of the Church. We have decided now to show also how they strive in other ways to corrupt the same faith, so that the faithful, mindful of their fallacious arguments, can avoid the traps of error. They labour to pervert holy scripture under the guise of philosophical or natural teachers. …

Book 3, ch. 2

Item, some heretics say, 'What is contained in the New and the Old Testaments is true if it is understood according to mystical understanding. Taken literally, however, all the things contained in them are nothing. For what is read about Christ, that he brought light to the blind and worked other miracles, is to be understood to apply to those who were in sin and backward in their minds, not to blindness of the body'. With these and many other errors they compose profane scriptures, decking them out with some flowers of philosophers,[19] as is that book that is called *The Perpendicular of Sciences*:[20] insofar as heresy finds a place in the hearts of those reading it, on account of the philosophical embellishment and also some sentences of holy scripture interposed <in it>. When those who carry around books of this sort are captured, they say, excusing their wickedness, 'Let the reader choose good things and cast aside the wicked things; good things should not be rejected because of bad things, nor true things because of false.' [*Another two sentences of excuse omitted.*]

Book 3, ch. 15

I learnt from the account of the same venerable man, Brother Elias,[21] when some heretics were spreading the virulent seeds of their error in the region of Burgundy and the brothers, Preachers of holy preaching, and the Brothers Minor were fighting manfully against the same heretics, indefatigably cutting down their wicked dogmas with the sword of the double-edged word of God,[22] at last they were captured by a judge of the region and consigned to the fire of flames, as they deserved, so that these malign authors [*or* originators] with their crime should be finished in a way that would terrify other men.

19 Flowers: quotations compiled in an anthology.

20 *Perpendiculum scientiarum*, which could also be translated as *The Plumbline of Sciences*, or *The Guide of Sciences*. Lucas's description does not fit the *Polypticum* often called 'The perpendicular' written in the tenth century by Atto of Vercelli; Lucas seems instead to be describing a contemporary heretic's work.

21 Lucas met Elias, the second Minister General of the Franciscan Order, when in Italy in 1234 or 1235, learning from him two stories about heresy, one in Lombardy (ch. 14, not translated here), and this one.

22 Rhetorical mutation of 'double-edged sword'.

A great abundance of wood was placed there, and when the fire was burnt fiercely suddenly there was an extraordinarily large toad – otherwise known as a 'crapaud'[23] – which cast itself into the middle of the flames, without anyone making it do this. One of the heretics, who was called their 'bishop' had fallen down into the fire and was lying face up. And the said toad sat on his face and in the sight of everyone who was there ate his tongue.

By the following day the whole of the heretic's body apart from the bones had turned into stinking toads, impossible to count because of their extreme numbers. Seeing this miracle, then, the local inhabitants glorified God and praised Him in his preachers, God who had deigned mercifully to liberate them from the horror of such a filthy pollution. The omnipotent God wanted to show directly through the filthiest and foulest animals how the dogmas of heretics are the foulest and filthiest things, so that all men can be diligent in avoiding a heretic like a toxic 'crapaud'. For just as the toad is reckoned the foulest among all quadrupeds, so heretical wickedness is worse and more sordid than all other sects.[24] Heretical blindness has exonerated Judaic perfidiousness, cleansed the insanity of Mahomet with its pollution and washed away Sodom and Gomorrah with its lasciviousness. For whatever is worst in the enormity of their wrongdoings is most holy when compared to the foulness and degradation of heretical wickedness. This is why the Christian must fly from such indescribable evil, which transcends the sin of all crimes.

Book 3, ch. 16

There was at the same time, in the region of Toulouse, a certain old man who was wealthy in the things of the world and very poor in the goods of the Catholic faith. When he saw death approaching, worn down with old age and illness of the body, he conferred all the things he had to a certain Catholic man, his son, and wretchedly surrendered himself to the heretics, renouncing the Catholic faith that he had promised at baptism, and through a minister of Satan he gave himself up to heretical wickedness. This was reported by talkers to Catholic judges, and they went to the house of this most lost old man, urging him to

23 Vernacular French, Latinised as 'crapaldus'.

24 'Sect', like 'law', was sometimes used to denote what we call a 'religion'.

return to the cult of Catholic truth. Since the said old man persisted, however, in his wickedness and heaped blasphemies on the religion of the Catholic faith, the judges decided to consign him to the flames. When his aforesaid son saw this, he was in turmoil, and he began vehemently to sympathise with his father and plead with the judges to take all his property and to burn him instead of his father and to spare the old man, who was perhaps about to die at that very moment through old age and illness. The judges were utterly amazed and did not believe the things that were said by the son, objecting that a Catholic ought not to die in place of a heretic and a very handsome youth in place of an old man. Replying to them he said, 'I am very sorry the old man fell into error, but he has not stopped being my father. And because the Lord commanded honouring a father, I want to die not instead of a heretic but instead of a father'. There was judgment, therefore, in favour of the petition of his soul, and the youth was brought to the place of burning. With a loud voice he anathematised all heresy, and professed the Catholic faith, and prayed the Lord Jesus Christ and Mary the Virgin Mother of God, with all the saints, to be there as a help to him. Some Friars Minor were present at the time, and they argued vehemently with the judges, saying a Catholic son should not die for his heretic father in this way. And they got hold of the youth to stop him being put in the fire. While this was happening the flame itself, in the sight of everyone who was there, leapt forth like a fiery arrow and went straight to the old heretic's bed and the visible flame burnt up and consumed the flesh of the execrable old man. A clamour went up from all those who had run along <to see this>, and together with the judges they glorified Lord Jesus Christ, who with such an evident miracle had liberated the Catholic youth and had struck down the most wicked old man with a worthy punishment. Imperceptible fire fights on behalf of the Catholic faith and rebukes the inertia of men who do not rise up to use all their strength in the defence of Catholic faith.

Book 3, ch. 17

In addition, a certain heretic called Arnold came into Spain from the confines of Gaul, 'sowing the weed' [Matthew 13.24] of heretical error. Among other works of wickedness was his application to the work of corrupting the minor short works of the holy fathers Augustine, Jerome, Isidore and Bernard, subtracting true things and adding false ones. He was an exceptionally fast writer, and he sold or gave the corrupted short works of the saints to Catholics, so that with this sort of fallacy he could deceive and trap the minds of careless readers. …

15. RAINERIO SACCONI OP, *SUMMA ABOUT THE CATHARS AND POOR OF LYON*

From Piacenza, Sacconi spent seventeen years as a Cathar before becoming a Dominican and acting as an inquisitor in Lombardy in the 1250s; the last reference to him is in June 1262. In this treatise, which he wrote in 1250, he was able to draw on his experience of being a high-ranking Cathar – a marginal note on one its manuscripts refers to him as a leader, 'heresiarcha'. His account of the places and numbers of Cathars (the full-fledged ones, not their believers) shows the effects of persecution on Cathars in France. They were reduced in numbers and the majority of them lived in exile in Italy. This fits what deponents interrogated in Toulouse in the 1270s recounted, their memories of travelling in Italy and meeting there many heretics from Languedoc, including bishops.[25] The computations reported here were done repeatedly by Cathars, and about all their churches, which suggests relations among them not quite so riven by the hostile divisiveness that Catholic polemicists liked to attribute to them. See C. Bruschi, 'Converted-turned-inquisitors and the image of the adversary: Ranier Sacconi explains Cathars', in A. Sennis, ed., *Cathars in Question* (York, forthcoming); M. Benedetti, *Inquisitori Lombardi del duecento* (Rome, 2008), ch. 2.

A translation of the whole treatise can be found in WE, pp. 329–51. Our translation is from the text edited in F. Šanjek, 'Raynerius Sacconi, Summa de Catharis', *Archivum Fratrum Praedicatorum* 44 (1974), 31–60 (at pp. 49–50).

How many are the churches of the Cathars

There are in all sixteen churches of the Cathars. Reader, do not blame me for naming them 'churches', but rather those who call them thus.

These are their names. The Church of the Albanenses or of Desenzano. The Church of Concorezzo. The Church of the Bagnolenses, or of Bagnolo. The Church of Vicenza or of the March <of Treviso>. The Church of Florence. The Church of the valley of Spoleto. The Church of France [= *northern France or Île-de-France*]. The Church of Toulouse. The Church of Carcassonne. The Church of Albi. The Church of Sclavonia. The Church of the Latins of Constantinople. The Church

25 See *Inquisitors and Heretics*, index entries for Apulia, Italy, Lombardy and individual Italian cities, pp. 1070–88.

of the Greeks in the same place. The Church of Philadelphia in *Romania* [= *in the East Roman (Byzantine) Empire*]. The Church of Bulgaria. The Church of Drugunthia.[26] And all of them originated in the last two.

The places in which they live

The first, that is to say the Albanenses, live in Verona and in many cities of Lombardy. In number they are roughly around 500 of both sexes.

Those of Concorrezzo are dispersed virtually throughout the whole of Lombardy. And of both sexes they are 1500 and more.

The Bagnolenses – they are in Mantua, Brescia, Bergamo and in the county of Milan, but few of them; and in Romagna, and <there> they are 200 [*or* 200 overall].

The Church of the March: they have nothing at Verona, and they are around 100.

Those of Tuscany and the valley of Spoleto: almost 100.

The Church of France: they live at Verona and in Lombardy. And they are around 150.

The Church of Toulouse and of Albi and of Carcassonne, together with some who were once of the Church of Agen, which has been virtually destroyed: they are almost 200.

The Church of the Latins in Constantinople: they are almost 50.

Item, the Church of Sclavonia, and of Philadelphia, and of the Greeks, of Bulgaria, and of Drugunthia: altogether they are almost 500.

Reader, you can safely say that in the whole world Cathars of both sexes do not add up to 4,000. And once upon a time this calculation was frequently made among them.

26 On the names of the churches, see Doc. 1 above, n.22.

PART IV: SERMONS

INTRODUCTION TO PART IV

For those interested in seeing how 'heresy' was constructed rhetorically by orthodoxy, sermons are an invaluable source. They were always very consciously directed towards an audience (even if the specific nature of that audience is often now impossible to recapture)[1] and some sermon collections were copied and circulated very widely (and particular stories extracted and circulated even more widely), making them the closest thing the medieval period had to 'mass media'.[2] One can highlight the importance of their use of imagery, rhetoric and storytelling, and the ways in which these elements of construction drew upon a variety of earlier tropes and ideas. But one can also note that one of their tools was to frame very carefully the truth-claim of each tale: that a particular story came from a particular witness, or that another tale was taken directly from the preacher's own experience in a particular time and place, and so forth. In short, the sermons needed to work for an audience, and in part that required elements of verisimilitude and historical specificity.

We present here a selection of extracts from two of the most important works of preaching in the thirteenth century, the tales collected by Stephen of Bourbon for use in sermons and a more technical guide for preachers written by Humbert of Romans.[3] We have also included two short sermons devoted specifically to heresy, because of their rarity, and because of their geographical interest, providing as they do a brief glimpse of heresy in *northern* France (Doc. 16), and connections

1 Though Doc. 19 specifies that it was delivered in the vernacular to a particular parish on a specific date.

2 See, in general, D. L. d'Avray, *The Preaching of the Friars: Sermons Diffused from Paris before 1300* (Oxford, 1985); B. M. Kienzle, ed., *The Sermon* (Turhout, 2000); as 'mass media', D. L. d'Avray, *Medieval Marriage Sermons: Mass Communication in a Culture Without Print* (Oxford, 2001). For sermons and *exempla* against heresy in particular, see Sackville, *Heresy*, pp. 53–75; B. M. Kienzle, *Cistercians, Heresy and Crusade in Occitania, 1145–1229: Preaching in the Lord's Vineyard* (York, 2001); C. Muessig, 'Les sermons de Jacques de Vitry sur les Cathares', *CdF* 32 (1997), 69–83.

3 For Stephen's treatise only five complete mss are extant, but various individual tales circulated more broadly. The treatise written by Humbert, as one might expect from his fame and importance, was more popular; twenty-three whole or part mss are still extant.

between northern Italy and southern France (Doc. 19); these, it should be noted, are unlikely to have circulated widely, but do give examples of specific preaching against heresy.

Witnesses in Languedoc interrogated in the 1240s (see Doc. 48) sometimes told inquisitors that, while they had not heard heretics preaching their errors, they did however know some of their doctrines – through having listened to the orthodox clergy preaching against them. The sermon-aids used by clerics and friars producing these sorts of anti-heresy sermons survive in some manuscripts containing neither stories nor imagery, simply bald statements of heretics' doctrines, followed in each case by their supporting biblical authorities and arguments and opposing biblical authorities and arguments advanced by the Church. These will have emerged from the simple knock-each-other-on-the-head-with-authorities polemical tracts used in the public debates between Catholics and heretics that were so common in the years before the Albigensian crusade started in 1209 (see Doc. 5 §22–4, 26, 47–8, 51–2, 54). We have inserted an example (Doc. 11) into Part III, Treatises; see the discussion of this area in its introduction.

16. A SERMON FROM C. 1200

This text comes from a collection of sermons preserved in a Latin manuscript originally from the Benedictine abbey of St-Vaast in Arras. The modern editor suggests that the author's methods and mastery of the rhetoric of biblical exegesis, alongside his citations of Ovid, Priscian, Martianus Capella and medical authors (Hippocrates, Galen and Johannitius) indicate someone who had frequented the schools in Paris around 1200. He addresses lay and married people, filling his sermons with French terms, and he was interested in castigating usurers, prostitutes and heretics. Translated from Bernard Delmaire, 'Un sermon inédit sur les "bougres" du nord de la France (vers 1200)', *Heresis* 17 (1991), 1–15.

Sermon against heretics

> 'Take for us these little foxes that demolish the vine of the Lord' [Song of Songs 2.15]

These little foxes are those that Samson tied together by their tails in order to set fire to the harvests of strangers [*see* Judges 15.4–5] – they [*the foxes*] came together by their bottoms but they had diverse faces. For the heretics, who are signified by foxes, come together by their bottoms, that is to say in the evils of error. They set fire to harvests, that is to say faithful souls, with the fire of their perversity. But having diverse faces – that is to say, holding diverse sects of their error – they confound themselves. They rend the seamless coat of the Lord [*see* John 19.23], that is to say, the unity of the Church, and, struggling thus among themselves, they bring about the Church's victory. On account of this, therefore and in order to confound and confute all the cunning of all these people, it is necessary to delineate distinctly all their points and positions.

It should be known therefore that the Bulgars [Bulgari] of La Charité and all their accomplices, in whatever part of the world, and all the disciples of the awful Oton[4] who soil all the borders of this kingdom with the poison of their wickedness, transmit these absurdities of their utterly insane doctrine.

4 A heretical leader not mentioned in other sources.

First they assert that baptism does not save babies and that confession of sins is silly and of no profit to the person who confesses.

For all those who are imperfect,[5] they adjudge that they should engage in sex randomly. And in this way they vilify the sacrament of marriage.

They say that holy orders were instituted not by God but by men. Thus they neither believe that priests or bishops can bind or loose, nor that anyone ought to obey – so they teach – the prelates of the holy Church.

These diabolic people say that the making of the eucharist is diabolic work.

The resurrection of bodies is nothing to them, but the resurrection of souls is believed by them.

That which keeps vigil [*i.e. dominates*] among them is all the perversity of those who keep vigil.[6] For they take pride in ignoring in this life the souls of the saints and <in regarding> as pointless the tears with which we pray to the saints to pray for us.

Following Mani and his accomplices, they assert that God made nothing that was not transitory and fleeting.

They prattle that the sun, the moon and all the stars and the four elements were devised by the one who said, 'I shall ascend to heaven and place my throne to the north etc.' (Saint Augustine),[7] and, to despatch this matter briefly, they impudently preach that there are two principles of things.

They receive nothing from the Old Testament, asserting that the devil was the giver of the law of Moses.

Among the accomplices of such a perverse doctrine, there are some who call themselves 'Perfected',[8] who impose their hands on others and their story is that in this way they confer the Holy Spirit.

When speaking, in order to be credited as truth-tellers, these evil givers of the Spirit always proffer 'Yes' or 'No' [Matt. 5.37]. And they

5 Imperfectus – perhaps meaning 'not fully-fledged' heretics; see Doc. 40 for 'perfectus' as fully-fledged.

6 Conjectural translation of a passage where the ms. has several deletions and the text seems corrupt.

7 Augustine, *Enarrationes in Psalmos*, Ps. 88; Corpus Christianorum 39, p. 1228. See Isaiah 14.13–14.

8 'Perfecti' is conjectured by Delmaire in place of the manuscript's 'perversi'.

would force no-one to take an oath. Even if someone were dealing with them about faith, they would not confirm by oath that they believed properly.

They pray, so to say, on bended knees when in the presence of their believers, murmuring I don't know what between their lips. With raised voices, they adore the Father and the Son and the Holy Spirit, through saying the 'Our Father'.

They do not eat meat or eggs or cheese. They take pride in living splendidly on vegetables prepared with oil and pepper, every kind of fish, the best preserves and fruit.

They drink delicate wines <and> very strong wines, holding baptism in such hatred that they are unwilling to baptise wines with water.

They hide themselves in lay people's clothing, walking around with a simple air in order thus to deceive the simple, so that those who are wolves should be thought to be sheep, and in order more easily to destroy … [*ms. breaks off at this point*].

17. STEPHEN OF BOURBON: TALES ABOUT HERESY

Bernard Gui tells us that

> Brother Stephen of Bourbon, originally from Belleville[9] in the diocese of Lyon, compiled the *Book* or *Treatise on the Gifts, about Various Preachable Materials*, which he divided into seven parts, in accord with the seven gifts of the Holy Spirit and their effects, distinguishing materials by causes and effects; and he filled <the book> with authorities, arguments and tales [*exempla*] for the edification of souls. Its prologue begins thus: 'Because many have laboriously accomplished in various ways, subtly and usefully, etc.' The *Treatise of the Seven Gifts of the Holy Spirit* begins thus: 'Since the beginning of wisdom is fear of the Lord', etc. It is, further, a very big volume, even though it deals only with five gifts.[10] Its original exemplar is in the library of the brothers at Lyon. Many have drawn from it as though from a 'well running over' [4 Esdras 2.32], composing other shorter treatises about the seven gifts of the Holy Spirit. This Brother Stephen died in the convent at Lyon in 1261 or thereabouts.[11]

The convent in Lyon was the second centre after Paris for preaching,[12] the base at various times of Humbert of Romans, William Peyraut and Stephen himself. In the prologue to his vast *Treatise* Stephen argues for the usefulness of tales (*exempla*) to the preacher, and the rest of the work was intended to be a resource-book for preachers, as Bernard Gui describes above. Though the material on heresy and inquisition is scattered, most of it appears in the account of the fourth gift, Fortitude, under the sub-section Pride.

Sometimes, with Stephen, there is less overt concern for precision than in other Dominican writers of his time: see, for example, the slapdash use of and reference to Church texts in his first account on the names of sects – see below, extract (ix). It is particularly evident in his hotch-potch accounts of heretics' doctrines, spread across a number of different *exempla*; as these do not yet have the benefit of a modern edition that would enable us to precisely delineate what Stephen was doing, we have not translated them. However, we

9 Belleville-sur-Saône.

10 Stephen ended his work part way through the fifth gift.

11 Gui's note, copied in the seventeenth century from a no-longer extant ms. of his works, is translated here from *Tractatus de diversis materiis predicabilibus*, ed. Berlioz and Eichenlaub, I, p. xvi, n.5.

12 See D. L. d'Avray, *The Preaching of the Friars* (Oxford, 1985), pp. 147–9.

have provided one example in Stephen's second account of heretics' names, with annotation showing the complexity of Stephen's mix of patristic reading and stories derived from recent experience and history, all being converted into 'preachable materials' – see below, extract (xii). See J. Berlioz, 'La prédication des cathares selon l'inquisiteur Étienne de Bourbon (mort vers 1261)', *Heresis* 31 (1999), 9–35, and Berlioz, '"Les erreurs de cette doctrine pervertie …". Les croyances des cathares selon le Dominicain Étienne de Bourbon (mort v. 1261)', *Heresis* 32 (2000), 53–67. On Stephen's life, see *Tractatus de diversis materiis predicabilibus*, ed. J. Berlioz and J-L. Eichenlaub, Corpus Christianorum Continuatio Mediaeualis 124 (Turnhout, 2002), I, pp. xxi–xxxi.

Extracts from parts 1 and 3 of the treatise are translated from the complete edition currently in progress, *Tractatus de diversis materiis predicabilibus*, ed. Berlioz and Eichenlaub, and for other parts from A. Lecoy de la Marche, ed., *Anecdotes historiques, legendes et apologues tirés du recueil inédit d'Étienne de Bourbon, dominicain du XIIIe siècle* (Paris, 1877).

(i) [from Berlioz, **Prima Pars**, *p. 3]*

Beginning

Treatise on various preachable topics, organised and divided in seven parts, according to the seven gifts of the Holy Spirit and their effects, going through distinctions [= *sections*] of topics, and through their causes and effects, packed with authorities [= *quotations from authoritative texts*] and reasons [= *arguments*] and various tales that pertain to the edification of souls.

Prologue

Many have laboured in many ways, subtly and usefully to compile various authorities from the Old and New Testaments, their commentators, and various saints, under various titles and on various topics, and also to connect various arguments with the authorities. They have done these things in order to instruct men; to admonish, move and encourage them to fear and avoid future evil things, and through this to retreat from sins and desire the good, and to be truly penitent about evil things they have done and to manfully reject temptations; so that they may persevere in what is good, live worthily, act prudently; so that they may distinguish good things from evil things and select them; so that they may choose and place goods that are better and more pertinent to salvation above other things; so that they may understand, believe and think rightly; so that they may recall and acknowledge the gifts of God; so that – through tasting good things as good – they may appreciate, desire and love them; so that they may patiently bear the evils, as it were, of the present for the sake of God; so that they may despise transitory and vain goods, ardently desire and pressingly and prudently seek after eternal goods, and through perseverance obtain them. The salvation of men is at issue here, their whole way of life, and salutary preaching, which is what the present work is about. For it is *exempla* that are the most forceful in bringing up these things and impressing them and imprinting them in human hearts, *exempla* that instruct most effectively the ignorance of simple men, and impress and imprint them so that they are remembered more easily, longer and more tenaciously. Deeds teach more than words, as Gregory shows in the book of *Dialogues* [Gregory the Great, *Dialogues*, I, prol. 9], and *exempla* move people more than categories [= *the language of logic*]. And it was with the highest divine wisdom, therefore, that Jesus Christ taught first of all with deeds rather than words and rendered the subtlety of preaching and doctrine into a form that was as it were gross, physical and visible, investing it and clothing it in various similes, parables, miracles and *exempla*. He did this so that his teaching could be grasped more quickly, known more easily, retained in memory more strongly and implemented in action more effectively. In fact, since he himself was eternal wisdom, incorporeal, invisible and also incomprehensible to men, he willed this, to be embodied in time and clothed in flesh, so that he could be more easily known by men and comprehended by human senses. Therefore: 'The Word was made flesh and dwelt among us' [John 1.14]. The blessed Denis said on this: 'Wise philosophers give body to their statements, clothing them with similes and *exempla*. For a statement that has been fleshed out makes an easier journey from sense [= *being heard*] to the imagination and from imagination to memory'.[13]

And therefore I, Brother R.,[14] the least in the Order of Brothers Preacher, desiring in my littleness to be useful in some way to the salvation of men, leaving more elevated, subtle and profound things to more elevated, subtle and profound minds, for the honour of God and his mother and saints and for the salvation of souls and the edification of my fellow men: to achieve the aforesaid useful things, trusting in

13 Berlioz finds no exact source for this, but parallels in the writings of John of Damascus and Augustine.

14 Most probably a scribe's wrongly transcribing S as R; Berlioz, pp. xix–xxi.

the help of my fellows and not without a great deal of time and labour, I have assembled various *exempla*, from various books and on various topics and under various headings – and from various worthy and learned men, from whom I have heard many things. [*Part of Stephen's 'bibliography' then follows, a list of his written sources but not of his oral ones.*]

(ii) [from Berlioz, Prima Pars, *pp. 114–15]*

Part 1: On the Gift of Fear

Fourth Title: On Hell

Chapter 6: On the 12 conditions and miseries of the bodies of the dead after judgment. …

The sixth is stench. There will be a real stink from the fumes where the bodies of all heretics, lechers and other fetid sinners are being burnt. I was in a city when an extraordinarily horrible and very stubborn heretic, called the Auvergnat [*i.e.* 'the man from Auvergne'], was being burnt a long way outside the town. Although burnt human flesh is not wont to stink but rather, so it is said, to give off fragrance, an unexpected and abominable stench spread through the city and over those who had not gone out to burn him, as those who were with me said. And it seemed to me as though it was showing how fetid and horrific he was.

(iii) [from Lecoy de la Marche, pp. 78–9]

Part 2 On the gift of piety

The first title is on the word of God ….

What sort of people preachers of the word of God should be.

The teachers and hearers of the word of God ought first of all to be humble.

…

Item, when Diego, the Bishop of Osma, came to the land of the Albigensians, with beasts of burden and episcopal horses, he heard that the land was infected and he preached against heresies in a certain town. The heretics rose up against him. Having no stronger argument in the defence of their error than the luxury of the episcopal equipage, they spoke thus to their believers. 'How could you believe in these people and others like them? They who have such sumptuousness, wealth, beasts of burden and mounted retinues preach to you that Christ was humble and poor! By contrast', they said, 'we preach to you in poverty and humility and abstinence. What we say with our mouths we show in our actions'. Confounded by this, the bishop sent away and abandoned the horses, the sumptuousness and the equipage, and together with the blessed Dominic he began to preach in that land on foot and as a poor man. And this was the cause of the institution of our order, and I heard this from the brothers who were in that land with the blessed Dominic.

(iv) [from Lecoy de la Marche, pp. 96–7]

The sixth title, on the Blessed Mary

Why the Blessed Mary should be hailed devoutly and freely praised …

She should be hailed and praised because she restores and repairs what has gone amiss, when it is good for those who praise her. When a certain cleric had his tongue amputated by the Albigensian heretics, he went to Cluny to the church of the Blessed Virgin and although he could not praise her with his tongue he could and did praise her with his heart, and she willingly heard his praises. And so on a certain feast day when he heard others praising her he strove to praise alongside them, the Blessed Virgin quickly formed a new tongue for him in his palate and restored speech to him. And suddenly he began to praise with the others! The newness of this tongue was apparent when it was stuck out. I saw him when he had become a monk, and many who saw the new tongue and its place beforehand declared that they had been present at a miracle.

(v) [from Lecoy de la Marche, p. 140]

On the piety of parents

When I was preaching the cross against the Albigensian heretics at Vézelay, …

(vi) [from Berlioz, Tertia Pars, *pp. 41–2]*

Part 3 On the gift of Knowedge

Book 3. On those things which pertain to the gift of Knowledge and Penance

Chapter 5. Let it be seen here how penance ought to be, and how it ought not to be. …

And it is to be noted first of all that penance ought to be faithful: that it should not be the penance of infidels, that is to say heretics, or other infidels. Hebrews 11th: 'Without faith it is impossible to please God' [Hebrews 11.6].

About a jongleur's horse. On this theme, I heard from brothers <in Provence>[15] that there were certain heretics in the land of the Albigensians who were boasting among their believers about their external mortifications. A certain jongleur was present, and he said he would prove that his horse was better than them. For if they did not eat meat neither did his horse, nor did he drink wine or even eat bread. If their bed was bad, his was worse. But all these things and all other harsh and austere things ought to profit his horse more than them, because they did not believe in the articles of faith, rather they disbelieved them. Since 'without faith it is impossible to please God', nothing they did could please God. But his horse's actions could please God more, because although he did not believe he did not disbelieve in anything, and thus both in actions and faith his horse was in a better state than they were.

Note this about a heretic. I heard that there was a certain old woman called Alberea, a Manichaean, in the diocese of Châlons towards Mont-Aimé. On account of her error she did not eat meat or eggs or cheese, and she abstained from many things, not for the sake of God but in accordance with the doctrine of her sect. She was so renowned that all the inhabitants regarded her as most holy for doing this. To conceal her error she took communion every Sunday – she did not however have faith in or devotion towards the Lord's body. She was taken and burnt. She confessed in law[16] that all these things were the devil's works,

15 Latin is corrupt; could also be Brothers of Penitence.

16 That is, as part of legal process against her.

infected works and intended to infect souls. And therefore the aforesaid penance [*her abstinence*] not only did not profit her but harmed her, in accord with this passage of apostle to the Romans, 14: 'All that is not of faith is sin' [Rom. 14.23]. I heard this from those who had earlier convicted her of this and had adjudicated her a heretic, and from her son, called Theobald, who was a Manichaean heretic and burnt at Mont-Aimé, after the sentence that was delivered there against more than 80 Manichaean heretics. I was present at this sentence, as were also almost all the bishops of <northern> France.

(vii) [from Lecoy de la Marche, pp. 192, 213–14]

Part 4: On the Gift of Fortitude

Fifth title: On bad example and scandal

On the argument of heretics against Catholics

I heard from the brothers of Provence that in the land of the Albigensians, when heretics are being overcome by <objections from> the scriptures and reasoning, they have no stronger argument to use in defending their error and subverting the simple than the bad examples of Catholics, and above all of Catholic prelates. So, when other arguments fail, they still have recourse to this argument. They say, 'Look at the sorts of people these or those are, and above all the prelates. Look at how they live and how parade around, not walking as the men of old did, such as Peter and Paul and the others'.

Item, I heard from brothers at that time about some legates and thirteen abbots who were sent to the land of the Albigensians to preach against the Albigensian heretics. Since they had with them a retinue of horses to carry their clothes and other necessities for the road, while preaching against the heretics and errors, the heretics rose up against them, preaching back to them, especially weaving their sermons about the bad examples and extravagance of the way of life of the Catholics and the corruption of clergy and religious. The abbots were very dismayed by this, desisted from preaching which had been not very fruitful, and left the country. The heretics said, 'Look at how these horses preach to you of Christ their Lord, the man on foot! Look how these rich people preach of Christ the poor man! Look at how these men of rank preach of Christ the humble and rejected!' And more of the same.

(viii) [from Lecoy de la Marche, pp. 274–7]

<Part 4,> Seventh Title: On the seven deadly sins and their kinds … first, on pride and its kinds

On presumption

…

On heresy

Since presumption is the mother of error, we should now talk about heresy or error, which especially darkens and blurs the human intellect. We propose, then, to say these five things about heresy. Firstly, through what arguments against heresy the Catholic faith is demonstrated to be true and heresy refuted and faith strengthened in the hearts of believers. Secondly, how error in its bad effects acts against the good effects of faith. Thirdly, the evil circumstances that envelope a heretic deviating from the faith. Fourthly, the errors that infect the heretics of our time, that is to say, the Waldensians and the Albigensians, called Patarenes or Bulgars [Patareni, Bulgari]. Fifthly, the sophisms they use to try to conceal themselves, and how they are to be detected …

[Firstly] Item, reason proves and approves our faith through comparison with other sects, when one sees the writings containing their position and claims … For many Saracens, when comparing the Gospels with the Qur'an and finding the law of Mahomet laughable and inconceivable to natural reason, have converted to God. The wiser men among them also, when in secret conversation with our lot, judge our faith the better and admit this in secret. But they do not dare admit this in public, through fear of the death they would incur if caught out, or because of love of the pleasures with which they have been brought up, so I have heard from those brothers who have been among them. And many received baptism in secret …

Item, I heard that there was in recent times a great prince in Auvergne, called the Marquess of Montferrand,[17] a man of remarkably penetrating natural intelligence and exceptionally advanced age, believed to be of a good six score years [*sic*]. He had produced many poems about kings and princes and the estates of various men of his time, and for

17 Robert IV, Count (known as the Dauphin) of Auvergne, c. 1150–1234.

forty years he had applied care and effort to the collecting of books of all the sects, whatever ones he heard existed throughout the world – doing this at great expense. He loved to read these, and <also> had them read to him. When he was ill with the illness from which he died, some of our brothers visited him, who <later> told me these things. When one particular thing, among other stuff they said to him, came to his ears – that there had been worry about him possibly being a heretic, since they had heard that he both read and listened to these books being read, and also because of the proximity of his land to the lands of the Albigensians – he made this reply. 'It is true that for forty years I have been concerned to collect at great expense books of all the sects, and to read and study in them. For the more I would look there, the more I would be strengthened in the Catholic faith and more I would abominate heresies, seeing the fallacy of what they provided. And as an expression of the contempt I had, for sects other than the faith, I had a wooden box made <to contain these books> and placed under my feet where I would sit when on a seat in my privy. It was as though I could not show more contempt for these sects than by having them under my feet when I was sitting down and about to carry out a task of a foul nature. But I have always observed the Gospels of my Lord with great honour. I read the books of various sects, however, for this reason: since the Albigensian heretics border my land, <I did this> in order to know how to be on my guard against their cunning tricks if they talked to me about their errors, to know how to turn back their own spears, and refute them by <using> their own propositions and assertions.' He had the said heretics' books extracted from the said place, and burnt in front of his eyes. Many years before his death, he had borne the stigmata of our Lord Jesus on his own body, in memory of his Passion and faith. Together with other penances that he carried out in memory of the Lord's Passion, on each sixth ferial day he used to drive nails into his flesh until they drew blood.

(ix) [from Lecoy de la Marche, pp. 279–81]

Item, when some heretic came to the village called Jonvelle-sur-la-Saône, disguised as a crossbowman [*he was captured*] ... When questioned ... he acknowledged that he had known a good seventeen sects at Milan, divided among themselves and hostile to each other, all of them condemned by those of his sect. And he named them to me, along with their differences. The first sect, to which he belonged, is called 'the Poor of Lyon', who also call themselves 'the Poor in Spirit', and they are called 'Waldensians' after <the name of> their heresiarch. Together with their other errors they condemn all those who possess worldly goods. Item, 'the Poor of Lombardy', who received possessions, about whose errors we shall talk below. Item, others called 'the Loaflets' [Tortellini], who say that consecration can only be done once a year, and only by a perfected master of theirs. They make a little round loaf [tortellum], and receive it from him in communion. … Others say that all good men are priests – not women.

<On this point> others do not distinguish by sex. Others were called 'Communists', because they say all things should be in common. Others 'the Rebaptised', who say those <baptised> by the Church should be rebaptised. Item, the Arnoldists, Speronists, Leonists, Cathars, Patarenes, Manichees or Bulgars [Burgari]: <these> are named thus after their originators. If someone wants to look, however, at their division and variety, he should read Isidore, *On the Etymologies*, and there he will find a good 67 or 68 names of sects which have preceded our times, which is <also to be found> in the *Decreta* [*sic*], chapter 24, the third question, at the end.[18] …

(x) [from Lecoy de la Marche, pp. 282–3, 286]

Secondly, to talk about the good effects of the faith … because faith is true … one gains everything one asks for. … By contrast, infidelity does not gain what it asks for. …

Item, I heard that when some heretic was burnt, a certain believer of theirs gathered his ashes as relics. Someone was suffering a tiny bit in his eyes, and placed some of the said dust on his eyes, on the advice of the said believer, who promised him recovery. Immediately he became totally blind. …

Faith provides comfort … Comforted by this faith, martyrs went to their death gladly, like someone going to a wedding. By contrast heretics go to their death sadly.[19] I heard that when a certain Catholic knight was watching heretics being burnt, he saw they were always looking down to the ground, in the way wolves do, as they were being led to the fire, and always sad. Wondering about this, he asked some

18 Isidore, *Etymologiarum dive originum libri xx*, ed. W. M. Lindsay (Oxford, 1911), Book 8, iii.5, unpaginated; Gratian, *Decretum*, Case 24, question 3, chapter 39 (Friedberg, I, 1001–6).

19 Compare the comments of William of Auxerre and Roland of Cremona, Docs 12 and 13.

wise man why this was so. He said, 'Because they do not believe in God, they do not raise their faces up, they do not raise their eyes to the heavens, nor do they take any consolation from heavenly things, nor do they believe in heavenly things nor do they aim at them: rather, they aim at hell, where their lot and inheritance is, together with the apostate Judas. By contrast the holy martyrs, like blessed Stephen, and blessed Lawrence, Vincent and Martin, look upon heaven, because they believe the heavens are open to them after death'.

Faith proves the man; in tribulation the faithful man is proved … Item, the Lord also sometimes proves and approves faith through fire, disproving heresy, as one reads happened at the time of the blessed Dominic in the land of the Albigensians [… *the story of heretics trying to burn Dominic's schedule of theological propositions*].[20] …

(xi) [from Lecoy de la Marche, pp. 287, 288–90]

[Thirdly], here we should look at the evil qualities and conditions in which heretics are wrapped. … Firstly, then, heretics are blind … They are liars. Timothy 4 [1 Tim. 4.1–2]: 'Some shall depart from the faith, giving heed to spirits of error, and doctrines of devils, speaking lies in hypocrisy'. … For now, seeing they cannot prevail by arguments and debates, they clothe their lies with duplicities and twists and sophisms and covers and evasions of words, to avoid their falsity being apparent: as though the addition of lies to fraud would remove rather than increase their guilt; and as though they were not perjurors, although they deceive intentionally, and perjure fraudulently.

Like a certain woman heretic: though she swore she had not gone to the land and schools of the Albigensians, when she was convicted of this, she pleaded innocence of the perjury, saying she had not gone there, because her journey by boat had been delayed. Another woman, though she swore on the Gospels and was convicted of perjury, said she was not a perjuror for swearing on a missal, for that book, so she said, was not the Gospel but dead skins.[21] When another woman was handing over her daughter to the heretics, on their advice she pretended to be going on pilgrimage to some holy <place>, taking her daughter with her. They received her in an underground house, clothing her in their

20 See Doc. 5 §54, and medieval lives of St Dominic in general.

21 Notion attributed by Paul of St Père of Chartres, writing in the late eleventh century, to those accused of heresy in Orléans in 1022; WE, p. 81.

habit and returning her old clothes to the mother, saying, 'Now you can declare to your neighbours that your daughter has passed out of this world and it has buried her. Having passed from the world, she has <come> to us and has been received in an underground house: and she is dead to the world'. Which she did, as <they told her>. Although she paid the priest for a burial <service>, as though she were dead, and spoke about her in this way, when the daughter left the heretics' community after seven years and returned, she revealed the fraud. The mother, remaining obstinate in her infidelity, was burnt …

<Heretics> are impure and depraved, and for this reason without a divine miracle cannot return to their earlier condition, like metal waste that cannot become silver and lees that cannot become wine. In the land of the Albigensians a certain heretic was putting to a Catholic a point of opposition <in debate, saying> that his sect was better than the faith of the Roman Church, because our Catholics sometimes became heretics, but not heretics Catholics. The Catholic replied that this was rather evidence of an excess of wickedness and rottenness. For the best wine sometimes becomes vinegar, not the other way round, especially when it has gone off; and grain turns into tares and weeds, not the other way round.

(xii) [from Lecoy de la Marche, pp. 290, 299–300, 301–2]

Fourthly, to talk about the heretics of our time, that is to say, the Waldensians and Albigensians, whence they originated, and from what, and how and why they have their names, and with what errors they involved and fight against the true faith. The Waldensians are so named from the first author of this heresy[22] …

According to what the blessed Augustine and Isidore say, the *Manichees*, whose plague still infects many places, took *their origin from a certain Persian called Manes*,[23] who was truly a maniac together with his followers, both in name and reality, and a demoniac, as the apostle says in the first <Epistle> to Timothy, 4: 'In the last times some shall depart

22 Stephen's account of the origins of the Waldensians, partly based on his talking with priests who knew Valdes, is translated in WE, pp. 208–10.

23 Augustine, *De haeresibus*, xlvi.1, ed. R. Vander Plaetse and C. Beukers, Corpus Christianorum Series Latin, 46, Aurelii Augustini Opera XIII.2 (Turnhout, 1969), p. 312; translated Peters, *Heresy and Authority*, p. 33. Isidore copied the first line of Augustine exactly in his *Etymologies*, only turning 'Manis' into 'Manes'.

from the faith, giving heed to … the doctrines of devils … forbidding to marry, to abstain from meats, etc.'[24] He arose after the times of the apostles in the early Church, like a plague, saying he was the Paraclete spirit whom the Lord promised to send to his disciples [John 14.16]. His <followers> called this Manes 'Manicheus' to avoid the word for insanity, and called themselves 'Manichees' after him, though they should rather be called 'Maniacs'. These are named by different people in different ways.

They are called 'Albigensians' for this reason, that they infected first of all that part of the province <of Narbonne>[25] that is towards Toulouse and the city of Agen, around the river *Alba* [*perhaps:* Tarn]. By the Lombards, also, they are called 'Cathars' [Gazari] or 'Patarenes' [Pathari]. By the Germans, 'Cathars' [Katari] or 'Catharists' [Katharistae].[26] They are also called 'Bulgars' [Burgari], because their special lair is in Bulgaria [Burgaria]. …

Item, they regard all meats as impure. Nor do they eat them, saying they are impure because they are procured through sexual intercourse and sleeping together; and because when they are killed all good nature leaves them;[27] and because they are the work of the prince of darkness.

24 Stephen selects parts of verses 1 and 3.

25 'Province' indicates the ancient Roman province, equivalent to modern-day Languedoc and Provence.

26 High medieval authors looked at the names of patristic sects and heresies and brief expositions of their doctrines mainly in (i) Augustine's *De haeresibus* CCSL 46, pp. 263–358, (ii) Isidore of Seville's *Etymologiarum sive originum libri XX*, ed. W. M. Lindsay, 2 vols (Oxford, 1911, unpaginated), viii.5, and (iii) Gratian's *Decretum*, which copied Isidore, thereby securing massively wider dissemination (Case 24, question 3, chapter 39, Friedberg, I, 1001–6). Modern scholars dispute what medieval authors meant when they applied the names of historical heresies to their contemporaries, but it did not necessarily mean they thought the new heresies were identical to the old; nor does it mean that all authors had the same view of them. In Augustine they would find 78 named sects, two of which are relevant here. (i) His no. 38 is the heresy of the 'Catharœ', who are a sub-group not of the Manichees but of the Novatians. 'The Cathars (Catharœ), who with great pride and odiousness call themselves by this name, do not allow second marriages, reject penance and follow the heretic Novatus, whence they are called Novatians'; Augustine, *De haeresibus* xxxviii, CCSL 46, pp. 306–7. (ii) His no. 46 is the heresy of the Manichees, and he describes three sub-groups, one being the 'Catharists' (Catharistae). The name was thereby associated with Manichaean doctrines, and also with obscene practices, described immediately before their name occurs; *De haeresibus* xxxviii, CCSL 46, p. 315; translated Peters, *Heresy and Authority*, p. 35.

27 This ground – but not the other two – is derived from Augustine, *De haeresibus* xxxviii.11, CCSL 46, p. 316; Peters, *Heresy and Authority*, p. 36.

They permit their Auditors [Auditoribus][28] to eat them, but forbid them utterly from killing them.

I heard that the Gallic [*northern French*] Catholic knights used to examine heretics in the land of the Albigensians in this way. They gave suspects chickens or other animals to kill, reckoning that those who were unwilling to kill them were heretics or their believers.[29] …

(xiii) [from Lecoy de la Marche, pp. 307–8]

Lastly [= Fifthly], we should look at the signs that mostly characterise heretics and <enable them> to be detected.

There are four signs by which heretics can be known, first their unwarranted usurpation to themselves <of the offices of preaching and teaching>, secondly the poison of their diffusion, thirdly the business of their hiding, fourthly their use of sophisms. …

Fourthly, when they used to dare to do this, and when men in the Church were less educated and there were <in the Church> fewer learned men, they were accustomed to defend themselves with arguments – fictitious ones – and in debates. Now, however, because they cannot <any longer> protect themselves in arguments or debates without their stupidity becoming clear, and <also> because they are frightened of being arrested, they wrap themselves in lots of sophisms, through the use of these trying to escape and deceive those who question them.[30]

28 Term from Augustine, *De haeresibus.* In the immediately following exemplum, Stephen moves from the patristic term 'Auditors' to the contemporary 'heretics' believers'.

29 In 1273 a woman recalled this test being applied to her grandmother's first husband. See *Inquisitors and Heretics*, p. 273.

30 The examples Stephen then provides were copied by Bernard Gui in the early fourteenth century in his description of the Waldensians; translated WE, pp. 400–1.

18. HUMBERT OF ROMANS ON INQUISITION AND HERESY

Born in the late twelfth century in the small town of Romans in the Dauphiné, Humbert studied canon law and theology in Paris, entering the Dominican Order there in 1224, and later serving as lector and prior (by 1237) of the convent in Lyon before becoming Master-General of the Dominican Order (1254–63). He died in 1277. His instructional treatise for preachers was compiled after 1263. Part of it was 'Materials for sermons', some for groups of persons and some for particular occasions. On Humbert, see E. T. Brett, *Humbert of Romans: His Life and Views of Thirteenth-Century Society* (Toronto, 1984); A. Murray, 'Religion among the poor in thirteenth-century France: the testimony of Humbert de Romans', *Traditio* 30 (1974), 285–324; for many additions to our knowledge of Humbert, see the editorial matter in Humbert of Romans, *Legendae sancti Dominici*, ed. S. Tugwell (Rome, 2008), pp. 325–8 dealing with the text provided here; and D. L. d'Avray, *The Preaching of the Friars: Sermons diffused from Paris before 1300* (Oxford, 1985), pp. 52–5, 147–8, 159. Translated from *On the Instruction of Preachers*, Book 2, chap. 62; *Maxima Bibliotheca Veterum Patrum*, ed. M. de La Bigne (Geneva, 1677), vol. 25, p. 555. We have used numbering and italics to emphasise that these are a set of notes designed to be expanded by a preacher giving an actual sermon based upon them.

61. On the inquisition of heretics

One should note that just as among angels there are some good and some bad ones, who sometimes transform themselves into the form of the good ones, following this passage, 2 Corinthians 11 [11.14], 'For Satan himself transformeth himself into an angel of light'; and among prophets there were some good ones and some false ones, pretending they were good, following this passage, 2 Peter 2 [2.1], 'There were two pseudo-prophets among the people'; and among the apostles there were some true ones and some false ones, pretending they were true, following this passage, 2 Corinthians 11 [11.13], 'Such are pseudo-apostles, deceitful workers, transforming themselves into apostles of Christ' – likewise, among Christians there are some true Christians holding true faith about Christ, and some false Christians holding false faith. They are both similar in their Christianity [*in their behaviour and apparent devotion*], and the false ones are similar in external appearance. These false ones, however, are those ministers of Satan about whom Paul speaks, 2 Corinthians 11 [11.15], 'The ministers of Satan are transformed as ministers of justice'.

One should note, further, that these false men are those 'tares' in the good field which 'the enemy' of man – that is to say, the devil – 'sowed over' the good seed, Matthew 13 [13.25]. They are those 'false prophets who come to' men 'in sheep's clothing, but inwardly are ravening wolves', as appears 'from their fruits' [Matt 7.15–16] <that they bear> for those who believe in them. They are the worst of men in any sort of sin, on account of the hope which they give <to their believers> about the ease of gaining mercy through the imposition of hands, Matthew 7. These are also that Antichrist who will pretend to be the true Christ, who will however be against him, just as they pretend to be true Christians but are however against them. Whence it is well said in 1 John 2 [2.18], 'Now there are many Antichrists'.

Item, one should note that they commit many serious evil things. They condemn the holy scriptures. 2 Peter, penultimate and ultimate chapters [2 Peter 2–3], 'The unlearned and unstable wrest' Paul's epistles 'and other scriptures to their own destruction' [2 Peter 3.16].

Item, just as Paul was building the Church during the time of his persecution, so also do they <build theirs>, scurrying through various places. 2 Timothy 3 [3.6]: 'Of this sort are those who creep into houses, and lead captive little women'.

Item, they corrupt the faith through false doctrine, which they mix with true doctrine, just as cancer corrupts one's flesh. 2 Timothy 2 [2.17]: 'Their speech spreadeth like cancer'.

Item, it should be noted that heresy always has stubbornness tied to it. It is not error that makes someone a heretic, but stubbornness. The difficult-to-break rope that draws man towards good is threefold: that is to say authority, reason and example. But these men are so obstinate that authority <such as scripture> does not move them, because they interpret it wrongly. Nor do reasons [*arguments*] move them, because they are unreasonable cattle, not understanding reason. Nor do examples move them – so many examples and of such great men who were and are in the Church, like great lights: for they prefer their few to all the people of this holy multitude. The Church therefore, having no other effective remedy against them, relies on their capture.

Conclusion. Therefore I ask all of you faithfully to help me, all of you, in finding and capturing them – <which is> the object of my being sent here.

Three things ought to move you to this.

The first is the zeal for the faith which ought to flourish in everyone. The Lord permitted heresies for this reason, that the faithful should be proved in their persecution. 1 Corinthians 11 [11.19]: 'For there must also be heresies among you, that they which are approved may be made manifest among you'.

The second is the great indulgence which we give to such people, namely, 'So and so',[31] etc.

The third is avoidance of the penalty of excommunication and such like, which henceforth we bring to bear on all who do not tell the truth that they know on this matter.

Text. Song of Songs 2 [2.15]: 'Take for us the little foxes that demolish the vines'. *Note,* that foxes scurry craftily at night-time through various places to take hens: thus heretics hide themselves for the taking of souls. And they are called 'little' on account of their pretended humility. Further, they 'demolish vines' when they spoil the holy scriptures, which are 'the vines of the Lord', proffering instead inebriating wine. And when they lay waste to the Church, which is also 'the vines of the Lord', possessing countless branches of good morals. And when they corrupt the faith, which is another 'vine' possessing precious shoots of good works. Such people are taken for the Lord, when they are taken, not out of hatred but for His honour.

One should note that just as among angels, etc.

62. On the solemn condemnation of heretics

Men are usually assembled together in public on the occasion of the <solemn> condemnation of heretics, when sentence is delivered against them. And because there are many who are moved by a false compassion with regards to them and judge the Church for excessive cruelty towards them, it is worthwhile explaining in a public sermon (i) why the Church inquires about heretics more thoroughly than about

31 'So and so' to be replaced, within a form for the giving of an indulgence, by the name of the individual to whom it is granted.

other sinners, and (ii) why it punishes them more heavily, and (iii) why it receives them back to repentance with more difficulty.

(i) On the first issue, *one should note* that heretics are more harmful in the Church than other sinners. For thieves and robbers are only harmful as regards temporal goods, and murderers in matters of the body. But heretics are harmful in spiritual matters, that is to say faith, which is the foundation of all goods, so that when it is destroyed everything collapses, like a tower when its foundation is removed. Therefore, just as sappers of towers are the most harmful to a castle, so are these to the Church – and they are more consistently harmful than thieves and murders, who commit their crimes infrequently. These assiduously run around various localities, both night and day pressing on with the business of drawing people into their sect. Furthermore they are more fraudulently harmful, through the appearance of piety that they pretend, as the apostle says, 2 Timothy 3.[32] Under this guise they administer poison, just like a treacherous doctor, according to this passage from 1 John 1: 'These things I have written to you concerning them that seduce you' [1 John 2.26]. Therefore because they bring about disaster, so seriously, so consistently and so fraudulently, it is just that there should be inquisition to root them out, carried out more thoroughly than against other sinners: just as there is a more thorough inquiry about a more harmful, more frequent and more cunning thief.

(ii) On the second point, *one should note* that heretics along with their supporters – for through the favour they show them the supporters make themselves part of all their evils – are punished without exceptions of persons. Whence, even if the pope were a heretic, he would be deposed.

Item, <they are punished> harshly: here there are some condemned to wearing some signs, here some condemned to prison for ever or for a fixed period, here some relinquished to the secular arm.

Item, <they are punished> in public, for they do this in the presence of everyone. And so, in this way, all of them are punished harshly and in public, to instil into every soul fear of perpetrating similar things. And we have an example of this sort of heavy punishment in this passage from the apostle, 1 Tim. 1: 'Some have made shipwreck concerning the faith, of whom is Hymeneus and Alexander, whom I have delivered up to Satan' [1.20]. Augustine, in the gloss on this: 'The apostle was

32 2 Tim. 3.5: 'Having the appearance indeed of Godliness, but denying the power thereof'.

of such great power that he would hand over to the devil those who retreated from the faith just by his word alone'.[33]

(iii) On the third point *one should note* that the infection of heresy is so great – arising from the heretic thinking that he believes well and that he has arguments in support – that hardly any one of them truly converts, even though sometimes they pretend to.

Item, this sort of vice is contagious, for the heretic infects the faithful.

Item, vicious men of this sort, even when they convert, easily relapse.

Therefore, although the Church never finally closes its bosom to anyone who is truly penitent, in a heretic's case the Church makes things very difficult, because of its lack of confidence in the truth of his confession, and because of its fear of contagion – as of one once infected with leprosy, who is scarcely reconciled – and because of the incentive to lapsing afforded by easy pardoning.

Conclusion. Let it be known to all of you that, because of ill report ⌜infamia⌝ and probable suspicions, we came to this place to inquire about heretics, as belongs to us by virtue of our office. And, proceeding according to the order of law, we found certain things which if we could in good conscience overlook we would willingly do. But because the counsel we have had from many wise men says that we cannot do this, it is our duty to proceed to some punishments, moderated according to the same men's counsel.

We ask God therefore and we ask you that you ask Him with me, that with the gift of His grace He makes those who are to be punished bear with such patience the punishments, which, as justice demands, we (though with anguish) propose to impose on them, that it redounds to their salvation.

On N. on account of X we impose the punishment of Y.

Material on the aforesaid things:

Text, Deuteronomy 7: 'When there shall be found among you within any of thy gates man or woman that serve strange Gods, and this is told

33 The *Ordinary Gloss* (*Glossa ordinaria*) on the Bible, a systematic collection of excerpts from patristic and early medieval comments on phrases and verses in the Bible, produced by Anselm of Laon and his followers in the early twelfth century, became a standard work of reference. This gloss comes just after one attributed to Augustine, but in the edition consulted here is ascribed to the ninth-century monk and commentator on Paul's epistles, Haimo of Auxerre, *Bibliorum sacrorum cum glossa ordinaria*, 6 vols (Venice, 1603), VI, p. 692, accessible on the website of the Lollard Society.

thee, and hearing it thou hast inquired diligently, and found it to be true, thou shalt bring forth the man or the woman who have committed that most wicked thing, to the gates of thy city, and they shall be stoned'.[34]

Note, however

– that this abbreviated passage in a few words touches upon the diligent inquiry to be made into infidel idolatry on a mere report, where it says 'When there shall be found' and as far as 'diligently';

– *item*, <*note*> their heavy punishment, where 'to be true' is said, and from there up to the end;

– *item*, <*note*> the exclusion of mercy, for there is not any mention of it. There is the *argument* that the same should be done to a heretic, who in many things is worse.

But, 'because there are many who are moved by a false compassion',[35] etc.

[63. On the preaching of the cross, in any sort of way]

…

64. On the preaching of the cross against heretics

It should be known that in many ways heresy is the worst among all kinds of sins.

Many other sins do not have obstinacy, but heresy has this. For, according to Augustine, error does not make a heretic. Whence he says, 'I could err, but I shall not be a heretic'.

Further, there are many other sins which stay only in the subject [*i.e. the sinner*], this one however goes into other people, because it is infectious. On account of this it is often signified in scripture by leprosy. It is not ridiculous to understand as leprous those who do not have the knowledge of true faith and profess various doctrines of errors.

Further, there are many other sins that do not cover themselves, and therefore those who perpetrate these things clearly acknowledge that

34 Deuteronomy 17.2–5, abbreviated.

35 Referring back to the second sentence of this chapter.

they are acting badly. This, however, covers itself up under the likeness of good. So, no heretic says he believes badly – rather that he believes well. And therefore it is said about heretics, Matthew 7 [7.15]: 'They come to you in the clothing of sheep, but inwardly they are ravening wolves'.

Item, one should note that among all sins this one is very harmful. For other sins harm either just the person who is committing them or a few others. This sin, however, aims to destroy the whole Church. On account of this heretics are signified in the 15<th chapter> of Judges [15.4–5] by Samson's foxes, which had tails tied together but faces turned in different directions.[36] For although heretics are divided among themselves, all of them are tied together in their objective of destroying the Church. Further, they multiply the paths that lead down to hell when they invent new sects of errors through which one can descend thither. 2 Peter 2 [2.1]: 'There shall be among you lying teachers, who shall bring in sects of perdition'. Further, like thieves who turn pilgrims away from a good path, they turn away from their route those who are ascending to heaven by the path of true faith, holding out the hope of a better life. Whence it is said about them, 1 John 3 [*recte* 1.4.1]: 'Many false prophets have gone out into the world'. For where is there greater leading astray than diverting from their path those who are walking in a good way? Look at the enormous damage here, the struggle to destroy the Church, to make new paths to hell, to turn men away from the straight path to heaven!

Item, one should note that the Church uses many remedies against heretics. It uses doctrine, in preaching, debating and discussion. But this does not work among many people. For they [*the heretics*] expound authorities perversely, and although they are few and illiterate [idiotae], they believe their own sense <of these> rather than the whole multitude of saints and wise teachers who have been and are in the Church.

Item, it uses the remedy of excommunication, for all heretics are ipso facto excommunicate. But they do not care about this, because they do not hold that prelates of the Church have this sort of power.

Item, where it has the power, it uses penalties against them. With regard to honours, they are punished by removal from office, as regards to temporal goods by confiscation, as regards to the body by brandings

36 See 4th Lateran Council (1215), can. 3, Tanner, *Ecumenical Councils*, I, 233, lines 13–14.

and even by death, when they are relinquished to the secular arm. But sometimes they defend themselves against these with the secular power that they have themselves or via their supporters. Then, when all milder remedies do not work, the Church uses military persecution against them – like a wise doctor, who uses iron to cut away a rotten member that is infecting others, when lighter remedies do not work. For it is better for the member to be destroyed by iron or fire than for it to corrupt healthy members.

And *note* that according to the Old Law there are three kinds of men who are worthy of <being put to> death. One is that of the blasphemers, 24 Leviticus: 'He that blasphemeth the name of the Lord, dying let him die' [24.16]. Another is of those committing an offence against the good of the community [respublica], 22nd chapter of Exodus: 'Evildoers thou shalt not suffer to live' [22.18]. For those are called 'evildoers' [malefici] who do harm to others.[37] Another is those who are pythonical, who have a python in their belly, Leviticus 20: 'A man or a woman, in whom there is a pythonical or divining spirit, dying let them die' [20.27]. Since therefore the heretics are the highest among blasphemers, saying many inappropriate things about God, and to the highest degree harm the good of the community, that is to say the Church, as was shown above, and have the spirit or evil of divination, by whose inspiration they undoubtedly divine many things and produce dreams about the scriptures – what is be done with them in the New Law? For in the New Law one ought to strive with even more zeal on behalf of the faith, and for every truth and for what is worthwhile.

Conclusion. Look therefore, most beloved, and behold how great is the wickedness of heretics, look also at how much harm they do in the world, and look again at how piously and in how many pious ways the Church labours to call them back. But none of these things will be able to work with them, and in fact they defend themselves with secular power. And therefore holy mother Church, reluctantly and with sorrow, summons a Christian army against them. Whoever therefore has zeal for the faith, whoever there is whom God's honour touches, whoever there is who wishes to have this large indulgence: let him come, and let him take up the sign of the cross. Let him join himself to the militia of the Crucified.

37 In this period, *malefici* came also to have the specific meaning of 'evil magic worker' or 'witch', but that is not necessarily intended here.

Material on the aforesaid things.

Text, Psalm 93: 'Who shall rise up for me against the evildoers? Or who shall stand with me against the workers of iniquity?' [93.16]

And *note*, that this was once said by King David, but now is said by Jesus Christ. For heretics are those evildoers about whom it is said: 'I have hated the assembly of the malignant' [Ps. 25.5].

Workers of iniquity are their believers, who rashly expose themselves to all iniquity in the hope of the easy forgiveness <of sins> that the heresiarchs promise them.

It is to be *noted* further, as above.

19. A SERMON FROM ITALY

Born into a noble family in Pisa around 1200, Federico Visconti studied in Bologna, became a chaplain of Pope Innocent IV and attended him at the Council of Lyon in 1245, and was Archbishop of Pisa from 1254 until his resignation, shortly before death, in 1277. This sermon was delivered during this period, taking as its theme Matthew 5.14, 'You are the light of the world', and explicating this in regard to the history of St Dominic and the Dominican order. We include an extract from it here because of its explicit mention of links between northern Italy and southern France. On Visconti, see R. Brentano, *Two Churches: England and Italy in the Thirteenth Century* (Princeton NJ, 1968), pp. 192–204, and A. Murray, *Conscience and Authority in the Medieval Church* (Oxford, 2015), ch. 4. Translated from N. Bériou et al., eds, *Les sermons et la visite pastorale de Federico Visconti, archevêque de Pise (1253–1277)* (Rome, 2001), pp. 670, 673, 675, 677–8.[38] The numbering is from this edition.

Sermon on the feast of St Dominic [5 August], master of the Preachers, which the same Lord <Federico Visconti> made in the vernacular at Santa Caterina[39]

You are the light of the world, Matthew 5[.14]

… [7] Following the five properties of the light of the sun, so the blessed Dominic is said to be the light of the world: namely the light of the world is firstly of the heavens, secondly it illuminates the whole world, thirdly it gives itself continuously, fourthly <it gives itself> freely, fifthly it expels darkness.

… [12] Item, just as light illuminates the whole world, so was the whole world illuminated by his [*Dominic's*] preaching. For there was not a race [gens] to whom the Preachers would not go to preach the word of God and illuminate their hearts in the faith; and indeed they even went to the Tartars, returning to the lord Pope Innocent IV at

38 See also André Vauchez, 'Les origines de l'hérésie cathare en Languedoc d'après un sermon de l'archevêque de Pise Federico Visconti († 1277)', in *Società, istituzioni, spiritualità: Studi in onore di Cinzio Violante* (Spoleto, 1994), pp. 1023–36.

39 Conventual church of the Dominicans in Pisa.

Lyon and bringing with them <news of> their way of life and customs written in a certain little book, which the same lord pope gave to us ...[40]

[The sermon turns now to Dominic's protection of the flock – the laity – from the wolves – the heretics; and his constant and freely given preaching, matching the third and fourth properties of light]

... [16] Item, the fifth property of light is that it drives out shadows and darkness ...

Thus the blessed Dominic drove out double shadows and darkness, namely the ignorance of heretical wickedness and of sinners, with the light and clarity of his preaching, as is shown in the example of a certain Lady of Toulouse: when staying in her house and knowing she was a heretic, he converted her by his preaching to the Catholic faith. Item, since in those parts of Toulouse and also in the Albigeois, the heresy of the Manichaeans was growing extraordinarily, so that this passage from the Psalm could be said about them: 'They have not known nor understood, they walk on in darkness, <all the foundations of the earth> shall be moved' [Ps. 81.5].

[17] But why had heretical wickedness grown there? Mainly for this reason. The heretics knew that the nobles living in those mountains were full of two vices, that is to say, avarice and lust. For they were thieves, preying on the public highways, and they also had sex indiscriminately with both married women and others. Under the pretence of piety they [*the heretics*] began to preach that they [*the nobles*] were doing very bad things, totally despoiling men in this way and making them poor. Done in this way, this was against the will of God. Although one man may take from the goods of another man in case of necessity, since according to the will of God all things are common [*in time of necessity*], one ought not to take away goods in this way, in order to be enriched by the act. 'Thou shalt not steal' [Ex. 20.15], that is, in order to enrich yourself. And therefore they [*the heretics*] were saying: 'We grant you this. When the carts of the merchants' cloths from <northern> France come through Marseille or to Montpellier, do not take them all but just take one or two pieces, as much as each of you needs, for yourself, your wife and your household'.

40 The *Historia Tartarorum* of Simon of St-Quentin; see J. Richard, *Simon de Saint-Quentin, Histoire des Tartares* (Paris, 1965).

They talked to them in a similar way about women, that they were not allowed to commit adultery with other men's wives, because this was against the will of God who forbade this in the Old Testament, Ex. 20, 'Thou shalt not commit adultery' [20.14]; again, 'Thou shalt not covet thy neighbour's wife' [20.17]. But you can safely do this without sin with single women, since it is natural, for the Lord said, 'Increase and multiply and fill the earth', Gen. 3 [1.22]. And so many of them often came together in one house, ten or twenty men and the same number of unmarried women, and after putting out the light of candles they had sex with each other, as though in love [quasi in caritate]. For, as the Lord said, 'They loved darkness more than light', John 3 [3.19], 'for their works were evil', as 'The eye of the adulterer observeth darkness', Job 24 [24.15]. And they are like thieves who are hypocrites, and bats, that is, unable to see the world's light, and similar beasts.

Because of this, the heretic preachers were regarded with great reverence and honour, and there was belief in them and their sermons. And so they began to preach, harmfully and fraudulently, that there were two principles, God and the devil, and that all these visible things and even our flesh were from the evil principle, that is from the devil. The soul, however, and all spiritual things were from the good principle, in fact from the good God. And they persuaded them of many other errors, and people believed them. And so it came about that that great region came to be full of heretics, both male and female, to such an extent that, because of the multitude of heretics, they preached publicly, even under the eyes of Catholic prelates.

[18] [*The sermon goes on to relate the tale of St Dominic's debate with the heretics, and the bonfire expelling the text of authorities which Dominic had supplied*][41]

41 See Doc. 5 §54.

PART V: LETTERS AND PAPAL BULLS

INTRODUCTION TO PART V

In this part we present a variety of letters, from a very public letter, widely circulated with the aim of stirring prelates into action against heresy (Doc. 21), to administrative letters, sent in the course of dealing with the practicalities of prosecuting heresy (Docs 25, 26), to a petitionary letter sent by the townspeople of Carcassonne complaining about an inquisitor (Doc. 27B).

The bulk of material here comes however from papal bulls – letters and decretals (the latter cannot be defined, but the term is sometimes used of a letter deliberately and explicitly settling issues of law).[1] There are several very famous papal letters which sit at the heart of the Church's prosecution of heresy, from *Ad abolendam* (1184)[2] and *Vergentis in senium* (1199)[3] to Gregory IX's 'founding' bulls commissioning inquisition against heresy (1231)[4] and the bull addressed to rulers of Italian cities, permitting them to use torture, *Ad extirpanda* (1252),[5] not to mention various other papal bulls relating to the Albigensian crusade.[6] These texts are all well known from secondary literature, and full or partial translations can be found elsewhere.

The papal texts we have chosen here provide some different and additional perspectives, and in particular cast light on geographical areas where other source materials are largely or wholly lacking. We have chosen material that tells us of activity against heresy in northern France (Doc. 20), with a particular focus on the Inquisitor Robert Lepetit (Docs 22, 23), which can be set alongside documents in Part

1 On the composition and style of these letters, see Léglu, Rist and Taylor, *Cathars*, pp. 25–8; and on the language used of 'peace', in an Italian context, A. Piazza, 'Paix et hérétiques dans l'Italie communale: les stratégies de langage dans les registres du pape Grégoire IX', in R. M. Dessi, ed., *Prêcher la paix et discipliner la société: Italie, France Angleterre (X^e^–XVe siècles)* (Turnhout, 2005), pp. 103–21.

2 Translated in Peters, *Heresy and Authority*, doc. 29, pp. 170–3.

3 See Sackville, *Heresy*, p. 224 (index entry) on the language of this.

4 Trans. in Peters, *Heresy and Authority*, doc. 38, pp. 196–8; Sibly, *William of Puylaurens*, appendix D, p. 145.

5 Translated in Léglu, Rist and Taylor, *Cathars*, pp. 68–72. Also available at www.documentacatholicaomnia.eu/01_01_1243-1254-_Innocentius_IV.html (accessed 8 December 2014).

6 Translated in Léglu, Rist and Taylor, *Cathars*, pp. 37–67.

II: Chronicles (cf. Docs 3, 4, 6, 7, 8); and we have included a rare piece of evidence for the operation of inquisition in south-*east* France, for an area where there are virtually no inquisitorial records. We provide also material that illustrates some of the complexities of conducting 'inquisition into heretical wickedness', from the necessity of providing sufficient prison space – again in a period where we lack accompanying deposition evidence (Docs 25A, 26) – to the initially successful way in which a town could fight inquisition politically (Docs 27, 28).

20. INNOCENT III, BULLS CONCERNING LA CHARITÉ-SUR-LOIRE

Innocent III (1160/1–1216) was born into a Roman noble family, studied theology at Paris, probably coming under the influence there of Peter the Chanter, and canon law at Bologna, was appointed cardinal-deacon by Gregory VIII (1187) before becoming pope at the age of 37 in 1198. Over 6,000 letters attest the extraordinary range and size of his activity. He was the pope who presided over the Fourth Lateran Council of 1215, who launched the 'Albigensian crusade' against heresy in Languedoc after the murder of the Cistercian legate Peter of Castelnau in 1208, and who brought the legal process of *inquisitio* into the Church's repertoire of powers. See C. Morris, *The Papal Monarchy: The Western Church from 1050–1250* (Oxford, 1991), ch. 17; J. Sayer, *Innocent III: Leader of Europe, 1198–1216* (London, 1994). Analysis of Innocent III's policy towards heretics appears in C. Thouzellier, *Hérésies et hérétiques: Vaudois, Cathares, Patarins, Albigeois* (Rome, 1969); W. Malecsek, 'Innocenzio III, papa', in A. Prosperi et al., eds, *Dizionario storico dell'Inquizione*, 4 vols (Pisa, 2010), I, 795–7. The letters selected here concern heresy in northern France; see their analysis in Maisonneuve, *Études*, pp. 158–63, and see also Docs 3–4. Translated from *Die Register Innocenz' III*, ed. O. Hageneder et al. (Rome and Vienna, 1964–), vol. 5, pp. 61–4; vol. 10, pp. 365–6.

A. Letter 35/6 from Innocent's fifth pontifical year, 1202/3

To [William] Archbishop of Bourges,[7] [Walter] Bishop of Nevers,[8] and Hugh Abbot of Cluny.[9]

Certain burgesses from La Charité recently came to the Apostolic See, putting forward a complaint against our venerable brother [Hugh], Bishop of Auxerre.[10]

Some time ago this same bishop had promulgated a sentence of excommunication against them as suspects of heresy. They came later on into the presence of our beloved son Peter, Cardinal-Priest with

7 William of Donjon, Archbishop of Bourges 1200–9.

8 Bishop 1196–1202.

9 Hugh of Anjou, Abbot 1199–1207.

10 Hugh of Noyers, Bishop 1183–1206.

the title of St Marcello, then Legate of the Apostolic See,[11] and they swore they would obey the commands of the Church. Whereupon in the council which was held at Dijon[12] and in the presence of many archbishops and bishops the same cardinal absolved them completely from both the excommunication and the accusation. And he imposed upon them an appropriate penance, which they later humbly carried out. And after they had come into our presence, as they had been ordered to do, and we had been informed by the same cardinal about the proceedings in this business, we sent letters on their behalf to our venerable brother bishops, ⸢William⸣ of Autun,[13] ⸢Robert⸣ of Châlons[14] and ⸢Reynold of Vergy⸣ of good memory of Mâcon,[15] and to you, our son the abbot, instructing you to proclaim by our authority that those who had come into our presence are Catholics and faithful, and not to permit them to be attacked by anyone with the accusation of error, so long as they do not henceforth plot anything by word or deed against the Catholic faith. There were certain women also from La Charité who had presented themselves to us for a similar reason, to whom we had extended the same favour of absolution. We entrusted these to your discretion – together with some old people and invalids and <other> women whom this point of accusation had stained and who had therefore been bound by the chain of excommunication – for you to decide what you thought ought to be decided, according to God and the Catholic faith. But the said Bishop of Auxerre did not lay off molesting them, and he obtained letters against them ⸢sent⸣ first of all to our venerable brother bishops ⸢Eude of Sully⸣ of Paris,[16] ⸢Nivolo⸣ of Soissons[17] and ⸢Geoffrey⸣ of Senlis,[18] and secondly to our beloved sons ⸢Hugh Clement⸣ Dean of Paris,[19] ⸢Jovin⸣ the Master of the scholars of Orléans,[20] and Master P. Vuerel. These second judges, learning from the letters addressed to them that the first letters had not been revoked, completely absolved these burgesses from their

11 Peter of Capua was legate in France from the end of 1198 to the beginning of 1200.

12 Council of Dijon, 6–13 December 1199.

13 Bishop 1189–1222.

14 Bishop 1185–1216.

15 Bishop 1185–98.

16 Bishop 1196–1208.

17 Nivolo of Chérisy, Bishop 1176–1207.

18 Bishop 1185–1213.

19 Attested as Dean of the cathedral chapter 1195–1215.

20 Died by early 1203.

jurisdiction. The burgesses themselves, understanding that the same bishop was acting maliciously against them – since he was obtaining letters to be sent to various judges to aggravate the accusation and was not subsequently prosecuting the case in their presence – appealed to our <Court of> Audience.

Coming down on this, however, the aforesaid bishop put forward the following against <this complaint>. Some time ago, because the aforesaid burgesses had been stained with the ill fame of heretical wickedness and were unwilling to present themselves for his inspection, he had for this reason often gone together with many religious men to their town of La Charité, and he promulgated a sentence of excommunication against them. Subsequently he took with him to their town [Michael] of good memory, Archbishop of Sens,[21] together with some of his suffragan bishops, but these burgesses got wind of their visit beforehand and absented themselves at that time. After the archbishop assigned a day for them <to come> to Auxerre and they were unwilling to appear in his presence, he received witnesses against them and eventually condemned them as heretics. And although the said burgesses took care to appear at the Council that the legate held at Dijon, what was done there was not their condemnation but only their excommunication. Furthermore, these burgesses did not observe the penance that had been imposed upon them. Rather, their most recent error was worse than their earlier error: for they acted against their own oaths in presuming subsequently to participate with heretics. For since in <their words of abjuration before> their absolution these burgesses petitioned to be shunned as heretics and publicans [publicani] if they did not obey the Church's commands and did not observe the penance that was imposed upon them, they had deserved to be excommunicated and to be shunned by everyone. For although the said burgesses positively claimed that they had participated with heretics neither before or after, as they had been accused, eventually some of them confessed that they had participated <with heretics> before they presented themselves for the legate's inspection – but afterwards they had taken care to keep clear of all contact with them, and had carried out the penance imposed on them. The bishop therefore urgently demanded that either they should openly state the articles in which they had erred, confessing that they had erred, or that witnesses should be received – whom he would produce – against them.

21 Michael of Corbeil, Archbishop 1194–9.

One ought to proceed in these matters all the more carefully, insofar as without the foundation of faith what is built upon it can prevail less: indeed, it cannot prevail at all, 'because without faith it is impossible to please God' [Hebrews 11.6]. Therefore through these apostolic writings we command and order your prudence to do this. Unless the said burgesses confess their error and profess the truth of the Catholic faith publicly and clearly, and provide a caution that is sufficient in your judgement, and exhibit appropriate repentance, you should arrange to receive those witnesses – chosen by the bishop himself or someone else – whom you think should be received on heretical wickedness, contact with heretics, non-observation of penance and other things relating to the business. And if something of the aforesaid things seems to you to be clearly proved – or something else that suffices for their condemnation – you are to take them back to the sentence that was imposed on them earlier, and you should order them to be shunned by all people as heathen and publicans. You should assiduously advise and strongly encourage the secular prince to do what pertains to his office when we have done what pertains to ours – if you love the faith, carefully and faithfully managing to carry out what we have ordered.

If not all <of you> etc., two etc.

Given at the Lateran, 12 May 1202.

B. Letter 206 from Innocent III's tenth pontifical year, 1207/8

To the bishops of Auxerre[22] and Troyes[23]

From the tenor of your letters, brother of Auxerre, we gather that, although your predecessor Hugh[24] of good memory, acting like a far-seeing and wise shepherd keeping watch over his flock through the vigils of the night, laboured with anxious care to eliminate heretical wickedness from the town called La Charité, he was still unable fully to cure that Babylon of this kind of sickness. For many people of both sexes, who had abjured every heresy before your aforesaid predecessor, 'returned like dogs to their vomit' [*see* Proverbs 26.11]. Giving themselves over to perdition was not enough for them, they also strove to drag others with them to perdition, secretly bringing into 'the kine of

22 William of Seignelay, Bishop of Auxerre 1207–20, Bishop of Paris 1220–3.

23 Hervé, Bishop 1206/7–23.

24 Hugh of Noyers, Bishop 1183–1206.

the people' [Psalms 67.31] certain heresiarchs whom they call 'consolaters' [consolatores],[25] for them to kill the sheep with the poison of their pestiferous doctrine.

As you know, actually, Hervé of Lorris and Hugh Ratier and some others fled from the town during the period of your predecessor, since they were heretics. Under the guise of carrying out trade they now travel, with their relatives, to suspect places, and stay there for three or four months. And then, when they return – this is what is said – they bring with them the pervertors of healthy doctrine. Your predecessor had excommunicated Thomas Morant on account of heresy that he confessed. Keeping quiet about the truth he obtained some letters from us, and through these the benefit of absolution from an Archdeacon of Paris. Afterwards he did not apply himself through the display of good works to putting an end to the notoriety he had gained. Therefore since you thought that like an *Ethiopian* he had not *changed his skin* [*see* Jeremiah 13.23], you requested him to be brought back to his earlier sentence, until it should become clear that he had rendered himself worthy of the benefit of absolution. Furthermore when, during the time of your predecessor Geoffrey, William of Munot, Stephen Pastourel and the widow of William of Sennevières were accused of heresy, they left the diocese of Auxerre. Now, when they have now returned, you wish to acquire certain knowledge about their faith, as pertains to your office. Although they have residences in your diocese, with malign trickery they are claiming at one moment that they are of diocese of Nevers, at another moment the diocese of Bourges. For this reason you have supplicated and entreated for the scythe of the Apostolic See to be wielded against these pestiferous people and against others who are suspect of heretical wickedness, lest their *plantations of trees* come to *overwhelm the cedars of God* [Psalms 79.11].[26] Since, therefore, your predecessor acted like a good farmer, pressing on carefully and wisely with the job of *catch*ing these *little foxes*, that sought to demolish *the vine* [Song of Songs 2.15] entrusted to him, you ought likewise to keep careful watch over your flock, lest the *ravening wolves* [Matthew 7.15] *catch and scatter* your *sheep* [John 10.12] – doing all this in the realisation of how you have succeeded him in honour and in responsibility.

25 A rare reference among evidence about heretics in the north to the administration of the Cathar rite, betraying knowledge of its name. Note that Ps. 67.31 is Ps. 68.30 in other versions of the Bible.

26 Note that Ps. 79.11 is Ps. 80.10 in other versions of the Bible.

Providing benevolent assent to your requests, through these apostolic writings we command your fraternity <you, our brother>, in whom we place complete trust, to proceed by apostolic authority against the aforesaid beasts, acting according to what you will be inspired to do on this matter, with the obstacle of appeal removed, uprooting the 'over-sowed cockle' [Matthew 13.25] from the field of the Lord and planting in it the purity of orthodox faith, and using ecclesiastical censure to restrain objectors.

Given at Rome, at St Peters, second day before the Ides of January, in the tenth year [12 January 1208]

21. CONRAD OF PORTO'S LETTER ON BARTHOLOMEW OF CARCASSONNE

After becoming a Cistercian in 1198, Conrad of Urach was elected Abbot of Clairvaux (1214) and then Cîteaux (1217), was made a cardinal (1219), acted as papal legate in southern France between 1219 and 1222, and died in 1227.[27] His convocation of a Council at Sens in 1223 is known through the Archbishop of Rouen's copy of the letter of summons. Conrad and the letter are discussed by Y. Dossat, 'Un évêque originaire de l'Agenais, Vigouroux de la Bacone', in his *Église et hérésie en France au XIIIe siècle* (Aldershot, 1982), no. xiii, pp. 635–9. The views of modern scholars range from those who regard the letter as based on observation of things that were actually there – albeit clothed in biblical language, and perhaps partly mistaken – to those who regard the letter's contents as pure fantasy, dreamt up to stimulate crusade. For an example of the former, see J. and B. Hamilton, eds, *Christian Dualist Heresies in the Byzantine World, c. 650–c. 1405* (Manchester, 1998), pp. 263–4; for an example of the latter, J.-L. Biget, 'Un faux du xiiie siècle? Examen d'une hypothèse', in M. Zerner, ed., *L'Histoire du Catharisme en discussion: Le 'Concile' de Saint-Félix, 1167* (Nice, 2001), pp. 104–33 (at 110–12).
We have translated the text given by F. Šanjek, 'Albigeois et "chrétiens" bosniaques', *Revue d'Histoire de l'Église de France* 59 (1973), 251–67.

Theobald, by the grace of God Archbishop of Rouen,[28] greeting, grace and honour to the venerable brothers, all of his suffragans. We have received a letter from the venerable father Conrad, Bishop of Porto and Santa Rufina, Legate of the Apostolic See, in these words:

> To the venerable brothers, to the (by the grace of God) Archbishop of Rouen, and to his suffragans, abbots, priors, deans, archdeacons <and> chapters constituted in the province of Rouen, Conrad, by His mercy Bishop of Porto and Santa Rufina, Legate of the Apostolic See, greeting in Christ Jesus. Although we are forced to implore your help on behalf of the bride of the true crucified, we are forced even more to be rent apart, sobbing and groaning. …
>
> Behold what we have seen within the confines of the Bulgars, Croatia and Dalmatia, near to the nation of Hungary. It is certain – there is no doubt – that, because of an Antipope, delays <in the coming> of the Antichrist will

27 F. Neininger, *Konrad von Urach (✝ 1227). Zähringer, Zistercienser, Kardinallegat* (Paderborn, 1994); on this letter, see pp. 226–8 and 374–5.

28 Theobald was Archbishop of Rouen 1222–9.

now be shorter, while the new Lucifer, bursting with the poisons of new arrogance, endeavours to establish his seat 'in the sides of the north' [Isaiah 13.14]: not so much in order to resemble the highest successor of the prince of the apostles [= *the pope*], rather to bring him down and annihilate him, together with the universal Church. Hence it is that the pope of perfidy, who has already to a large degree dragged down into ruin the wall of the *vineyard* [Song of Songs 2.15] of the Lord of Hosts, a wild boar is *devouring* the vine and trampling on it [Ps. 79.14].[29]

The Albigensians come in abundance to him, to get him to reply to their <requests for> advice, eager for his teachings, and embracing the opinions of the sect of this damned man. This Satan has made a certain man of his perverse persuasion known as far as the diocese of Agen – a man by the name of Bartholomew of Carcassonne (for he originates from Carcassonne) – and <he has him> acting for him so that the poison of the dragon in the chalice of Babylon [*see* Apoc. 14] might be more abundantly offered to those corrupted regions. Showing baneful reverence towards him, a bishop of the heretics, Vigouroux of La Bouconne,[30] handed over his see and his place to this Bartholomew in the town that is called Pujols, and took himself off to the region of Toulouse.

This is the Bartholomew who, in the salutation at the beginning of his letters (which circulate all over the place), entitles himself thus: 'Bartholomew, servant of the servants of the hospital of the holy faith, to so and so, greetings'. Further – something that is hateful to say and horrible to hear – this man creates bishops and endeavours to organise churches of perfidy.

... Wherefore we strongly advise you, pressingly ask and, on the shedding of Jesus Christ's blood, urgently demand, and, by the authority of the lord pope which we discharge in this matter, we formally command you to come to Sens on the next octave of the apostles Peter and Paul [6 July 1223], where with God's favour other prelates of France will also gather, prepared to give counsel on the aforesaid business of the Albigensians and to make provision, together with the others who will be present there: otherwise we shall take care to report your disobedience to the lord pope.

Given at Provins, sixth day before the nones of June.[31] By the authority of this mandate, we command you to come in person to Sens on the aforesaid day.

[The Archbishop of Rouen's own letter now resumes; it repeats this order to attend]

29 Note that Ps. 79.14 is Ps. 80.13 in other versions of the Bible.

30 On this Cathar bishop, see Doc. 2 and index.

31 A mistake, since this is not in the Roman calendar. If IV has been taken as VI – a plausible error – the date is 2 June.

22. GREGORY IX AND THE INQUISITOR ROBERT LEPETIT

A nephew of Innocent III, Gregory (1170–1241) studied in Paris and (probably) Bologna. He became cardinal-deacon in 1196 and cardinal-bishop in 1206, thereafter often acting as legate, going to Germany in 1207 and to northern and central Italy in 1217/19 and 1221; he also took part in the preparation of the Fourth Lateran Council. Elected pope in 1227, in the early 1230s he oversaw the entrusting of inquisition to the mendicant orders in Germany, France, Italy and Aragon. See C. Thouzellier, 'La répression de l'hérésie et les débuts de l'inquisition', in A. Fliche, C. Thouzellier and Y. Azais, *La chrétienté romaine* (1198–1274) [= A. Fliche and V. Martin, *Histoire de l'église*, 21 vols (Paris, 1934–52), vol. 10], pp. 291–324; Dossat, *Crises*, pp. 111–18; Maisonneuve, *Études*, ch. 5; F. Mores, 'Gregorio IX, papa', in A. Prosperi et al., eds, *Dizionario storico dell'Inquizione*, 4 vols (Pisa, 2010), II, 728–30. It is from his pontificate that many key early texts regarding the practice of inquisition are drawn, and it has been calculated that the word 'heresy' appears in 235 of his letters. On the *Five Books of the Decretals* of Gregory IX, see the introduction to Doc. 34. Here we translate texts relating to one of the earliest known inquisitors, Robert Lepetit, also known as Robert le Bougre, on whom see also Docs 6, 7 and 8, and the analysis of Gregory's letters about heresy in northern France by Maisonneuve, *Études*, pp. 266–70. Translated from *Les Registres de Grégoire IX*, ed. L. Auvray et al., 4 vols (Paris, 1896–1955), vol. 1, cols 707–9, 1194–5; vol. 2, cols 144–5, 361–2.

A. Gaudemus *('We rejoice') (19 April 1233)*

To Brother Robert, of the Order of Brothers Preacher. We rejoice in the Lord …[32]

Some time ago we gave letters to our beloved sons … the Prior of Besançon and Brother William, of the Order of Brothers Preacher, and to you, with the orders that with them you should search out the truth about the aforesaid crime <of heretical wickedness> in Burgundy, with diligent care and following set procedure.

Acting in these matters in place of your prior and not wishing to appear negligent in carrying out the office, you entered the town of La Charité in the diocese of Auxerre, which had a very bad reputation for this vice.

32 We omit some of the prefatory text.

And there you put forward and preached the doctrine of Catholic and evangelical truth, taking great pains to urge the inhabitants entirely to abandon this sort of vice and to return to Catholic unity. When this had been done, you managed to get many among them to reveal candidly to you the species of various kinds and the many kinds of species of the aforesaid crime and error in which they had been heinously involved: such that a father did not to any degree spare his son or wife, nor the son himself his father, nor a wife her own children or husband, nor <anyone> their fellows in this crime – or, in a certain measure, themselves. More – they offered to say this aloud in public and from the bottom of their hearts, if you so demanded. And of their own free will they put wooden fetters or chains round their necks, each and everyone of them abandoning themselves to whatever sort of satisfaction was to be imposed upon them by the Church.

From their testimony and certain account, you learnt and discovered with greater certainty that there was a fetid nest of the aforesaid wickedness in that town. It was infected with the corruption of this aforementioned crime, above and beyond its earlier reputation and men's general opinion and to such an extent that it could hardly or ever be recalled to the path of rectitude. For the inhabitants there had rejected the Catholic faith from the bottom of their hearts, ruining it by holding secret conventicles and throwing off the yoke of ecclesiastical discipline. Those who had at no time been disciples of truth had made themselves teachers of villainy and also of error.

Their fallacious knowledge or doctrine – which ought rather to be called the opposite of knowledge – extended its branches everywhere, bringing forth not flowers but the stench of pestiferous death, and it gave contagious draughts to drink to inhabitants of those regions, draughts of fatal and damnable plague. And thus the ministers of Satan 'oversowed' [*see* Matthew 13.25] wicked seed in the Lord's crop through the provinces of Bourges, Reims, Rouen, Tours and Sens, also throughout the whole of Flanders and many other places, especially those nearby in the kingdom of France [= *northern France*]. Deceiving the clever, seducing the simple and 'having the appearance of Godliness but denying the power thereof' [2 Timothy 3.5], they have damnably infected the unbridled multitude with the aforesaid blight. Their 'words are smoother than oil and the same are darts' [Psalm 54.22],[33] for with their tails they sting like a scorpion [*see*

33 Ps. 54.22 is Ps. 55.21 in other versions of the Bible.

Apocalypse 9.10], and in the end they 'bite like a snake' and like an asp, spreading abroad poison like a basilisk' [Proverbs 23.32]. Those who drag more people down to the lower hell with them [*see* 2 Peter 2.4] think that they are giving greater service to God and are also given higher praise in the opinion of others. Anyone who is not a participant in their wickedness is driven out of their company, as someone unworthy. Furthermore, if anyone starts to hunt down these foxes, they transfer themselves to another region in order to flee and avoid his jurisdiction.

To avoid danger incurred by delay in these things, we have decided to entrust this business to your prudence, carefully asking for and exhorting you to pious zeal, and imposing this task upon you for the remission of your sins. Together with your aforesaid colleagues, or one of them if both cannot be present, and in consultation with the diocesans, you are to apply zeal, diligence and efficient effort to the extirpation of heretical wickedness from the aforesaid town and neighbouring regions, in accord with the contents of earlier letters, and to the *capture* of this sort of *little foxes*, which are striving with tortuous coils *to destroy the vine* of the Lord of Hosts [Song of Songs 2.15]: summoning, if necessary, the secular arm, promulgating sentences of excommunication against their receivers, defenders and supporters, and sentences of interdict upon their lands, and proceeding otherwise as seems to you expedient; attentively watching out to prevent any reverting and *destroying* even more the *vine* of the Lord.

To this end, you can examine the statutes of the Apostolic See which we have decided to have promulgated on this matter and which have been sent to you under our seal, and you can use the wisdom given to you by God to be on your guard against their traps. If some of them completely abjure the stain of heresy and want to return to ecclesiastical unity you are to extend to them the benefit of absolution, according to the form of the Church and in consultation with diocesans, and impose upon them what is customary to impose on such people. So that in all these things stated above you can more freely and effectively carry out the office entrusted to you, together with your colleagues, we indulge twenty days of penance per week for all those who come to your and your companions' preaching, alongside those who give you help in these things, and counsel or support.

Given at the Lateran, thirteenth day before the calends of May, in the seventh year [19 April 1233]

B. To the prior and Brother Robert of the Order of Preachers, of Paris (23 November 1234)

Accuri, son of Aldebrandino and a Florentine merchant and citizen, appeared in our presence and described how he was once in <northern> France and spoke several times to some heretics who, he thought, were Catholics. He gave 10 Tours shillings to someone who was serving them, and he often bowed his head to them as a sign of respect. Later on, learning that they were heretics and worried that danger might arise from this and threaten his body and soul, he went to the Holy See and humbly requested us to make provision for him in this matter. We therefore gave letters to our venerable brother … the Bishop of Florence and his colleagues, instructing them to inquire thoroughly into the truth about the sincerity of his faith, his life, morals and reputation, and to despatch to our presence the <record of the> inquisition, enclosed and under their seals. The same bishop together with one of his colleagues – the third was legitimately excused – carried this out faithfully, and had the inquisition held against him sent to our presence, with their letters, containing an ordered account of the matter. On our command these were opened by our beloved sons, the elect of Ostia and Palestrina, and nothing could be found against him on account of which he should incur disrepute or the danger of any other harm. In fact, since we had a salutary penance imposed upon the said merchant by our beloved son, Brother Raymond, our penitentiary,[34] through these Apostolic writings we order your prudence not to allow Accuri to be molested by anyone on account of this matter; if you can find anything else against him, report it faithfully to us.

Given at Perugia, ninth day before the calends of December, in the eighth year of our pontificate [23 November 1234]

C. To Brother Robert, of the Order of Preachers (23 August 1235)

Some time ago, in response to the noise from some who would not put up with you or your brothers proceeding to inquiry into heretical wickedness in French parts which had not been, so they said, infamed of heresy,[35] we wrote to you and other brothers who were with you,

34 Raymond of Peñafort; see Doc. 34 below.

35 We are translating 'infamata/infamatus' as 'infamed' rather than 'defamed'. The modern sense of 'defamed' is that something has been said unjustly about someone,

deputed to go about this business, that you should desist from the business you had begun, to avoid somewhere that had not previously had the reputation of heresy now acquiring this slur. Later, in fact, such a multitude of venomous reptiles is said to be bursting out from all parts of the kingdom of France and such a pus of heresies is gushing forth, that, saving one's conscience, these cannot now be tolerated, nor can they be hidden through turning our back on them. Therefore, through these Apostolic writings, we command your prudence to proceed everywhere against heretics, in the provinces of Sens, Reims and other provinces in the kingdom of France, in consultation with prelates and your religious brothers and learned men, acting with care to avoid innocence perishing and wickedness going unpunished.

Given at Perugia, tenth day before the calends of September, in the ninth year [23 August 1235]

D. To the Bishop of Orléans – Archbishop-elect of Bourges[36] *– and the Prior of the Order of Brothers Preacher in France, and the Archdeacon of Châteauroux in the diocese of Bourges (10 April 1236)*

Appearing in our presence, Évrard, cleric of La Charité, demonstrated to us in his petition that some time ago,[37] when we entrusted the inquisition of heretics in France to Brother Robert of the Order of Preachers, the same brother suspected sinister things about his mother, Petronilla. The Archbishop of Bourges[38] and the Bishop of Auxerre,[39] whom we had deputed as inquisitors to inquire into the vice of heretical wickedness in the town of La Charité, had not found her culpable or suspect in this matter but zealous for Catholic purity – as he [*Évrard*] claims. Brother Robert imposed upon her the obligation of purgation with the fourth hand [*i.e. canonical purgation with four compurgators*]. Following this, Petronilla appeared in front of the said brother at the specified time and place, together with her compurgators, and humbly requested to receive the purgation imposed on her by him. Because some envious people were falsely suggesting to him that the said cleric [*Évrard*] had

whereas the medieval sense is a negative public reputation, sufficient to justify a process of inquisition or arising from such a process.

36 Philip Berruyer.

37 In 1231.

38 Simon of Sully.

39 Henry of Villeneuve.

defamed him at the Apostolic See, Robert claimed that she had failed to carry out her purgation, and wrongly ordered her to be handed over to a strict prison. Without reasonable grounds he did the same to Landry, the same Petronilla's son-in-law, even though he had received purgation from him about the same accusation. In their simplicity the two of them did nothing to try to recover from this injury.

Therefore the said cleric, taking up the prosecution of the case in law of the said Petronilla and Landry, made a humble supplication to us: that, while he was prepared to take on the penalty of a convicted person if the aforesaid accusation was proved, or would be proved in the future, against them, we should deign to come to their support with paternal provision in their side in this matter.

Wherefore through these apostolic writings we command your prudence, upon which we place complete reliance in the Lord, to inquire diligently about the truth concerning the aforesaid things and their reputation and purity of faith and to report faithfully to us in your letters what you find, so that on the basis of your account we can safely ordain what ought to be ordained in this matter. Meanwhile, if nothing crops up against them that is contrary to the Christian faith, see to it – as seems expedient to you – that they are kept in lighter custody, from which however they cannot escape.

Given at Viterbo, fourth day before the ides of April, in the tenth year [10 April 1236]

23. URBAN IV, REGARDING ROBERT LEPETIT AND LA CHARITÉ IN 1234/5 (BULL OF 25 OCTOBER 1263)

Jacques Pantaléon was born in Troyes around 1200, studied theology and law at Paris, was a canon of Lyons, later Archdeacon of Liège, participated at the Council of Lyons in 1245, acted as legate in many countries from 1247, and became Patriarch of Jerusalem in 1255. Elected pope in 1261, he died in 1264. See on him E. Amann, 'Urbain IV', *Dictionnaire de Théologie Catholique*, 15 vols (Paris, 1903–50), vol. 15, pp. 2288–95. On his letters concerning inquisitors in Languedoc, see Dossat, *Crises*, pp. 196, 200–2, and concerning Provence, Doc. 24 below. Translated from *Les registres d'Urbain IV (1261–1264)*, ed. J. Guiraud et al., 4 vols (Paris, 1892–1958), vol. 3, pp. 137–8.

To brothers of the Order of Preachers deputed by apostolic authority inquisitors of heretical wickedness in the kingdom of France.

Appearing in our presence John called the Knight,[40] of La Charité, a layman of the diocese of Auxerre, described to us that he had been passionately and illicitly in love with a certain woman from that place who was a suspect of heretical wickedness. He left that same place, together with the same woman, and went off to distant parts, and two months later he left the said woman and returned to the aforesaid place. At any rate because of this the late Brother Robert, called Lepetit ['the Small'] – who at that time belonged to the Order of Brothers Preacher and was inquisitor in those areas of this sort of <heretical> wickedness – regarded the said John as suspect of the said wickedness, and proceeded to inquisition against him. And although he found nothing else against him, nevertheless, in the end the said Robert imposed a public penance on the aforesaid John for this reason, and ordered him to fast for ever on bread and water every Friday, and on Lenten foods at certain times of the year, at these times confessing his sins and receiving holy communion, and to confess his sins once a year to his bishop or to someone else designated by him. And the said Brother Robert condemned him as a heretic, <the condemnation to take effect> if he were proved not to have done this. The same John

40 Surname rather than rank.

devoutly carried out this public penance, but he omitted to do what had been imposed upon him by the same brother in relation to other <sins>.

Concerning <sins>: the said Brother Robert, following his own inclinations, ordained that public penitents should not bear arms and that those who were usurers should restore their usuries; and if they carried on exercising the wickedness of usury or bearing arms and were convicted of this, they would be regarded and condemned as heretics. If such public penitents entered Lombardy, the said Brother Robert judged them to be heretics, as opponents of and rebels against the sentence of excommunication that had been promulgated <against those who did this>. The said John, however, went against this statute, taking himself to over the seas <to the Holy Land> and to various other areas, often bearing arms for his own defence, and he spent many years in parts of Lombardy, engaging in that sort of usurious wickedness.

Wherefore the said John made humble supplication to us: that – since he is and always will be a Catholic and was never a heretic or believer or supporter of heretics and wishes to return the aforesaid place of La Charité, which he left more than twenty-eight years ago – we should have a salutary penance imposed upon him for his transgression of these statutes and the other aforesaid things, and have him absolved, according to the form of the Church, from the sentence of excommunication. And that we should not regard him as someone to be stained with the disgrace of this heretical wickedness because of the aforesaid.

In this connection, then, if this is the case, by apostolic authority we command your prudence, to punish the aforesaid John for the excesses stated above, diligently taking into account all the relevant circumstances. You are to proceed with him, providing to him mercifully those things that he is asking, as seems to you expedient according to God for the promotion of the business of the faith and John's salvation. If however it becomes clear to you, through those things that have been found against him so far or happen to be found in the future, that the said John transgressed in this matter more seriously than he stated above, you should not only not provide for him in the aforesaid matters, you should in fact punish him more severely as a deceiver and liar, to the extent his guilt demands.

That if not all.[41]

Given at Viterbo, eighth day before the calends of November, in the third year [25 October 1263]

41 In a papal bull, the formula 'Quod si non omnes' was an instruction to proceed with only two judges if three were not available.

24. URBAN IV, REGARDING FRANCISCAN INQUISITORS IN PROVENCE (BULL OF 25 NOVEMBER 1263)

What little is known about inquisition in south-eastern France has been put together by Jacques Chiffoleau.[42] Dominican inquisitors are glimpsed before the resumption of inquisition by bishops (1249–55), but from the 1260s the inquisitors in these areas were Franciscans. Their activities can be traced mainly through papal bulls rather than through inquisition acts. The transition between the two orders is illustrated by this bull, devoted to a Waldensian follower in Arles who confessed to a Dominican inquisitor around 1237 and was to be dealt with by Franciscan inquisitors in 1263. Translated from G. G. Sbaraglia, *Bullarium Franciscanum, Romanorum pontificum constitutiones, epistolas ac diplomata continens*, 4 vols (Rome, 1759–68), II, p. 527.

To our beloved sons ...[43] brothers of the Order of Minors, deputed inquisitors of heretical wickedness by apostolic authority in the counties of Provence and Forcalquier, greetings and apostolic benediction.

Constituted in our presence, <our> beloved son William of Jonquières, citizen of Arles, stated that when he was fifteen years old or thereabouts, he was led astray by his late mother and often frequented heretics of the sect of the Waldensians, sometimes in his parental home but also elsewhere, greeting them and receiving the kiss of peace from them, and together with them eating bread blessed by them. He also frequently heard their admonitions. He did not however commit these to memory, nor did he notice at the time whether they said anything against the Catholic faith. For this reason the said William did not believe he was doing wrong with them; he did not see more than four or five them together; also, he believed they were good men. Later, in fact, the same William's said mother was convicted of this sect of the Waldensians, and penance was imposed on her on account of this, that is, that she

42 'L'inquisition franciscaine en Provence et dans l'ancien Royaume d'Arles (vers 1260–vers 1330)', *Frati minori e inquisizione* (Spoleto, 2006), pp. 151–284. See also H. J. Grieco, 'Franciscan inquisition and mendicant rivalry in mid-thirteenth-century Marseille', *Journal of Medieval History* 34 (2008), 275–90.

43 The names, blank here, are given in other bulls to Franciscan inquisitors in these areas in 1265–6 as William Bertrand and Maurin.

should go to the Holy Land and live there for five years. In addition, the same William's late father was convicted of the aforesaid sect and condemned to perpetual prison, where the same father ended his last day. Of his goods, two parts were confiscated by Archbishop John,[44] of good memory, and the commune of Arles, while the third part at least was reserved for his children. Afterwards the said William, observing that the Church persecuted the Waldensians and totally condemned their sect, without anyone denouncing him on this charge, accusing him or citing him or initiating proceedings, and also not induced by fear of proofs but simply by the pricking of his conscience, humbly confessed these misdeeds to the said Archbishop and to Brother William of Jouques of the Order of Preachers. He underwent no relapse thereafter, nor did anyone proceed against him on these matters. On the contrary, afterwards the said citizen, through zeal for the Catholic faith, was often minded to persecute infidels of this sort.

Because, however, the aforesaid archbishop did not absolve the same citizen for this crime, since it was secret, and did not impose salutary penance on him on account of it, though his confession was written down – and twenty-six years, he reckons, have now elapsed – the aforesaid citizen has humbly supplicated us to provide for him in this matter, with fatherly care.

Wherefore we entrust this to your discretion, that – if he has not been denounced, accused, cited or proceeded against by anyone, and does not return to the unity of Catholic faith through fear of proofs, taking into account all the circumstances you should provide the aforesaid citizen with the benefit of due absolution for his aforementioned misdeeds, which he claims that he has hitherto confessed – even though the <fact of> the aforesaid confession cannot be established; and you should impose upon him with mercy a salutary penance – as seems to you <right> according to God and as you know to be expedient for the business of his faith – through which penance, however, if the offence was, as he claims, secret, it does not become in any way publicly known. If however it becomes clear to you, through the things that have been found so far or perhaps happen to be found later, that he transgressed more seriously than he reported above, you are to punish the said citizen more severely, as a deceiver and liar, insofar as his guilt demands.

Given at Orvieto, on the seventh day before the calends of December in the third year of our pontificate

44 John Baussan, Archbishop of Arles 1233–58.

25. ROYAL LETTERS CONCERNING INQUISITION

The practicalities of prosecuting heresy always required support from secular powers, as we see briefly in the first letter here, issued by King Louis IX of France (born 1214, reigned 1226–70); though this also meant that secular authorities could be petitioned by those subject to inquisition, as per the second letter. On Louis IX's ordinance of 1229 on measures to repress heresy, *Cupientes*, see Maisonneuve, *Études*, pp. 238–41, and in regard to heresy and inquisition more generally, W. C. Jordan, *Louis IX and the Challenge of Crusade* (Princeton, 1979), pp. 83–4, 154–8. The first letter is translated from *HGL*, VIII, 1435–6, the second from a partial edition in M. Mahul, *Cartulaire et archives des communes de l'ancien diocèse et de l'arrondissement administratif de Carcassonne*, 6 vols (Paris, 1857–71), V, 628.

A. Louis IX, 14 October 1258

Louis, by grace of God, King of France, to the Seneschal of Carcassonne,[45] greetings. We command you to this extent, that you take care to provide safe and secure conduct to the brothers Preacher, inquisitors of heretical wickedness in your area, as often as the need should occur and they, consequently, ask you for this; and that you provide them with help and assistance in an efficient way in the expenses and needs that crop up in relation to the moving forward and carrying out.of the said business – to expedite it. You are to have the rest of the work on the prisons, now already begun, finished without delay.

On our behalf, further, you are to require and persuade (in an effective way) the barons, prelates and landholders – of those areas where it is clear that they have incursions of heresy – that they provide appropriately for the needs of those coming from their lands who have been imprisoned and immured. In order to avoid any impediment or delay to the business of the aforesaid inquisition arising from this, if need be we wish to provide for them at our own expense, requiring and levying

45 Peter of Auteuil, Seneschal of Carcassonne 1254–63; see on him L. Delisle, 'Chronologie des baillis et des sénéchaux royaux, depuis les origines jusqu'à l'avènement de Phillipe le Valois', *Recueil des Historiens des Gaules et de la France* 24 (Paris, 1904), pp. 250*–251*.

<the money> later on from those lords from whose lands they have come, as has been said: warning the same prelates, landholders and barons that they are not to hold or place in *bailliages* or public offices the sons of heretics, or their nephews [*or* grandsons], or their believers, or those suspect or indeed defamed of heresy.

Done at Vincennes, on the Monday after the feast of St Denis, AD 1258, in the month of October [14 October]

B. Royal commissioners, March 1261

… Brunissendis, daughter of Bernard Talle, of Villesèquelande, petitions for the return to her of the two pieces of land and a vineyard within the bounds of the said village that were given to her as a dowry when she married, which the lord king holds, because her husband was imprisoned and she was signed with double crosses <for heresy>. Having seen the petition … we find that she should be restored to the petitioned <properties>, especially because the king does not want the fact of husbands being found guilty of heresy causing their wives to be deprived of their goods.[46] … Therefore we order you to this, that you restore to her the said two pieces of land and vineyard, if the king holds them.

46 See on Louis IX's policy *HGL*, VII, p. 484.

26. TWO LETTERS OF ALPHONSE OF POITIERS

Born 1220, Alphonse of Poitiers was the younger brother of the future Louis IX. The terms of the Peace of Paris, arranged between Louis IX and Raymond VII, Count of Toulouse, in 1229, specified that Raymond VII's daughter Joan was to be given into the king's custody and married to one of his brothers, and that on Raymond's death they would inherit the town and diocese of Toulouse. Alphonse married her (in 1236 or 1237), and became Count of Toulouse in 1249 following Raymond VII's death; he and Joan were childless and after they both died in 1271 the holdings of the Count of Toulouse passed to the French crown. Alphonse's dealings with inquisition in Languedoc can be traced through his correspondence, and they have been studied by Dossat, *Crises*, ch. 12.ii, 'Alphonse de Poitiers et l'inquisition'. These letters are among the rather scarce evidence for inquisition in these years.[47] The first is to an official who from late 1256 was in charge of the confiscation of property from those convicted of heresy, throughout Alphonse's southern domains, and thus of the operations that financed the inquisition.[48] Translated from Auguste Molinier, ed., *Correspondance administrative d'Alfonse de Poitiers*, 2 vols (Paris, 1894–1900), I, pp. 610–11 (nos. 948–9).

(A) To James Dubois, 13 January 1268

Alphonse etc, to his beloved and faithful clerk James Dubois, greetings and affection.

From the series of your letters, which we have recently received, we understand that the brother inquisitors into heretical wickedness are proceeding in the business of inquisition at Toulouse, and are incurring great expense in carrying out the same business there. Therefore, if they thought it expedient, they could incur less heavy expenses carrying out inquisition at Lavaur, or elsewhere. We shall provide appropriately – from the castle of Lavaur or another suitable castle – for the persons who happen to be arrested and have to be imprisoned, if the castle [*Château Narbonnais*] at Toulouse does not suffice – whether

47 See *Inquisitors and Heretics*, pp. 37–41.

48 See Dossat, *Crises*, pp. 284, 293–302, 305, 317.

these persons will be poor or wealthy we do not know, but time will tell. … [*the letter then turns to other matters*].

Given at Gournay-sur-Marne, Sunday in the octave of the Epiphany, AD 1268 [13 January 1268]

(B) To the inquisitors Pons of Pouget and Stephen of Gâtine, 13 January 1268

Alphonse etc., to the religious men and beloved to him in Christ, brothers Pons of Pouget[49] and Stephen of Gâtine,[50] of the Order of Brothers Preacher, inquisitors into heretical wickedness in the region of Toulouse, greetings and sincere affection.[51]

We commend, in the Lord, the zeal that we utterly trust you have – for the promotion of the business of the faith and the repression of the stain of heresy in the region of Toulouse – knowing that our desire, with all our bowels, is for this business to prosper with the help of the Lord. As to the matter on which you wrote to us – that we should wish to assign our castle at Lavaur to the custody of people infected with the said stain who happen to be arrested – we have decided to respond to you thus: that, since at present we do not have our own seneschal in the region of Toulouse, when we have appointed him (which we plan to do shortly) and when we have got to know the number and quantity of people who have been arrested, then, if our castle at Toulouse is not enough, we shall arrange for them to be in safe custody, God willing, making use of the castle at Lavaur or some other suitable castle for their custody, and ensuring that no danger can arise from the lack of a prison. For the rest, we ask your prudence this, that you proceed diligently and faithfully with the advancement of the business of the faith, as we trust you will.

Given [*as the preceding, 13 January 1268*]

49 Pons of Pouget was active as inquisitor 1262–71; Douais, *Documents,* I, pp. 167–9; *Inquisitors and Heretics,* pp. 38–9; cf. Doc. 39, forms of sentences no. 11.

50 Stephen of Gâtine was active as inquisitor 1264–76; Douais, *Documents,* I, pp. 169–72; *Inquisitors and Heretics,* pp. 38–9; cf Doc. 39, forms of sentences no. 11.

51 See Dossat, *Crises,* pp. 194–5, on this letter.

27. JOHN GALAND OP, INQUISITOR 1282–93

Evidence about John Galand's activities as an inquisitor, mainly at Albi and Carcassonne, survives in two unpublished manuscripts, BnF MS Doat 26 and BnF MS Lat. 12856, whose contents are analysed in Douais, *Documents*, I, 30, 81, 182–91, 208. We have not included any of these records in this collection, but he is mentioned in Doc. 51; and the second document below, protesting against his activities, is the subject of a deposition translated as Doc. 52. Unlike most inquisitors active in Languedoc, Galand did not come from the area, and his inquisitions were contested at the time, and continued to be contested until a papal commission of inquiry in 1330. For the little that is known about him see the references listed in his index entry in J. Roche, *Une église cathare: l'évêché du Carcassès, Carcassonne, Béziers, Narbonne, 1167–début du XIVe siècle* (Cahors, 2005), p. 542.

Translated from Charles Molinier, *L'Inquisition dans le midi de la France au XIIIe et au XIVe siècle: Étude sur les sources de son histoire* (Paris, 1880), p. 446 n.1; and Jean-Marie Vidal, *Un inquisiteur jugé par ses "victimes": Jean Galand et les Carcassonnais (1285–1286)* (Paris, 1903), pp. 39–43. The numbering is Vidal's, which he added to his edition of a manuscript copy from 1715 of a lost medieval original.

A. Galand's prison instructions, 1282

[4 July] AD 1282, on the sixth ferial day, Saturday, within the octave of the apostles Peter and Paul, Brother John Galand, inquisitor, imposed a strict injunction and command upon Ralph, warden of the prisoners – on Ralph's oath – and upon Bernarde, his wife, in the presence of Brother Peter Rey, prior,[52] Brother John of Falgous and Brother Archimbaud.

Henceforth they are not to hold [*or* maintain] any scribe in the Wall, or horses, nor are they to receive a loan or any gift from anyone among the prisoners.

Item, they are not to keep the money or anything else of any of those who die in the Wall, but they are to report and hand these over immediately to the inquisitors.

Item, they are not to take out of the prison anyone who is imprisoned and detained within it.

52 Prior of Brothers Preacher in Carcassonne, 1277–86.

Item, in no way nor for any reason are they to take prisoners outside the first [outer] gate of the Wall, nor are they to enter their house [cell], nor are they to eat with them.

Item, the servants who are designated to serve others are not to be involved in their work, nor are they to send these or others to any place without the special permission of the inquisitors.

Item, the said Ralph is not to play with them at any game, nor is he to put up with them playing among themselves.

And if they are found to be guilty in any of the aforesaid things, they will be expelled immediately and for ever from the wardenship of the Wall.

Done in the presence of the aforesaid inquisitor and with the witness of the aforesaid and also of me, Pons Prevôt, notary, who wrote these things.

B. The complaints of Carcassonne against John Galand, 1285

Complaints of the city of Carcassonne against Brother John Galand, Inquisitor

[1] Let everyone know that we, the consuls of Carcassonne, that is to say, Bertrand Luce, Arnold Isarn, William Serre, Peter William of Cornèze, Lord Raymond of Palaja, knight, Pons Barrot, Raymond Espinasse, Roger Carcassès, Roger Ferroul, squire, perceive the extraordinary extent to which the town of Carcassonne, the community of men of this place and each and every man in this community are being injured and irreparably harmed by you, Brother John Galand, of the Order of Brothers Preacher, deputed by apostolic authority inquisitor of heretical wickedness in the kingdom of France, and by your colleagues. Against the law and form or <the form> of the commission made for this, worked out and handed down for the carrying out of inquisition, and against the accustomed and usual practice observed hitherto by your predecessor inquisitors of heretical wickedness, you proceed in the business of inquisition – as far as Catholic, religious and other persons are concerned – too harshly and dangerously; perhaps seduced by the advice of some of your fellow brothers in your order and of some men plotting against our community and mauling its property, and unduly, against the order of law, and to the great scandal and defamation of the whole of the said town and those living in it.

[2] Without a previous summons you take persons who are of good and praiseworthy reputation and from a family that is, going a long way back, Catholic. And you hold these people as prisoners in a harsh and terrible prison until – whether through fear of tortures or prison or through the grace promised to them about the penance that is to be imposed – they confess whatever is asked of them, either about themselves or others, on the aforesaid accusation. You do not admit any defences put forward by them or by their relatives or friends.

[3] Item, if you find through the deposition of a witness or witnesses – of whatever condition they are, enemies, disreputable, vile or malevolent people – that someone has been hereticated in their illness, which will be utterly false, you proceed against all those said to have been present at the aforesaid heretication, seizing them and putting them into the aforesaid prison. In no way do you allow them to be freed from this prison or captivity, and you are unwilling to receive their defences. Rather, you have them given over to very severe tortures, as is contained below, until they have confessed whatever is asked about themselves and others. After they have been freed from prison and tortures, virtually all of them declare and say that they made the aforesaid confession through fear of tortures. Among these many guiltless ones many have died because of tortures or prison.

[4] We regard ourselves as being oppressed, because, going against the former usual and accustomed practice of your predecessors in the inquisition, you have made a new prison. It is called the 'Wall' but really it ought to be named 'Hell'. In this you have constructed many cells, houses for torturing and tormenting men with various kinds of tortures. Some of these are so dark and airless that those living in them cannot tell whether it is night or day; the whole time they are without air and virtually any light. The miserable wretches living in other cells have shackles of wood or iron. They cannot move, and have to do their thing and urinate underneath themselves. They can only sleep lying on the cold earth. And thus they pass the time – long times – night and day, always with these sorts of tortures. Not only are those living in other places in the prison deprived of air and light but they are also deprived of food, apart from the *bread of grief*[53] – and water, which is provided rarely.

53 See 1 Kings 22.27: 'Put this man in prison, and feed him with the bread of affliction and water of distress'.

[5] Some, in truth, are placed on the rack and many of these lose limbs through the severity of the tortures and are rendered utterly without capacity. Too much suffering and pain bring some of them to end their days with the cruellest of deaths. In the said prisons continuous crying is heard, *weeping* and groaning and immense *gnashing of teeth* [Matthew 8.12, etc.]. What more? Life is a punishment for them, death a solace. And under this coercion they declare what is false to be true, choosing to die once rather than be tortured often like this. And through these untrue and extorted confessions not only do those who confess perish unjustly, but also those named by them, even the innocent. Those who have seen and participated can provide testimony to the truth of all these things.

[6] This is how it has come about that those who are newly cited, hearing of the suffering and sickness of those who have been delivered to the Wall and these prisons, want to save their own blood. Some of them have fled and taken refuge with unknown kings [*in remote kingdoms*]. The others say what is false is true. In making this declaration they not only accuse themselves but also other innocent people, in order to flee in whatever way possible from the aforesaid punishments, choosing rather to fall with infamy into the hands of God rather than into those of perverse men. Later on, those who confess in this way reveal to their close friends that the things they have said to the brother inquisitors are not true, in fact they are false, and that they confessed them because of fear of imminent death. Occasionally some of those who have been summoned are provided by you with security so that they more freely and fearlessly engage in the wicked incrimination of others.

[7] Item, you made an announcement in the churches of Carcassonne about William Martin – who had been hereticated, so you said, during the illness from which he died: whoever wanted to and could defend him was to appear before you at an hour specified by you. One person from the people and community of Carcassonne presented himself in his defence, one of the kin of the said William Martin. And when he appeared before you accompanied by some of his friends, you wore a look of evil, like a savage lion, making many menaces against them, saying that if from now on people appeared in front of you on this business or accompanied the defendant, you would have them put in the Wall or prison. And you asked for the names of the others who were accompanying him, wanting to write them down. Through fear of this the person who had offered himself in his defence desisted from defence. And in this way, against God and against justice, defence

was denied to the friends of William Martin, who could have defended him.

[8] Item, through fear of you, no learned man [*lawyer*] dares to provide counsel and to support us in justice, and in this way justice perishes completely and wickedness rules.

[9] Item, when those summoned by you or put into your prisons, acting themselves or through their friends, urgently ask you about admitting just and legitimate defences, they offer securities, perhaps, and <say> that they are prepared concerning someone to stand in <for them> in an appropriate legal action, when and as often as they are summoned by you. You unduly and unjustly refuse to admit <the defences>, and in fact, what is worse, when the summons is first issued, you proceed straightaway to seize the person and have all his goods seized, placing him in the aforesaid prisons; and with the severity of tortures or violent fear of them you force the person to confess things that are not true against himself, thereby completely removing from him the opportunity of both defence and appeal.

[10] Item, what is wicked to hear, <there are> some people who are vile and infamed of heresy and are condemned for giving false evidence; and it is reported that prison guards, sons of iniquity, led on by a spirit of malevolence and prompted by the devil, say these things to these imprisoned and tormented people. 'Wretched, why do you not talk so as to get free? Unless you talk you will never get out of this place, nor will you be able to avoid torment!' And they reply, 'Sirs, what shall we say? What should we say?' And they tell them, 'Say this, say that'. And what they suggest is false and wicked. And these wretched people say it, as they have been instructed, as though it were true,[54] so that they can avoid the continual torments. And yet, in the end, they themselves perish and make the innocent perish too.

[11] Item, from the time of its foundation the city of Carcassonne and its inhabitants have acted well and praiseworthily in building churches, hearing masses and sermons, making offerings and giving alms, feeding and supporting religious persons, worshipping God and the holy mother Church, and in expelling all heretical wickedness so thoroughly that a heretic was never found or heard there. In fact, as far as steadfastness in divine cult and the Catholic Christian faith is concerned, it is regarded as one of the most praiseworthy among the cities

54 Text actually says: false.

of the province of Narbonne. Despite this, you and your assistants have slandered it, asserting that heresy flourishes in it, as much among clergy and lay people as among religious persons, which is against the opinion shared by all the prelates and other good Catholic men of the whole province of Narbonne.

[12] Item, the people of Carcassonne have been so shaken by your threats, acts of terror, arrests and tortures, that they are giving up on the truth, and they are beginning secretly to take away <their things> from the city and to export and transfer themselves elsewhere, beyond the district and jurisdiction of the lord king – to such an extent that it is feared that, unless the lord provides counsel, the whole place will crumble and come to irreparable ruin.

[13] Item, since it is well known throughout the land that there are no heretics or their believers or supporters in the city, and that they cannot be seen or heard there or named, it is not to be presumed nor is it credible that such great corruption as you claim exists in the said city. And the witnesses that you say you find attest what is untrue either through enmity or fear of arrest and tortures, as has been indicated above.

[14] Because of these injuries and each single one of them and many other things, which we shall state at a time and place, made and threatened by you against us and our community and every person of the same, we are fearful about this, on the basis of clear evidence, and we reckon – on probable and plausible grounds – that you are going to inflict worse on us in the future. In these writings, therefore, we appeal to the Apostolic See or to the Prior of the Preachers in Paris, against you and your processes and sentences, on behalf of ourselves and the whole aforesaid community and each of its councillors and our adherents and all who wish to adhere to us. We place ourselves and all who adhere to us under their protection.

[15] Item, to the most serene prince, our lord King of the French, whose men we are, we appeal, by name as above, in relation to servants, bailiffs and other officials of the court of the lord king carrying out your orders for the seizure of persons and goods, which takes place unduly and unjustly. We petition again and again and with fitting urgency for letters of appeal, placing ourselves and the said community and individuals in it and our goods, councillors and those adhering and wishing to adhere to us under the protection and defence of those to whom we have decided to appeal.

[16] We declare, furthermore, that we do not make the present appeal in order to obstruct or hold back the due and proper carrying out of the office of inquisition against heretical wickedness, so long as it does not proceed by seizing and torturing but rather according to the form of the power given to you by apostolic authority, with the consultation of prelates and the admission of the defences of those who wish to defend themselves in a just way. In fact, we offer ourselves to help and obey you in hunting down and capturing heretics and their supporters and receivers wherever they can be found.

[17] The consuls of Carcassonne indicate to you honourable men, lords William[55] and Sans,[56] archdeacons of the church of Carcassonne and vicars or procurators during the vacancy of the see, that – although the highest pontiff entrusted to the religious man, the Prior of the Order of Brothers Preacher in Paris, the carrying out through four brothers of his order of inquisition against heretics or those erring in heretical wickedness throughout the kingdom of France – he nevertheless reserved this: that the diocesans of places should and could inquire, each in his own diocese, concerning the crime in question, doing this through their delegated or episcopal power. About Brother John, called Galand, the inquisitor given by the Paris prior to act in the province of Narbonne: the truth is that although he may be in himself a good man – as is said – he has no knowledge of the men, living or dead, of this land, nor does he have the appropriate expertise in law. Because of this he is easily deceived by the secret dispositions of evil-doing and faithless men who are trying to make Catholic and faithful men their companions in the punishments and torments which they are acquiring through their own guilty acts. On account of this, the aforesaid consuls are concerned not only that any stain of heresy – if there is any in their community, which they do not believe – should be removed, for the honour of God, the exaltation of the Catholic faith, the conservation of the your episcopal <jurisdiction> and dignity, and the safe-keeping and freeing of Catholic men, but also that Catholic and faithful men are not harmed when this is done. Therefore the consuls supplicate and ask that you attach to yourselves persons both intelligent and skilled in law, and religious and other God-fearing men. With their help, inquire into the said crime so diligently, carefully and solicitously and proceed in this business of inquisition in such a way that through your industry

55 William of Castillon.

56 Sans Morlana.

and diligence and the mature counsel of wise men any stain of heresy is wiped out utterly from your diocese: and that Catholic and faithful men remain uninjured and unstained by the fraudulent testimonies and false, crafty and made-up assertions of malevolent and faithless men – especially those Catholic and faithful men who have striven in the past to sustain and strengthen the Catholic faith and to fight heretics. For it would be hard and very terrible if the good name of such men were to be harmed through the statements and depositions of malevolent and faithless men – which is what often happens in front of the Brother John named above.

28. CLEMENT V'S COMMISSION TO INVESTIGATE INQUISITION, 1306

The years around and just after 1300 saw the peak of controversy about inquisition and its methods in Languedoc: popular anti-inquisition propaganda by the Franciscan Bernard Délicieux (see Doc. 57), who persuaded the king to bring about the deposition of the Toulouse inquisitor, Fulk of St-Georges, in 1302; the papal commission of inquiry into the Carcassonne inquisition in 1306 translated here; and measures at the Council of Vienne (1311–12) to reform the inquisition. The two cardinals entrusted here with the commission to investigate inquisition were then present at the Council of Vienne, which suggests their input into decrees 26–7[57] reforming the operations of inquisition. On the council, see J. Lecler, *Vienne* (Paris, 1964), and on both Clement V (1305–14) and the more prominent contemporary *cause célèbre*, M. Barber, *The Trial of the Templars*, 2nd edn (Cambridge, 2006), and S. Menache, *Clement V* (Cambridge, 1998). Translated from J-M. Vidal, *Bullaire de l'inquisition française au xive siècle jusqu'à la fin du grand schisme* (Paris, 1913), pp. 9–11.

Clement the bishop, servant of the servants of God, greeting and apostolic benediction to the beloved sons Peter [of La Chapelle-Taillefert], Cardinal-Priest of St-Vitale and Berengar [Frédol the Elder], Cardinal-Priest of Saints Nereo and Achilleo.

The tearful complaint of some men from the areas of Carcassonne and Albi and Cordes has often thrust itself into our hearing. This is that many men from those areas were sentenced to the Wall [= *prison*] for ever and deprived of all their goods by our venerable brother Bernard, Bishop of Albi, and by the beloved sons who are or were for a time inquisitor or inquisitors of heretical wickedness in those regions. This was done against God and justice and wickedly, since those men were Catholics and were up to that point commonly regarded in those regions as true and good Christians, as the said plaintiffs offer themselves to prove – and to demonstrate sufficiently concerning the wicked proceedings of the bishop and of the many inquisitors who were in those areas.

In truth, while this question is pending, they worry, so they claim, about the persons pursuing this matter: that they will be oppressed by

57 Tanner, *Ecumenical Councils*, I, 380–3.

the aforesaid inquisitors, and that no-one will dare to appear to bear witness against the same inquisitors – if they appear the inquisitors will act savagely against them. For those whose unjust condemnation is at issue, who are detained in the walls or prisons of the said bishop and inquisitors, and have been and still are so greatly oppressed by the harshness of imprisonment, the absence of beds and scarcity of food and the cruelties of tortures, that they are forced to render up their spirits [*die*]: <worrying> that these <conditions> will be aggravated more, <they are asking> us to make appropriate provision …[58]

Although we could wish the case or question of the proceedings of the said bishop and inquisitors to be dealt with in our court in front of our venerable brothers, the cardinals of the Roman Church deputed to this both by us and by our predecessor of blessed memory, Pope Benedict XI, because you – who possess more knowledge than other cardinals about the people and matters of those regions and have <soon> to travel through them – for some sound reasons can more easily make provision about the occurrences of the aforesaid articles, we entrust and command your discretion to provide security, on our authority, while the aforesaid business is going on, to brothers Bernard Blanc and Francis Aymeric, of the Order of Preachers, as well as three or four others from each of the aforesaid places, that is to say, from Carcassonne and Albi and Cordes, who are to proceed with the said business; and that in the meantime you should be willing to provide for the said imprisoned and immured people, if you see that they are in need, in such a way that they are not – against justice – oppressed.

And because it is of public advantage to know the truth, about whether, as we hope, inquisitors proceeded rightly, or whether, God forbid, they acted wrongly and wickedly, so that any witnesses can come forward to provide evidence, we order the inquisitors of heretical wickedness in those regions and the aforesaid Bishop of Albi, while the inquiry into these proceedings is going on or at least until the Apostolic See orders it to be done otherwise, not to hand over to hard or strict imprisonment anyone arrested or due to be arrested for the matter of heresy, nor to expose them to tortures, nor to proceed to inquisition except together with the diocesan bishop or with some other good man deputed by him. As far as these things are concerned, we would like you to appoint our beloved son the Abbot of Fontfroide, of the Cistercian Order in the diocese of Narbonne, or some other good man

58 The edition we use omits the next part.

who seems to you expedient, to act as substitute in the place of the aforesaid Bishop of Albi, since the affair is about his proceedings – the mode of inquisition remaining in other things undiminished and free, in particular that whoever were held suspect of heresy by the aforesaid inquisitors can be arrested.

As to the fact that some time ago the cancellation, or suspension or alteration of some books of inquisition produced at Carcassonne was put forward before us, we order you to make yourselves informed about the aforesaid things, and to report this information when you return to us – to avoid that inquisitor having to bring the said books into our presence.

Further, you are to proceed with our authority in all the aforesaid things and in others, if they should crop up, concerning the aforesaid things, notwithstanding any privileges whatsoever, which we wish to assist no-one <in going> against the aforesaid things; any appealing put aside, and only having God before your eyes; through ecclesiastical censure having what you decree or ordain in the aforesaid matters firmly observed; peremptorily assigning to the procurators or procurator of the said Bishop of Albi and the oft-mentioned inquisitors, and also to the said brothers Bernard and Francis and other impugners of the aforesaid process a specific date on which they are to appear in Bordeaux in our presence or that of the aforesaid cardinals to whom the matter has been entrusted, to proceed in this matter as is just.

Given at Charolles, the third day before the ides of March, in the first year of our pontificate [13 March 1306]

PART VI: COUNCILS AND STATUTES

INTRODUCTION TO PART VI

The wars of the Albigensian crusade (1208–29) were brought to an end by the Peace of Paris[1] in 1229, by which Raymond VII, Count of Toulouse (d. 1249), capitulated and swore to persecute heresy. He was allowed to keep for his lifetime a third of the lands his father had held. His daughter Jeanne was to marry one of the French king's brothers – she married Alphonse of Poitiers in 1236 or 1237. They were to inherit on Raymond's death, and if they died childless – as they did in 1271 – the county of Toulouse was to pass to the French crown.

In the wake of the Peace of Paris, a series of ecclesiastical councils provided for the prosecution of heresy in Languedoc, beginning with one in Toulouse held by the papal legate to whom Raymond VII had sworn his surrender (1229), backed up by statutes that Raymond issued in 1233. These set out remedial provisions for the ecclesiastical and secular policing of the region, focusing particularly on locating and arresting heretics, but dealing also with wider issues pertaining to the Peace. What informed the content of these provisions was a mixture of contemporary circumstance and practical measures – such as payment for capturing heretics – and the inherited framework of ecclesiastical legislation, notably the bull *Ad abolendam* (1184) which had established the need for secular support in persecuting heresy,[2] and the legislation against heresy (canon 3)[3] and wider pastoral provisions of the Fourth Lateran Council (1215).

In conjunction with texts that we have included in Part VII, these ecclesiastical materials set the basis for the conduct of inquisition into heretical wickedness in the region. There are many studies of the history of the development of inquisition. The foundational historiography tends to split down confessional lines between condemnatory Protestants (the greatest of whom was undoubtedly Henry Charles Lea) and exculpatory Catholics (Thomas de Cauzons being the most

1 Translated in Sibly, *William of Puylaurens*, appendix C, pp. 138–44. See Wakefield, *Heresy*, ch. 7.

2 Peters, *Heresy and Authority*, pp. 170–3.

3 Tanner, *Ecumenical Councils*, I, pp. 233–5.

subtle, from the generation following Lea). More recent scholarship has continued to debate the relative brutality or moderation of medieval inquisitors, but has focused also more closely on the changing political climate of its operation, and the developing ways in which it was understood and practised. To analyse these aspects, historians have looked not only at the materials produced by inquisition – the depositions and sentences – but the materials that framed and guided the process of inquisition, setting out its ground rules, providing the practical detail and problem-solving that arose as it was carried out. Fundamental here are two French works, by Henri Maisonneuve and Yves Dossat, both of which concentrate on inquisition in France in the mid-thirteenth century.[4] Maisonneuve worked carefully through each ecclesiastical council to track the development of anti-heresy legislation, whereas Dossat pieced together from these and other sources the difficult period of establishment of Dominican-conducted inquisition (during which inquisitors and Dominican friars were temporarily expelled from Toulouse by its consuls in 1235; see Doc. 9, no. 3), a further crisis (its apparently total suspension between mid-1238 and 1241) and then a period c. 1249 to 1255 when the business of inquisition was conducted by the bishops rather than the Dominicans (for examples of which, see Doc. 49).[5]

This Part VI, in conjunction with Part VII, provides a substantial portion of the documentary sources from which the early history of inquisition is written. These two parts contain much detail relevant to particular issues: on the relative degree of organisation and 'institutionalisation' of inquisition into heretical wickedness as it progressed across the thirteenth century; the kind of power that it wielded, with a particular question regarding its relative brutality or moderation; and the way that it set about the pursuit of those it sought to condemn as 'heretics' and the much larger group of 'supporters' whose punishments and penances required management, both with regard to the penitents themselves but also with regard to the wider audience in the public penitential message they conveyed.

We have, for editorial convenience, included here the provisions of Dominican provincial chapters, which cast interesting light on relations between ordinary Dominican brothers and Dominican inquisi-

4 Maisonneuve, *Études* and Dossat, *Crises.*

5 Maisonneuve, *Études,* chs 5 and 6; Dossat, *Crises,* chs 5 and 7; note also the Introduction to Doc. 49. On these councils, see also Arnold, *Inquisition and Power,* chs 1 and 2, and Sackville, *Heresy,* ch. 3.

tors. These are of course a very different sort of document from the ecclesiastical councils or Raymond VII's Edict; but it can be said that all are concerned with setting out rules to be obeyed. As they do so, they reveal as much about the concerns of those in authority as they do about the subsequent outcomes and behaviour of those subject to the rules.

29. COUNCIL OF TOULOUSE, 1229

This Council was held under the auspices of the papal legate Romanus Bonaventura, Cardinal of Sant'Angelo (1216–36), later Cardinal of Porto, who died in 1243 – see W. Malecsek, *Papst und Kardinalskolleg von 1191 bis 1216* (Vienna, 1984), pp. 189–95. It was attended by the archbishops of Narbonne, Bordeaux and Auch, various other bishops, Raymond VII, Count of Toulouse, two consuls from Toulouse and the royal seneschal for Carcassonne. The council and its setting are described in chapter 38 of William of Puylaurens's Chronicle (see translation in Sibly, *William of Puylaurens*, p. 83). William makes clear the importance of the secular powers in effecting the provisions of the council. The text of the council is found in, or prefacing, a variety of later inquisitorial handbooks. Its context is investigated in P. Bonnassie and G. Pradalié, *La Capitulation de Raymond VII et la fondation de l'université de Toulouse, 1229–1979: Un anniversaire en question* (Toulouse, 1979), where a modern French translation is provided, pp. 43–51. On its debt to Louis IX's ordinance for measures repressing heresy, *Cupientes*, see Maisonneuve, *Études*, pp. 238–41. Translated from Mansi, *Sacra concilia*, 23, cols 194–204. Where a canon does not relate to heresy or inquisition, we have translated the title only.

These statutes were promulgated in a council at Toulouse, AD 1229, in the month of November, by Lord Romanus, Cardinal-Deacon of Sant-Angelo, Legate of the Apostolic See.

Although from the Apostolic See's various legates there have emanated various laws directed against heretics and heretics' believers, supporters and receivers, and dealing with the preservation of the peace in the diocese of Toulouse, the province of Narbonne, and adjoining dioceses and neighbouring lands, and other matters known to pertain to the good state of the land – we however see that, after the dangers of long and wretched turmoil, the aforesaid lands are now almost miraculously enjoying peace, and this with the consent and will of the notables. With the counsel of archbishops, bishops and prelates, and barons, and knights, we are moved to ordain and decree things which we know are expedient for the purgation of heretical wickedness and the preservation not only of peace but also of, as it were, a newly converted land.

1. That a priest and three lay people should be designated in every single place to search carefully for heretics

Accordingly we ordain that archbishop and bishops or bishop shall <appoint> one priest and two or three lay people of good repute, or more if needs be, in every single parish, both in cities and beyond. They are to bind these by oath to search for heretics in these same parishes carefully, thoroughly, faithfully and frequently, inspecting every single house and underground room that gives rise to some suspicion, and searching buildings appended or attached under these roofs and other hiding-places – all of which we order to be demolished. And if they find heretics, their believers, supporters and receivers or defenders, after taking care that they cannot escape, they should make sure they notify the archbishop or bishop or lords of the place or their *baillis* with all haste, so that they can be punished by the appropriate penalty.[6]

2. That exempt abbots are to do the same

Exempt abbots shall do this same thing for their places, which are not subject by diocesan law to the bishops.

3. That lords of places should search[7] for heretics

The lords of lands shall also take pains to carry out the search for heretics in towns, houses and woods, and to demolish outhouses, attached buildings and underground hiding-places of this sort.

4. Of the penalty for the person who permits a heretic to stay on his land

We ordain, further, that in future anyone who knowingly permits a heretic to stay on his land, whether because of money or some other

6 *animadversione debita puniantur*. In later councils – e.g. Tarragona, 1242 (Doc. 34) – this certainly means the death penalty. It is not clear, however, whether that is intended in this text.

7 The word used here and below (e.g. statute 9) is *inquirere*; given the specific usage in this and other statutes, we choose to translate it as 'search for' rather than 'inquire' or 'conduct inquisition'.

reason (whatever it is), and has confessed this or been convicted of it: he shall lose his land for ever, and his body shall be in his lord's hands, to do with it what he ought.

5. Of the person not convicted of knowing that heretics were on his land

When either heretics are frequently found on someone's land or he is defamed for this: if he is not convicted of knowledge but lax negligence is proved, he should be punished with the lawful penalties.

6. That a house in which a heretic was found should be demolished and the ground confiscated

We decree that the house in which a heretic has been found should be demolished, and the place itself or the ground is to be confiscated.

7. Of a *bailli* who is not diligent against heretics

Further, if a *bailli* who is permanently resident on the land – in a place about which there is suspicion – is not found to be very thorough and diligent <in acting> against heretics, he shall lose his goods, and in the future he shall not be appointed *bailli* either there or elsewhere.

8. That no-one shall be punished as a believer or a heretic, unless he is judged to be such by ecclesiastical authority

In order to avoid innocent persons being punished instead of the guilty and the <stigma of> heretical wickedness being attached to anyone through the calumny of others, we ordain that no-one shall be punished as a believer or heretic, unless they have been judged to be a believer or heretic by the bishop[8] of the place or another ecclesiastical person who has that power.

8 Note that inquisition still fell under the authority of a bishop.

9. That anyone can search for or capture heretics on someone else's land

We ordain moreover that anyone can search for or capture heretics on someone else's land, and that the *baillis* of these places are obliged to lend them help and support – such that the king's *bailli* can do this on the Count of Toulouse's and others' lands, and the Count of Toulouse and others can do it on the king's land.

10. How to deal with heretics who have returned to the faith voluntarily

Item, we ordain that if vested heretics have voluntarily left heresy and returned to the Catholic faith, recognising their error, they should not stay in the town in which they had lived earlier, if that town is held to be suspect of heresy. Rather they should be placed in a Catholic town not noted for any suspicion of heresy. Henceforth and as a mark of detestation of their former error, they shall wear two prominent crosses, high up, of a different colour from the colour of their clothes, one on the right and the other on the left. Nor may anyone be excused from wearing these crosses, without a testimonial letter from his bishop about his reconciliation. Nor henceforth shall public offices be entrusted to such people, nor shall they be admitted to actions in law, unless they have been restored to their standing by the lord pope or a legate *a latere*[9] and after suitable penance has been imposed on them.

11. How to deal with heretics who have not converted voluntarily but through fear or some other reason

Further, heretics who have returned to Catholic unity through fear of death or some other cause (but in any case not voluntarily) are to be confined to prison by the bishop of the place to do penance, with this caution, that they should not have the opportunity to corrupt others. Their material needs shall be provided for by those who have taken hold of their goods, as prescribed by the prelate. If however they have no goods, they are to be provided for by the prelate.

9 Legate *a latere* (from the side) of the pope: a cardinal legate given enhanced jurisdiction by the pope.

12. Of the oath to be taken by every Catholic

Everybody, both men and women – males from their fourteenth year, females from their twelfth[10] – is to abjure any heresy, by whatever name it is called,[11] that raises itself up against the holy and Catholic Roman Church and the orthodox faith. They must also swear to observe the Catholic faith that the Roman Church holds and preaches, and to persecute heretics with all their strength – and they will be conscientious in revealing them. Further, the names of all the men and women in whatever parish are to be written down, and all of them shall take the aforesaid oath in the presence of the bishop or in the presence of worthy men who have been asked to do this. And if someone was absent and has not taken the oath within fifteen days of his return – inspection of the <roll of> names can make this clear – he is to be regarded as a heresy suspect. This type of oath should be renewed every two years.[12]

13. That every person should confess and receive communion three times a year; otherwise they are to be regarded as suspects of heresy

Moreover: 'All <the faithful> of either sex'[13] after they have reached the age of discretion[14] shall make confession three times a year of their sins to their own priest or to another priest with their own priest's consent and mandate. They are to carry out the penance imposed on them humbly and with all their strength. And they shall receive the sacrament of the Eucharist with all reverence three times a year, at Christmas, Easter and Pentecost – in such a way that confession precedes communion.

10 The ages at which males and females were regarded as able to contract marriage in canon law.

11 'omnem haeresim... quibuscunque nominibus censeatur', altering to plural the phrase 'omnem haeresim, quocumque nomine censeatur' in the decree *Ad abolendam* of 1184.

12 No roll survives, or any direct evidence of the implementation of this statute; see Doc. 37 §31 below. Nevertheless, it is worth noting resemblance between this and the long lists – drawn up by parish – of individuals denying heresy on oath that are to be found in one set of inquisitions from 1245–6; see Doc. 48 (Toulouse 609).

13 Canon 21 of the Fourth Lateran Council of 1215 was known by these, its opening words (Tanner, *Ecumenical Councils*, I, 245), and the Toulouse canon continues to quote or paraphrase Lateran. Where it stipulated a minimum of once a year, here there is the more demanding minimum of three times, an older tradition found in many dioceses before 1215.

14 The age of discretion was taken by canonists to begin at seven.

<And they shall do this> unless <they think> that on some reasonable ground and with the advice of their own priest they should abstain from participating for a while. In addition, priests are to take care through the inspection of <the roll of> names, as was explained above, to ascertain whether any people are secretly avoiding communion. For anyone who abstains from communion, other than with the counsel of his own priest, is to be regarded as suspect of heresy.

14. That no lay people should have books of scripture, other than the Psalter and the Divine Office; and they should not have these books in the vernacular tongue

We also make this prohibition: lay people shall not be permitted to have books of the Old or New Testament; except perhaps for the Psalter or a Breviary for the Divine Office, or Hours of the Blessed Mary – someone may want to have these out of devotion. But we most strictly forbid them having the aforesaid books in vernacular translation.

15. How to deal with ill people who are defamed of heresy or known to be under suspicion

We also decree that any persons who are defamed of heresy or known to be under suspicion may not in future carry out the office of a doctor. And when an ill person happens to have received holy communion from the hands of his priest, there should be careful watch over him until the day of his death or recovery, so that a heretic or heresy suspect cannot gain access to this ill man. For we are given to understand that from the access of such people, wicked and terrible things have often happened.

16. That wills should be made in the presence of one's own priest or another ecclesiastic

When someone in fact wants to draw up a will, he shall do this with the witness of his priest or some other ecclesiastical person if his own priest is not available, with other men of good opinion there whom he has wanted to come along. And wills made in another way are to have no force, nor are they of any moment.

17. That no administrative position should be entrusted to heretics or people defamed of heresy, and that such people should not be retained in a household or in counsel

We also prohibit prelates, barons, knights or any lords of lands from entrusting *bailliages* or administrative positions on their lands to heretics or their believers. Nor shall they dare to have or retain heretics or even those defamed of heresy or those they believe to be heresy suspects in their household or counsel.

18. Who is to be regarded as 'defamed'

Moreover, those people ought to be regarded as 'defamed' against whom public rumour [fama] cries out, or those whose defamation was legitimately established among good and serious men before the bishop of the place.
[*From this point on the statutes only occasionally bear upon heresy and its repression*]

… 25. That every Sunday and feast day all must come to church; and the penalty for those who are absent[15]

… 35. That one should not have familiarity or a truce with fugitives

Item we order that no-one should have any friendship, familiarity or truces with fugitives [faiditi],[16] or others who have made war. From his [= *a person who has had such friendship etc.*] goods he is to deal with the expenses <of acting> against them or make reparation for the damage they have caused; otherwise his punishment <in this use of his goods> should be to his lord's profit.

15 The penalty is a monetary fine of 12 pennies Tournois.

16 'Faiditus' or 'feiditus', in Occitan 'faiditz', denoted an outlaw or rebel. It was used very frequently in Languedoc in the thirteenth century about knights and soldiers who had fled on account of the crusade, and later simply to denote fugitives. See L. M. Paterson, *The World of the Troubadours: Medieval Occitan Society, c. 1100–c. 1300* (Cambridge and New York, 1993), p. 59.

36. That no-one should receive thieves or mercenaries [‘routiers’]

37. That there should be an oath against the enemies of faith and peace, some of whom are designated by name

Moreover we order that, when anyone has made war, there should be a new oath against him. Anyone who refuses to implement this will be regarded as a breaker of the peace. In its form, the oath is to be explicitly ‘against the enemies of the faith and peace’, namely William, called Lord of Peyrepertuse, Gaucerand, who held Puylaurens, Raymond of Niort,[17] and they are to be excommunicated and perpetually disinherited, nor can they be absolved from this sentence except by the Apostolic See, or by a legate with full powers sent out by the pope.

… 42. That women who have castles and fortresses should not marry enemies of the faith and peace

Women who are widows, and noble women who are heirs, who have fortresses or *castra*, should not knowingly marry enemies of the faith and peace. That if they do, their *castra* and fortresses should be seized by the lords of the land – eventually, however, lawfully to revert to their heirs.

… 45. That these statutes should be expounded to parishioners four times a year

Moreover we order that these statutes should be diligently expounded by parish priests to their parishioners four times a year, namely on the Sundays following the four periods of fast.[18]

17 In Mansi’s text the name is Mort. In emending to Niort, we follow the suggestion of Bonnassie and Pradalié, *Capitulation de Raymond VII*, p. 49 n.6. On this famous family of heresy supporters, see W. L. Wakefield, ‘The family of Niort in the Albigensian Crusade and before the Inquisition’, *Names* 18 (1970), 97–117 and 286–303.

18 Ember days were four major fasting days spread across the liturgical year, falling in Advent, Lent, Whitsun and September.

30. EDICT OF COUNT RAYMOND VII OF TOULOUSE, 1233

In the treaties concluding the Albigensian crusade (1229) Raymond VII had promised to pursue heretics in his lands, and in the context of his efforts in the early 1230s to regain favour with Pope Gregory IX he issued this edict: see the texts translated in Sibly, *William of Puylaurens*, Appendix D. The Edict includes some references back to the Treaty of Paris, but is otherwise more obviously the product of episcopal direction on canon law regarding heresy, and the practical support which the secular authorities were to provide in this regard. See Maisonneuve, *Études*, p. 272. In his *Crises*, pp. 271–5, Dossat provides a succinct survey of Raymond VII's policy with regard to inquisition. Translated from Mansi, *Sacra concilia*, 23, cols 265–8; we have added the numbering.

In the name of the holy and indivisible Trinity. For the exaltation of the Christian faith, and the extirpation of heretical wickedness and the preservation of the peace and the conservation of the good condition of the whole land, and its improvement: we, Raymond, by the grace of God count of Toulouse, with the counsel and assent of the bishops and other prelates, counts and barons, knights and many other prudent men of our land, after earlier mature deliberation and careful study, have decided to ordain these salutary statutes in the lands of our people.

[1] Since it is our firm intention to purge heretical wickedness from our land and the lands of those subject to us, and as we propose to work both carefully and faithfully towards this end, we ordain that all barons, knights, *baillis* and other men of ours should bring great vigilance and painstaking care to bear on the task of pursuing, searching for, capturing and punishing heretics, as was promised by us in the Peace made at Paris.[19]

[2] Item, we ordain that there should be immediate legal inquisition[20] against those who have killed the hunters of heretics, or perhaps – let us hope not – kill them in the future, and against all towns and men of our lands under our jurisdiction who have consented to their killing or

19 The Treaty of Paris (1229) ended the crusade: it is translated in Sibly, *William of Puylaurens*, appendix C.

20 'Inquisitio' can be translated as 'enquiry' as well as 'inquisition'. Here it means 'legal secular inquiry'.

may consent in the future. Let due justice be done to all of these, both the men and the towns. And this we wish to be faithfully observed both by us and by our barons and *baillis.*

[3] Item, we ordain that wherever heretics are found in our lands or jurisdiction, whether within cities, castles or towns, or on holdings outside them, the men of that city, town or castle, in which they were found (or the man on whose holding they were found), must pay marks to the men who captured the heretics: namely for each heretic, one mark.

[4] Item, we ordain that suspects in faith should not be appointed as seneschals or *baillis.* And if by chance some happen to be appointed, they are to be removed immediately.

[5] Item, concerning the houses in which since the time of the Peace made at Paris a heretic has been found alive or buried, or in which a heretic preached: if this was with the knowledge and consent of the master of the house and he was of legitimate age, we ordain that these houses are to be destroyed and all the goods of those who inhabited these houses then <when the heretic was in them> are to be confiscated, unless they can clearly prove their innocence and legal ignorance. The inhabitants, however, are to be captured and punished with the lawful penalty. And all suspect cabins, remote from the common habitations of *castra,* and <also> fortified caves and secluded places[21] in suspect and notorious districts should be destroyed or closed up. And in future no-one should be so bold as to construct such dwellings in the aforesaid places, or to live in the same. If anyone is caught in these after our edict, all his moveable goods are to be confiscated, while castellan lords, in whose lordships such dwellings happen to be found after our edict, will be fined 25 Toulousan pounds.

[6] Item, we ordain that all the inheritances of those who have made themselves heretics, or who do so in the future, are to be confiscated and seized: such that the aforesaid goods cannot (via sale or gift or any other way) come down to those children of theirs or other heirs, who – if they had been of orthodox faith and in cases where there was no will – would by right be succeeding to these things. And if the aforesaid goods have been rendered to such people or are otherwise being retained by them, they should be totally removed from them. Further, houses of those who have become heretics since the time of the said

21 The Latin (clusellum, plural -a) appears in *Inquisitors and Heretics,* p. 306.

Peace, or will become heretics in the future, which they inhabit at that time, are to be destroyed without mercy.

[7] Item we ordain that all who have prevented inquisitors of heretics from entering towns or houses or hidden places or woods, or who have defended heretics who have been discovered, or who have abducted captured heretics, or who have been unwilling to provide these inquisitors with help in capturing heretics, when asked by them for this, or who have not hastened to the aid of <inquisitors'> cries for help, or who have not when asked supplied help in guarding those whom they have captured, or who have allowed those entrusted into their care to abscond – and most of all if these were suspect of heresy: such people, who have the power of custody <and fail to exercise it>, are to be punished by having all of their goods confiscated. Nevertheless they are also to be subject to other penalties in law.

[8] Item, we ordain that if any are found who are suspected of heresy, they are to swear peace and allegiance to the Catholic faith, abjuring all heresy. And if they have refused to swear allegiance to the Catholic faith and to abjure heresy, they are to be punished by the declared penalty against heretics. And if after taking this oath they have been found to be receivers, supporters or counsellors of heretics, or knowingly to have participated with them in something, they are to be liable to a similar penalty.

[9] Item, we ordain, that if someone is discovered after his death to have been a heretic and this has been proved in law before the bishop of the place, all his goods are to be confiscated. And the houses of those who have become heretics after the Peace was made at Paris, or the houses of those who become heretics in the future – in which they lived or will live – are to be destroyed.

[10] Item, we ordain that the goods of those who were vested heretics are to be confiscated, even if they have freely left off from the observances of the heretics – unless they have presented testimonial letters about their reconciliation or have proved it otherwise through Catholic and honest persons. And even if this reconciliation has been established, if they have not adopted the crosses they have been asked to wear for their reconciliation by their bishop, or if they have adopted them and then on their own authority taken them off, or they have been found to be concealing them within their clothes (for they are bound to wear them on the outside of their clothes and they are to be prominent, outside at the front part of the chest): they are to be punished with a

similar penalty. And whether they have goods or not, they are to be compelled to do this in the right way.

[11] Item, because we understand that when believers of heretics are planning to make themselves perfected heretics according to their detestable rite, during the time preceding this they sell or give away their possessions or inheritances, or pledge them as securities or dispose of them in other ways, thereby cheating <our> treasury. Notwithstanding these sorts of contracts – which are <in any case> reduced to invalidity – we ordain that the said goods are to be seized. This action is to be taken if it seems to us, after considering the circumstances of the said contracts in which these goods were transferred and their contracting parties, that the contractors were participants in the fraud.

[12] Item, we understand that certain believers give themselves to the heretics under the pretence of mercantile activity or pilgrimage, so that through such an absence they defraud the fisc and remove their goods from it. The bishop of the place will have admonished and questioned on this matter their neighbours, or those holding the goods of people who are absent in this way. If the past and also present absence of these people has not been proved in law in front of the bishop to be for a just and reasonable cause – proved by these same neighbours or by those holding the goods, and within a year (to be counted from the date of the same bishop's admonition) – we ordain that if they are otherwise suspected of heresy there should be a presumption against them as against heretics: and their goods are to be confiscated. If in fact after the confiscation of the goods or beforehand, they or their successors or those holding their goods have been able to prove a just and plausible cause for their absence beyond the aforesaid period of time: the goods can be lawfully left with them or restored to them.

[13] Item, because we are unwilling for the keys of the Church to be held in contempt in our land, we ordain that anyone who has contumaciously remained in excommunication for a year is to be compelled to return to the bosom of the holy mother Church through the seizure of their goods, as is more fully stated in the Peace made at Paris.[22]

[*The remainder of the statutes deal with other aspects of justice and peace in the Toulousain, including actions against mercenaries and robbers, those doing evil magic, those acting against the material interests of religious houses (especially the Cistercians), those instituting new tolls.*]

22 Treaty of Paris, item 5: Sibly, *William of Puylaurens*, p. 139.

31. COUNCIL OF BÉZIERS, 1246

William de la Broue, Archbishop of Narbonne (1245–57), held a council on 19 April 1246 which resulted in two documents, one containing canons – many of them directed against heretics, translated here – the other a set of instructions for inquisitors, translated in Part VII (Doc. 37). Both of these are discussed by Dossat, *Crises*, pp. 163–7, and together with the Council of Narbonne (Doc. 36) they are analysed by Maisonneuve, *Études*, pp. 293–307. William also provided a consultation in 1248, in response to questions from the inquisitors Bernard of Caux and John of St-Pierre; it is edited in Douais, *Documents*, pp. lxix–lxx, and discussed by Dossat, *Crises*, pp. 166–7. There are many details about William in R. W. Emery, *Heresy and Inquisition in Narbonne* (New York, 1941). Translated from Mansi, *Sacra concilia*, 23, cols 689–704.

1. That there should be laymen who are to search diligently for heretics

Wishing to extend the cult of the Catholic faith and in order to extirpate completely the madness of heresy from the province of Narbonne,[23] acting with the advice of the suffragan bishops of the church of Narbonne and the approval of all the council, we ordain that bishops should appoint two or three laymen of good repute in suspect places in their diocese, to act with the rector of the <parish> church or the person who exercises the cure <of souls> in his place. They are to bind these laymen with the pledges of oaths to apply diligent attention and care to the searching out of heretics and likewise their *believers, receivers, supporters* and *defenders.* If they find such people, they must focus on reporting them with as much speed as possible to the bishop of the place or the lords of the places, or their *baillis* or officials.[24] Further,

23 The importance of Narbonne in Roman times, when it was the capital of the region, has its high medieval counterpart in Narbonne as the the ecclesiastical capital, with its archbishops ruling a province extending from the Rhone to the Garonne: more or less, modern Languedoc.

24 Like the first canon of the Council of Toulouse, 1229 (Doc. 29 above), this loosely adapts part of canon 3, 'We excommunicate', of the Fourth Lateran Council (1215); Tanner, *Ecumenical Councils*, I, 233–5.

if they cannot detain the heretics they must take care that they cannot flee.

2. That someone who allows a heretic to stay on his land should be excommunicated

We ordain moreover that whoever knowingly allows a heretic to remain in his land because of payment or any other cause should thereby incur the sentence of excommunication, in addition to the other penalties against such people set forth in the Council of Toulouse.[25] If anyone is convicted of or confesses to this, he is to continue to be denounced by name and in public as excommunicate until it comes to the knowledge of the diocesan bishop that he has made proper satisfaction for such a crime against holy mother Church.

3. When the goods of those who are accused of the crime of heresy are to be confiscated

The goods of those who are accused of the crime of heresy should not be confiscated until they have been condemned by a formal sentence, unless they have knowingly clung to criminals in the same crime, after they knew they were infected by this sort of crime. And we say that the same thing should be observed in regard to those who in good faith deposit or entrust something to, or in some other way make a contract with, people of this sort who are publicly reputed to be Catholic. Completely putting aside <the question of> dishonesty <in these dealings>, those who contract in this way should not lose anything, even if those with whom they contract are secretly heretics, unless they knew what they were when they contracted with them.

4. That heretics' goods which they held from churches should revert to the churches

Because many people are being condemned for heresy who held possessions, rents or other moveable or immoveable goods from churches, monasteries or ecclesiastical men, we ordain that these sorts of goods

25 See canons 4 and 5, Council of Toulouse (1229), Doc. 29 above.

should freely revert to the churches or monasteries or ecclesiastical men from whom the said goods are, in whatever way, held, notwithstanding the terms of the agreement. Further, anyone who has presumed to violate this statute should be excommunicated forthwith, unless after legitimate warning he lays off this presumption. We order the same to be observed regarding the goods of fugitives [faidits].

5. That pardoners should preach nothing, except what is contained in their letters from the pope or bishop

In order to reform the arrogance of some people and to prevent the advancement of the faith being held back, we order that pardoners should not be permitted to preach anything to the people in churches other than what is contained in the lord pope's letters of indulgence and the diocesan bishop's letters. Nor are their little charters or schedules to be received from them. Nor in future is anyone to be let in to do this, unless he is a friar or other suitable person, carrying with him testimonial letters from his superior. For it is certain that many scandalous things have arisen from venal and mercenary pardoners, sometimes from their depraved way of life, at other times from their erroneous preaching, promising the damned liberation from hell for a modest payment.

6. That there should be no mocking of penitents, who have had a cross imposed upon them for the crime of heresy

Since sinners should be called to penance according to the voice of the Lord [*see* Luke 5.32], it is right to rejoice if they receive and undergo the penance willingly. Wherefore, in order to avoid the conversion of sinners being delayed and public discredit making converts reject their penance and relapse, we ordain and by virtue of the Holy Spirit we forbid mockery being made of penitents upon whom crosses are imposed for the crime of heresy. Nor are they to be excluded from their own places or common dealings. And if, having been warned, <such mockers and excluders> refuse to desist, they must be compelled by ecclesiastical censure.

7. That parish priests should teach the articles of faith simply, on Sundays[26]

We also ordain that on Sundays parish priests should take pains to explain simply and clearly to the people the articles of faith, so that no-one thereafter can put forward as an excuse the cover of ignorance. And at synods they should be ordered to do this. From their seventh year and above children should be taken by their parents to church on Sundays and feast days, and they should be instructed in the Catholic faith, and they should teach them the Salutations of the Holy Mary [Ave Maria], Our Father [Pater Noster], and I believe in God [Credo in Deum].[27]

8. That heretics, and their *supporters* are to be excommunicated every Sunday

Adding that heretics, or their *believers, supporters,* and *receivers* and *defenders,* are to be excommunicated every Sunday. And if any one of the aforesaid *believers, supporters, receivers* and *defenders* is personally warned and named as excommunicate and refuses to come to his senses within forty days, while persisting in their [*i.e., the heretics'*] defence or impeding their inquisition, then he is to be punished as a heretic. For among such people persevering and defence of error produces the adjudication of a man as a heretic.

9. That secular powers are to aid the Church against heretics

Further, we advise counts, barons, rulers and consuls of cities and other places, and all other secular powers discharging whatever office, that, following a reminder from their diocesan bishops, they are to take a

26 Raymonde Foreville has argued that the statutes of councils and synods in Languedoc were thirty years behind their equivalents in northern France and England in legislating for the pastoral needs of the laity. For her, it was this canon of Béziers in 1246 that initiated the process of catching up; 'Les statuts synodaux et le renouveau pastoral du xiiie siècle dans le midi de la France', *CdF* 6 (1971), 119–50.

27 On the requirement of these three in England, see N. Tanner and S. Watson, 'The least of the laity: the minimum requirements for a medieval Christian', *Journal of Medieval History* 32 (2006): 395–423.

corporal oath.[28] This is that they will faithfully and efficiently help the Church against heretics and their accomplices, doing this in good faith, in accordance with their office and to the best of their abilities. And that they will take care with all their strength to drive out all the heretics censured by the Church from the lands subject to their jurisdiction. And if it is necessary, they should be compelled by ecclesiastical censure to do this.

10. On those who extend counsel or patronage to heretics and supporters

Item, <this also applies> to all the others who secretly or openly are going to extend counsel, patronage or *support* to heretics and their *receivers* and *believers*.

11. On notaries who draw up documents for the same people

We ordain the same as regards notaries or scribes who knowingly draw up legal documents for heretics or their *supporters*, in life or at death.

12. On the same people's doctors

We ordain that the same should be observed as regards the same people's doctors.

13. That heretics or those suspected of heresy should be removed from the office of *bailli*

We order that those who were in fact formerly fully-fledged heretics or designated as heretics, or are rightly *suspect*, are to be removed totally from all public offices, including that of *bailli*, if they hold these, and in the future they are not to be appointed to such offices.

28 In physical contact with a holy object, for example the Bible.

14. That those who appoint them to the office of *bailli* are to be excommunicated

If in fact there are any who appoint these sorts of persons in their *bailliages*, unless they remove them when lawfully warned to do so, they are to be excommunicated.

15. That the rectors of churches should frequently explain this to the people

Rectors of churches or those acting in their place should be solicitous in frequently publicising and explaining to the people the penalties decreed against the aforesaid people.

16. That the peace oath should be renewed

In a time of peace faith can be more freely preached, inquisition against heretics carried out and ecclesiastical sacraments administered. Rejoicing together in the tranquillity of peace, we ordain the renewal of the oath of peace in *castra*, towns and cities, in accordance with the statutes of the Council of Toulouse[29] and following the form previously observed. Furthermore, with reverence to God and embracing ecclesiastical liberty according to canonical statutes, we command bishops, abbots and all other ecclesiastical men, together with their men, to support peace (when they have been asked by you) against the disturbers of the peace – reserving, however, bishops' rights over those subject to them.

[*The canons that follow relate to the general governance of the Church, reinforcing or amplifying the canons laid down by the Fourth Lateran Council. Alongside various canons on the governance of the parish and the behaviour of clergy and monks, these include a number of canons against the Jews, e.g. against their 'usury', against them having Christian servants, ordering that they wear an identifying badge, ordering them to remain inside during Holy Week, and prohibiting Christians from going to Jewish doctors*].

29 Council of Toulouse (1229), canon 28.

32. ACTS OF THE PROVINCIAL CHAPTERS OF THE DOMINICAN ORDER

These are taken from the 'Acts', the decisions taken at the meetings of Dominicans called 'provincial chapters', held each year in different cities and towns of Languedoc.[30] Most of the business concerned ordinary Dominican friars, especially the assignment of individuals to studying, preaching and teaching; we focus here on what they have to say about those who were acting as inquisitors. The acts of the provinces of Toulouse and Provence – laboriously and scrupulously compiled by Bernard Gui, and edited by him several times – are an example of the character of his scholarship, as is also Doc. 9. Translated from *Acta capitulorum provincialium*, ed. C. Douais, 2 vols (Toulouse, 1895), I, pp. 22, 23, 27, 28–9, 69.

Chapter of Montpellier, 1242

9. Item, we will and command inquisitors not to ride, except where there is great and clear need, for example if they are travelling through a dangerous locality and during the time they are in that locality, or if they need to go to a council or legate, and if they <are in a hurry and> have little time. And this they are to do after receiving licence from their superiors, if this can be conveniently acquired. Nor are they to carry money for spending or handle cash, nor is anyone to do this in their name. Rather, horses and their expenses should be provided for them by outsiders. Nor are they to keep horses, or to have grooms for horses. And if they have sometimes lapsed in these matters, they are to be corrected by their superiors. And whenever they wend their way to their convents, they are to come to chapters [= *regular formal meetings in the convents, attended by all*].

Item, <they are also to come> to the chapters of 'Visitors'[31] when they are summoned by their superiors.

30 The clearest account of these chapters remains M. D. Knowles, *From Pachomius to Ignatius: A Study in the Constitutional History of the Religious Orders* (Oxford, 1966), ch. 6.

31 Designated inspectors.

Item, by virtue of the obedience <by which they are bound>, we strictly prohibit them from imposing monetary penalties either on the dead or on the living, nor are they to exact or receive ones that have already been imposed.

Item, by the same prohibition we command them to abstain entirely from the implementation of sentences, for instance the constructing of prisons, the guarding of people who have been arrested, imprisoning people, digging up the dead and burning: except when this has been permitted to them.

Chapter of Narbonne, 1243

2. Item, that the books of inquisition are not to be carried around.[32] And that priors or other brothers are not to make inquisitors <act as> pardoners.

Chapter of Cahors, 1244

7. Item, that inquisitors should not put up with anything being given <to them> in relation to the business of inquisition: because this could give us a bad reputation.

Chapter of Avignon, 1245

6. Item, when inquisitors come to a place where we have a convent, they should come once a week to the chapter – or, if they are hindered for some reason, seek licence <for their absence>.

10. Item, priors and other brothers are to receive inquisitors charitably, and they should not believe easily those who defame the office of inquisition.

32 This is in the light of the loss of such books when inquisitors were killed the year before at Avignonet; see Doc. 46.

Chapter of Bordeaux, 8 September 1257

4. Item, in places where we have a convent no brother should eat with inquisitors.

PART VII: LEGAL CONSULTATIONS AND INQUISITORS' MANUALS

INTRODUCTION TO PART VII

As mendicant inquisitors got under way in the 1230s, they rapidly developed their procedures. This process was helped along by consultations with legal experts and ecclesiastical councils on many technical questions about definitions of different sorts of support for heresy, how to set up an inquisition, and the work of interrogation and sentencing. We provide here two consultations of lawyers (Docs 33 and 35) and sets of responses and guidance from three councils (Docs 34 and 36–7). Note that Doc. 37 is one of two distinct texts from the Council of Béziers. In order to avoid confusion, we have attributed the legislation of this assembly to the 'Council of Béziers' (Doc. 31) and called the guidance it issued to inquisitors the 'Consultation of Béziers' (Doc. 37).

These consultative documents were themselves the roots of inquisitors' manuals. It is important to note that the fame and accessibility of one example of this genre – Bernard Gui's early fourteenth-century *Treatise on the Practice of Inquisition* – has produced a somewhat misleading perspective on inquisitorial literature overall. Gui's treatise is a five-part work containing formulae (for things like sentencing) in its first three parts, an account of the office of inquisitor in its fourth part, and descriptions of different sects and how to interrogate their members in the fifth part.[1] However, Gui's treatise was assembled when inquisition had virtually finished its job in Languedoc, and this coherently organised, polished and, above all, very lengthy work is not representative of the everyday realities of inquisitors in the mid- and late-thirteenth century, and the textual aids *they* used. Surviving manuscripts suggest that in the thirteenth century an inquisitor usually used a rather small book, suitable for being carried around. It would contain an anthology of useful texts, the selection varying, but most often including the following:

(a) a few papal bulls dealing with inquisition,
(b) some formulae for sentences for different sorts of crime in heresy and different penalties (such as those in Doc. 38),

1 There is a tiny extract from part 4 in Doc. 40(b), on the meaning of 'perfectus', and most of the fifth part is translated in Wakefield and Evans; see WE, pp. 373–445.

(c) legal consultations on particular questions, most frequently those of the Avignon lawyers of 1235 (Doc. 33) and Guy Foulques (Doc. 35), and
(d) a selection of the consultative councils (Docs 34 and 36–7), as also of the Council of Toulouse of 1229, Raymond VII's statutes of 1233 and the Council of Béziers of 1246 (Docs 29–31).

Here we address our readers directly with a suggestion: you can assemble the documents listed above from the contents of this source book, and you will then be looking at an anthology very much like the typical 'inquisitor's aid' of the mid- to late thirteenth century.

Where the texts in Part VII discuss or define technical terms for types of heretic or suspect – believer, receiver, supporter, defender, counsellor, suspect, vehemently suspect – these terms are italicised.

Alongside the anthologies, the genre did include more unified manuals. Since the brief manual *Narbonne Order of Procedure* from the 1240s, often regarded as the earliest, is available in translation in Wakefield, *Heresy*, Appendix 6, pp. 250–8, we have translated a longer and later manual, from the 1270s, in Doc. 39.

On the genre and its uses see Sackville, *Heresy*, pp. 135–53, and Sackville, 'The inquisitor's manual at work', *Viator* 44 (2013), 201–16. While the fundamental account remains A. Dondaine, 'Le manuel de l'inquisiteur', in A. Dondaine, *Les hérésies et l'inquisition, XIIe–XIIIe siècles* (Aldershot, 1990), ch. II, much more work has since been published, including studies by R. Parmeggiani, such as *Explicatio super officio inquisitionis: origini e sviluppi della manualistica inquisitoriale tra due e trecento* (Rome, 2012), and V. Bivolarov, *Inquisitoren-Handbücher: Papststurkunden und juristische Gutachten aus dem 13. Jahrhundert* (Wiesbaden, 2014).

33. A LEGAL CONSULTATION, 1235

As in various other texts – including for example the Council of Tarragona 1242, which follows below – we see here experts being consulted on questions arising from the pursuit and prosecution of heresy. We have italicised the key words that are being defined. The specific case here is believers in the Waldensians, but the principles discussed also applied to approaches to believers in heretics of other sects. The jurists consulted were all well known in Avignon at the time, and it is worth remembering that one of the earliest inquisitors, William Arnold, came from Provence (Montpellier) and was also a jurist (*legista*). On the Avignon jurists, see G. Giordanengo, 'Hérétiques et juristes (juin 1235)', *Avignon au Moyen Âge: Textes et Documents* (Avignon, 1988), pp. 53–8; further evidence about them is provided by S. Balossano and J. Chiffoleau, 'Valdesi e mondo communale in Provenza nel Duecento', *Valdesi medievali*, ed. M. Benedetti (Milan 2009), pp. 76–82. On the consultation, see Arnold, *Inquisition and Power*, pp. 41–2. Translated from A. Patschovsky and K. V. Selge, eds, *Quellen zur Geschichte der Waldenser*, Texte zur Kirchen- und Theologie-Geschichte 18 (Gütersloh, 1973), pp. 50–4.

Opinion of the <juris>-consults of Avignon, in which is stated who should be called *believers*

Let it be known to all who will see the present page, that on June 20 in the 1235th year ad, Brother John, Prior of the Brothers Preacher in Avignon,[2] and the jurisconsults Geoffrey Gaucelin, Bertrand Cavalier, Bertrand Guillem, William Isnard, were questioned by Brother William of Valence, of the Order of the Preachers. <He questioned them> on behalf of himself and of Lord Bertrand, provost of Arles,[3] and Brother William of Jouques, who were jointly delegated by the lord legate[4] to impose penances or punishments on those people who were found to be guilty of the matter of heresy in the city of Arles. A careful and clear exposition was given to them of the variety <of things constituting>

2 Their convent was founded in 1224.

3 Bertrand Malferrat, canon of the cathedral chapter from 1225, provost (1231–58), archbishop (1258–62).

4 John of Bernin, Archbishop of Vienne (1219–66), papal legate (1233–8), who also provided a consultation, 15 May 1235; Parmeggiani, *Consilia*, pp. 8–10.

guilt, in the ways that are written below. Counselling firmly and faithfully, they said that those who confessed that they had the faith of the Waldensians, or that they believed that the Waldensians were good or holy men, were *believers* of the Waldensians and their errors, and should be judged as such. For they said firmly that they regarded it as the same thing to believe in the Waldensians or to believe in their errors or to believe them to be good men.

In a similar way they said that those who have confessed their sins to the Waldensians, in the way that they ought to confess to priests, were *believers*.

Similarly, those who have eaten bread and fish blessed by the Waldensians according to their accursed custom on the day of the <Lord's> supper – since the counsellors are firmly of the opinion that the Waldensians believe that they are then consecrating the body of the Lord.

And similarly those who have learnt the epistles and gospels from the Waldensians, and other things from divine scripture.

And similarly those who have often visited the Waldensians and heard their preaching and have been their benefactors; and also those who have only visited them and have often heard their preaching, <doing this> without the intention of apprehending and betraying them.

In the same way all the aforesaid counsellors said that a general excommunication applies to everyone as much as a particular excommunication applies to an individual. Therefore those who know that the Waldensians, their *believers*, their *receivers*, their *defenders* and their *supporters*, have been excommunicated by the Church, but presume to go against <this>: these people, although they have not been excommunicated individually and by name, should be understood to come under this particular sub-clause of the statutes of the lord pope, 'We strictly ordain that, if any such person has been marked out by excommunication etc.'[5] And similarly under any other similar sub-clause contained in any law, statutes or letters.

They also said that when anyone has been shown by their confession or other lawful proofs to be guilty in the aforesaid ways, even though the grace of absolution from excommunication may be granted to him, he

5 From canon 3 of the Fourth Lateran Council, repeated in Gregory IX's statute against heretics of Feb. 1231; Tanner, *Ecumenical Councils*, I, 234; *Texte zur Inquisition*, ed. K.-V. Selge (Gütersloh, 1967), p. 41.

must first be condemned with a definitive sentence and then punished, and it must be pronounced that he was a *believer*, or guilty in some other way, according to the degree of his crime.

They said furthermore that those <should be regarded> as having *come freely* who, though not cited by name, came forward within the limits <of time> generally and publicly assigned <for coming forward>, neither knowing nor suspecting that their error had been revealed by another person, and immediately confessing this error or sin, all of it, fully and freely. Others, however, are firmly to be presumed not to have *come freely*.

It should be known, in truth, that it was declared by the aforesaid Brother William, after asking for counsel from the afore-named counsellors, that all those are called guilty who knew that those in whom they believed, those whom they favoured and to whom they gave things, or that those whom they received, visited or heard, were Waldensians or the Poor in Spirit or the Poor of Lyon, and that the Waldensians or the said Poor Men had been denounced as heretics by the Church, and that both they and also their *believers* and *receivers* had been excommunicated, and that they have in this way knowingly and contumaciously lapsed in the aforesaid matters.

The said counsellors desired to attach their seals to this little charter as witness to the aforesaid things.

34. COUNCIL OF TARRAGONA, 1242

The council was conducted under the direction of Raymond de Peñafort (c. 1180/85–1275), the most important canon lawyer of the mid-thirteenth century. Raymond was born near Barcelona, studied and taught law at Bologna, and entered the Dominican Order around 1223 before writing a very influential short treatise on penance (first edition 1224–6). In 1230 he went to the court of Pope Gregory IX (1227–41), serving there as papal penitentiary. At Gregory IX's request he drew up a large collection of canon law, *The Five Books of Decretals,* which gained official status in the Church when the pope issued it in 1234. Leaving the papal court, Raymond served for two years as Master-General of the Dominican Order (1238–40), revising its constitutions.

On Raymond, see the introduction to Raymond of Peñafort, *Summa on Marriage,* trans. P. J. Payer (Toronto, 2005). The publication of proceedings of a conference devoted to Raymond includes an article on the text translated here, *Magister Raimundus,* ed. C. Longo (Rome, 2002), pp. 165–91; see also Arnold, *Inquisition and Power,* pp. 42–4, and Sackville, *Heresy,* pp. 93–100. The text is sometimes presented as Peñafort's directory of instructions for inquisitors, and appears in various later inquisitorial handbooks. It was again focused primarily on Waldensians – as some of the details in the lengthy oath of abjuration below make clear – but the wider principles applied to all heretics. We have again italicised the key words being defined. Translated from *Texte zur Inquisition,* ed. K.-V. Selge (Gütersloh, 1967), pp. 50–9; there is also a partial translation in Peters, *Heresy and Authority,* pp. 198–9.

As time passed, while we, Peter, by divine mercy Archbishop of Tarragona, were trying to bring to a successful result the inquisition against heretical wickedness in the city of Barcelona that had been begun by the Archbishop of Barcelona, Berengar, of good memory, with the assent of the chapter, during the vacancy of the see, various doubts arose here and there among the lawyers who were there with us. Therefore, in order to have clearer procedure in the matter of heresy and of inquisitions to be carried out in the future in the province of Tarragona, we have had discussions here and there with the venerable Brother Raymond of Peñafort, penitentiary of the lord pope, and other prudent men. We have decided to act in a certain way in the procedure of sentences on heretics, supporters, suspects and the relapsed, the punishments imposed on them, in accordance with the discretion given to them [*i.e. the prudent men*] by the Lord, that we may proceed more easily according to the statutes and provision of the Holy See against heretics, the Sandalled, or others.

1. First, the question is raised, who should be called *heretics*, who *suspects*, who *believers*, who *supporters*, who *receivers*, who *defenders*, who the *relapsed*, for these categories of men are spelled out within the canon.[6] And it seems that those who persist in their error are *heretics*, such as the Sandalled [=Waldensians], who say one should not take a oath for any reason, that ecclesiastical or secular powers are not to be obeyed, and that the penalty of the body [*execution*] is not to be inflicted in any case, and similar things. *Believers* in the said heresies, indeed, are also to be called *heretics*.

A person who has heard the preaching or reading of the Sandalled, or who has genuflected, praying with them, or who has given them the kiss <of peace>, or who has believed that the Sandalled are good men, or has done other things which can probably arouse suspicion, can be said to be a *suspect* of heresy. And a person who has prayed or done any other of the aforesaid things with them once can be called *simply suspect*. If however a person had often heard preaching or reading, or had prayed, or had done any other of the aforesaid things with them – he could be called *vehemently suspect*. If in fact a person had done all of the aforesaid things, especially if often – he could be called *most vehemently suspect*. And we are saying these things so that the discerning judge can make the purgation heavier or lighter, as he sees fit.

Those who have seen the Sandalled in a square or house or other place, recognising that they were the Sandalled, and have not revealed them when they had the opportunity to reveal them to the Church or a justiciar or other people who could and wanted to capture them – we believe they are *concealers*.

Those who have made a pact not to reveal heretics or the Sandalled, or have otherwise arranged for them not to be revealed, are *hiders*.

Those who have knowingly received heretics or the Sandalled in their houses or other places of theirs two or more times are *receivers*.

And we believe that a house or lodging in which heretics or the Sandalled have convened twice or more often for preaching or reading or prayer, or also where heretics or the Sandalled are often lodged, is a *place of reception*.

6 Gregory IX's decree against heretics, February 1231; see *Texte zur Inquisition*, ed. K.-V. Selge (Gütersloh, 1967), p. 41.

Those who knowingly defend heretics or the Sandalled, by word or deed or whatever clever ploy, on their lands or elsewhere, to the detriment of the Church's ability to carry out its task of eradicating heretical wickedness – these we call *defenders.*

We believe that all of the above, more or less, can be called *supporters,* and also those who have otherwise and in whatever way given them help, advice and support. And we believe that all *supporters* can be said to be *suspects,* such that they must purge themselves and abjure all heresy and all *supporting.* And they must be reconciled to holy mother Church.

Those who, after having abjured or renounced heresy, revert to their former heretical belief, we call *relapsed.* Those who after abjuring heresy or *support* do good to heretics or conceal them – in the same way we call them those who have *relapsed into support.*

And we say that all the aforesaid are excommunicated by major anathema, apart from those who are *suspect* without engaging in *support,* if any such happen to be found.

A sentence against *supporters* will be formulated as follows:

> Let it be known to all that it is clearly established to us, through what was found, proved and enacted in inquisition, that N. has been convicted for *support.* We pronounce him excommunicate and *suspect* of heresy. And if he is not absolved, and if within a year he does not make satisfaction, he is to be subject to the penalty of the general council.[7] And if he is deficient in purgation, and remains in excommunication for a year, he is to be condemned as a *heretic.*

2. Among some people doubt arises about those who have relapsed into belief and about heretics who dogmatise – if after they have been convicted they wish to repent, whether they should be relinquished to the secular arm? And it seems to us that they should not be; but in both cases they should be condemned to imprisonment.

3. Item, if there is at issue a really great number of heretics or believers and they are prepared to abjure heresy, a discerning judge will be able to impose canonical penalties on such people to a greater or lesser extent, in accordance with the provision of the Apostolic See, and thus avoid imposing the penalty of imprisonment. With *believers,* even if the number is not so great, the discreet judge may moderate the penalties

7 Canon 3 of the Fourth Lateran Council (1215): those under excommunication for one year who fail to give satisfaction for their faults and receive absolution are condemned as heretics; Tanner, *Ecumenical Councils,* I, 233.

as he sees fit, after considering the circumstances. This does not apply to fully fledged heretics [perfecti heretici], or the Sandalled, or dogmatisers of their errors, or to *believers* who have relapsed into belief after abjuring or renouncing heresy. Having first of all utterly abjured heresy and after receiving absolution from excommunication, these are to put into perpetual imprisonment, so that they may save <their> souls there and henceforth not corrupt others.

4. Item, a question is raised about someone who has given a kiss to a Sandalled or a heretic, believing or knowing him to be a Sandalled, or has prayed with him, or concealed him, or has heard preaching or a reading from him, and has believed such a person was a good man: whether he should be adjudged a *believer* in his errors? And we believe not. But such a man should be condemned as a *supporter*, *hider* and *benefactor*, and *vehemently suspect* that he believes in their errors, unless he is so literate and discerning that he cannot claim ignorance. We have decided that this should be left to the arbitration of the discerning judge.

5. Item, before inquisition begins, someone has confessed his heresy or *support* to his priest, and now is summoned by the inquisitors: in this case, his confessor is to be believed. If it is found that he has indeed confessed – through confession to his priest – and although the priest has done ill in not sending him on to the bishop[8] – the person confessing is nevertheless to escape temporal punishment through this confession: unless he is found to be in false penance [*is pretending to repent*] or to have relapsed after penance, or is publicly defamed. Further, if he claims public penance or reconciliation, he is to prove this through two witnesses.

About those with whom it is clear that they confessed before inquisition began: they must abjure heresy publicly and carry out any other due ritual, unless the matter was so secret that they do not have ill fame or witnesses against them. And in either case they are immune from all temporal penalty.

If any persons summoned by the inquisitors deny <things> during their depositions, and afterwards – because of the inquisitors' persistence or because they are frightened about <other items of> evidence – reveal the truth, but say that they kept silent about the truth through shame or fear: such people we believe are perjurers, because those who

8 That is, the priest has not referred the confession to his bishop. Confessors' manuals reiterated various 'reserved' sins, which could only be remitted by a bishop: preeminent were murder, major sexual sins such as incest and sodomy, and heresy.

knowingly speak falsehood or are silent about the truth are perjurers. And therefore a heavier canonical penance should be imposed on them. 6. Item, from time to time in general inquisition for the sake of security the due rituals of the law of the Church are held in reserve and heretics or those who have relapsed are absolved in secret. Doubt is raised: how should the sentence be formulated? And we say that since the person is not now a heretic, it should be formulated thus:

> Let it be known to all that it is clearly established to us, through what was found, proved and enacted in inquisition, that N. was convicted for heresy and afterwards returned to the unity of the church. Proceeding with mercy towards him, we condemn him to perpetual imprisonment according to canonical statutes.

If he is not yet absolved, it is formulated thus:

> Let it be known to all, etc., that N. was convicted of heresy, and wishes to return to the unity of the church. Proceeding with mercy towards him, etc.

If he does not wish to repent, but persists in error, the sentence should be formulated thus <and delivered> in the presence of a secular judge:

> Let it be known to all that it is clearly established to us, through what was found, proved and enacted in inquisition, that N. was convicted for heresy as condemned by the church. We condemn him as a heretic.

A heretic who is truly penitent after absolution will abjure his heresy publicly as is contained below, and moreover in the presence of many who belong to the diocesan bishop's jurisdiction.

> I, N., recognising the true, Catholic and apostolic faith, abjure, and in abjuring detest all heresy, particularly the sect of the Waldensians, the Sandalled, or the Poor of Lyon, into which driven by my sins I fell.
>
> This sect tries to affirm that one should not obey the Roman Church or prelates subjected to it or secular princes, holding the keys of the Church in contempt and asserting that prayers or alms cannot help the dead, and that remissions <of sins> or indulgences, that are granted by the lord pope or other prelates, have no power to help anyone.
>
> It asserts, further, that one should not swear an oath for whatever necessity or utility. Item, it asserts that the penalty of the body[9] should not be inflicted in <the course of> justice.
>
> Item, <it asserts that> in the sacrament of the altar, after the bread and wine are consecrated they are not made into the body and blood of Christ, if the priest is a sinner. And they regard everyone as a sinner, unless he is of their sect.

9 Capital punishment.

Item, <it asserts that> that the consecration of the body and blood of Christ can be done by any just man, even a layman, provided he is of their sect, even though he is not a priest ordained by a Catholic bishop.

I abjure, detest, and condemn these and all their other errors.

I consent moreover to the holy Roman and Apostolic See. And with my mouth and in my heart I profess that I hold and observe that same faith, in the articles stated above and all the others, that the blessed Pope Gregory, or whoever is the father of the Roman Church [= *the current pope*] and all other prelates of the holy Roman and Apostolic and Catholic Church hold, preach publicly and affirm. And because you, lord Archbishop, and other prelates, deliver to me and assert …[10] and in particular on the following <articles>: I believe and recognise that one should obey the lord pope, the Roman Church and its other prelates and Catholic secular princes.

And I affirm that the power of the keys for binding and loosing was given by the Lord to the blessed apostle Peter and to the other apostles, and through them to all the prelates of the Catholic Church.

I believe firmly that their indulgences and remissions, and also alms and prayers help the living and the dead.

Item, I believe firmly and attest that one can swear an oath for necessity and utility without sin, and that in justice punishment of the body ought to be inflicted.

I confess moreover that the sacrament of the body and blood of Christ can be performed by no-one except a priest ordained by a Catholic bishop, who is obedient to the lord pope and the holy Roman Church. And if such a priest is a sinner, although it is a sin for him to approach such a sacrament, I nonetheless believe and firmly confess that it is a true sacrament, and that after consecration by such a priest the bread and wine are made into the true body and true blood.

Whence, upon my oath I say by almighty God and these four holy gospels of God that I hold in my hands, and under the liability of anathema I promise to you lord Peter, by the grace of God Archbishop of Tarragona, and Bernard of La Granada, Archdeacon, and all the Chapter of Barcelona (during the vacancy of the see), and through you I promise to the chief of the apostles and to his vicar, the most blessed Pope Gregory, and to his successors.

I promise that – regardless of anyone's persuasions or anything else – I shall never believe otherwise or hold <any faith> except according to what the true and holy Roman Church teaches and holds and what I have declared above.

I swear moreover that I shall not have any association, familiarity or participation with the Sandalled, the Waldensians, the Poor of Lyon, or heretics of whatever kind, nor shall I render them aid, counsel and support

10 Something is missing here. What was handed over was probably a copy of the gospels, upon which the oath would be taken.

> through receiving, hiding, supporting, giving to them or <helping> in some situation.
>
> And if I learn or get to know where one or some of the aforesaid <heretics> or their supporters are, at the earliest opportunity I shall reveal him to the bishop or prelate or judge or rector of that place, assuming these are Catholic and observe the faith of the holy Roman Church.
>
> And if I do anything against this – God forbid – and do not observe each and every one of the aforesaid things, let me be subject to canonical severity, and, as one incurring the crime of perjury, let me be found liable to eternal damnation, and let me have my reward in the world to come together with the originators of heresy.[11]

A suspect will purge himself publicly in the jurisdiction of the bishop of the diocese in this manner, as is given below:

> I, N., swear by almighty God and by these four holy gospels that I hold in my hands, before you lord Peter, by the grace of God Archbishop of Tarragona, and before all those sitting with you, that I neither am nor was a Sandalled or a Waldensian or a Poor Man of Lyon, nor a heretic of any other heretical sect that is condemned by the Roman Church. Nor do I believe in their errors nor did I believe nor shall I believe at any <later> stage of my life.
>
> Rather I profess and declare that I believe and for ever after shall believe in the Catholic faith that the holy Roman and apostolic Church publicly holds, teaches and preaches, and that you, lord Archbishop, and the other prelates of the holy universal Church hold, publicly preach and teach.

Compurgators will swear in this way:

> I, N., swear by God and by these four holy gospels which I hold in my hands, that I firmly believe that N. was not and is not a Sandalled, a Waldensian or a Poor Man of Lyon, nor a heretic or believer in their errors; and I firmly believe that in this he swore the truth.[12]

Once the judge has fixed the number of compurgators to be assigned to someone, he should take care – it is not proper to change it later, in order not to make a mockery of the Lateran Council.[13]

11 'Originators of heresy' meaning originators of particular heresies, as Mani of Manichaeism.

12 Compurgators, used extensively in medieval law, were asked to attest that they believed the accused to have sworn truly, rather than attesting directly on the facts of the matter themselves. However, the first clause here suggests that, in the case of heresy, there was an element of factual attestation.

13 Allusion to the stipulation in canon 4 of the Fourth Lateran Council: that purgation should be 'appropriate', presumably not brought into disrepute by abuses of number, character or variation of compurgators; Tanner, *Ecumenical Councils*, I, 233.

7. Item, if through inquisition any heretic or Sandalled or believer is found to have been buried in a cemetery, his bones are to be exhumed and burnt, if they can be identified.

8. Item, if, after the beginning of an inquisition, the *support* of some people who have gone the way of all flesh becomes clear to the inquisitors, on the basis of confession or witnesses, and these people, if they had lived, would have been condemned for *support*, unless they had been secretly or publicly absolved in that inquisition: such people are to be left to divine judgment.

Item, because in general inquisition many are found to have died in *support* [*i.e. while being supporters*], since *support* is a corollary and accessory to heresy, we believe that such people should be exhumed if their bones can be identified. They should not however be burnt for dying excommunicate, in case perhaps their absolution may be proved, or because signs of penance may have been showing, according to canonical statutes.[14] If in truth any *supporters* are found to have relapsed into some type of *support* after the abjuration or renunciation of *support*, they should be punished more heavily than others, according to the decision of a discerning judge. For a wound inflicted a second time is slower to heal.

9. Item, priests are instructed to inquire diligently in confession about heretics and the Sandalled and their *believers* and *supporters*. And if they find anything, they have to write it down faithfully. And immediately – together with the person or persons who have confessed – they have to show what they have found to the bishop or his vicar. If however the person who has confessed is unwilling to agree to what he has said being revealed to the bishop or his vicar, the priest should nevertheless consult learned and God-fearing men, without identifying the person in question, about how to proceed further.[15]

10. Item, when preaching to Catholic people, exhorting them or having conversations with them, one of the Sandalled says some good words that contain no error, or at any rate not an explicit error, for

14 As the following sentence makes clear, the point here is *relapsing* into acting as a *supporter*: if someone 'died as a supporter' having no previous absolution, they have died excommunicate but have not relapsed. If, however, they were previously absolved, and then returned to being a supporter and died in that state, they are liable to be dug up and burned.

15 Priests were not supposed to reveal that which they had heard in confession; although, as noted above, they are also supposed to 'refer' major sins to the bishop for absolution.

example, 'Do not lie or swear', 'Do not fornicate', 'Render to each what is his', 'Go to church', 'Pay to the clergy tithes and their rights', and suchlike. Those listening – and knowing or believing this man is one of the Sandalled – believe he is a good man because of the good words they hear from him. Further, they believe that these men's sect is good, and that men can be saved in this sect. Doubt arises here, whether on account of this they can be condemned as though they were the Sandalled, or as *believers* in their errors (especially if they know or believe that the Church persecutes the Sandalled as heretics), and thus (unless they convert) be relinquished to a secular judge to be burnt?

After careful consultation and discussion, this is how it seems to the experts. Such people are to be regarded most vehemently as *suspect* – suspect that they are *believers* in the errors of the Sandalled. And purgation of this should be ordered through many compurgators, according to the rank of the person in question. However, he should not be adjudicated to be a Sandalled or *believer* on these grounds, unless he is so educated [litteratus] and discerning [discretus] that simplicity and ignorance can in no way be a valid excuse – something which it seems should be left to the decision of a discerning judge.

However, it seems to be otherwise in the case of someone who says or believes that the Sandalled who are already condemned by the Church as heretics, or even because of this already burnt by secular justice [*i.e. specific individuals*], were good men and saved, and that any other people, of any sort, could be saved in that sect or faith in which or for which they were condemned and burnt. The adjudication is that such people cannot be excused in any way, so long as they are adult and capable of reason.

11. All *supporters* moreover are *suspect* to a greater or lesser degree, as has been said. And for that reason they must publicly purge themselves and abjure heresy, according to the number of compurgators.[16] The form for purging and abjuring heresy for supporters will be very like the form for heretics, as written above. One thing however should not be passed over. This is that those who confessed and were absolved in secret before an inquisition <started>, should be reconciled and abjure in secret before some witnesses – and the names of these witnesses are to be preserved in the acts [*i.e. written legal records*]. This is unless

16 Perhaps meaning that the number should vary according to the degree of suspicion, greater for example when suspicion is most vehement.

what they did is openly known through fame or witnesses, and then they should abjure and be reconciled publicly. In either case, they are immune from all penalty. Further, solemn penance is to be imposed on all *supporters* and *believers*, to greater or lesser degrees as we shall define below.

12. Heretics who persevere in error are to be relinquished to secular judgment.[17]

After they have abjured and have received absolution, perfected heretics and those who dogmatise [*preach heresy*] and those who have relapsed into belief are to be placed in perpetual prison.

Believers in the errors of heretics, however, should do solemn penance, namely in this way. They should be in processions at the episcopal seat or cathedral, on the next feast of All Saints, and on the first Sunday of Advent, on Christmas Day, on the <feast days of> Circumcision, Epiphany, St Mary in February [*Candlemas*], St Eulalia, St Mary in March [*Annunciation*], and on all Sundays in Lent. And they are to be there, barefoot, clad in breeches and shirt (except on St Mary in February and Palm Sunday). After being disciplined [*beaten*] publicly in the processions they are to be reconciled to the Church in the church of Santa Maria del Mar by the bishop or a priest.

Item, on the Wednesday at the beginning of the fast [*Lent*] they are to come similarly to the episcopal see in the same manner, barefoot and in breeches and shirt, and according to the lawful form then expelled from the church, and thus be placed outside the church for all of Lent; however <they should come> to the doors of the church, so that there they can hear the office <of the Mass>.

And on Holy Thursday, barefoot and in breeches and shirt, <they should come> before the doors of the church, then be reconciled publicly to the church following canonical statute. And they must do this penance – of the fourth day and standing outside the church for all of Lent and on Holy Thursday – every year for as long as they live.

And on Sundays in Lent, after the reconciliation, they are to leave the church and stand outside the doors until Holy Thursday. And they must always wear two crosses on their breast, that are not of the same colour as their clothes, and they should wear such things that all can see they are doing solemn penance. However, they should not abstain from entering church during Lent for more than ten years.

17 By this stage, this is clearly understood to mean the death sentence.

It is to be understood that women should come and be disciplined <fully> clothed.[18]

The penance for those who have relapsed in *support* is similarly solemn, as that of *believers* set out just above, on all the aforesaid days, apart from this, that they are to wear crosses and do penance in the same way on Ash Wednesday and Holy Thursday only for ten years.

The penance for those who have not relapsed into *support* but are *supporters* and *most vehemently suspect*, will be in the same way solemn, on the feast of All Saints, Christmas Day, Epiphany, Saint Mary in February, and all Sundays in Lent. And they must do for seven years the penance on the fourth day of Lent, and standing outside church for all Lent, and reconciliation on Holy Thursday, as stated above.

The penance for those who are *supporters* and *vehemently suspect* will be solemn in the same way, on the feast of All Saints, Christmas Day, Saint Mary in February, Palm Sunday. And they must do for five years the penance of the fourth day of Lent and standing outside the church for all Lent, and reconciliation on Holy Thursday, as stated above.

The penance for those who have been *supporters* will be solemn in the same way, on the feast of All Saints, Saint Mary in February, Palm Sunday. And they must do for three years the penance of the fourth day of Lent and standing outside the church for all Lent, and reconciliation on Holy Thursday.

Further, all the aforesaid people must do the penance on the prescribed feasts and days in this city, and not elsewhere, until the feast of Easter – those, that is, who are citizens. Outsiders are to do it in their parishes, and not elsewhere, except on the Wednesday at the beginning of Lent and on Holy Thursday, when all of them are to come to the episcopal see of Barcelona. For the subsequent Lenten times, all of them, whether citizens or outsiders, must do the penance they have to do – on the fourth day after the beginning of Lent and on Holy Thursday, for ten years, seven, five or three according to the varying degree of guilt, as has now been defined – at the episcopal seat of the city Barcelona and not elsewhere. This is unless with just and rational cause and special licence from the Bishop of Barcelona or someone acting in his place if he is absent, they have gone elsewhere, and then in the places where they have gone with the permission of the bishop they are to do the same penance in the presence of the bishop of that place or the person

18 This qualifies the earlier specification for men – barefoot, etc.

acting in his place, carrying letters from the bishop or his deputy containing the penance they have to do. And the persons who have done this penance are to carry letters back to the Bishop of Barcelona from the bishop of that place, containing testimony about the penance that has been done. And if it happens that, without fraud or deception, when they return they cannot come to the cathedral church on those two days,[19] on two solemn feast days assigned to them according to the will of the bishop, they will be publicly disciplined at the see of Barcelona, following the form of those two days.[20]

19 The fourth day of Lent and Holy Thursday.

20 A phrase is probably missing, which is qualified by 'following the form'.

35. THE *CONSILIUM* OF GUY FOULQUES

Guy Foulques (c.1195–1268) was a lawyer of Louis IX, married, and after being widowed entered the Church, becoming Bishop of Puy, Archbishop of Narbonne and finally in 1265 Pope Clement IV. His consultation was the most widely copied of all in inquisitors' handbooks, perhaps because of papal prestige as well as subtlety of thought. Scholars used to think it was written in the 1250s, but it has recently been established that it had been written by August 1243. We have selected the sections dealing with key points of definition, as found in other texts given here. Q. 9 is discussed by P. Biller, 'Deep is the heart of man, and inscrutable: signs of heresy in medieval Languedoc', *Text and Controversy from Wyclif to Bale: Essays in Honour of Anne Hudson*, ed. H. Barr and A. M. Hudson (Turnhout, 2005), pp. 267–80. On Foulques, see Y. Dossat, 'Gui Foucois, enquêteur-réformateur, archevêque et pape (Clément IV)', *CdF* 7 (1972), 23–57. Translated from V. Bivolarov, *Inquisitoren-Handbücher. Papsturkunden un juristische Gutachten aus dem 13.Jahrhundert mit Edition des Consilium von Guido Fulcodii*, MGH Studien und Texte 56 (Wiesbaden, 2014), pp. 239–45.[21]

The Ninth Question, <On *believers*>

The next question is, who ought to be called *believers* in the errors of heretics?

Certainly those who confess they believe, are therefore *believers*, just as they say they are. For they judge themselves out of their mouths, and 'the case of someone who has confessed cannot be defended'.[22] And this is without doubt.

Those who have adored, shown reverence according to their custom, or received confession or communion from them according to their rite, or did similar things which pertain to their rite, undoubtedly are convicted of having been their *believers*.

For attitude is presumed from <someone's> external acts, as is argued:

21 Bivolarov gives an account of Guy's life (pp. 206–13), and new arguments for the work's date (pp. 214–17).

22 Ovid, *Poems from Exile*, Ex Ponto, 2 'To Messalinus', line 54.

– in 32.q.5, the chapter 'Whosoever shall look' ['on a woman to lust after her, hath already committed adultery with her in his heart', Matthew 5.27];[23]

– in the *Codex*, *On evil intent*: ['it is appropriate for evil intent to be proved by transparent <acts of> deceit'];[24]

– 'Nor does it matter whether someone makes their will known through the things they say or the things they do', *Digest*, *Concerning the laws and decrees of the Senate*, <chapter> 'About some cases';[25]

– 'For we can deny and confess not only by what we say but by what we do', eleventh Case, question 3, *Some think*.[26]

I say this about those deeds in which error is expressed, as in the examples I provided above which pertain to the rite of those who err. However, if someone has visited them, provided alms, escorted them and done similar things, in which nothing pertaining to their rite is explicitly manifested, I do not believe such a person can be judged a *believer*, even though others have written the opposite.[27] For all these things occur sometimes through physical affection, sometimes at the behest of friends, sometimes through the intervention of money. And since the pope says that not simply *believers* but 'believers in their errors are to be condemned as heretics',[28] I am driven to the opinion that there is some sign of error in them. For this reason I do not adjudge those I talked about earlier – whom I commented upon just above – to be *believers* of heretics, but rather their *supporters* and *receivers*, as I shall demonstrate below. Though a *believer* may be adjudged a heretic, do not be quick – I beg you – to punish someone as a *believer* and, consequently, as a heretic. For in this crime no-one is condemned,

23 Gratian's *Decretum*, Case 32, question 5, chapter 13 (Friedberg, I, 1136), quoting Gregory's *Moralia* xxi.9.

24 Justinian, *Codex*, book 2, title 20(21), § 6; *Corpus Iuris Civilis*, ed. T. Mommsen, P. Krüger, R. Schoell and W. Kroll, 3 vols (Berlin, 1872–95), II, 109.

25 Justinian, *Digest*, book 1, title 3, § 32; *Corpus Iuris Civilis*, I, 6.

26 Gratian, *Decretum*, Case 11, question 3, chapter 84 (Friedberg, I, 666). Gratian uses St Jerome's commentary on Titus I.16, 'They confess that they know God, but in their deeds they deny him'.

27 See Doc. 33 above.

28 Gregory IX, *Five Books of the Decretals*, Book 5, title 7, chapter 15 (Friedberg, II, 789); the bull *Excommunicamus* (1231), repeating first words of Fourth Lateran Council canon 3.

even on the grounds of vehement suspicion, in the *Liber extra, On presumptions*, 'Your letters'.[29]

And if someone objects: how therefore do you call those who adore and do similar things *believers*, if you condemn no-one from presumption? I reply: I do not condemn them only from presumption, rather from true proof. For this is the strongest proof which happens through the deed itself. Otherwise, in fact, one cannot establish anything about the mind, for 'deep is the heart of man, and inscrutable'.[30] But signs of this sort, that cannot be twisted <to mean something> good nor to anything other than what they expressly indicate, are to be regarded as proofs. And therefore they are called 'manifest <acts> of deceit' in the *Codex*, 'On evil intent'.

What therefore are we to say about those who have heard their sermons and preachings? I reply: If they have heard only once and never afterwards wanted to return, they seem to be blameless, and as far as this is concerned not to be adjudged *believers*; nor do they seem to have approved what they afterwards avoided. And I say this, following the argument in Case1, question 1, 'It is clear'.[31] However, those who have come the first time and then later on frequent <them> at suspect times and places can be regarded as *believers*. I argue from the opposite case in the said canon 'It is clear' and similarly from the *Liber extra, On presumptions*, 'By his inclinations' ['a child is known', Proverbs 20.11].[32]

Those that I have said above cannot assuredly be *judged* to be *believers*: I do admit, however, that they are not without great suspicion, and therefore that the obligation of purgation [*clearing of name under oath*] can be imposed upon them, according to apostolic mandate and canonical sanctions, according to this, 'Those who are only found suspect of heresy', etc., the *Liber extra, On Heretics*, 'We excommunicate'.[33]

29 Gregory IX, *Five Books of the Decretals*, Book 2, title 23, chapter 14 (Friedberg II, 357); letter from Pope Innocent III instructing the Bishop of Nevers and the Archdeacon of Berry not to condemn as a heretic a man from La Charité on the grounds only of considerable suspicion.

30 From a variant Latin translation of Jeremiah 17.9; discussed by Biller, 'Deep is the heart of man', pp. 278–9.

31 Gratian, *Decretum*, Case 1, question 1, chapter 111 (Friedberg, I, 401–2). The case concerns persons whose attendance at a heretical ceremony occurred only because they were forced.

32 Gregory IX, *Five Books of the Decretals*, Book 2, title 23, chapter 3 (Friedberg II, 353).

33 Gregory IX, *Five Books of the Decretals*, Book 5, title 7, chapter 13, § 2, reproducing canon 3 of the Fourth Lateran Council of 1215.

Item, and those who retain heretics' books: I say these are similarly suspect, and should be purged. However, if they have burnt the books they are in the clear; the argument: Case 5, question 1, chapter 3, at the end.[34]

The tenth question: <On the *supporters* of heretics>

The next question is on the *supporters*, that is to say, who should be regarded as *supporters.* In this matter my judgement is that <we need to distinguish> – there is not one condition for everyone: some people are private persons, whereas others hold office with public power.

Those who exercise office by the power of the sword [*secular authority*] can be regarded as *supporters* just through omission – if, for example, they do not drive out and punish as they ought those who have been condemned by the Church.[35] And these canons show that from this they are to be understood to be *supporting* them: Case 23, question 3, 'Who can'[36] and question 5, 'Who by vices',[37] and question 8, chapter 'Furthermore'.[38]

However, private persons in this case, if they do not arrest, <or> if they do not detain someone who is getting away, cannot be said to be *supporters.* For these things pertain to those who exercise power. And there is argument in support in Case 26, question 2, chapter 'If from the threshing floor'.[39] And this I am declaring about private persons, who are not bound by oath to this. If however they have sworn to point them out, as many people do, and <instead> hide them: I do not deny that this is to *support* them, since they are bound to this by the duty imposed by their oath and it is a mortal sin in this case to hide the truth; Case 11, question 3, 'Whoever'.[40]

34 Gratian, *Decretum*, Case 5, question 1, chapter 3 (Friedberg, I, 545).

35 That is, if they fail to execute them.

36 Gratian, *Decretum*, Case 23, question 3, chapter 8 (Friedberg I, 898): 'Who can obstruct and confuse the perverse and does not do it – this is nothing other than favouring their impiety'.

37 Gratian, *Decretum*, Case 23, question 5, chapter 38 (Friedberg, I, 941), on 'the person who spares and favours the feeding of vices'.

38 Gratian, *Decretum*, Case 23, question 8, chapter 12 (Friedberg, I, 955), whose rubric is 'The person who does not correct crimes which he could set right commits them himself'.

39 Gratian, *Decretum*, Case 26, question 2, chapter 10 (Friedberg, I, 1023–4).

40 Gratian, *Decretum*, Case 11, question 3, chapter 80 (Friedberg, I, 665).

I have stated, therefore, how someone may seem to *support* through omission: but someone can also *support* through words. So, if someone makes excuses for heretics, not through a slip of the tongue or by way of a joke, but in gatherings or among lay people, as many people do, often saying, 'These men are not the kind they are said to be, nor do they deny these things or those things'; or perhaps because some of them are advocates, and in their defence make excuses for their transgressions: these people can be called *supporters*, after consideration of the persons, time and places in question. Not all of these things, however, can be strictly defined. For it is often the case that these words arouse simple men to the love of heretics, and diminish and weaken the devotion they have for the Church. Case 11, question 3, chapter 'Fearing' suggests that excusers of what is false *support* it.[41] And those bishops who supported Lothar [II] were condemned as supporters; Case 2, question 1, last chapter,[42] and elsewhere the pope, explaining the mode of *supporting*, says that they tried to cover up his crimes with trumped up defences; Case 11, question 3, 'Thus'.[43] And it is inferred from these two chapters that someone who uses these sorts of trumped-up defences is understood to *support*. Of course, I am speaking about those who do this deliberately, not those who, as often may be the case, slip into this just by stumbling or by way of a joke. For 'a slip of the tongue ought not to be made into the grounds for a punishment or penalty'; *Digest*, 'On the Julian law of lese-majesty', 'The infamous'.[44] And similarly those things that are said by way of a joke do not bring liability; *Digest*, 'On actions and liability', 'The substance of liability',[45] and Case 22, question 2, chapter 'What he said'.[46]

Item, someone *supports* by action, and this seems clear enough. And I say this about the person who escorts, who arranges, who sends alms, who sets free, who organises the things by which they are set free, and does things similar to these. And though this needs no proof, there is

41 Gratian, *Decretum*, Case 11, question 3, chapter 85 (Friedberg, I, 666–7).

42 Gratian, *Decretum*, Case 2, question 1, chapter 21 (Friedberg, I, 449); the divorce of Lothar II from Theotberga in 857 was a famous test-case in canon law.

43 Gratian, *Decretum*, Case 11, question 3, chapter 96 (Friedberg, I, 669–70).

44 Justinian, *Digest*, book 48, title 4, § 7; *Corpus Iuris Civilis*, I, 794.

45 Justinian, *Digest*, book 44, title 7, § 3; *Corpus Iuris Civilis*, I, 713.

46 Gratian, *Decretum*, Case 22, question 2, chapter 18 (Friedberg, I, 872); quoting the comment by St Augustine that what Joseph said in Genesis 44.15 was not meant seriously and was only a joke.

supporting argument in Case 23, question 4, chapter 'There is unjust',[47] and the *Digest*, 'On thefts', 'If by security', § 'If iron tools'.[48] I say the same about a person who sets free <a heretic> because of the entreaties <of others>. Supporting argument: Case 14, question 6, chapter 5, in that short verse, 'I may have said this very confidently'.[49] Nor should we be swayed by the fact that someone is called in this verse 'companion in the crime'. 'Companion' is not understood as though to mean that the person committed that crime himself. Rather, 'companion' is taken to mean being a participant in the corruption. Case 2, question 7, chapter 'To neglect'[50] talks about this sort of companionship, where it says, 'One should be worried about secret companionship <in the case of someone who fails to stop an obvious crime'>.

But what should we say about prelates who are unwilling to construct prisons or do similar things that pertain to the progression of this business? I reply thus. Since they do this not in *support* of heretics but through avarice, I do not call them *supporters.* And therefore I advise the brothers <Preacher> not to involve themselves directly with them but to consult the Apostolic See.

47 Gratian, *Decretum,* Case 23, question 4, chapter 33 (Friedberg, I, 915).

48 Justinian, *Digest,* book 47, question 2, chapter 55(54), § 4; *Corpus Iuris Civilis,* I, 770.

49 Gratian, *Decretum,* Case 14, question 6, chapter 3 (Friedberg, I, 743); quoting St Augustine defining as a 'companion in the fraud and crime' someone who intervenes to stop the restitution of stolen goods or does not compel someone who has taken refuge with him to restore the goods.

50 Gratian, *Decretum,* Case 2, question 7, chapter 55 (Friedberg, I, 501).

36. COUNCIL OF NARBONNE, 1243/4

Held in late 1243 or early 1244, the council was presided over by Peter Amiel, the Archbishop of Narbonne, and had the participation of the archbishops of Arles and Aix and the bishops of Carcassonne, Elne, Maguelonne, Lodève, Agde, Nîmes, Albi and Béziers. These prelates considered questions put to them by Dominican inquisitors and drew up their replies in 29 canons. Those to whom the replies were sent will have included Brother Ferrier, on whose activities see Docs 41, 43, 44, 46, and various references in 48. On Peter Amiel, see R. W. Emery, *Heresy and Inquisition in Narbonne* (New York, 1941), ch. 3. The council is discussed by Arnold, *Inquisition and Power*, pp. 44–5, Dossat, *Crises*, pp. 159–61, Maisonneuve, *Études*, ch. 6, and R. Parmeggiani, *I* Consilia *Procedurali per l'Inquisizione medievale (1235–1330)* (Bologna, 2011), pp. 22–4. Translated from *Texte zur Inquisition*, ed. K.-V. Selge (Gütersloh, 1967), pp. 60–9.

Peter, by the grace of God Archbishop of Narbonne, John and Raymond,[51] Archbishops of Arles and Aix respectively, and other prelates,[52] whose seals are appended to this document: greetings in the Lord to the beloved faithful sons in Christ, the brothers of the Order of Preachers, constituted inquisitors of heretics in the above-mentioned and surrounding provinces.

1. On the punishment of heretics who have acquired immunity

Cutting short your doubts, as far as we can, we have decided to counsel your zealousness thus. Some of you promised immunity from prison to those heretics and their *believers*, *receivers*, *defenders* and *supporters* who were coming of their own will, before the set day, to tell the whole truth both about themselves and others – promised with due deliberation and praiseworthily (for one should deal more gently with those who have confessed of their own will) and because you were hoping that through this the hidden pus of heresy would be better and more easily detected: rightly, as the outcome of the matter clearly showed.

51 Peter Amiel, Archbishop of Narbonne 1226–45; John Baussan, Archbishop of Arles 1233–58; Raymond Audibert, Archbishop of Aix-en-Provence 1223–51.

52 The bishops of Carcassonne, Elne, Maguelonne, Lodève, Agde, Nîmes, Albi, Béziers.

You are to impose penances on these people: namely that they are to wear crosses. Every Sunday they must appear stripped of some of their clothing – as fits the conditions of the season – and carrying rods in their hands. And they must present themselves to the priest of their parish who is saying Mass, between the Epistle and the Gospel: and there they are to receive discipline.[53] And they must to do this on every solemn procession. Further, on the first Sunday of every month, after procession or Mass, they must visit – similarly stripped and with rods – all the houses in the same city or town in which they saw heretics. And they must attend Mass and vespers every Sunday, and a general sermon[54] if it takes place in a town; unless they have some honest impediment <to doing this>.

If by chance the town was under interdict or they were excommunicated, they must visit all the churches and the houses where they saw heretics, on specified days. And they must attend general sermons. They must fast. They must visit saints' shrines, instead of going overseas <on pilgrimage to the Holy Land>, which used to be imposed on such people. They are required to defend the faith and the Church against Saracens, or heretics, or their supporters, or people who are otherwise rebels, for a fixed number of years, or months, or days, with arms and at their own expense, doing this themselves or via others who are more suitable. They are to follow your instructions, doing this by the lord pope's command and decision or his legate's or ours.

2. The journey across the sea <on pilgrimage to the Holy Land> is not to be imposed upon them

The journey mentioned earlier is not in future to be imposed upon them, because of a recently produced papal prohibition about this – 'Lest the very basis of the faith should be violated by their perfidy', at the point where it began, 'Because there could be reasonable anxiety <about the effect> of this sort of penance bringing together over there people who would otherwise be dispersed'.[55] However, the lord pope himself wants those who had this journey imposed upon them before his prohibition to carry it out.

53 That is, be beaten with the rods by the priest.

54 Ceremonial sentencing of heretics.

55 These seem to be quotations from this otherwise unknown papal bull.

3. That, where it seems expedient, they should be sent to other towns or provinces

And where it seems expedient, they should be thrown out of the town in which they have been living, and dwell in another town or province for a while or forever.

4. That prisons should be constructed to contain poor converts

Prisons should be constructed to contain poor people who have been converted from heresy. And they should provide with them their needs properly, so that prelates are not burdened excessively by such people or become unable to provide, perhaps because of their numbers.

5. That penances are permitted to be at the discretion of inquisitors

And here we touch one point, that you are not to impose all the penances detailed above everywhere, or all of them on everyone. Rather, using the discretion granted you by the Lord and bearing in mind the quality of guilt, person, time, place and other circumstances, you should apportion the penances with such care and shrewdness that by either punishing or indulging the lives of guilty people are reformed; or at least, that it can be clear who *walks in darkness*, who *in light*,[56] who is truly penitent, and who feigns conversion, to avoid scandal being generated from this <use of discretion> among true Catholics. Nor can it be that heresy is defended or nurtured on the pretext of <avoiding> scandal or for any other <reason> among you, however important it may be.

6. That those who have been converted should confess their guilty acts in public

Further, after summoning clergy and people, you should make all who have been converted confess their guilty acts and abjure and swear

56 Scriptural; see, for example, 1 John 1, 6–7.

in public, as is contained in the apostolic mandates and more fully in the statutes of Lord Romanus,[57] except where the slightness of guilt or the enormity of scandal suggest drawing back from full rigour in <implementing> this. And let public instruments [*official documents*] be drawn up containing the guilty acts, abjurations, promises and penances of each individual, so that the truth – so long hidden but now both wonderfully and mercifully revealed by God – can no longer perish or hide.

7. That inquisitors can add to or take away from penances that have been imposed

There is always in reserve one thing that may be called upon, with care, by you or other inquisitors or those to whom the Roman Church has decided to commit <inquisition> or a person who has the job by virtue of his position. You and they are at any time allowed by your or their own judgement and will, on reasonable grounds, to add to or take away from the penances that have been imposed.

8. Supervision of the carrying out of their penances should be entrusted to their own <parish> priests

Further, you are to entrust supervision of their penances to their own <parish> priests. These priests – in this way having under their control the penances of each of their parishioners and carefully monitoring their carrying out – should immediately report these parishioners to you (or to others you have appointed), if there are any who hold these penances in contempt. You or your appointees will proceed against them in a way that is specified below.

9. What is to be done about those who are to be placed in prison, if there is an excessive multitude of them

Further, concerning heretics or their believers who are not worthy of the aforesaid immunity, because they suppressed the truth about themselves or others, or because they did not come forward within the

57 The statutes of Toulouse (1229), Doc. 29 above.

time of indulgence, or for some other reason – people however who are prepared unreservedly to obey the mandates of the Church and to admit the truth they had either suppressed or denied: there is no doubt that such people should be placed in perpetual prison, in accordance with the statutes of the lord pope. However, we understand that you have found such a great multitude of these people that not only the money but also the stones and cement could scarcely suffice for the construction of prisons. We advise you to defer their imprisonment, where this seems fit, until fuller consultation of the lord pope about their great numbers. However, if there are by any chance some whose wickedness is so acute as to give good grounds for anxiety about their impenitence or flight or relapsing, or corrupting or confusing others, you should assign these without any delay to a strong and suitable prison.

10. On those who rebel against the penance of prison or do not carry out another penance

Further, there are those heretics who, after swearing to obey the mandates of the Church and acquiring (or not acquiring) the benefit of absolution, present themselves as rebels, either not entering prison (the penance imposed on them) or leaving after entry, or refusing to observe or carry out whatever other penance, or obstinately absenting themselves from receiving it – and thus they openly demonstrate their lack of repentance and the falseness of their conversion –

[11. On those who have fallen back into the heresy they abjured]

– and there are those who, after abjuration or purgation of error, are found to have fallen back into the heresy they had abjured. Without any hearing, you are to relinquish them to secular judgment for punishment by the due penalty [*i.e. execution*]. For it is enough for such people to have deceived the Church once, especially where their numbers have grown so great! Nevertheless, if they repent, penitence is in no way to be denied to them.[58]

58 They are allowed to confess and receive absolution before execution.

12. Let us state who are to be said *to rebel*, who *to have fallen back* into heresy

Certainly those who have been lawfully warned and do not apply themselves freely to emending their contempt – without a doubt we say that they are *rebelling*. At the same time we rightly understand as having *fallen back* into heresy those who, after their abjuration or purgation (as stated above), have presumed inexcusably, knowingly and willingly to *receive* heretics or otherwise *support* them. For then one ought not to doubt that they have done this as a consequence of their earlier error – most of all if they had specially abjured what they <then> did and had freely made themselves liable to this sort of penalty <if they relapsed>. And if they have some grounds that can excuse them from so vehement a presumption <of this degree of guilt>, at the very least and without any delay they are to be assigned to perpetual prison.

13. On *receivers* or *supporters* who have either *fallen back* or have fled from receiving their penance

Further, there are those who – although they have only been found to be *receivers* or *defenders* or *supporters* and have been reconciled or have sworn to obey the mandates of the Church – have *fallen back* into their abjured guilt or have obstinately fled from receiving or carrying out their penances. And because of this they are bound by the second chain of excommunication, either through their oath or by a sentence. If they wish to return <to the fold>, in addition to a sworn caution you should get from them sureties of such a sort and size that will deter them from straying in this way <again>, because of their fear of the temporal penalty. You should send them, with your testimonial letters containing the whole truth, to the lord pope, to get absolution and to receive penance.

14. Let us state who should be regarded as *supporters* of heretics

Clearly, we take to be among *supporters* both those who impede the extirpation or correction of heretics or believers and also those who do not provide help for this, when not providing help cannot take place without obvious guilt. One can ascertain the greater or lesser degree of guilt in such people through careful consideration of the circumstances. For someone provides much *support* to heretics or believers, in concealing them when he could and ought to point them out. He provides even more *support* when, through concealing them or in some other way, he maliciously tries to impede their examination or imprisonment or punishment. He provides most *support* who releases those who have been captured or imprisoned, against the wishes of the Church; or gives them counsel or help, whether ordered or sworn to do such things, or when these things are perpetrated through his counsel, help, command or <exercise of power in> law.

15. That someone who does not take punitive action against them, although he has the power to do so, should be regarded as their *supporter*

Someone with temporal jurisdiction who puts off persecuting, or expelling from his land or province, or delays taking punitive action against the aforesaid pestiferous heretics or rebels censured by the Church – he is to be regarded as guilty of this crime, and beyond compare in this! A man who avoids preventing a crime that is so great and so obvious to him in law, through the Church's denunciation or otherwise; a man who avoids this, even though he is bound to do it and can do it – and especially if this is a man who has obliged himself by his own oath to do it – this man is not immune from suspicion of keeping wicked company.

16. On those who, though they can, do not capture the aforesaid or help those capturing them

Nor are those people free of crime who wickedly fail to capture heretics or the *rebels* specified above, or who fail to help those who are trying to capture them when they have the opportunity of time and place and the power to do this – and most of all if they fail when they have been asked to do this by those capturing or wanting to capture them. The ways of harming used by heretics and their believers and supporters, when they are striving to *tear down the vine of the Lord of Hosts,*[59] are many, and they are more or less untraceable: and one must

59 Combination of Song of Songs 2.15 and Dominus Sabaoth (Bible, *passim*), here perhaps derived from the opening words of Innocent III's bull of 1213 summoning

work against them with both shrewdness and manly strength. With the grace given you by God, let your zeal attend to the recognition of their evils and to the application of salutary medicine. And let your discernment make up for what cannot be easily contained in writing.

17. That brothers Preacher should abstain from monetary penances

Once the bishop of a place, acting by virtue of his office, has exacted pledges of goods (taking them in similar fashion from those acting as guarantors of heretics or believers who have fled, or from the deceased who did not carry out their penances, or from their heirs or guarantors) and has deposited them in some sacred place, the imposition of penances is a matter to be referred to the lord legate. For the honour of your order you are to abstain and to keep yourselves away from such monetary penances and exactions. For otherwise the full carrying out this sort of business would overwhelm you and bring you to the ground.

18. That the aforesaid guilty persons are not permitted to enter a religious order

Unless there is an indulgence from the pope or his legate, you are not to permit any of the aforesaid guilty people to enter any religious order, so as to avoid the corruption of the order's simplicity by such people. And if some of them have entered an order after an inquisition has started or before an inquisition (when they have not confessed or been canonically absolved), doing this without the pope's permission or the legate's or yours, you are to get them out.

19a. That no-one is to be excused from prison on account of age etc.

Further, concerning people who are to be imprisoned: we have decided to add this. Without special indulgence from the Apostolic See, no man is to be excused from prison because of his wife, even if she is

the Fourth Lateran Council, *Vineam Domini Sabaoth: Select Letters of Innocent III*, ed. C. R. Cheney and W. H. Semple (London, 1953), p. 144.

young,[60] nor a wife because of her husband, nor anyone because of their children or parents or people otherwise closely tied to them, or because of physical weakness, old age or some other similar cause.

[19b]

If some guilty or suspect people pertaining to your inquisition are not or were not, in fact, present, and if, within the suitable time limit you have accordingly assigned to them (and which has been publicised within churches), they have not bothered to appear or to provide an excuse in law: you are to proceed against these unhesitatingly, just as against those who are present.

20. Who are to be subject to inquisition

We understand that these people are subject to your inquisition:

– those who did wrong within the bounds of this <particular> inquisition;

– or those who have their residence there, or had it when the inquisition began;

– or those who were cited by you <to appear>, either while they were staying there by reason of some public or private task <they were carrying out>;

– or those without a fixed residence who were found there <within these bounds>;

– or there are those who have or have not been bound by some sort of caution – you have begun to make inquisition against them, or have perhaps imposed purgation on them.

So, you can and you ought to proceed against such people, whether they are present or absent – unless perhaps, because of some major or minor crime committed elsewhere or because of their place of residence or on some other grounds, other inquisitors have begun to proceed against them.

60 Here the excuse rejected is that of looking after a girl who may have got married for the first time near the canonical minimum age of twelve.

And whereas with God's sanction inquisition is carried out in various places and by various inquisitors, it is safer and more beneficial for anyone who has done wrong, in whatever places, to stay tied to the one and only inquisitor who – acting on some of the grounds that have been written above, and doing this without fraud or danger to the business in hand or to souls – was the first to deal with him.

21. That if other inquisitors get to know something, they should write to the <inquisitor> to whom the guilty person is bound

Thus – that if other inquisitors have been able to get to know about this person, they should nevertheless inquire and they should write to those inquisitors to whom this guilty person should be bound. And in this way you will fight as though you are one man, and you will conquer.[61]

22. That the names of witnesses are not to be made public by word or sign

Further, in accord with the foresight and will of the Apostolic See, you are to take care that the names of witnesses do not become public through any word or sign. However, if it happens that there is inquisition against someone, and he says perhaps that he has enemies or that some people have conspired against him, the names of the enemies and the cause and truth of the hostilities or conspiracy are to be got out of him, so that consultation should be taken about the witnesses as well, themselves also convictable of error.

23. That no-one should be condemned unless convicted

You are not to proceed to the condemnation of anyone without clear and open proofs or their own confession. For it is better to leave a crime unpunished than to condemn the innocent.

61 That is, inquisitors should act collectively, in unison.

24. That all are to be allowed to make an accusation or give evidence

Because of the enormity of this sort of crime, all are to be allowed to make an accusation or give evidence, even criminals and people of ill repute and also accessories to crime.

25. What objections remove the credibility of witnesses

The only objections that completely remove the credibility of witnesses are those that seem to come not from zeal for justice but the fire of malice, such as capital[62] conspiracies and hostilities. In truth although other crimes weaken credibility they do not exclude it, especially if the witnesses have reformed <and no longer engage> in crime.

26. On the person who is convicted, but obstinately denies

If however someone obstinately does not fear to deny their guilt, and it is completely clear on the basis of witnesses or some other proof that he can be judged to be a *believer* or a *heretic*: without any doubt this person is to be regarded as a heretic for as long as he persists in this sort of denial, even though he may otherwise pretend conversion. For someone who does not wish to confess his sin evidently does not repent it.

27. That those who have made a deposition once should not be questioned again, unless about circumstances

Further, witnesses who have made a deposition once, when questioned generally about themselves and others: if later on, after this sort of deposition an inquisition is initiated against someone about whom they said what they knew, it is not necessary for them to be produced again – unless, perhaps, it seems that they ought to be questioned on some circumstances about which they had not been questioned.

62 Probably meaning murderous.

28. Whether to believe a confessor,[63] regarding anyone's absolution or penance

<The question is raised>, whether one ought to believe in a confessor, on his own, on the matter of the absolution or penance of a person, dead or alive: although it seems that the answer should be 'no', lest this have some impact on the Church, one must await a response from the lord pope. However, when dealing with people who belong to your inquisition (according to the definition given above) and who have been absolved by those who do have the power to absolve, you are not to <re->impose upon them the penance that <had previously> been imposed by them.

29. Of what and from what can people be judged to be *believers*

In order to remove any further doubt about which guilty matters are those on the basis of which people can be judged to be *believers*, we are giving our firm judgment that they are these:

If people have made reverence to heretics, where *believers* – begging for their prayers and calling them 'Good Men' – virtually adore them.

If they have been *present*, but not with the intention of betraying or finding fault or for some other good reason or excuse,

– at the <heretics'> consolation, where they treacherously lie, saying that the person whom they consolate and receive as a heretic can save himself through the imposition of hands;

– or at their 'Service', where the senior person holds a book open and where they understand that there is remission of sins, as though in a general confession;

– at the Waldensian supper, where on the day of the Supper [*Holy Thursday*] a table is set up and bread placed upon it. And the Waldensian who blesses the bread, breaks it and gives it to those who are present, accords with his damnable sect in believing that he is making the body of Christ.

63 That is: a parish priest or mendicant friar to whom someone had confessed, and received penance and absolution, for a heretical sin.

If they have confessed their sins to these Waldensians, as one is accustomed and ought to confess to one's own priest.

If they have knowingly or damnably *received*

– the Peace from the heretics or the Waldensians,

– or bread blessed by them and sent or given to them by anyone.

If they have *believed* that they can be saved in their sect,

– or that they are holy men, or the friends or messengers of God, or that they are men of good conversation and way of life,

– or that their persecutors are sinning <in persecuting them>,

– or if they have praised them in such a way (or shown through any sign or word when confessing in law or elsewhere) that they had faith or belief in them.

If they received them willingly and often, heard them, visited them, gave or sent them food or other things, or learnt from them prayers, or the epistles or gospels.

Though individual items may not amount to proof, these and similar things provide a lot of support <for the adjudication of people as *believers*>, especially as John says in his Epistle, 'If any man come to you, and bring not this doctrine, receive him not into the house, nor say to him, "God speed you". For he that saith unto him, "God speed you", communicateth with his wicked works' [1 John 10–11].

We realise all these things when those who are guilty in this way are found. They knew that the people to whom or by whom these things took place were heretics or Waldensians. Nor were they ignorant of the fact that the holy Church denounces such people (who because of their own errors and damnable sects are segregated from the unity of the Catholic faith), and that it excommunicates them, persecutes them and condemns them. Nor should one without good reason believe someone who says he was ignorant of this. Who is the lonely traveller who does not know the condemnation of heretics and Waldensians, carried out so justly and so long ago? So famous, made so public and so much preached about? Followed by so much expenditure and the sweat and toil of the faithful? And so firmly sealed by so many deaths of those infidels who have been solemnly condemned and punished in public?

In any case, such an evident disciple of the masters of lying, who denies such a notorious truth, should not be tolerated but rather condemned along with <the heretics or Waldensians> who are condemned. For the very size of this past history demonstrates and proves that it could not have been ignored.

Those who want to hide, and strive to have the heretics and Waldensians concealed, entrust themselves to their *believers*, perpetrating with them the aforesaid evils and similar things in their lairs. Even though some of these people may similarly deny having heard their errors or believing in what they heard, these things do not allow them to be immune from participation in believing – at least implicitly – in their errors. For although these people may say nothing explicitly against some particular article of faith, nevertheless silently and by logical consequence they do in fact talk [against the faith], since they say and think, by word or sign, that these perfidious men who are known to be rejected by the Church are good men. And furthermore, since they believed that the aforesaid things help the salvation of their souls, either believing that there was salvation outside the Church or believing that those whom the Church condemns are not outside the Church: without any doubt they have erred.

For our part we are writing these things to you, beloved sons in Christ, since both the lord pope and the lord legate have provided that this business <of inquisition> should be entrusted to you in many provinces. We do not wish to bind or confine you with our advice, for it would not be right for the specific liberty of making decisions, that has been granted to you, to be restricted – to the prejudice of this business – by the advice, forms and rules of people other than the Apostolic See. Rather we hope to help your zeal <in pursuing this business>, as we are commanded by the Apostolic See: so that you who bear our burdens may take back from us, in mutual love, advice and help in this business of ours.

37. CONSULTATION OF BÉZIERS, 1246

We have translated the proceedings of the Council of Béziers in Part VI (Doc. 31); here we provide the guidance issued by the council in response to questions arising in the prosecution of heresy. Translated from Mansi, *Sacra concilia*, 23, cols 715–24, and Parmeggiani, *I* Consilia *Procedurali*, pp. 34–46. See Dossat, *Crises*, pp. 163–7; Maisonneuve, *Études*, pp. 293–306.

The consultation of the provincial council of the Archbishop of Narbonne and his suffragans, held at Béziers, on how one should proceed in inquisition against heretics.

William, by God's grace Archbishop of Narbonne,[64] to our beloved in Christ, brothers of the Order of Preachers, constituted by apostolic authority inquisitors against heretics in the provinces of Arles, Aix, Embrun and Vienne, greetings in the Lord. We have received letters from the most reverend father Peter, by God's grace Bishop of Albano,[65] in this form:

> To the venerable father in Christ and most dear friend, by the grace of God Archbishop of Narbonne, P., by His mercy Bishop of Albano, greetings in the Lord.
>
> Although we wrote to you once when acting in place of the lord pope in the regions of Provence, asking you to order inquisitors of heretics to proceed in the inquisition of heretical wickedness, in consultation with you and the diocesan bishops (with whom they thought it expedient to do so), following the customary form in imposing penances that has been handed down to them in these matters: bearing in mind the nature of the business, we wish and with the authority of the lord pope we order you to enjoin the aforesaid inquisitors not to desist from proceeding in the business of heresy, in consultation with you, diocesan bishops and other prelates (with whom this seems expedient), following the customary form in such things and the apostolic letters sent to them. For the expenses necessary in these matters, you are to provide for these same inquisitors in accordance with

64 William de la Broue, Archbishop 1245–57.

65 Peter of Collemiers [usually given as Collemieu], Archbishop of Rouen, 1237–44, Cardinal and Bishop of Albano, 1245–53, produced in late 1245/early 1246 a consultation on inquisition which is edited in Dossat, *Crises*, pp. 348–9.

> the Council held at Montpellier by the most reverend father the Bishop of Avignon, then Legate of the Apostolic See.[66]
> Given at Lyon, 7 March

By the authority of this mandate, therefore, we enjoin you to attend without any delay to proceeding in the aforesaid business of inquisition that has been entrusted to you according to the tenor of the same mandate.

To these things: we – the aforesaid <Arch>bishop, Raymond of Toulouse, Clarin of Carcassonne, Berengar of Elne, William of Lodève, Peter of Agde, <Raymond> of Béziers, Raymond of Nîmes, <Pons> of Uzès,[67] by God's grace bishops, abbots and other prelates of the province of Narbonne gathered together in a provincial council at Béziers, whose seals are attached to these present <letters> – willingly accede to your zealous requests, with which you humbly entreated us to be directed and strengthened by our advice in the whole of the business in question, settling as far as we can your questions, at the same time wanting to help your zeal, as is commanded us by the Apostolic See itself: so that you who bear our burdens may take back from us, in mutual love, advice and help in this business of ours.[68]

1. Our advice is this. Following the apostolic mandate, you should stay at what you see as a suitable place within the bounds of inquisition that have been assigned to you, so that you can carry out inquisition of this locality and – since it is not safe for you to go to every single place – to carry out <from there> inquisition of other localities <as well>. And there you are to gather together the clergy and people and preach the word of God. After that, you are to explain to them the mandate given to you and the reason why you have come, and, as you think opportune, read out the letters by which you have authority to proceed. And then you are to order all those who know that they themselves or others have fallen into the crime of heretical corruption, to appear before you to tell the truth.

2. A suitable period of time, which you usually call a 'Time of Grace', is assigned to these people, who will not otherwise receive this

66 Zoën Tencarari, bishop 1242–64(?), apostolic legate July 1243–March 1245.

67 Raymond of Fauga OP, bishop 1232–70; Clarin, bishop 1226–48; Berengar VI, episcopal dates not known; William of Cazouls, bishop 1241–59; Peter III Raymond Faure, bishop 1242–71; Raymond III de Sale, bishop 1245–7; Raymond d'Amaury, bishop 1242–72; Pons of Becmil, bishop 1239–49.

68 Identical to closing words of Doc. 36 above.

grace. Those who come within this period, repenting and saying the full truth both about themselves and others, are to have immunity from the penalties of death, prison, exile and the confiscation of their goods.

3. Since the carrying out of inquisition will have been needed in other localities, you should make this sort of general citation and assign the Time of Grace. Clerics and lay people should be assembled in that locality, where there is to be a summons, by some ecclesiastical person to whom you have entrusted this task by your letters patent.

As testimony to his reception of the mandate he is to append his seal to these letters, while at the same time writing back (in his own letters patent which are similarly to have his pendant seal) in what way, in whose presence and when he has carried out the mandate that had been given to him.

4. From those who have appeared in front of you thus, within the assigned Time <of Grace>, you are to receive oaths that they will say the absolute and whole truth, that they know, about the matter of the stain of heresy, both about themselves and also about others, living and dead.

Afterwards, while you or the scribes are questioning them carefully about each of the things which will seem to need inquiry, you are to have their confessions and depositions faithfully written and set down in the acts of inquisition. This is to be done either by a public person [*a public notary*], if you can obtain one, or some other suitable person, sworn in to the task, acting together with another suitable man, likewise sworn in: so that a text of this sort, either done by a public hand or (as we have mentioned) two suitable men, and set down and written out in the acts, and recited to the person who is confessing and deposing in the presence of the inquisitor and the notary, or the said two suitable men, obtains the force of <legal> validity.

You should arrange the reception of the aforesaid oaths publicly and in the presence of all who come together to confess: so that in accordance with what is demanded by the form of the oath, everyone is bound to say the truth about both himself and others.

Each and every person is to understand that inquisition is being carried out against them, and about what things, in such a way that the headings <of those points>, about which there will be inquiry, will be seen to be, as it were, explained to each person.

On account of this, when witnesses have attested once in such a general and commonly known inquisition, it is not necessary for them to be produced again if, after this sort of deposition, an inquisition starts <that is> specially directed against someone about whom they have <already> said what they knew. This does not apply if it seems that they should perhaps be questioned about some circumstances upon which they had not been questioned, especially since (as we shall touch upon later) the names of witnesses in this favoured legal proceeding – as it is privileged business – are in no way to be made public.

5. You are to bestow the benefit of absolution, following the mode prescribed by the Church, on these people who confess fully and of their own will within the Time of Grace and say that they are returning to ecclesiastical unity. Specifically, you are to make them

– abjure every heresy that raises itself up against the Holy and Roman Church and the orthodox faith, by whatever names it is called;

– and swear that they will, correspondingly, observe and defend the Catholic faith that the same sacrosanct Roman Church holds and preaches;

– and that they will pursue with all their strength heretics of whatever sect, as much the condemned vested ones as the […],[69] <and> their *believers*, *receivers*, *defenders* and *supporters*: tracking them down, accusing them and capturing them, or at least in good faith pointing them out to inquisitors or other faithful men who want to and can capture them and are in a more favourable position to do so.

And those that are found and have been found to have fallen into the same crime on these matters shall abide by the commands of the inquisitors and the Church. And they shall receive and carry out the penance that, at whatever time, had been imposed on them[70] – solemnly pledging all their goods to the inquisition and the Church to guarantee the reception and carrying out of the penance.

6. You are to summon by name <to appear> at their time [*each at the time designated by the inquisitor*] those who, though they are guilty, scorn to appear within the Time of Grace, or wickedly suppress the truth.

69 We suggest that there is a missing word or phrase here, indicating perfected – i.e. fully-fledged – heretics from another group condemned by the Church – probably Waldensians.

70 A conditional penance which they had bound themselves to receive if they failed to fulfil the oath.

7. If they have not wished to confess the truth (that has been found against them), you are to set out for them the headings of the things upon which they have been found guilty. And, similarly, you are to make known what has been said by the witnesses.

8. After giving suitable adjournments and granting opportunity for defence, you are to be generous in admitting their counterpleas and objections.

9. And if some have failed in their defence, unless they have wanted to confess freely the guilt that was proved, you are to assign an appropriate concluding date for the sentence and you are to condemn them. And while they persist in their denial they are not to be admitted to mercy, however much they may place themselves under the will of the Church.

[*chapters 10–13 copy Narbonne (1243), canons 22–5, without the rubrics; 12 omits the opening words of Narbonne c. 24, 'Because of the enormity'; see Doc. 32*].

14. You are to have those who defiantly absent themselves solemnly summoned in their parish or cathedral church and in the localities where they have, or used to have, their domicile. And after thus lawfully making known the points presented in the case, and after a reasonable period of waiting, and after a careful discussion based on the acts <of inquisition> and receiving counsel under seal from prelates you deem suitable, you are to proceed to the condemnation of such people, as their guilty acts require: God's and the Gospels' presence makes good their absence!

15. With regard to those who later on want to return and obey, and generally all those who earlier on were defiant or disobedient or whose flight you were right to be worried about: you should get from these people the guarantees of sureties, or have them detained where you think most suitable.

16. You are to examine perfected and vested heretics in secret and in the presence of some discreet and faithful men, encouraging them to convert insofar as you can. And you are to show yourselves benign and favourable to those who want to convert, since much light is cast upon the business through them, and it [*the business*] is moved forward. And you are to moderate and reduce their penances in accord with the character of their conversion and merit, and to the degree that you see fit.

17. Where you can do this without difficulty, you are to be slow in condemning those who are unwilling to convert, frequently encouraging

them to convert, doing this yourselves or through other people. But in the end you are to have those who stubbornly persist in their wickedness confess their errors in public, to promote detestation of these errors: relinquishing those who are thus condemned in the presence of the secular powers and their *baillis*, according to the apostolic mandate.

18. In the case of the condemnation of heretics or believers who were not canonically reconciled before their deaths, you are to summon their heirs or others who by law ought to be summoned, and, after granting them ample opportunity for defending, you are to proceed similarly.

19. You are to exact appropriate satisfaction from the heirs of those who confessed and were reconciled but died without receiving penance – lest such, and such a great crime, that they also confessed publicly in court, should remain in some ways unpunished. And you are to do the same with those who died after receiving penance but without completing it, if they began to delay, or pledged their goods <to guarantee> the carrying out of the penance, as we touched on above, or if the journey overseas was imposed on them.

20. By apostolic mandate, you are to place perpetually in prison heretics condemned as relapsed, obstinate heretics and fugitive heretics, who want to return <to the Church>, similarly also those who were captured, that is to say, those who after the Time of Grace did not bother to appear except when summoned by name, or those who knowingly and against their oaths suppressed the truth. Nor are you to impose on any of them the penance of a period of prison. But after they have been detained in prison for some time, humbly obeying your orders, and after signs of obedience have appeared in them that move you to mercy – and if at the same time you know this to be expedient – you can mitigate or commute the penalty or penance of this sort of perpetual prison, by the lord pope's indulgence, granted to you in this, and with the consultation of the prelates under whose jurisdiction they are.

21. <You are to do this> after having received from them good sureties that they will carry out the penances imposed upon them to the best of their abilities, and oaths about persecuting heresy and defending the Catholic faith, as was described above in relation to those who are to be reconciled; also, after delivering the sentence on them, that if in future there should be found <even> a slight suggestion that they are deviating from the faith, they are to be mercilessly punished with the due penalty:

22. always reserving to yourselves this power that, if it seems expedient to you for the business of the faith, you can put the aforesaid people back in prison, even without a new reason for this. In the case of those condemned as fugitives, relapsed and obstinate, the caveat about oaths and sureties mentioned above should also apply before their imprisonment.

23. You are to make provision for there to be little rooms for such people who are to be imprisoned, according to the ordinance of the Apostolic See, insofar as is possible in each of the cities of the corrupt dioceses – separate and hidden rooms, to prevent mutual perversion or the perversion of others. And the great rigour of prison is not to extinguish them [*kill them*], because you are to have them <supported> by those who hold their goods, and have their necessities provided, in accord with the statutes of the Council of Toulouse.

24. Further, at the beginning no-one of the aforesaid guilty people should have this penance or penalty of perpetual prison remitted or commuted into another, unless he gives away heretics, or imminent danger of death threatens his children or his parents because of his absence, or for some other cause which seems very just and reasonable.

25. A wife should have free access to an imprisoned husband, and vice versa, lest they be deprived of cohabitation – whether both are imprisoned or just one of them.

26. You are to impose these sorts of penances upon those who are not to be imprisoned, either because of the promised Grace, or the character of their wrong-doing, or some other reasonable cause.

That is, that they are to defend the faith and the Church that they have in such a way offended, doing this for a period decided by you and acting either themselves or via others who are more suitable over the seas [*in the Holy Land*] or this side of them [*here*], against Saracens, or heretics and their supporters, or people who are otherwise rebellious against the faith and the Church.

Further, in detestation of their former error, they are to wear on their upper clothing two yellow-coloured crosses, two and a half palms in length and two in width, and having in themselves [*the dimensions of the fabric*] the width of three fingers, one in front on the chest, the other behind between the shoulders. The clothes on which they wear the crosses: these clothes are not themselves to be yellow-coloured – meaning the upper clothing – and they are not to wear other clothing on top, whether inside or outside their houses.

And if they were vested or condemned heretics, they should wear a third cross of the appropriate size and the same colour on their hat or veil.

And if by chance they had perjured or encouraged others to perjure, they should have a second horizontal arm, of a palm's width or thereabouts, on the upper part of the two crosses that they have to wear (on the chest and between the shoulders).

Those obliged to travel overseas are to wear these crosses until they have arrived. And they are not obliged to wear them thereafter until they enter a ship on a shore overseas to return, and then they are to resume the crosses and wear them forever thereafter, at the coast, at sea and when on islands.

They are to be present at Mass and vespers and the sermon on Sundays and feast days, if these take place in the town where they are. And similarly on other days they are either to hear masses or at least come to church before lunch to pray – unless they have a genuine impediment.

And at Mass on every Sunday and feast day, between the <readings of> the Epistle and the Gospel, they are to present themselves to the priest who is celebrating, in public and in the presence of the people, having taken off their upper clothing and veil or hat (unless they have to wear crosses on their veil or hat) and carrying rods in their hands. And there, after discipline has been given to them, the priest is to explain that they are doing this penance because of the guilt of heretical disgrace.

They are also to follow the processions that take place in towns where they are at any time, in this way. That is, after taking off their upper clothing and baring their heads of veil or hat (unless they wear crosses on these), they should be between clergy and people, and from the beginning holding up long rods, high in their right hands. And at the last station they are to present themselves to the person in charge of the procession, for him to explain to the people that they are doing this sort of penance because of the things that they committed in the crime of heretical wickedness.

27. Similarly, you are to impose on the guilty people who have been mentioned pilgrimages, and pecuniary penalties and penances, on behalf of the constructing of prisons and the provision of necessary expenses for poor people who are to be imprisoned, and to the persons who are necessary for the business of inquisition. And <you are to order> them not to carry out usuries, and to make restitution of usuries already received.

28. And they are not to hold *baillages* or administrative offices, nor are they to be in the counsels or households of powerful men. Nor are they to exercise the job of either a doctor or a notary. Nor are they to have access to other public offices, or legal proceedings. Nor are they to wear orphreys, or similar ornaments, or yellow headbands, or silk, or belts studded with gold or silver, or grooved or painted shoes. And where this seems to be expedient, they are to be thrown out of the town in which they had been living, to stay for a while in a certain other town or province.

29. We have brought together these discretionary penances not for you to impose all of them and equally on everyone. Rather, you are to dispense them carefully and with foresight, according to the discretion granted you by the Lord <pope>, and after thinking about what is useful in the business, the quality of the persons, the amount of the guilty acts and other circumstances: so that, by punishing or indulging, the way of life of the guilty may be corrected, or at least that one can make clear *who walks in darkness*, who *in light*, who is truly penitent, who fictitiously converted.

You are to impose these sorts of penances publicly, except in a case where the sin was secret, which was not revealed or expected to be revealed by someone else. After the clergy and people have been called together, you are to make them confess their guilty acts publicly, and to abjure and swear, as was described in relation to those who are to be reconciled.

Each of them is to mandate the drawing up of public instruments drawn from these things, containing the guilty acts of these same people, their abjurations, promises and penances. And your testimonial letters, containing these same things, are to be given to each of them.

The power is always reserved to you, to be able on a reasonable ground to add to the penances that have been imposed, or take away from them, or even to commute them. And we advise you who are going to employ this power, to do this as often as seems to you expedient for the salvation of souls or for the advantage of the business.

Those upon whom pilgrimages were imposed: they are bound to show the said testimonial letters on every pilgrimage to the person in charge of the church they are visiting, and to bring back to you his letters about the carrying out of that pilgrimage. Those in fact who have travelled overseas: as soon as they can, when they have arrived overseas, they are to present themselves with your letters to the venerable fathers or patriarchs of Jerusalem or Acre or to some bishop or someone acting in their place, and, when they return from the pilgrimage that has been praiseworthily carried out there, they are to bring back to you letters from whichever overseas bishop.

30. You are not to allow any of the aforesaid guilty people to enter any religious order, to avoid the simplicity of religion [= *monasticism*] being corrupted by such people, unless there are open signs of conversion and you know that scandal and danger are absent. If however this has happened, you are to revoke it.

31. You are to have the statutes and laws published on these things by the Apostolic See and its legates and princes observed to the hilt, so that with the Lord's help heresy may be better and more quickly extirpated and the faith implanted in this country.

Further, you are to make everyone, both males and females, abjure all heresy – males from the fourteenth and females from the twelfth year and above – and to swear to observe and defend the Catholic faith and to persecute heretics, as is stated above more fully and comprehensively on these things in the oath that those who are to be reconciled have to take: the names of each one of these having been written down both in the acts of inquisition and also in their own parishes.

And those who are present within the designated time and do not take the oath – and those who are absent and do not take it within fifteen days after their return – are to be regarded as suspect of heresy. You are to bring about this universal abjuration as soon as possible, either through yourselves or through your notaries or scribes, or through other ecclesiastical men to whom you have decided to entrust this.

32. This being added in the oath taken by counts, barons, rulers and consuls and the *baillis* of cities and other places: that when asked they will help the Church against heretics and their accomplices, faithfully and effectively according to their office and power, and that they will devote themselves in good faith and using all their strength to the extermination from the lands subject to their jurisdiction of all those designated by the Church as heretics.

33. Those who lapse after this sort of abjuration and those who do not observe and carry out the penances imposed upon them are to be punished with the due penalty for the relapsed.

34. Further, in every single parish, both in cities and outside, one priest or two or three laymen of good reputation – or more if needs be – are

to be bound by an oath (to be removed or altered as seems right to you) that they will look for heretics – diligently, faithfully and frequently – in towns and outside, hunting through people's houses, underground rooms, huts and little enclosed places and other hiding-places: all of which you are to have blocked up or destroyed.

You are to entrust the supervision of the carrying-out of the penances, that have been imposed on individuals in the parishes, to the aforesaid sworn priest and laymen. Thus these men – having in front of them the penances of individual parishioners and keeping careful watch on their carrying-out – may denounce to you without delay those who hold their penances in contempt, if there are any such, for you then to proceed against them as against the relapsed, as has just been said.

35. Further, you are to have those houses destroyed in which heretics are or were found, alive or dead, vested or condemned, with the knowledge and consent of the lords of these houses, where these lords are of lawful age, and you are to have the goods of all those living there at the time confiscated: unless they can manifestly prove their innocence and just ignorance. Similarly you are to have confiscated the goods of both heretics and believers whom you have condemned, either as heretics or to prison. And you are to have marks paid, to those capturing heretics, by those who will be bound to pay according to the statutes.

36. You are to have observed to the full whatever you know to be just and bound by law: about negligent or suspect *baillis* and other culpable people not being placed in administrative or public offices or in the counsels or households of powerful men; and about people not possessing theological books (laymen not having them in Latin and neither laymen nor clergy having them in the vernacular), and about the penalties against the aforesaid people; and also <about acting> against priests who are negligent around these matters to which they are bound by office or commission, and about confession of sins and communion three times a year, and also hearing masses and sermons in their entirety on Sundays and feast days, and about all the other things that pertain to the extirpation of heresy and the implantation of faith; and particularly about the offspring of heretics, of *receivers* and of defenders, up to the second generation, not being admitted to any ecclesiastical benefice or office.

37. Among other things which are part of your laborious and very broad office, you are to take the utmost efforts in applying yourself to the observation of the order of the law, except insofar as this business

is privileged and insofar as we have declared above and counsel. And you are to have written down all the things that you do, that is to say summonses, graces or indulgences, interrogations, confessions, depositions, abjurations and guaranteeing, sentences and penances and all the other things that occur: written down in such a way in the acts of inquisition, either by public hand [*notary*] or two suitable men on oath, as we said earlier, in the appropriate order and with the detailing of places, times and persons. For if a dispute on something arises about your process, through these <written acts> the truth can be declared.

Given at Béziers, 19 April 1246

38. FORMULAE FROM A LATER INQUISITOR'S HANDBOOK

As noted in the introduction to Part VII, the commonest 'how to do it' books used by inquisitors were not systematic treatises, but manuscripts containing an anthology of useful texts. These included formulae for procedure, in particular for sentencing. It is the latter which we translate here, from one particular handbook compilation. The compilers also copied out sentences that had actually been delivered, sometimes removing names or other details, to be used as models by other inquisitors. The formulae were adaptable to both Waldensians and Cathars. Although the Waldensians were far less numerous than the Cathars, the eight examples given below show a preference for models relating to them, something we have also seen in the Avignon consultation and the Council of Tarragona (Docs 33–4), on the definition of a believer.[71]

The contents of this particular anthology are described in A. Dondaine, 'Le manuel de l'inquisiteur', pp. 140–54, who dates it to 1265. We have translated the texts from *Quellen zur Geschichte der Waldenser*, ed. A. Patschovsky and K.-V. Selge, Texte zur Kirchen- und Theologiegeschichte 18 (Gütersloh, 1973), pp. 55–69.

(1) Penance on a person who confessed of their own accord

To the reverend father and lord in Christ and by the Grace of God Bishop of Nîmes, Brother William of Valence and Pons Garin of the Order of Preachers,[72] constituted by the Apostolic See inquisitors against heretical wickedness, reverence and greeting.

You will have got to know that your parishioner, B. Sayssa, came to us and humbly and devoutly confessed how he had been guilty for a good forty years in the matter of the Waldensian heretics, visiting them and handing over to them money and other things. Whence we, wishing to deal with him mercifully – partly because he came neither called nor cited, but rather of his own free will, partly because he acknowledged his crime humbly, and thenceforth, after the said time, neither saw nor visited the Waldensians and has not as far as this is concerned relapsed

71 See L. J. Sackville, 'The inquisitor's manual at work', *Viator* 44 (2013), 201–16.

72 These inquisitors were active together in the diocese of Narbonne in 1237. There is some information on both in Douais, *Documents*, I, 138–43.

on any point, and partly because the Church did not at that time pursue them so publicly – we, I say, are remitting him to you, as someone absolved according to the form of the Church. And we have enjoined on him on this count a salutary penance: namely that within the year he should visit the Church of St-Mary at Le Puy, and that in consultation with you he should expend as much for the benefit of good poor men as he believes, according to his conscience, that he handed over to the Waldensian heretics.

(2) Penance of perpetual imprisonment to be imposed on those who were perfected <heretics>

Whereas you, John of Burgundy, who were a perfected Waldensian heretic [perfectus … Valdensis hereticus] for thirty years and more, believing in their errors, and conducted yourself as a Waldensian heretic in the presence of the friends and familiars of the Waldensians, now, with the eyes of your mind opened and after abjuring the deadly stain of Waldensianism and all heresy, by whatever name it is called, wish to convert and to return to the unity of the sacrosanct Roman Church, since you have obtained the benefit of absolution according to the form of the Church through us, brothers William of Valence and Pons Garin, of the Order of the Preachers, constituted by the Apostolic See inquisitors against heretical wickedness – we, I say, the aforesaid inquisitors, supported by the authority of the high pontiff, enjoin on you the salutary penance of perpetual prison. Adding, nevertheless, that if – let us hope it does not happen! – it should come about that you relapse, preaching or teaching the errors of those Waldensians, or in any other way, or if you should break prison or in any other way flee, going off without the permission either of us or of someone acting in our stead, we would then relinquish you – as a perjured heretic and one who has falsely converted – to the secular court, binding with the chain of excommunication each and every person who lent help, counsel or support to your liberation. Adding moreover that whoever knowingly received, protected or hid you, or knowingly showed aid, counsel or favour to you in any way after you had been liberated in this way – lest they should be seen to derive advantage from their wickedness – would be subject to the aforesaid excommunication, as receivers, defenders and protectors of Waldensian heretics. Done, etc.[73]

73 Place and date omitted by the person copying this into the inquisitors' anthology.

(3) On houses to be demolished

In the name of Our Lord Jesus Christ.

Whereas in this year Raymunda of Les Balines and Alazais Calosa, Waldensian heretics [female], were found this year in the house of Bernard Olivar of Durban, and he fled a first and a second time, and was twice cited by us and, as a man aware that this would be bad for him, was unwilling to appear, we denounce him; and with the authority which we discharge we command the said house to be utterly demolished, never in the future to be rebuilt, and, in accord with Apostolic statute, there should be there forever a receptacle of filth, where there was once a den of heretics. We bind with the sentence of excommunication, however, anyone who rebuilds the said house or lends counsel, help or support to its rebuilding. Done, etc.

(4) On those who are to be imprisoned

In the name of Our Lord Jesus Christ. On such and such a year and day.

Whereas I, N., Inquisitor of heretical wickedness, have found through the inquisition which I am making about heretics and also about those defamed of heresy, that:

you, A., so and so, were a believer and [female] friend and often, on many occasions in the past, knowingly a [female] receiver of the Waldensian heretics; and moreover that many heretics have been found recently, in your presence, hiding in a very suspect place in your house with books and sandals and various items of equipment. However, although you were frequently required by me to tell every bit of the truth about the aforesaid things, on oath and according to the form of the court, you impudently held in contempt the religious tie of the oath, and with effrontery you totally denied everything. At last, however, following wiser counsel, when you saw that I was preparing to proceed against you as against a heretic and as far as I could according to law, you admitted your guilt and the aforesaid perjuries, and, abjuring again all heresy and especially that of the Waldensians, in which you had been found guilty, and swearing to tell the whole truth without any fiction both about yourself and others, living and dead, you acknowledged you were a heretic.

And you conceded and exposed yourself to be punished by the due punishment of the secular court if henceforth you should be caught in any lie in your confessions. Nevertheless, however, you can be convicted once again of perjury and manifest lies in the confession you made afterwards in court in front of me; item, since you asserted there [*in court*] that you have knowingly and on many occasions received many Waldensian heretics, eaten with them, received the Peace from Waldensian women, and have also eaten the bread blessed by these Waldensians on the day of the Lord's supper and in your house, and have heard and in part believed their pestiferous teachings, in particular against the <taking of an> oath, <killing in> justice, purgatory, and offerings for the dead; you also say that you believed, from eight years ago and thenceforth, that the Waldensians were good men and friends of God and in a state of salvation and that they taught this salvation to others who wished to learn from them, and for this reason you used to receive them, because you used to believe these were good men, although you heard that the Church persecuted them and drove them out as heretics, and that the secular court was burning them if they would not convert;

– although, I say, you have been like this, and have been discovered to be like this, however, because you have returned to your heart and want to return to ecclesiastical unity with a pure heart and a faith that is not pretended, as you say, abjuring all heresy and promising and swearing that you will observe all the things just as they are contained more fully in the form of the oath; and have bound yourself by your own free will to the penalty that is for heretics should you do something contrary to or hold in contempt the penance which has been enjoined on you; recognising that you have been absolved, from the excommunication by which you were bound because of the aforesaid things, on this condition and with this reservation, that if you are found knowingly to have suppressed the truth about yourself or about another or if you do not humbly and observantly follow the penance and commands which have been imposed on you, from that point onwards the aforesaid absolution will be of no profit to you, but will be completely regarded as something that has not been done;

I, the aforesaid inquisitor [*we omit the final section containing the sentence to perpetual imprisonment*].

Done, etc.

(5) On crosses that are to be imposed

To all of Christ's faithful who will see the present letters, Brother Ferrier and Peter Durand, constituted by apostolic authority inquisitors of heretical wickedness in the province of Narbonne and in the dioceses of Albi, Rodez, Mende and Le Puy, send eternal greetings in the Lord.

Whereas such and such a woman, the bearer of these letters, as we have found from her own confession, which was made in court in front of us:

on many occasions gave and sent to the Waldensians bread, wine, fruit, coins and other things; frequently heard the words and dogmas of the Waldensians, who were preaching and saying that simply to take an oath and to kill anyone in justice is a sin; received Waldensians in her house for a long time; gave her dead daughter's shirt to a Waldensian woman; ate and drank (together with the Waldensians at the same table and familiarly) some of the things which they had blessed in their manner; when she was ill, allowed the Gospel of John and the 'Whosoever wishes' [= *Athanasian creed*] to be read over her head by Waldensian women; further, for many years believed the Waldensians and their errors, firmly hoping she would be saved through them;

– we, following in the footsteps of Him who wishes no-one to perish, have imposed on this woman – reverting of her own accord to the bosom of holy mother Church, utterly abjuring heretical disgrace and at last attaining the benefit of absolution according to the form of the Church – that in detestation of the old error she should forever wear on her outer clothes two crosses, yellow in colour, two and a half palms in height and two in width, <the arms of the cross> three fingers in size, one in front on her chest, the other behind between the shoulder-blades – never using clothing, on which she wears the crosses, that is yellow in colour. While she lives she is to attend Mass and vespers and the general sermon,[74] if one takes place in the town where she is, unless there is a genuine obstacle. For seven years she shall follow general processions, between clergy and people, holding high in her hand long rods, and presenting herself in some position in relation to the person leading the procession, to display to the people that she is carrying out this penance on account of those things that she committed against the faith. In this current year she is to visit the shrine of Blessed Mary of

74 General sermon to gathered clergy and people at the beginning of an inquisition, also for the declaration of sentences.

Le Puy, and the following year the shrine of St-Gilles, and the third year the shrine of Blessed Mary of Montpellier, and in the fourth and fifth years the shrine of Blessed Mary of Sérignan. And on each of the aforesaid pilgrimages she is obliged to show our present letters, which we wish her to have and to carry, to the person in charge of the church she is visiting, and she is to bring back to us testimonial letters from the same prelate, about her pilgrimage there duly completed.

Wherefore, dearly beloved, if you come upon the aforesaid such and such a woman, having our letters and wearing the crosses and observing those things we have imposed upon her and behaving in all things as a Catholic, you are in no way to molest her or permit her to be molested on account of those things which, as we recorded above, she committed against the faith. If however you see her doing or trying to do the opposite, you are to regard her as a perjured excommunicate and bound by her earlier guilty acts. We decree that the reconciliation and mercy accorded to her cannot from that point on benefit her, and, by the authority with which we carry out our office, we bind with the chain of excommunication her, as a heretic, and all those who knowingly either receive or defend or otherwise provide her with counsel, aid or support, as supporters, receivers or defenders of heretics.

Given at Narbonne, ides of May [8 May], the 1244th year

(6) On heretics judged and relinquished to the secular arm

Let it be known to all that when such men of Carpentras as Pons Lombard, John of Marseilles and Guiraud of Cahors were presented to us, William, by the mercy of God Bishop of Carpentras,[75] by such and such a noble man, as men who were publicly professing the Waldensian error, so it was said, we, following in the steps of the man who convicted the wicked servant from his own mouth [Matthew 18. 23–34], questioned them individually, asking if they wanted to hold to the way of those who are called 'Waldensians' or 'the Poor of Lyon'. Although they confessed in the presence of many, we, nevertheless, who are not ignorant of their tricks, descended to particulars and extorted from them among other things the confessions which are written below, completely different from the faith and averse to Catholic truth. Two of them, that is to say, John and Guiraud, publicly confessed that those

75 William Beroardi, bishop 1231–63.

who are called the 'sandalled' among them can, where necessity impels, consecrate the body of Christ, even if they have not obtained the sacerdotal order through the rite of the Church. The third, however, Pons Lombard by name, wished neither to assert nor deny this. The three were unanimous and in agreement in confessing that they firmly believed and held that no-one ought to confirm the truth with an oath, even in order to save his neighbour, and they asserted that taking a legal oath was forbidden in every case. Further, they also added that it was not licit for any power or judge to hand over to death people found guilty of whatever crime; if he did this, then for this alone, they assert, he will merit the punishment of hell. The purgatorial fire – in which the sincerity of our faith holds and preaches that souls which, although they died in charity, remained however debtors for something, are purged by divine justice – they denied it was anything or in any place, confessing by the same error that the offerings of the living were of no profit to the dead, unless these offerings had been imposed on the survivors, by name, by them while they were alive.

Since in fact these things have been openly maintained by them, for the sake of salvation and piously we advised them to profess and believe in these and other matters only what the Roman Church teaches about them, explaining to them the purity of Christian faith. And although we believed on the basis of very probable signs that they were rather stiff-necked, having compassion for them, with fatherly feeling and with all our innermost parts desiring their salvation, we gave them a day of deliberation, and space for just repentance from last Saturday until today.

Since therefore the aforesaid children of darkness are in fact rebels against the light, and cannot be won over by coaxing or broken by lawful terrors,[76] and are obdurate in their errors and will believe neither in accord with the counsels of the learned nor the testimonies of scripture, we, who are bound by the office rightfully entrusted to us to use all our strength in purging the diocese of heretical wickedness, after consultation with religious and other prudent men, adjudge the same Pons, John and Guiraud to be heretics and – with justice intervening – alien from the Catholic faith.

76 One of the very rare references – in this period – to torture. See also Doc. 48, fol. 134r.

(7) Penance of imprisonment to be imposed on a believer

Whereas it appears by the confession of the woman that she saw and knew Waldensians of both sexes from her 16th to her 18th year, and heard them and their benefactors excommunicated in church, and nevertheless afterwards they were received in her house, and on many occasions she heard their preachings from the Gospels and the Epistles, and that it was a mortal sin to take an oath; and ate with them very many times, and ministered to them, and went from house to house of the Waldensians' friends begging for bread and wine and pennies to help support the Waldensians; and believed they were good men, and that people could be saved in their belief and sect and way of life; and received the Peace from them on many occasions; and ate the bread and fish blessed by the Waldensians on the day of the supper [*Easter Thursday*]; and finally was cited and appeared: we pronounce that she should be handed over to perpetual prison.

(8) On a believer who is to be exhumed

Because it is clear through witnesses that such and such a woman, during the illness from which she died, bequeathed her cloak to the Waldensian Anagelina and 20 shillings to the society of the Poor of Lyon, we pronounce her to have been a believer of the Waldensian heretics, and that therefore she should be disinterred and cast out of the cemetery of the faithful.

39. AN INQUISITORIAL MANUAL: *INSTRUCTION ABOUT THE WAY IN WHICH ONE SHOULD PROCEED AGAINST HERETICS*

The earliest inquisitors' manual from southern France, the little compilation known as the *Narbonne Order of Procedure* (*Ordo Processus Narbonnensis*), was drawn up in 1248 or 1249.[77] The longer manual translated here (the *Doctrina de Modo Procedendi contra Hereticos*) draws upon it and other, earlier texts.[78] It begins with a description of procedure in the southern provinces, and then includes the entire text of the directives of the Council of Tarragona of 1242 (Doc. 34 above) and the list of questions to put to a heretic or Waldensian from the *Narbonne Order of Procedure*, making a few small additions at the beginning and end. The manual concludes with formulae used by inquisitors, which fall into two groups that are distinct in origin and date. The first group (nos. 1–12) draws upon inquisition in Languedoc, including place-names, inquisitors and one prominent heretic (Raymond of Mas-Saintes-Puelles, active in the 1240s and 1250s) from that region; the last dated form comes from April 1271. The second group (nos. 13–18c) draws upon inquisition in northern France, with place-names from northern France and Belgium, and dealings not only with heretics but also Jewish converts and a famous philosopher from the arts faculty in Paris. Where they are dated, the forms in this second group are later, coming from 1277 and 1278.

It appears, therefore, that there were two editions of this manual, the first from southern France, compiled after April 1271.[79] There was then a cardinal's request (19 May 1273) to southern inquisitors to send documentation to their northern French colleagues to help them in the job, which may have sent the manual north. There in northern France a second edition was produced which incorporated the northern inquisition forms (nos. 13–18c). The revision left another mark on the southern text, specifying that sentences be read *in gallico*, 'in northern French'. It is only this second edition that survives.

What of the first edition? The work carried out vigorously in Toulouse by the two inquisitors Pons of Parnac and Renous of Plassac, beginning in 1273, has the air of a re-launch of inquisition. The compilation of the first, southern edition of this procedural manual could have been one of the initiatives associated with this and with Pons of Parnac, a trained lawyer; on him, see Doc. 9 §20. On

77 Translated by Wakefield, *Heresy*, pp. 250–8.

78 Dossat, *Crises*, pp. 203–4; Dondaine, 'Manuel de l'inquisiteur', 108–11.

79 Dossat's suggestion, *Crises*, pp. 203–4.

the re-launch and this suggestion about the manual, see *Inquisitors and Heretics*, pp. 41–8, 49, 60–2.

We translate the edition found in *Thesaurus Novus Anecdotorum*, ed. E. Martène and U. Durand, 5 vols (Paris, 1717), V, cols 1795–1814; for the question-list, however, we use the edition in *Inquisitors and Heretics*, pp. 67–70, and for form 16 we follow the emendations suggested in its re-edition by P. Fredericq, *Corpus Documentorum Inquisitionis Haereticae Pravitatis Neerlandicae*, 5 vols (Ghent, 1889), I, pp. 140–1.

This is the way inquisitors in the regions of Carcassonne and Toulouse proceed. First the person accused or suspected of heresy is summoned. When he comes, he takes an oath on the holy gospels to tell the whole truth that he knows about the crime of heresy or Waldensianism, both about himself and also about others, living and dead. And if he conceals or denies, he is placed and detained in prison until he confesses. However, if he tells the truth, his confession is carefully written down by a public notary. And if the person who is confessing errs when talking, he can alter himself [*i.e. what he says*], and his confession is corrected. After his confession, two religious persons[80] are called, and in their presence his confession is repeated to him. Once he has acknowledged this and the deposition has been done,[81] he abjures heresy.

He is to swear that he will observe the faith of the Roman Church and abide by the mandates of the Church and of the inquisitors and carry out the penance imposed on him by the inquisitors. After this has been done he is absolved and reconciled.

And at the end of his deposition it is written thus: 'These things he attested in such and such a place, in the presence of N. and N. inquisitors, in the presence and testimony of N. and N. and of me, notary N., who have written this'.

The relapsed, however, who are to be relinquished <to the secular arm> are not reconciled, even if they seek this, nor the perfected heretics, for they neither seek nor want this.

And when many have confessed, whose numbers suffice for the making of a <general> sermon, the inquisitors are then to summon to a place determined by them lawyers, brothers Minor and brothers Preacher, and ordinaries [*bishops*], without whose counsel (or that of their

80 Members of religious orders.

81 That is, once his confession has been turned into a formally attested deposition.

delegates) they never condemn anyone. When the council has gathered, the inquisitors put forward in the council a brief abstract containing the substance of a confession, without stating the name of the person confessing, speaking thus: 'A certain person of diocese N. did such and such'. Then the advisers reply, 'Penance is to be imposed on him at the discretion of the inquisitors', or 'This person is to be imprisoned', or '<This person> is to be relinquished <to the secular arm>'.

After this has been done, all are to be summoned: that they are to appear on such and such a day in the presence of the inquisitors, to acknowledge their guilty acts, and on the following Sunday to receive penances for their guilty acts. Then the inquisitors are to call prelates, abbots, priors, guardians [*heads of convents of Franciscans*] <and> *baillis.* And in their presence and that of all the people, summoned and gathered there for this, all of those who had confessed and who abide by their confessions are called first – otherwise, if they deny <their confessions>, they are put back into prison.

The records of their guilty acts[82] are recited to them, firstly of those who ought to have discretionary penances. And crosses are to be given to them, and major or minor pilgrimages, as their guilty acts require. And double crosses are to be given to perjurers, simple crosses to others.

Afterwards, when those with crosses depart, the records of the guilty acts of those who are to be imprisoned are recited. One person gets up after another, and stands until his confession has been read out and recited. When they have been recited the inquisitor sits down and while he is seated he gives the sentence, first in Latin and immediately after it is recited in <northern> French. Afterwards the records of the guilty acts of the relapsed are recited, and after a sentence has been given the person is relinquished[83] in a similar way.

And at the end of the sentences it is written and pronounced thus: 'This sentence was delivered in such and such a year on such and such a day, in such and such a place, and in the presence and witness of N., N.'

Those however who are relinquished, because of their relapsing, ought not to be burnt on the day when they are judged: but they are to be

82 We have been translating *culpa* (guilt) as 'guilty act'. The word came to mean also a document – the *culpa* – containing extracts from a deposition of the principal guilty acts of a person, as in Doc. 42. Where it has this meaning we translate it as 'record of guilty acts'.

83 The legal act of relinquishing: not yet its consequence.

encouraged to confess. And the eucharist ought to be given to them, if they ask for it and if signs of repentance appear. Thus the lord pope wills and counsels.

[*The* Instruction *now contains the entire text of the Council of Tarragona of 1242 – translated above as Doc. 36 – minus the preamble, and then continues thus:*]

Some agreements between inquisitors

There are two things upon which brother inquisitors come together, for the sake of proceeding uniformly. These are that – in the case of localities that are very suspect and of bad reputation – there should be a universal inquisition and summons to abjure heresy and tell the truth, with the giving of a Time of Grace – where otherwise this is not given. In the case of places not <very> suspect, all should be summoned who know that they and others have fallen into the crime of heretical disgrace, and this should be done generally, with the said limitation [*i.e. without a Time of Grace*] and without mentioning names.

Form of taking the oath and questioning

Those who have been found by inquisition to be suspect of the matter or guilty, as it seems to the inquisitors, are summoned individually by name or generally <to appear> and tell the truth and abjure heresy. At the beginning they are to swear to tell the whole and absolute[84] truth about themselves and others, both living and dead, on the crime of heresy and Waldensianism, putting aside the entreaties <of others>, monetary gain, fear, hatred and love, and notwithstanding sworn pacts or oath.[85]

Then[86] they should be questioned individually about all of these and about more if it seems expedient. To be specific, he <should be questioned> carefully if he had seen a heretic or Waldensian, and

84 The edn has *veram* (true), a mistake for *meram* (absolute).

85 That is, sworn agreements with others to say nothing; see Doc. 48 for some examples.

86 Here our translation switches to the text edited in *Inquisitors and Heretics*, pp. 67–70.

where, and when, and how often, and with whom, and about other circumstances.[87] And repeat these for each of the <other> questions.

If he heard their preachings or admonitions.

If he gave them lodging.

If he escorted them from place to place, or otherwise kept them company or arranged for them to be taken or accompanied.

If he ate or drank with them, or received from them some of their blessed bread.

If he gave or sent them anything.

If he was their money agent, or messenger, or assistant.

If he had their deposit or anything else of theirs.

If he adored a heretic or bowed his head, or genuflected or said, 'Bless us' in front of them.

If he was present at their *consolamenta* or *apparellamenta.*

If he was present at the Waldensian supper.

If he confessed his sins to them, or received penance or learnt anything from them.

If he had familiarity or participation with a heretic or with a Waldensian otherwise, in whatever way.

If he took upon himself or made a pact or entreaties or threats about not saying the truth about himself or about others.

If he advised or encouraged anyone to do any of these things.

If he believed in a heretic or a Waldensian, or in their errors.

And note that in each case there should be inquiry about the person in question, and about their circumstances, that is to say, about their name, country, parent, age, physical disposition and similar things.[88]

Item, <there should be questioning> about the action that is at issue, and its circumstances.

Item, about its place.

Item, about the date.

87 What follows are the questions of the *Narbonne Order of Procedure,* translated by Wakefield, *Heresy,* pp. 252–3.

88 This sentence and the next four items are additions to the question-list in the *Narbonne Order of Procedure.*

Item, about those people who were present and the circumstances, or about other matters that relate to these five things – in fact, about all these things, and sometimes about more.

Finally, after the faithful writing down of what he has been questioned about with regard to all these things – and sometimes (not without reasonable cause) with regard to other things – you should confirm all that he has confessed or attested in the presence of two of us, or at least one.

1. Form for receiving heretics and their believers who are returning <to the faith>[89]

In the name of Our Lord Jesus Christ. Amen. In such and such a year and day, we, N. and N. of the Order of Brothers Preacher, inquisitors, etc.

Because it is established in law and clear to us that N. from such and such a place saw and adored a heretic, etc.

Item, because N. from such and such a place saw and adored a heretic, and did these things and those from such and such and date, and later.

Now following saner counsel they wish to return to the unity of the Church, as they assert. After they have, first of all, abjured all heretical wickedness, following the form laid down by the Church, we absolve them from the chain of excommunication – by which they had been bound and tied, by reason of the aforesaid crime – if they have returned in good heart to the unity of the Church and have carried out the mandates imposed upon them.

And a day was assigned for them to appear before us to receive penance for the crime of heresy, because they shamefully wronged God and holy mother Church in the aforesaid ways. After taking the counsel of good men, we condemn them to carry out the suitable penance for those convicted of such a crime – to the prison of the Wall[90] for ever – reserving to ourselves the power <to mitigate the sentence> etc.

89 We have inserted the numbers of the following forms.

90 The prison (*carcer*) was called the Wall (*murus*). Usually *carcer* and *murus* are simply alternative ways of saying prison, but here both words are used.

2. Form of sentence against heretics' believers who are unwilling to appear

On the aforesaid year and day, we the aforesaid inquisitors:

Because it is established in law and clear to us that William Peter from such and such a place saw and adored a heretic, and he committed this from the eighth year.

Item, because Arnold Rigaud of St-Nauphary[91] often saw a heretic, led him and kept him company etc.

After they had been legally summoned on account of this, to receive penance for these things, a day was assigned to them, but they did not appear.

After they had been peremptorily summoned to appear before us and receive definitive sentence, they were contumaciously absent. After receiving the counsel of good men we condemn them with a definitive sentence, excommunicating them and all who henceforth will have knowingly given them counsel and help, or support.

Done, etc.

3. Form of sentence against a suspect of heresy who, when summoned, is unwilling to defend or purge himself

On the aforesaid year and day, we the aforesaid inquisitors:

Helena, the wife of N. from such and such a place, was defamed of heresy and to the highest degree suspect, saw and adored a heretic etc., as is established in law and clear to us through witnesses, and when she was offered the opportunity of defence she was unwilling to defend herself. After careful examination of the witnesses and publication of the facts of the evidence and doing other things according to form, we peremptorily assigned to her a day to hear definitive sentence on the crime of heresy. After receiving counsel from men of good understanding, we condemn this same Helena, with a definitive sentence, as – according to what we have heard of her – a heretic, excommunicating her and everyone, etc.

91 Tarn-et-Garonne dpt.

4. Form of sentence against a dead believer in heretics, who was unwilling to acknowledge the truth when called before the inquisitors

On the aforesaid year and day, we the aforesaid inquisitors:

It is established in law and clear to us that N., from such and such a place, saw and adored heretics, led them and received them in his house, the truth of all of which things he hid when in front of inquisitors N. and N., etc.

All who ought to have been called for his defence were called, law and due order in other things were observed, the aforesaid day was peremptorily assigned for <the hearing of> definitive sentence, etc.

Since not a whit of confession or penance is established or clear to us, we regard him as a believer in heretics and therefore, although he is dead, we condemn him for heresy, in addition ordering his bones to be exhumed and totally cast out of the church and cemetery.

If there are any objectors, etc.

5. Form of sentence against someone who fell back into the heresy he had abjured

On the aforesaid year and day.

After James of Odars[92] abjured all heresy in front of inquisitors and received penance from them for those things he had committed in the crime of heretical wickedness, he saw and adored a heretic, etc.

Since therefore the aforesaid James, 'as a dog that returneth to his vomit' [Proverbs, 26.11], fell back into that heresy which he had abjured, not observing the promise he had made nor also the oath, often forgetting and ungrateful for the grace afforded him by the Church, we brothers N. and N., inquisitors of heretical wickedness, with definitive sentence pronounce you James to be relapsed – as we have said above – and we hold you as no longer belonging to the court or jurisdiction of the Church.

Done, etc.

92 Haute-Garonne dpt.

6. Form of sentence against dead heretics whom – after a lawful sentence – no-one defends

On the aforesaid year and day, we the aforesaid inquisitors:

Because it is established in law and clear to us that Galhard and his brother Vernier of Séguenville[93] were hereticated during the illnesses from which they died and they died as heretics, and those who should have been called for their defence were called and the order of law in other things was observed: after these things a day was peremptorily appointed for the hearing of the definitive sentence, <and> having received the counsel of good men, we pronounce that they were heretics at death and died as heretics, and with a definitive sentence we condemn them as heretics.

Furthermore, we order their bones to be exhumed and totally thrown out of the church and cemetery, subjecting objectors or rebels – if there are any – to the sentence of excommunication.

Done, etc.

7. Form of sentence of excommunication against someone who is presumed to have relapsed and when summoned did not come

On the aforesaid year and day, we the aforesaid inquisitors:

Because on the basis of those things we have found in inquisition against Raymond of Mas-Saintes-Puelles[94] we hold him to be vehemently suspect (that after his confession of heresy which he made about heresy, he committed <things> against the faith), and because when he was summoned lawfully and peremptorily on account of this to reply about the faith in front of us, he did not bother to reply, though for a long time he was awaited: we bind him with the chain of excommunication as a suspect of heresy and contumacious, under pain of excommunication ordering that no-one henceforth should dare to receive him and give him counsel, help and support.

93 Haute-Garonne dpt.

94 Aude dpt. On this prominent heretic, deacon of the heretics of Vielmur in 1250, see his index entry in *Inquisitors and Heretics*, p. 1047.

8. Form of sentence against converted heretics who accepted usuries after their oath <of abjuration>

On the aforesaid year and day, we the aforesaid inquisitors:

Because Isarn of Fontenilles[95] and Pons Ranga of the diocese of Toulouse, when they were judicially arraigned, swore in the presence of the then inquisitors of heretical wickedness that they would do every penance which the same inquisitors or whoever was acting temporarily for them decided to impose, and that they would obey the mandates of the inquisitors and the Church, and among other things this was imposed upon them by the inquisitors, that they should not engage in usuries, either in person or through others, and should make restitution if they have extorted <money in this way>: and because, after a while, as though heedless of their own salvation and in contempt of their own oaths, they lent their cash in person or through others for the sake of usuries, and extorted a lot from many people: after receiving the counsel of good men, we wish them to be put into the perpetual prison of the Wall, and we order them to remain there in perpetuity, to carry out their penance; reserving the power.[96]

9. Penance of heretics when one believes[97]

To all the faithful in Christ who will see the present letters, brothers William Bernard and John of St-Benoît[98] of the Order of Preachers, inquisitors of heretical wickedness in the communities and lands of the noble man, the Count of Toulouse, greetings.

Because N. from such and such a place in the diocese of Toulouse saw and adored a heretic, heard their admonitions, <and> believed that the heretics were good men and had a good faith, and committed this from such and such a time and thereafter, as he acknowledged on oath in front of us in court, we impose upon him as penance for the aforesaid things that he shall forever wear on the front and back of all his clothes, apart from his shirt, two yellow-coloured felt crosses, and that he will

95 Haute-Garonne dpt.

96 Of altering the sentence.

97 Text corrupt at this point.

98 William Bernard of Dax, active as inquisitor 1258, 1263 and 1267; cf. *Inquisitors and Heretics*, p. 415 n.38; Doauis, *Documents*, I, pp. 166–7. John of St-Benoît, active as inquisitor in 1256; Dossat, *Crises*, p. 193.

not be in his house or go around outside his house without these displayed. Their size: the height of one arm should be the length of two and a half palms, and the other arm, the horizontal one, should be the length of two palms, and the width of each arm should be three fingers. And if they get torn he is to repair them.

And he is to go once this year to St James of Compostella and St-Denis in <the Île-de-> France, <for> solace, etc. And for each of the pilgrimages he is to bring back testimonial letters.

Item, every year he is to visit the church of St-Stephen in Toulouse on <the feast of> his invention [*3 August*], and the church of St-Sernin <in Toulouse> on the octave of Easter.

Item, he is to confess three times every year before Christmas, Easter and Pentecost, and to take communion on these feasts, unless the counsel of his own priest is that he ought to abstain.

Item, on all Sundays and feast days he is to hear Mass and be present at sermons if he is in localities where these are taking place, unless he can be lawfully excused.

Item, during the Lord's Advent he is to fast on Lenten food.

He is not to observe auguries, divinations <and> sorceries.

He is not to be involved in usuries or extorted goods, by himself or through another person, and if he receives <any such> he is to make restitution.

Henceforth he is not to hold public office, to wear grooved or painted shoes, or to use gilded saddle, harness <and> spurs.

Item, he is to pursue heretics and with all his strength protect the Catholic faith. The power of changing, commuting and also increasing things in the aforesaid penance, as seems expedient, is reserved to us and other inquisitors, etc.

10. Granting the laying down of crosses

Know all men that we, N. and N., brothers <Preacher>, by apostolic authority deputed inquisitors of heretical wickedness in the lands and communities of the Lord Count of Toulouse, give and grant to N. of such and such a place, permission to lay down the felt crosses that had been imposed upon him for the crime of heretical wickedness: reserving to us and to other inquisitors the power of re-imposing on the same person these same or other crosses, without any new cause, as seems expedient.

We are changing nothing, however, in any other things that were imposed upon him as penance for the aforesaid crime.

Done, etc.

11. Commutation of imprisonment in the Wall to another penance

Let it be known to all that we, Brother Pons of Pouget and Brother Stephen of Gâtine,[99] of the Order of Preachers, by apostolic authority deputed inquisitors of heretical wickedness in the lands and jurisdiction of the illustrious King of France that are in the provinces of Narbonne and Arles and in the cities and dioceses of Albi, Rodez, Carcassonne, Périgord, Mende and Le Puy, acting with the counsel of good men, have decided mercifully to liberate Bernard of Sourouillac of St-Cels[100] in the diocese of Toulouse, from the imprisonment in the Wall which had been imposed upon him for the things he committed in the crime of heretical wickedness, where he had lived for some length of time, humbly obeying our and the Church's mandates.

In commutation and mitigation of the said penance of imprisonment and the Wall, and for the detestation of his old error, we impose on him this. He is to wear on his clothes, apart from his shirt, two crosses of yellow felt crosses, one in front on his chest and the other behind between his shoulders, and that he will not be in his house or go around outside his house without these displayed; and if they get torn he is to repair them. Their size: the height of one arm should be the length of two and a half palms; the other arm, the horizontal one, one and half palms <and> that the arm should have the width of three fingers.

In addition, over the course of four consecutive years he is to visit the holy places of blessed James of Compostella, Blessed Mary of Rocamadour, Le Puy, Vauvert, <Our Lady> of the Tables in Montpellier and of

99 Pons has left traces of his activity as inquisitor at Carcassonne 1262–4, Stephen in 1264, and together the two were also inquisitors for Toulouse from late 1268; see Doc. 26(B). Dossat, *Crises*, p. 194; index entries, *Inquisitors and Heretics*, pp. 1040, 1055; Douais, *Documents*, I, pp. 34 n.8, 167–9.

100 Tarn dpt.

Sérignac, St-Gilles, St-Guilhem-du-Désert, St-Antoine-de-Viennois, and St-Vincent of Castres, bringing back testimonial letters from people in charge in the said places, <stating> that he had completed the stated pilgrimages.

In addition he is to confess three times every year before Christmas, Easter and Pentecost and to take communion on these feasts, unless he is to abstain on the counsel of his own chaplain [*parish priest*].

And with the same frequency he is to have the present letters read and explained to him in the vernacular, so that through this he can be better informed what to do and what not to do.

For as long as he lives, on Sundays and feast days he is to hear parish masses in their entirety and to be present at sermons that occur in places he happens to be, unless he can be lawfully excused. And during the masses between the <reading> of the Epistle and the Gospels he is to present himself with rods in his hand to the celebrant priests, and he is to receive discipline from them.

Carrying rods, he is also to follow processions which occur in places where he is, between clergy and people, and at the last station <of the cross> he is to receive discipline from the man who was at the head of the procession.

And on Sundays he is to abstain from all servile work and cultivation.

Henceforth he is not to discharge any public offices whatsoever, in any way, in his own name or anyone else's.

And he is not to be involved in usuries or extorted goods, by himself or through another person, and if he receives <any such> he is to make restitution.

He is not to observe auguries, divinations and sacrilegious things.

Further, he is to pursue heretics, by whatever name they are called, and with all his strength he is to protect the Catholic faith and ecclesiastical persons and ecclesiastical rights.

The power of changing, commuting and also increasing things in the aforesaid penance, as seems expedient, is reserved to us and other inquisitors, etc.

We impose on him these things, therefore, reserving to ourselves and to our successors in this office the power at any time of adding to, commuting or changing the stated penance and sending the same Bernard back to the said prison, without any new guilty act or cause, if it seems expedient, granting to him the present letters, sealed with our seals, as testimony of the aforesaid things.

Done at Carcassonne, 12 April AD 1271

12. Form for calling together clergy and people for a <general> sermon

Brother Simon Duval[101] of the Order of Brothers Preacher, deputed by apostolic authority inquisitor of heretical wickedness in the kingdom of France, greetings in the author and completer of the faith, Jesus Christ, to the distinguished and beloved men, all the priests and chaplains established within Caen and its suburbs, to whom the present letters have got through.

By the aforesaid authority we impose this on you: that on this next Sunday after the feast of St Vincent the Martyr, after breakfast you are to come together with the people who are subject to you in a procession to the house of our brothers <Preacher> in Caen, to hear the word of God and the apostolic mandate. You are to do this <not> to the extent needed to avoid being censured for negligence, but rather with the promptness in obeying that would merit commendation.

You are to put your seal on the present letter as an indication that you have received the mandate.

Given at Caen, AD 1277, on the feast of St Agnes [= 21 or 28 January]

13. Another form for calling together clergy and people

Brother Simon Duval of the Order of Brothers Preacher, deputed by apostolic authority inquisitor of heretical wickedness in the kingdom of France, greetings in the author and completer of the faith, Jesus Christ, to the distinguished and beloved men, all the priests and chaplains established within Orléans and its suburbs, to whom the present letters have got through.

Since you ought to show yourselves equally obedient and zealous in those things which relate to the exaltation of the faith, by the aforesaid

101 At this point the examples cited switch from southern to northern French towns. Simon is not known outside these texts. Form 17 below indicates he was empowered by the King of France, Philip III.

authority we strictly impose this on you. On this next Thursday [7 July] after the octave of the apostles Peter and Paul, and at the first ringing of prime <by the bells of the cathedral> of the Holy Cross you are to take pains to come in person, together with the people who are subject to you, to the court of the lord king, to hear our and the apostolic mandate and to have a great indulgence.

To indicate that you have in fact received the mandate you are to have your seal appended to the present letters.

Given at Orléans, AD 1278, on the third ferial day after the feast of the blessed Peter and Paul [2 July]

14. Form for citing those who were summoned but did not come

Brother Simon Duval, Inquisitor of heretical wickedness, greetings in the author and completer of the faith, Jesus Christ, to the distinguished men lord R. and master J., curates of Louviers[102] in the diocese of Évreux.

Because your parishioner Ralph Alavy, summoned by us to provide testimony in the business of the faith, did not come on the day assigned to him, as he should have done, by the aforesaid authority we mandate and command you to summon the said Ralph to appear before us, first of all, on the fourth ferial day after the next feast of blessed Mary Magdalen [27 July], in order there to receive just penalty for his failings and to do satisfaction for his disobedience and contempt.

To indicate that you have received and carried out the mandate, you are to have your seal appended to the present letters, which you are to send back to me via one of those who are summoned for Sunday.

Given at Évreux, AD 1277, on the sixth ferial day before the feast [15 July]

15. Form for citing suspects of heresy

Brother Simon Duval, by apostolic authority deputed inquisitor of heretical wickedness in the kingdom of France, greetings in the author

102 Haute-Normandie dpt.

and completer of the faith, Jesus Christ, to the distinguished men lord Reynold and lord John, curates of Louviers in the diocese of Évreux.

By apostolic authority and for the remission of sins we strictly impose this on you, that you summon before us tomorrow at Évreux, in the house of our brothers, Galtier called 'the Par.' [*abbreviation unclear; possibly 'the Parisian'*], Richard Mercier, William and Reginald called 'the Brittany' <and> Ralph Alavy, so that they appear before us to provide testimony in the business of the faith.

In the same way you are to summon Peter Clement and Isabelle la Fauveil,[103] even though she has been heard previously.

In a similar way and for the same reason and at the same hour you are to summon – for next Sunday – Alice la Hardie,[104] Plaisance called 'Aspera',[105] Matilda la Rouarde,[106] Peter and Robert of Corbeil and their wives.

The aforesaid summonses should be done in secret and, being summoned, they are to leave other things aside and come in person, to avoid incurring heavy treatment for disobedience.

To indicate that you have received and carried out the mandate, you are to have your seal appended to the present letters.

Given at Évreux, on the fifth ferial day before the feast of blessed Mary Magdalen, AD 1277 [16 July]

16. Form for citing those who left the realm and who <had> committed <heresy> within the realm

Brother Simon Duval of the Order of Brothers Preacher, by apostolic authority deputed inquisitor of heretical wickedness in the kingdom of France, greetings in the author and completer of the faith, Jesus Christ, to the religious men <the prior>[107] of the brothers Preacher and the guardian[108] of the brothers Minor and those acting in their place.

103 'La Fauveil' has a variety of meanings in Old French, including dun in colour, and talking.

104 The Bold.

105 Sharp, rough or bitter.

106 Perhaps reddish. If the text is corrupt we could conjecture fox (roublarde).

107 The prior: not in the edn; our conjecture.

108 Title of superior of a Franciscan convent.

Since it is explicitly contained in the authoritative apostolic document sent to us, the inquisitors, that we can entrust summonses, examinations of witnesses <and> pronunciations of sentences to brothers of the Order of Preachers and Order of Minors, notwithstanding any privilege given them by the Apostolic See, and also that we may freely proceed against those who have sinned in the crime of heresy in the kingdom of France and transferred themselves to other parts, by the authority that we exercise we order and command you and everyone of yours to do this. In the presence of trustworthy witnesses you are to summon peremptorily Master Siger of Brabant,[109] canon of St-Martin in Liège, and Master Bernier of Nivelles,[110] canon of the same place, who are probably and vehemently suspect of the crime of heresy and are said to have committed <sins> in this crime in the kingdom of France, to appear in person in front of us on Sunday after the octave of the Epiphany [16 Jan 1278] at St-Quentin in Vermandois in the diocese of Noyon, there to reply to us about the faith and to tell the pure and whole truth both about themselves and about others, living and dead, on the crime of heresy and on things relating to this crime.

To indicate that you have in fact received and executed this mandate, you are to have your seal appended to the present letters.

Given AD 1277, on Monday, the feast of blessed Clement [23 November]

17. Form of writing to capture fugitives[111]

Simon Duval of the Order of Brothers Preacher, by apostolic authority deputed inquisitor of heretical wickedness in the kingdom of France, greetings in the author and completer of the faith, Jesus Christ, to all those who will receive the present letters.

Since – by the apostolic authority and also the royal power that I exercise in capturing heretics and perfidious Christians who have con-

109 Siger of Brabant (c. 1240–84) was a prominent master in the Arts faculty in Paris in the 1260s and 1270s. He and Boethius of Dacia were held to be responsible for many of the 219 articles condemned by the Bishop of Paris, Stephen Tempier, on 7 March 1277. See *La condamnation Parisienne de 1277: Texte latin, traduction et commentaire*, ed. D. Piché (Paris, 1999); the articles are translated in *Medieval Political Philosophy: A Sourcebook*, ed. J. Parens and J.C. MacFarland, 2nd edn (Ithaca and London, 2011), pp. 335–54.

110 Or Nijvel, in the province of Walloon Brabant.

111 On Jews in Normandy in the 1270s, see N. Golb, *The Jews in Medieval Normandy* (Cambridge, 1998), pp. 507–9; he does not discuss forms 17–18c.

verted or reverted to the damnable rites of the Jews – I am sending Copin, a servant of the *bailli* of Caen, to capture a certain Jewess called Bonnefille, wife of Copin of Samois,[112] whom I am having detained at Caen for apostasy from the Christian faith, I ask each and every one of you – further, by the aforesaid authority and power I particularly require you – to this: you are to supply counsel and useful help, as they are asked of you. You are to do this ⌜not⌝ to the extent needed to avoid being censured for negligence, but rather with the promptness in obeying that would merit commendation.

The present letters are to be valid until the next octaves of blessed Vincent the Martyr.[113]

18a. Summons, against a dead man who had himself circumcised and handed himself over to the damnable rites of the Jews

Inquisitor N., greetings to the person in charge N.

Since through the acts of lawfully carried out inquisition it is found that the dead man N. damnably handed himself over to circumcision of the flesh of the foreskin and other rites of the Jews, denying the truth of the Catholic faith and the sacrament of baptism which he had earlier received (something which is known to be the more reprehensible the more freely the most holy name of Christ comes to be blasphemed, through a sort of casual hostility); and because, according to the high pontiff's commission on this entrusted to us, one is to proceed against reprobates of this sort as one does against heretics – and their crime, whether among the living or the dead, is to be judged by the quickest justice: by the authority that we exercise we order and command you to this. After gathering trustworthy witnesses, you are to summon peremptorily N. and N., sons and heirs of the said dead man, to appear on such and such a day and in such and such a place in front of us, to say and put forward, if they <can> put forward something, in defence of the said late man N., and to …[114] of the same <sons and heirs> on the aforesaid things, why he should not be condemned as a heretics.

Given, etc.

112 Samois-sur-Seine, Seine-et-Marne dpt.

113 His feast-day was 22 January.

114 Text missing here in the edn. Context suggests questioning of the sons and heirs.

18b. Second summons of this sort, which is added after the aforesaid one

In your church in the presence of the people you are publicly to set forth the published act of summons, that if there are any men, apart from the aforesaid sons and heirs of the aforesaid dead man, who want to defend the aforesaid defunct man and to whom the defence of the same man pertains by law, they are to appear on the said day to put forward <things> about the said dead man, as described above, and to proceed in the way and to the extent that there should be proceeding in law.
Given, etc.

18c. A third, in which there is addition – to the aforesaid things – in what is said

Indicating publicly that if anyone appears on the said day who wishes to – and by law can – defend the said dead man on the aforesaid things, we are to proceed against him to a definitive sentence, in the way that there should be proceeding in law.

Given, etc.

19. Summons on one's own case

You are to summon <someone> to appear to reply about the faith and to tell the pure and whole truth both about himself and about others, living and dead, on the crime of heresy and on things pertaining to this crime.

Given etc.

40. BERNARD GUI ON *PERFECTI*

The fifth book of Bernard Gui's manual has been translated several times, but just as important is the fourth part of his *Treatise on the Practice of Inquisition* [*Tractatus de Practica Inquisitionis*], where Gui discusses the authority and powers of inquisitors, using previous texts and adapting them to his purpose. Prominent among these is an anonymous treatise written in Italy between 1280 and 1288–92, *On the Authority and Form of Inquisition*.[115] The texts translated here are relevant to modern anglophone and French historians' habit of calling the elite among Cathar heretics 'perfects', although the Latin *perfectus/i* is not generally used to denote the Cathar elite in the inquisition registers of thirteenth-century Languedoc. Paramount in Gui's use of *perfectus* is someone who has been completed – 'perfected' – and it is in this sense that his register of sentences permits the use the term *perfectus* to apply to a Waldensian Brother. Where it is found in other texts (and occasionally in fourteenth-century registers), the first meaning to be explored is Gui's: 'full', 'completed' or 'fully-fledged'. Compare the definitions made at the beginning of the *On the Life and Deeds of the Poor of Lyon* (Doc. 53). See the appendix in Sackville, *Heresy*, pp. 201–2, '*Perfecti* as a term to denote heretics'. Translated from Doat 36, fol. 17v, and Bernard Gui, *Practica inquisitionis* iv, ed. C. Douais (Paris, 1886), p. 218.

A. from On the Authority and Form of Inquisition

Among heretics, some are fully fledged [perfecti], and some not fully fledged [inperfecti]. Those who hold the faith and <follow> the way of life of the heretics are called 'fully fledged'. Those, however, who have only the faith but not the way of life – they are properly said to be 'believers'.[116]

B. from Gui, Treatise on Practice *[his additions italicised]*

It should be known, then, that some heretics are *called* 'fully fledged', some *however* 'not fully fledged'. Those are called 'fully fledged' *heretics* who *have professed* the faith and way of life, *in accordance with their rite, and*

115 This is edited in an unpublished University of Bologna PhD dissertation of 2008 by Stefania Pirli, '*De auctoritate et forma officii inquisitionis*'.

116 Doat 36, fol. 17v.

hold *or observe them and teach them to others.* Those are *called* 'not fully fledged' heretics, however, who *in fact* have the faith *of the heretics*, but do not *follow* the way of life *of the same – as far as their observances and rites are concerned.* And these are properly *called* 'believers' *in the errors of heretics, and they are judged as heretics.*

PART VIII: INQUISITION TRIALS

INTRODUCTION TO PART VIII

The 1270s inquisition manual translated in Part VII (Doc. 39) provides an ideal version of the inquisitorial actions that generated the records translated in this final part. A suspect was questioned (note the list of questions the manual supplies), a notary recorded what was said and his notes were written up, an abstract of guilty acts called a 'culpa' (literally 'guilt') was composed, and this was used in drawing up a sentence imposing penalties, for which there were models provided (as in Doc. 38 also).

Where the records survive, they are the richest of all sources for the study of 'heretics' and 'sects' and the Church that labelled them thus and tried to repress them. But their survival was patchy. Looking at Latin Christendom as a whole, we see few, for example, surviving from early fourteenth-century Austria and Bohemia, although we know from the statistics of executions and a few fragments of interrogations that inquisition was probably a larger affair there than in Languedoc at the time.[1] In thirteenth-century France the records survive from the south, not the north, a reminder of how precarious is our knowledge. How different would be our view if we had interrogation records from northern France, rather than just passing references in a chronicle, a sermon collection and certain formulae in the aforementioned inquisition manual (Docs 6, 17 and 39)?

The comparatively abundant southern French records survive in different modes and include various different kinds of document. Some medieval manuscripts are extant (Docs 48–9, 53–7), but vary in their proximity to the original interrogation, ranging from one which includes sections written in the original hand of a notary who took down his own deposition (Doc. 54) to a copy made around 1260 of records of enquiries from, mainly, 1245–6 (Doc. 48).

There are also numerous early modern copies of now-lost medieval manuscripts (a selection here translated as Docs 41–7, 50–2). A word is needed about the trustworthiness of the copying: they were all

1 *Quellen zur böhmischen Inquisition im 14. Jahrhundert*, ed. A. Patschovsky, MGH, Quellen zur Geistesgeschichte des Mittelalters 11 (Munich, 1979), pp. 18–24.

produced in the 1660s by a team of scribes working for Jean de Doat, whose surname still identifies them in the French National Library.[2] The commission was asked to record documents bearing upon the rights of the crown and those of historical interest, the inquisition registers falling into the latter category. Doat's scribes made their copies according to contemporary orthography, and there are occasional mistakes in transcription, but there is no evidence of deliberate tampering and there is no general problem of authenticity.[3] This can be demonstrated by the myriad interconnections between depositions preserved in medieval manuscripts and early modern copies – an example here is the medieval manuscript of Peter of Mazerolles's deposition (Doc. 48 fols 124r–v) and the early modern copy of the deposition of his mother, Helis of Mazerolles (Doc. 44).

One problem that remains with the early modern documents is that the no-longer extant medieval document was created somewhere within a line of production of texts: but, given its absence, we can only conjecture its precise position in the sequence. The forms of the records that survive vary, from the agreed record of interrogation – a 'deposition' like Docs 41, 43, 48, 49 (II), 50–2, 54 and 57(b) – to extracts produced for the inquisitor to assess guilt and draw up sentences (Doc. 42 – there given very succinctly – and Doc. 55). We have juxtaposed deposition and sentence in two cases, Docs 45 and 48, and the reader will note the contrast: the length and detail of the deposition as against the brevity and lack of detail of the sentence. Finally, Doc. 53 shows depositions being used to construct an inquisitor's account of a sect.

A fundamental concern with these records has long been the truth or otherwise of what the deponents confessed when interrogated by inquisitors. Suspicion about inquisition records has its own history, especially in southern France. Inquisitions in the 1280s, including the depositions represented here by Doc. 51, came under suspicion not only from opponents of the inquisition (Doc. 57) but also within the Church. To the papacy itself, around 1300, some of these records were called the 'suspect books' (libri suspecti); see Friedlander, *Hammer*, pp. 17–18, 59–63. However, this highlights the relative *lack* of general suspicion in the 1270s, and a general contrast between the reputation

2 *Inquisitors and Heretics*, pp. 20–6, 117–20.

3 See C. Sparks, *Heresy, Inquisition and Life Cycle in Medieval Languedoc* (York, 2014), p. 15 n.70.

for dodginess of Robert Lepetit (see Doc. 7) in northern France and the implacable, cruel but more sober image of inquisition in Languedoc before the 1280s.

There is an abundance of modern scholarship on inquisition records. Recent work has tended to concentrate not on irregularity of procedure but rather on how this procedure itself shaped and constricted what the records contain, imposing the Church's vocabulary on 'heretics' and their rites, taking spoken vernacular into written Latin, and dictating via questions a record that would contain mainly that which interested inquisitors. Sackville (*Heresy*, pp. 121–35) has provided a general survey of this genre of texts and literature on them. Dossat (*Crises*, pp. 58–61) detailed notaries' actions in producing records of proceedings, and Sneddon has analysed the influence of individual notaries' linguistic habits on the records (*Inquisitors and Heretics*, pp. 83–106). Arnold has analysed the different voices of the records, the balance between inquisitorial categorisation and the excess of detail generated within each deposition (Arnold, *Inquisition and Power*, chs 3, 4 and 5). In a parallel vein, Bruschi's study, suggesting how to read depositions, restored some agency to the person under interrogation and emphasised what she called the 'surplus' of evidence provided in depositions, material not derived from or shaped by the inquisitor's questions – see 'Magna diligentia est habenda per inquisitorem: precautions before reading Doat 21–26', in C. Bruschi and P. Biller, eds, *Texts and the Repression of Medieval Heresy* (Woodbridge, 2003), pp. 81–110; see also her account of interrogation in the 1270s, *Inquisitors and Heretics*, chapter 3 (i).

We suggest to the modern reader – keen to know what people thought and felt, and frustrated by depositions' concentration on actions rather than thought – that it is useful to look at the discussion of a 'believer' by Guy Foulques (Doc. 35) and literature cited in its introduction. See also Biller's analysis of the reasons for a minimalist range of doctrines for questioning in the enquiries of 1245–6, as seen in Doc. 48: Biller, 'Intellectuals and the masses: oxen and she-asses in the medieval Church', in J. H. Arnold, ed., *The Oxford Handbook of Medieval Christianity* (Oxford, 2014), pp. 323–39 (at 328–31).

The compendious surviving material from inquisitorial registers therefore provides evidence of the operation of inquisition through the thirteenth century; but also, of course, evidence for the nature of the heretics they were persecuting. We have tried to provide in our selections a balance between representative examples and unusual moments of particular interest. The first deposition below (Doc. 41) recounts, among other things, the holding of a 'Cathar' council in 1225, the business of which was with heretics with the titles of 'Bishop', 'Elder Son' and 'Younger Son'. These are encountered throughout the depositions of the late 1230s and 1240s, but thereafter the hierarchy of the southern French Cathars was to be found in exile in Italy (see Doc. 15), and there were no bishops in the Catharism briefly revived in Languedoc by a small group under Peter Autier in the early fourteenth century (of which there are some glimpses in Docs 54–5).

The castle of Montségur was rebuilt at the request of Cathars around 1204–6 (see introduction to Doc. 47) and was re-adopted as their headquarters in 1232.[4] The ordinations within this safe haven are the clearest glimpse we get of the through-flow of ordinations and the system of succession, as described by witnesses interrogated about life within the castle. Here, for example, is Raymond of Péreille, co-lord of Montségur: 'he received and maintained at Montségur Gaucelin, Bishop of the Toulousan heretics, and Guilabert of Castres who succeeded him in the episcopate [in episcopatu[5]] of the heretics of Toulouse, and John Cambiaire and Bertrand Martin, bishops of the heretics, who succeeded <in the episcopate> similarly' (Doat 22 fols 217v–218r). And Berengar of Lavelanet: 'the aforesaid heretics made their ordinations [ordinationes] there. They ordained John Cambiaire <Younger>[6] Son, and Bernard Bonafos Deacon of Toulouse, and Tento Bishop of the heretics of Agennais, and they made Raymond of Montouty, whom they called Raymond Donat, deacon of heretics' (Doat 24 fol. 44v).

Overall, then, the depositions provide a variety of perspectives and an extraordinary wealth of material on heresy – including Waldensian

4 Berengar of Lavelanet, interrogated in 1244: 'He saw that Guilabert of Castres, Bishop of Heretics, and Bernard of La Mothe, Elder Son, and John Cambiaire, <Younger> Son of Vigouroux [ms: Hugh] of La Bouconne, Elder Son of the heretics of the Agennais, and Pons Guilabert, Deacon of the heretics of Vilamur, and Tento, Bishop of the heretics of the Agennais, and many other heretics, went into the *castrum* of Montségur and petitioned and supplicated Raymond of Péreille, former lord of said *castrum*, to receive heretics within the *castrum* of Montségur to this end, that the Church of the heretics could have its residence and headquarters [caput] in the said *castrum*, and could send out from there and protect its preachers'; Doat 24 fols 43v–44r.

5 Accounding to Feuchter, *Ketzer*, p. 429 n.338, the only time the term episcopate [episcopatus] is found.

6 Ms: et.

heresy – in southern France. We have provided cross-references to some important events and people, but the index will also be of use in this regard.[7]

7 For the most important noble families, see also the family trees provided in Mark Gregory Pegg, *A Most Holy War: The Albigensian Crusade and the Battle for Christendom* (Oxford, 2008), pp. xiii–xix and M. Roquebert, *L'Epopée cathare 3: Le lys et le croix, 1216–1229* (2nd edn Paris, 2007), pp. 603–8.

41. RAYMOND JEAN OF ALBI, 1238: THE COUNCIL OF PIEUSSE AND BISHOPS

This is one of the earliest depositions still extant, and it contains a remarkable description of a Cathar council (fols 269v–270v), which should be compared to Doc. 1. The inquisitor, the Dominican Ferrier, was a Catalan.[8] He was already at work in 1229, authorised by the Archbishop of Narbonne – thus acting as inquisitor well before this task came to be specifically entrusted to the Dominicans and Franciscans (see below, Doc. 48 fol. 5r–v) – and traces of his activity continue up to 1247. Although his fame as an inquisitor procured his entry into an Occitan poem (see introduction to Doc. 45 below), and persisted into the fourteenth century (see Doc. 8 §§9 and 21, and the introduction to Doc. 45 below), nothing is known about when he died, other than it being after two priorates he held, 1250–4. See on him W. L. Wakefield, 'Friar Ferrier, inquisition at Caunes, and escapes from prison at Carcassonne', *Catholic Historical Review* 58 (1972), 220–37, and 'Friar Ferrier, inquisitor', *Heresis* 7 (1980), 33–41. Translated from Doat 23, fols 260v–273v.[9] We include folio numbers thus: /261r/.

AD 1238, 12 days before the calends of March [18 February], Raymond Jean of Albi, nephew [*or* grandson] of John Seminoret, was required to tell the truth about himself and about others, both living and dead, on the accusation of heresy and Waldensianism. And he was sworn in as a witness.

He said that he saw Bernard of Lamothe[10] and his companions, heretics, at Villemur in the diocese of Toulouse, /261r/ in the house of Peter of Cos, preaching there. The same witness and Peter of Cos, who was ill at the time, were present at this preaching.

8 He is sometimes confused with another Dominican called Ferrier, also from Catalonia, who taught theology in Paris in the 1270s.

9 Part of the deposition has been edited by Feuchter, *Ketzer*, pp. 491–3.

10 Bernard, seen administering the *consolamentum* in Montauban in 1209 or earlier (Doat 23 fols 3r–5v), noted as 'Elder Son' of the Cathar diocese of Toulouse in 1232 (see n.1 above) and then bishop in various records, was notably active up until the fall of Montségur in 1244. A widow called Esclarmonda attested that she and other ladies had seen him 'confirmed as bishop' [confirmatus in episcopum], without being asked about the date; see below Doc. 48 fol. 62r. He is mentioned a number of times in Doc. 48 below. There is an account of him in Feuchter, *Ketzer*, pp. 206–7.

He also says that the same heretics came away – and the same witness with them – and they went into Guinha's house, where the aforesaid heretics stayed. And the same witness adored the same heretics there, saying 'Bless' three times while kneeling before them, and adding after the last 'Bless', 'Senior, pregat Deu per aquest pecador que adducat me ad bonum finem' [‘Lord, pray God for this sinner that He may lead me to a good end’]. And to each 'Bless' the heretics replied, 'May God bless you', and added after the last 'Bless', 'May God be implored'.[11] He also said that he saw that Brun Gairaud of Villemur came there to see /261v/ the said heretics, and adored them, as said earlier. He also said that Bernard Grau and Peter Raymond, inhabitants of Villemur, came there in similar fashion to see the said heretics, and they adored these heretics, as contained <in the description of the rite> above. He says that Rogafres and his sister Alamanda came to the aforesaid house in a similar way to see the said heretics, and adored them, as said earlier.

He also says that the aforesaid heretics – and the same witness with them – went away from there and into the house of Bernard the Smith Stibance [*probably family name*, ‘Ploughmanson’]. And there Bernard the Smith and his wife Guillelma adored these heretics. When this had been done, the heretics and the same witness went away from there, and went into the house of the knight Isarn of St-Michel-de-Lanès, and they were there for seven days. /262r/ The villagers Brun Gairaud, and Bernard Grail, and Peter Raymond son of Pagan, and Rogafres and his sister Alamanda, and Bernard of *Petra Fossor*, and Bernard the Smith, and Guinha, and his wife, and Abalin, came there to see these heretics, and others whose names he does not know. And all of them – both the same witness and also the others – adored the said heretics there. <Asked> about the time, <he said> that it was 16 or 17 years ago.

Item, he said that the aforesaid heretics, and the same witness together with them, left the *castrum* of Villemur and came to Montauban, and there they entered the house of Joanna of Avignonet, mother of Bonet

11 'Adore' (*adorare*) was the word used by inquisitors for the performing of this rite, which the heretics called *melioramentum*. There is evidence that the heretics taught their followers how to carry it out (see below, Docs 42, 257v; 45, 211r; 48, 5v etc.) and that they should not do it unless they believed in the heretics (Doc. 48, 90v). See B. Hamilton, 'The Cathars and Christian perfection', in P. Biller and [R.] B. Dobson, eds, *The Medieval Church: Universities, Heresy and the Religious Life*, Studies in Church History subsidia 11 (Woodbridge, 1999), pp. 20–1; Wakefield, *Heresy*, p. 41; J. Duvernoy, *La Religion des Cathares* (Toulouse, 1976; repr. 1989), pp. 208–11; Feuchter, *Ketzer*, pp. 214–16.

of Avignonet of *Mocpestler*, and her companion, [female] heretics. And they were there for two or three days. /262v/ And the brothers William Aribert and Engelbaud, and their wives Dulcia and Folcauda, and the son of Bernard Capellis, came there to see the heretics. And there all of them adored these heretics, as said earlier.

He also says that the same witness and these heretics together with him left there and went into the house of Engelbaud, and they ate and lay there. And the same witness and Engelbaud and his wife Dulcia <ate> at the same table together with them. And at this point the heretics blessed the bread, in their manner.[12] All who were at the table ate some of it. And every single time they started eating and drinking something, they would say, 'Bless', and the heretics would reply, 'May God Bless you'. He also says that Engelbaud, and his wife Dulcia, and his sister Dulcia, who had come there to see these heretics, adored /263r/ these heretics there, as contained above.

He also says that the heretics left there and went into the house of Andreva and her daughter, [female] heretics, and they ate there, as said earlier. And Joanna, wife of Guitard, came there to see the said heretics and adored them, as said earlier. About the time: when Carcassonne was besieged by the Count of Toulouse.[13]

Item he said that the aforesaid heretics – and the same witness together with them – <left> the said town of Montauban and entered the town of Moissac, and there they entered the house of Peter Escudier. And there they ate, and lay. And then Arnold of Mothe, and Raymond of Lagarde, and Jean of Lagarde, and Peter son of Petronilla of Bergerac, and Stephen, brothers, /263v/ came there to see these heretics. And the same witness, and the brothers Peter Escudier and Raymond Escudier, and their mother Guillelma were there. All of them – both the same witness and also the others – adored these heretics, as said earlier.

He also says that the aforesaid heretics and the same witness with them left there and went into the house of Arnold of Lamothe, and they were there for two or three days. And they ate and lay there. And they blessed bread, and the same witness and Arnold of Mothe ate some of it. And Raymond of Lagarde, and John of Lagarde, and Peter and Stephen, the sons of Petronilla of Bergerac, and their mother,

12 On the Cathars' blessing and distribution of bread, see Hamilton, 'Cathars and Christian perfection', pp. 16–17; Duvernoy, *Religion des Cathares*, pp. 212–16; Feuchter, *Ketzer*, pp. 217–18.

13 Raymond VII's siege of Toulouse in 1223.

Petronilla herself, and others whom he does not remember, came there to see them. And all of them – both the same witness and also the others – adored these heretics there, as said earlier.

He also says /264r/ that these heretics and the same witness together with them <left> there and entered the house of Falquet. And they ate and lay there, and they were there for a good three days. And the brothers William Augier and Peter Augier, and Raymond of Garde, and Peter of Garde, and the brothers Peter Escudier and Raymond Escudier and Peter and Stephen, the sons of Petronilla of Bergerac, were there to see them. And all of them – both the same witness and also the others – adored these heretics, as said earlier.

He also said that the aforesaid heretics and the same witness together with them <left> there and entered the house of Petronilla of Bergerac, and they lay there. And there were there for a good two days. And Pons Guiraud, and Raymond of Garde, and John of Garde, and the brothers Peter Escudier and /264v/ Raymond Escudier were there at night-time to see the heretics. And all of them – both the same witness and also the others – adored these heretics there. And the same witness, and Petronilla of Bergerac, and her sons Peter and Stephen were there. About the time: it was a little after <the date stated> above.

Item, he says that the aforesaid heretics and the same witness together with them left there and <entered> into Castelsarrasin, and they entered the house of Stephen Saux, and they were there for four days, and they ate and lay there. And Raymond of *Campaira*, who wore the habit and cross of the Hospital of St-Jean, and William the Smith, and his mother, and his sister Guirauda were there to see these heretics. And there all of them – both the same witness and also the others and Stephen Saux – adored these heretics, as said earlier.

He also said that the said heretics and the same witness with them <left> there /265r/ and entered the house of the aforesaid William the Smith. And they were there for about 8 days, and they ate and lay there. And Bernard of Ca<sta>gnac, knight, and Pons Guctard [*perhaps* Guintard] came there to see the said heretics. Questioned, he said that they did not adore the said heretics. He also said that Vital Guintard, and Raymond William of *Bareio*, and his brother came there to see the said heretics. And there all of them – both the same witness and also the others – adored these heretics. About the time: 14 or 15 years ago; and then Bernard of Castagnac … [*sentence not completed; probably the seventeenth-century copyist missed a line*].

Item, he says that these heretics and the same witness together with them <left> Castelsarrasin and went to Toulouse. And there they entered the house of Sicard of Gameville, <which is> in front of the house of Bernard of Mons.[14] /265v/ The heretics stayed in this house. And Sicard of Gameville, and Aymeric the Elder of Castelnaudary, and his wife Constance – who made a feast that day for the heretics – and Fayens the mother of William of Toulouse, and others whom he does not remember came there to see them. And all of them adored the said heretics there.

He also says that that the said heretics and the same witness together with them from there went on the road <called> *De posa raiba*, and entered the house of a certain woman who was the mistress of Raymond Roger, who lived next to the house of Pons of Capdenier, and they were there for about 8 days.[15] And Bernard of *Murello* and his wife Na Tholosa,[16] and their children, and the father-in-law of Bernard of *Murello*, and others whom he did not know came there to see them. And all of them adored these heretics there.

He said also that the /266r/ aforesaid heretics and the same witness together with them entered the house of Alaman of Roaix, and they were there for four days.[17] And the heretic Guilabert of Castres[18] was there. He also says that Alaman of Roaix, and his wife, and their sons Alaman and Bec, were there in the aforesaid house. And both of them, Alaman of Roaix and his wife, adored these heretics there, as said earlier.

He also says that the aforesaid heretics and the same witness together with them <left> there and entered the house of the Lady of Moissac, and they ate and lay there. And there were there the Lady of Moissac,

14 The wealthy Mons [*De Montibus*] family had their house in the north-east of the city.

15 Pons Capdenier [Capitedenario] was one of the wealthiest men in Toulouse, with a house by the basilica of St-Sernin.

16 'Na', short for 'Domina', Lady.

17 The Roaix were another family from the elite of Toulouse, and Alaman a famous supporter of the heretics, whose sentence to life imprisonment in 1248 is translated in Wakefield, *Heresy*, pp. 239–41.

18 Noted as 'Elder Son of the heretics of Toulouse' when seen at Fanjeaux in 1204 (Doat 24, fol. 42r). Took part in debate at Montréal in 1207 (*Chronicle of William of Puylaurens*, p. 26); Cathar Bishop of Toulouse 1220–37, named as such fol. 270r below, and noted at various points in Toulouse 609 and elsewhere in the surviving sources. See J. Duvernoy, 'Guilhabert de Castres', *Cahiers d'Études Cathares* 34 (1967), 32–42.

and her daughter Na Ondrada, and two sons of the said Na Ondrada, and Bertrand and Arnold William. And all of them adored the said heretics there. About the time: 14 years ago.

Item, he says that leaving Toulouse the aforesaid /266v/ heretics and the same witness with them came into the Lantarais and into the fort of William Costau. And there they entered the house which the heretics who lived there had constructed. And William Costau, and his wife, and their son Guiraud Costau, and similarly their daughters came there to see these heretics. And all of them adored these heretics there, as said above.

He said also that from there they came to Tarabel, and there they entered the house of Na Longa of Tarabel, and they ate and lay there. And Lady Longa of Tarabel, and her sons Arnold Stephen and Galhard Stephen were there. And some whom he did not know came from the said fort to see them. And all of them adored these heretics there, as said earlier.

He also said that from there /267r/ these heretics and the same witness with them came to Fourquevaux, and there they entered the house of Lady Marchesia of Fourquevaux, mother-in-law of Sicard of Montaut.[19] And the ladies Marchesia and her daughter-in-law Gauda and their household were there. And they adored them there. And the aforesaid heretics ate there and the same witness together with them.

He also says that there the same witness parted company from the same heretics, and came to Caraman to Guiraud of Gourdon of Caraman, heretic and heretic-deacon of Caraman.[20] And the same witness was with this heretic for a good year. And the aforesaid Guiraud of Gourdon and his companion, heretics, and the same witness together with them, came away from Caraman <and went> to Labécède, and they entered the house of Guilabert of Castres, heretic, and they were there for three days. /267v/ And many men of Labécède – among whom there was [*blank*], <and> he did not know the others – came there to see those heretics. And all of them adored the said heretics there.

He also says that from there the aforesaid heretics and the same witness together with them came to Laurac, and entered the house of Raymond Bernard, deacon of the heretics, and they were there for two

19 Lord, knight and co-lord of Esperce.

20 Possibly the same as Gualhard of Gourdon (Doc. 48, fol. 159r); active as early as 1205.

days. And the knights Miro of Camplong and Roger of [*blank*] and the brother of Amiel of Beaufort, knights, came there to see the said heretics, and many others whom the same witness did not know. And all of them adored the said heretics there. About the time: 14 years ago and more.

Item, he says that the aforesaid heretics and the same witness with them left Laurac <and went> to Fanjeaux. And they entered the house which Guilabert of Castres, heretic, was making there /268r/ under the houses of Bernard Hugo of Festes. And they were <there> from the beginning of Lent, which was just starting, to the middle of that Lent. And the knights Peter of St-Michel-de-Lanès, and Isarn Bernard of Fanjeaux, and Bernard Hugo of Festes came there to see these heretics, and many others, whose names he does not know. And all of them adored these heretics there. About the time: it was 14 years ago and more.

Item, he said that these heretics and the same witness together with them <left> Fanjeaux <and> came to Montréal, and there they entered the house of Peter Durant, deacon of the heretics of Montréal. And they left in the morning and came to Pech-Aldebert, and there they were lodged with the wives of Bernard and Pons of Villeneuve, daughters of the late Hugh /268v/ of *Romeges* of Montréal. And they ate there, and the aforesaid ladies adored these heretics there. And when this had been done they left and came through Aragon, and entered the house of Alazaicia of Aragon and her baby daughter and another of the heretics [male]. And they lay there. And Lady Saura, mother of Roger of Aragon, and another lady of the said *castrum* came there to see them. And they adored these heretics there.

He also says that from there they came to Montolieu, and Fabrissa, wife of Jaubert of Parazols, received them there at the top of the *castrum.* And they lay there. And the said Fabrissa adored these heretics there. About the time: as above.

Item, he says that from Montolieu they came to Saissac, and there they were lodged with William Bernard of Airoux.[21] And they lay there, and ate. And from there /269r/ they entered the house of Alamanda Mirpuenta and her companion, [female] heretics. And from there they entered the house of Arnold Raynaud and his sister, and there both Arnold Raynaud and his sister adored these heretics. And from there

21 Famous Good Man and medical practitioner; it is peculiar that 'heretic' is not given after his name.

they came <back> into the house of William Bernard of Airoux, and they were there for two days. About the time: as above.

Item, he said that these heretics and the same witness together with them <went away> from Saissac <and> came to Verdun. And there they were lodged in the house of two heretic women. And they lay there, and ate, and in the morning /269v/ they went away. About the time: as above.

Item, he says that the same witness and the other heretics <left> Verdun <and> came to Limoux in the Razès area. And they entered the house of two heretics who were skinners, and they lay there for one night, and in the morning /269v/ they left. About the time: a little after <the date given> above.

Item, he says that he says that from there the aforesaid heretics and the same witness together with them came to Pieusse, and they entered the house of heretics. And they found there many heretics congregated, up to a hundred. Among them were Guilabert of Castres, and Pons Bernard,[22] and Benedict of Termes,[23] and Bertrand Martin of Tarabel,[24] and Raymond Agulher,[25] and Bonfils of Cassès,[26] and others whom the same witness did not know. And there and then the heretics held a general council ⌜concilium generale⌝.[27] In this council the heretics of Razès petitioned and requested ⌜petierunt et postularunt⌝ for a bishop to be given to them. For <they said> it was not

22 See below.

23 See below. Already a leader in 1207, when participating in a debate at Montréal (*Chronicle of William of Puylaurens*, p. 26); Cathar Bishop of Razès from 1225 to an unknown date.

24 See introduction above. Bertrand Martin was active in Mas-Saintes-Puelles by c. 1225–6 (Toulouse 609, fols 21v–22r), noted as deacon by c. 1229 (Doat 23 fol. 141v), as Elder Son of Guilabert of Castres c. 1231 (Doat 24 fol. 111r), succeeding him as Bishop of the heretics of the Church of Toulouse (see introduction above). He held another council in the early 1240s (Doc. 48 fol. 214r). Mentioned often by those who deposed about Montségur (e.g., Doc. 46), he was executed there after its capture; *Chronicle of William of Puylaurens*, p. 108. See J. Duvernoy, 'Bertrand Marty', *Cahiers d'Études Cathares* 39 (1968), 19–35.

25 See below – earlier Deacon of heretics of Tarascon; Elder Son of Razès from 1225; bishop by at least 1232 (Doat 24, fols 94r, 98r; cf. Doc. 46 fol. 180v), until 1244.

26 Cathar Deacon of St-Félix; mentioned as such 'when the Count of Montfort held this land' (up to his death in 1218), Toulouse 609, fol. 216v.

27 Some examples are provided of the Latin words, which are ecclesiologically and legally formal. It is useful to compare them with the vocabulary of the Acts of St-Félix (Doc. 1) and the *On the heresy of the Cathars*, probably written by an Italian former Good Man. See L. Paolini, 'Italian Catharism and written culture', in *Heresy and Literacy 1000–1530*, ed. P. Biller and A. Hudson (Cambridge, 1994), pp. 88–90.

expedient for them that, when necessities arose among them, heretics had to come or be free <to come> from the Toulousain or Carcassès [= *Carcassonne area*]. For they did not know to whom they should be subject or obedient. And some of them /270r/ would go to the heretics of the Toulousain, others to the heretics of the Carcassès. And so it was determined [fuit deffinitum] that a bishop should be granted to these heretics of Razès, and that a person should be taken from the Carcassès heretics and that they should provide for this person the *consolamentum* and imposition of hands or ordination of the bishop of the Toulousan heretics.[28] When this had been done they granted, to the aforesaid <heretics> of Razès, Benedict of Termes as bishop. Guilabert of Castres, bishop of the Toulousan heretics, provided him the *consolamentum* and imposition of hands or ordination [ordinationem]. When this had happened, they made Raymond Agulher Elder Son and Peter [*should be* Pons] Bernard Younger Son.

He also says that the knight William the Elder of Villeneuve, was there, and many others /270v/ whom he does not remember. And the same William and the others adored them there. About the time: it was 13 years ago.

He also says that there the same witness left these heretics with whom he was going about, and he came to Peter of Corona,[29] Deacon of the heretics of Catalonia. With him and his companion, heretics, the same witness came from there to Mirepoix. And they were lodged in the house of the Barbas, that is to say, Berengar Barba and Peter Barba. And they ate and lay there. And the brothers Berengar Barba and Peter Barba were there, and these two Barbas adored them. And in the morning the aforesaid heretics and the same witness with them left there, and came to Quié in the Sabartès, and there they were lodged in some great house. And at the suggestion of Peter of Corona, heretic, Arnold of Serres of Quié escorted there to these heretics /271r/ Roger the Elder of Comminges, father of that one – <Arnold> – who talked

28 This rite is described in detail elsewhere below, and in the Occitan 'Cathar Ritual' text, translated WE, pp. 488–91. It was used, as here, to create 'perfected' or 'fully fledged' heretics (cf. Doc. 40 on possible meaning of 'perfected'), and was also administered to believers on their deathbed, to 'lead them to a good end', i.e. salvation at the hands of the heretics, as frequently attested in some of the following documents. See Wakefield, *Heresy*, pp. 36–9; Hamilton, 'The Cathars and Christian perfection', in Biller and Dobson, *The Medieval Church*, pp. 12–14, 16, 21; Barber, *Cathars*, pp. 90–4; Duvernoy, *Religion des Cathares*, pp. 146–70; Feuchter, *Ketzer*, pp. 218–20.

29 probably: 'of the Crown [of Aragon]' = of the kingdom of Aragon.

too much with the said heretic Peter of Corona there.[30] However, he did not adore them in his the witness's sight. He also says that many men from the said *castrum*, came there to see these heretics, and Peter Lombart, and Peter Pons and others whom the same witness did not know.

He also says that from there the aforesaid heretics and the same witness came to Carol. And they lodged there with a certain person who provided lodging, and they lay there. And in the morning they left there, and came to Josa, and they were lodged in the house of Raymond of Josa at the head of the *castrum*. And they were there for four days. And they saw Raymond of Josa, and his other knights and his household, who adored these heretics. He also says /271v/ that at that time the wife of Raymond of Josa was lying in childbirth.

He also says that from there, passing through Cervera and Berga, they came into the mountain<s> of Cerdagne. And there they stayed in the house of Arnold of *La Sencia*. And they were there for a year. And the aforesaid heretics – and the same witness with them – very often went from there into the town of Lérida. But he does not know the names of those whose houses he entered. The aforesaid heretics had many goods [*gifts*] from these houses. He also says that when a year had gone by, and after the peace was made between the Church and the king and the Count of Toulouse,[31] the same witness left … of the heretics.[32]

He came into the Lantarais. And there the same witness was ill in a certain manse which was called Pujagou. And there Pons Guilabert and his companion,[33] heretics, consolated[34] him and received /272r/ the same witness, in this manner. After white cloths had been placed on a certain table and on top <of them> a book which they called *The Text*, they asked the same witness, who was a little distance away from the book, whether he wished to receive the ordination of the Lord. And the same witness said, 'Yes'. Afterwards he rendered himself to God and the gospels. And he promised that henceforth he would not be, nor would he eat, without a companion and without prayer. And that if he

30 The lack of clarity here reflects the Latin.

31 Peace of Paris, 1229.

32 Ms: *discessit apud facis* [some crossing out or correction] *haereticorum*; perhaps originally *a*[something not now recoverable] *faci*[*ebu*]*s haereticorum* – 'left the company of the heretics'.

33 Pons Guilabert was named as Cathar Deacon of Villemur in 1232 (Doat 24, fol. 43v)

34 That is, performed the ritual of the *consolamentum*.

were captured without <his> companion, he would not eat for three days. Nor would he eat meat henceforth, nor eggs, nor cheese, nor anything fatty apart from oil and fish. Nor would he lie, nor swear nor indulge in any lust. When this had been done, he came in front of them – with some intervals – genuflecting <and> saying three times, 'Bless'. And afterwards he kissed the said heretics' book. And when these things had been completed, /272v/ they placed the book and <their> hands on his the witness's head, and they read the Gospel. Following this, the heretics did the *apparellamentum*, and they did the Peace there, kissing each other crosswise.[35] About the time: it was 7 years ago.

He also says that he stayed in this sect for three years in a certain hidden place in a little enclosure. And William Costau and his son Arnold and a certain woman of Pujagou, Raymonde, wife of Peter of Pujagou, would bring food there for the same witness and the other heretics.

Item, he says that earlier the same witness, together with Guiraud of Gourdon and Bonfils, heretics, came to Lombers, and entered the house of Arnold Berengar and other heretics. And someone whom the same witness did not know came to see these heretics, and adored them, as said /273r/ above.

He says that he saw other heretics with these heretics at Graulhet. About the time: it was 14 years ago.

He also says that he was often present at the service of the heretics which they call the *apparellamentum*, which they do from month to month.

He also says that when the seven years described above had passed, the same witness came to Albi and was reconciled by the venerable father the Bishop of Albi.[36] And he had his letters of reconciliation <from him> and following this from Brother Arnold of the Order of Preachers, given <to the diocese as> inquisitor of heretics.[37]

35 *apparellamentum*: term used by the Catholic Church to denote what the Good Men appeared to call 'Service', a monthly meeting at which the Good Men confessed minor faults; believers were allowed to attend. See also Doc. 45, fol. 215r below. The liturgical form is provided in the Occitan 'Cathar Ritual' text, translated WE, pp. 484–5. See Hamilton, 'Cathars and Christian perfection', pp. 18–19, and Duvernoy, *Religion des Cathares*, pp. 203–8.

36 Durand of Beaucaire, Bishop of Albi 19 July 1228 to 7 August 1254.

37 Arnold Catalan OP, nominated Inquisitor to the diocese of Albi in 1234, and mentioned in the chronicle of William Pelhisson: see Wakefield, *Heresy*, pp. 141–2, 211, 226–8.

These things he gave witness to in the presence of brothers Ferrier and Peter of Alès, inquisitors,[38] witnesses brothers Pons and Bernard, and Lord Bernard of Vermeils.

This is the confession which he made to Brother Arnold on 30 April AD 1235.[39] /273v/ Raymond Jean, nephew of John Seminoret, confessed on oath, in front of Brother Arnold, that it was a good 5 years before that Peter of Corona, deacon of the heretics, and Bernard of Lamothe, heretic <and> deacon of the heretics, received him. Questioned about the place, he said it was in a wood. And from there he went into the city which is called Lérida. And Arnold of *La Sencia* and his companion, heretics, <also went there>. And they stayed in the same city for a good 8 days.

Item, he said that he stayed with them for 3 years.

38 Peter of Alès OP was prior of the Dominican convent in Toulouse, 1232–3. He is visible acting as inquisitor only in 1237–8; see Douais, *Documents*, I, pp. 130, 136, 141.

39 This brief appendix presumably indicates an entry which the Inquisitor Ferrier has located in an earlier register, made by the Inquisitor Arnold Catalan, and had copied out again.

42. SELECTIONS FROM THE PENANCES OF PETER SEILA, 1241–2

Peter Seila (d. 1258) – sometimes named as Peter Cellan or Sellan – was one of the first two recruits to the incipient Dominican Order in Toulouse in 1215, and he looms large in Bernard Gui's account of early Dominicans; see Doc. 9 §§2–4.[40] He was a rich citizen, and gave them houses to occupy. He was also one of the earliest inquisitors, and considerable evidence arising from his inquisitions in towns in Quercy in 1241–2 survives in one of the seventeenth-century copies now in the French National Library, BnF MS Doat 21. Peter Seila's register(s) of depositions no longer survive, either in original form or copies, although we see a cross-reference to a register of depositions in one of the sentences translated here (see fol. 307r below). What survives are the extracts drawn up to assess the degree of guilt (described in the Introduction to Part VIII above), and penances. Notably absent from these are imprisonment and execution, probably the result, as persuasively argued by the remarkable study of Jörg Feuchter (see below) in the case of Montauban, of a deal done by the city elite with the inquisitors.

We have translated mainly from J. Duvernoy, ed., *L'Inquisition en Quercy: Le registre des pénitences de Pierre Cellan, 1241–1242* (Castelnaud La Chapelle, 2001). Where the penances are on deponents from Montauban we have translated from the later edition in Feuchter, *Ketzer*, pp. 454–89. We include folio numbers thus: /185r/.

/185r/ From Gourdon. AD 1241, first week of Advent

Huga, wife of the late Raymond Giraud, was a receiver of heretics, heard their preaching many times and adored them many times. And she gave them things of hers, and often visited them at the hostels [hospitia] where they were, where she often heard their preaching. And at the time she believed they were good men. And she was present at the heretication of her said husband.

40 He is mentioned frequently in Wakefield, *Heresy* and in biographies of St Dominic, for example M.-H. Vicaire, *Saint Dominic and His Times*, trans. K. Pond (London, 1964), pp. 168–70, 235, 245–6, 250. The fundamental account of his activities as inquisitor is Feuchter, *Ketzer*, ch. 5. See also C. Taylor, *Heresy, Crusade and Inquisition in Quercy* (Woodbridge, 2011).

She will go to Le Puy, to St-Gilles, to St James <of Santiago de Compostella>, and to San Salvador ⌜Oviedo⌝ of Asturias, to St-Martial de Limoges, St-Léonard, St-Denis, St Thomas of Canterbury. And she will wear in front two crosses, two palms in length and two fingers in width, for one year. And she will support a pauper for as long as he lives.

Stephen Galtier was a receiver of heretics, and escorted them, and heard their preaching many times, /186r/ so often that he does not remember <the number>, and adored them many times, and ate with them many times, and gave them things of his. And he believed they were good men.

He will stay for 2 years in the land of Constantinople, and he will wear crosses measuring a palm across his shoulders, and he will set out on the journey between the first Sunday of Advent and the <end of the> year.

Stephen Palmier heard the preaching of heretics many times and in many places, and adored them many times, and escorted them.

Same <penance> as Huga, except for the pauper.

Alazaicis of *Laquiebra* kept heretics in her house for a long while at diverse times, and often heard their preaching, and gave them things of hers, and many times adored them. And she went to their hostels many times.

Item, as Huga.

Bertrand, knight of Gourdon, saw heretics in his *castrum*, and spoke with them in his own house, /186v/ knowing they were heretics. And he heard their blasphemies. Item, he saw one day Vigouroux of La Bouconne,[41] and spoke with him, and let him depart. Item, he said that some time he had in his company Bartholomew of Carcassonne.[42] At the time he did not hear he was a heretic – he knew this later, however, before he left him.

William Ichier saw Peter of Vals, Waldensian, once.

He will go to Le Puy.

41 'Elder Son' of Agen in 1232 (Doat 24, fol. 43v), later Cathar Bishop of Agen. Mentioned by Durand of Huesca around 1223 (cf. Doc. 2). See Y. Dossat, 'Un évêque cathare originaire de l'Agenais: Vigouroux de la Bacone', in Dossat, *Eglise et hérésie en France au XIII siècle* (London, 1982), XIII.

42 On this heretic, see Doc. 21.

Raymond Arpa was a host and escort for many heretics for a long time, and heard their preaching, and believed they were good men, and that one could be saved by them.

And he was captured for heresy, and this was not during the period of grace.[43]

He will stay in Constantinople for 8 years. Regarding cross and journey, just as the others.

William Peregri ate with heretics, and received blessed bread /187r/ and the Peace, and for part of a night they were in his house. And he heard their preaching many times and in many houses, and gave them things of his, and also two little tunics, and he adored them many times.

He will stay in Constantinople for 3 years, and provide for a priest as long as he lives. Regarding cross and travel, just as the others.

Peter Peregrine adored heretics so many times that he does not know the number, and heard their preaching many times, and was present at the heretication of two believers, and two *apparellamenta*, and gave them things of his. And he escorted them, and received them in his barn, and also in his house at Gourdon.

William Bonald said that he believed the heretics were good men, and he heard their preaching /187v/ many times, and he often read for them the Gospel in 'Roman' [*in the Romance vernacular*], and adored them many times, and heard their preaching many times. He often escorted others to the heretics. He ate and drank with them, often received little gifts from heretics, and also he bought grain from heretics, and gave heretics the kiss of peace, and was present at *apparellamenta*, and was present at some heretication. And he gave heretics two loaves. Item, he perjured himself before Brother Bernard of Caux,[44] when asked to swear on oath whether he had seen heretics. He carried letters for heretics. Item, he went to the Waldensians twice, and heard their preaching, and gave them things of his.

He will stay for 3 years in Constantinople. Regarding cross and travel, just as the others.

43 That is, not during the first two weeks of inquiry, when the inquisitors invited confessions in exchange for more lenient sentences; see e.g. Doc. 37.

44 On this inquisitor, see Doc. 48 below.

Bernard of Latour heard the preaching of heretics many times and in various places, and he adored them once, and ate with them, and carried a certain ill woman to be hereticated, and he was present at a heretication in the house of Rothas. And he escorted women heretics for two days' journey or more, and went to many and various places /188r/ with the heretics.

Bertrand of Lascroux heard the preaching of heretics many times and in many places. And on Christmas night he visited heretics, and he was present at the heretication of Ranulph of Goulème 'the scabby', and the heretication of William Molinier, who bequeathed the heretics 100 shillings, which the said witness received and passed on to En Roques for him to pass on to the heretics. Item, he gave corn to the heretics.

At the time he also believed they were good men. He adored heretics many times and ate with them. And he also saw Waldensians, and sometimes heard their words.

He will stay in Constantinople for 3 years, and provide for a priest for as long as he lives. Regarding cross and travel, just as the others.

William of Montgaillard was present at the heretication of Ranulph of Goulème the scabby, and he was a receiver of heretics, /188v/ and heard the preaching of heretics many times and in many places. And he adored them often, and escorted them many times. And he said he would receive them a hundred times if they came to him a hundred times, because he loved them very much, and he served them, as he said, just as though he was serving God, and he received the Peace from the heretics. And on the instruction of heretics he sold their cloths, and he received a loan from them. Item, he said that his sister made herself a Waldensian in his house, and <lived there> in her own room for a month.

He will stay for 3 years in Constantinople. Regarding cross and travel, just as the others.

… /190r/ Guiralda of Rieu left her husband, and made herself a perfected heretic ⌜hereticam perfectam⌝,[45] and stayed with the heretics for half a year.

She is to resume two crosses, and she will go to Le Puy, St-Gilles and St James.

45 See Doc. 40: this could be translated as 'made herself a fully fledged heretic'.

.../198r/ Rocas saw heretics often, and he was a receiver and host of the heretics for a long time. And from the moment he saw them he believed in them. And he provided them with necessities. And he adored them often, and ate the bread blessed by heretics. And believers in heretics often came together to his house to hear their preachings and adore them, in his presence, and he ate with them. And he was present at three heretications, one of which was done in his house. And he escorted heretics, and received heretics' bequests. And he believed in the heretics as though they were messengers sent by God. /199r/ He received heretics so many times, ate with them so many times, and they with him, and adored them so many times, and heard their preachings so many times, and saw so many men and women with the heretics that he does not remember. And he cried when the heretics left. He kept them company on Easter Day. Item, he said that if he died he wanted to die in their hands.

He will stay for a period of 3 years in Constantinople. Regarding the cross and travel, just as the others.

... /199r/ Item, in the year as above [1241], on the Lord's Advent. From Gourdon.
Amalvin of Fénelon [*or* Fénelou] was a receiver and host of heretics, adored heretics so many times he does not know how often, and heard their preaching many times, and saw heretics in various places, and, as he said, he adored them whenever he saw them. And /199v/ he gave them things of his often, and ate bread blessed by the heretics, and was present at an *apparellamentum* done in his house, and received the Peace from them.

He will stay in Constantinople for 3 years, and provide for a priest for as long as he lives. Regarding cross and travel, just as the others.

Bertrand of St-Clair of Milhac saw heretics so many times and in so many places, and he adored them and heard their preachings so many times that he does not remember. And he escorted them.

He will stay in Constantinople for 2 years. Regarding cross and travel, just as the others.

Fortanier of Gourdon heard the preaching of heretics and adored them so often that he does not remember, as he said. And he escorted them, and he got 7 Cahors pounds for getting them escorted. And he ate with heretics. Item, he had heretics in the *castrum* /200r/ above Gourdon, and gave them corn and money. And he got from the heretics shirts and an angel [*a gold coin*]. He also said that wherever he saw heretics he adored them; and he believed they were good men.

Raymond Pomels escorted heretics many times, and saw heretics so many times and adored so many times and heard their preaching <so many times> that he cannot remember, and he also ate with heretics many times. And he gave beans to heretics, and ate bread blessed by heretics many times. And at the time he believed there was no salvation for other men than with the heretics, and that whenever he should die he wanted to die in their hands.

He is to stay for 3 years outside the six bishoprics of Cahors, Agen, Toulouse, Albi, Rodez, Carcassonne. And he is to wear a cross on his front for a year.

/200v/ William of Lasvignes often received, escorted, <and> heard the preaching of heretics, <and> adored once.

He will stay for a year in Constantinople. Regarding cross and travel, just as the others, and he will support a pauper for a year.

Bertrand Bresier saw heretics in many places in Toulouse and in Gourdon, and he heard their preachings and adored them.

As above, except for the pauper.

Ranulph Giraud sometimes escorted heretics, and heard their preaching many times.

The same as his mother,[46] except for the cross and the pauper.

Raimunda, wife of the late Ranulph of Goulème, heard all of the Passion in her house from heretics, and was a receiver and host of the heretics, and adored them many times, and heard their preaching, and was present at her husband's heretication. And she believed they were good men. /201r/ And she also saw Peter of Vals, the Waldensian, and asked him for counsel about her maidservant's illness. She also said that she received heretics in her own house after her husband died.

She will go to Le Puy, to St-Gilles and St-James, San Salvador of Asturias, St-Martial, St-Léonard, St-Denis, St Thomas of Canterbury. Regarding crosses, the same as Huga.

46 See very first penance.

... /203v/ Pana received Waldensians so many times that she does not remember, and she was a host of the Waldensians, and she sent them bread and wine and other things to eat so many times that she does not know the number. And a debate was carried out in her house between Waldensians and believers in the heretics. And she loved Peter of Vals like an angel of God.

Just as the previous one, apart from the pauper and the cross.

.../206r/ Guiraud Molinier saw heretics often, adored them and wrote a will for them, and for this he got shirts and sandals.

Same as the previous one, apart from the cross.

... William of Pradels saw heretics, heard their preaching, gave them things of his, and saw heretics often and in various places, and believed they were good men. And he often saw a Waldensian, and believed the Waldensian was a good man, and he once gave him something to eat, and heard his preaching.

He will wear a cross for 2 years.

Joanna of Ribière saw heretics twice.

She will go to Le Puy.

Raymond Bernard saw heretics twice, and accompanied them.

He will go to Le Puy, St-Gilles and St James.

Elias of La Valade saw heretics twice.

The same as the previous one.

Bernarda of Ribière saw women heretics many times, /208v/ and heard their preaching, and gave them things of hers and believed they were good women.[47]

The same as the previous one.

47 This is a very rare – and frustratingly vague – mention of female heretics preaching; see also Doc. 48, fol. 239v. On Cathar preaching, see J. H. Arnold, 'The preaching of the Cathars', in C. Muessig, ed., *Medieval Monastic Preaching* (Leiden, 1998), pp. 183–205.

William Ricart saw heretics many times and in various places, and often heard their preaching, and was present at an *apparellamentum.* He received the kiss of peace from them, ate with them, received them in his house often, gave them things to eat, received a pair of tongs [*or* shears] from them, gave them a cape, a shirt, a tunic, a quart of grain. He escorted Waldensians to heretics to debate, he kept heretics company on Easter Day, he was their depositary, and he heard the preaching of the heretics many times. He believed they were good men, and if he died he wanted to die in their hands. He adored them so many times that he cannot remember.

He will stay in Constantinople for 3 years. Regarding cross and travel, just as the others, and he will maintain a pauper for as long as he lives.

... /201r/ Raymond of Péreille knowingly read in a book of the heretics.

He will go to Le Puy.

... From Montcuq, AD 1241 /214r/ in Lent

/215r/ Arnold Vital saw Waldensians four or five times, and he made sandals for some Waldensian, and he gave them 10 shillings.

The same as the previous one.

... /217r/ Peter of Penne saw heretics many times and in many places, and he ate and drank with heretics many times, and he sent heretics bread and fruit and other things. And he believed they were good men and that one could be saved in their sect. And he ate bread blessed by heretics. He said also that the routier [= *bandit*] Lobaix could do as much in heaven as Martin of Tours, and he said this to clergymen who were buying wax in honour of the blessed Martin. He believed no-one could take an oath or kill without sin. Item, he disbelieved the sacraments of the Church, and he believed there was no Church but the heretical Church, and no-one was saved in the Roman Church but everyone was saved in /217v/ the heretical Church. Item, he said that God does not destroy what He has done, nor will it pass away. He also said that he adored heretics, which he had earlier denied, on oath and when questioned. Item, he said that he himself had preached heresies many times to other men.

He will stay in Constantinople for 7 years. Regarding cross and travel, just as the others.

… /219r/ … N'Algartz of Villar rented her house to Waldensian women, and they were there for two years. And she gave them things of hers, and believed they were good women.

She is to go to Le Puy, St-Gilles, St James, St Thomas of Canterbury.

Bertrand of La Roque of Montcuq received William of Caussade and his brother G., heretics, in his house. And he also received another heretic with them in his house. And he saw heretics in the house of Arnold of Primes, and adored them there.

Item, he sent heretics to the house of Vigouroux, and he saw them there. Item, he saw heretics /219v/ at Paris.[48] Item, he saw heretics, namely Vigouroux and his companion at Moissac, and the said Vigouroux asked him for escort. Item, he committed all the things that have been said against him <in others' testimony> in the domain of Mercuès, and in all the other places as specified above.

He will stay in Constantinople for 3 years, and provide for a pauper as long as he lives. Regarding cross and travel, just as the others.

Sebilia of Montcuq saw heretics often and in various places, and adored them often, and escorted a certain person to heretics.

Francis Clergue [*or* the clerk] was present at a debate between heretics and Waldensians.

Item, he escorted Vigouroux and his companion, heretic, from the manse of Lacoste to the manse of Prignac. And he sent the same heretics bread and wine and apples and a new pot, on the instructions of Guilhamassa. Item, he gave the same heretics things to eat /220r/ from his own stuff, in the said manse. Item, he saw heretics in the house of Bernard of Cazelles. Item, he received a certain book from the heretic Vigouroux, and a certain sum of money which he passed on to William of *Baussan* on the instructions of the said heretic. Item, he sent greetings to the said Vigouroux via a certain lady. Item, he sent the said heretics at the manse of Prignac a blanket and two sheets. Item, he sent greetings to the same heretic via a certain woman, since the same heretics had sent greetings to him beforehand. Item, he saw other heretics, and gave them things to eat. Item, he saw Waldensians preaching publicly in the *castrum* of Montcuq. Item, he believed the heretics were good men. Item, he did not come during the period of Grace.

48 There are several places called Paris in Languedoc.

… /222v/ … Na Sauriz, wife of Bertrand de Montcuq, saw Waldensians, and heard their preaching, and <one of them> taught her some prayers, so she says.

She will go to St James.

N'Aymara of Montlauzun saw heretics and heard their preaching. She said also that she gave Waldensians wine and wood and flour, and believed they were good women.

She will go to Le Puy, St-Gilles, St James, San Salvador, and provide for a pauper for a year.

Gaillarda of Lagarde said she had given some of her things to Waldensian women, and believed they were good women.

She will go to Le Puy, St-Gilles and St James.

Guillelma of Labarthe saw Waldensians and gave them things of hers, and heard their preaching, and believed /223r/ that they were good women.[49] And she heard from them that a man ought not to take an oath, nor kill; and she believed this was good.

She will go to Le Puy, St-Gilles, and St James and San Salvador.

Stephen of Roquefort received Waldensians in his house, and gave them things of his, and heard their preaching, and believed they were good men.

The same as the previous one.

William Bernard d'En Arces said that at some time he believed that the good God did not make visible things. Item, he said that at some time he believed the body of Christ was not the body of Christ [*sic*],[50] and that no-one could know his wife <sexually> without sin. He also said that Guillemassa taught him all of the aforesaid errors. He also said he had seen a heretic.

He will stay in Constantinople for a period of 2 years. Regarding cross and travel, just as the others.

49 See P. Biller, 'The preaching of the Waldensian Sisters', in P. Biller, *The Waldenses, 1170–1530* (Aldershot, 2001), VIII.

50 Perhaps: 'what appeared to be Christ's body was not really a body', or 'that the consecrated Host was not really Christ's body'.

... /224r/ Alazaisia, En Guillemassa's maidservant, saw up to 20 heretics at various times in En Guillemassa's house, and she prepared food for them and served it to them.

She also said that she loved the Waldensians very much, and heard their preaching, and believed they were good men, and gave them some of her things.

She will go to Le Puy, St-Gilles, St James, St-Denis, St Thomas, and wear a cross in front for a year.

... /225v/ ... The Cahorsin[51] Rigald saw debates of the heretics and Waldensians.

The same as the previous people.

... /226r/ ... Arnold of Peyre saw heretics often. At the request of William of Caussade, heretic, he accompanied the sister of the said heretic and his niece to Cremona, and he believes that they made themselves heretics. And he invited another person to see /226v/ heretics, and with their money he bought for them and carried to them two ells of linen cloth.

He will go to Le Puy, St-Gilles, St-Denis, St James, St Thomas.

.../227v/ ... From Beaucaire

William of *Frussenet* said at some time that God did not make man, nor bread, nor wine, nor grain, but the 'wantonness of the original earth'.[52]

He will go to Le Puy, St-Gilles, St James, San Salvador.

William of Moulin said that when women came to his mill and said that God and the blessed Martin made the mill go well, he replied that he himself was the St William who makes and had made the mill <work>.

He will go to St James.

51 Here meaning from Cahors rather than usurer.

52 This is in the vernacular in the record – putaria de la terra ogerina [*perhaps* origina]. Compare the formulation in *Inquisitors and Heretics*, pp. 232–3: pinguedo terrae, quam ipse vocabat 'putiam', dabat bladum (the fertility of the earth, which he called 'wantonness', gave the corn).

/228r/ William of St-Michel bought cameline cloth from heretics. Item he saw heretics twice. Item, he said that he believed that the Waldensians were good men. Item, he said that he was a believer of the Waldensians. Item, he gave a certain Waldensian some boots.

He will go to Le Puy, St-Gilles and St James.

Ostaca went to a certain heretic who had asked him to, and he was with him for five days, and ate with him, and stayed with him in a certain house, and heard their preaching and adored them, and received from the same heretic 20 shillings which he gave him. Item, he saw heretics elsewhere, and escorted a certain heretic and adored him. Item, he saw heretics elsewhere. Item, he said that William of Caussade, the heretic, sent greetings via him to Francis Clergue [*or* the clerk].

Bernarda Fabrissa rented a certain /228v/ house to Waldensians, and they were there for a year. Item, she said that the same Waldensian women came to a certain house where she was staying, and vice versa. And they taught her that one should not take an oath or lie. Item, she said that she believed they were good men,[53] and she often gave the Waldensians bread or wine.

Crosses for two years.

Peter Vital of Val Tauran said that Geoffrey of Caussade sent him to his brother William of Caussade, the heretic, to fetch him. And the said witness went to him and told him to go. And the said heretic said he could not come at that time. And coming to Montcuq the said witness found the heretic there, with another one.

He will go to Le Puy, St-Gilles and St James.

William of Burc saw heretics and adored them three or/229r/ four times, and heard their sermons often, and he wanted to give them 2 pence, and they were unwilling to take them. And he received from the hands of the heretics two quires containing their errors, which he kept for 8 days and more, and they pleased him. He said, however, that he returned to a heretic [*corr.:* someone] who later made himself a heretic; and he lent him four gold coins for three months, which he later got back. Item, he saw heretics and heard their preaching.

From Montauban, AD 1241 in the week before Ascension Sunday

53 Note switch of gender in the formula about belief.

Bernard Capel saw the heretics many times and in many places, and heard their preachings, and bent his knees before the heretics, dragged along /229v/ by someone <pulling him> by his clothes, so he said. Item he saw Waldensians two or three times.

He will go to Le Puy, St-Gilles, St James, St-Denis, San Salvador and St Thomas.

... /232v/ Peter Lanes the Elder said that he saw Waldensians, and gave them alms. And at her death his wife gave herself to the Waldensians and was buried in their cemetery. However he was absent, so he said. And he saw Waldensians elsewhere.

He will go to Le Puy, St-Gilles and St James.

... /233v/ Pons of Vacaresse said that he saw heretics and spoke with them. Item, during a certain illness he was hereticated by heretics, and in his will he bequeathed them a hundred gold coins, which he did not pay, so he said.

He will stay in Constantinople for 2 years. Regarding cross and travel, just as the others.

Raymond Toset said that he often saw heretics and adored them.

Item, he got counsel from some Waldensian /234r/ for an illness in his hand.

He will stay for a year in Constantinople. Regarding cross and travel, just as the others.

John Fournier Faure said that in his illness he had some Waldensian as a doctor. Item, he heard the preaching of the Waldensians many times, and they often gave him things to eat. And he was present at the Waldensians' supper, and ate bread and fish blessed by the Waldensians, and drank their wine.[54] Item, he believed the Waldensians were good men.

Item, he said that he had received penance for these things from Brother William of La Cordelle.[55]

He will go to Le Puy, St-Gilles, St James, St Thomas.

54 On the Waldensians' supper, see E. Cameron, *Waldenses: Rejections of Holy Church in Medieval Europe* (Oxford, 2000), p. 77; Feuchter, *Ketzer*, pp. 228–9.

55 William of La Cordelle was a Franciscan friar, papal penitentiary and crusade preacher in northern France; see Feuchter, *Ketzer*, pp. 326–30.

Raymond Carbonel gave Waldensians 4 pence.

He will go to Le Puy, St-Gilles.

Raymond Carbonel saw the Waldensians many times and in various places, and he induced his brother to pay /234v/ 200 shillings to the Waldensians that had been bequeathed to them. Item, he was present at a debate of the Waldensians and the heretics.

Item, he was present at the Waldensians' supper, and ate bread and fish blessed by them, and drank their wine, and heard their preaching.

He will to go to Le Puy, St-Gilles, St James, St-Denis, St Thomas.

James Carbonel said that he had frequently gone to the schools of the Waldensians and read with them. Item, he was present at a disputation of Waldensians and heretics, and ate bread and fish blessed by them, drank their wine, and he was then 12 years old or thereabouts. And he believed the Waldensians were good men up until the time that the Church condemned them.

He will go to Le Puy, St-Gilles, St James and St-Denis.

... /240v/ Guillelma of Sapiac stayed with a certain woman heretic, her aunt, with whom she was raised for some years. And she saw heretics and adored them so many times that she cannot recall. And after she had been reconciled by the Bishop of Cahors, afterwards she saw heretics and adored them and heard their preaching. Item, afterwards she saw elsewhere Peter Abit, heretic, and his companion. Item, she and her husband received Joanna of Avignonet and her companion, women heretics, in her house and adored them often. And she received other heretics in her house, whom she adored often, and she often heard their preaching there. Item, when they wanted them the heretics received the goods of her house. Item, she believed the heretics were good men, and she believed in their faith, and she received the Peace from the women heretics. Item, she often ate bread 'signed' by the heretics.[56] Item, when she was a young girl, she was a vested heretic for 2 years and more.

She will go to Le Puy, St-Gilles, St James, San Salvador, St-Denis, St Thomas and lastly to Rome, and she will wear a cross for 7 years.

Fabressa of Sapiac saw heretics, and adored them, and heard their preaching, and received some /241v/ women heretics in her house,

56 The 'sign' made by heretics when blessing bread is not spelled out.

who were there for many days, and she ate with them at the same table. Item, she sent the heretics bread.

She will go to Le Puy, St-Gilles, St James, St Thomas, and wear a cross for a year.

The Lady of Coutès saw Waldensians preaching publicly, and gave them alms, and went to the house in which they were living, and heard their preaching, and went to them many times on behalf of a certain ill man. Item, on Good Friday she went to the Waldensians twice, and heard their preaching, and she confessed her sins to some Waldensian, and received penance from the Waldensians. Item, she believed they were good men. Item, she saw heretics and ate cherries with them; and it was said that they had been reconciled. Item, she saw many heretics elsewhere. Item, she ate bread 'signed' by the Waldensians.

/242r/ As the previous, except for the cross.

Geralda, daughter of the said Lady, went to the Waldensians often for the sake of her ill son, and gave them alms of bread and wine. Item, she went once on Good Friday to the house of the Waldensians, and heard their preaching. Item, she heard the preaching of the Waldensians in her house, and escorted them to a certain other house, and heard their preaching. Item, some women heretics sent her rissoles and she ate them. Item she ate, as she believes, some bread signed by Waldensians, and she heard their preaching.

As above.

William Martin saw heretics and heard their preaching. Item, he believed at some time that the heretics were good men.

He will go to Le Puy, St-Gilles, St James, St-Denis.

Bernard Remon saw Waldensians and /242v/ heard their preaching, and he believed they were good men. Item, he went to the heretics, wishing to test who was better, the Waldensians or the heretics, and there he heard the preaching of the heretics. Item, he spoke with heretics elsewhere and heard their preaching. Item, he adored them, after he had confessed some of the aforesaid things to Brother William of Belvès [*or* Belvèse, Belvèze].[57] Item, he escorted his sister, a heretic,

57 Otherwise unknown friar. Duvernoy, *Inquisition en Quercy*, p. 147, suggests Beauvais.

from Toulouse to Montauban, and escorted his sister and other women heretics to a certain manse. Item, he went to her, and brought them fish, and drank with them. Item, he asked a certain woman to receive these women heretics in her manse, which she did, and he promised her 50 shillings. Item, another time he ate with the heretics. Item, he made a gift to the said heretics, and heard their preaching and ate with them. Item, he carried fruit to the heretics. /243r/ Item, he made a tunic and a cape for his sister, the heretic. Item, he saw heretics. Item, he believed they were good men and had a good faith. And he ate bread 'signed' by them. Item, he debated with someone about the faith of the heretics and the Waldensians, and he supported the faith of the heretics.

He will stay in Constantinople for 3 years. Regarding cross and travel, as the others.

… /245r/ Arnold Folcautz saw Waldensians in his house many times, and they had the care of his brother in his illness and of himself and his brother's wife <in their illnesses>, and he gave them bread and wine, and the Waldensians frequently had alms from his house and his brother's house. Item, <he said> that he believed they were good men. He saw heretics and spoke with them, and heard from them expositions of authorities.[58] /245v/ And he received heretics in his house, who slept there and ate in his house, and he heard their admonitions. Item, he saw other heretics, and spoke with them. And, when asked by another heretic, he promised his service to one of them. And he often heard their admonitions.

…/249r/ Pons of La Jonquière saw Waldensians, and heard their preaching, and was present at the supper of the Waldensians, and ate bread and fish blessed by them.

Item, he said that he often /249v/ went to the Waldensians and to <their> hospital, and there often he heard their preaching, and gave them alms. And he believed they were good men, and that a man could be saved in their faith.

He will go to Le Puy, St-Gilles, St James, San Salvador, St-Denis.

… /257v/ … Peter Saliners saw heretics twice, and heard their preaching. And the heretics taught him <how to> adore heretics. And they gave him the 'Our Father' of the heretics, written. Item, he saw heretics

58 'Authorities' = texts from the Bible, possibly also writings of the Fathers.

elsewhere, and heard their preaching, and adored /258r/ them. Item, he saw heretics elsewhere. Item, he said he believed the heretics were good men.

The same as the previous one.

… /260r/ Stephen Gras saw the Waldensians many times, and some Waldensian taught him how to make a loaf. Item, he saw the Waldensians twice, and heard their preaching.

He will go to Le Puy, St-Gilles, St James.

… /253r/ Arnold Rufet saw heretics in two places, and ate with them, and adored them. Item, he saw heretics many times at Milan. Item, he saw four heretics elsewhere, and he ate with them. Item, he saw heretics elsewhere. Item, he said he saw heretics often and in various places.

He will stay in Constantinople for 2 years. Regarding cross and travel, just as the others.

William of Brouil saw Waldensians and heard their preaching. Item, he saw heretics elsewhere, and he was at a discussion about some will in the presence of Waldensians.

Item, he saw heretics, and heard their preaching, and he debated with them about the creation. Item, he saw heretics.

He will go to Le Puy, St-/263v/ Gilles, St James, St-Denis.

… /269v/ Bertrand Bodo saw Waldensians, and heard the sermon of some Waldensian woman. Item, he often heard the preaching of the Waldensians in the squares at Montauban. Item, when they came to him he knew they were rejected by the Church. Item, a certain Waldensian came to his house.

He will go to Le Puy, /270r/ St-Gilles, St James.

… /274r/ When he was a boy, Pons Seguin dined with the Waldensians, and heard their preaching. Item, he saw them elsewhere, and heard their preaching, and he was with the Waldensians so many times that he does not know the number, and he gave them bread and wine many times, and he believed they were good men. Item, sometimes he read in the books of the Waldensians. Item, he received a certain [*blank*] in his house, and there … [*gap in manuscript*].

He will go to Le Puy, St-Gilles, St James, San Salvador, St Thomas.

… /275v/ … Bernard of *Valcel* handed over to the Waldensians a quarter of grain his brother had bequeathed them in his will.

He will go to Le Puy, St-Gilles.

… /280r/ … William Cabat went to see the heretics to see if they were as bad as was said, so he said. Item, he saw four heretics elsewhere, and he greeted them, and he could not talk with them because they were eating.

He will go to St James.

… /282v/ … From Moissac. AD 1241, in the week of the Lord's Ascension

… /286v/ William Augier saw two /287r/ heretics in some cellar. Item, he said the heretics had a good law.[59]

He will go to Le Puy, St-Gilles, St James.

… /290r/ Bernard Stephen saw heretics, and he prayed with them on bended knees and beating his breast. Item, he saw heretics in three places at Cremona. Item, he saw heretics and gave them 12 pence. Item, he saw heretics in three places elsewhere, and drank with them. Item, he saw heretics elsewhere, and in the heretics' house he ate their food. Item, he gave some heretic 3 shillings for boots.

He will stay in Constantinople for a year.

… /295v/ … Ramunda, wife of Bernard of Quercy, saw heretics. Item, she saw heretics elsewhere and sat with them. Item, without being aware of it [nesciens] she was consolated by heretics, according to what bystanders told her.[60]

… /300r/ William of Barbe saw heretics, and drank with them, saying 'Bless'. Item, he saw heretics /300v/ there, and saw there someone reading the Apocalypse. Item, he escorted heretics as far as Port <de la Montagne sur G>aronne.[61]

59 'Law' here is broadly equivalent to the modern meaning of 'religion'.

60 Presumably on her sickbed, being thought likely to die.

61 Conjectural reading.

He will go to Le Puy, St-Gilles, St James, San Salvador.

… /301r/ Ramon Guiraud saw heretics when he was a boy, and he was /301v/ with them for a large part of the day and night. And he heard someone reading the books of the heretics, and the heretics expounding.

He will go to St James.

… /303v/ … Raymond of Gaillard saw heretics, and he escorted them by boat to Montauban. Item, he saw heretics elsewhere. Item, he saw heretics elsewhere. Item, another time, summoned by some heretic he went to him, and on behalf of that heretic took some letters to some <other> heretic. Item, asked by someone, he went to Villemur to see some heretic, and he then stayed with the heretics for a long time. /304r/ Item, he adored heretics, and he gave heretics <sums ranging> from 12 pence to 2 shillings.

Item, elsewhere he gave someone 2 Provence shillings to support the work of the heretics.

He will stay in Constantinople for 2 years. Regarding cross and travel, just as the others.

Raymond of Bénac saw heretics in a certain house. Item, when some women heretics were captured, someone who had heretics in his house, fearing for himself, told him to go to his house and tell someone who was there that the Good Men who were in his house should go up in the tower; which he did. Item, he ate with heretics.

He will go to Le Puy, St-Gilles, St James.

Arnold del Huc saw heretics in a certain house. Item, another time he saw heretics, and gave them 10 Morlaàs shillings

The same /304v/ as the previous person.

Raymond of La Garde saw heretics and adored them. Item, he saw heretics elsewhere, and heard their preaching, and adored them. Item, he saw heretics in the same place, and adored them. Item, heretics were in his cellar for part of one night. Item, another time he went to the heretics, and adored them, and spoke with them. Item, he saw heretics in his house and his brother's. Item, he saw heretics elsewhere, and adored them. Item, he said that there was a time when he believed that all Cistercians and all the religious [*members of religious orders*] were heretics.

He will go to Constantinople for 3 years. Regarding crosses and travel, just as the others.

Humbert Escudier saw heretics in a certain house. Item, another time he saw heretics, and brought /305r/ them fish twice, on behalf of someone. Item, he saw heretics elsewhere, and he brought them grapes on behalf of someone.

He will go to Le Puy, St-Gilles, St James, San Salvador.

Raymond of Loc took a certain heretic in his boat as far as Villemur, not knowing he was a heretic; but he knew afterwards when he got the fare. Item, another time he took two heretics to Montauban, and when they got into the boat he did not know they were heretics, but afterwards, when they were in the boat, he did. He did the same another time, with other heretics whom he took to Agen.

He will go to Le Puy, St-Gilles, St James.

Na Gassacs of La Motte [*or* Lamothe, La Mothe] received a certain woman heretic in her house, and served her, and blessed her stay in her husband's house. Item, she saw heretics in the house of her husband, Arnold of La Motte, and they were there for two days. Item, she saw heretics in the same place often, at various times. Item, she adored heretics in the same place. Item, another time she saw and adored heretics in the same place. Item, she saw heretics elsewhere, twice, and she adored them twice, and heard their preaching. Item, she heard the preaching of the heretics many times, and adored them often in her house and in other houses, but she does not remember the number of times. Item, she gave them a seam [*measure*] of wine.

She will go to Le Puy, St-Gilles, St James, San Salvador, St-Denis, St Thomas, and wear a cross for 2 years.

Garcia of the Bonafous[62] often said in the hearing of other men that nobody could be saved except with the heretics. Item, he heard their preaching many times. Item, /306r/ when someone told him that he [*the someone*] would willingly confess his sins to the brothers Preacher

62 Family name, not a place name.

or brothers Minor if he could find them, he replied that if he spoke with one of the Good Men he could be saved.

He will go to Le Puy, St-Gilles, St James.

From Montpezat, AD 1241, during Lent

… /307r/ Ramunda of Mazérac, Prioress of La Lécune,[63] was in the heretic habit[64] for four or five years. Item, she asked the nuns if the Blessed Virgin had breast-fed her son just as carnally and had suffered in childbirth just as other women. Look in the book[65] for the other things which they depose against her.

She is to leave the place, and enter a stricter monastery.

From Almont, the year as above, in Lent

… /309v/ Bernarda of Rô was a perfected heretic [heretica perfecta] for seven years.

She will go to Le Puy, St-Gilles, St James, St-Denis, St Thomas, and <wear> a cross for 5 years.

… /310v/ Arnold of La Roque, priest, went to heretics in a certain vineyard, and read in a book of the heretics, and ate pears with them.

He will go to St James, and to Rome, with our letters, and he is to be suspended from office.

From Castelnau d'Hélène[66] Item, in the year as above, in Lent

Petrona of *Prestis* said she received Waldensians in her house many times, who slept there, and ate and drank, and she believed they were good men, and often gave them things of hers, and heard their preach-

63 Augustinian Priory at St-Paul de Loubressac.

64 The heretics' religious 'habit', i.e. clothing. See Doc. 5 §13.

65 No longer extant register of depositions.

66 Modern Castelnau-Montratier.

ing. She said, however, that she was absolved by the archdeacon on the instructions /311r/ of the bishop.

She will go to Le Puy, St-Gilles, St James, St-Denis, St Thomas.

William of Lamothe [*or* La Mothe, La Motte] saw heretics many times and in various places. He said also that a certain heretic took care of him while he was ill.

He will go to Le Puy, St-Gilles, St James, San Salvador, and to maintain a poor man so long as he lives.

Ademar Raymond often saw heretics, and heard their preaching, and he received in deposit [*i.e. for safe-keeping*] 15 gold pieces from some heretic. Item, when he held Belcastel, next to Lavaur, from the late Count of Toulouse, he provided for two heretics there for three years.

He will go to Le Puy, St-Gilles, St James, St-Denis, St Thomas, and to maintain a poor man for as long as he lives.

... /311v/ Bigordana saw heretics, and heard their preaching, and adored them, and on somone's instructions gave them bread and wine and fish. And she adored heretics as often as she saw them. She also said she saw two women heretics, to whom she gave thread from which they made two headbands. Item, she took in two men in her house one night, with the appearance of pilgrims, and in the morning when leaving they told her they were heretics. She also said that whenever nasty things were said about the heretics she defended them, and she loved the heretics.

She will go to Le Puy, St-Gilles, St James, San Salvador, St Thomas.

43. MARQUESA THE SPY, 1243

From a family deeply implicated in heresy, Marquesa came to work as a spy, and from her depositions we gain a sense of how an inquisitor could infiltrate communities of believers. Her village of Pauligne is about 30 km south-west of Carcassonne, near Limoux. Translated from Doat 23 fols 94r–99v. We include folio numbers thus: /94v/.

In the year as above, 7 days before the calends of September [26 August 1243], Marquesa, wife of the late Bertrand of Prouille, formerly of Fanjeaux, now of Pauligne, required to tell the truth about herself and others, living and dead, on the accusation of heresy and Waldensianism, was sworn in as a witness.

She said that when Augeric Isarn, her brother, was ill at Fanjeaux in the house of the same witness's sister, Juliana (and <the house of> her son Aimeric, a sergeant) – ill with the illness from which he died – the same witness saw that Bega of Fanjeaux, a knight, and William of L'Île and Galhard of Festes, knights, and Arnold of Ou, came into the aforesaid house to see /94v/ this ill man. And each one of them individually preached at and counselled this ill man to render himself to the good men, that is to say, to the heretics, because they were good men, and holy, and gave salvation, and no-one could be saved without them. And since they said and insisted that in all ways he should render himself to the heretics, the ill man gave assent to their will and demand, promising that he would render himself to the heretics when they were brought to him. When they heard this the aforesaid knights left the house, and the following night Bega of Fanjeaux and William of L'Île and Gallard and Jordan Picarella came back again to the aforesaid house, armoured [muniti] and wearing swords, doublets and iron helmets. And after them there came into the aforesaid house Peter Marcel and Arnold d'Oeuf, and they brought in Bertrand /95r/ Martin and his companion, heretic, to consolate the ill man. And they consolated and received the ill man in this way. First, the same ill man, on the petition of the heretics, rendered himself to God, and to the Gospel, and to the Good Men. And he promised that henceforth he would not eat meats, or eggs, or cheese, or anything fatty, apart from oil and fish; he would not swear or lie, or indulge in any lust, for the whole time of his life, nor would he desert the sect through fear of death by fire or water, or any other kind of death. Then he said the prayer, that is, the 'Our Father', according to the rite of the heretics. Afterwards the heretics placed their hands and a book on the head of the ill man, and read. And they gave him the Peace, and they prayed to the Lord, making many bows and genuflections. And there were present at this *consolamentum* the same witness, and the same witness's sister Juliana (wife of Peter Baudriga /95v/ of Lasbordes), and Jordan of Roquefort, the same witness's son, and Aymeric the sergeant, nephew of the same witness, and the aforesaid knights, and Peter Marcel, and Arnold Oeuf, and Aladairia Oliba (wife of Arnold Oliba). And there after the *consolamentum* had been done, all of them, both the same witness and the other men and knights, adored these heretics, each person saying on his behalf 'Bless', genuflecting three times before them, and adding, after the last 'Bless', 'Lords, pray to the Lord on our behalf, that he make us good Christian [men] and good Christian [women], and lead us to a good end'. And the heretics replied to each 'Bless', 'May God bless you', and they would add after the last 'Bless', 'Let God be implored, and let him make you good Christian [men] and good Christian [women], and lead you to a good end'. And after the adoration they received the peace from the heretics, in such a fashion that the women received the peace first from the book of the heretics, and then kissed each other, /96r/ each one kissing the other once on the mouth, and similarly the men received the kiss from the heretics, and afterwards kissed each other, each kissing the other on the mouth. She also added that Gallard of Festes was instructing the same witness, and the witness's son, and Aladaicia Oliba, how to adore the heretics, and how to receive the peace. She also said that the aforesaid ill man then bequeathed 400 Melgueil shillings <to the heretics>, in this fashion, that this legacy should be paid to them when his land had been restored to his heirs. <Asked> about the time, <she said> that it was 10 years ago.

Item, she said that the same witness's mother Ermengarde left the *castrum* of Fanjeaux with the [female] heretic Turcha, and she went to Lavelanet, and there she had herself hereticated, and she took on the habit [*religious clothing*] of the heretics. And when the same witness heard this she rushed there to her mother, and brought her back with her to Fanjeaux, and there she abandoned the said sect, and was reconciled by Brother Dominic.[67] Questioned, /96v/ she said that she did

67 St Dominic. The evidence for Dominic's activity in this regard is collated and edited in *Monumenta Diplomatica S. Dominici*, ed. V. J. Koudelka (Rome, 1966), pp. 177–80; he is mentioned again in Doc. 48 below, fols 20v, 160r–v.

not then adore her mother, or other heretics. <Asked> about the time: it was 32 years ago.

Item, she says that she saw Calvet of Bélesta and other heretics living and maintaining in public a house in the *castrum* of Roquefort, and there the same witness often adored these heretics, as said before. She added also that she often saw that Vezian of Roquefort, and Sicard of Roquefort, and the same witness's husband William of Roquefort, and Arnold Corb, lord of the *castrum* of Roquefort, came very often into the house of the heretics, to see them and to hear them; and they would adore them, as said before. She also said that the aforesaid Calvet of Bélesta, heretic, often gave the same witness comfort while she was eating. About about the time: it was before the first coming of the crusaders.

Item, she said she saw Peter Isarn, her sister's husband, who had been made a heretic, /97r/ living with his companion, heretic, at Fanjeaux in his own house, where both lived for almost one year.[68] And there the same witness often saw these heretics, and ate some of the bread which they would bless, and she would say, 'Bless', and the heretics would say, 'May God bless you'. Questioned, she said that the same witness did not adore them. <Asked> about the time: it was 14 years ago.

Item, she says that when Arnold Gros of Pauligne, who lived at Fanjeaux with Peter of Rouzégas, *bailli* of the Count of Toulouse, at Fanjeaux, was ill at Fanjeaux in the Count of Toulouse's Hall – ill with that illness from which he died – the same witness was called by Peter Gros, the said ill man's son, and came into the said hall to see this ill man. And then the aforesaid ill man begged for the heretics to be brought to him to consolate him. And there were there Raymond Sicard, and Peter Raymond Batailler, and Bernard /97v/ of Navarre. And while they were standing there in front of this ill man, Pons Rigaud the younger of Fanjeaux came into the hall, and he brought there before the ill man, in order to consolate him, Raymond Rigaud and his companion, that is to say, a heretic. In truth however they did not consolate the ill man, because he was already dead; but all there – both the same witness and the others – adored these heretics, as said above. And when this had happened the heretics left, with Pons Rigaud, and went on their way. About the time – it was 2 years ago this year, in the last Lent.

68 A not uncommon name; this is not the bishop Peter Isarn, who was executed in 1226.

Item, she says that she saw in Fanjeaux, in the house of Peter Recort, Peter Recort's brother Arnold Recort, and five other heretics, and then the same witness handed over to them fish, fruit and wine, and they adored them, as said above. And there were there Peter Recort, and his wife Guillelma, and William /98r/ Recort, and Raymond Recort, and others whom she does not remember, and there they adored these heretics, as said above. She also added that the same witness came to see these heretics for this reason, because she was an investigator of heretics [exploratrix haereticorum] on behalf of Master Ralph,[69] for whom the same witness sought out these heretics. She did not take them [*arrest them*], although she came into the said house at the time when the aforesaid heretics were there in order to take the heretics <who are> discussed here; for the heretics then hid themselves in some sewer. About the time: it was about 8 years ago.

Item, she says that she saw nine heretics, whose names she does not know, in the mill of Isarn of Fanjeaux of *Rocatud* [*perhaps* Roquetour] by Couelle [*or* Queille]. And there came there similarly, together with the same witness, Chartres of Couelle, who was burnt. And there both the same witness and the aforesaid Chartres adored these heretics, as said above. And there the same witness gave to these heretics /98v/ fish which she had bought with the money of Master Ralph, for whom the same witness was seeking out these heretics. On account of this the same Master Ralph of Narbonne came there and took one of the heretics; the others escaped through a wood. He will get their goods and things, however. <Asked> about the time: it was 8 or 9 years ago.

Item, she says that Pictavin Arveu and William of Palaja of Fanjeaux had escorted the same witness to Miramont to see a heretic there, and when they were there they found in Hugh of Durfort's hall Raymond Mercier and his companion, that is, a heretic, and all there – both the same witness and the others – adored the said heretics, as said above. And there were there Hugh of Durfort, and his wife Richa, who similarly adored these heretics, as said above. She also added that the same witness sought out these heretics /99r/ for Master Ralph; and on this account Master Ralph came to Prouille; however the heretics had gone on their way. <Asked> about the time: it was 10 years ago.

Item, she says that she saw that Auda, mother of Isarn Bernard of Fanjeaux, and her daughter Braida, and Raymonde of St-Germain, mother of Peter of St-Michel-de-Lanès, and Raymonde of Durfort,

69 On Master Ralph, see the introduction to Doc. 49 below.

mother of the mother of Bernard Hugh of Festes, and Guirauda, and Raina her daughter's daughter, and Esclarmonde the mother of Bernard of Festes, and Orbria mother of Gaillard of Festes, and the brothers Roger and William of Festes, and Saura the mother of Amiel of Le Mortier, were ⌜male⌝ heretics and ⌜female⌝ heretics. And Guillelma of Tonneins, mother of William Assalit, and Comdors mother of William of Villeneuve, and her daughter Agnes, and Lombarde, daughter of William Assalit, were ⌜female⌝ heretics, similarly <both> before and after the first coming of the crusaders.

Item, /99v/ she says she saw at Fanjeaux, Lombarde, daughter of Isarn of Montolieu and her companion, ⌜female⌝ heretic, in the house of William Arnold Jubileu; and there were there Auda, wife of William Arnold Jubileu, and Elise wife of William Faure of *Faris*, sisters of this ⌜female⌝ heretic. Questioned, she said that the same witness did not adore these ⌜female⌝ heretics, nor did she see other <women> adoring them. About the time: it was 10 or 12 years ago.

Questioned, she said she was a believer of the heretics from around the age of reason onwards, such that she believed she would be saved if she died in the sect of the heretics.

These things she attested in the presence of Brother Ferrier and Pons Garin,[70] Inquisitors. Witnesses: William Basterius and Bonmancip, clerics, and Peter Grandis.

70 On this inquisitor, see Doc. 38, No. 1.

44. HELIS OF MAZEROLLES, 1243

Helis came from Mazerolles-du-Razès, in the Aude dpt, and was the wife of Arnold of Mazerolles, a knight. Both were from powerful noble families, and most of the people she mentioned were nobles; M. Barber, *The Cathars*, 2nd edn (Harlow, 2013), pp. 42–9, provides a fine short introduction. The deposition of her son, Peter of Mazerolles, is found below (Doc. 48, fols 124r–125v). Translated from Doat 23, fols 162r–180r. We include folio numbers thus: /162v/.

AD 1243, 3 days before the nones of August [3 August] Helis of Mazerolles, wife of the late Arnold of Mazerolles, asked to tell the truth both about herself and others, living and dead, on the charge of heresy and Waldensian<ism>, was sworn in as a witness.

She said she saw that Guilabert of Castres, heretic, used to maintain his house openly at Fanjeaux, with many other heretics. And the same witness went often to the house of the said heretics there. And /162v/ the said heretics preached there. And there were present at this preaching the same witness, and Auda, the same witness's mother, who later was a heretic, and Fays of Fanjeaux wife of the late Peter of the Île [*or* Lahille], and Raymunda wife of the late William of Durfort, and Saura wife of Raymond Amiel, and Raymunda wife of the late Roger Peter, and Endia, mother of Coch of Fanjeaux, who was later a heretic [*i.e. Endia was*], and many others whom she does not remember. And after the preaching the same witness and all the other aforesaid ladies left there and went on their way. Questioned, she said that the same witness did not adore the said heretics, nor genuflected before them, nor did any other woman in the same witness's sight. <Asked> about the time, <she said> that it was 50 years ago.

Item, she said she saw the same witness's late grandmother Guillelma of Tonneins who was a vested heretic. And while she held the said /163r/ sect the same witness saw that the same witness's said grandmother Guillelma with many other female heretics maintained their house openly at Fanjeaux. And the same witness, who was then a girl, often went there to see the said heretic. And then the said heretic often gave the same witness bread, wine, nuts and other fruits. Questioned, she said that the witness neither adored the said heretic nor genuflected before her. About the time: that it was 50 years ago.

Item, she said she saw at Montréal that Bernard Cot of *Fi* and Arnold Guiraud, heretics, maintained their house openly at Montréal with many other heretics. And the other aforesaid heretics often preached there. At which preaching there were present the same witness, and Fabrissa Cata, and Raymonda of Sanches, and Lady Rataria wife of Maur/163v/ of Montréal, and Ermengardis of Rebenty wife of the late Peter of Rebenty, and Berengaria of Villetravers wife of the late Bernard Hugo of Rebenty, and Saurina wife of the late Isarn Garin of Montréal, and his sister Dulcia, and Guirauda Darava of Montréal, and Poncia Rigauda wife of Rigaud of Montréal. And after the preaching the same witness and all the other aforesaid adored the said heretics, each on her own account saying three times, 'Bless' while genuflecting in front of them. And after the last 'Bless' they would add, 'Lords, beg the Lord on behalf of this sinner to make me a good Christian and to lead me to a good end'. And the heretics would reply to each 'Bless', 'May God bless you'. And after the last 'Bless' they would add, 'May God be implored and make you good Christians and lead you to a good end'. And when this had been done the same witness went away from there /164r/ and left the heretics there. About the time: that it was 40 years ago.

Item, she said she saw that the witness's sister-in-law Fabrissa of Mazerolles, heretic, maintained her house openly at Montréal with many other heretics. And the same witness often went there to see the said heretics. And coming there to see the said heretics were Aimeric of Montréal, and Raines of Mazerolles, and the brothers Peter of Mazerolles and Arnold of Mazerolles, and Bertrand of Mailhac the husband of Vesiada, and Bernard of Arzens, and Malpuel, his brother, and Monk [*or* a monk] of Arzens, and Peter Rigaud, and William Rigaud, and the brothers William Peter of *Vilandegut* and Plausso of *Vilandegut* and Gallard of *Vilandegut*, and Raymond Goch of Montréal and his brother-in-law Arnold of Cailhavel. And the same witness, and all the other aforesaid came there often to see the said female heretics. And sometimes /164v/ on the occasions when the witness and all the other aforesaid came, they would eat there with the aforesaid heretics. The aforesaid [female] heretics however did not eat there together with the aforesaid knights. Questioned, she said that sometimes when the same witness was beginning to eat she would say, 'Bless', and likewise at the first drink. However, the aforesaid knights did not say 'Bless' in the same witness's hearing. And the same witness often adored the said heretics there, in the way that has been said. Questioned, she said that the aforesaid others did not adore the said female heretics in the same witness's sight. About the time: that it was 35 years ago and more.

Item, she said she saw that Bernard Cot of *Fi*, heretic, often preached at Montréal in the house which the same heretic maintained in the said *castrum*. And there would come to this preaching the same witness, and Aimeric of Montréal, and Raines of Mazerolles, and Peter of Mazerolles and Arnold of Mazerolles, brothers, /165r/ and Bertrand of *Viallac*, and Bernard of Arzens and his brother Malpuel, and Monk of Arzens [*or* a monk of Arzens], and Peter Rigaud, and William Rigaud, and the brothers William Peter of *Vilaudegut* and Plausso of *Vilaudegut* and Guallard of *Vilaudegut*, and Raymond Gach of Montréal and his brother-in-law[71] Arnold of Cailhavel, and Fabrissa Cata, and Rateria wife of Maur, and Alamanda mother of Bertrand Malpuel, and Adalaicis of Malviès the mother of the same Alamanda, and Ermengaudis of Rebenty, and Guirauda of *Arana*, and Veziada wife of Bertrand of Mailhac, and Adalaicia Cata, and many others she does not remember. And after the preaching the witness, and all the aforesaid, both men and women, adored the said heretics, in the way that has been said. And when this had been done the same witness went away from there and left the said heretics there. About the time: that it was 40 years ago or thereabouts.

Item, she said /165v/ she saw at Montréal that Peter Durant, heretic, together with his companions, heretics, maintained their house openly at Montréal. And the said heretic often preached there. And coming there on various occasions to hear the sermon of the same heretic were the same witness, and Veziada wife of the late Bertrand of Mailhac, and all the other aforesaid men and women who are <written> in the nearest place above. And the same witness and all the other aforesaid adored the said heretics there on these occasions, in the way that has been said. When this was done, the same witness left there and went on her way. About the time: that it was as above.

Item, she said she saw that Arnaud Terrat and his companions, heretics, maintained their house publicly at Montréal; and the same witness often went there to see the said heretics at the same time as Fabrissa Cata, and together with Rateria wife of Maur, and with Alamanda mother/166r/ of Bertrand Malpuel, and with Adalaicis of Malviès, and

71 Ms. has *socius* (companion), probably a mistake for *sororius* (brother-in-law).

with Adalaicis Cata, and with many other ladies of Montréal. And the same witness and all the other aforesaid ladies adored the said heretics there, in the way that has been said. About the time: that it was as above.

Item, she said she saw that Ferranda, and Serona, and Bona Filia, and Romeva and her daughter Pagana, heretics, maintained their houses openly at Montréal. And the same witness often went there to see the said heretics, together with the aforesaid ladies who are written down in the nearest place above. And the same witness and all the other aforesaid ladies often adored the said heretics there, in the way that has been said. About the time: that it was as above.

Item, she said she saw at Gaja<-la-Selve> in the diocese of Toulouse Peter of Bélesta and his companion, heretic. And the same witness often went to see /166v/ the said heretics there. And Aladaicis of Mirepoix, at that time the same witness's damsel [*lady-in-waiting*], went with her to see the said heretics. And the same witness, and the said Aladaicis of Mirepoix, often adored the said heretics there, in the way that has been said. And sometimes the aforesaid heretics lent the same witness 20 shillings, sometimes 10, sometimes more, sometimes less. However, the same witness returned to them all that they had lent to the same witness. About the time: that it was 35 years ago and more.

Item, she said she saw that the same witness's sister-in-law Fabrissa of Mazerolles, while she adhered to the said heretical sect, went to Gaja in the diocese of Toulouse. And the said Fabrissa and her companion, heretic, maintained their house there openly. And the same witness often went to see the said heretic there. And she often adored her, /167r/ in the way that has been said. And the same witness often ate there with the aforesaid heretic and her companions, at one table, <eating> blessed bread and other things placed on the table. And at each kind of food [*at each course*] and at the first drink, when it had just been drunk, the same witness would say, 'Bless'. And the heretics would reply to each 'Bless', 'May God bless you'. And the same witness often adored the said heretics there, in the way that has been said. And there came there to see the said heretics Mir of Camplong, and Roger of La Tour of Laurac, and Stephen of Calmont, and Hugo of Léra, and Peter Roger of Mirepoix the brother of the current Peter Roger,[72] and the same witness's husband Arnold of Mazerolles and his brother Raines of Mazerolles. And all the aforesaid spoke with the aforesaid

72 From 1234 to 1244 co-Lord of Montségur together with Raymond of Péreille.

heretics there. And sometimes they ate there, but not at one table with the aforesaid female heretics. Questioned, she said that /167v/ the aforesaid knights did not in her sight adore the aforesaid heretics there. About the time: that it was 35 years ago.

Item, she said she saw Raymond Imbert, and his companion, heretic, in the house of Peter of Bélesta, heretic, at Gaja in the diocese of Toulouse. And they preached there. And present at this preaching were the same witness, and Bernard of Raissac of Gaja, and Guiraud of Gaja. And there the said heretics 'apparellated' the same witness's sister-in-law Fabrissa, heretic. Present at this *apparellamentum* there were present the same witness and all the other aforesaid. And the same witness and all the other aforesaid adored the said heretics there, in the way that has been said. And they received the Peace from the said heretics, in the way that has been said. And when this had taken place, the same witness left there, and went on her way. About the time: that it was 35 years ago.

Item, she said /168r/ that Raymond Bernard of St-Martin and his companion, heretic, came one day to Gaja to the same witness's house. And they stayed there for a little while. And the same witness, and Guirauda Darava, and the rest of the same witness's household, whose names she does not remember, <were there then>. And the same witness and the said Guirauda Darava adored the said heretics there, in the way that has been said. About the time: that it was 35 years ago.

Item, she said she saw Guilabert of Castres and his companion, heretic, in the house of heretics at Montségur. And the same witness, and the same witness's sister Gaia, and Fabrissa the wife of Bernard of Villeneuve, and Gaussion wife of Pons of Villeneuve <were there>. And the same witness and all the other aforesaid adored the said heretics there, in the manner that has been said. About the time: that it was 34 years ago.

Item, she said /168v/ she saw Raymond of Simorre, and his companion, heretic, in the house of the knight Bernard Garsi at Montolieu. And they preached there. And there were present at this preaching the same witness, and the same witness's sister Gaia, and Constancia the wife of the late Arnold, and the same Constancia's sister Guillelma Garda, and Fabrissa the wife of Bernard Garsi, and Marquesia the wife of the late Peter Roger of Mirepoix the father of the current Peter Roger, and Auda the late wife of Peter Roger of Mirepoix, and Aicelina of Montolieu, and many others whom she does not remember. And after the preaching, the same witness and all the other aforesaid adored the said heretics, in the way that has been said. When this had taken place the same witness went away from there and left the heretics there. About the time: that it was 18 or 20 years ago.

Item, she said she saw Bartholomew of Na Lauressa,[73] and his companion, heretic, in the house of Aicelina of Montolieu at Montolieu. /169r/ And they preached there. And present at this preaching were the same witness, and the same witness's sister Gaia, and Constancia wife of the late Arnold Raymond, and the same Constancia's sister Guillelma Garda, and Fabrissa wife of Bernard Garsi, and Marquesia the wife of the late Peter Roger of Mirepoix the father of the current Peter Roger, and Auda once wife of the current Peter Roger of Mirepoix, and Aicelina of Montolieu. And after the preaching the same witness and all the other aforesaid adored the said heretics, in the way that has been said. When this had been done, they went away from there, and left the said heretics there. About the time: that it was 18 or 20 years ago.

Item, she said she saw Raimunda of Montfort, with three daughters of the same Raimunda, heretic, in the house of Na Femariers at Montolieu. And the same witness, and the same witness's sister Gaia, who went with /169v/ the same witness, spoke with the said heretics. And the same witness, and the same witness's sister Gaia, and Longa Bruna the wife of Peter Raymond of Tonneins, and Marquesia the wife of the late Peter Roger of Mirepoix adored the said heretics there, in the way that has been said. And the aforesaid Femoriers was in the said house with the aforesaid heretics, and she adored the said heretics there, in the way that has been said. When this had been done, the same witness went away from there and left the said heretics. About the time: that it was as above.

Item, she said she saw the same witness's mother Auda, and her companion, heretic, in the house of William Arnold of Arras[74] at Alaigne. And the same witness, and the same witness's sister Gaia, and Marquesia wife of the late Peter Roger of Mirepoix, and Mathelia of Alaigne wife of Roger of Alaigne, and Comdors wife of William Arnold of Arras, and William Arnold of Arras of Alaigne spoke /170r/ with the aforesaid heretics there. And the same witness and all the other aforesaid adored the said female heretics there, in the way that has been said. About the time: that it was 17 years and more ago.

73 Ms: Laurelissa.

74 Perhaps Vieil Arras, in Aude dpt.

Item, she said she saw Raymond Mercier [*or* the Mercer], and his companion, heretic, in the house of William Arnold of Arras at Alaigne. And they preached there. And present there at this preaching were the same witness and the same witness's sister Gaia, and Cecilia the wife of Arnold Raymond, and Bernarda the wife of Bernard of *Capia*, and Marquesia the wife of the late Peter Roger of Mirepoix, and Mathelia of Alaigne, and William Arnold of Arras, and Comdors his wife. And after the preaching the same witness and all the other aforesaid adored the said heretics, in the way that has been said. About the time: that it was 18 years ago.

Item, she said she saw William Bernard of Airoux and his companion, heretic, at Montolieu in the house of Constancia of Montolieu. /170v/ And the said heretic used to preach there sometimes. And coming there to hear the sermon would be the same witness, and Constancia of Montolieu, and Fabrissa wife of Bernard Garsi, and Guillelma of Lagarde, and Marquesia wife of the late Peter Roger of Mirepoix father of the current Peter Roger, and Auda the former wife of the current Peter Roger. And after the preaching the same witness and all the other aforesaid adored the said heretics, in the way that has been said. When this had happened they left there and went on their way. About the time: that it was 18 years ago and more. She added also that she sent a trout to the aforesaid heretics via the same same witness's late son Pons of Mazerolles.

Item, she said she saw that Adalaicis of Aragon,[75] and her daughter Essanta, heretics, maintained their house openly at Montolieu. And the same witness, and Marquesia wife of the late Peter Roger of Mirepoix /171r/ the late father of the current Peter Roger, and Auda the wife of this Peter Roger, and Constancia of Montolieu, and her sister Guillelma of Lagarde, and Fabrissa the wife of Bernard Gaissi, and Aicelina of Montolieu[76] often came there to see the said heretics. Questioned, she said the same witness did not adore the said heretics, nor did others in the same witness's sight. About the time: that it was as above.

Item, she said she saw Arnold of Verfeil and his companion, heretic, at Montolieu in the house of Montolieu. And they preached there. And there were present at this preaching the same witness, and Constancia of Montolieu, and Aicelina of Montolieu, and Guillelma Garda, and

75 Either the Aragon in the Aude dpt or the one in the dpt of Haute-Garonne; not the Iberian kingdom.

76 Ms. here mistakenly has 'questioned'.

Adalaicis of Falgous, heretic, and Fabrissa the wife of Bernard Garsi, and the said Fabrissa's father Arnold of Aragon, and Montolieu of Montolieu, and Longabruna wife of Peter Raymond of Tonneins. And after the preaching the same witness and all the other aforesaid adored /171v/ the said heretics, in the way that has been said. And when this had been done the same witness went away from there, and left the said heretics in the said house. About the time: that it was 18 years ago and more.

Item, she said that she saw Guilabert, and his companion, heretic, in the house of Turcha, heretic, at Fanjeaux. And they preached there. And there were present at this preaching the same witness, and Lady Canaeis of Fanjeaux, and Gensers wife of Peter of St-Michel, and Veziada the wife of Isarn, Bernarda of [*blank*],[77] <and> Longa Bruna wife of Peter Raymond of Tonneins. And after the preaching the same witness and all the other aforesaid adored the said heretics, in the way that has been said. And when this had been done they went away from there, and left the said heretics in the said house. About the time: that it was 18 years <ago> or 20.

Item, she said she saw that the heretic Esclarmunda the mother of Bernard Hugo of Festes, and her companions, female heretics, maintained their house openly /172r/ at Fanjeaux. And the same witness, and Vesiada the wife of Isarn Bernard, and the same witness's sister Gaia, often went there to see the said heretics. And the same witness, and the other aforesaid ladies, adored the said heretics there, in the way that has been said. And when this had been done the same witness, and the other aforesaid ladies, went away from there and left the said heretics in the said house. About the time: that it was as above.

Item, she said she saw at Fanjeaux, in the house of Gallard of Festes, Orbria the mother of the said Gallard, and her companion, a female heretic. And the same witness often, and the same witness's sister Gaia, and Veziada the wife of Isarn Bernard, and Gensers the wife of Peter of St-Michel, and Gallard the wife of Raymond Garsias, and Lady Cavaers, went to see the said heretics there. And they would speak with them. And the same witness and all the other aforesaid ladies /172v/ often adored the said heretics there, in the way that has been said. And when this had been done the same witness and all the other aforesaid ladies went away from there, and left the said heretics there. About the time: that it was 18 years ago, or 20.

77 Probably the Bernarda of Belmont who appears below.

Item, she said she saw at Fanjeaux that Guilabert of Castres, heretic, maintained his house openly there. And the same witness often went there to see the said heretic. And the aforesaid heretic sometimes preached there. And there were present at this preaching the same witness, and Veziada the wife of Isarn Bernard of [*blank*], <and> Gensers wife of Peter of St-Michel, and the same witness's sister Gaia, and Gallarda the wife of Raymond Garsias, and Lady Cavaers of Fanjeaux, and Bernarda of Belmont, and Longa Bruna wife of Peter Raymond of Tonneins, and many others whom she does not remember. And after the preaching the same witness and all the other aforesaid /173r/ adored the said heretics, in the way that has been said. And when this had happened they went away from there and left the said heretics there. About the time: that it was 18 years ago. She also added that she sent an eel to the aforesaid heretic Guilabert of Castres via the same witness's messenger Peter John.

Item, she said she saw Raimunda of Cuq and her companion, heretics, near Gaja. And the same witness, and Guillelma of Belpech – at that time the same witness's damsel – spoke with the aforesaid heretics there. And then the same witness gave the aforesaid heretics a pound of pepper. And after they had stayed there a little while the aforesaid heretics left there, and went on their way. Questioned, she said that the same witness did not adore the said heretics, nor did others adore them in the same witness's sight. About the time: that it was 6 years ago.

Item, she said that at Gaja in the house of Gallarda Laurentia of Gaja she saw /173v/ two [male] heretics whose names she does not know. And the same witness, and the same witness's daughter-in-law Ermengardis, spoke with the said heretics there. And the aforesaid Gaillarda Laurentia was there. And the same witness and all the other aforesaid adored the said heretics, in the way that has been said there. When this had been done, they went away from there and left the said heretics there. About the time: that it was 3½ years ago.

Item, she said that she saw Bertrand Martin, and his companion, heretic, in a certain meadow outside Gaja. And they preached there. And present at this preaching were the same witness, and Peter of Mazerolles, and Three Measures, knight, who is otherwise called Peter William,[78] and Peter Fort, knights. And after the preaching the same

78 Concerned to precisely identify people in their records, inquisitors sometimes specified aliases and nicknames. See W. L. Wakefield, 'Pseudonyms and nicknames in the inquisitorial documents of the Middle Ages', *Heresis* 13 (1990), 9–22.

witness and all the aforesaid adored the said heretics, in the way that has been said. About the time: that it was 6 years ago.

Item, she said that on another occasion she saw in a certain /174r/ meadow near Gaja Bertrand Martin, and his companion, heretic. And they preached there. And present at this preaching were the same witness, and Fabrissa of Mailhac, and Guirauda Darava, and Pons of La Chapelle and Bernard Laurence, and Guillelma, wife of Pons of La Chapelle, of Gaja. And after the preaching the same witness and all the aforesaid adored the said heretics, in the way that has been said. When this had happened, they left there and went on their way. About the time: that it was 5 or 6 years ago.

Item, she said that she saw at Gaja in the diocese of Toulouse, in the house of Pons of La Chapelle, [...][79] the father of Jordan of Lanta, heretic, and his companion, heretics. And the same witness spoke with the said heretics there. And there came there to see the said heretics Peter of Mazerolles, and his brother Arnold of Mazerolles, and Three /174v/ Measures, knights, and Escout of Roqueville, knight. And the same witness and all the other aforesaid adored the aforesaid heretics there, in the way that has been said. And there were there Pons of La Chapelle, and his wife Guillelma, who adored the said heretics,[80] in the way that has been said. And then the same witness sent the aforesaid heretics there something to eat via Peter Aymeric, at that time squire of Peter of Mazerolles. About the time: that it was 7 years ago.

Item, she said that at Gaja in the house of Pons of La Chapelle she saw Vigouroux of La Bouconne, and his companion, heretic. And they preached there. And present at this preaching were the same witness, and Peter of Mazerolles, and Three Measures, and Bernard of Roqueville, knights, and Bernard the elder of St-Martin and Mir of Camplong, and Peter of Olmes, crossbowman, and Arnaud of Verzeille, and Bernard Laurence, and Pons /175r/ of Calès, and Pons of La Chapelle, and his wife Guillelma, and Raymond Aicart. And after the preaching the same witness and all the other aforesaid adored the said heretics, in the way that has been said. When this had happened the same witness went away from there and left the said heretics there. And then the same witness sent the said heretics bread and wine and apples [*or* fruit]. About the time: that it was 7 years ago and more.

79 No gap in ms., but a name is missing here: William Bernard Unaud.

80 Ms. incorrectly uses female gender – unless a passage has been omitted by mistake.

Item, she said that she saw at Gaja, in the house of Gaillarda Laurencia of Gaja, Peter Polhan, and his companion, heretic.[81] And they preached there. And present at this preaching were the same witness, and the same witness's daughter-in-law Ermengardis the wife of Peter of Mazerolles, and the same witness's daughter-in-law Ermessendis the wife of Arnold of Mazerolles, and Bernard Laurence, and his wife Gallarda, and Raymond Aicart. And after the preaching the same witness and all the aforesaid adored the said heretics, /175v/ in the way that has been said. When this had been done they went away from there and left the said heretics there. About the time: that 3 years will have passed by around the next feast of All Saints.

Item, she said that she saw Bernard of Mayreville, and his companion, heretic, in a certain cottage of Gallarda Laurencia near Gaja. And the same witness, and Ermengardis the wife of Peter of Mazerolles, and Pons of La Chapelle, and his wife Guillelma, and Pons of Calès, and Gaillarda Laurencia, spoke with the said heretics there. And there the same witness and all the other aforesaid adored the said heretics, in the way that has been said. When this had happened they went away from there and left the said heretics in the said house. About the time: that 3 years have elapsed.

Item, she said that she saw Raymond of Montouty, and his companions, heretics, beside the spring of Gaja.[82] And the same witness, and Raymond Aicart, /176r/ and Pons of La Chapelle spoke with the said heretics there. And there the same witness and all the aforesaid adored the said heretics, in the way that has been said. About the time: that it was 6 years ago.

Item, she said that she often saw Peter of Mas and his companion, heretic, in the house of Pons of La Chapelle in Gaja. And the same witness and the same witness's daughter-in-law Ermessendis spoke with the said heretics there. And Pons of La Chapelle's wife Guillelma was in the said house. And there the same witness and all the aforesaid adored the said heretics,[83] in the way that has been said. When this had happened the same witness went away from there, and left the said heretics in the said house. About the time: that it was 5 years ago.

81 Peter Polhan, or Pollan: on this Cathar bishop, see Doc. 1.

82 See introduction to Doc. 41.

83 Ms. mistakenly uses female gender.

Item, she said that she often sent things to eat to the aforesaid heretics at the house of Pons of La Chapelle <and to the house> of Gallard Laurencia via Peter Aimeric.[84] About the time: that was 7 years ago and more.

Item, she said she often saw at Gaja in /176v/ the house of Pons of La Chapelle of Gaja Peter of Mas and his companion, heretic. And sometimes the said heretic would preach. And coming to listen to the sermon would be the same witness, and Pons of La Chapelle, and William Gaubert, and Pons of Calès, and Bernard Laurence, and his wife Gallarda, and Pons of La Chapelle's wife Guillelma, and many others whom she does not remember. And after the preaching and before the preaching the same witness and all the aforesaid adored the said heretics, in the way that has been said. When this had happened, the same witness went away from there, and left the said heretics in the said house. About the time: that it was 7 or 8 years ago and more.

Item, she said she saw in Montolieu in the house of Aicelina of Montolieu Peter Roger and his companion, heretic. And they preached there. Present at their preaching were the same witness, and Fina of Aragon, and /177r/ Saura of Aragon, and Constancia of Montolieu, and her daughter Arnauda, and Guillelma Garda, and Marquesia the wife of Peter Roger of Mirepoix (now dead), and Fabrissa the wife of Bernard Garsi, and Longa Bruna the wife of Peter Raymond of Tonneins, and her sister Alompias, and the same witness's sister Gaja, and Aicelina of Montolieu. And after the preaching the same witness and all the other aforesaid adored the said heretics, in the way that has been said. When this had happened the witness went away from there, and left the said heretics in the said house. About the time: that it was 18 or 20 years ago.

Item, she said she saw at Montréal that the same witness's sister, Braida, heretic, maintained her house openly at Montréal with many other female heretics. And the same witness often went there to see the said heretics. And there used to come there to see the said heretics Pons of Villeneuve, and /177v/ Bernard of Villeneuve, brothers of the said Braida's son-in-law, and Veziada wife of Bertrand of Mailhac, and Fabrissa the wife of Bernard of Villeneuve, and Gaussion the wife of Pons of Villeneuve, and Berengaria of Villetravers, and Guirauda Darava. And the same witness and all the other aforesaid ladies adored the said heretics there on the occasions when they came. Questioned,

84 Ms: P. Raimundum Aicart. Perhaps 'P' was 'per' in the original ms.

she said that her brother Pons of Villeneuve[85] did not adore the said heretics in the the same witness's sight. About the time: that it was 25 years ago or thereabouts.

Item, she said that when the boy Isarn of Aragon, nephew [*or* grandson] of Isarn of Aragon, was ill at Montolieu in the house of Bernard Garsin of Montolieu, ill with that illness from which he died, there came to visit him there William Bernard of Airoux and Bartholomew of Na Lauressa, heretics. They consolated the said ill man in this manner. First, /178r/ the aforesaid heretics asked the said ill man whether he wished to render himself to God and the Gospel. And the said ill man replied that he did. Then, in response to questioning by the said heretics, the said ill man promised that henceforth he would not eat meat or eggs or cheese or anything fatty, except oil and fish. And that he would not swear or lie or engage in any act of lust for the whole length of his life. Nor would he desert the heretical sect through fear of fire or water or any other kind of death. And then the aforesaid heretics placed their hands and a book on the head of the said ill man, and they read. And they made many genuflections in the presence of the said ill man. And they prayed. And there were present at the said *consolamentum* the same witness, and Fabrissa the wife of Bernard Garsi, the said ill man's sister, and Bernard Garsi, and Arnold of Aragon, and /178v/ many others whom she does not remember. When this had been done the aforesaid heretics left there and went on their way. Questioned, she said that the same witness did not adore the said heretics, nor did others in the same witness's sight. Nor did the same witness receive the Peace from the heretics, nor did others in the same witness's sight. About the time: that it was 20 years ago.

Item, she said that <when> Roger Isarn, the same witness's late brother, was ill with the illness from which he died at Fanjeaux, in the house of Gaillard of Festes, she went to see the said ill man. And before the same witness entered the house in which the said ill man was lying the said ill man lost his <power of> speech. And there were present in the house Guilabert of Castres and his companion, heretic, and the same witness's sister Braida, heretic. Questioned, she said that the aforesaid heretics did not receive or consolate the said /179r/ ill man in the same witness's sight. About the time: it was 18 years ago and more.

85 Pons of Villeneuve is described as (i) the brother of the son-in-law of Braida, who is Helis's sister, and (ii) as Helis's brother. Unless there are two of the same name, there is corruption in the text here.

She added also that in the said house there were together with the aforesaid heretics, when the same witness entered, Genser the wife of Peter of St-Michel, and Vesiada wife of Isarn Bernard, and Longa Bruna the wife of Peter Raymond of Tonneins, and Gallarda wife of Raymond Garsias, and Raymond Garsias, and Lady Cavaers, and Isarn Bernard, and many others, up to a hundred. Questioned, she said that the same witness did not adore the said female[86] heretics, nor did others in the same witness's sight. About the time: that it was as above.

Item, she said she saw at Laurac, in the house of Blanche of Laurac,[87] Isarn of Castres and his companion, heretic. And the same witness, and Guillelma of Mireval, and Guillelma of Camplong, and Marcella wife of William of La Tour, and Blanche of Laurac /179v/ who was a heretic <were> there. And the same witness and all the aforesaid[88] adored the said heretics there, in the way that has been said. When this had taken place, they went away from there and left the said heretics in the said house. About the time: that it was 35 years ago and more. Questioned, she said she had sworn before Brother William Arnold[89] and Brother Stephen,[90] Inquisitors, that she would say the full truth about herself and others, and she had not done this. In fact she had knowingly hidden <things> from them, and knowingly perjured herself in front of them. And after the abjuration of error she has often relapsed.

Questioned, she said she was a believer of heretics from the years of discretion onwards – such that she believed that if she died in their sect she would be saved.

She attested these things in the presence of brothers Ferrier and Pons Garin, inquisitors. Witnesses: Brother William Sauci and Brother Raymond Arnold of the Order of Preachers, and Bernard of Vermeils, /180r/ and Bon Mancip, cleric.

86 Probably a mistake; two of the previously noted heretics were male, one female.

87 Widow of Sicard II, co-lord of Montréal, who died c.1200.

88 Ms. mistakenly has male gender.

89 Killed at Avignonet on the night of 28–29 May 1242; two accounts of this are in Docs 46 and 48 fol. 140r–v below. See Doc. 9 §§3–4, Wakefield, *Heresy*, ch. 8, and his translation of William of Pelhisson's chronicle in appendix 3. William was one of the earliest and most active of inquisitors, and traces of his activities – references by a deponent to an earlier confession to William Arnold – are found in a high proportion of the mid-thirteenth-century inquisition registers.

90 Stephen of St-Thibéry OFM, deputed to act alongside William Arnold in 1236; killed with him at Avignonet. On him, see Wakefield, *Heresy*; Douais, *Documents*, I, pp. 144–8.

45. WILLIAM DONADEU OF *ELVES*, 1244

Elves may be Elbes in the Aveyron dpt; but see the sentence on William that follows this deposition, where his alias 'Nebias' is given. The Donadeus were a great merchant family in Cahors, where one Peter Donadeu was a citizen and banker for heretics.[91] Notable in William Donadeu's deposition are the heretics' workshop and three heretics, Sicard Figuiers, Peter Capellan and John of Collet. All three feature in a near-contemporary Occitan poem containing a debate between a Catholic called Izarn and the heretic Sicart Figueiras, which among other things depicts noble female heretics spinning their distaffs while expounding scripture and mentions the inquisitors Ferrier and Bernard of Caux. The poem was edited by P. Meyer, 'Le débat d'Izarn et de Sicart de Figueiras', *Annuaire-Bulletin de la Société de l'Histoire de France* 16 (1879), 233–85, with a modern French translation (265–84); there are extracts in English translation in Léglu, Rist and Taylor, *Cathars*, pp. 208–13. Notable also in Donadeu's deposition are the heretics' journeys to and from northern Italy, and the appearance of the heretic Sicard Lunel, who worked for many years after his conversion as an inquisitor's agent; see on him *Inquisitors and Heretics*, index entry p. 1054. We have translated from Doat 23, fols 209r–217v, emending more often than usual because of the carelessness of the copy. We include folio numbers thus: /209v/.

AD 1244 on the nones of March [3 March], William of *Elves*, who by his own name is called William /209v/ Donadeu of Mazérac in the diocese of Cahors, required to say the truth about himself and others, both living and dead, on the accusation of heresy and Waldensianism, was sworn in as a witness.

He said that he saw Peter of Caussade and Grimald Donadeu, the same witness's brother, and Peter of Camp, heretics, at Najac in the diocese of Rouergue, in the house which the aforesaid heretics publicly maintained there. And then the same witness ate there things which the same heretics gave to the same witness; and after eating the same witness left there and went on his way. <Asked> about the time, <he said it was> 20 years ago.

Item, he said that later he saw the same heretics at Cordes, when they were entering their residence – they lived there publicly, maintaining

91 The deposition is discussed by Taylor, *Quercy*, pp. 139–40, and Feuchter, pp. 305–6 n.191.

a weaving craft workshop. And he saw once, in the workshop of these heretics, William /210r/ of Virac, a knight of Cordes, who was standing there together with these heretics. And then the same witness adored the heretics there, once – saying 'Bless' three times, genuflecting in front of them, adding after the last 'Bless', 'Lords, pray to God for this sinner, that he make me a good Christian and lead me to a good end'; and the heretics would reply to each 'Bless', 'May God bless you', and they would add after the last 'Bless', 'Lords, pray the Lord for this sinner, that he make him a good Christian and lead him to a good end'.[92] He also added that there were then in this workshop Sicard of Figuiers, who was a heretic and was living with other heretics, and Talafer of St-Marcel and Peter of Gironde of Mazérac, who were learning weaving there with these heretics. He also said /210v/ that the same witness twice ate in these heretics' workshop, but not together with these heretics at the same table. About the time: about 20 years ago.

Item, he said that in his house at Mazérac he received Hugh of *Maorle* [*perhaps* Majourals] and his companion, heretic, whom Peter Donadeu, the same witness's brother, brought there. And Ratairon, brother of Bernard of Belfort, and Bernard of Belfort, his brother, knight, and Peter of L'Aile, and Arnold of Lagarrigue, and Raimunda La Do<n>sella [Damzel – *noble lady-in-waiting*] came in there to see these heretics; and there all adored these heretics, as has been said. And the same witness, and Peter Donadeu, the same witness's brother, were there. He also added that the aforesaid heretics then ate in the house of the same witness, and the same witness's aforesaid brother gave them <things> to eat; and the aforesaid heretics /211r/ blessed bread in their manner at the beginning of eating. And they gave the same witness some of the blessed bread, which the same witness ate after the heretics ate. And when the same witness began to eat this blessed bread, he then said 'Bless', just as the heretics taught the same witness to do; and the heretics replied, 'May God bless you'. He also said that the same witness's brother, Peter Donadeu, adored these heretics, as was said above. He added, further, that in the morning of the following day the same witness's brother, Peter Donadeu, and Arnold of Lagarrigue, took the aforesaid heretics from his the witness's house, and went away with them. About the time: it was 16 years ago.

Item, he said that when the same witness came into the *castrum* of Najac, the brothers Peter of Laussedat and Raymond of Laussedat,

92 Ms. has 'me' rather than 'him'.

shoemakers, brought /211v/ the same witness into the house of Hugh of Muret to see heretics. And when they were there, they found, in the house of the aforesaid Hugh of Muret, William of Caussade, and three other heretics with him. And there were there the aforesaid Hugh of Muret together with these heretics, and Hugh Massella, and Raymond of Combelles of Najac, and Raymond of Verdié. And there the same witness and all the others adored these heretics, as has been said. When this had happened, the same witness and the aforesaid brothers, shoemakers, went away from there, and left the aforesaid heretics. About the time: about 16 years ago.

Item, he said that he saw in the manse of Somplessac William of Caussade, and Sicard of Figuiers, and Daide of Laussedat, Bernard Carbonier [*or* the charcoal-maker],[93] and other heretics. And there were there Guiraud of Somplessac, and his wife Petronilla, and their son Guiraud. And immediately the same witness /212r/ left there, and gave the news to Peter Donadeu, the same witness's brother, that heretics had come to the aforesaid manse; and then the same witness's aforesaid brother went to the aforesaid manse, alone, and the same witness stayed behind. About the time: about 8 years ago.

Item, he said that he saw the same heretics in the manse of Lapradelle in the honour [= *administrative area*] of Caussade. And there were there together with these heretics Arnold of Lapradelle, and Arnold and Guiraud and Raymond, sons [*ms:* son] of this Arnold of Lapradelle, and Bertrand of Lagarde, knight of Montalzat, and Peter of Lacombe of this manse, and William of La Séjalié of Caussade, who brought fish to these heretics. And the same witness and William of La Séjalié of Caussade adored the same heretics, as has been said. He also said that the same witness then ate there, but not together with these heretics /212v/ at the same table. And afterwards the same witness left there, and went on his way, and the heretics stayed behind. About the time: that this was 4 years ago.

Item, he said that when the same witness came into the *castrum* of Najac, Peter of Laussedat, shoemaker, told the same witness to go to the *castrum* of Parisot 8 days later, to pick up heretics from there and accompany them, and that he would be well remunerated for this. And after a lot of words the same witness promised to go to the same *castrum* of Parisot. And then, when the aforesaid 8 days had elapsed, the same witness went to the *castrum* of Parisot, and found there, in the house of

93 Perhaps the Bernard Carbonel who appears below.

Sebilia Estiva, William of Caussade, and Aimery of Collet, and Sicard of Figuiers, and other heretics. And there were there Peter of Salles of Parisot, and Sebilia Estiva, and Estiva her daughter. And there the same witness adored /213r/ these heretics, as has been said. And when this had been done the same witness and Donadeu of Gironde, who had come with the same witness and similarly adored the same heretics, picked up the same heretics and brought them away from the aforesaid house, and accompanied them, intending to bring them to the manse of Somplessac. However, while they were on the journey, Guiraud of Caussére, and Raymond and knights from Penne d'Albigeois, and a certain <northern> Frenchman, and Guiraud of *Senesellas* found the witness and the heretics, and they captured the witness and the heretics noted above. About the time: that it was 5 years ago.

Item, he said that <when> the same witness came by chance one day into the house of Matfred Amiel of Penne d'Albigeois, he found there John of Collet[94] and Aimery of Collet, and /213v/ Peter Capellan,[95] heretics, who were standing there and warming themselves by the fire. And there were there Berengaria, mother of Matfred Amiel <and> ⌜*others whose names are missing*⌝. And there the same witness <and the others> adored the same heretics. And when this had been done, the same witness left there, and the heretics stayed behind. About the time: about 4 years ago.

Item, he said that he saw the same heretics twice in the aforesaid house. And there were there Matfred Amiel, and Berengaria his mother; and there the same witness on each occasion adored these heretics, as has been said. About the time: as above.

Item, he said he saw at Penne d'Albigeois in the house of William of Cassagnes, Sicard Lunel, and his companion, heretic<s>. And there came there to see the same heretics William At, the husband.[96] And there were there William of Cassagnes, and his wife Raimunda. /214r/ About the time: as above.

Item, he said that he saw at Caussade, in the house of William of Bouzinac, merchant adventurer,[97] four ⌜female⌝ heretics, whose names

94 'Débat d'Izarn', lines 272, 640: Joan del Colet.

95 'Débat d'Izarn', lines 146, 271, 639: P. Capela.

96 Ms: at maritus. The explanation – 'husband of', with woman's name missing – suggests itself, but runs up against the rarity of identification of a male by marital status.

97 Ms: auenturarii.

he does not know, and there were there William of Bouzinac, and his maidservant, whose name he does not know. About the time: as above.

Item, he said that he saw in the manse of Lagarrigue in the honour of Caussade, Grimald, the same witness's brother, and Arnold his companion, heretic<s>. And there were there Bernard of Lagarrigue, lord of the said manse, and his wife, whose proper name he does not know. And there the same witness adored these heretics, as has been said. About the time: as above.

Item, he said that at the request of William of Caussade, heretic, the same witness and Stephen of Lagarrigue of Najac escorted and accompanied Garsendis and her daughter Guillelma, heretic, during /214v/ Lent, into Lombardy, and they left these ⌜female⌝ heretics in the city of Cremona.[98] And for this the same witness and Stephen of Lagarrigue got 100 Cahors shillings from these heretic women. About the time: it was 15 or 16 years ago.

He also added that when they were on their journey between Susa and Turin they came upon Raymond Bruguier, barber, of Najac, who was coming back from Lombardy; and he spoke to one side with these heretic women. He also said that in the city of Piacenza they were given hospitality by Giovanni Cappelani, citizen of Piacenza, who received these heretics, and the same witness and Stephen of Lagarrigue. And he provided for these female heretics, and for the same witness and all the others on Easter Day.

Item, he said that the same witness's father, /215r/Arnold Donadeu, when he was in his old age, went to the *castrum* of Najac, and there he made himself a heretic, and he finished his days among the heretics. However, the same witness was not present when he received the *consolamentum* from the heretics. About the time: it was 16 years ago.

Item, he said that he saw, in the manse of Somplessac, William of Caussade and Fulconel of Dernaceuillette, and other heretics. And there the aforesaid heretics carried out an *apparellamentum*, which they call a 'service' ⌜servicium⌝. And present at this *apparellamentum* were the same witness, and Peter Donadeu, the same witness's brother. And there both the same witness and Peter Donadeu, the same witness's brother, adored these heretics, as has been said. And after the adoration they received the Peace from these heretics, kissing them twice, on the

98 Emending corrupt text 'et Lombardam ...in civitate Tremonsi' to 'in Lombardiam ... in civitate Cremonensi'.

mouth sideways, then each of them kissing each other in a similar way. About the time: about 4 /215v/ years ago.

He added also that Bernard of Castelnau of St-Cirq came to the same manse, and there hereticated himself. And the same witness saw the same Bernard of Castelnau, made a heretic, in the said manse, together with other heretics, holding and observing the sect of heretical wickedness.

Item, he said that he saw, in the manse of La Lautardié in the honour of Caussade, Sicard Lunel, and Deodat of Aussedat, and Bernard Carbonel, heretics, and two heretic women. And there were there Deodat Lautard, and William Lautard, brothers, and the wives of the said brothers, whose names he does not know. About the time: 6 years ago.

Item, he said that he saw in the manse of Maurimont in the Caussades <area>, William of Caussade and William of Fourques, heretics. And there were there Bernard Hugh, Lord of the manse, and a certain woman who was said to be the niece [*or* grand-daughter] /216r/ of this Bernard Hugh, whose name he does not know. About the time: as above.

Item, he says that he saw at Laguépie, in the house of Bernard Helias, Isarn and his companion, heretic<s>. And there were there Bernard Hoelias, and Esquilada his wife. About the time: it was 10 years ago. He added also that the same witness had gone to the aforesaid house to the same heretics on the instructions of William of Caussade, to announce to these heretics that they should go to the same William of Caussade, heretic, in the area of the Caussades.

Item, he said that he saw on another occasion, in the said manse of Somplessac, William of Caussade, and other heretics, and with them Bernard Helias of Laguépie, who had carried there on his ass the same William Bernard of Caussade, who was ill at the time, according to what the same Bernard /216v/ Helias told and recounted to the same witness. About the time: about 6 years ago.

Item, he said that he saw at Najac, in the house of William the pelterer, Raimunda of Roumagnac, [female] heretic, and her companion. The wife of William the pelterer, the mother of the same [female] heretic, Raimunda of Roumagnac, whose proper name the same witness does not know, was maintaining them there. About the time: it was 10 years ago.

Item, he said that the same witness's brother, Peter Donadeu, handed over to him certain letters on behalf of William of Caussade, heretic, ordering the same witness, on behalf of this heretic, to carry the aforesaid letters to Cahors and deliver them to Peter Donadeu,[99] citizen of Cahors, on behalf of this heretic. And then the same witness carried these letters to Cahors, and delivered them to the aforesaid citizen. He also added that he heard it said often by the same witness's brother/217r/ and by other believers of the heretics, that the aforesaid Peter Donadeu, citizen of Cahors, had an infinite amount of money on deposit by the heretics and their believers. About the time: it was 10 years ago.

Item, he said that the same witness went into the city of Cahors to Brother Peter Seila, Inquisitor, in order to confess, and was required by him on oath to say the whole truth. He knowingly suppressed the truth, however, on many things, and knowingly committed perjury. About the time: it was within the last 3 years.[100]

Item, he said that when the same witness was required on oath <to tell the truth> by some scribe of Brother Bernard of Caux, Inquisitor, at Montpellier, where he was held a prisoner, he knowingly suppressed many things, and he knowingly perjured many things in the confession which he made. About the time: it was within the 9 years before the feast of [... *gap in ms*].

Item, he said and confessed that he was a believer of the heretics /217v/ for 18 years, such that he believed that if he died among them and in their hands and faith he would be saved. And from the time when he confessed to the aforesaid Brother Peter Seila he did not believe in the heretics.

These things he attested in front of Brother Peter Durant,[101] who read all the aforesaid things to him at Lagrasse, in the monastery. Witnesses: Lord Bernard, chaplain of the Lord <Bishop> of Albi, and Raymond Codainh, Bon Mancip, and Guiraud Trepat [*or* Frepat], public notary, who wrote these things.

Appendix: Sentence on William of Elves

[Only a handful of sentences given by John of St-Pierre and Bernard of Caux survive, in a separate manuscript, BnF MS Lat. 9992. Translated from Douais, *Documents*, II, pp. 31–4.]

99 Another of the same name, Peter Donadeu.

100 See Doc. 42 for selections from Peter Seila's penances; William Donadeu of *Elves* is not in the surviving evidence however.

101 Peter Durant [or Durand] OP, Inquisitor in Toulouse region until 1248; see Wakefield, *Heresy*, pp. 174, 187; Douais, *Documents*, I, pp. 138–43.

In the name of our crucified Lord Jesus Christ, Amen. In the year as above, 8 days before the ides of July [8 July 1246]. We, brothers of the Order of Preachers, Bernard of Caux and John of St-Pierre, deputed by apostolic authority inquisitors of heretical wickedness in the cities and dioceses of Toulouse and Cahors –

whereas it has been established, through the judicial confessions made by Gaubert of Puylaurens, knight, and Ermersendis, wife of Bernard Mir Arezad, of St-Martin-de-Lalande, of the diocese of Toulouse, <and> Bernard Raymond Arquier of Montauban and William Donadeu otherwise Nebias, of Mazérac in the diocese of Cahors, –

that the aforesaid Gaubert … also the aforesaid Ermersendis … also the aforesaid Bernard Raymond … also the William Donadeu otherwise Nebias, of Mazérac often saw and adored heretics, believed they were good men, heard their preachings, often ate with them, escorted and accompanied heretics[102] as far as Lombardy, –

these people, now following a wiser path, have first of all abjured heresy and declare they want to return to the unity of the Church: we free them, according to the form of the Church, from the chains of excommunication, with which they have been strictly bound by reason of the aforesaid crime, so long as they return to ecclesiastical unity, however, in a good heart, and carry out the commands imposed upon them; lawfully cited, they <now> appear before us, on the day peremptorily assigned to them, to receive penance on the crime of heresy: because they have scandalously offended against God and the Church, in the ways stated earlier, after getting the advice of many prelates and other good men our will and command is that to work through the appropriate penance they be thrust into perpetual prison, to remain there for ever; and we order them to carry out this penance by virtue of the oaths they have taken. If however they prove unwilling to do the aforesaid penance, we bind them with the chain of excommunication.

Done at Toulouse, in the common house, in the presence of Arnold, Prior of St-Sernin, Fort, chaplain of the same place, Amiel, chaplain of St-Stephen, Raymond, chaplain of Daurade, Sylvester, chaplain of Verfeil, Arnold, chaplain of Puylaurens, Arnold, chaplain of Cazères, Nepos, clerk, Raymond Rainier and Stephen Maistre, consuls <of Toulouse>, and many others, etc.

102 hereticos: the notary uses male gender to cover both genders.

46. IMBERT OF SALLES, 1244: MONTSÉGUR AND THE MASSACRE OF THE INQUISITORS AT AVIGNONET

We have translated two of the depositions relating to the events at Avignonet, this one and Bertrand of Quiriès's (Doc. 48 fol. 140r–v). The events are narrated in Wakefield, *Heresy*, pp. 168–71, and their context provided in M. Barber, *The Cathars*, 2nd edn (Harlow, 2013), pp. 150–64.[103] Initiatives to get the murdered inquisitors canonised failed, in contrast to the Dominican inquisitor Peter of Verona, who was canonised a year after his murder in 1252. Imbert's deposition also casts light on the *castrum* of Montségur and its final siege by the northern French in 1243–4. See the introductions to Docs 41 and 47 on the origins of Cathars' use of Montségur; Wakefield, *Heresy*, pp. 171–3 for an account of the siege, and M. Roquebert, *L'Épopée cathare 4: Mourir à Montségur* (Toulouse, 1989) for an exhaustive and precise account. Translated from Doat 24, fols 160v–181v. We include folio numbers thus: /161r/.

AD 1244, 14 days before the calends of June [18 May], Imbert of Salles, son of Gaucelin of Salles, by Cordes in the diocese of Albi, living at Montségur, required to say the truth about himself and others, both living and dead, on the accusation of heresy and Waldensianism, was sworn in as a witness.

He said that he saw that Peter Raymond of Plaigne, brother of William of Plaigne, come to the *castrum* of Montségur to Peter Roger of Mirepoix,[104] on behalf of Raymond of Alfaro, *bailli* of the Count of Toulouse.[105] And he gave him letters from the said Raymond of Alfaro, *bailli* of the Count of Toulouse. However the same witness did not see the letters nor did he hear their tenor. And afterwards the same Peter Roger of Mirepoix called together all the knights and sergeants of the *castrum* of Montségur, saying /161r/ that they could do something to great profit, and all of them should follow him. And after this, the same Peter Roger of Mirepoix and William Ademar of Lasvals and

103 See also Y. Dossat, 'Le massacre d'Avignonet', *CdF* 6 (1971), pp. 343–59.

104 Lord of Montségur alongside his father-in-law, Raymond of Péreille.

105 His parents were a leader of mercenaries in Navarre and an illegitimate daughter of Count Raymond VI of Toulouse, the half-sister of Raymond VII, for whom he was seneschal, and *bailli* for Castelsarrasin.

Bernard of St-Martin of Laurac and Raymond Willam of Tournebouix and Raymond of Corbières, and Gaillard Ot, and William of L'Île [*or* Lahille], and Perrin of Pomas and Peter Aribert and John Asermat and Arnold Roger and Guiraud of Rabat and William of Plaigne and the aforesaid Peter Raymond of Plaigne and the same witness and Otho of Massabrac and Alzieu of Massabrac, brothers, and Peter Vital and Peter Roger of La Tour de Lissac, and Brasillac of Cailhavel and Ferro, and Peter of Alzeu, and John Cathalan and Arnold Got and many others whom he does not remember, /161v/ went together into the wood next to Gaja. And when they were there Bernard of St-Martin arranged bread, wine, cheeses and other things to be brought there, which the same Peter Roger, the same witness and the others ate. And then Peter of Mazerolles came there, and with him Peter Viel and Jordan <of> Villar and Verseia, a crossbowman, and another crossbowman whose name he does not know, and others whom the same witness did not know. And then the same Peter of Mazerolles talked – to one side, secretly – to Peter Roger <of Mirepoix>. And after a bit the same Peter of Mazerolles went off on his own, and left there Peter Roger of Mirepoix, the knights Jordan of Villar and Peter Viel, and 2 crossbowmen, namely Verseia and the other one, whose name the same witness does not know, and 25 men from Gaja, /162r/ some of whom carried battle-axes and other arms, whom the same witness did not know.

He also said that afterwards the same Peter Roger together with John Acermat remained in a certain *castrum* of William of Mas – the same witness does not know the name of the *castrum*. And Guiraud of Rabat and Bernard of St-Martin and the same witness and all the aforesaid others went together onto a certain ridge next to the *castrum* of Mas. And when they were there, Jordan of Mas the younger came alone to the said place, and he talked there – apart, to one side – to Bernard of St-Martin, and to Balaguier, knight of Laurac. And afterwards Bernard of St-Martin called Peter Vital, and told him to select 12 sergeants with battle-axes. And then the same Peter Vital picked out Sicard of Puivert /162v/ and William den Marti and Peter Aura and William Ademar and others from Gaja whom the witness did not know. And afterwards the same Bernard of St-Martin and Balaguier and Jordan and the aforesaid sergeants, with battle-axes, arranged themselves on the road and went off in front. And the same witness and all the others, both knights and sergeants, followed them, and they went thus to the house of butchery [*abbatoir*] at the *castrum* of Avignonet. And when they were there,

William Raymond Galairan came out of the *castrum* – after two others – and talked to Bernard of St-Martin and Jordan of Mas, and asked them if they had picked out sergeants with battle-axes, and they told him yes. And after this all of them together – both the same witness and the aforesaid others – approached the *castrum* of Avignonet. And then the said William Raymond Galairan entered the *castrum* /163r/ of Avignonet to find out what the brother inquisitors were doing; and after some time he came back and said they were drinking. The same William Raymond Galairan went back again into the said *castrum*, and after a short time came out, and said that the brothers were going to bed. When they had heard this, Balaguier and Jordan of Mas and Jordan of Quiriès of Mas and William of Plaigne and Peter Vital and Sicard of Puivert, and William den Marti and Peter Aura and William Ademar of Lavals and Ferro and Arnold Vital and the others from Gaja, whose names the same witness does not know, all with battle-axes, went to the gate of the *castrum*, and some people of Avignonet who were inside the *castrum* opened the gate of the *castrum* for them. And the same witness and the others, both the knights and also the sergeants after them, entered the *castrum* of Avignonet and found in the *castrum* /163v/ Raymond of Alfaro and a certain squire who belonged to the brother inquisitors' household – and who that night had served drinks to the inquisitors – and 15 other men of Avignonet with battle-axes and staves. And then all those aforesaid who were carrying battle-axes, and Raymond of Alfaro, and those from Avignonet went to the Hall of the Count of Toulouse, where the brother inquisitors were sleeping. And breaking down the door they entered, and killed Brother William Arnold and Stephen, inquisitors, and their companions and household. However the same witness remained outside, and Arnold Roger said to the same witness, 'Imbert, why did do you not go into the place where the others are? For maybe they will be using the opportunity to grab stuff and other things for the heretics!'[106] And then the same witness said to him 'Sir, where shall I go? I do not know where I should go'. And then two men from Avignonet /164r/ said to the same witness, 'We will take you there'. And when they had heard this, the same witness and all the foot-sergeants who had come to the *castrum* of Avignonet, together with those two men from Avignonet, went up to the top of the *castrum*. And when they were there, they found the brother inquisitors, and their companions and household, killed. And there were in the Hall, at that time Raymond of Alfaro and William Raymond Golairan and

106 Arnold Roger is calling inquisitors 'heretics'. See also Doc. 2.

William of L'Île [*or* Lahille] and Jordan of Mas and Jordan of Quiriès of Mas and William of Plaigne and Vital, and Sicard of Puivert and William den Marti and Peter Aura and William Ademar of Lavals, and Ferro and Arnold Vital and others from Gaja and Avignonet whom the witness did not know, who were grabbing the things and stuff and books of the inquisitors, /164v/ and breaking into chests. And then the same witness got from there a little box of preserved ginger and more than 10 pence for the transport of the things which – with some others – he got from there.

The same witness also added that he then heard that Raymond of Alfaro – who was then wearing a long tin-plated iron doublet – was bragging that he had struck the brother inquisitors with some wooden mace, saying, 'This is great! Terrific!' ['Va be! Esta be!'].[107] And William Ademar of Lavals, similarly, bragged strongly about the same brothers' deaths, and William of Plaigne similarly. And Peter Aura, similarly, bragged about the same <brothers'> deaths – that he had struck them with some Segovian <sword>. And, similarly, Balaguier, and Sicard of Puivert, and Ferro, and Peter Vital, and William den Marti, and Arnold Vital, and William Raymond /165r/ Galairan, and Jordan of Mas the younger, and Jordan of Quiriès of Mas bragged strongly about the slaughter of the same brothers.

The same witness also added that those who had entered first with battle-axes, as said earlier, killed two of the same inquisitors' household who had climbed up above the Hall – they threw them down.

The same witness also said that the sergeants from Gaja got and carried away from the house where the brother inquisitors were a Bible and other books and a lot of stuff. And Raymond Bernard Barba of Queille got from there a book which was sold for 40 Toulouse shillings; and William of Plaigne got a candle-holder; and Agut Catalan a blue shirt of perse [*a kind of dark-blue cloth*] with yellow silk; and William Laurent of Castelbon two satchels for containing /165v/ books; and the same witness white boots, which he bought for 6 Toulousan pence; and Peter Aura a Segovian <sword>; and Peter Vital shoes and boots lacking uppers; and William of Plaigne some hangings and sheets; and Sicard of Puivert sheets; and Ferro bloody sheets; and Barra, squire of Bernard of St-Martin, a belt and knife belonging to Brother William Arnold; and William of Plaigne, a palfrey belonging to Raymond

107 Our thanks to John N. Green on this vernacular phrase, and its proximity to various modern demotic phrases.

Scriptor [*or* Raymond, a scribe]; and Bernard of St-Martin a cap; and Peter Vital a scapular; and a certain official clerk, Galhard of Calmont, who lives with Bernard of Arvigna, bought another scapular from Sicard of Puivert; and William den Marti got large shoes.

The same witness added also that after the slaughter/166r/ of the brothers had been carried out and their things grabbed, Raymond of Alfaro – together with those who had killed the brothers and the same witness and the other sergeants – left the Count of Toulouse's Hall, where the said slaughter had been carried out. And with lit candles which Raymond of Alfaro had had given to them – Peter Vital carried one lit torch and William of Plaigne the other – they went to Arnold Roger and to Guiraud of Rabat and the other knights who were standing in the streets within the *castrum* of Avignonet. And then Arnold Roger shouted out 'Chatbert, William Fort – get yourselves here with armed horses!' And then the same Arnold Roger and Guiraud Rabat and the other knights asked Raymond of Alfaro, 'Has it all gone well?' And Raymond of Alfaro said, 'Yes! Go – and good luck!' And when they had heard this, the same Arnold Roger/166v/ and Guiraud of Rabat and the same witness and all the aforesaid others left the *castrum* and went on their way. And those who were with Raymund of Alfaro shouted out, 'To arms!' And when Arnold Roger and Guiraud of Rabat and the same witness and the aforesaid others had got next to Anthioche (which belonged to William of Mas), where Peter Roger of Mirepoix and John Acermat stayed behind, they found there the same Peter Roger and John Acermat. And then the same Peter Roger of Mirepoix asked William Ademar, 'Traitor, why did you not bring me the cup of Brother William Arnold's head?', saying that he would have drunk wine from it. And William Ademar told him that no-one had wanted to carry it to him.

He also added that they all went together into the scrubland of Mazères of Boulbonne,[108] and from there they went /167r/ to the *castrum* of St-Félix, where the men of St-Félix gave the same witness and the other sergeants things to eat. And the chaplain of the said *castrum* gave things to eat to Peter Roger of Mirepoix and one of his companions, and at the time the aforesaid chaplain and men of the said *castrum* knew perfectly well that the brother inquisitors had been killed by the same Peter Roger's companions.

He added also that he had heard at Avignonet that Raymond of Alfaro said to Arnold Roger and Guiraud of Rabat and to the other knights,

108 A Cistercian abbey.

that if the brother inquisitors had not been killed at Avignonet, there would have been 20 armed men on horse-back ready to kill them between Castelnaudary and the *castrum* of St-Martin. And the same witness heard this said by Peter Roger, after the deed.

The witness also said that Raymond of Alfaro gave Raymond Scriptor's palfrey to William of Plaigne, in the Count of Toulouse's Hall at /167v/ Avignonet – he had earlier promised it would be given to him on account of the letters that William of Plaigne had carried to Peter Roger of Mirepoix at Montségur, to bring about the slaughter of the brother inquisitors.

Item, the same witness added that when the aforesaid Peter Roger of Mirepoix and all the aforesaid others left the *castrum* of Montségur to kill the brother inquisitors, Roger of Bousignac and Peter of Roumégoux of Queille, knights, came out to meet the same Peter Roger of Mirepoix, and talked to the same Peter Roger of Mirepoix. And both of them –namely Roger of Bousignac and Peter of Roumégoux – knew about the death of the brother inquisitors. About the time: it was 2 years before the most recent vigil of the Ascension of the Lord.

Item, he said that Peter Roger of Mirepoix sent John Catalan /168r/ and Arnold of Bensa to Péreille to certain man called Butiro, for this <reason>: he was to tell the same Butiro to go on behalf of the same Peter Roger of Mirepoix to Isarn of Fanjeaux, and tell the same Isarn of Fanjeaux to provide assurance to the same Peter Roger of Mirepoix about the Count of Toulouse, <namely> that the same count was carrying out his business. And then the same Butiro – and with him Raymond Domerg of Laroque – went to the same Isarn of Fanjeaux, and told him what the aforesaid sergeants had told them. And then the aforesaid sergeants, namely John Catalan and Arnold of Bensa, went back into the *castrum* of Montségur, and they said that Isarn of Fanjeaux sent word that the Count of Toulouse was carrying out his business well, and had taken a wife,[109] and that he would come before the feast of Christmas, and that meanwhile the same Peter Roger and those who were inside the *castrum* /168v/ of Montségur should keep themselves well. About the time: that it was a year ago.

Item, he said that Isarn of Fanjeaux sent Raymond of La Combe, and William Miri of Queille, and Matthew, heretics, to Peter Roger of Mirepoix at the *castrum* of Montségur. And on behalf of Isarn of

109 Early in 1243, Raymond VII married Margaret of Lusignan, daughter of Hugh X of Lusignan and Isabella of Angoulême.

Fanjeaux they told Peter Roger of Mirepoix and others of the *castrum* of Montségur to hold themselves <steady> until Easter, for the Count of Toulouse was coming to these parts, <bringing> great assistance from the emperor.[110] About the time: this side of the last beginning of Lent.

Item, he said that Bernard of Aliou, and Arnold of Usson promised to give Corbair Catalan 50 Melgueil pounds, for Corbair to go into the *castrum* of Montségur with 25 sergeants to provide help against the <northern> French /169r/ and those who were holding Montségur under siege. And then, after the 50 Melgueil shillings had been received from the aforesaid knights, Corbair got himself ready to enter the *castrum* of Montségur; but he did not enter because he did not have all his sergeants. But Matthew, a heretic, and the aforesaid sergeants, namely Raymond of La Combe and William Miri of Queille, did enter the *castrum* of Montségur, and they passed by the sentries of the men of Camon, who promised them the passage, knowing they were entering the *castrum*. About the time: as above.

Item, he said that when the same witness, together with his companions, was in the *castrum* of Usson, intending to go into the *castrum* of Montségur, Bernard of Aliou and Arnold of Usson handed over to the same witness Raymond of Belvis, crossbowman, /169v/ so that he could go into the *castrum* of Montségur together with the same witness, against the French. And then the same witness and Raymond of Belvis – sent by Arnold of Usson and Bernard of Aliou – and the same witness's companions entered the *castrum* of Montségur against the French and the Gascons who held the said *castrum* under siege.

He added also that Raymond of Belvis told the witness that he, Raymond of Belvis, had 40 Melgueil shillings and grain and arms in the *castrum* of Usson. About the time: around 1 year ago.

Item, he says he saw that William of Bellecombe, who was one of Raymond Maury's sergeants, went into the *castrum* of Montségur and ate there and stayed there, and spoke to Peter Roger of Mirepoix; but the same witness does not know about what he spoke. About the time: that it was a year ago.

Item, he says that Escot of Beaucaire, who was one of Fortinhol's sergeants, dragged out Tarascon of Alet and had him captured, and when the same Tarascon was ransomed the same Escot entered /170r/ the *castrum* of Montségur and had a share of the same captive's ransom.

110 Frederick II, 1194–1250.

And he stayed in the said *castrum* of Montségur for two days and nights. And then the same Escot adored heretics in the said *castrum* – that is, in the house of Bertrand Martin, bishop of the heretics – saying 'Bless' three times on bended knees before them, and adding after the last 'Bless', 'Sirs, pray God for this sinner, to make me a good Christian and lead me to a good end'. And to each 'Bless' the heretics replied, 'May God bless you'. And after the last 'Bless' they added, 'Let God be entreated, and let him make you a good Christian and lead you to a good end'. And the same witness was there, and others whom he does not remember. About the time: that it was as above.

He also added that then the same Escot agreed with Peter Roger of Mirepoix that if Escot made a signal /170v/ with fire – <visible> to the same Peter Roger – the same Peter Roger of Mirepoix would know that the Count of Toulouse had conducted his business well. And afterwards the same Escot made a signal with fire twice, from the hill-top of Bidorles, to the same Peter Roger and the others of the *castrum* of Montségur.

Item, he said that Arnold Teulin of Limoux entered the *castrum* of Montségur and said to Peter Roger of Mirepoix and others of Montségur that if they could smash the Bishop of Albi's siege machine they would have nothing to fear afterwards. About the time: this year, before the beginning of Lent.

Item, he said that the engineer Bertrand of La Vacalerie of Capdenac entered Montségur at night, and there he made machines <for use> against the king's machines. And one day on the ramparts the same Bertrand of La Vacalerie spoke publicly in front of everyone. 'Men, it should not now be hidden from you. You should know that Sicard Alamand /171r/ and Bertrand Roca, the Count of Toulouse's *baillis* – to whom the Count of Toulouse sent letters about this – on behalf of the same Count of Toulouse sent me into the *castrum* of Montségur, to provide you with support. And if we can resist the army and hold out against them for seven days we shall be liberated'. And the same witness was there, and Arnold Gorz, and Peter Vital, and Raymond of Marseille, and Raymond Monit, and William Peter, and Maurin William of Bouan, and John Cathalan, and Arnold Gorz [*sic*], and others whose names he does not remember. About the time: before the middle of last Lent.

He added that after the surrender of the *castrum* of Montségur into the hands of the king and the Church, Peter Roger of Mirepoix handed over his horse to the same Bertrand of La Vacalerie, and sent him with his horse to /171v/ Montgaillard.

Item, he said that Matthew, heretic, told the same witness that when the same Matthew, heretic, and Peter Bonet, deacon of the heretics of Toulouse, left the *castrum* of Montségur and got out of there gold and silver and an infinite <amount of> money, they made their way via the place over which the men of Camon were keeping watch (who gave the same heretics the opportunity and the route to pass through freely and get away), and that the aforesaid heretics then went on to the <fortified> grotto in the Sabartès that is held by Pons Arnold of Châteauverdun. About the time: this year, around last Christmas.

Item, he says that John Reg of St-Paul Cap-de-Joux entered Montségur with letters from the bishop of the heretics of Cremona,[111] and gave them to Bertrand Martin, bishop of the heretics of Toulouse. /172r/ And the letters said that the church of the heretics of Cremona was in tranquillity and peace, and that Bertrand Martin should send two of his brother heretics to the Bishop of Cremona, through whom he ⌜*Bertrand*⌝ could inform him ⌜*the bishop of the heretics of Cremona*⌝ about the state they were in.[112]

The same witness also added that the same John Reg said that Alaman (crossbowman of the Count of Toulouse, who lives in the area where Bartac[113] lives) and heretics from the Sabartès grotto (to whom the same Alaman had gone) had sent the same John to the *castrum* of Montségur. About the time: at the last feast of the Circumcision of our Lord, this year.

Item, he says he saw that Peter Raymond Sabatier of Queille often carried bread, wine, honey and other food to the heretics of Montségur, and the same Peter Raymond Sabatier often adored /172v/ heretics there, in the way described above, in the sight of the witness. About the time: that it was a year ago.

Item, he says he had heard it said by Bertrand Martin, bishop of the heretics of Toulouse, that when Peter Gitbert, heretic, left the *castrum*

111 This designates the bishop of a specific Lombard church of heretics, not a southern French bishop living in exile. Compare bishops referred to in 1274 (*Heresy and Heretics*, pp. 474–5), where a heretic may be living in Lombardy, but is still designated 'Bishop of the heretics of Toulouse'.

112 Though 'brothers' could be siblings, it probably here means fellow heretics, as if 'friars' in an order.

113 Alias of William-Matfred of Puylaurens, co-Lord of Palajac and famous fugitive.

of Montségur, Amicus of Fougax received the same heretic in his house. About the time: this year, between the feasts of All Saints and Christmas.

Item, he says that when the Gascon and French sergeants who held the *castrum* of Montségur under siege wanted to take the *castrum* by surprise and were getting ready the ladders by which they wanted to climb up, Claustra of Lavelanet shouted out to those who were inside the *castrum* of Montségur, 'Watch out for the ladders!' And thus those who were inside, hearing this, stopped others who were about to climb up and enter the *castrum* – from climbing up the ladders. About the time: this year, between Christmas and /173r/ the beginning of Lent.

Item, he says that Bertrand Martin, bishop of the heretics, asked the same witness to tell the same heretic's brother, Raymond Martin, that he would find information – about those 40 Toulousan shillings which the same Raymond Martin knew about – either in the church of the heretics of Fanjeaux or <the church of the heretics> of the Lauragais.[114] About the time: this year, about half-way through last Lent.

Item, he says he saw that Raymond of St-Martin, and Amiel Aicart and Clement, and Taperell, and Limoux and William Peter, heretics, brought Peter Roger of Mirepoix a cover[115] full of pieces of money belonging to the heretics and they gave these to the same Peter Roger of Mirepoix. About the time: that it was as above, namely after the promise of the surrender of the *castrum* of Montségur into the hands of the king and the Church.

/173v/ Item, he says that the same Peter Roger of Mirepoix got hold of pepper, oil and salt and wax and a covering of green perse from the house of Bertrand Martin, bishop of the heretics, and kept all of them. About the time: that it was as above.

Item, he says he saw that Peter Roger of Mirepoix got hold of an enormous quantity of grain from the heretics, and 50 doublets that the heretics had had made at their own expense. About the time: that it was as above.

Item, he says that Peter, a servant of the heretics, gave the same witness an iron helmet and other livery that had belonged to Jordan of

114 'Either in the church to which the heretics of Fanjeaux belong, or to the one to which the heretics of the Lauragais belong'. See Docs 1 and 15 for 'church' denoting a Cathar bishopric, roughly comparable to a diocese.

115 flaciata: woollen cover – the coins presumably wrapped in it.

Mas. And Peter Roger took all these away from the same witness, for this reason – because the same witness had spoken to the seneschal. About the time: this year between Christmas and the beginning of Lent.

Item, he says he saw that William Ademar of Lavals got hold of a chest full of wheat /174r/ that belonged to Raimunda of Cuq, heretic. About the time: before the middle of the last Lent, this year.

Item, he says that Raymond of Marseille, and the witness with him, and Raymond of Belvis twice ate in the house of Bertrand Martin, bishop of the heretics; not, however, together with the heretics at the same table, but they did eat bread blessed by them and other things laid out on the table. And at the beginning of each course of food and at the first drink, they said, 'Bless', and the heretics replied, 'May God bless you'. And after eating all of them, both the same witness and also the others, adored the same heretics, in the way described above. About the time: that it was half a year ago.

Item, he says that the same witness, and William Ademar, and Raymond of Belvis, and Bertrand of La Vacalerie ate three times in the house of Raymond of St-Martin, deacon of the heretics, /174v/ at Montségur; but not at the same table with the heretics nor of bread blessed by them. And after eating the same witness and the others left. Asked, he said that they did not adore the same heretics, neither the same witness nor the others, that he saw. About the time: this year, around the feast of the Circumcision of the Lord.

Item, he says that the same witness, and the same witness's wife Bernarda, and William Miri of Queille ate for 8 days in the house of Donata of Toulouse, [woman] heretic, but not at the same table with her nor of bread blessed by her. Asked, he said that he did not adore the same heretic, neither the same witness nor the others, that he saw. About the time: this year, before the middle of Lent.

Item, he says that the same witness and Bernard of Carcassonne ate one day in the house of India of Fanjeaux, female heretic, but not at the same table /175r/ nor of bread blessed by her, nor did they adore her. About the time: this year, between the feasts of All Saints and Christmas.

Item, he says that the same witness and Raymond of Belvis, and Borde of Barbaira, and William of Plaigne, and Bernard Roan, and William of Bouan often ate in the house of Raimunda of Cuq, woman heretic, but not at the same table with her nor of bread blessed by her; nor did they adore her, neither the same witness nor the others, that he saw. About the time: around 2 years before this year's Christmas.

Item, he says that the same witness and William Miri, and Raymond Monit, and Bernard of Scopont, and Maurin, and William Peter of Narbonne, and Brasillac, and Raymond of Las Coumes, and Arnold Gorz ate in the house of Peter of Mas, heretic, at Montségur, /175v/ but not at same table together with the same heretic, nor of bread blessed by him. Asked, he said that he did not adore the same heretic, nor did the others, that he saw. About the time: this year, before the middle of last Lent.

Item, he says he saw Bertrand Martin, bishop of the heretics, preaching in the house of the said Bertrand Martin, bishop of the heretics, at Montségur on Christmas Day. And there were present at his sermon the same witness, and Peter Roger of Mirepoix and his wife Philippa, and Arnold Roger and his wife Cicilia, and Marquesia, mother of the same Cicilia, and Gallard of Congost, and Berengar of Lavelanet, and Bertrand of Bardenac, and William Ademar, and Raymond William of Tourneboix, and Raymond of Corbières, and Gallard Ot, and Hot /176r/ of Massabrac, and Adalaicia of Massabrac, and Fays wife of William of Plaigne, and Peter Robert, and John Catalan, and William Guitbert, and Bernard of St-Martin, and William of L'Île [*or* Lahille], and Balaguier of Laurac, and William Peter, and Maurin, and Bertrand of Congost, and Arnold Roquier, and Pons of Narbonne, and Pons Fiac, and Peter Vital, and Comellas, and William Raymond of Larocque, and Sicard of Puivert, and William den Martin, and Arnold Vital, and Arnold Domerg, and others whom he does not remember. Asked, he said that the same witness did not adore the same heretic nor did the others that he saw – for the same witness and William Arnold Belfol left there. About the time: it was a year before last Christmas.

/176v/ Item, he says that the same witness adored heretics about 20 times in the *castrum* of Montségur, in the way described above, and the same witness saw that Peter Roger of Mirepoix and the others adored the aforesaid heretics many times, in the way described above. About the time: from within the year up to the day when the *castrum* of Montségur with the heretics was surrendered into the hands of the King of France and the Church.

Item, he says that the same witness and Peter Vital and other sergeants escorted and accompanied Raymond of Mas and three other heretics from the *castrum* of Montségur as far as Gaja. And when they were near Gaja the heretics entered the *castrum* of Gaja, and the same witness and the others went on as far as Génébrières. Asked, he said that the same witness did not adore the same heretics, nor did the others, that the same witness saw. The same witness also added that /177r/ Raymond of Mas, heretic, was riding at the time on Bernard of St-Martin's horse. About the time: it was a year ago this year, between Christmas and the Circumcision of the Lord.

Item, he says that when the same witness was in the *castrum* of Laurac, John den Arnauda brought the same witness into a certain house to see heretics there. And when they were there, they found there two female heretics, namely Peirona and her companion. And there the same witness and John den Arnauda ate things that the aforesaid heretics gave to the same witness and John den Arnauda. And the same John den Arnauda adored the same heretics there, in the way described above. Asked, he said that the same witness did not adore the same heretics nor ate with them at the same table nor of bread blessed by them. /177v/ About the time: it was a year ago around last August. Asked whose the aforesaid house was, he said he did not know.

Item, he said he saw Raimunda of Cuq and Flors, women heretics, in the house of Roquier at Queille. And there were there the wife of Bernard of Boutier, and Arnauda the wife of Arnold Roquier, <and> William the son of Arnold Roquier. Asked, he said that the same witness did not adore the same heretics, nor did the aforesaid women, that the same witness saw. About the time: that it was as above.

Item, he says that the same witness and Raymond of Marseille, and Bernard of St-Martin escorted and accompanied Raymond of Couiza and Peter Guibert from the *castrum* of Montségur to Campels.[116] And when they were there, they left the same heretics there and returned to the *castrum* of Montségur; and the heretics kept on their way towards Lordat. /178r/ Asked, he said that the same witness did not adore the same heretics. But the others adored them, in the way described above. About the time: that it was 1½ years ago.

Item, he says he saw Berengar Tornier and his companion, heretics, in the house of Petit at Niort. And there were there Guillelma Gasca, the mistress of Bertrand of Auriac, and Arnold Maurin of Prades, and someone called Albat, who rides with Raymond of Cabaret and is from

116 A passage is missing here, since the references in the following three sentences are to female heretics.

Caunes. Asked, he said that he did not adore the said heretics, nor did the others in his sight. About the time: that it was 3 years ago.

Item, he said he saw that Raymond of Niort [*or* of the Niorts] of Bélesta, heretic, came to the *castrum* of Montségur and brought letters to Bertrand Martin, bishop of the heretics, on behalf of the bishop of the heretics of Cremona. About the time: this year, before the feast of All Saints.

/178v/ Item, he says he saw Peter Paraire, and William of Bugarach, and Ferrar, and another heretic whose name he does not know, at Villetritouls, in the Val de Daigne, in the house of a certain person whose name he does not know. And there came there with the witness, Arnold of Monastiès [*or* Le Monastère]. And then the same witness and Arnold of Monastiès ate there with the same heretics at the same table. And at each course and at the first drink they said, 'Bless', and the heretics replied, 'May God bless you'. And both of them, the same witness and Arnold of Monastiès, adored the same heretics there, in the way described above. And there were there the lord of the house, and his wife, whose names he does not know. He also added that he saw that two women carried to the heretics a foccacia [*fogassia*] and figs and grapes. About the time: 2 years before the August of this year.

/179r/ Item, he said that Pons Roger of Salza of Val de Daigne escorted Peter Paraire and the other aforesaid heretics from Villetritouls as far as Puylaurens. About the time: that it was as above.

Item, he says he saw the aforesaid heretics in the house of Raymond Laurence at Puylaurens. And present there were Domerg of Roussillon, who is an engineer, and Raymond Laurence, and Durantel of Roquefeuil, and Peter Embri of Puylaurens, and Bernard Effort, and Bernard Monier of Alzau [*or* Axat]. And all them there – both the same witness and also the others – adored the same heretics, in the way described above. About the time: around 2 years ago.

Item, he said that he saw Peter Jacob and Berengar Malcuit and Peter Brunet and Marquesia and Berengar of Dourgne and Prima and two other women heretics whose names he does not know, at Puylaurens – /179v/ Peter of Cucugnan was providing them with food. And all the aforesaid heretics were living in the *castrum* of Puylaurens. About the time: that it was as above.

Item, he says he saw Marquesia and Prima, women heretics, in the house of Bernard of Viviers at Fenouillet. And there were there Caranat, a lame shoemaker whose personal name he does not know, and Peter Textor [*or* a weaver], and Peter of Villeraze, and Bernard of Viviers and his mother, whose name he does not know, and Raymond Martin of Fenouillet. Asked, he said he did not adore the same heretics nor did the others that he saw. About the time: that it was 2 years ago.

Item, he said that Bertrand Martin, bishop of the heretics, gave the witness 20 Melgueil shillings, and gloves and a linen hat, and a corset, and a tunic, and /180r/ pepper and salt and oil. About the time: in the last Lent, this year.

Item, he says that the same Bertrand Martin gave all the knights and sergeants of Montségur oil, pepper and salt at the beginning of Lent.

Item, he says that some heretic from Toulouse, a purse-maker, gave the same witness shoes. About the time: the middle of last Lent.

He added also that Peter Sabatier, heretic, gave the witness 2 Melgueil shillings, and Donata of Toulouse <gave him> a linen cap and a purse and a pin-box, and Guirauda, a woman heretic from Caraman, <gave him> some breeches and 10 Melgueil shillings as a pledge.

Item, he says he saw that Raymond of Marseille, and Brasillac, and Raymond of Tournebouix hereticated themselves and received the *consolamentum* from the heretics /180v/ at Montségur. And Bertrand Martin and Raymond Agulier, bishops of the heretics, consolated them in this way. First, at the prompting of the heretics, they surrendered themselves to God and the Gospel. And they promised that they would hold to the sect of the heretics throughout their lives. They would eat neither meat, nor eggs, nor cheese, nor anything fatty, apart from oil and fish. They would not swear, nor lie, nor engage in any sex. They would not desert the sect of the heretics through fear of death by fire or water, or any other sort of death. And when all of these promises had been made, they [*the bishops*] placed their hands and a book on their heads. And they read and prayed to God, making many bows and genuflections. And present at this *consolamentum* were the same witness, and William Miri, and Pons of Narbonne, and Roger/181r/ of Sautel, and Raymond Monit. Asked, he said that same witness did not adore them nor receive the Peace from them, nor did the others that the same witness saw. About the time: that it was as above.

Item, he says that Raymond of Niort and his wife Marquesia sent Escot of Belcaire with letters for Peter Roger of Mirepoix to the *castrum* of Montségur. And then the said Escot stayed in the *castrum* of Montségur for two days and nights. And then the same Escot recounted how the Count of Toulouse was conducting his business well. He also said that

Peter Roger of Mirepoix gave the same Escot coins. About the time: this year before the feast of All Saints.

Item, he says he saw Peter Paraire, deacon of the heretics of Fenouillèdes, and Raymond of Narbonne and Bugaraig, /181v/ heretics, in the *castrum* of Quéribus – Chatbert was maintaining them there in some vault. And there were there Borde of Barbaira, and Domerg. Asked, he said that the same witness did not adore them, nor the others that the same witness saw. About the time: that it was 3 years ago.

He also added that Peter Paraire, heretic, told the same witness that Peter Suavis of St-Paul-de-Fenouillet was received and consolated by the heretics in his illness from which he died.

Asked, he said that he was a believer in the heretics for three years, such that he believed he would be saved if he died in their sect.

He attested these things in front of Brother Ferrier. Witnesses: Peter Aribert and Guiraud Trepat, Notary, who wrote these things.

47. PETER WILLIAM D'ARVIGNA, 1246

Peter came from Arvigna, in the canton of Varilhes, near Pamiers, in the Ariège, and with his brothers he was co-Lord of Dun. The huge Cathar council he reports taking place in Mirepoix forty years earlier has been linked to a statement by the co-Lord of Montségur, Raymond of Péreille, in his deposition of 1244, that forty years earlier 'he rebuilt the castle of Montségur, which had previously been in ruins, at the behest and the requests of Raymond of Mirepoix and Raymond Blasquo and other heretics' (Doat 22 fol. 217v); see also the Introduction to Part VIII above. Translated from Doat 24, fols 240r–245r. We include folio numbers thus: /240v/.

AD 1246, 15 days before the calends of November [18 October] Peter William d'Arvigna, brother of Bernard d'Arvigna, asked to tell the truth about himself and others, living and dead, on the accusation of heresy and Waldensianism, was sworn in as a witness.

He said that he saw, at Mirepoix, Jordana of Marliac, the same witness's mother, and Flandina of Marliac, the same witness's grandmother, and their companions, that is to say the heretics, /240v/ living publicly in the houses of these heretics. And the same witness often ate, drank and stayed with the said heretics, and so many times that he does not remember how often. But he did not adore them or see them adored. And this was 40 years ago or thereabouts.

Item, he saw at Mirepoix Raymond Blas and many other heretics, both male and female, <and> up to 50 hostels of heretics. And he saw there with the said heretics Peter Barba, Pons Barba, Peter Raymond Roger, and Raymond of Rau, <now> dead, and large numbers <of others>. The same witness adored the said heretics there, bending his knees three times in front of them saying, 'Bless, good men, pray for this sinner'. And this was 10 years ago or thereabouts.

Item, he said that he saw at Mirepoix a great gathering of heretics, up to 600 heretics who had come there /241r/ to decide some question which the heretics were dealing with among themselves. But the same witness did not adore them nor see them adored. And this was 40 years ago, or thereabouts.

Item, he said that he saw, at Dun, Philipa, mother of Roger Bernard the Count of Foix,[117] and her companions, heretics, in the heretics'[118] own houses. And he saw there with the said heretics Alamanda of Nougairol, and Cecilia, wife of Arnold William d'Arvigna, the same witness's father. And the same witness often ate and drank with the said heretics. But he did not adore them or see them adored. And this was at the same time.

Item, he saw at Dun William Clergue [*or*, the Cleric], deacon of the heretics, and his companion, heretic, in the general square at Dun. And the said heretics preached there. He saw there with the said heretics Raymond /241v/ of Tourtrol, Raymond of Les Pujols <and> Bernard of Léran, dead men, and many others whom he does not remember. And the same witness and all the others heard the preaching of the said heretics. But he[119] did not adore them nor did he see them being adored. And this was 40 years ago or thereabouts.

Item, he saw at Mirepoix in the house of the Prior of Manses[120] Guilabert of Castres and Raymond Agulher and their companions, heretics. And he saw there with the said heretics Arnold of Castelbon,[121] Roger of Cominges the elder the Count of Pailhès,[122] Raymond d'Arvigna, the same witness's uncle, and the said Prior of Manses. But he did not adore them or see them adored. And this was 25 years ago or thereabouts.

Item, he said that <when> Lord Raymond d'Arvigna, the same witness's uncle, was ill at Dun with a grave illness, /242r/ he was hereticated. And Guilabert of Castres and Bernard of Lamothe and Gerald of Gourdon, heretics, hereticated him. And there were present at this heretication the same <witness>, and Pons Ademar, Bernard Durfort,[123] Raymond Tourtrol, Peter Barba of Mirepoix and Carbonel,

117 And wife of Raymond Roger, count of Foix (1188–1223).

118 'Heretics' mistakenly given in male gender.

119 Here, and again below, the scribe first wrote the singular 'he' (adoravit) and this was later corrected to 'they' (adoraverunt).

120 Priory dependent upon the Benedictine abbey of Montolieu in the diocese of Carcassonne.

121 Viscount of Castelbon, d. 1237. In 1202 his daughter, heiress to the viscounty, married Roger Bernard II of Foix.

122 Viscount of Couserans, nephew of Raymond Roger, Count of Foix, still alive in 1244.

123 Pons and Bernard were brothers, and co-lords of Saverdun.

scribe of Mirepoix.[124] But he [/they] did not adore them nor did he see them adored. And this was 22 years ago or thereabouts.

Item, he said that the same witness accompanied the said Raymond d'Arvigna, heretic, from Dun right up to the grotto of Ornolac. And the same witness carried the money the said heretic Raymond had with his pack-horse. But he did not adore him nor did he see him adored. And this was at the same time.

Item, he saw at Queille, in a certain house outside the town, Vigouroux of La Bouconne and his companion, that is to say, heretic. And he saw there with the said heretics /242v/ Peter Raymond of Queille and Chartres and two youths from Mirepoix whose names he does not recall. They led a horse there for the said Vigouroux, and they brought for the same Vigouroux two fish pasties and a blue cape. And then the same witness and all the others ate there with the said heretics. And the same witness and the others adored the said heretics there. And the same witness escorted the said heretics from there and as far as Calmont. And he brought them into the house of Bernard d'Arvigna. And the said heretics were there for a night and half a day, and they ate there. And he saw there with the said heretics Peter of Mazères and [*name missing*] of Saverdun, and a certain maid of the house called Bernarda. And then the same witness sent his messenger to Saverdun to his brother, Bernard /243r/ d'Arvigna and to the said Bernard's wife Gauda, and he told them to come to see the said Vigouroux. And the said Bernard, occupied with many matters of business, could not come. And he saw there with the said heretics Gauda, Bernard d'Arvigna's wife, and Arnold of Villemur[125] (the one still alive), Bernard Durfort, Arnold of Mazerolles <and> Gui of Marliac. And all the aforesaid talked there with the said Vigouroux and his companions, heretics. And they heard their preaching. But they did not adore them, nor did he see them adored. And from there the same witness and the said Bernard Durfort escorted the aforesaid heretics at night-time as far as Montgiscard. And there two brothers from Rouze came out and received the said heretics there. But the same witness did not see the ones who received the heretics, but he understood that they were /243v/ the ones from Rouze. And then the said Vigouroux gave the same witness a felt hat. And likewise the two companions, also

124 Carbonel of *Alsono* – one of several places in Languedoc called Alzonne or Aussonne – was public notary of Mirepoix, and drew up the confirmation of the customs of Mirepoix in 1207.

125 Co-lord of Saverdun.

heretics, gave him some gloves and a linen hat. But he[126] did not adore them, nor did he see them being adored. And this was 14 years ago or thereabouts.

Item, he saw at Saverdun, in the house of Alazaisis, wife of Guilabert of Pechauriol, Raymond Peter and his companion, heretics. And he saw there with the said heretics the same Alazaisisia, and Guilabert of Pechauriol, Bertrand of Pin, Peter of Villemur, and the same witness's brother, Bernard d'Arvigna. And when the same witness entered the said house, the heretics were preaching. And the same witness and all the others heard the preaching of the said heretics. But they did not adore them, nor did he see them adored. /244r/ And it was 15 years ago or thereabouts.

Item, he said that when Bertrand of Durban, brother of the Abbot of Foix, was ill with the illness from which he died, at Pamiers, in a certain low room where no-one lived, two heretics came there whom the same witness did not know. And then the heretics hereticated the said Bertrand of Durban. And there were present at the said heretication the same witness, and the men who brought the said heretics there, Pons Roger the bastard, brother of Peter Roger of Mirepoix, and someone else who was called William. And then the said ill man bequeathed his horse to the aforesaid heretics. But they did not adore them, nor did he see them adored. And this was 19 years ago or thereabouts.

Item, he said that he saw, at Dun, Philippa, wife of Raymond Roger/244v/ the Count of Foix, and her companions, heretics, in the same heretics' own houses. And he saw there with the said heretics the aforesaid Raymond Roger, and William Amiel of Pailhès, both now dead, and many others <whose names> he does not recall. And all ate there with the said heretics, fish and other things the heretics gave them. But they did not adore them, nor did he see them adored. And this was 40 years ago or thereabouts.

He believed the aforesaid heretics were good men and that they had a good faith and that one could be saved through them, though he knew that the Church persecuted them. And he heard them saying that God did not make visible things, that the consecrated host was not the body of Christ, that there was no salvation in baptism or marriage, and that the bodies of the dead will not rise again. And the same /245r/ witness believed just as the same <heretics> said. And it is 30 years and more

126 Ms: they.

since he first believed that the heretics were good men. But he did not believe after he made his confession about heresy to Brother Peter of Cendres of the Order of Preachers at Foix. And he confessed to Brother William Arnold and his companion, inquisitors,[127] at Foix. And afterwards he did not see heretics.

These things he attested at Pamiers, in front of brothers Bernard of Caux and John of St-Pierre, inquisitors.[128] And he took an oath and abjured, and bound himself, as above.

Witnesses: Raymond of Aure, Prior of St-Antonin and Peter Fresapan, public notary, who received a public act from the same Peter William <d'Arvigna>.

127 Ms: socium suum inquisivit; mistake for socio suo inquisitoribus.

128 On these inquisitors, see information in Doc. 48.

48. DEPOSITIONS BEFORE BERNARD OF CAUX AND JOHN OF ST-PIERRE, 1245–6

The depositions below are a selection from a manuscript held in the municipal library in Toulouse, MS 609. This is a copy made around 1260, on paper (one of the earliest surviving paper manuscripts from France), of the 4th and 5th books of a set of inquisition registers; there were originally over ten volumes, but the others are no longer extant. Most of the depositions were made in front of two Dominican inquisitors, Bernard of Caux and John of St-Pierre, in 1245–6.

We know virtually nothing about John, other than the dates of his work as inquisitor (1243–8) in collaboration with Bernard; see Doc. 9 §7. Bernard was at work as an inquisitor in the Agenais before May 1241, working with John in the dioceses of Agen and Cahors between November 1243 and March 1245.[129] The two moved to Toulouse, where they started on 1 May 1245, beginning an enormous inquiry, planned to cover the diocese of Toulouse, which lasted until 1 August 1246. Summonses were read out in parishes, and people travelled to Toulouse to be questioned in St-Sernin. The fact that MS 609 contains over 5,000 depositions and yet is only a copy of a fraction of the original attests the extraordinary size of the enterprise. Only a few of the inquisitors' sentences survive, in a separate manuscript. Among them is one on Esclarmonda of Bret: we translate her deposition below (fol. 62r), and include her sentence in an appendix.

Although the manuscript was given a definitive study in 1959 by Yves Dossat,[130] and has been interpreted extensively by Mark Pegg more recently,[131] it has never been edited, because of its size and the difficulty of reading parts of it, where water damage has caused the ink to spread. The reader should be warned of the significance of this for our translation, which is not based on a physical re-examination of the manuscript itself, but rather a provisional reading of a microfilm copy, with additional reference to the low-resolution digitised version made by the Bibliothèque Municipale de Toulouse, eked out by reference to other (imperfect and incomplete) modern transcriptions.[132]

129 On Bernard, see Y. Dossat, 'Une figure d'inquisiteur: Bernard de Caux', *CdF* 6 (1971), pp. 253–72 and Douais, *Documents*, I, pp. 148–60. On Bernard's fame and posthumous veneration, see the introduction to Doc. 45 above and Doc. 9 § 10.

130 Dossat, *Crises*.

131 M. G. Pegg, *The Corruption of Angels: The Great Inquisition of 1245–1246* (Princeton, 2001).

132 A digitised version of the ms. is available online at http://numerique.bibliotheque.toulouse.fr/cgi-bin/superlibrary?a=d&d=/ark:/74899/B315556101_MS0609#.

In our selection from this manuscript of over 400,000 words, we have two aims. The first is to provide a representative view of its organisation and character. The document is arranged via parishes: their names are provided throughout the manuscript as headings, and each is followed by the depositions of the parishioners. We have given each parish name in bold when it appears, and we have selected one parish (Mas-Saintes-Puelles) for the translation of a large number of depositions, in order to illustrate one of the document's salient features: that there are folios that contain many depositions, each occupying only one line, as deponent after deponent is recorded as taking an oath, denying any involvement, and abjuring heresy.[133] These however flow seamlessly into longer and sometimes very lengthy depositions. Mas-Saintes-Puelles was chosen because the selections given here can be studied alongside an exemplary article by Walter Wakefield, 'Heretics and inquisitors: the case of Le Mas-Saintes-Puelles', *Catholic Historical Review* 69 (1983), 209–26.[134]

Secondly, we have tried to illustrate the document's extraordinary riches, by picking out fuller depositions from across the whole manuscript. These provide many glimpses of the Church's earlier dealings with heretics, including the efforts of Dominic, Bishop Fulk of Toulouse and the Archbishop of Narbonne before the job of inquisition was conferred on the mendicants. The light cast on the Cathar and Waldensian sects also goes back a long way, the furthest reach here being a claim to remember back to around 1175 (fol. 159r). Bernard and John used a question-list, to which was tacked on a quintet of doctrines for suspected believers in Cathars, imposing a formulaic character to these depositions. At the same time the process permitted much that is not formulaic to be recorded, such as an immoral dice- and chess-playing parish priest who loved heretics, or a condemned criminal choosing to receive the *consolamentum* before being buried alive.

Finally, as a manuscript that comes from the middle of the thirteenth century and is the largest and most detailed of all inquisition records from this period, MS Toulouse 609 has a special position in showing the authenticity and value

VX3EsvlVhBd. Two typescripts exist, both with errors. One, prepared by the late Jean Duvernoy, is in three files online at http://jean.duvernoy.free.fr/text/listetexte.htm (under 'Sources inquisitoriales'). The other, a photocopy of a typed transcript made at Columbia University, lacking fols 200v–225r, is in Columbia University Library, Butler Collection, BX4890. B47 1255g; its short title is 'Interrogatoires subis par des hérétiques albigeois'.

133 Compare the provisions in the Council of Toulouse of 1229 [Doc. 29, canon 12] and the Consultation of Béziers of 1246 [Doc. 37, no. 31] for the annual written recording of abjurations of heresy of adults in each parish.

134 Most of ch. 10 of Wakefield, *Heresy* is based on this manuscript. Some of the evidence from Cambiac translated below (fol. 239v) was used in another article by Wakefield, 'Heretics and inquisitors: the case of Auriac and Cambiac', *Journal of Medieval History* 12 (1986), 225–37. On what the interrogations contain of Cathar doctrine, see P. Biller, 'Cathars and the material world', *Studies in Church History* 46 (2010), pp. 89–110.

of those records that survive only in seventeenth-century copies and whose contents overlap. Translated from Bibliothèque Municipale, Toulouse, MS 609. We include folio numbers thus: /1r/.

[*On the reverse of the front end-paper, in script contemporary with the ms.*] Confessions from the 5th book of Brother Bernard of Caux's <inquisitions in> the Lauragais, transcribed in this book up to folio 158.

Item, from the said folio thereafter <transcribed> from the said Brother Bernard's 4th book.

/1r/ From Mas-Saintes-Puelles

Item, on the year and day as above [27 May 1245], William of La Selve, sworn in as a witness, said that he saw, in the house of Peter Cap-de-Porc, Peter Volvena and his companion, heretics. And he saw there with them Peter Bernard Mazeler. And both of them adored the said heretics there. And this was 10 years ago or thereabouts.

Item, he saw, in the house of William Bru of Canast, Bernard Martin and his companion, heretics. And he saw with them there Raymond den Amelh[135] and Peter Bernard of Mazel. And the same witness adored the said heretics there, and he saw the others adoring them. And this was 12 years ago.

Item, he saw, in the house of Na Rica, Bernard, the son of Na Rica, and his companion, heretics. And he saw with them there Peter Gauta, the elder, Peter Bernard Mazeler, William Bru of Canast <and> Arnold Maiestre. However, he does not recall whether he and the others adored the said heretics there. And this was 12 years ago or thereabouts.

Otherwise he did not see heretics, that he recalls. He also said that he believed heretics were good men, and had good faith, /1v/ and were truth-tellers and friends of God. But he did not hear the heretics talking about visible things, about baptism, about the consecrated host, nor about marriage. However, he heard members of the clergy describing the errors that the heretics say. However, the same witness never believed the aforesaid errors. And it was 15 years ago that he first believed the heretics were good, and 10 years ago that he stopped believing this.

135 Of the Amielhs, a family.

And he <had> confessed to Brother Ferrier, but he did not have penance from him. And he abjured here, and took an oath, etc.

Witnesses: the aforesaid. [*given earlier, at the end of the first deposition*: Arnold, Prior of St-Sernin, Arnold Cerda, and Brother William Pelhisson of the Order of Preachers,[136] and Brother Bernard of Caux, Inquisitor].

... Item, on the year and day as above [27 May 1245], Bernard of Baziège, sworn in as a witness, said that he never saw heretics, nor did he believe in them, nor did he adore, nor give or send anything, nor did he escort, nor receive, nor did he hear their preaching.

Item, on the year and day as above, Peter of Baziège, sworn in as a witness, said the same on everything as the just mentioned Bernard of Baziège said.

Item, on the year and day as above, Pons of Mas or of Loubère, sworn in as a witness, said that he kept Rixenz Bruna in the same witness's house for a month. However, the same witness did not know she was a heretic until the lord Bishop of Toulouse[137] took her prisoner in the same witness's residence. And the same person who is speaking [*i.e. Pons*] was similarly taken prisoner because of this. He also said that afterwards the said heretic was reconciled by the said Bishop of Toulouse. And this was 12 years ago or thereabouts.

Item, he said he saw heretics living openly in the land. And this was 30 years ago or thereabouts.

He did not otherwise see heretics, nor believe, nor adore, nor give or send them anything, nor escort, <nor> hear their preaching. And he abjured heresy, and took an oath etc.

Witnesses: the aforesaid.

... /3v/ ...

Item, on the year and day as above [22 June 1245], Bernard Garriga, sworn in as a witness, said that he saw heretics living openly in the land. And this was 36 years ago. Otherwise he never saw heretics, apart from captured ones, nor did he believe, nor adore, nor give or send them anything, nor did he escort, nor hear their preaching.

136 His chronicle, recounting the early years of the Dominicans in Toulouse and inquisition, is translated in Wakefield, *Heresy*, pp. 207–36. See Doc. 9 §3.

137 Raymond of Le Fauga OP, Bishop 1232–70.

Item, on the year and day as above Arnold of *Mozier* [*perhaps* Mazières], sworn in as a witness, said he never saw heretics, apart from captured ones, nor did he believe, nor adored, nor give or send anything, nor hear their preaching.

Item, on the year and day as above, Bernard Lapassa, sworn in as a witness, said the same in all things as the said Arnold of *Mozier*.

Item, on the year and day as above, Bernard Lapassa, sworn in as a witness, said the same in all things as the said Bernard Garriga.

Item, on the year and day as above, Peter Lapassa the younger, sworn in as a witness, said the same in all things as the said Arnold of *Mozier*.

Item, on the year and day as above, Arnold Lapassa, sworn in as a witness, said the same in all things as the said Bernard Garriga.

Item, on the year and day as above, William Paraggos, sworn in as a witness, said the same in all things as the said Bernard Garriga.

/4r/ [*On this leaf there follow 32 depositions, 28 of which occupy one line each, containing similar negatives.* /4v/ *There follow 17 depositions, mainly similar negatives, ending in Stephen's, the last in a long sequence whose date, 'as above', suggests hearings on 22 June 1245.*]

Item, on the year and day as above, Stephen of Rouzégas, sworn in as a witness, said that he saw heretics living openly at Mas and throughout the land. And this was 30 years ago and more.

Item, he said that he saw at Mas, in the house of Bernard of Quiriès, John Cambitor and his companion, heretics, who preached there. Present at their preaching were the same witness, and Bernard of Quiriès, and Moreta, and Bernard of Mas, knight, and others he does not recall. And there all of them – and the same witness – adored the said heretics, each of them on his own behalf saying three times, on bended knees in front of them, 'Bless', and adding, 'Lords, pray God on behalf of this sinner, that he may make me a good Christian and lead me to a good end'. And this was 18 years ago.

Item, he says he saw at Mas, in the house of Bernard of St-André, Peter Bolbena and his companion, heretics, who preached there at night. And present at the same preaching were the same witness, and Peter Gauta the Elder, and William Vidal, and Bernard of Mas, knight, and Bernard of Quiriès, knight. And the said Bernard of St-André, and all of them, and the same witness adored the said heretics there. And this was 16 years ago or thereabouts.

Item, he says that Peter of St-André and Arnold Godalh brought along by night two heretics – whose names he does not know – to the same witness's house, when the same witness's wife, Willelma was ill, in that illness in which she died. And then the aforesaid ill woman did not allow herself to be hereticated by the aforesaid heretics. And there were there the same witness, and Peter Roger, and Garnier, and Raymond Garnier. However, the same witness did not adore, nor did he see them adored. And this was 10 years ago or thereabouts.

Item, he said that he saw at Mas, in the house of Na Ricca, Raymond of Mas, heretic. And he saw there with him Jordan of Mas, knight. However, the same witness did not adore, nor did he see him adored.[138] And this was 10 years ago or thereabouts. He never otherwise /5r/ saw heretics.

The same witness also said that he believed the heretics were good men, and had a good faith, and were truth-tellers, and friends of God. However, he did not hear the heretics talking about baptism, nor about the consecrated host, nor about marriage. He did however once hear from a certain heretic that God had not made visible things, and that flesh and blood will not possess the kingdom of God. And the same witness never believed the aforesaid errors. And it was 20 years ago that he first believed that the heretics were good men, and 10 years ago that he finally left this belief.

And he confessed to Brother Ferrier, but he did not have penance from him. And he abjured heresy, and took an oath, etc. Witnesses: the aforesaid.

Item, in the year as above, on the calends of July [1 July 1245], Bernarda, wife of Garnier, sworn in as a witness, said that she saw, in the house of Raymunda of the Amaniels [*a family name*], Fabrissa [*missing word: relative, probably* mother *or* aunt] of the said Raymunda, heretic. And she saw there with them Maria the wife of Bertrand of Quiriès, and Willelma Meta the mother of Bernard of Quiriès, and the same Raymunda of the Amanels. But she did not adore, nor saw her adored. And this was 20 years ago or thereabouts.

138 This often repeated formula is represented in the ms. by 'nō ado nc vidit ado', in which it is not clear whether the second 'ado' is a passive or active infinitive, 'adorari' or 'adorare'. We have preferred the first, transcribing as 'non adoravit nec vidit adorari' and translating as above. If the second 'ado' is taken as 'adorare' along with conjectural addition of 'alios' and 'eos', we would translate the resulting 'non adoravit nec vidit <alios eos> adorare' as 'did not adore nor saw others adore them'.

Item, she saw, in her and her husband Garnier's house, Peter Bolbena, heretic, who had come to visit the said Garnier, the same witness's husband, who at the time was ill. And she saw there with him Stephen of Rouzégas and William Vidal, who had come there with the said heretic. But she did not adore or see him adored. Rather, as soon as she saw the heretic she was overcome with so much anger that she left the house. And this was 18 years ago or thereabouts.

She did not otherwise see heretics, nor did she ever believe they were good men, nor did she adore them, nor hear their preaching, nor did she give or send them anything, nor did she escort nor did she arrange for them to be escorted.

She confessed the aforesaid things to Brother Ferrier at Saissac.

She also said that that Albaric, her first husband, was not a heretic.

And she abjured heresy, and took an oath, etc. Witnesses: Arnold of Mas-Stes-Puelles, Arnold the Prior of <St->Sernin, and Brother Bernard, Inquisitor.

Item, on the year and day as above, Willelma Companha, sworn in as a witness, said that she saw in her house Rixen and Stephana, heretics. And she saw there with them Bernard of St-André <and> Peter of St-André, who were later heretics, and Arnold Maiestre, the same witness's concubine, who escorted the said female heretics there, and the same witness's mother Aymengarda Companha, who was lying ill. And then the said female heretics counselled the said Aymengarda, the same witness's mother, to make herself a heretic, which she did not want to do. And the said brothers Bernard of St-André and Peter, brothers, adored the said female heretics. However, neither the same witness nor her mother adored them. And this was 14 years ago or thereabouts.

Item, on another occasion she saw, in the same witness's house, Bernard of Mayreville and Raymond of Na Riqua. And she saw with them there Bernard of St-André, and Peter of St-André, Roger Sartre [*or* tailor], William Tesseire [*or* weaver], Bernard Aichart, William Pons of Roque Haute, Aymeric of Molleville, Bernard Cogot, and the same witness's concubine Arnold Maiestre, who was lying there ill. And then the said heretics hereticated the said Arnold Maiestre. And the same witness and all the others adored the said heretics there, three times on bended knees saying, 'Bless, good men, pray to God on our behalf'. And this was 12 years ago or thereabouts.

She believed that the aforesaid heretics were good men, and had good faith, and one could be saved through them, although she knew that the Church persecuted them. However, she did not hear them saying errors about visible things, nor about sacraments; nor did she believe in the aforesaid errors. And it was 20 years ago that she first believed the heretics were good men, and 10 years ago that she did not believe them [*started not believing*].

She confessed the aforesaid things to Brother Ferrier at Limoux.

She abjured, and took an oath, etc.

Witnesses: the aforesaid, and Arnold Cerda.

Item, on the year and day as above, Ramunda, the wife of the late Gondaubou, sworn in as a witness, said that she saw Willelma Audena, the same witness's aunt, heretic, at Cabaret. And she lived with her for 3 years. And she often adored her. And this was 20 years ago or thereabouts.

Item, she said that William Bertrand of Lanta together with four other men came to Narbonne, into the same witness's house, and ate and drank in the same house. And the said men were heretics' messengers, as she heard later. And they had escorted heretics to Narbonne, into the house of Raymond John. And then the *bailli* of the lord Archbishop of Narbonne arrested the same witness and the same witness's sister Florencia, because he believed that the heretics, whom the aforesaid men were escorting, were in the same witness's house: but they were not. And then Brother Ferrier, who was then inquisitor by the authority of the lord Archbishop, reconciled the same witness and the same witness's sister Florencia. And Brother Ferrier then went together with the same witness as far as Mas, and reconciled her, and handed her back to her husband at Mas. And she had letters of the said reconciliation from the said Brother Ferrier. And this was 16 years ago. And afterwards she did not see heretics.

She believed that the aforesaid heretics were good men, and had a good faith, and one could be saved through them. And she heard them saying that God had not made visible things, and that the consecrated host was not the body of Christ, and that there was not salvation in baptism and marriage, and that the bodies of dead men /5v/ will not rise again – and at that time she believed as her said aunt Willelma taught her.

And she abjured, and took an oath, etc.

Witnesses: the aforesaid.

Item, on the year and day as above, Florensa, the wife of the late Peter of Fournès, sister of the aforesaid Ramunda, sworn in as a witness, said that she lived for half <a year> at Laurac with Willelma Audena, the same witness's aunt, heretic. And she ate and drank with her. And she often adored her, just as the said heretic taught the same witness to adore. And this was 20 years ago or thereabouts.

Item, she said that she lived with her husband at Cabaret for two years. And she saw many male and female heretics there, and often adored them. And she heard their preaching. And she saw that all the men and women from the town used to go to the heretics' preaching in public, and adored them. And this was 18 years ago and thereabouts.

Item, she said that while the same witness and her sister Ramunda were living at Narbonne, someone called William Bertrand together with four other men came to the same witness's and her sister's house. And they ate in the same witness's house. And they said they were the heretics' messengers, and they had escorted two heretics to the house of Raymond John of Narbonne. However, neither the same witness nor her sister knew this, but later they heard it said when the said Raymond John was arrested. And then the *bailli* of the lord Archbishop of Narbonne arrested the same witness and her sister Raymunda, and took them to the court of the lord archbishop. And then Brother Ferrier, who was then inquisitor by the authority of the lord archbishop, reconciled the same witness and the same witness's sister, Raymunda, and let them go away. And then the same Brother Ferrier went with her sister Raymunda as far as Mas, and handed her back to her husband. And this was 16 years ago, or thereabouts. And afterwards she did not see heretics.

She believed that the aforesaid heretics were good men, and had a good faith, and one could be saved through them, although she knew that the Church persecuted them. And she heard them saying errors: about visible things, that God had not made them; and that the consecrated host was not the body of Christ; and that the bodies of dead men will not rise again; and that there was not salvation in baptism and marriage. And she believed as they said. And it was 22 years ago that she first believed the heretics were good. However, she did not believe after Brother Ferrier reconciled her. Nor did she see heretics afterwards, apart from captured ones.

She confessed all the aforesaid things to Brother Ferrier at Saissac.

And she swore, and took an oath, etc.

Witnesses: the aforesaid. …

/20r/… Item, on the year and day as above [19 May 1245] Ramunda, wife of the late William Germa, sworn in as a witness, said that she saw many heretics living openly at Mas. However, she had no familiarity with them. And this was 60 years ago.

Otherwise she did not see heretics, nor believed, nor adored, nor gave, nor sent, nor escorted, nor received, nor heard their preaching.

Later, she said that the same witness was an open heretic for 3 years or thereabouts, then at that time when heretics lived openly at Montmaur. And this was 60 years ago or thereabouts.

And she was reconciled by the Toulousan lord bishop – it was 10 years ago. And the lord bishop gave her two crosses. And after a year the same witness left off the crosses, without the Church's permission.

And she abjured heresy, and took an oath, etc.

Witnesses: the ones in the confession of Ermengardis.

Item, on the year and day as above, Na Segura, wife of William Vital, sworn in as a witness, said that she saw in her own house Bertrand Martin and his companion [*in margin*: heretics]. And she saw there with them Bernard of Mas <and> Galhard, brothers, and Saurimunda, Bernard of Mas's wife, and Raimunda Barrava, and Fabrissa, William of Mas's wife, and Pons Gran, and Pons Rainart, and Aribert and Jordan of Mas, brothers <and> knights, and William Gasc and his wife, and Raymond Iazaut, and many others whom she does not recall. And the same witness /20v/ adored them. And she believes that the others adored, but she does not remember. And this was 12 years ago or thereabouts.

Item, on another occasion she saw in the said house Peter Bolbena and his companion, heretics. And she saw there Arnold Donat, and Garnier, and Bernard Barrau. And the same witness adored, and believes that the others adored. And this was around the aforesaid time.

Item, in the same house she saw Raymond <son> of Na Richa, and his companion, heretics. And she saw there with them the said Richa. And the same witness and the said Richa adored the said heretics there. And this was 8 years ago or thereabouts.

Item, in the same house she saw Arnold Prader and his companion, heretics. And she saw there with them Jordan of Quiriès, and Raymond

Gauta, and Arnold Garner. And the same witness and the others adored them there. And this was around the aforesaid time.

Item, she said that when she was a girl about 10 years old she was a vested heretic. And she stayed a heretic for a good five years, and later she went out of this. And this was 40 years ago, and then the heretics lived openly at Mas.

Item, she said she believed the heretics were good men, and truth-tellers, and friends of God. And she heard the heretics saying that the consecrated host was not the body of Christ, and the same witness believed as they said. About other errors: she did not hear them speaking.

And she confessed to other inquisitors – and did not afterwards see heretics, nor send them anything nor receive anything from them – which confession she believes was true.

And blessed Dominic reconciled the same witness from heresy. The said Toulousan bishop gave the same witness two crosses. And on many days she did not wear the crosses, and on many occasions she wore them covered rather than uncovered. And she abjured, and took an oath, etc.

Witnesses: the ones in the confession of Ermengardis. …

/30r/ From St-Martin-de-Lalande …

/32v/ … Item, on the year and day as above [30 May 1245], Raymond Jocglar, sworn in as a witness, said that while he was going to the place called Lapeyre near Beaupuy, he left behind in his house his daughter Ramunda and his son Raymond. And when he came back to his house he found Willelma, wife of Ramond Faure of Camplong, and her companion, heretics. And then the same witness asked his said son and his daughter who sent the said heretics there? And when the same witness questioned the said Ramunda, the same witness's daughter, she replied that Isarn Gibel had brought the said heretics in there. And he [*Isarn*] had promised the said Ramunda, the same witness's daughter, that, if she let them stay in the said house, they would do a large good thing for her [*or* would pay her a lot]. And then this sent the same witness into a great rage, <and> he beat his daughter and threw her out of the house naked, without any clothing. And while he was hitting his daughter, Isarn of Gibel came there, and his wife Andriva, and the same witness's brother Pons, and they threatened the same witness, and got the said heretics out of the house and took them off to their house. And then his said daughter made herself a heretic, and afterwards he did not see her, though he heard it said that she had converted. But he did not adore the said female heretics there, nor did he see them adored. And this was 3 years ago or thereabouts.

He did not see heretics otherwise, nor did he believe or ever adore them, nor did he give or send anything, nor did he hear their preaching.

And he confessed to Brother William Arnold at Castelnaudary. But at that time he had not seen the said female heretics nor did he know anything about heresy.

And he abjured heresy, and took an oath, etc.

Witnesses: the aforesaid. …

/40v/ … In the year as above, 14 days before the calends of January [19 December 1245], Ramunda, the daughter of Raymond Jocglar, converted from heresy, sworn in as a witness, said that when her said father threw the same witness out of his house for heresy, <and> because he believed she was a whore, William of Gouzens and Ermengarz, his wife, and Martina Villaudina and Finas, her daughter, and Na Melia, and Arnalda of Garridech comforted the same witness …[139]

She said that the said William of Gouzens /41r/ and Ermengarz, his wife, often sent to the said female heretics bread, wine and fish and other eatables via the same witness. And this was 3 years ago or 4.

Item, she saw Fabrissa and her companion, heretics, at St-Martin, in the house of Martina Villaudina. And she saw there with them William of Gouzens and Ermengarz, his wife, and the aforesaid Martina and Finas, her daughter. However, the same <witness> did not adore the said female heretics nor see them adored. And this was 3 years ago or thereabouts.

Item, she saw the just-mentioned heretics in the house of Arnalda of Garridech, and she saw the said Arnalda there with them. However, the same witness did not adore them or see them adored. And this was at the same time.

Item, she saw two heretics[140] whose names she does not know at St-Martin, in the house of Isarn of Gibel. And she saw there with them

139 'comforted' is uncertain. Because of difficulty in transcription we omit the next fourteen lines of this leaf.

140 We cannot be sure the ms. has *hereticos* (male) rather than *hereticas* (female).

the said Isarn and Andriva, his wife. However, the same witness did not adore the said heretics, nor saw them adored. And this was 5 years ago or thereabouts.

Item, she saw Fabrissa and her companion, heretics, in the house of Raymond Jocglar, the same witness's father. And she saw there with them the said William of Gouzens and Ermengarz, his wife, who had escorted the said heretics there, and Martina Villaudina and Arnalda of Garridech, and the said Raymond, the same witness's father. And all of them and the same witness adored the said heretics there and heard the preachings and admonitions of the said heretics. And this was at the same time.

Item, she said that Bernard Alzeu escorted the same witness, together with the said heretics, out of St-Martin. And he escorted them right up to some little village near Laurac, where he brought them into the house of Raymond Arnold. And she saw there with the said female heretics the said Raymond Arnold, brother of the said Fabrissa, heretic, and Raymond Jocglar, the same witness's brother, who similarly kept company with the same witness and the said heretics and the said Bernard Alzeu. And there the same witness adored the said heretics often, and ate the bread blessed by them. However, she did not see others adore them. She also said that the same witness had promised the said heretics <that she would> deliver herself to them whenever they agreed to this. And this was at the same time.

Item, she said that the same witness lived with the said heretics at Laurac, in two houses, but she does not know whose they were. And Fanjeaux and his companion, heretics, came there. And she saw there with them many men and women from Laurac, whose names she does not know. And all of them and the same witness heard the said heretics' preaching and adored them. However, the said heretics were unwilling to hereticate the same witness until she was fully trained in respect to the ways of the heretics [donec bene esset instructa secundum mores hereticorum] and did, first of all, three 40-day fasts.[141] And this was 3 years ago or thereabouts.

Item, she said that when the same witness had lived at Laurac in the aforesaid houses for a month or thereabouts, the said heretics left there and went on their way towards Montségur. And they were unwilling to take the same witness with them, because the same witness was not

141 On the three forty-day fasts of the Cathars, see J. Duvernoy, *La Religion des Cathares* (Toulouse, 1976; repr. 1989), p. 175.

yet fully trained nor properly established in the heretics' sect, and for this reason they left the same witness there. And then a certain young man from Laurac – who lived as a prisoner this year in the Château Narbonnais – escorted the same witness to Gaja, where he brought the same witness into some house. And the master of this house, whose name she does not know, escorted the same witness by night to a certain woodland, where he left the same witness with Arnalda and her mother, heretics. And there the same witness was captured with the said heretics. And the said heretics were burnt at Toulouse. And when she was taken right up to the fire, the same witness through fear of the fire converted to the Catholic faith. And this was 2½ years ago.

She believed the aforesaid heretics were good men, and truth-tellers, and friends of God, and one could be saved through them.

She also that the same witness was with the heretics from the feast of blessed Martin up to around Pentecost. And she was hereticated at Laurac, <in the house> of some knight, but she does not remember his name. And this was 3 years ago.

She also said that she saw Arnold[142] of Mazerolles, Lord of Gaja, adoring Arnalda and the mother of the same Arnalda, heretics, on bended knees, saying 'Bless' three times. And this was at the aforesaid time, or thereabouts.

And she abjured heresy, and took an oath, etc.

Witnesses: Brother William Pelhisson, and Arnold <Auriol>, Prior of St-Sernin, and Brother Bernard of Caux, Inquisitor, who received this confession. …

/41v/ From Mas-Saintes-Puelles …

/43r/ From Montgaillard …

/47v/ These two from Trébons, from the parish of Montgaillard …

/48r/ From Barelles just by Montgaillard …

142 Ms: Bertrand or Bernard.

/50r/ From Renneville

/58r/ From Baziège

/62r/ From Gourvielle

Item, on the year and day as above, on the calends of July [1 July 1245], Esclarmonda, wife of the late Pons Bret, sworn in as a witness said that she saw heretics living openly in the land. And this was 35 years ago or thereabouts.

Item, at the same time she often saw the same witness's mother-in-law, Raymunda Bret, heretic, in the same witness's and her husband's own house. And she often ate with her. But later her said mother-in-law was reconciled <to the Church>.

And she never believed, nor adored them, nor gave or sent them anything, nor heard their preaching.

Afterwards she said she believed the heretics were good men, and had a good faith and were friends of God, although she knew the Church persecuted them. And she heard the heretics saying that God did not make visible things, and that the consecrated host is not the body of Christ, and that marriage does not have value for salvation, and the same witness believed as the heretics said. But it is more than 30 years since she did not believe [*i.e. stopped believing*], and 40 years since she first believed.

She also said that she once went to a sermon of heretics at Montesquieu. And then Bernard of Lamothe was confirmed as bishop of the heretics. And there many ladies adored Bernard of Lamothe, bishop of the heretics, and other heretics, on bended knees saying, 'Bless'. However, the same witness never adored him, although the same witness's mother-in-law begged the same witness many times <to do so>. And she abjured heresy, and took an oath, etc.

Witnesses: Brother Arnold, Prior of St-Sernin; Raymond Ferriol; Arnold Cerda.

She also said that she saw in her husband's house Bertrand of Roqueville and his companion, heretics. And she saw there with them her husband Pons Bret, and her household. And everyone, and the same witness, heard the heretics' preaching. And she believes her husband adored them. And this was 15 years ago or thereabouts. She also said that her husband was not hereticated.

Witnesses: the aforesaid.

And she <had> confessed to inquisitors at Avignonet.

In the year as above, 5 days before the nones of July [3 July 1245], Esclarmonda, wife of the late Pons Bret, sworn in as a witness, adding to her confession, said she saw Bernard Columbassa and his companion, <heretics>. in the yard of Raymond of Gourvielle, her son-in-law. And she saw with them Raymond Bret,the same witness's son, Septalina, the same witness's daughter, adoring them on bended knees, saying 'Bless' three times. And this was 6 years ago this summer.

She said also that she heard it said by Peter Dominici, prisoner in the Château Narbonnais, that Bertrand of Brantalou and Raymond of Gourvielle, her son-in-law, had seen the aforesaid heretics in the said place.

She also said that she believed the aforesaid heretics were good men and had a good faith and were friends of God and truth-tellers. And she heard them saying that God had not made visible things, and that the consecrated host is not the body of Christ, and that marriage is prostitution. And the same witness believed as they said, and if she died in their hands she believed she would be saved, and if she died without their hands she believed she would be damned. But it is more than 5 years since she did not believe.

And she acknowledged that she had done ill, because recently when arraigned in court she had sworn <to tell the truth>, and when questioned she denied the aforesaid things. And she said that she denied through shame.

Item, she acknowledged she had done ill because she denied the aforesaid things in front of Brother William Arnold at Avignonet.

She also said, again, that her husband was not hereticated, nor did he ask for the heretics, nor did the same witness advise him to have heresy.

And she swore, etc.

Witnesses: The Prior of Mas-Stes-Puelles; Arnold, Prior of St-Sernin; Arnold Cerda; William Barasc; and Brother Bernard, Inquisitor.

AD 1246, 5 days before the ides of March [11 March 1246] this confession was read out to the said Esclarmonda at Toulouse in the presence of brothers Bernard of Caux and John of St-Pierre, inquisitors, which confession she acknowledged was true.

Witnesses: Arnold, Prior of St-Sernin in Toulouse; Bernard Isarn, chaplain of Saubens; William, chaplain of Baziège; brothers Otho and William Gari, of the Order of Preachers; and Peter Fresapa, public notary, who wrote this. …

/64v/ From Montgiscard …

/69r/ From Lagarde …

/71v/ From Laurac …

/75v/ … In the year as above, 6 days before the ides of July [10 July 1245], William Rigaut, leper, said that he saw Raymond of Carlipa and his companion, heretics, in the house of his uncle William Médicin at St-Paul Cap-de-Joux. And he saw there with them William Aycard, and Bernard Gui and Peter Gui and Raymond Gui, brothers, and William Fisa and Bernard Fisa, his son (to whom the whole business of the heretics was disagreeable), and Bernard Rigaut, the same witness's brother, and Ricarda Aicarda, the said William Aicard's mother. And the said William Médicin, who was ill with the illness from which he died, was hereticated by the said heretics, in the sight of the same witness and all the people named earlier, apart from Bernard Rigaut who was not present at the heretication – but he did adore them – and apart from Bernard Fisa, who covered his face because he did not want to look. But all the others adored the said heretics. And this was 17 years ago.

Item, he saw the said Raymond of Carlipa and his companion William Richart, heretics, at St-Paul, outside the town in the lepers' house. And they came there to hereticate the leper Calvet, who was then ill with the illness from which he died. And he himself had sent for them, and they hereticated him. And present at the said heretication were Bernard of Toulouse, and Willelma of Laurac, who was looking after the said leper. However, the same woman did not have faith in them, so the same witness says. And the same witness and the said Bernard of Toulouse adored the said heretics there. And this was 16 years ago.

Item, he said that while the same witness was at Laurac in the lepers' house there was there a certain woman called Bernarda – who at the time was ill – the concubine of Raymond Bartha. And the said Raymond Bartha was at that time a fugitive, and stayed by day in the said leprosary. And he wasted all the goods of the said house, to the ill will of those who were there. Urged and begged by the said Raymond Bartha, fugitive, John of Arnalda, fugitive, and Arnold Mazeler – now burnt[143] – escorted Peter of Mas and Pons Tolsan to the said ill woman. They hereticated her, though first she received the body of the Lord. The same witness, however, was not present, but he heard some words said by the aforesaid heretics which led him to believe that the said ill woman was hereticated. The same witness, however, did not adore them, but Raymond Barta did. And they were there for a day and a night. But afterwards the aforesaid Peter did adore them there, many times. And this was 3 years ago.

Item, he saw in the garden of the lepers' house Tolsana, and the mother of Bernard Aymeric, and another woman, heretics, whom Pons of Capelle brought there from Gaja. And he saw with them there the sister of Bernard Aymeric, and the wife of Bernard Flamas, and William Sartre, and Peter of *Mauloc*. But the same witness did not adore, nor did he see <others> do this. And Bernard Garsias and Arnold Mazeler took the said heretics out of the house. And this was near the time of the most recent grape-picking.

He believed that the aforesaid heretics were good men, and had a good faith, and were friends of God, and truth-tellers, and one could be saved through them or with them.

Asked about errors, he said that he had often heard it said by the heretics that God had not made visible things, and that baptism of water and marriage were not of value for salvation and that the consecrated host was not the body of Christ. And the same witness believed then just as they said.

Item, he said that the said Raymond /76r/ advised the same witness to love the heretics, and he recommended the heretics to him a lot.

Item, he said he heard from the said Raymond Barta that baptism and marriage and the consecrated host were of no value for salvation, and that there will not be resurrection of bodies, and that the said Raymond did not believe in <anything> except the New Testament. And the same witness's wife Ramunda, and his son Isarn, and the leper woman Aimengars heard this.

143 That is, subsequently executed for heresy.

Witnesses: Stephen, Archpriest of Laurac, and Centoul the chaplain [*parish priest*] of St-Léger, and Brother William Pelhisson of the Order of Preachers. …

/77r/ … On the year and day as above [10 July 1245], Petrona Fizela, sworn in as a witness, said that she saw Ramunda and the said Ramunda's daughter, heretics, in the same witness's own house. But she saw no-one there with them, nor did she adore them thus [*in heretical mode*]. And this was 17 years ago or thereabouts.

Item, she said that after she confessed to Brother William Arnold, Inquisitor, and abjured heresy, she saw two heretics whom she did not know in John Afailer's hut, where the said John's son Lawrence Afailer lay ill. And she saw there with the said heretics Bonet Faure, Bernard Cuilha <and> Arnold Cuilha, brothers, John Afailer, Arnold Mazeler and Arnold Babot who escorted the heretics there, Bernard Roco, <and> Bernard Delbosc. And then the ill <boy> asked the aforesaid heretics to receive him. But they were unwilling to receive him, because he was very young. And when the ill <boy> heard that they were unwilling to receive him, angered he closed his eyes as though he were dead. And as quickly as possible the said heretics placed a book on the head of the said youth. And the same witness[144] and all the others the adored the said heretics there, on bended knees. And this was 4 or 5 years before summer this year.

She believed the aforesaid heretics were good men, but she did not hear them saying errors. She did the aforesaid things after she abjured heresy in the presence of Brother William Arnold, Inquisitor.

And she abjured heresy, and took an oath, etc.

Witness: the aforesaid. …

/80r/ From St-Michel-de-Lanès of the Lauragais

AD1245, 2 days before the ides of June [12 June 1245] Peter of St-Michel, sworn in as a witness, said he saw heretics living openly at Laurac, but he had no familiarity with them. And this was 20 years ago or thereabouts.

Item, in the house of Bernard of St-Michel, knight, he saw Bertrand Martin and his companion, heretics. And he saw there with them

144 Ms. has witness in the genitive.

Bernard of St-Michel, and William Bernard, son of Galhard Roger, and Bertrand Raymond, brothers, and Raymond Maire, keeper of the count's treasure, and Raymond of Lanès, *bailli* of Bernard of St-Michel, who [*plural*] had brought the said heretics there; and the wife of the said Bernard of St-Michel, called N'Albia, and N'Ot of Rival, and Pons Magrefort, and Pons of Bosc Mir, and Gualharda the wife of John Amielh of Mas-Saintes-Puelles, and Arnold Baro, the chaplain of St-Michel, and Raymond of Malvezie, and Bernard and Arnold, brothers, and Peter Ros the elder and Peter Ros the younger, and Pons Balans, and Stephen of Avigno<net>, and many others he does not recall. However, the same witness did not adore; but all the others adored the said heretics. And all of them, apart from the same witness, took an oath and made a pact among themselves – apart from the aforesaid chaplain Arnold Baro, whom he did not see taking the oath, or adoring, but he did see him going in to the aforesaid heretics – that they would reveal the aforesaid things to no-one. And the said heretics did the *apparellamentum* there, in the sight of all the aforesaid. And they preached. And this was 12 years ago.

Item, when he was in the house of Raymond Maire, the same Raymond Maire asked the same witness to eat with him some eel pasty which he had got from Brun and his companion, heretics, who were in the said house at the time, as the same witness heard said by the said Raymond Matfre [= Maire]. And this was at the same time.

Item, at Labécède, in the house of Arnold Caudera, knight, he saw William Vital and his companion, heretics. And the same witness saw there with them Pons of St-Michel, the same witness's brother, and William Raymond,[145] notary of Labécède, and Peter Rigaut, Lord of Labécède, and Sanche, the same Peter Rigaut's brother, and Peter Cathalas, knight, and Arnold Caudera, knight, and Andorras, knight, brothers, and Na Caudera, the said Andorras's mother, and many others whom he does not recall. And there the said heretic expounded the Passion of Christ, and the said notary William Raymond read out the Passion. However, the same witness did not adore, nor did he see that Peter Rigaut and Sanche, brothers, and Peter Cathalas adored the said heretics there. And all the others heard their preaching. And this was 11 years ago or thereabouts.

Item, when Roger of La Tour, the same witness's uncle, was ill at Laurac in the house of Bernard of St-Martin, he entreated the same witness to

145 Ms: William Arnold.

get heretics to come to him, because he wanted to be hereticated – and the same witness replied that he would not do it. And the same witness left immediately and went to Castelnaudary. And later he heard it said that the same Roger was made a heretic. And the same witness returned to the same Roger and found him at the point of death. And he saw there two heretics, whose names he does not know. And he saw there with them Adelasia, the said Roger's wife, and Pons of La Tour, and William of Lahille [*or* L'Île], and Balaguier, brothers, knights, and Arnold Faure, and Pons Fort, and Bernard of St-Julien, knights, and Pons of St-Michel, the same witness's brother, and Adelasia and Ermessen, the same witness's sisters, and many others whom he does not recall. However, the same witness did not adore, nor did he see them adored. And this was 7 years ago.

Item, he said that Bernard of St-Michel sent some messenger to the same[146] witness that the same witness should go to Na Fizas, the aforesaid Bernard of St-Michel's mother, who was ill and preparing to be hereticated. However, the same witness was unwilling to go. But later he heard that the said ill women had been hereticated, and he heard it said that at the time Raymond Matres, and William, son of Galhard Negre, and Raymond of Lanès escorted Bernard of Maire and his companion, heretics, to the said ill woman. And this was 7 years ago or thereabouts.

Item, he said that he often saw in Bernard of St-Michel's house the heretic Adelasia, the same witness's father's sister, and two other female heretics. And he often saw there <with them> the same Bernard of St-Michel, and Albia, the same Bernard's wife, and Gualharda, the wife of John Amielh of Mas-Stes-Puelles. However, the same witness did not adore, nor did he see them adored. And this was 15 years ago or thereabouts.

Item, in the house of Alaman of Roaix in Toulouse, when Raymond of Château de Roussillon [*or* Roussillous] was ill there, <the same witness saw> [*missing here: name of heretic, and companion, 'heretics'*] the said Alaman, and many others whom he does not recall. And the same witness talked with the said heretics there. However, he did not adore them nor see them adored, nor did he see that they hereticated the said Raymond of Château de Roussillon [*or* Roussillous]. And this was at the same time.

146 Ms: 'there' (ibi) instead of 'to the same' (ipsi).

Item, he saw Bernard of Lamothe and his companion, heretics, living openly at Lamothe, who [Bernard] asked the same witness not to do them ill. And the same witness replied that he would never do them either ill or good. And this was 20 years ago.

Item, in some house at Toulouse he saw the said heretic, sister of the same witness's father, and many other female heretics, and Bernard /80v/ of Lamothe and his companion, heretics. And the said heretics asked the same witness to listen to their preaching, and the same witness was unwilling. And he saw there Joanna, the wife of Bernard Raymond Tozetz of Toulouse. However, the same witness did not adore, nor did he see them adored. And this was at the same time.

Item, at Vaudreuille Peter Rigaut, the Lord of Labécède, said to [*asked*] the same witness if he wanted to see the heretics he had in his house, and the same witness said he did not. And this was 12 years ago or thereabouts.

He also said that he heard the heretics saying that God had not made visible things, and that the consecrated host is not the body of Christ, and that marriage is not of value. However, the same witness did not believe as they said. He did not otherwise see heretics, nor did he believe, nor adore, nor give, nor send, nor escort, nor hear their preaching.

And he confessed to other inquisitors at Limoux, and afterwards he did not see heretics.

Item, he said that he heard William Tort of Issel saying in the barber's shop at Pomarède that Arnold Baro, the aforesaid priest, had imposed a penance of six ferial days on the said William. And later the said William played chess with the said priest Arnold Baro, and won the aforesaid six ferial days.[147]

Item, he heard that although the said Arnold Baro was a priest he loved the said heretics, and he used to eat together with them at Labécède.

Item, the said witness said that the said priest made many false marriages at St-Michel, and that he is very much an associate of Bernard of St-Michel, and that he is a blasphemer and plays dice, and that because of gaming he abandons ill people to die without unction or penance.

And he abjured heresy, and took an oath, etc.

147 Presumably: won the cost of commuting the penance.

Witnesses: Arnold, Prior of St-Sernin; William Peter of St-G [*perhaps* Germain], and [*missing name(s)?*] brothers of the Order of Preachers, and Arnold Gasc, and Brother Bernard, Inquisitor.

He also said that Raymond of Lanès, and Pons of Bosc Mir, and his brother William of Bosc Mir, Gualharda the wife of John Amielh of Mas-Stes-Puelles, and Pons William of Gourvielle, and Bernard of Montesquieu, the bastard, who lives at Cailhavel, know heresy in St-Michel and surrounding parts of the country, and Arnold Baro the chaplain of St-Michel-de-Lanès, and <as do also> William the son of Galhard Negre, and all the aforesaid, and Pons Negre. …

/82r/ From Maurémont …

/82v/ From the Bastide of Arnold of Falgar [La Bastide Beauvoir] …

/84v/ From Plaigne …

/86v/ These are from Blazens of the parish of Plaigne …

These are from Belle Combe of the parish of Plaigne …

/87r/ From Auriac …

/90v/ On the year and day as above, 8 days before the ides of November [6 November 1245], Lady Honors, wife of Gerard of Castelnaudary [*note in ms. margin:* This is the mother of Bernard of Auriac, who killed Guilabert <of> Carbonel], said that she saw at Toulouse, in the house of Na Bernart, Bernard Bonafos[148] and Raymond Gros and two other companions, heretics. And she saw there with them the same Bernarda, lady of the house,[149] and Hugo Vital, the said Bernarda's son, and the housemaid Joanna of Verfeil. And the same witness had come into that house to heal her arm, with which she was ailing, because she could

148 See introduction to Doc. 41 above.

149 Where the deponent and her circle are ladies, 'lady of the house' has a more formal sense than it does in modern English.

not get advice at Auriac. But neither the same witness nor the said Vital adored the aforesaid <heretics>. However, she did see the said Bernarda and the housemaid Joanna adoring. And Bernarda told the same witness to adore the said heretics and taught her <how to>. And the same heretics then told the same witness that she should not do this [*i.e. adore them*] unless she had faith in them. And this was 10 years ago or thereabouts.

Item, she said that at Lascombes in the diocese of Albi, in the house of Na Galharda of Lascombes, she saw Ademar of Roquemaure and his companion, heretics. And she saw there with them the knight Bertrand of Roquemaure – who was accompanying the same witness, who was then travelling to her own parts, that is to say to Montaigut in the diocese of Albi, near Rabastens, from where she originated – and Gualharda, the lady of the house, and Raimunda, the same Gualharda's daughter, and Matfres of Lascombes, the same Raimunda's husband. However, they did not adore, nor did she see others adore. And then the said knight Bertrand of Roquemaure, who was there with the same witness, went out of the house, because he had found heretics there. And he did not want to go back in there until the said heretics had gone away from there. And then the said heretics told the said knight Bertrand of Roquemaure that he had a very bad understanding [*of what was appropriate*], because he had never refused this to any of his kin. And this was 15 years ago or thereabouts.

Item, she said that she saw the son of William Raymond Golairan of Avignonet living openly at Auriac, in the house of Guilabert of Carbonel; and <she saw> some horse of the same William Raymond Golairan, which the same Guilabert of Carbonel kept after the brother inquisitors were killed at Avignonet. And she heard it said that after he fled from Avignonet the said William Raymond Golairan stayed in hiding in the said William of Carbonel's house.[150]

Item, she said that she never believed the heretics were good men, nor friends of God, nor truth-tellers, nor that one could be saved through them, nor did she ever adore them. However, she heard the heretics saying errors, that there was no salvation in marriage; but she did not hear them talking about other errors.

She also said that she confessed to inquisitors at Toulouse.

And she abjured, and took an oath, etc.

150 On these events, see Doc. 46 above.

Witnesses: the aforesaid [*scribal mistake*], Arnold, Prior of St-Sernin, and brothers of the Order of Preachers William Pelhisson, and Brother Bernard, Inquisitor. …

/94 v/ … [*This note follows depositions from February 1246. It has no date or names of deponents and witnesses.*]
It is said that Andreva, wife of the late Raymond Isarn of Vaure, spoke with the women heretics whom William Carbonel captured in the house where the chaplain of Auriac lives: and on her own.

Item, it is said that the said chaplain's pupil, Peter of Devèze, made himself familiar to the said heretics to such an extent that they had a will, that is to say the disposition of their goods, written by him. And when this had been done the said heretics retained the aforesaid script. And when the said heretics had to be brought out of the aforesaid house and taken off to Toulouse, one of them put the aforementioned deed [carta] or script between two fence-posts of the said Andreva<'s house> that were outside the enclosure of the fencing on the side of William of Prés's house. And the said heretics were in the said chaplain's yard. And when Martin the sub-chaplain of Auriac learnt through talk what had happened with the said deed, straightaway he went to the said Andreva and asked her for the aforesaid instrument, in the presence of Lady Brunisen, daughter of Oliver of Cuq, and Raymond Pons and Lady Mary, wife of the said Raymond Pons, and the daughter of Raymond Pons, and many others. And then the said Andreva denied, <saying> that she had not had the aforesaid deed. And then in the presence of the aforesaid people the chaplain put his hand into the said Andreva's bosom, and found the said deed there, which he displayed to everyone. …

/96r/ … AD 1245 on the nones of July [7 July] Arnold Rodelh sworn in as a witness said that he saw heretics living openly at Auriac. However, he did not adore them nor did he see them adored. And this was 30 years ago.

He did not otherwise see heretics, nor did he believe, nor did he adore, nor did he give nor did he send them anything, nor did he hear their preaching.

[*There follow twenty people swearing as witnesses on the same date and denying, often in the form* 'said the same as the aforesaid Arnold about heresy'.]

/96v/ … In the year and day as above Willelma Michaela, sworn as a witness, said the same as the aforesaid Arnold about heresy.

Item, she said that she lived with the Waldensians at Castelnaudary for three years. And at that time the Waldensians were living openly in the land. And she dressed, ate, drank, prayed and did other things just as they did.[151]

[*There follow seventeen more people swearing as witnesses on the same date, most of them denying.*] All the aforesaid abjured heresy.

Witnesses: Arnold, Prior of St-Sernin, Peter Aymes, chaplain of Montgey.

Item, in the year as above, 4 days before the nones of July [4 July], Willelma Michaela was again sworn as a witness.[152] She said that she saw Waldensians, and she lived with Bernarda of Pomas, and Rixen of Limoux, and Christiana, Waldensians, for four years or thereabouts. And she heard them saying that no-one ought to swear, for the truth or for a lie, nor ought they to make a binding oath, in law or outside law. …

/99r/ From Montesquieu …

/109r/ From Gardouch …

/114r/ From Vieillevigne of the parish of Gardouch …

/114v/ From Las Bordes …

/117r/ From Maurens by Cambon …

On the aforesaid year and day [13 December 1245], Durand of Las Bordes, sworn in as a witness, said that he saw in the Cugnet wood two heretics whom he did not know. /117v/ And he saw there with them Bernard Garrigas, and Peter of Massalens, of Villeneuve, who had escorted the said heretics there. However, the same witness did not adore the said heretics there, nor see them adored. And this was 5 years ago or thereabouts.

151 See 250v for memory of Waldensians living openly at Castelnaudary before 1209. Taken with Willelma's further testimony, this evidence suggests Waldensian women clothed in a religious habit, and following regular conventual life very early in the thirteenth century. Compare Doc. 53.

152 Since this is her second appearance, there is a mistake in the dates.

Item, he saw in some hut by Villeneuve four heretics whom he did not know. And he saw there with the said heretics Bernard Garriga and Peter of Massalens, who had escorted the same witness there. However, he did not adore them nor saw them adored, though the said heretics demonstrated to them the form of the adoration [modum adorationis] many times. And this was 4 years ago or thereabouts.

Item, he said that he saw, in some hut in the vineyard of Peter of Garrigues or <of> Audet, two heretics whom he did not know. And he saw there the same Peter of Garrigues and Vital of Le Faget. And all, and the same witness, heard the heretics' preaching. And the same witness and Peter of Garrigues adored them on bended knees, saying 'Bless'. However, Vital of Le Faget did not adore them, in the same witness's sight. And this was 3 years ago or thereabouts.

He believed at the time that the aforesaid heretics were good men, and had a good faith.

And he heard them saying errors: about visible things, that God had not made them; and that the consecrated host is not the body of Christ; and that there was not salvation in baptism and marriage; and that the bodies of dead men will not rise again. However, the same witness did not believe in the aforesaid errors.

And he confessed to Brother William Arnold, Inquisitor, at Lavaur. And <it was later that> he saw and adored heretics, as is stated above, in the vineyard of Peter of Garrigues. …

/118r/ From Génerville by Laurac …

/118v/ From Labécède …

/121v/ From Gaja …

/124r/ … AD 1246, 3 days before the ides of July [13 July] Peter of Mazerolles, Lord of Gaja, condemned for heresy, required to tell the truth both about himself and others, living and dead, on the accusation of heresy and Waldensianism, was sworn in as a witness.[153]

153 See his mother's deposition in Doc. 44 above.

He said that when he was a boy he saw at Montréal many heretics, male and female, whose names he does not recall. And he often ate the bread and fruit the heretics gave him. But he did not adore them or see them adored. Nor does he remember the time.

Item, he saw two heretics, whom he did not know at the time, at the castle of Bernard of Aliou and Raymond of Niort. But later he heard that they were Guilabert of Castres and his companion, heretics. And he saw the aforesaid Bernard of Aliou and Raymond of Niort there, and Hysarn of Taysse and Bernard of Taysse, brothers, who were from Limoux. And then the aforesaid heretics preached there. And then all of them and the same witness heard the preaching of the said heretics. And all of them, apart from the same witness, adored them. And this was when the Count of Montfort held this land.[154]

Item, he said that later he heard it said that the aforesaid heretic was Guilabert of Castres.

Item, he said that he saw at Miremont in the Sabarthès Guilabert of Castres and his companion, heretics, in the hall of Raymond Sans of Rabat. And he saw there with the said heretics Hysarn of Castillon, the same witness's relative, Lord of Mirepoix, <now> dead, Gualhard of Festes of Fanjeaux, and the same Raymond Sans and Athon of Castillon of Rabat. And then the same witness and the aforesaid others heard the preachings of the aforesaid heretics. And the same witness, and Raymond Sans of Rabat, and Hysarn of Castillon, and all the aforesaid others adored the aforesaid heretics there.

And this was around the <time of the> Peace [*1229*].

Item, he saw at Labécède, in the house of Raymond Garsias of Labécède, Guilabert of Castres and his companion, heretics. And he saw there the same Raymond Garsias and Belengaria, his wife – both <now> dead – and Pagan of Labécède who was later a heretic, and Three Measures of Roqueville. And then the same witness – asked <to do it> by the said heretics and taught how to do it – /124v/ adored the said heretics there, <as did also the others>, genuflecting, each of them saying three times on their own behalf, 'Good men, bless. Pray to God on behalf of this sinner'. And this was 15 years ago or thereabouts.

Item, he saw at Toulouse in the house of Estult of Roqueville many heretics whom he did not know. But he did not adore them nor did he see them adored. And it was the time of the war.

154 During the crusade and up to Simon de Montfort's death, 1209–18.

Item, he often saw in the same house of the Roquevilles Braida, the same witness's aunt, and her companions, heretics. And he saw there with the said heretics Geralda, Estult of Roqueville's wife. However, he did not adore the aforesaid heretics nor did he see them adored. And this was at the same time.

Item, he said that when Raines of Mazerolles, the same witness's uncle, was ill at Toulouse in the Roquevilles' house, the said William Salamon and his companion, heretics, wanted to hereticate him. But the said Raines was unwilling to put up with being hereticated. And the same witness saw the said William Salamon and his companion, heretics, there. And he saw there with the said heretics Estult of Roqueville and Begon, the same Estult's brother. And then the same witness got the said heretics William Salomon and his companion out of Estult's house, and transported them in his mounted equipage right up to the outside of the town of Toulouse. And the said Estult of Roqueville was there with the same witness. But he did not adore the said heretics then nor see them adored. And this was at the time of the war.

Item, he saw at Villeneuve-la-Comptal, in the house of Pons of Villeneuve, formerly the seneschal,[155] two heretics whom he did not know. And he saw there with the said heretics the same Pons of Villeneuve and some man who was said to be from Rieutort, whose name he does not recall, who escorted the said heretics there. And then the same witness and the said Pons and the one who had escorted the said heretics there adored the said heretics there. And this was around the time of the Peace.

Item, he said that Bernard of Roqueville and Three Measures, brothers, asked the same witness to escort Vigouroux of La Bouconne and his companion, heretics, to the wood of La Selve by Gaja. And then the same witness and Three Measures escorted the aforesaid Vigouroux of La Bouconne and his companion, heretics, right up to the wood of La Selve by Gaja. And the said heretics were in the said wood for a day and a night. And there the same witness and the said Three Measures adored the aforesaid Vigouroux and his companion, heretics. And this was since the Peace.

Item, he saw Pagan of Labécède two or three times, and William Bernard Unaud, the father of Jordan of Lanta, and many other heretics, in the vaults of the Sabatats in the Lantarais. And he saw there the

155 Seneschal of the Toulousain from at least April 1235 to February 1241.

aforesaid Jordan of Lanta and Gerald Unaud, the said Jordan's brother. And the aforesaid heretics gave the same witness and the aforesaid Jordan and Gerald Unaud bread. And the same witness and the aforesaid Jordan and Gerald Unaud adored the aforesaid heretics there. And this was at the time of the war.

Item, he saw the aforesaid William Bernard Unaud and his companion, heretics, in a place which is called Le Bousquet in the house of Jordan of Lanta. And he saw there Jordan of Lanta and Gerald Unaud, the sons of the said heretic, and Guy of Castillon, the same witness's relative, who is from Mirepoix. However, he did not adore them then, nor see them adored. And this was since the Peace.

Item, he saw the aforesaid heretics in the same place on the paving by the house of the said Jordan. And he saw there with the said heretics the aforesaid Jordan of Lanta and Gerald Unaud, brothers, the sons of the said heretic. However, he did not adore them, nor did he see them adored. And this was at the same time.

Item, he saw at Montréal, in the same heretics' house, Raines of Mazerolles, the same witness's uncle, <and> seven heretics whose names he does not recall. And he saw there with the same heretics the same Raines and Bertrand of Mailhac, both now dead. And then the aforesaid Raines and Bertrand of Mailhac adored the aforesaid male heretics there, but the same <witness> did not adore them. And it was at the time of the war.

Item, he saw Bertrand Martin and his companion, heretics, in the wood of La Selve by Gaja. And he saw there with them Begon of Roqueville and Estult of Roqueville, brothers, and Three Measures of Roqueville, <and> Pons de La Chapelle of Gaja. And the same witness and all the others heard the preachings of the said heretics. And they adored them. And this was since the Peace.

Item, he saw the aforesaid Bertrand Martin and his companion, heretics, at Gaja in the house of Pons of La Chapelle. And he saw there with the said heretics Arnold of Mazerolles, the same witness's brother, and Peter Fortz, and Amiel of Camplong, knights of Laurac, and Three Measures, and Pons of La Chapelle and the same Pons's wife, who were later burnt. And then the same witness, and all the others, apart from Peter Fort and Amiel of Camplong, adored the aforesaid heretics there. And all of them heard their preaching. And this was since the Peace.

And then Bertrand Martin, heretic, lent the same witness 200 Toulouse shillings. And he asked the same witness to be a friend of the heretics, and to love them, and with all his strength to defend them, so as to stop anyone doing bad things to the heretics. And the same witness then promised the said Bertrand Martin, heretic, /125r/ that he would defend and keep guard over him and other heretics with all his strength. And this was since the Peace.

Item, he said that when the *castrum* of Montréal was besieged by the King of France's Seneschal, John of Beaumont,[156] the same witness saw there in the said *castrum* Peter Pola,[157] bishop of the heretics, and his companion, heretics. And then Jordan of Lanta entered the said *castrum*, and Peter of Coucagne, Lord of Calan, entered with the said Jordan. And then the two of them spoke with the said heretics in the house of En Bres, who was living near Montréal. And then the said Jordan of Lanta asked the same witness to get the said heretics out of the *castrum*, by whatever means. And then the same witness, on the insistence of the said Jordan, handed over the aforesaid heretics to his sergeant, Raymond Aychart. And then the said Raymond Aychart escorted the said heretics right up to Gaja into the house of a certain woman who is called Laurencia. And the said heretics were there for two nights until he came from Montréal. And that night there came to Gaja, Gerald Unaud, the brother of Jordan of Lanta, and Pons of La Tour the Elder of Laurac, then *bailli* of the lord count,[158] and Balaguier, now dead. And they ordered the same witness to go and talk to them at the church of Arbonnens, which the same witness did. And then the aforesaid Gerald Unaud told the same witness, on behalf of Jordan of Lanta, the same Gerald's brother, to hand over to them Peter Pola, the aforesaid bishop of heretics. And then the same witness passed the said heretic on to the aforesaid Gerald via Raymond Aychart, the same witness's sergeant. And the same witness then lent a mule to the said heretic, on which the said heretic rode. And then the said Gerald Unaud, and Pons of La Tour, and Balaguier escorted the said heretics right up to Besplas. And they sent them to the headquarters of the *castrum*, so he heard it said by Raymond Aychart and someone else whose name he does not recall. And this was five years ago or thereabouts. However, he did not adore them, nor see them adored.

156 John of Beaumont-Gâtinais (c.1190–1255), Grand Chamberlain of Louis IX 1240–55. The siege was late October 1240.

157 Elsewhere Peter Pollan, Peter Pollain, etc; see also above and Doc. 1.

158 Raymond VII of Toulouse.

Item, he saw at Laure[159] in the house of a certain lady, the mother of Amiel of Rustiques, the aforesaid Peter Pola and his companion, heretics. And he saw there with them Arnold of Mazerolles, the same witness's brother, and Amiel of Rustiques, and the said Amiel's mother, whose name he does not know. And then the heretic gave the same witness a felt hat. And the same witness adored them there. And he saw them adored by others. And this was 7 years ago or thereabouts.

Item, he saw the heretic Bernard of Plas in the wood of La Selve by Gaja. And he saw there Raymond Aychart and Jordan of Villars, of the diocese of Carcassonne. And then Bernard had come from Lombardy. And then the same witness spoke with the said Bernard for this <reason>: that he wanted to know any news from Lombardy. However, he did not adore, nor see him adored. Nor did he know he was a heretic until he heard it said later that he had been burnt and that he had brought about the destruction of the town of Gaja.

And this was 5 years ago or thereabouts.

He believed that the aforesaid heretics were good men, and had a good faith, and that one could be saved through them, although he knew that the Church persecuted them. And he heard the heretics saying that God had not made visible things, and that the consecrated host was not the body of Christ, and that there was no salvation in baptism or marriage, and that the bodies of the dead do not rise up again. And he heard them saying that each soul of a man went around so many bodies until it could be saved. And the same witness believed the aforesaid errors, except that he did not believe that the consecrated host was not the body of Christ and he did not believe that when the soul left the body it could enter another body. And it was 16 years and more that the same witness believed that the heretics were good men. But he did not believe after he confessed to Brother William Arnold and his companion, inquisitors, though he often saw heretics afterwards.

Asked if he saw heretics after he was condemned, he said no. Asked if he ever gave anything to heretics, he said no, nor did he ever eat with them, except when he was a boy. Nor was he present at an *apparellamentum* of the heretics, apart from once at Gaja in the house of Pons of La Chapelle. And then the same witness, and Peter Fortz of Laurac, and Amiel of Camplong, and Three Measures, and Arnold of

159 Ms: *Laura* – though there could be a copyist's omission of final *-cum*, i.e. *Lauracum*, Laurac.

Mazerolles adored Bertrand Martin and his companion, heretics, there. And they received the Peace from them.

These things he attested at Toulouse in front of the brothers Inquisitors Bernard of Caux and John of St-Pierre.

And he abjured heresy, and took an oath, etc. And he bound himself and his things to the obedience of the commands of the inquisitors. And he agreed to the drawing up of a public instrument.

Witnesses: Raymond of Foix, Prior of the brothers Preacher of Toulouse;[160] William of Boissoles, Sub-Prior;[161] brothers William Pelhisson and Peter Barrau of the Order of Preachers; Arnold, the Prior of St-Sernin; Brother Bernard of Auriac, Senior Cellarer from Boulbonne;[162] and Peter Fresapa, public notary, who drew up from this a public instrument.

/125v/ Item, in the year as above, 2 days before the ides of July [14 July 1246], the aforesaid Peter of Mazerolles, sworn in as a witness, added to his confession, saying that, after he was condemned for heresy, one night he ran into Arnold Prader and his companion, heretics. And Raymond Aychard and Pons of Calès were with the same witness. And immediately – when the same witness heard the aforesaid heretics coming – he believed they were other men, strangers. And without delay the aforesaid heretics fled. And the same witness and his companions chased after the said heretics, and they got hold of two of these heretics. And Arnold Prader got away and he could not get hold of him. But afterwards the same witness had the said Prader called, and then the said Prader came back to the same witness. And then the same witness told the aforesaid heretics that in future they should not dare to come near to the *castrum* of Gaja. And he did not adore them, nor did he see them adored. And this was 4 years ago or thereabouts.

Item, he said that he saw Bernard of Mayreville and his companion, heretics, in the cemetery at Gaja. And he saw there with the said heretics Estult of Roqueville and Three Measures, brothers, who were escorting the said heretics, and Raymond Aychart, who had come there with the same witness. And then the said Estult asked the same witness to provide the said heretic Bernard of Mayreville with a nag, which the

160 Prior after 1242, d. 1258.

161 Later Prior at Béziers (1254–6) and Castres (1263–5), d. 1271.

162 A Cistercian monastery.

same witness was unwilling to do. And at the time the said heretic was going to Montségur. And he did not adore them, nor did he see them adored. And this was 4 or 5 years ago.

Item, he saw at Castres, in a house built of stone – he does not know its name – a certain heretic called Bartholomew, and his companion, heretics. And he saw there with the heretics Arnold of Villemur, Lord of Saverdun, and William Bernard of Estanove. But he did not adore them, nor see them adored. And this was at the time of the war.

Witnesses: Arnold the Prior of St-Sernin; Brother Bernard of Auriac, Senior Cellarer from Boulbonne; Pagan, chaplain of St-Martin-de-Lalande; and Peter Fresapa, public notary.

In the year as above, 17 days before the calends of August [16 July 1246] the aforesaid Peter of Mazerolles, sworn in as a witness, said that Gerald Unaud, Jordan of Lanta's brother. and Pons of La Tour the Elder told the same witness, on behalf of the said Jordan of Lanta, to hand over to them Peter Pola and his companion. And then the same witness handed over the aforesaid Peter Pola and his companion, heretics, to the aforesaid Gerald Hunaud, and Pons of La Tour, and Balaguier.

Item, he said that he heard that Peter Rigaud and his brother Sans, and Raymond of Vaure, Bertrand of Montmaur, Arnold Boter of Vaure, Pons Alamand, Peter Alamand, and Bertrand Alamand, brothers, were believers in and supporters of the heretics.

Item, AD 1246, 5 days before the ides of October [11 October], the said Peter [*text of the deposition stops at this point*]

/126r/ From Issel, a league from Castelnaudary …

/127v/ … In the year and day as above [9 June 1245] Bernard Durand, sworn in as a witness, said that all that he did with heretics, or saw being done, or knows in any way, is contained in the writing he composed together with Pons Garriga. And he believes that it is true throughout, and everything is contained there.
[*After eleven brief depositions on the same day:*]
All the aforesaid abjured heresy, and swore, etc.

Witnesses: Stephen, Archpriest of Laurac; Master Peter of Caraman; Silurius, chaplain of Verfeil; and Brother Bernard, Inquisitor.

/129r/ From Beauteville …

/130r/ From Avignonet …

/134r/ … These are suspects of heresy:[163]

– Stephen of Villeneuve, who is an escort and receiver of heretics; and three heretics were captured in his house. And he holds heretics' deposits [comendas].

– Raymond Gros: and he knew beforehand about the death of the inquisitors,[164] along with the aforesaid Stephen of Villeneuve. Because Raymond of Na Richa, who was present and was racked [tractus] at Toulouse, revealed it to them. But they were unwilling to be part of it.

– William Baudric the elder;

– Raymond Segans; /134v/

– Pons Faure of Lagarde, who is an escort of heretics;

– Peter Brus;

– Ademar of Navarre; it is said that he was a heretic, and he left [= *stopped being a heretic, or left the sect*]. …

/136r/ … In the year as above [1245], 18 days before the calends of December [14 November], Bernard Ribairencs was sworn as a witness. He said that he saw the heretics living publicly at Avignonet and in many other places in the land. But he did not adore them, nor did he see them adored. And this was 30 years ago.

163 These notes, preceded and followed by depositions, contain one of only two references to torture in the 1240s depositions. The other is in Doat 22, 6v–7r: captured heretics gave away to the Count of Toulouse the whereabouts of Arnold Bordeler, who was captured, 'et fuit levatus in eculeum, sed nihil dixit nec potuit ab /7r/ eo extorqueri, ut dixit' ('and he was raised on the rack, but said nothing nor could anything be twisted out of him, so it was said'). In the only instances of torture in a register of depositions from Toulouse, 1273–82, the seneschal Eustace de Beaumarchais had two brothers 'put to the question' in 1274; *Inquisitors and Heretics*, p. 46. The scant evidence about one of the two cases in the 1240s points to action by an official of the Count of Toulouse; in the two cases from 1274 a named royal official acts. It is only in the years around 1300 that explicit evidence of direct involvement by inquisitors proliferates; for two examples, see Docs 55A and 57A (4). See also possible reference to torture in Doc. 38, no. 6.

164 The killing of inquisitors and their household, 28–29 May 1242; see Doc. 46, and the account in Wakefield, *Heresy*, pp. 169–71.

Otherwise he did not see heretics, apart from captured ones, nor did he ever believe, nor adore, nor give, nor send, nor escort, nor did he hear their preaching.

[*Similar denial from next witness*]

On the aforesaid year and day Michael Verger was sworn as a witness. In all things he said the same as Bernard Ribairencs. He also said that he saw in William Ademar's house John Cambiaire and his companion, heretics.[165] And he saw there with them William of Cailhabel, Arnold Negre, Stephen of Villeneuve, Hysarn Ademar, <and> Bernard of Gardouch, knight, now dead. And the same witness then heard the said heretics saying that no-one in marriage could be saved. And he stayed there for a little while. But he did not adore, nor did he see them adored. And this was 10 years ago or thereabouts.

Item, he said that the Waldensians were persecuting the said heretics. And he often gave alms to the said Waldensians, when they sought it for the love of God. And because at the time the Church was supporting the said Waldensians, and they were together with clerics, singing and reading in the same church, he believed they were good men. And this was 25 years ago.

And he abjured heresy and took an oath etc. …

/139v/ …[*The words placed in rounded parentheses in the following are interlinear in the manuscript, placed above names. They were originally additional notes entered into the record by the inquisitor about a particular person named by the deponent – that he or she was dead or a fugitive etc.*]

AD 1245, 8 days before the ides of February [6 February], Bertrand of Quiriès, sworn in as a witness, said that he saw at Avignonet in the house of the same witness and Blancha, his mother (dead), Belengaria and her companion, heretics, who stayed there for 8 days and more. And there were there the same witness, and the said Blancha, his mother, who had received the said heretics while the same witness was away. However, the same witness did not adore the said heretics, nor see them adored. And he heard it said by his said mother that Bernard of Gourvielle, the brother of the said Berengaria, heretic, got the said heretics out of there. And this was 15 years ago or thereabouts.

165 John Cambiaire named as 'Minor Son' of Cathar diocese of Toulouse c. 1232 (Doat 24, fol. 43v) and possibly earlier (Doat 22, fols 226v–227r); burned c. 1233 (Doat 24, fol. 46r–v).

He also said that he saw with the said heretics Willelma, wife of William Baudric, and Ermessen, the same witness's sisters. But he did not see them adoring the said heretics.

And this was at the same time.

Item, he saw in Avignonet in the house of Stephen of Villeneuve, Raymond Sans, deacon of the heretics, and two other heretics, whose names he does not know. And he saw with them there William Ademar (dead) and Bernard of Gardouch (dead) of Avignonet. And there the same witness and the aforesaid others adored the same heretics on their arrival and departure. And they heard their preaching, and ate bread blessed by them and other things placed on the table. And Willelma the wife of Stephen of Villeneuve was there then, <but> at the fireside in another house. And this was 15 years ago or thereabouts, and it was on Easter morning.

Item, on the insistence of his aforesaid mother he saw at Avignonet [*first name missing*] Bernard and his companion, heretics, in the house of Pons Rangis. And he saw there with them the said Pons Rangis and his wife. And all of them, and the same witness, adored the heretics and heard their preaching. And this was at the same time.

Item, he said that when the same witness was gravely ill in his house at Avignonet, the said Blancha, his mother, kept on advising him and begging him to love the Good /140r/ Men, and, if he happened to be dying, to surrender[166] himself to them. And then Stephen of Villeneuve and Donat of Villeneuve, the same witness's brother-in-law, brought there Raymond of Sans, the deacon of heretics, and his companion, heretics, on the orders of the said Blancha, his mother. And then the said Raymond Sans touched the same witness's pulse, and said he had the strength <to live>.[167] And all of them there, and the same witness, heard the said heretics' preaching. However, they did not adore them. And then the same witness, instructed by the said Blancha, his mother, and by the aforesaid others, promised the said heretics that if he were dying he would die in their hands. And he bequeathed them 50 shillings, which the said Blancha his mother would be bound to pay to them after the same witness's death. And this was 14 years ago or thereabouts.

Item, he said that he saw at Avignonet in the house of William Richard (fugitive) and Bernard Richard (fugitive), brothers, Bernardin and his

166 Ms: crederet; we take this as a mistaken version of 'cederet' or 'traderet'.

167 Ms transcription problematic here.

companion, heretics. And he saw there with them the said William Richard and his brother Bernard Richard, and Ademar of Avignonet (dead), who escorted the same witness there. And all of them, and the same witness, adored the said heretics there. And they ate some hare, and other things the heretics gave them.[168] And this was 12 years ago or thereabouts.

He also said that at that time the mother of the said William Richard was in another house, by the fire, when the same witness and all the aforesaid were eating with the heretics. And this was at the same time.

Item, he said that when Macip of Toulouse captured heretics in three houses at Avignonet – that is to say, in the house of Tholosan of La Salle and in the house of Stephen of Villeneuve and in the house of William of Cailhabel – the noise and rumour went out that the same witness had given away the said heretics, though it was not true. And on account of this the said Blancha, his mother, kept on crying and hating the same witness, because she believed he had handed over the said heretics. And this was 8 years ago or thereabouts.

Item, at Asti in Lombardy he saw Raymond Hymbert of Moissac, heretic, who went with the same witness from Asti right up to Alba. And there, when they wanted to eat, the same witness realised that Raymond was a heretic. But the same witness did not adore him.

And this was 3 years ago.

Item, he said that William Raymond Golairan told the same witness that Bernard of St-Martin and William of Lahille [*or* L'Île] and Balaguier of Laurac (suspect), knights, were about to come to Avignonet at night-time, to talk with the same witness and some other men from Avignonet. And when it was night, the said witness and the said William Raymond went out of the town to the said knights – which knights asked the same witness to be an assistant in the capturing of Brother William Arnold and Brother Stephen, the inquisitors, who were ruining and destroying the whole land. At their request the same witness and the said William Raymond then promised them that they would do their will, and they would protect them from the men of Avignonet with all their strength. And they entreated the said knights to give them a good share of the said inquisitors' money, and they readily promised to do this. After this had been done, the same witness

168 Although the heretics were forbidden to eat meat, their followers were not. We cannot find another example in inquisition records of heretics providing followers with meat to eat.

and the said William Raymond went into the town of Avignonet, and revealed it to Donat, the same witness's brother-in-law, who was overjoyed, and to William Richard and Bernard Richard, brothers. And they asked them to be involved in the capturing of the said brothers, and they replied, 'Gladly!' And then the said William Raymond went through the town of Avignonet in a similar way, and he revealed the said matter to Raymond of Na Richa (hanged), and William Faure (hanged), and Peter Esquieu, and Raymond of Auset, and Peter of Bovila [*or* Beauville], and Cardinal, the same William Raymond's squire. And he asked them to be involved in the capturing of the said brothers. On hearing this all the aforesaid were delighted. And they gathered together at the same William Raymond Golairan's house, and there they planned how they would carry out the matter, fixing on certain places and streets – to avoid any man being able to come upon it, if there turned out to be a lot of noise and disturbance. After this had been done, the said knights, and Jordanet of Mas (dead), and Galhard Othon (dead), and Verseila, and Peter Vielh, and William of Plaigne, and others – up to 80 <altogether> – entered the said *castrum*. And when they were in front of the aforesaid William Raymond's house, Cardinal, the same William Raymond's squire, brought out of it two lit torches. And then all of them and the same witness went with the said lit candles to the hall where the said brothers were. And then Bernard of Na Vidal (dead) entered the said hall through some unlocked part of the same hall, and opened the hall's main gate to all the aforesaid. And when the same witness and the said William Raymond saw the said knights smashing the brothers' doors, they went away. And the same witness fixed on one crossroads and kept watch, and the said William Raymond <kept watch over> another, so that no-one could come upon the death of the brothers. And after the slaughter of the brothers, when the aforesaid knights and their retainers left, the same witness, and William Raymond (in prison), and Peter of Bovila [*or* Beauville] and some others from Avignonet called <people> to arms, and the same witness /140v/ put on chain mail and an iron helmet. And they went to the hall where the said brothers had been killed: as though to appear as being uninvolved in that killing. And this was 3½ years ago.

Item, he says he believed the heretics were good men, and truth-tellers, and friends of God, and that they had a good faith and one could be saved with them, though he knew that the Church persecuted them. And he heard the heretics saying that God did not make visible things, and that there was not salvation in baptism and marriage, and that the bodies of the dead will not rise again. And the same witness firmly believed just as the heretics said. And it was 15 years ago that he first believed, and he stayed in this belief for 10 years and more.

Item, he said that after the aforesaid killing of the inquisitors the same witness and the said William Raymond saw Bernard of Mayreville and his companion, heretics, in some wood near Montmaur. And both of them adored the aforesaid heretics. And then he got 8 shillings from the aforesaid heretic for some book which had been of ⌜*belonged to*⌝ the inquisitors killed in the said place.

Asked why he wanted to be involved in the killing of the said inquisitors, he said he believed – and it was said by others – that <through the killing> the business of the inquisitors would be snuffed out, and the whole land would be liberated, and there would be no more inquisition.

Item, he said that a certain tall, hard and thin young man received the same witness and the same William Raymond at Châteauverdun, and he bought necessities for them – and he knew that they were fugitives because of the killing of the said inquisitors.

He also said that he confessed about heresy to the brother inquisitors, before their killing, and was reconciled. And he abjured heresy, and swore to persecute heretics. And he recognised that he had done ill, because later he consented to the killing of the aforesaid brothers, and provided help, and because later – as has been said – he adored the heretics.

Item, he said that after he went to the Roman curia[169] he <still> believed the heretics were good men.

And he abjured heresy and swore, etc.

Witnesses: brothers of the Order of Preachers Raymond, Prior of the brothers Preacher of Toulouse, and William of Bessol, and Peter Aribert; and the brothers Bernard and John, inquisitors.

Item, 7 days before the ides of February, in the year as above ⌜7 February 1245⌝, the aforesaid Bertrand of Quiriès, sworn in as a witness, said that when Blancha, the same witness's mother, was suffering at the point of death, she asked the same witness and the Ermessen and Willelma, the same witness's sisters, to bring about the same Blancha having the Good Men, that is to say the heretics. And then the same witness and the said sisters Ermessen and Willelma told her that they

169 To the papal court, which was peripatetic.

could not find heretics; and for this reason she was not hereticated. He also said that the same witness's mother Blancha advised the same witness to be involved in the capturing of the brother inquisitors. He also said that he was never hereticated, ever.

Item, he said that he never assented to the killing of the inquisitors, just their capture: and this as an obstruction to the inquisition of heretical wickedness.

Witnesses: Arnold, Prior of St-Sernin; Peter Aribert; and brothers Bernard and John, inquisitors.

The aforesaid confession was read out to the said Bertrand of Quiriès in Toulouse, in front of the brother inquisitors John of St-Pierre and Reginald of Chartres.

And he swore, and abjured, and bound himself and his things [*i.e. property*], etc.

Witnesses: Master Giles, clerk of the Lord Count of Toulouse; and Peter, chaplain of Dreuilhe, public notary, who wrote this. AD 1255, calends of July [1 July]. …

/140v/ From Gibel of the Lauragais …

/141r/ From Montauriol …

/142v/ From Cumiès …

/143r/ From Villeneuve-la-Comptal …

/144r/ From Montferrand …

/145v/ From Cazalrenoux by Laurac …

/149r/ From Vibram by Laurac …

/149v/ From Fanjeaux …

/159r/ … In the year as above, 6 days before the calends of June [27 May 1245], Bernard Gasc said that for a good year he lived with his mother, Marquesia, next to the house of William of Carlipa, heretic. And he often ate in their house [*probably meaning the house of William and his companions*], and they [*sic*] gave him bread and wine and nuts. But he did not adore, nor did he see <them *or* him > adored. And this was 70[170] years ago or thereabouts.

Item, he said that he saw Raymond of Lavaur and his companion, heretics, in the house of Raymond of St-Gaudéric. And he saw there with them the same Ramond of Lavaur, and Filhol, and William Brus, and William of Lavaur, Raymond Sirvent, Bernard Isarn and Bernard Guirault, Peter Borrel and William of Lusignan. And everyone, apart from the same witness, adored the said heretics there. And this was 40 years ago or thereabouts.

Item, he saw Peter Belhomme and his companion, heretics, in the heretics' own house. And he saw there with them Dominic of Pexiora, and William, the said Dominic's brother, and Peter of Pexiora, and William Escarit, <and> Bego of Fanjeaux. And everyone, apart from the same witness, adored the said heretics there. And it was at the same time.

Item, he saw Arnold Clavel and his companion, heretics, in the same heretics' house. And he saw there with them William Hugon; Richa Bruna, heretic; Peter Fornier and Isarn, his brother; Raymond of Valats; William of Na Neus; Pons Agulher and Pons Pairoler and William of Fanjeaux; Arnold Faure; William Faure. And the same witness and everyone adored there the said heretics on bended knees, saying, 'Bless, Good Men, pray to God for us'. And this was 40 years ago or thereabouts.

Item, he saw Arnold of Verfeil and Gualhard of Gourdon, heretics, at Caraman, in the same Gerald [= Gualhard] of Gourdon's house. And he saw with them there Bernard of Lamothe, heretic. And the same witness adored the said heretics there. And this was 40 years ago or thereabouts.

He believed the aforesaid heretics were good men, and had a good faith, and were friends of God, though he knew the Church persecuted them. /159v/ And he heard them saying errors: about visible things, that God had not made them; and that baptism and marriage were of no value for salvation; and that the consecrated host is not the body of

170 This remarkable number is perfectly clear in the ms: LXX.

Christ or the Lord, and that the bodies of the dead will not rise again. However, he himself did not believe the aforesaid errors.

He confessed the aforesaid things to Brother William Arnold and his companion, inquisitors, at Fanjeaux.

Item, he said that within three years after the aforesaid confession he entered the house of Peter Fornier, barber, and he wanted to light some candle. And he saw there Raymond Rigaut and his companion, heretics. And he saw there with them the same Peter Fornier – who was lying ill with the illness from which he died – and Arnold Tornier and Stephen Piquer and Ramunda, the same Peter Fornier's concubine. And then the said ill man asked the said heretics to hereticate him. And they said they would not do it until he handed over to them what his father and his mother gave to them at their deaths. And the said Peter Fornier said to the said heretics that he had 26 sesters of wine; and that he would give wine and corn until they regarded themselves as having been paid up with regards to his father and his mother and himself; and that they should receive him. But they were unwilling to do this, because it was not the custom in the heretics' sect.[171] And then the said ill men had them thrown out of the house; and he said many abusive and insulting things to them. But the same witness did not adore them nor see them adored.

And he was absolved from excommunication. And he abjured heresy and swore, etc.

Witnesses: Arnold, Prior of St-Sernin; Arnold Cerda; and Brother Bernard, Inquisitor. …

/160r/ … On the year as above, 4 days before the ides of March [12 March 1246], Willelma Martina, wife of the late William Lombard, sworn as a witness on heresy, said that while she was young she saw many heretics and women heretics at Fanjeaux. And the said heretics often gave her bread and nuts, and [*another gift missing?*] for the love of God. And the same witness often carried the heretics' spools to weavers. And she often adored the said heretics, in the way that they taught her to do. And this was 40 years ago or thereabouts.

She also said that she confessed the aforesaid things to Brother Dominic of the Order of Preachers. /160v/ And she had penance from him, that she should carry two crosses on the front for two years, and that during

171 See the rules in the Occitan 'Cathar ritual' about administering the *consolamentum* to the sick when they were still in debt to the heretics' church; WE, p. 492.

these two years she should not eat meat except at Christmas, Easter and Pentecost. And the same witness carried out this penance. And she had letters from the same Brother Dominic about this penance, and she lost them when the *castrum* of Fanjeaux was burnt by the Count of Montfort.[172] And thereafter she did not see the aforesaid heretics.

At the time she believed the aforesaid heretics were good men, and had good faith, and were friends of God. And she did not hear them expressing their errors.

She confessed the aforesaid things to William Arnold, Inquisitor, at Fanjeaux, and to Brother Ferrier at Saissac.

And she abjured, and took an oath, etc., in the presence of Brother Bernard of Caux, Inquisitor.

Witnesses: Arnold, Prior of St-Sernin; Arnold, chaplain of Péchaudier; Bernard Pons, notary; and Brother Peregrine of the Order of Preachers.

On the aforesaid year and day, Arnalda of *Fremiac*, wife of the late Arnold of *Fremiag*, sworn in as a witness on heresy and Waldensianism, said that when she was young Hysarn Bola, the same witness's uncle, forced her to enter the heretics' sect. And she was a vested heretic for 6 years. And when the same witness was hereticated, present at the said heretication were Saura, now dead, <former> wife of Raymond Amiel of Mortier, Curta, now dead, <former> wife of Raymond Ferrand, and Raymond Ferrand, now dead. And she saw many men and women of Fanjeaux, who are now dead, adoring the heretics.

And she confessed to Brother Dominic. And he reconciled her, and gave the penance that she should wear two crosses in front until she took a husband. And she wore them for one year, and afterwards took a husband.

She also said that the Abbot of St-Papoul[173] gave her penance, and enjoined the same witness to wear two crosses in front. And she wore them for two months. Asked why she left them off, she said that everyone marked with the cross left off the crosses, and on account of this the same witness left off the crosses.

She confessed the aforesaid things to Brother Ferrier at Saissac, except that she did not confess that she left off the crosses imposed by the Abbot of St-Papoul.

172 Fanjeaux was burnt in 1209, probably by inhabitants rather than de Montfort.

173 Benedictine abbey.

And she abjured heresy, and took an oath, etc., in the presence of Brother Bernard, Inquisitor.

Witnesses: the aforesaid. …

/165v/ … On the aforesaid year and day [6 March 1246] Raymond Novelli, sworn in as a witness, said that after his confession that he made at Fanjeaux to Brother William Arnold, the late inquisitor, he did not see heretics, nor believed, nor adored, nor gave, nor gave, nor sent, nor escorted, nor heard their preaching.

He said however that before the said confession he saw heretics three times, and adored them once. And twice he had heretics brought to his house to hereticate his father and his mother during the illnesses from which they died. But the said parents of the same witness were not hereticated, because they did not have the heretics at an opportune time [*perhaps*: in time].

Item, he said that the same witness kept watch in front of the gate of a certain house when a certain murderer, who was due to be buried alive, was being hereticated there, to make sure no-one could chance upon the said heretication.

And he believed that the heretics were good men. But it is 17 years since he did not believe this.

And he confessed to Brother Ferrier at Limoux. And afterwards he did not see heretics.

And he abjured heresy.

Witnesses: the aforesaid. …

/169v/ From the parish of Folcarde: <those> from Rieu Majou …

/170r/ From Trébons …

/170r/ From Veilhes …

/171r/ From Baraigne …

From the parish of Baraigne: <those> from Cailhabel …

/172r/ From Pexiora …

/174r/ From St-Germier of the Lauragais …

/176r/ From Séran by St-Germier …

/177r/ From Puybertier …

From Mayreville …

From Villepinte …

/181r/ From Villesiscle …

/183v/ From Villeneuve-la-Comptal …

/184v/ From the parish of Montgaillard: from Lavelanet, from Barelles, from Trébons …

/185r/ From the parish of Montgaillard: from Barelles …

/185v/ From Lavelanet …

From Barelles …

/186r/ From Montauriol …

From St-Martin-de-Lalande …

/189r/ From Bram …

/190r/ From Pexiora …

/191r/ From Laurac ...

/196r/ From Gaja ...

/197v/ From Barsa ...

From St-Sauveur by Gaja ...

/198r/ From Mireval ...

AD 1245 on the nones of December [5 December], Pons Amiel, an old man, notary of Mireval, was sworn as a witness. He said that he saw Isarn of Castres, the heretic, debating with Bernard Prim, the Waldensian in the square at Laurac, in the presence of the people of the town. But the same witness did not adore the said heretics, nor did he see them adored. And this was 37 years ago.

Item, he said that when the same witness took the oxen of some heretics of Le Vaux, Peter Roger of La Tour and Roger of La Tour, knights from Laurac, took the said oxen away from the same witness and restored them to the said heretics. And this was 40 years ago. Otherwise he never saw heretics, apart from captured ones, nor adored, nor believed, nor gave, nor sent, nor escorted, nor heard their preaching.

He also said that, before he took her as his wife, Dias – who is now the wife of the same witness – lived at Labécède with Rossa, the aunt of the same Dias, and her companions, heretics. And she was brought up there with them.

And he confessed to Brother William Arnold at Laurac.

And he abjured heresy and swore, etc.

Witnesses: Brother <William> Pelhisson, Nepos the cleric, and Brother Bernard, Inquisitor.

In the year as above, 4 days before the nones of March [4 March 1246], Amiel Bernard the younger, student [scolaris], sworn in as a witness, said that while the same witness was walking down the street, he heard two truants [trutanni][174] arguing in the hospital at Laurac.

174 Could be translated as 'vagabonds'.

Item, he said that one of the truants was saying that a tree leaf or an ass's turd was just as good to take for communion as the body of Christ, so long as it was done with good faith. And the other truant was arguing against him. And later the same witness heard from the boy Peter Adalbert, in the church at Mireval, that John Adalbert, the same Peter Adalbert's father, had taken the leaf of a herb [*or* grass] as communion when the sun died [*at sunset?*] or was eclipsed. And when he had heard this, he recounted all of the aforesaid, just as he had heard from the truants, in the presence of Stephen Cleric, Bernard Donat and Morgat [*perhaps*], students, present. And this was 2 years ago.

Item, he said he never saw heretics, nor believed, nor adored, nor gave, nor sent, nor escorted, nor/198v/ heard their preaching.

And he abjured, and took an oath, etc.

Witnesses: Peter Aribert, Peter Fresapan, and brothers Bernard and John, inquisitors. …

/198v/ From Airoux …

/199r/ From St-Sauveur, from Marzens …

/199v/ From Lanta …

/201v/ From Montauban …

/203v/ From Odars …

/205r/ From Tarabel …

/206r/ Préserville …

/206v/ From Fourquevaux …

/208r/ From Damiac …

/208v/ From Varennes by Caragoudes …

/209r/ From Les Varennes …

/210r/ From St-André-de-la-Landelle by Varennes …

/210v/ From St-Anatoly: addition …

/211v/ From Prunet, from St-Paulet, and from Saussens …

From Gauré, from Vallesvilles, from St-Léonard, and from St-Jean – of one parish …

/212r/ From Vallesvilles …

/212v/ From Drémil [*or perhaps* Tréville] …

/213v/ From Pujol, from the parish of Ste-Foy …

/214r/ From Mayreville, from Peyrefitte

AD 1247 [*no further date given*] William Salomon, sworn in as a witness on the accusation of heresy and Waldensianism, said that he never saw heretics or Waldensians, except as captives, nor did he believe, nor adore, nor give or send anything, nor heard their preaching.

He said, however, that he heard it said by Cathalan, Pons Magrefort of Pech-Luna's squire, that the said Pons Magrefort kept in his house for two nights Bernard of Mayreville and his companion, heretics. And this was 3 years ago or thereabouts.

Item, he said that the said Cathalan told the same witness that the said Pons Magrefort handed over the aforesaid heretics to Ralph Serrut of Pech-Luna, and the said Ralph kept the said heretics in his house for a day and a night. And afterwards the said Ralph Serrut accompanied the said heretics as far as Mayreville, and that he would say [*in order to say?*] to John Raymond about the aforesaid brothers [*no previous speci-*

fication of brothers] and Bernard Allegre, that they should go to the said heretic Bernard of Mayreville. And then the said John Raymond went to the said heretic, as the same witness heard from the said Cathalan. But he does not know whether or not Pons Raymond and Bernard Allegre went to the said heretic. And then the said John Raymond and Ralph Serrut escorted the aforesaid Bernard of Mayreville and his companions, heretics, as far as Mas-Stes-Puelles, into the house of Peter of <Cap-de->Porc. And this was at the same time.

Item, he said that the aforesaid Cathalan, who lives at Peyriac, told the same witness that Bertrand Martin and Bernard of Mayreville and their companions, heretics, held a council [fecerunt concilium] at St-Sernin near Bélesta in the land of the Count of Foix.[175] And there were present at this council Pons Magrefort of Pech-Luna, Bertrand of Peyrefitte, the late Arnold Olme, Gualhard of Villar, Estout of Fonters, Aimengardis the wife of Bernard Servat, the maidservant of Hugh of Mayreville, who prepared food to help support the heretics.

And it was two years ago or thereabouts that the said Cathalan told all the aforesaid things to the same witness. And the said Aimengardis, the wife of the Bernard Servat, faithfully recounted to the same witness all the things that were done at the said Council of St-Sernin.

And he confessed to Brother Ferrier and his companion, inquisitors, at Conques, but he did not say the aforesaid things to them because at the time he did not know them. …

/214v/ From St-Félix …

/218v/ From Roumens, from the land of St-Félix …

/220v/ From Montégut …

/222r/ From Les Cassés …

175 This council took place at a date after William's confession to the Inquisitor Ferrier and before the execution at Montségur in March 1244 of Bertrand Martin. Including the Bishop of the heretics of Toulouse, Bertrand Martin, the deacon Bernard of Mayreville and some local nobles, the list suggests both importance and difficulty in gathering many people.

/227r/ From St-Paul Cap-de-Joux …

/229r/ From Pomarède …

From Nogaret …

/230r/ From Juzes and from Mourvilles: from the parish of Juzes …

/230v/ From Montmaur …

/232r/ From Vaudreuille …

/233r/ From Dreuilhe …

/234r/ From St-Julia …

/234v/ From Hautpoul …

/235v/ From Lavaur …

/237v/ From Cambiac by Auriac …

/239v/ … In the year as above, 11 days before the calends of January [22 December 1245], Aimerssens, the wife of William Viguier of Cambiac, sworn in as a witness, said that it was a good 23 years ago that Geralda of <St-Martin-de->Capuer, the same witness's aunt, took the same witness to Auriac to the house of Na Esquiva, wife of William Aldric, knight. And she saw, in the said house, two female heretics. And she saw with them there the said Esquiva, and the said William Aldric, and William Aldric, their son, and the said Geralda. And all of them and the same witness, taught by the said Esquiva, adored the said heretics, three times on bended knees, saying, 'Bless, good ladies, pray to God for us sinners'.

She also said that later that same day Raymond of Auriac <and> [*missing one or several names*] went to the said heretics. And all of them and the same witness heard the preaching of the said female heretics for a long time. And they adored them, in the way said above. And in front of everyone the said heretics said to her, because she was an adolescent girl and pregnant, that she was carrying the devil in her belly. And the others began to laugh at this.

Item, she said that she often saw heretics at night-time entering the house of Raymond Vassaro. And she saw going into the said house, when the heretics were there, Bernard Deodat, and Arnold of Caubel, and Arnold Sabatier, Peter Arnold, Helyas Gausbert, Stephen Augier and his wife Bernarda, and Valencia, wife of Peter Valence, and Peter Viguier and William Viguier, the same witness's husband, and William Girbert and his sister, Aicelina, and William Sais, son of Jordan Sais, and the same Jordan, and Pons Aim of Francarville, son-in-law of Jordan Sais. All the aforesaid she saw going often into the said house when the heretics were there, from two years ago onwards. And in the sight of the same witness they adored the said heretics and heard their preaching. And the same witness observed this through the barrier which is in the said house, which house is next to the same witness's house. She said, however, that it was only twice that she saw the said Pons Aym with the heretics there, but all the others on many occasions, as has been said. She also said that William Viguier, her husband, often admonished her to love the heretics, just as he did and others from the town. But the same witness did not want to love them, after the heretics said to her that she was pregnant with the devil. And for this reason her aforesaid husband beat the same witness often and said many abusive things, because she did not love the heretics.

Item, she said that it was a year ago this summer that the same witness found a sack with 23 fresh eels, and a man's shirt, and half a quart of onions, and a bowl of chickpeas, and one and a half loaves of bread, and a gourd, in some ditch near Cambiac and near Maurens, in a wood where the heretics sometimes used to live. And then she took the whole sack away with her. And she sent immediately for the chaplain, that is to say, Martin of Auriac. And she showed the lot to him and told him where she had found it, so that he could look there for the heretics.

Item, she said that it was a good 3 years ago that Jordan Sais brought a certain book to the same witness's house. And he said to William Viguier, the same witness's husband, that he should take the said book into safe-keeping. And he said that the said book was Lord[176] Raymond Fort's, the deacon of heretics. And then the same witness told him, no way would she put up with that book staying in the said house. And then the said Jordan said abusive things about this to the same witness, and in the same witness's sight gave the said book for safe-keeping to Peter Viguier. She also said that later, after a month, a certain messenger of Bertrand Alamann came to the same witness's house and told the same witness that, on behalf of Austorga of Rouzégas, he was looking to get back a book of Raymond Fort, deacon of the heretics, from William Viguier, the same witness's husband. And then the same witness told him he should look for Peter Viguier, who could give him advice about the said book. And she believed that that is how he recovered the said book.

Item, she said that this year, between Pentecost and the feast of St-John the Baptist, Jordan Sais came to the same witness, and William Sais his son, and Helias Gausbert, and Raymond Vassaros, and Peter Arnold, and William Viguier, the same witness's husband. And the said William Sais said to the same witness, in no way should she tell the truth to the inquisitors about the things she had seen done by them in the matter of heresy, and that she should not want to destroy them by telling the truth. For none of the inquisitors would force her to say <anything> except those things she herself wanted to say.[177] And all the aforesaid others said this same thing to her, threatening. And then the same witness replied to them that she would tell the truth about the things they were doing. And then the said William Sais took the same witness and put her into some cask, and similarly the same witness's son, because he was supporting her. To him they said, 'Boy, do you <really> want to help this old woman[178] who wants to destroy all of us?' And all the men of Cambiac saw and heard this. And she remained in the said cask for a night, and in the morning she redeemed herself from the said lords of Cambiac for 3 shillings and 7 /240r/ pence.

Item, she said that this year in August, when William Sais left the Château Narbonnais prison, he came to Cambiac and asked William Viguier, the same witness's husband, to give the Good Men – the heretics – a quarter of grain. And the said William Viguier was unwilling

176 Prelate's rather than noble's title, comparable to 'Lord' Bishop.

177 Ms: nullus compelleret eam – de inquisitoribus – quod diceret nisi ea que ipsamet vellet dicere.

178 vetula: perhaps better translated as 'wretched' rather than 'old'.

to give <it>. And then, in the presence of the same witness, the said William Sais said to the said William Viguier, 'Let me pay you for now and pay me back when you can'. But the said William Viguier was unwilling. She said that afterwards the said William Sais often asked the same witness's husband for the said grain.

Item, she said that William Viguier, the same witness's husband, told the same witness that Helyas Gausbert gave one measure of grain to the said William Says for the heretics, and Peter Arnold another quarter, and Arnold Sabatier another, and Raymond Bassaro another, and William Girbert a half of a quarter and Stephen Augier the other half, and William Sais himself one quarter on his own account and another on behalf of William Viguier. And then William Sais had all the corn gathered together in his house, saying that two worthy men were due to come that night for the said grain – one of them was Philip of Auriac. And the said William Sais had the said grain carried by his nag to Stephen Augier's straw barn. And he made a messenger <go> to the chaplain of Auriac, to come for the said gain. And then the said chaplain came with his companions, and took away all the said grain from the said place. And <it was> the same witness that showed him the grain.

And the same witness abjured heresy, and took an oath etc.

Witnesses: brothers of the Order of Preachers William Pelhisson, Peter Tosoirer and Stephen Rachaut, and Brother Bernard of Caux, who received this confession.

Item on the same year and day, the aforesaid Ermessens said that Bertrand Alamann came to Cambiac and made a collection for the redemption of Raymond Fort, deacon of the heretics, who had been captured. And the men of Cambiac gave 7 shillings, and William Sais 12 pence, and in her sight, in the same witness's house, her husband gave 6 pence.

Item, she saw Fabrissa, Raymond Vassaro's wife, carrying a woollen blanket and bread and wine to some woodland which is between Cambiac and Maurens. And the same witness reported this to the chaplain, and the said chaplain went there and took <the grain> away from the said heretics who were in the said hut.[179] And because he had few companions – Peter Cleric <and> John Bosquet of Auriac – he did not dare to seize the aforesaid heretics, through fear of the heretics' believers. And she said the two just mentioned saw when the said chaplain had the aforesaid grain.

179 No hut has been mentioned. Omission of text earlier?

Witnesses: the aforesaid, apart from Brother Stephen.

Item, on the same day and year, the said Armessens, sworn in as a witness, said that she heard Stephen Augier saying to Peter Valence – in the same Peter Valence's house – that the heretics were brought to Peter of Rouzégas during his illness, but the said Peter did not want to be hereticated: at which his wife Austorga was very grief-stricken. About the time: she said it was after the said Peter of Rouzégas's death.

Item, she saw and heard Willelma Torneria and Valencia, wife of Peter Valence, saying that on behalf of Jordan Sais they were carrying linen and canvas to Falgayrac, to Austorga, Peter of Rouzégas's wife, so that the Austorga could sew the said linen and canvas for the women heretics that the said Austorga was lodging. And it is a year ago that the same witness heard the aforesaid things and also saw the said women carrying the said linen.

She also said that Willelma Torneria, the said Jordan Sais's concubine, lives in Toulouse.

Witnesses: Brother William Pelhisson; Bernard of Caux; Raymond, chaplain of Cambon.

AD 1246, 11 days before the calends of July [22 May], Aimersens, wife of William Viguier, added to her testimony saying that recently, on the day after Pentecost, at night-time, when the same witness was going to Auriac, she found on the road Englesia, wife of Peter Ratier, and Domestica, wife of Gerald of Auriac, carrying bread and wine. And then the same witness asked them where they were going. And they were unwilling to tell her, but they asked the same witness not to reveal to anyone that she had found them. And because of this the same witness believed that the said women were carrying the said bread and wine to heretics.

Item, she said that William Sais carried a certain book, which he had given as surety, to William Bonet of Auriac. <By this surety> Peter Arnold, Helyas Gausbert, Raymond Vassaro, Arnold Sabatier, Peter Viguier took an oath – and similarly the said William Sais, who made all the other aforesaid men take oaths and agree among themselves not to reveal to the brother inquisitors – that is to say, to Bernard of Caux and John of St-Pierre – <about> the grain which the same men had given to the church of the heretics: that it was gathered together in Stephen Augier's barn, where the grain was later found. The chaplain of Auriac had it. And this was during the last grape-picking. …

/240r/ From St-Léonce …

From St-Paul Cap-de-Joux …

/242r/ From Cambon …

/245v/ From Scopont [Maurens-Scopont] …

/247r/ From the parish of St-Martin, from Massac by Lavaur …

/247r/ From Guitalens, from the territory of Puylaurens …

/247v/ From Saix, and from Montespieu, and from Viviers in the parish of Saix …

/249v/ … Item, on the aforesaid year and day [7 March 1246], Peter Martin, sworn in as a witness, said that the same witness received for two or three nights William Montaner and his companion, Waldensians. And there were there the same witness, and Ramunda, the same witness's wife, and Raymond Beadz, the same witness's herdsman. And all of them and the same witness ate with the said Waldensians at the same table and of bread blessed by them. And they heard their preaching. They said, among other things, that one should not take an oath in any eventuality, nor kill, even for justice [= *capital punishment of criminals*]. And the same witness believed as they said. And twice he gave things to eat to the said Waldensians, or three times. And this was 10 years ago or thereabouts.

He also said that the same witness received the Peace from the said Waldensians. And this was at the same time.

Item, he saw Adam and Berengar, Waldensians, in some hut in the wood of Rouffie. And he saw with them there John Cochafieu, who came with the same witness. And this was 12 years ago or thereabouts.

Item, he said that the same witness and the same witness's brother Raymond Martin, the witness's brother, brought two Waldensian women – that is, Arnalda and Good Lady – out of the house of Galharda Bruna of Castres, begged to do this by the said Galharda. And when they were outside the town of Castres the said Waldensians were taken away from them. And one of them was burnt. And this was 8 years ago or thereabouts.

He also said that the same witness learnt a prayer from the said Waldensians.

Item, he said that he believed the Waldensians were good men, and truth-tellers, and friends of God, and that they had a good faith and one could be saved through them, although he knew that the Church persecuted them. And it is 14 years since he first believed the Waldensians were good men. And he stayed in this belief for only 7 years or thereabouts.

He never saw heretics or Waldensians otherwise, nor did he believe, nor adore, nor give, nor send, nor escort, nor did he hear their preaching.

And he confessed to inquisitors at Toulouse.

And he abjured, and took an oath, etc., in front of brothers Bernard Peter and John, inquisitors.

Witnesses: Bernard, Prior of Lavaur, and Peter Aribert.

Item, he said that Sichard Niger, Bernard Gatha <and> John Cochafieu are believers ion the heretic, so the same witness believes. …

/250r/ From Castelnaudary

… AD 1245, 16 days before the calends of March [14 February], Raymond Arrufat, sworn in as a witness, said that Bernarda, the same witness's mother, was hereticated. And he saw that Raymond Bernard and his companions, heretics, carried her in death from Castelnaudary to St-Martin-de-Lalande, when the same witness was 8 years old or thereabouts. And this was 40 years ago or thereabouts.

Item, he said the same witness's brother John Arrufat was hereticated. And the just mentioned heretics carried him to St-Martin. And he died there in their hands. However, the same witness did not adore them or see them adored. And this was at the same time.

Item, he said that when Peter Arrufat was ill with a deadly wound, in the house of Peter Arrufat, the same witness's father, William Aolric, knight, had the said ill Peter carried to the same William's house. And Estout of Roqueville, knight, escorted there Arnold Arrufat and his companion, heretics, in the same witness's sight. There they hereticated Peter Arrufat, the same witness's brother, with the consent of the same witness's father Raymond Arrufat, as he heard it said. However, the same witness was not present at the heretication. This was before the coming of the crusaders [*i.e.* before 1209].

Item, he often saw Waldensians and heretics in the house of the same witness and his father Raymond Arrufat, and they slept and ate there very often. And he saw there /250v/ with them Raymond Arrufat, the same witness's father, and the whole household. However, the same witness did not adore the said heretics, nor saw them adored. And this was at the same time.

Item, he said that he saw heretics and Waldensians living openly at Castelnaudary. However, he did not adore them. And this was before the coming of the crusaders.

Item, he heard it said that Johanna and Ermengardz, the same witness's sisters, now dead, were heretics. And Raymond Arrufat, the same witness's father, extricated them from heresy and gave them husbands. However, the same witness did not see them while they were heretics. And this was 38 years ago, and more.

Item, he saw at Las Bordes, in the house of Alazaissia Rogeria, the same witness's relative, three heretics whose names he does not know, sisters of the said Alazaicia. And he saw there with them the said Alazaicia and her husband Peter Roger, who was a heretic later on. However, the same witness did not <adore> the said heretics nor saw them adored. And this was 25 years ago or thereabouts.

Item, he saw at Las Bordes, in the house of Peter Baudriga, the same Peter's mother and <her> sister, heretics. And he saw there with them the same witness's niece [*or* grand-daughter] Guirauda, and the wife of the said Peter Baudriga, and the whole household. However, the same witness did not adore the said heretics, nor saw them adored. And this was at the same time.

Item, he saw at Castelnaudary, in the house of Na Minha, the aforesaid [*missing here: first, the name of a male heretic, and companion, secondly, the name of a woman*], who called the same witness, while he was walking in the street, <to come> there. And there the same witness, and the said Pons[180] adored the said heretics on bended knees, three times saying, 'Bless, worthy men [probi homines], pray to God on our

180 The lack of any previous mention of Pons indicates missing text, no longer recoverable.

behalf'. However he does not recall about the said Na Minha, whether she adored the said heretics. And then the said witness sent to the said heretics via Na Minha, the daughter of his nurse Bernarda, three rotten salted fish[181] by way of mockery.

And this was at the time the army left off the siege of Castelnaudary,[182] and it was 23 years ago or thereabouts.

He said also that the said Pons of Le Verger often asked the same witness not to reveal this matter to Brother William Arnold, Inquisitor, and that he would give the same witness whatever he wanted – to whom the same witness replied, no way would he hide this from the aforesaid inquisitor. And this was when Brother William Arnold was doing inquisition at Castelnaudary.[183]

Item, he said that while Castelnaudary was being besieged,[184] Raymond of Roqueville was there, seriously wounded. And, at the time, he heard it said that before the spear was drawn out of his body the said Raymond was hereticated in the house of William Arnold and his wife's niece. And the same witness saw there in the said house, through some hole in the door, two heretics, one of whom was called Vadassac. And he saw there with the said heretics Bernard of Roqueville, and William of Issus, and others whom he does not recall. However, the same witness did not adore the said heretics, nor saw them adored. And this was 23 years ago or thereabouts.

Item, he said that when the same witness, and Peter Salomon, and Peter Simon, and Pons Amiel were coming from Las Bordes to Castelnaudary, they found two men at night-time at the gateway to Castelnaudary. And since they could not enter through this gateway the said men went together with the same witness and the aforesaid others to the Mercadil gateway. And then the said Peter Salomon and Peter recognised that the said men were heretics, and they took them and beat them badly. And afterwards, through fear, they let them go. And the same witness took them to the house of Bernarda Provincial, the same witness's nurse, and brought them inside. And he saw with them there the said Bernarda, and William Provincial, her brother. And in the morning the said heretics went away from there. However,

181 Ms: pices; conjecturally, pisces.

182 February 1221.

183 The two periods of William Arnold's itinerant inquisition that included Castelnaudary were 1236–8 and 1241–2; the precise sequence cannot be reconstructed.

184 July 1220–February 1221.

the same witness did not adore nor saw them adored. And this was at the same time.

Item, he said that he often saw William Provincial and his companion, heretics, at Castelnaudary in the house of the said Bernarda, the same witness's nurse. And he saw there with them the said Bernarda, and Bernard Provincial, her son, and Na Minha, and Ermessens Perina, the said Bernarda's sister. However, the same witness did not adore the said heretics, nor did he see the others adoring. And this was 20 years ago or thereabouts.

Item, he said he saw the other one of the heretics[185] talking two or three times with Raymond Arrufat, the same witness's father, in the same Raymond's house. However, he did not see his said father Raymond adoring the said heretics. And this was at the same time.

Item, he said that when the same witness was living among hostages at Narbonne alongside other men from Castelnaudary in the house of Dulcia Ferreira of Narbonne, Pons of Gibel of Castelnaudary was ill to the point of death in the said Dulcia's house at Narbonne. And during the same witness's absence two men, whose names he does not know, came there to hereticate the said Pons. And when Mercadier of Castelnaudary found the said heretics there, he said that he would reveal this to John Valle, the precentor. And then the same witness went there, and saw the said heretics leaving the house. And there were there Bernard Peter, the aforesaid Pons of Gibel's nephew [*or* grandson], and Stephen Valles, and William Bord of Castelnaudary, and others whom he does not remember. And he heard it said that /251r/ at his death Pons of Gibel was not hereticated by the aforesaid heretics, because he was unwilling to be hereticated by the aforesaid heretics, since they were not of the faith of the heretics of the Toulousain. And he saw that the said Pons sent for the religious solitaries of Boulbonne,[186] and surrendered himself to them. And this was 20 years ago or thereabouts.

Item, he saw a certain Waldensian whose name he does not know, the sister of the said William Bord, often coming to the house of the said Dulcia at Narbonne.

Item, he saw at Castelnaudary, in the house of Pons of Villeneuve, Catbert of Barbaira, knight, condemned for heresy, whom the same

185 See above for the other one, Vadassac.

186 Cistercian monastery.

witness asked to provide escort to William Arnold Bord, the messenger of William Arnold, the same witness's nephew [*or* grandson]: which he did. And this was 5 years ago or thereabouts.

Item, he saw Raymond of Puy and others condemned for heresy coming and going openly in Castelnaudary. And this was at the time of the war[187] of the Viscount of Béziers.[188]

Item, he said that he never believed the heretics were good men, nor that they had a good faith, nor were truth-tellers, nor friends of God. And he had often heard errors from captive heretics about visible things and the Church's sacraments. However, he did not believe in the said errors.

And he confessed to Brother William Arnold at Castelnaudary, and again to Brother Ferrier at Saissac.

And he abjured, and took an oath, etc.

Witnesses: Arnold, Prior of St-Sernin; Peter Aribert; Centoull, chaplain of Gauré; Raymond, chaplain of St-Paul; Brecas; and Brother Bernard, Inquisitor.

Appendix: Sentence on Esclarmonda Bret

Esclarmonda's deposition is above at fol. 62r. Translated from Douais, *Documents*, II, pp. 10–16.

In the name of our crucified Lord Jesus Christ, Amen. AD 1246, 3 days before the ides of May [13 May 1246]. We, brothers of the Order of Preachers, Bernard of Caux and John of St-Pierre, deputed by apostolic authority inquisitors of heretical wickedness in the city and diocese of Toulouse.

Whereas it has been established, through the judicial confessions made by Aldriga, sister of Peter Laurence, Bernard of Prat, Joanna, wife of William of Soulier, Willelma of Mas of Toulouse, Stephen Garric of Lavaur, Esclarmonda, wife of the late Pons Bret, of Goudourville, Arnold of Na Borgesa of Roqueserière, Stephen Faber, Peter Faber, Arnold Faber, Peter Folc, Jordan Ugole, Pons Jordan, Arnold Andree, William of Gouzens, of St-Martin-de-Lalande, William Sermenha, Pons of Piquel, and William of Sérignan, of Fanjeaux, of the diocese of

187 1240.

188 Raymond II Trencavel, who had once held this viscounty.

Toulouse, that … [*each person is named, with brief details of their crimes, the sixth being Esclarmonda:*] Also, Esclarmonda, named earlier, wife of the late Pons Bret of Goudourville, saw heretics, adored, believed they were good men, and believed she would be saved in their faith, and believed she would be damned if she died otherwise than in the hands of the heretics, and ate with a woman heretic, and denied the truth before other inquisitors, and afterwards before us, against her own oath; [*twelve more names follow*] …

[*paragraph follows, on condemning them to prison, identical to that given in Doc. 45 above, appendix*]

Done at Toulouse, in the cloister of St-Sernin, in the presence of Raymond, Provost of <the Cathedral of> St-Stephen, Master Arnold Pelisso, canons of St-Stephen, Arnold Auriol, Prior of St-Sernin, Peter of Drudas, William Raymond, canons of St-Sernin, Amiel, chaplain of St-Stephen, Raymond, chaplain of Daurade, Fort, chaplain of St-Sernin, Raymond, chaplain of the Blessed Mary of Daurade, William Ade, *bailli* of the Lord Count of Toulouse, Pons Astre, Raymond of St-Cézert, Raymond Rainier, William Hugo Pellicier, Bon Mancip Maurand, and Jordan of Villeneuve, consuls of Toulouse, and many others.

49. INQUISITION IN CARCASSONNE, 1250–9

Translated here are extracts from Bibliothèque municipale de Clermont-Ferrand MS 160, from its edition in Douais, *Documents*, II, pp. 115–301.[189] The manuscript contains material emanating from inquisition in Carcassonne, in two distinct parts. The first part contains 278 short texts (under 270 titles in Douais), which are minutes taken down at the time by notaries, with a view to later drafting more formal documents. Blank spaces were left for later additions. Most of the texts deal with cautions (pledging money to guarantee someone's appearance), temporary releases from prison, commutation of penalties and an accused person's list of enemies whose testimony would be vitiated by this. They cast considerable light on the day-to-day operations of the inquisition, which at this point was under the authority of the bishops of Carcassonne, William Arnold (1248–55) and William Radulphe (1255–64).[190] The three judges, acting sometimes alone, sometimes in pairs, were Ralph, Raymond David, chaplain of St-Vincent and Peter Aribert, notary. All bore the title Master, and were therefore probably Masters of Canon Law or Theology, and they seem to have been members of the secular clergy of the diocese, not of any religious order. Master Ralph is also seen at work above, in Doc. 43, fols 98r–99r. See J. Paul, 'La procédure inquisitoriale à Carcassonne au milieu du XIIIe siècle', *CdF* 29 (1994), 361–96. We have translated twenty-four of these notarial minutes, and just one of the fifty-one records of interrogations found in the second part of the manuscript. The numbers in square brackets are from Douais's edition.

189 See also J. Roche, *Une église Cathare: L'évêché du Carcassès, Carcassonne, Béziers, Narbonne* (Cahors, 2005), pp. 48–9.

190 From the late 1240s to the mid-1250s, mendicants seem to have ceased to act as inquisitors, and the task passed to bishops. This 'crisis' is the main focus of Dossat, *Crises*, and is summarised in Wakefield, *Heresy*, pp. 186–8. Although relating directly to a different southern French archbishopric, it is instructive to note the key provision of the council of L'Isle-sur-Sorgue, 19 September 1251: 'Item, concerning the inquisition of heretics: what has been decreed in the canons and statutes of councils is to be observed. And the said inquisition is to be done by each bishop in his own diocese. And by the authority both of the bishop and also this council, earlier records are to be demanded from the Preachers [*Dominicans*] and others who are holding them.' J. H. Albanès, ed., *Gallia christiana novissima*, 7 vols (Valence, 1900), III, cols 443–4 (no. 1158).

<Register of the notary of the inquisition of Carcassonne, Part I>[191]

[2] AD 1251, 7 days before the calends of February [26 January 1252], the inquisitors imposed upon Ulix as penance for perjury, because he did not resume the crosses as he had sworn to do, that on Sunday after this coming Septuagesima Sunday[192] he should come to Carcassonne to visit all the churches of the Bourg of Carcassonne, with bare feet and in shirt and breeches, with rods in his hand, going from one church to another; and he should do the same thing on the first Sunday of every month, until he goes to Outremer [*the Holy Land*]. And this was enjoined upon him by virtue of the oath he has taken.[193]

[3] AD 1249, 16 days before the calends of April [17 March 1250], Peter of *Caucers,* Vital of Cavanac (who lives in Carcassonne), William Aigabeu of Malviès, and Raymond Tocaire of Cavanac pledged surety to the Lord Bishop of Carcassonne for Sicred of Cavanac under pain of 30 Melgueil pounds, <to guarantee> him coming on the day and days specified by his [*the bishop's*] mandate, and doing the penance he would decide to impose on him. And the aforesaid guarantors swore this on the holy gospels of God, and each one made himself liable with all of his goods, without the contribution of another, for the whole sum.

[10] In the year as above, 7 days before the calends of April [26 March 1250], Cavaier Portier [*or* a porter] of Carcassonne, Raymond Goiric of Clermont-Dessus, William Bosca of Vignevieille, Arnold Arquier of Termes, Peter Graudomic of Lairière, and William Leves and William Arnaud pledged surety to the lord Bishop of Carcassonne for Raymond Gastaire, and for Arnold of Lairière, under pain of 50 Melgueil pounds, <to guarantee> him not leaving the city without our permission. And the aforesaid guarantors swore this on the four holy gospels of God, and each one made himself liable with all of his goods, without the contribution of another, for the whole sum.

This was done in the presence of the lord Bishop of Carcassonne, Master Peter, the Official of Carcassonne, and Master Raymond David and Mota, Castellan of Montréal, and of Bon Mancip, notary, who wrote these things.

191 Modern title.

192 The third Sunday before Lent.

193 See no. 88 below on Ulix.

[18] In the year as above, 12 days before the calends of September [21 August 1250], Peter Hot, son of Raymond Hot, of Villetritouls, appeared before the lord Bishop of Carcassonne. And asked if he wished to defend himself on those things that have been found against him in inquisition, he said yes. Item, asked if he has enemies, he said yes. And he was assigned the next sixth ferial day [*Friday*] on the feast of St Anthony [2 September] for the naming of his enemies, and for saying the causes of enmities with those who have deposed against him in inquisition. Witnesses: Peter of Vaure, Master Raymond David, and Peter Aribert, notary, who wrote these things.

[22] In the year as above, 5 days before the ides of August [9 August 1250], William Ralph of Villarzel and William of Rentières the elder, of the bourg of Carcassonne, pledged their surety, under oath, to the lord Bishop of Carcassonne, under pain of 50 Melgueil pounds, and they made themselves and their property liable, each for the whole sum without the contribution of the other, for Bernard Mourgue of Villarzel, who is ill in prison; to whom the aforesaid lord bishop gave permission to leave until he is free of the same illness. And within 8 days after his recovery he is to return to his original status [*in prison*], without <the further exercise to this end of> our authority.

Witnesses: Brother Raymond Barravi, of the Order of Friars Minor, and Brother Raymond of Canet, of the same order, and Bon Mancip, notary, who wrote these things.

[28] In the year as above, 3 days before the ides of September [11 September 1250]: Peter Hot, son of the late Raymond Hot, of Villetritouls. For him and on his instructions, William Arnold of Taurize, Raymond Requin and Bernard Hot, brother of the said Peter, pledged surety to the lord Bishop William, Bishop of Carcassonne, and under oath they made themselves and their property liable – each for the whole sum – under pain of 50 pounds, <guaranteeing> that the same Peter Hot would come on the day or days assigned to him, and that he will obey each and every one of the mandates of the lord bishop, and that he will do and accomplish every penance that the aforesaid lord bishop decides to impose upon him, and that he will conduct his case in front of the same lord bishop; and if he were not to do <these things>, all of the afore-named would pay the said amount of money, at the will of the said lord bishop, such that none of them could be excused for his part. And he is assigned the vigil of the next feast of St Matthew [20 September] to present before the same lord bishop all his

legitimate objections and defences – if he has any – against those things that have been found against him in inquisition.

Witnesses: Peter of Vaure, chaplain, Master Peter, Official <of Carcassonne>, Raymond Peter, Bon Mancip, and Peter Aribert, notary public, who wrote these things.

[29] In the year above, on the ides of September [13 September 1250]. At the request of William, Abbot of St-Hilaire,[194] Lord William, Bishop of Carcassonne, gave permission to Alazaicia Sicred of Cavanac, of the diocese of Carcassonne, to leave prison, where she had been imprisoned for the crime of heretical wickedness; and that she be outside prison wherever she wished until the next feast of All Saints, such that she would return to prison that day, without waiting for a <specific> order from the same lord bishop, to stay there for ever for the carrying out of penance for the said crime. And the aforesaid Alazacia swore on the holy gospels of God to do this and accomplish it, in the presence of the aforesaid abbot and [*name blank*], his monk, Master Peter, Official <of Carcassonne>, Bruno, warden of the prison, and many others, and Peter Aribert, public notary, who wrote these things.

[30] AD 1250, 2 days before the ides of October [14 October 1250]. Peter of Lagarde, of Conques, appeared at Villars [*or* Villar] before Lord William, Bishop of Carcassonne; and, asked if he wishes to defend himself regarding those things that have been found against him in inquisition, he said yes.

Item, asked if he wishes to receive these things in writing, he said yes.

Item, asked if he has enemies, he said yes; and he supplied them in writing; and he does not wish to name more enemies, but rather he wishes to renounce the naming of enemies. Witnesses: Lord Guiraud, Peter of Vaure, Master Raymond David, and Peter Aribert, notary public, who wrote these things.

Item, the same day he was given in writing the things that had been said by the witnesses who had deposed against him in inquisition. And he was assigned the following Friday to appear before the lord bishop, wherever he may be in the diocese of Carcassonne, to propose and object and state what he wishes in his defence.

Witnesses: Master Raymond David, Peter of Vaure, and Peter Aribert, notary public, who wrote these things.

194 William Peter, Abbot (1237–63) of the Benedictine monastery of St-Hilaire.

[36] AD 1250, 2 days before the calends of December [30 November 1250], permission was given to Peter Pelha of Couffoulens, to lay down the crosses imposed upon him for heresy, until he returns from <northern> France where he wishes to go. And within 8 days after his return he must present himself to the lord Bishop of Carcassonne, and with all his will resume those or other crosses, without any new case <being brought against him>; and must show him testimonial letters about the pilgrimages he has carried out. And he swore on the holy gospels of God to observe and carry out the aforesaid things; and he consented to the drawing up of a public instrument <about this>. As regards the other things that have been imposed upon him, however, nothing has been changed.

The witnesses are Lord Guiraud, chaplain of Aiguesvives, Peter of Bezins, Raymond Peter, William Pons, and many others, and Peter Aribert, notary, who wrote these things.

[80] On the same day [5 October 1251], Viguier [*or* the viguier] of Montolieu and Bertrand Malpuel made themselves and their property liable for the payment to inquisitors of 150 shillings at three times, that is to say 50 shillings next Thursday, another 50 the following Thursday, another 50 the Thursday after that, on behalf of Peter At of Moussoulens, who received the said money from heretics. And they swore to observe and carry this out in that way, and they consented to the drawing up of a public instrument about it.

Witnesses: Sanche Morlana, Peter Raymond of Ventajou, and Peter Aribert, notary, who wrote these things.

[81] On the same day, in the church of St-Michel in the bourg of Carcassonne, the order was given by the inquisitors to the men of Preixan, Couffoulens, Cavanac, Cornèze, Leuc and Villeflour upon whom crosses had been imposed for heresy and to whom grace was given about the crosses [*to lay them down*], that they should begin to make the minor pilgrimages imposed upon them for the said crime within the next 8 days, and major ones within the next 15 days; and those that are bound to this should go overseas on the first available passage.[195]

[85] In the year as above, 2 days before the nones of October [6 October 1251] William Raymond of Ventenac, cited, appeared at

195 Minor pilgrimages could be local or within France, for example to Rocamadour or Le Puy, major ones to Compostella, Rome or Canterbury, while 'overseas', Outremer, means the Holy Land. Compare to the sentences of Peter Seila, above, Doc. 42.

Carcassonne before the inquisitor. And asked if he wished to defend Bernard of Ventenac, his late father (whose heir he showed he was by a written instrument), on <the charge of> heresy, he said that he wished to have a day to consider this; and he was assigned Monday <to return and respond>.

[87] In the year as above, 7 days before the ides of October [9 October 1251], the said William Raymond of Ventenac appeared. And asked if he wished to defend Bernard of Ventenac, his father, on those things concerning heresy which had been found in inquisition against him, he said no.

[88] In the year as above, 2 days before the nones of October [6 October 1251], grace was given by the lord bishop to Ulix of Cabaret regarding the crosses imposed upon him for heresy, until next Christmas. And then, without waiting for an order from him or anyone else, he must take up the crosses again. And he swore thus, and consented to the drawing up of a public instrument. Witnesses: Pons Benedict, Roger, Canon of Carcassonne, and Peter Aribert, who wrote these things.

[126] AD 1251, 7 days before the ides of March [9 March 1252]. Peter of Berriac appeared before the inquisitors. And asked if he believed the letter made regarding the purgation of William Nègre was true, he was unwilling to reply, <despite> being asked many times. And by virtue of the oath he has taken, he was ordered not to leave the episcopal house until he replied. And after some interval he replied, and he said he did not believe the said letter was true. He believed however that the two seals attached to it were true, and that the scribe who wrote it was true and lawful. And he was assigned the Monday after Passion Sunday to prove the causes of the falseness of the aforesaid letter.

[147] In the year as above, 15 days before the calends of July [17 June 1252]. William Roger of Villegly swore to take himself across the sea <to the Holy Land> on the next available passage, <to stay there> for two years, under pain of 100 pounds. And William of Tours and Raymond, his son, and Bernard Aosten of Pennautier pledged surety for him, under the same penalty, by oath and public instrument, each making himself and his property liable for the whole sum.

Witnesses: Bernard Digon, Peter Raymond and Peter Aribert, notary, who wrote these things.

[148] In the year as above, 15 days before the calends of September [18 August 1252], Pons Vital of Conques appeared before Master Raymond David, Inquisitor, and he acknowledged that he was the heir

(together with Peter Vital, his brother, now dead) of John Vital, his uncle, upon whom the passage overseas <to the Holy Land and staying there> for five years had been imposed. And he was ordered to make satisfaction on the following Saturday on his [*John Vital's*] behalf, as recompense for the same passage, with 20 pounds *tournois*.

[152] In the year and on the day as above [3 September 1252], Peter Brice of Montréal, to whom grace was given <of release> from prison in exchange for passage overseas <to the Holy Land>, swore to take himself overseas by the first passage in March. And this extension was granted to him at the request of the lord archbishop.[196] Otherwise he must then return to prison.

Item Brice, brother of the said Peter, swore that he will similarly take himself overseas on the first passage. Otherwise he will return to prison.

[154] In the year as above, 6 days before the nones of October [2 October 1252], Raimunda Manfere of Sauzens, wife of the late Raymond Copier, signed with crosses for the crime of heretical wickedness, appeared before Master Raymond David, Inquisitor, without crosses. And asked why she was not wearing crosses as she was obliged to do by her own oath, she said she was not wearing them on her tunic because the earlier ones were torn and she did not have the wherewithal to buy <new ones>. She also said that she was wearing crosses on her cloak. But her mistress Ava, the wife of Lawrence Chatmar, with whom she lives as a wet-nurse, ordered her not to wear the said cloak with the crosses, and gave her some other cloak, without crosses, to wear.

[160] In the year as above, 5 days before the ides of November [9 November 1252]. Raymond Autier <and> Raymond Amiel of Villemoustaussou swore and made themselves and their property liable for Arnold Narbonne, who is to be brought out of prison on the following day, under pain of 20 pounds, <guaranteeing> that the same Arnold will serve the nuns of Rieunette in their works well and faithfully for two years, in his office or trade, namely as a mason; unless he has legitimate impediment <to carrying this out>; otherwise they should replace him with someone who knows how and can complete this time for him.

Witnesses: the Chaplain of Verzeille, and his nephew,[197] and Peter Aribert.

196 William of La Broue, Archbishop of Narbonne (1245–57).

197 Or grandson.

The same Arnold Narbonne swore this.

[164] In the year as above, 5 days before the nones of March [3 March 1253], Gallard Vassal, of Salsigne – who has relapsed into heresy (adoring heretics from the feast of St Michael onwards), after penance had been imposed upon him previously for those things he had wickedly committed in the same crime, and who through his own arrogance has laid off the crosses that were imposed on him – swore to stand by each and every mandate of the inquisitors, and to carry out and accomplish whatever may be imposed upon him for the said crime. And Peter Cavaer of Fournès, Raymond Abbas, William of Villar, <and> William Bordes of Salsigne pledged surety for him on this, on pain of 25 pounds, each of them making himself and his property liable for the whole sum. And by virtue of his present oath, the said Gallard was ordered immediately to resume <and wear> the crosses which in his arrogance he had laid off. Moreover, for the relapse, since he has recently sinned in heresy, he is to wear in perpetuity two crosses on a hood, each of one palm's <width>, and he must not be either in his house or outside it without wearing the hood and the crosses there attached. And on every Sunday this Lent he is to visit all the churches in the Bourg, in shirt and breeches, with rods in his hand, barefoot, and wearing the aforesaid hood.

This order was given to the said Gallard by masters Ralph and Raymond David, inquisitors, who received the aforesaid instrument and <document of legal> obligation. Witnesses: Bernard Digon, Peter Raymond, and many others, and Peter Aribert, notary, who wrote these things.

[205] Witnesses whom Bernard Pons produced to prove hostilities between himself and his wife:

AD 1254, 15 days before the calends of July [17 June 1254], William Namdata, sub-chaplain of Saissac, sworn in as witness, said that he had heard it said – and it is reputed in Saissac and Puylaurens – that Arnaude, wife of Bernard Pons, was found at Puylaurens by her same husband with Raymond Gueirejat, who was having a thing with her. And she does not to this day, on his [*her husband's*] account, leave off having a thing with many more. And also a man at Montolieu regards her as a prostitute [*perhaps meaning 'keeps her as a prostitute' – indeed, he is probably the young man of Montolieu mentioned below*], as it is said and reputed at Saissac. Asked, he knew and could assign no other cause of hostilities between them, except as he has said.

Peter of *Opere* [*perhaps* Loupia] sworn <as witness>, said he had heard it said by Bernard Pons that someone from Puylaurens had gone away with Arnauda his wife, and that the same had [*gap in edn*] him; and on account of this he had beaten her, as he heard it said by others. He also said he had heard it said that the said Arnauda is a prostitute, and she does not on account of her same husband leave off having a thing with many men, and that a certain young man of Montolieu still holds her and commits adultery with her. Asked, he assigned no other cause of hostilities, other than as has been said.

Raymond Benedict, sworn as witness, said he had heard it said by Arnauda, wife of Bernard Pons, that she wished her said husband was dead, so that she could have Pugoler of Montolieu as her husband, and that she would even be willing to be made a leper if only she could have the same Pugoler as her husband. About the time: this year. About the place: at Saissac in the house of Bernard Pons. About bystanders: he said that a certain schoolboy of the said Bernard Pons <was there>. About her defamation: he said the same as the aforesaid others, through hearing <it>. Asked, he said he knows nothing else.

[211] In the year as above, 14 days before the calends of December [18 November 1254], William Megier, Peter Yalguier <and> Peter Pastor made themselves and their property liable by oath and public instrument, under pain of 50 pounds, for Rixenda, wife of William Hualguier, imprisoned for heresy, who has been given permission to leave the Wall and to be outside until she has given birth: such that when a month has gone by after the birth she must return to prison, without awaiting a specific order to do so, <and> without any contradiction or delay. And furthermore she will obey all and each of the commands of the inquisitors. Witnesses: William and Astruc Gaulassa.

[236] AD 1256, 4 days before the ides of April [10 April 1256]. Bernard of Latour, knight, sworn as a witness and questioned, said he did not know anything on the matter of heresy apart from what he confessed before the inquisitors of Carcassonne.

Item, asked, he said that when Raymond Sabatier was signed with crosses for heresy, he spoke with the witness very pressingly (because he knew that he [*Bernard*] was of the family of the lord bishop), asking that he intercede for him with the same bishop, so that the same Raymond might lay off the said crosses. And for this he promised him 100 Melgueil shillings, and in addition, as a token of service, in perpetuity an annual payment of 6 pence. The same witness accepted all these things, and made a pact with the same Raymond, that he would have him released[198] from <wearing> the cross by the aforesaid lord bishop. And on this business he worked hard on the lord bishop and inquisitors, to be able to bring it about. And he did what he could, but he could not manage to do it – although for this thing the same witness got 33 shillings from the aforesaid Raymond. Regarding these, the same witness later made an agreement with the same Raymond to repay him 20 shillings, because he had not managed it. And he ordered the precentor, his brother-in-law,[199] to give him one measure of barley; however the precentor only gave him 8 sesters and half a pint of grain, so he understood.

Item, he said that the aforesaid Raymond Sabatier gave him 5 shillings to convey to Master Peter Aribert for the aforesaid business. But the same master was unwilling to receive them. Asked if he restored those 5 shillings to the aforesaid Raymond, he said that he does not remember. He also said that on behalf of the same witness the sacristan of St-Nazaire and the archdeacon and precentor of the same place did a lot of asking of the lord bishop and the inquisitors, about getting the said grace <to lay off> the crosses. About the time: 2 years ago or thereabouts.

Item, the said Bernard of Latour, knight, placed himself entirely under the will of the venerable father William, by divine permission Bishop of Carcassonne, and of the inquisitors, to carry out or observe whatever they decided to impose upon him, if he committed <a crime> in anything in the aforesaid things. And for this he made himself and his property liable, by oath and public instrument.

He deposed these things before the said inquisitors Master Ralph and Peter Aribert, inquisitors [*sic*]. Witnesses: Peter Vasco and William, chaplain of Cuqserviès.

<Register of the notary of the inquisition of Carcassonne, Part II>[200]

[32] AD 1259, 2 days before the calends of November [31 October 1259], William Sicre, son of Adalaicia Sicre, of Cavanac in the diocese of Carcassonne, brought in as a prisoner, added to his testimony,

198 Ed: de cruce signari; probably mistake for 'de cruce resignari'.

199 Ed: sorori; mistake for 'sororio'.

200 Modern title.

saying that Amblard of Villelongue (sent by Bernard Acier, so he said) came to Cavanac and from there escorted the same witness to Belvèze into the house of Guillelma of Gramazie, to see heretics. And the same witness saw there the same Bernard Acier and his companion, heretics, in the presence of the same Amblard and Guillelma (his betrothed or his wife). And the same witness alone adored the said heretics there; but he did not see the others adoring. And then the aforesaid heretics asked the same witness about the state of his area, and of the heretics' believers. And the following day, after adoring the heretics and receiving from them as a gift 5 Melgueil shillings, the same witness left the heretics in the aforesaid house and went home. About the time: around 5 years ago.

Item, he said that on the instruction of the said Amblard the same witness went to the *castrum* of Rieux in the Val de Daigne into the house of Durant Gilles, and he saw there Peter Fatis, heretic, in the presence of the said Durant Gilles, [*gap in edn*] his wife, <and> [*gap in edn*] the daughter of the same Durant, 8 years old. And on arriving and leaving there the same witness adored the said heretics. And the aforesaid heretics asked the same witness to receive them. And he left them. And after some days had gone by, the aforesaid heretics came to the same witness's house at Cavanac, and they were there for two or three days, in the presence of the same witness and the same witness's mother Adalaicia, who gave them things to eat. And every day they adored the same heretics in the morning and in the evening, as above. And after the said days had gone by, the same witness escorted the said heretics to Cornèze into the house of Arnold Barbion, who received the aforesaid heretics, in the presence of Adalaicia, his wife. And there the same witness and the other two, in the same witness's sight, adored the said heretics, as above. And when this had been done, the same witness left the heretics there and went home. And this was around the aforesaid time.

Item, he said that on the instruction of Arnold Barbion of Cornèze, the same witness went out to meet the aforesaid heretics, and took them and escorted them to the same witness's house, where they were for a day and a night, in the presence of the same witness and his mother Adalaicia, who received them and gave them things to eat. And on their arrival and departure the same witness and the same witness's mother adored them. And after the said day had gone by, the aforesaid heretics left there and went on their way towards the Val de Daigne. About the time: around 4½ years ago.

He also added that after 8 days had gone by, the aforesaid heretics came back to the same witness's house at Cavanac, as they had arranged with the same witness. And they were there for two days, in the presence of the same witness and the same witness's mother, who received them and gave them things to eat. And each day they adored them twice, in the morning and in the evening. And William of Préchanel saw and visited the aforesaid heretics there, but he did not see him adoring. And after the said days had gone by, the same witness on his own took up the aforesaid heretics and accompanied them to the place called 'the hill of Cavanac', where the same witness adored the heretics and left them. About the time: as above.

Item, he said that on the instruction of Arnold Barbion the same witness went to near the water [*or* river] at Leuc, where he found the aforesaid Bernard Acier and his companion, heretics. After adoring them there, he escorted them to Servian in the Val de Daigne, into the house of Arsendis, who received them. And in the morning, after the same witness had taken breakfast in the house's cellar, where the heretics were and the said Arsendis with them, and had adored the heretics, he left the heretics there and went home. About the time: around 3 years ago.

Item, he said that on the instruction of the said Arnold Barbion, the same witness went to the water at Leuc, where he found the aforesaid <Bernard Acier and his companion>, heretics, whom he adored there and escorted to Comelles, into the house of Peter of Comelles, with the wife of the said Peter of Comelles. After leaving the heretics at some straw barn, he went home. And this was around the aforesaid time.

He also added that after 15 days had gone by, he went to the pass of Villaudry, as he had arranged with the heretics, and found the said heretics there. And after adoring them he escorted them to the road from Cavanac, where he left them and adored them, as above.

Item, he said that on the instruction of William of Pauligne of La Bézole the same witness went outside Cavanac to some vineyard of the same witness, where he found Bernard of Montolieu and Bernard Acier, heretics, whom he adored. And he escorted them into the same witness's house, where they were for a day and a night, in the presence of the same witness and the same witness's said mother, both of whom received the aforesaid heretics, gave them things to eat, and adored them. And after the said day had gone by, the same witness escorted the aforesaid heretics thence, and accompanied them to the pass of

Villaudry, where he adored them and left them. About the time: around a year ago.

Item, he said that William of La Bézole came to Cavanac and escorted the same witness to La Bézole and from there to the wood of *Mata* to see heretics. And from there, on the instruction of the aforesaid youth, the same witness climbed the hill above the said wood, where he found Bernard of Montolieu, heretic, and with him Vital of Pauligne of La Bézole, who recounted to him that Peter Pollan, bishop of the heretics, had left them secretly, and had hidden all the money and all the treasure.[201] After hearing this, the same witness remained there in the same place with them for three days. And on the first day, searching through the wood, they found under the earth a bottle[202] where there were, by number, 12 or 13 pounds sterling; and on the second day another bottle, in which there were 14 pounds sterling; and on the third day a third bottle, in which there were 18 Millau pounds. Taking hold of these, they went together to Cornèze, where Bernard of Montolieu, heretic, remained, together with Arnold Barbion, who had gone out to meet the same heretic. And the same witness and Vital of Pauligne went to Cavanac with the money, into the same witness's house. And after one or two days both of them, the same witness and the said Vital, went with the money to Casals, where they found Bernard of Montolieu and Bernard Acier and another heretic, and both of them adored them. When this had been done and they had returned the money to them, the same witness went away on his own, leaving the heretics and Vital of Pauligne, who stayed with them. About the time: around a year ago.

Item, he said that, as he had arranged with the heretics and Vital, after 15 days had gone by the same witness – with 2 pounds the heretics had left in the same witness's house – went to Servian into the house of Arsendis. And from there Peter, the son of the same Arsendis, escorted the same witness to Rieux, into the house of some woman (whose name he does not know) who lives by the town gate towards the south – where the same witness and the said Peter ate. And in the evening the aforesaid woman directed the same witness towards a certain road in the *castrum*, saying that he would find in the last house of that street what the same witness was looking for. When he had heard

201 Cf. Doc. 45, fol. 217r; Doc. 46, fol. 171v; and see A. Roach, 'The Cathar economy', *Reading Medieval Studies* 12 (1986), 51–71.

202 Usually leather.

this, the same witness followed that road and opened the door of the last house, where he found Bernard of Montolieu, Bernard Acier, and Peter of *Camia*, and two heretics – whom the same witness had first seen together with Peter, son of Arsendis, in some vineyard by Rieux, and he had spoken with them then about the thing to do with Vital of Pauligne, who had not come as he had promised the heretics. And then in the aforesaid house the same witness adored the said heretics. And he told them that Vital of Pauligne – whom the same witness had gone to see at La Bézole, on the heretics' instructions – could not come, because the same Vital had had a problem in a knee; and he [*Vital*] was saying that they should think for themselves, because the same Vital could do nothing for them. And after some delay, the heretics gave the same witness 20 Melgueil shillings for the labour he had undertaken and done on their behalf. Taking these and returning to the house of the said woman, he slept and overnighted there. And on his leaving the heretics, he promised them that if he got to know beforehand of anything that could be of concern to them, he would report it to them. He also added that in the vineyard where the same witness saw the aforesaid heretics, as said earlier, he adored them and returned the said 2 pounds to them. Asked if Peter, the son of Arsendis, adored the said heretics, he said he did not, nor did he see them together with the same witness. Item, about the time: as above.

Item, he said that on the instructions of Adalaicia, Arnold Barbion's wife, whom the same witness found in the Bourg of Carcassonne, the same witness went to the house of the same Arnold Barbion at Cornèze, where he saw and visited Bernard of Montolieu, Bernard Acier, Peter of *Camia* and another heretic, in the presence of Adalaicia, the wife of the same Arnold Barbion; and the same witness adored the said heretics there. And after this had been done, on the heretics' instructions the same witness went to La Bézole to Vital of Pauligne. The same witness told him, on behalf of the heretics, that if the same Vital knew <the whereabouts of> the money which they had hidden together with Vital and some other woman, which the heretics could not find, he should inform them. And the same Vital replied to the same witness that he had not been afterwards in the place where the money had been hidden, nor did he know anything about that money. On hearing this, the same witness gave up, and he told this to the heretics at Cornèze in the house of Arnold Barbion, in the presence of the said Adalaicia, Arnold Barbion's wife. And after adoring the heretics and leaving them there he went away from them. About the time: this year, around Christmas.

Item, he said that on the instruction of Arnold Barbion, coming from Montolieu, the same witness went to Cornèze, where he found Bernard Acier and Peter of *Camia*, heretics, in some little house, which Arnold Barbion's wife Adalaicia showed to the same witness; and the same witness adored the same heretics there. And when this had been done, the aforesaid heretics asked the same witness to leave with them and go into Lombardy. The same witness replied to them and said that he would not go, because he did not have the money ready, and he left them thus. About the time: this year in the middle of Lent.

He believed the aforesaid heretics were good men, friends of God and truth-tellers, and that they had a good faith and that he and others could be saved in their sect, and he was in this belief until the last time he left them. And he acknowledged that he had done and committed all the things added above (from the beginning of the addition), after he was released from the Wall where he had been imprisoned for those things which he had committed in heresy originally, and also after grace had been given him about <laying down> the crosses on his release; whence he confesses he knowingly relapsed into the heresy he had abjured.[203]

Item, he said that Dias and Johanna, female heretics, were in the same witness's and his mother's house for a year and more, continuously, eating and drinking at the same heretics' own <expense>. However, both the same witness and his mother sometimes bought grain for them, and sometimes bought grain from them. And both of them, the same witness and the same witness's mother, often adored the said heretics.[204] And he saw and visited the said heretics there. Many times and often William of Préchanel adored the same heretics, in the same witness's sight.

He also added that after the lapse of the said crime, the same witness and William of Préchanel together with Peter Paraire and other heretics escorted the aforesaid heretics[205] from there and accompanied them and escorted them out as far as the hill called *Carga Sobregii*. And after both the same witness and William of Préchanel – in the same witness's sight – had adored the heretics there, they left them. About the time: around 11 years ago. And when he first confessed he did not say this, because he did not recall it.

203 This made him liable to execution. Added later to one of William Sicre's earlier depositions is the interlinear note 'Burnt'.

204 Edition mistakenly has male gender, as also in the next two instances of heretics.

205 Edition: still male gender.

Item, he said that after Bernard Acier, heretic, was taken as a prisoner to Carcassonne and was converted, and when the same witness heard about his conversion, he went to Carcassonne into the marshal's house, where the inquisitors were living and interrogating. And the same witness found there, detained as a prisoner, Vital of Pauligny, whom the same witness advised about what had happened with Bernard Acier – who [*Vital*] told the same witness that the said Bernard Acier was confessing and he had spoken about the same Vital. And he had been taken prisoner on account of this. And he was presuming that if he [*Bernard*] had not yet spoken about the same witness, he would now speak and reveal the same witness and what he had done. And he counselled the same witness to take flight and leave the country. When they had heard this the same witness and William of Préchanel and the same witness's mother Adalaicia left the *castrum* of Carcassonne[206] and went to Malviès into the house of Adalaicia, the same witness's sister, wife of William Aigabeu, where they left the same witness's mother; the same witness and William of Préchanel went to Rocamadour to visit the church and oratory of the Blessed Virgin Mary. And departing from there they returned to Raymond Ferrand's fort, between Montréal and Fanjeaux. And they found there the same witness's mother, Adalaicia. And after a while the same witness's sister Adalaicia and her husband William Aigabeu, from Malviès, came into the house of William Aigabeu's brother-in-law, Bernard Deodat, where the same witness and William of Préchanel were. And they gave them the news that the convert Bernard Acier had revealed all that had been done by the same witness and the other one [*i.e. William of Préchanel*] – telling them they should take flight. When they had heard this, leaving the same witness's mother there (together with the same witness's sister and brother-in-law), the same witness and William of Préchanel fled and left the country.

He deposed these things at Carcassonne, before Brother Baldwin of Montfort, Inquisitor. Witnesses: brothers Peter Blegier, and Felix, and William Escobillo, a convert <from heresy>, of the Order of Preachers, and Reginald of Castres, notary, who signed <this>.

And he swore, and abjured and was reconciled.

206 Edition: Cavanac.

50. THE TWO CONFESSIONS OF JORDAN OF SAISSAC, 1279 (AND 1244)

Although Dominican inquisitors carefully kept records of earlier inquisitions in Toulouse and Carcassonne, it is rare to catch the sort of glimpse of their direct use that we are given in this case. Jordan of Saissac, knight, the son of the powerful nobleman Sicard, Lord of Puylaurens, had participated in the revolt of Raymond II Trencavel in 1240, and a record of his subsequent confession in 1244 to Brother Ferrier is still extant. Thirty-five years after that earlier interrogation Jordan was questioned again, this time by Brother Hugh of Bouniols,[207] who clearly had in front of him a record of the earlier confession, which is referred to several times. We have translated the text of the 1279 confession edited in *Inquisitors and Heretics*, pp. 920–30, and interleaved this with translations of relevant parts of the 1244 confession in Doat 23 fols 50v–57r.

In year as above, 16 days before the calends of May [16 April 1278], Lord Jordan of Saissac, knight, appeared of his own will to confess, with the hope of the grace which Brother Hugh of Bouniols, Inquisitor, promised in a public sermon in the church of Lagardiolle (the same witness was there and heard it). This grace was that the inquisitor would receive into grace and without imposing a humiliating penance whoever came forward of their own will to confess about heresy – whether or not he had previously been summoned to confess or not, whether he had concealed heresy knowingly or unknowingly. Received into this same grace by the said inquisitor – that is, without the Wall [= *prison*] or a humiliating penance – he was sworn in as a witness and he added to his confession. He said that he saw two heretics whose names he does not know in the bourg at Carcassonne, in the house of a certain woman from Saissac, at the time when the viscount[208] was holding Carcassonne under siege. And he saw Bartac of Palajac, Peter of Le Moulin of Saissac, and Raymond of Pexiora there with those heretics. All of these – and the same witness – heard the words and admonitions of the said heretics there. And they adored them, genuflecting, saying,

207 Hugh acted as inquisitor (1276–9) with Stephen of Gâtine, Pons of Parnac, Peter Arsieu and John Galand; Douais, *Documents*, I, pp. 181–2. Other interrogations: *Inquisitors and Heretics*, pp. 648–51, 691–7, 703–13.

208 Raymond II Trencavel, who besieged Carcassonne Sep.–Oct. 1240; see Wakefield, *Heresy*, p. 154.

'Bless' – apart from the aforesaid woman; he does not remember about her.

Item, he said that before the same witness, Peter of Moulin and Raymond of Palajac saw two heretics at Carcassonne – as was said in the first confession – the same witness and the aforesaid others adored other heretics.
[*This detail is not in the extant record of the first confession.*][209]

Item, he said that when he saw the aforesaid heretics at Carcassonne, in the house of the aforesaid woman, the same witness promised the said heretics that he would help them in those things where he could, and that he would do good to them.

Item, he said that the same witness and Bernard of Azille, Bartac, William Peter of Villotte, Raymond Peyrole of Boissézon, Peter of Le Moulin and Prebondes of Mireval, knight, and William Sobet, who was then ill, saw and visited two heretics [*or* those two heretics] at Montréal, in the house of Isarn of Villetravers and the aforesaid Bernard of Azille, knight. And there they heard the words and admonitions of the said heretics. And they adored them in the aforesaid way. About the time: when the stronghold of Montréal was being besieged.[210]

Item, he said that the same witness, Bernard of Azille, knight, Peter of Le Moulin, and Raymond of Peyrole, and Bric Sabatier [*or* Bric, shoemaker] saw Peter Polhan and his companion, heretics at Montréal, in the house of the said. And there they heard the words and admonitions of the said heretics, and adored them in the same way as above.

Item, he said that when the same witness saw heretics in the house of En Villota of Puylaurens – as was said in his first confession – the same witness and Sybil, the same witness's wife, adored the said heretics in the same way as above. About the time: as is specified in that deposition.

[*1244 confession*: He said that he saw Bernard Engelbert and his companion, heretics, at Puylaurens in the house of En Vilota … but the same witness did not adore the heretics, nor others in the same witness's sight. About the time: 11 years ago or thereabouts].

Item, he said that while the same witness had some illness,William Bernard of Airoux, heretic, took care of the same witness, and visited

209 See *Inquisitors and Heretics*, p. 920, n.3: Hugh's record was fuller than the copy that is still extant.

210 Early November 1240.

the same witness many times during the said illness: for he was a doctor. About the time: 47 years ago or thereabouts.

Item, he said that he saw Sicard Lunel and his companion, heretics, at Palajac. And he saw there, together with the said heretics, Bartac, and Preboide of Mireval, Raymond Peyrole, Raynard and Peter William, brothers of the said Bartac, and Guilabert of Cabanes. All of them – and the same witness – heard the words and admonition of the said heretics, in the house of the said Bartac. And they adored them, as above. About the time: it was 36 years ago or thereabouts.

Item, he said that the same witness received Peter Capellan, Aimery of Collet, and Sicard Lunel, deacons of the heretics, and Sicard Guilabert, heretic, in the same witness's tower at Caucalières. And they were in the said tower for some days – but he does not know for how many – and they ate there of the same witness's goods. And the same witness visited them there many times. And he heard their words and admonitions, and he adored them many times, in the same way as above. And Adémar, the same witness's *bailli*, Raymond Peyrole, Bonet Engilbert and Fura, together with the same witness, saw the said heretics there. All of them adored the said heretics there, in the same way as above. About the time: 40 years ago or thereabouts.

Item, he said that before, <when> he saw heretics in the house of Bonet Engilbert of Caucalières, as has been said, the same witness and all those named in the said deposition adored the said heretics, in the same way as above. About the time: as is specified in that deposition.[211]

⌈*1244 confession*: He said that he saw Aimery of Collet and his companion, heretic, at Caucalières, in the house of Bonet of Labruguière, the *bailli* of the same witness – and no-one was living in that house. And there the same witness, and Rainard of Palajac, and William Peter of Villotte, and Preboide of Mireval, and Roger of *Monserrat* spoke with the said heretics. And there the same witness and all the aforesaid others adored the said heretics, as has been said. After this, the same witness went away from there, and left the heretics there. About the time: that it was 2½ years ago.⌉

Item, he said that when he saw Aimery of Collet, heretic, at La Roque of Sémalens, the same witness, and Raymond Peyrole, and William Peter of Villotte, who had escorted the said heretic there, did adore him, in the same way as above. About the time: as is in that deposition.

211 Here Jordan confirmed rather than altered his earlier confession.

[*1244 confession*: He said that one night, when the same witness was at La Roque of Sémalens by Caucalières, William Peter of Villotte came to the same witness with Aimery of Collet and his companion heretic … Once again, he said that the same witness did not adore the said heretics, nor did the said William Peter in the same witness's sight. About the time: that it is half a year ago.]

Item, he said that when the same witness and Peter of Raviac escorted and accompanied Arnold Bos and his companion, heretics, from the river-bank of Hautpoul as far as Palajac, and brought them into the house of Bartac, the same witness and the said Peter did adore the said heretics, in the same way as above.

He also said that Peter Cernin and Potel, a servant, escorted the said heretics to the said place where the same witness and the said Peter received them. About the time: as is contained in that deposition.

[*1244 deposition*: He said that when Rainard of Palajac, brother of Bartac, was ill at Palajac, the said ill man sent a messenger to the same witness, that he should send him Arnold Bos, heretic, by whatever possible means. And then the same witness sent Peter of Raviac to Hautpoul, and he escorted the said heretic and his companion, heretic, to the same witness. And then the same witness, together with the said Peter of Raviac, escorted the said heretics to Palajac, to the house of Rainard and his brothers. After this, the same witness went away from there, and left the said heretics there. Once again, he said that the same witness did not not adore the said heretics, nor did he genuflect in front of them, nor did the said Peter <of> Raviac do so in the same witness's sight. About the time: 6 or 7 years ago.]

Item, he said that when the same witness saw Arnold Bos and his companion, heretics, by Hautpoul, the same witness adored them, as above.

Item, he said that in all the places where he saw heretics, the same witness adored them, when he could.

[*1244 confession: since Jordan had said in 1244 that he saw Arnold Bos near or at Hautpoul on two occasions, once four years before, the other three or four years, once adoring them, once not, this seems to be a general correction, concerning all his contacts with Arnold Bos and his companion.*]

Item, he said that when Pons Caus, knight, of Albi was ill with the illness from which he died, in the house of Sebaude at Puylaurens, two heretics – whose names he does not know – hereticated the said Pons Caus and received him into their sect, according to the manner of the heretics. And the same witness, and Lady Sybil, the same witness's wife, William Peter of Villotte, and Fura, and some others whose names he does not recall were present at the said heretication. And after the said heretication, the same witness and the aforesaid others did adore the said heretics, in the same way as above. About the time: 35 or 36 years ago or thereabouts.

[*1244 deposition*: He said that when Pons Caus was ill at Puylaurens in the house of some woman, with the illness from which he died, the same witness went to see the said ill man, and he found in the said house two heretics whose names he does not know. And William Lobat, squire, was with the said heretics in the said house, when he entered. And when the same witness had been with the said ill man for a while, he went away from there, and left the said heretics in the said house with the said heretics].

Item, he said that when Isarn of Dourgne,[212] knight, was ill with the illness from which he died, the same witness certainly knew that Sicard Lunel and his companion, heretics, were brought <to his house> near Puylaurens to hereticate the said ill man; but they did not enter it, nor did they see the said ill man, nor had the said ill man asked for the said heretics. And Raynald, the brother of Bartac, escorted them there, with the same witness's knowledge and consent. About the time: about 40 years ago.

Otherwise – so he says – he did not see heretics, nor did he commit any act of heresy that he remembers, apart from what has been said.

Asked why he did not say these things at the beginning, he said it was because of shame and fear.

He deposed these things at Carcassonne before Brother Hugh of Bouniols, Inquisitor. Witnesses: Brother Raymond Sicre, Prior of the Brothers Preacher of Castres, Brother John of Falgous, Brother Paul, of the Order of Preachers, and John of Essey, notary, who wrote these things.

He took an oath and abjured, and he was reconciled.

212 Lord Isarn, Jordan's brother.

51. THE PLOT AGAINST INQUISITORIAL ARCHIVES, CARCASSONNE, 1284

We have translated the last part of one of the lengthy depositions of a copyist of books from Carcassonne, which bears upon a plan to steal inquisition registers. In 1887, H. C. Lea raised questions about the credibility of the story,[213] and the debate continues.[214] See Given, *Inquisition*, pp. 118–19 for the broader context, and an interesting analysis in C. Bruschi, *The Wandering Heretics of Languedoc* (Cambridge, 2009), pp. 150–2. Translated from Doat 26, fols 211v–216v. We include folio numbers thus: /207r/.

/207r/ Item, AD 1285 on the ides of July [15 July], the aforesaid witness Bernard Agasse, returning after remembering more, added to his testimony, saying that …

/211v/ … Item, he said that a certain day – which he says he cannot remember – when the same witness was at Salsigne, on the day of the tax assizes, Bernard Faure of La Tourette came to the same witness, and told him he wanted to speak with him in private. And then the same witness and Bernard /212r/ Faure went out of the village of Salsigne to the area of the Durants, and there they found Bernard David <and> John David, brothers, Raymond Macellar, and Bernard Benedict of Villardonnel. And then they were all together, and Bernard David said to the same witness, 'Master Bernard, you know things in this land, and we want to confide in you, because you perhaps know them better than others. We have spoken with a certain person, who is to bring about and arrange us getting all the books of the inquisition which relate to this land, namely the Carcassès, in which confessions are written. However, this person does not know letters [*i.e. is illiterate*], and would not be able to recognise them nor pick them out among other books. And if you are willing to pick them out among the others, doing a great /212v/ good for the whole land, you will get a large reward for doing it'. And then the same witness replied to the said Bernard David, <asking> if that person was really sure, and if one could trust him in

213 H. C. Lea, *A History of the Inquisition of the Middle Ages*, 3 vols (New York, 1887), II, pp. 59–60.

214 There is a comprehensive account in Roche, *Une église cathare*, pp. 435–41.

this matter. And all the aforesaid replied: very much so, and that it was safe to trust him. After he had heard this, all of them together with the same witness agreed to set out immediately on the road towards Carcassonne: which they did. And when they got to Carcassonne it was around compline and after a little delay the same witness and the aforesaid Bernard Faure and Bernard Benedict went to the house of Master Arnold Matha. And when they were there, they found Master Arnold Matha, Bernard David, and John David, and Raymond Macellar, and with them William Pagès and Bernard /213r/ Costa his companion, heretics. And while they were all standing thus, there entered together Sans Morlana, the senior archdeacon, Arnold Morlana his brother, William Brunet, Official of Carcassonne, and Jordan Ferroll, Official of Razès. And all the aforesaid were gathered together in the room of Master Arnold Matha, and the same witness with them. And then the said Sans began to speak to the witness: 'Master Bernard, these worthy men who are here have spoken to you, since – in relation to some things you know – it seems to you that you are willing to do what they have told you'. And the same witness replied 'Lord, willingly, let me do it!' And after the said Sans added, 'Master Bernard, a certain person is supposed to hand over to us all the books of inquisition of this land, and because /213v/ that person does not know letters, it is necessary for you to pick them out among the other books and bring them to us'. And same witness replied that he would indeed do this. And immediately Bernard of Lagarrigue came in, who was then living with the inquisitors. And then the said Sans said to the said Bernard of Lagarrigue, 'Bernard, we have spoken to you about certain things, as you know, and we have arranged for Master Bernard Agasse – who is here – to go with you, and pick out those books that we want to have'. And then the said Bernard of Lagarrigue replied, 'Lord, I want to be sure about what has been promised me, and I want this to be very secret, and that we should all take an oath'. And then the said Sans, the archdeacon, said, 'That is fitting. I shall be the first to take an oath'. /214r/ And all of the aforesaid and the same witness swore on the holy gospels of God in the presence of the aforesaid heretics. And then the said Bernard of Lagarrigue said again, 'Lord, before doing anything I want first of all to be sure about the money promised me'. And then the said William Brunet replied, 'Bernard, do not fear, because if we can get the books tomorrow you should come immediately to our workshop and you will be paid'. The said William Pagès, heretic, then said 'Bernard, do not fear – because if you want I shall give it to you immediately'. And they decided and promised to give the said Bernard of Lagarrigue

150 pounds, and 50 pounds to the same witness. And afterwards the said Bernard of Lagarrigue said to the same witness, 'Master/214v/ Bernard, tomorrow, in the morning, come up, and you will find me in the house, and we shall carry out our business'.

And then, that morning, the witness went up inside the house of the inquisitors, and found there the said Bernard of Lagarrigue, who told the same witness that it could not be done now, because he could not find the key in a certain chest where he was supposed to be able to find it. However, Brother John Galand <the Inquisitor> was supposed to come that week from Toulouse, and when he had come, <Bernard said>, 'I shall bring it about that at least I get the key – or I shall have another key made, similar to it. And you should go'. And the same witness immediately left him. And later that same day the said Sans Morlana sent for the same witness, and asked him what he had done together with the said Bernard of Lagarrigue. And the witness related to him what he had done /215r/ and how the said Bernard of Lagarrigue had replied to the same witness. And then the said Sans asked the witness to be scrupulously careful about this.

The witness also said that the said Sans Morlana, seeing after three weeks that the same witness was doing nothing and believing that he would persist in this <inactivity>, took as a case against the same witness some decretals which the same witness was writing out for him – the allegation being that he was behaving badly in this writing <job> – and had him arrested and held prisoner for a good three weeks. Asked about the time, he said that after the next feast of St Michael it will be 2 years ago.

He attested these things in front of Brother John, Inquisitor. Witnesses: Brother John of Falgous, Bernard of Malviès, Arnold Archembaud, and I, Raymond /215v/ <of> Malviès, notary of the inquisition, who was present and received <the deposition>.

AD 1286, 16 days before the calends of May [16 April].
Because a certain rumour is said to have arisen within Carcassonne, to the effect as it were that witnesses <appearing> before the inquisitors of heresy were incited or forced to suggest in their depositions some false things against themselves or others, therefore we, Brother William of St-Seine, Brother John Galand and Brother John Vigouroux,[215]

215 See Doc. 9 §18. On all three inquisitors, see Douais, *Documents*, I, 186 and 190–1; on John Galand, see ibid., pp. 182–90, Doc. 27 and Doc. 52.

Inquisitors, wanting all falsity to be uncovered and for the truth to prevail – most of all in a matter such as this business – and <acting> in order to remove every kind of suspicion, have had all the depositions made by the aforesaid Bernard Agasse in front of us or one of ours, on various dates, carefully read out and explained, /216r/ to him, in front of us, in the presence and witness of the religious men <whose names are> written below, advising him many times <by> asking him and offering him this: that he exercise licence to correct errata – if there were any there – and freely remove falsities – if there were any there.

Item, after the reading out and attentive listening – as said earlier – he was carefully asked by the aforesaid inquisitors whether he had confessed the aforesaid things because asked to do so or for a price, or fear, hatred or love of any person, or incitement or the hardship of tortures. The said Bernard, on his oath, firmly declared that each and every thing he had deposed against himself or against others was true and did not contain any falsity. He added that he said and attested the aforesaid things not coerced by tortures or otherwise persuaded, but only /216v/ for the salvation of his soul and the defence of the Christian faith.

He attested these things in front of the aforesaid brothers, inquisitors, in the presence and witness of Brother Peter Regis, Prior of the Brother Preachers of Carcassonne, Arnold del Gras, Peter of Leva, of the Order of Brother Preachers, and me, Raymond of Malviès, Notary of the inquisition, who was present, wrote and received the deposition.

52. BARTHOLOMEW VESIAN, REGARDING THE CARCASSONNE APPEAL AGAINST THE INQUISITOR JOHN GALAND, 1291

This deposition relates to the complaints raised by the citizens of Carcassonne against the Inquisitor Jean Galand; see also Docs 27 and 28. The appeal is discussed in Friedlander, *Hammer*, pp. 16–18. Translated from Doat 26, fols 140r–141v. We include folio numbers thus: /140r/.

/140r/ AD 1291, 6 days before the calends of July [26 June], Bartholomew Vesian, notary of the bourg of Carcassonne, was brought out of prison and taken to the new room in the Wall of Carcassonne, and placed in judgment in front of William of St-Seine, Inquisitor.[216] He swore on God's holy gospels, and was asked by the said inquisitor to say /140v/ the truth about himself and others, both living and dead, on the matter of heresy and things relating to it. He replied and said that he knew nothing about the said crime and that he had never sinned in it.

Asked if he had publicly carried out the office of public notary at the time when some people from the bourg of Carcassonne had appealed against the inquisitors, either before or after the said appeal, he said that he read out the said appeal in the chapter house of the Brothers Preacher at Carcassonne, in the presence of Brother John Galand, who was then the inquisitor, and the consuls of the bourg and a large section of the people of Carcassonne. And he also read out the said appeal elsewhere, and he made it known. And at the request of the consuls he made a public instrument from it. Nor did he intend in these things to do anything against the inquisition – so he said. He said, furthermore, that he confessed about these things to Brother John Galand, the Inquisitor at the time, who then /141r/ discharged him from them.

Questioned, he also said that that when the consuls of Carcassonne received the counsel [*legal advice*] that they could not appeal against the inquisitors unless every individual in the town appealed, together with some of the consuls he made this public on the streets of Carcassonne

216 Inquisitor of Carcassonne, 1286–92.

on some Sundays and feast days. And there was discussion with the people there. After this, at the request of the consuls, he asked for and received the votes of men who wanted to appeal or to consent to the appeal against the inquisitors. And he took all these down in writing, and <drew them up> in public form [*i.e. as a notarial instrument*], intending – so he said – to carry out his office lawfully, especially since he was doing what he was asked to do. And he was prepared to abide by the ordinance of the inquisitors concerning all these things – so he said. He said, however, that the aforesaid Brother John Galand, to whom he confessed all the aforesaid things, as he said, absolved him in relation to all these things.

He attested this in front of /141v/ the aforesaid inquisitor on the aforesaid day and place, in the presence of lords William of Castillon, major Archdeacon in the church of Carcassonne <and> Arnold Bonhomme, sacristan in the said church, Procurators of the episcopate during the vacancy of the see, Pons Faure, Official of Carcassonne, and brothers Peter Berengar, Sub-Prior of the Brothers Preacher of Carcassonne, John of Faugoux, Fulk of St-Georges,[217] of the Order of Brothers Preacher, and me, Raymond of Malviès, notary of the inquisition, who wrote and took it down.

217 Later Toulouse inquisitor; see Doc. 9 and Doc. 57.

53. ANONYMOUS TRACT, *ON THE WAY OF LIFE ... OF THE POOR OF LYON*, C. 1300 (?)

We have inserted this tract on the Poor of Lyon (Waldensians) here, rather than among the treatises in Part III, in order to underline the fact that its author worked it up from a deposition or depositions. He cut and pasted, in order to turn an individual's testimony into a generalising text, but he did not finish the job. He left loose ends: there is reference to topics about which the person deposing ('iste qui deponit') was ignorant, and to a a missing seventh part, which included something about the crime and guilt of the deponent. The deponent's combination of very considerable knowledge and areas of ignorance suggests someone like John Philibert (the priest whose sentence by Bernard Gui is translated in Doc. 56). While the tract's use of 'perfected' for professed Waldensians fits the understanding of an inquisitor like Gui (see Doc. 40), its use of a term for a Cathar rite (consolare, 'to consolate') to denote the rite of profession of vows and reception into the Order of the Poor suggests someone was confused: but whether this was the deponent or author is not clear. The tract is very interesting for the light it casts on the Waldensians, presented here as a sort of underground religious order, international, and having a certain amount in common with the mendicant orders of Franciscans and Dominicans. It is also attests development in one genre of literature in the Church, the formal description of a sect or 'religion' not just as a set of doctrines but an entity with many facets: an ensemble of people, doctrine, teachings, rites and organisation. This was to reach a high point in the sect descriptions that Bernard Gui provided in the fifth part of his *Treatise on the Practice of Inquisition*, translated WE, pp. 375–445. Our translation is based on P. Biller, 'Appendix: edition and translation of the *De vita et actibus*', in C. Bruschi and P. Biller, eds, *Texts and the Repression of Medieval Heresy* (York, 2003), pp. 196–206; the date and origins of the tract are investigated ibid., pp. 163–93, and the genre of descriptions of sects at pp. 189–90.

There follows <a tract> about the way of life and doings, the faith and the errors of the heretics who call themselves the 'Poor of Christ' or the 'Poor of Lyon'.

First, about the same heretics and their friends, and the believers in their errors, and what the difference is between them.

§ Secondly, about the same <heretics'> belief and errors.

§ Thirdly, how they live in the <their> hospices.

§ Fourthly, how they celebrate their councils or chapters.

§ Fifthly, when and how some of them may profess or be consolated.

§ Sixthly, about the visitation of their friends and believers.

§ Seventhly and lastly, about the crime and guilt of the person who is attesting or confessing.

First, therefore, it should be known that in the sect of the aforesaid heretics there are some who are called 'perfected' ⌜perfecti⌝ and 'established' ⌜solidati⌝ heretics, <and> others <who are called> their 'friends' and 'believers'.

Item, among the 'perfected' heretics, some are called the 'Sandalled', others the 'novices'. The 'Sandalled' are those who are called 'priests', 'masters' and 'teachers' of all heretical wickedness. And they can, so they claim, consecrate the body of Christ just as Catholic priests do.

Item, the 'Sandalled' do not keep money, and they wear shoes with the tops cut off, or perforated above the feet, and boots perforated in a similar way, in accord with the authority, 'Have your feet shod with sandals' ⌜Mark 6.8–9: 'He commanded them … to be shod with sandals'⌝. And whatever is ordained, constituted or even commanded by the same 'Sandalled' <heretics> is inviolably observed by all those who are under them; and they are obeyed as heads. In this sect <both> men and women may be received, and they are called 'brothers' and 'sisters'. They do not possess any immovable goods, but renounce their property and follow poverty. They do not work, they do not acquire or earn anything to support themselves, but they are supported by and live off the goods and alms-giving of their friends and believers, while they apply themselves very zealously to their own concerns.

§ Item, their friends and believers own property, and marry, trade, do business, also buy things and make profit. And they are visited by the same perfected heretics, preached to and led by them into their belief, as will appear below.

Secondly, it should be known that the aforesaid heretics hold, believe and teach their believers and friends the seven articles of faith and also the seven sacraments – and for the most part the other things that Catholics believe – apart from the following errors.

§ They do not believe that the lord pope has power on earth as great as the power blessed Peter had, unless he is as good and holy as blessed Peter was.

§ Item, they do not believe that there is purgatory, except only in this world.

§ Item, they do not believe that alms-giving or prayers benefit the souls of the dead.

§ Item, they do not believe that anyone is allowed, for any reason in the world, to kill a man or take an oath, without committing mortal sin.

§ Item, they believe that one person can confess his sins to another, according to the authority of blessed James: 'Confess your sins one to another', etc. [James 5.16].

§ Item, they believe that those among them who are ordained – to become the 'sandalled' – can consecrate the body of Christ just as Catholic priests do.

Thirdly, one should know that the aforesaid heretics <live> in various places, provinces and kingdoms, both in Germany and in other parts, dwelling in houses and households, two or three of them in a hospice together with two or three women, who pretend to be their wives or sisters. Sometimes old women [*i.e. old female heretics*] live in hospices without men: but they are visited by other heretics often – very often – and food is provided for them. This is the sort of life they lead in the hospices. They rise often, and genuflecting in front of their beds apply themselves to prayer. And he who rules the hospice tells <them> that they should pray for the kings and dukes and governors of the world, that God may grant them to govern the world to His glory and their salvation: or similar words.

§ Item, they pray for their brothers and sisters, and for their believers and friends, for them to be able to do such good things and so much penance in this world that can win through to the joys of paradise: or similar words.

§ Item, they pray for their enemies and persecutors, that through God's help they may be converted to penance: or similar words. And on behalf of all of them they say the 'Our Father' six times.

§ After the praying, the one who rules the hospice is the first to rise. And he says, 'If it pleases Him, may God be with us'.

§ After this those who want to learn scripture, both men and women, <receive> a reading from their teachers. And afterwards, when they have received the readings and repeated them lots of times, they do what they want. And the women prepare food. If any of them publicly offend in some matter, they throw themselves to the ground in front of everyone in the hospice, begging for forgiveness and penance. And then they are raised up by those who are standing around, and penance is given to them. Before a meal they apply themselves to prayer, as is specified above, and often during the day. At a meal, the one who rules the hospice performs the blessing of the meal in this way. He says, 'Bless', and the others reply, 'Lord', and afterwards the 'Our Father' prayer is said. When this is over, the rector says in the vernacular, 'May God, who blessed five loaves of barley and two fish in the desert, bless this food and this drink and the persons about to receive them. In the name of the Father and the Son and the Holy Spirit, Amen.' Sometimes at a meal or at supper there is preaching by the one who rules the hospice. And when the supper and preaching are over he is thanked by someone who is there, and his preaching is confirmed. After a meal they give thanks, and the rector of the hospice says in the vernacular, 'Benediction, and glory, and thanksgiving', etc. [*see* Apocalypse 7.12]. And they apply themselves again to prayer, as <described> above.

And the members of the household of the hospice confess their sins to the rector when they want; they are not, however, compelled to do so unless they want to. If any of their friends or believers come to their hospice, there is a great feast for them and they are received with joy. And they are preached to and exhorted in the faith recorded above. And when they <want to> confess, penance is imposed upon them by the rector <or> by someone else from the hospice if he is not there.

Item, when some perfected heretics living in one town come to the hospice of some perfected heretics living in another town, on their arrival they give each other the kiss of peace, the men to the men, the women to the women. And they do the same when departing.

Fourthly, it should be known that once a year during Lent the aforesaid perfected heretics celebrate a General Council or Chapter in some place in Lombardy or Provence [= *southern France*], or in other regions where the 'Sandalled', or some of them, live. And this used to happen more in Lombardy than elsewhere. Three or four perfected heretics come to this Council from Germany, bringing together with them some cleric or other interpreter, and they pretend in some way that the purpose <of their journey> is visiting the holy places of the apostles Peter and Paul.[218] Virtually all the heretics who are governors of

218 That is, pilgrimage is their disguise.

hospices gather together in this General Council or Chapter. Believers, however, are not admitted into this chapter, nor young perfected heretics, nor women, however perfected and old they may be, nor any perfected [male] heretic, however old, unless he is totally subject to their will and obedience, and unswervingly observes that sect.

§ The aforesaid chapter, further, deals with the whole condition of the said sect. And there is questioning by anyone: as to what one has heard about the state of his household, and about how it is run. And if any of them have been disobedient or rebellious they have to be sent away and attached to other companions.

§ Item, if any perfected heretics have been among them for a long time, <living> according to the sect's rule, and have become knowledgeable in scripture, they are made 'Sandalled' at the same chapter. And from then on, together with the other 'Sandalled', they are called 'masters' and 'rectors' and 'priests'.

§ Item, the said chapter decides about those who wish to profess and to be consolated. And those who have this granted are consolated afterwards, and a residence or society[219] is assigned to them, where they are to live that year.

§ Item, the visitors of their friends and believers, whose job it is to visit them that year, are deputed and appointed in the said chapter. And two are sent into off into any region or province where some of their belief live.

§ Item, the money and alms that have been given and sent to them by their friends and believers are brought to this chapter. The money, in fact, is divided up according to the said 'Sandalled' <heretics'> decision. And each person is given a set portion for himself and his household, to maintain them in food and clothing for the following year. And if some of those who are due to run hospices <the following year> are not there <at the chapter>, money is sent via some who live in their areas. And the majority of the money upon which they live <and> are maintained is brought from Germany.

§ The person who is deposing this, however, does not know how they celebrate [*i.e. how they consecrate the eucharist*].

§ Similarly, he does not know how they ordain people to make them 'Sandalled'. But he has heard that they have their shoes removed by the

219 Societas: the community of a particular hospice.

other 'Sandalled'. And boots and shoes perforated above the feet – as specified above – are handed over to them.

Fifthly, it should be known that the profession of those who are received among them is done like this. Everyone who lives in the hospice, both men and women, gather together. A senior <heretic> or one who is very wise, from the society or hospice in which the one who is to be consolated is due to live that year – or some other heretic from elsewhere if he is there and is regarded as wiser – preaches, and after the questioning <of the novice>, they explain[220] to the person who is to be received all the observances of the said sect. And that the person who is to be received must believe what is specified above, and that henceforth he must observe chastity, possess nothing of his own, promise humility and obedience, and obey and comply with the counsel and will of the same heretics in all things. He must not take an oath, nor kill, and must do everything in his power to avoid committing any sin: in fact, he should rather suffer death than offend in any of the aforesaid things. Should he be unwilling to carry out the aforesaid things, he would not be received among them. The one who is to be consolated has to reply that he is prepared to do everything in his power faithfully to carry out and observe each and every one of the aforesaid things. And then he casts himself to the ground, and he is raised up by those standing around. And the kiss of peace is given by each person there, if he is a man by the men, if a woman by the women. And then the person who has been received in this way must pay the expenses of the meal (if the person has the wherewithal to pay).

Sixthly, it should be known that those who are deputed and appointed to visit believers go about it this way. They get to <the places> they have to visit. And before they arrive at the said places they send some believer, who knows those they have to visit, to them. And he notifies them that 'such and such'[221] brothers are coming. And then the aforesaid believers instruct and assign them a specific day and hour when they should come. They come at this time, together with the said <believer> who is escorting guides them, sometimes by day, sometimes at night.

§ Up to now they do not have great gatherings. But they visit the said believers, <going out> from a hospice – <or seeing them> in a hospice,

220 Perhaps a mistake for 'he explains'.

221 Naming them.

that is to say, whichever ones come into their hospices.[222] And they stay there in each hospice for two or three or four days, sometimes more, sometimes less. And they preach to and exhort and instruct these believers in the aforesaid faith and errors, telling them to avoid the aforesaid things: they should not kill, not lie, not take an oath, not do anything they do not want <to be done> to themselves.

§ Item, they hear the confessions of their believers. And they impose penances on them. And they receive alms from these same believers. And they teach them scriptures. And they visit in this way other hospices of the said believers.[223] And in many places the said perfected heretics bring to their believers, and to their children and households, some playthings, namely belts, knives, pin-cases and pins, to get a more enthusiastic and pleasant reception. And the said visitation happens more in winter than summer, since the believers are more able to have the time to spare. When believers are visited, the brothers greet them on behalf of all their brothers. And the said believers ask them to greet all their brothers on their behalf, and to pray to the Lord for them. And thus the visitors and the believers take the money and alms <given> to them to the coming general chapter and present them there, and they divide them up, as specified above.[224]

Seventhly, it should be known that … [*A blank space follows. Note the contents-list at the beginning*: 'Seventhly and lastly, about the crime and guilt of the person who is deposing or confessing'].

222 Conjectural translation of corrupt Latin which here, and in the last sentence below, suggests the possibility that the author was writing in a slapdash way towards the end of a text he did not finish.

223 Whereas earlier 'hospices' [hospitia] denoted the houses in which the Brothers and Sisters lived a formal religious life, in some ways comparable to that of Catholic religious in monasteries, nunneries and convents, here it seems to denote no more than the lodgings and houses of the ordinary 'lay' believers.

224 The Latin text of this last sentence is quite corrupt.

54. PETER OF GAILLAC OF TARASCON, NOTARY, 1308

The Inquisitor Geoffrey (d. 1316) was a northern Frenchman from Ablis (Yvelines dpt). He entered a Dominican convent in Chartres, whose library once contained his now-lost commentary on Peter Lombard's *Sentences.* Appointed inquisitor in 1303, he produced an anthology of documents useful for inquisitors (1306). Catharism had been revived by Peter Autier and his circle in the Sabartès region just after 1300 (see on this M. Barber, *The Cathars*, 2nd edn (Harlow, 2013), ch. 6, and Doc. 9 §16) and its destruction was brought about mainly by Geoffrey. But he has remained less famous than his contemporaries, Bernard Gui and Jacques Fournier, because all that survives of his work is a register of depositions made in front of him or his deputies between May 1308 and September 1309.

Selected here are the depositions of Peter of Gaillac. These are unusual in that as a notary he wrote much of them himself,[225] and his own hand survives in the manuscript, BnF MS Lat. 4269, fols 54r–59v. It can be seen online in the digitised image made available in BnF Gallica. Omitting the lengthy surrounding formulae of authentification of the confessions, we have translated from the edition by A. Pales-Gobilliard, *L'Inquisiteur Geoffroy d'Ablis et les cathares du comté de Foix (1308–1309)* (Paris, 1984), pp. 332–61, emending this occasionally against the ms.

AD 1308, 10 days before the calends of November [23 October], I, Peter of Gaillac, notary of Tarascon, cited, appearing and lawfully arraigned in front of the religious man Brother Geoffroy of Ablis, of the Order of Brother Preachers, appointed by apostolic authority inquisitor of heretical wickedness in the kingdom of France, in the House of Inquisition in the city of Carcassonne in the place called 'Audience' [*'hearing'*], swore on the holy gospels of God to say the whole and pure truth on the matter of heresy, as the principal regarding myself and as a witness about others both living and dead. As accused and a sinner in the aforesaid crime, I acknowledge and confess that I have erred and done wrong in the aforementioned crime, and that 3 days before the nones of August [3 August] AD 1308, arraigned in judgment in front of the religious man Brother John of Faugoux, of the aforesaid order, who was acting

225 Though see the earlier reference to a submission to inquisitors written by two men together: Doc. 48 fol. 127v.

in the place of the said lord Inquisitor, I made a confession about the things I committed in heresy. Earlier, however, having been for some time in the Wall or the prison of the Wall of Carcassonne, and having sworn in front of the said <inquisitor's> lieutenant to say the whole and pure truth on the said crime of heresy, as principal regarding myself and as witness about others living and dead, I said and confessed that it was 8 years or thereabouts before the recently past feast of the birth of the blessed John the Baptist [24 June, c. 1300] that I had come from the university of Toulouse. And when I was in my own house at Tarascon Lady Gaillarda, my mother, told me and indicated to me that Peter Autier and William Autier of Ax were in the town of Tarascon, and that they had come from the regions of Lombardy, and were in the house of Arnold Piquier of Tarascon, and that they held the faith and sect of the heretics, which they regarded as good and Catholic. And I was asked by the said lieutenant of the aforesaid lord Inquisitor if I then went to see them, at the instigation of the said lady, my mother, and I said and replied no. But a little while later, during the vigil of blessed John the Baptist, I went to the house of the said Arnold Piquier, together with the said lady, my mother. And in some room in the said house I found Peter Autier and James Autier, the aforesaid heretics, who described to me their faith and the sect, and the life they led, saying that at a first glance, as far as worldly men were concerned, their sect was thought of, talked about and regarded as bad and useless. However, for someone who believed perfectly and firmly both in its basis and in it, it was useful; and it led a man both to a good end and also to the path of salvation. At the time I said nothing to them in reply, I did not then respond anything to them, but after taking leave I went away, <feeling> within myself utterly astonished, dumbfounded and fearful. And I was asked who was there by the said lieutenant, and I said that <there were there> the said lady, my mother, and I, and the said heretics, and no-one else. Item, I was asked if at the time I made any reverence to them, and I said no.

Item, I said that after 15 days or so had passed after the aforesaid things, I bought a certain trout in the square in Tarascon, on the instructions of Alissendis, wife of the late Peter Martin of the said place, who gave me 12 pence to buy the said trout, and told me to carry it and give it on behalf of the said Alissendis to the aforesaid heretics, who were in the house of the aforesaid Arnold Piquier: which I did. And I was asked if there was any person with the said heretics when I presented the said trout to them, and I said no. Item, I was asked if I ate or drank at the time with the said heretics, and I said yes.

Item, I was asked what I ate, and I said that the said heretics gave me part of the said trout which they had cooked very well and had prepared with good spices; and I ate bread blessed by the same heretics. And I was asked about the manner of blessing, and I said that I did not remember. But I did see that they broke a loaf into strips and said certain words which I did not and do not now remember.

And I was asked if I heard their preaching or admonitions, and if I heard them saying anything against the faith of the Roman Church or against the articles of faith or the ecclesiastical sacraments, namely about the sacrifice of the Mass, about baptism, about marriage and about all other things which heretics believe and say against the Catholic faith: and I said and replied yes. And I was asked what the said heretics said about the Roman Church. And I said that they said that it did not have the power to pardon sins because, they said, it was besmirched and full of evil works and examples, because it did not hold to the path to salvation but rather to that of perdition.

Item, they said that the bread placed on the altar, and blessed with the words with which Christ blessed it on the day of the <Last> Supper with the apostles, is not the true body of Christ. Rather it is delusory and scandalous to say this, because that bread is the bread of corruption, propagated and born of the root of corruption. But that <other> bread about which Christ said in the Gospel – 'Take ye and eat … all of this all, etc.' [Matthew 26.26, 27] – is the word of God; and the blood, about which he says that it is like unto the word of God, according to the Gospel of the blessed John, who said, 'In the beginning was the Word, and the Word was with God and the Word was God' [John 1.1]. Whereby they concluded, from this, that the word of God is that bread that is spoken of in the said Gospel, and, from what follows after this, that the aforesaid Word is the body of Christ.

Item, they said that in the Roman Church marriage – about which the Gospel says, 'Let her marry in Christ',[226] and 'They two shall be in one flesh etc.' [Matthew 19.5; Mark 10.8; Genesis 2.24] – is done falsely and as a pretence and not following the word of God. For this reason: because, just as is said in the Gospel, God made marriage in paradise, *that* marriage was of the soul and spirit, as one would expect from a spiritual thing; and not from fleshly things nor from a cause of corruption, as through the Roman Church; for in paradise there never was corruption of the flesh, nor anything other than what is wholly

226 From the marriage rite, echoing 1 Cor. 7, 39.

and purely spiritual. And God made that marriage for this <reason>: that the souls which had fallen from heaven – in ignorance and through pride – and were in this world, should return to the life through marriage with the Holy Spirit, namely through good works and abstaining from sins, and 'they two' would 'be in one flesh', just as is read in the Gospel. But, as they said, that <marriage> which is done by the Roman Church, as they say, is the union of two different fleshes, and thus they are not two in one flesh, but rather male and female, each for itself in different fleshes.

Item, I said and deposed that they said that no-one should adore the cross, and that its sign [*i.e. signing oneself with the cross*] is of no value in any way, for this reason: because God suffered death there and great dishonour. And they put forward an example: if a man was hanged on some tree, that tree would always be hateful to the friends and relations of the man who had been hanged, and they would blame that tree and never want to see it. They would want this to be likened to the place where God, whom we ought to love, was hanged – we were bound to regard it with hatred, and we ought never to desire its presence.

Item, about baptism: they said that in the Catholic Church it was done in ignorance and not following the ordinance of God, for this reason: because, although it is read in the Gospel, 'He that believeth and is baptised' [Mark 16.16] in the water of the Holy Spirit etc. [*see* Matthew 3.11], that water with which children are baptised in the Roman Church is not the water of the Holy Spirit, but rather the water of scum and corruption, and such water has no power to absolve sins. But the water of the Holy Spirit, spoken of in the Gospel and commanded by God to be used in baptism, is the word of God and His good works; and whoever does this and believes the Word, he is baptised with the water of the Holy Spirit.

Item, the said heretics said that the journey across the sea <to the Holy Land> has no value, nor are men's sins remitted on account of this. For, although it is said in the Gospel 'If any man will come after me, let him deny himself, and take up his cross, and follow me' [Matthew 16.24], in fact, however, Christ does not talk about nor does he mean such a cross, whether one of the matter of corruption or the sort which those journeying over the sea wear.[227] But the cross which is good works and true penance and observing the words of God – that is the cross of

227 Sewn on, worn by crusaders, pilgrims, and converted heretics who had cross-wearing pilgrimage to the Holy Land imposed on them as penance.

Christ, and he who observes this follows Him and denies himself, and takes up his own cross: and not the cross of corruption, as said earlier.

Item, they said that the pope, cardinals, bishops, abbots and priests do not have the power to pardon sins, for this reason, because they are impure and of evil spirit: in brief, as you would expect, as people doing evil works and not holding or following the word of God. Instead they are people adoring idols and false prophets, <and> evil fruits, namely vanities and lies; talking as greedy people, avaricious, fornicators, and slanderers, flatterers of God, blasphemers, adulterers, gluttons, the unclean; and doing evil deeds, in accord with what is read, 'Beware of false prophets, who come to you in the clothing of sheep, but inwardly they are ravening wolves. By their fruits you shall know them' [Matthew 7.15–16]. And according to that, what is unclean cannot cleanse what is unclean; but the same heretics … [*An entire leaf is then torn out from the ms.*]

From Larnat: Philip of Larnat; Sibilia, his mother; Arnold Yssaura; Raymond, his son; Peter, son of the said Arnold;

From Alliou: Raymond Porcell; William Porcell; Raymond Azemar; Arnold Bayle; someone who is called Belot;

From Luzenac: Peter of Luzenac; William Bernard, his brother; Luzenac, his brother; Bernard, their brother; Lady Ramunda, their mother;

From Lordat: Raymond Arnold Tisserand <*or* the weaver>; Raymond Sabatier; William of Vernaux;

From Quié: Peter d'en Hugol [*family name*]; Ermengardis, his wife; William of Area; Raymond of Area; Bernard of Area; Guillelma, their mother; Raymond Peter the younger; Bachelor, son of Peter Benet; Peter of Area; James Cartier;

From Rabat: Atho of the Château; Lady Miracla, his mother; William Arnold of the Château; William Macar;

From Junac: Bernard of Junac the younger; William, his brother; Peter, his brother; Galhard, his brother; James, his brother; their mother; Peter Martin; Arnold Martin, his son; William Martin, son of the said Peter; Peter Grat.

Item, I said I had heard it said from some of the same believers – though I cannot remember from whom – that Jordan of Rabat, and Galharda, my mother, and Guillelma, wife of the late Bertrand Mercier, Bernard Tornier, Peter of Area, William Auger and the wife of the late

Arnold Piquier, all of Tarascon, were hereticated at their ends, and died in that faith.

Item, I said I heard it said commonly, both by the same heretics and by the said believers – by whom I do not remember – that, when among other believers, the same heretics frequented more and were more used to living with, and had greater friendship and familiarity with them in their houses, <these people> as follows: from Tarascon, <in the houses> of Arnold Piquier, Alamanda, wife of the late Arnold of Vicdessos, Bernard Ceravel, smith, Raymond Sutra, smith; and at Junac, in the house of Peter Martin; at Ax, in the house of Sibille d'en Bayle; at Larnat, in the house of the said Arnold Eyssaura; at Quié, in the house of William of Area and his brothers, item, in the house of Peter of Luzenac and his brother; at Lordat, in the house of Raymond Sabatier. And I believe and believed that they would be received there or in one of these places; and that at least they [*these followers*] knew the dwelling places they [*the heretics*] have outside the land of the Sabartès.

Item, I said that sometimes – as I heard it said – the aforesaid heretics lived at Carol in the house of en Berto, and sometimes at Mijanès in Donezan, and sometimes at Lavelanet in Mirepoix. And I was asked, in what hostels. And I said I had certainly heard it said, however I said I do not remember in which ones.

Item, I said I confessed I heard it said (by more than 20 believers in the sect of the heretics, whose names I said I do not remember) that a certain man from Val de Daigne who was one-eyed – to whose house James Autier, heretic, had fled at the time when he escaped from prison, and <at whose house>, it was said, he hid himself – died at Tarascon in the house of Bernard Ceravel, smith. And he was hereticated (and I said that I did not know by which heretic) and was buried in the cemetery of the church of the blessed Michael in Tarascon; and one could get to know the truth about this from the said Bernard Ceravel and his wife. Item, I said I heard it said by the late Bernard Tornier of Tarascon, that 4 years or thereabouts have passed since Peter Raymond, nephew of William Bayard of Tarascon, was so ill that it was feared for his life. And the same William Bayard sent Philip of Larnat, squire, his nephew (according to what the said Bernard Tornier told me) to the house of the said Bernard Tornier, where William Autier was hidden. And during daytime the same Philip left the said Bernard's house, together with the said William Autier, and led him through the barriers of the walls of Tarascon to the said William Bayard's house (as the said Bernard Tornier told me), where the said boy was lying in bed. I was asked if I heard it said that the said boy was then hereticated, and I said no, because shortly afterwards he recovered, and the said William Autier left the said house. However, as I heard it said by the said Bernard, he stayed there for three or four days.

Item, I was asked if I saw other heretics, or if I knew many other things about the matter of heresy, and I said no, not that I could recall. However, if I were to recall that I had committed some other wrong thing in the matter of heresy or that others had sin, I would come to confess these things and reveal them to the inquisitors as fast as possible: with this reservation, that I would not <thereby> incur perjury.

These things I deposed and said on the aforesaid said year and day and in the aforesaid place: that is to say, in the room of Master James of Poloniac, guardian of the prison of Carcassonne, AD 1308, 4 days before the nones of August [2 August], before Brother John of Faugoux, lieutenant of the said lord Inquisitor, in the presence and witness of Brother Pons of Tourreilles, Brother Pons of Marseille, Brother William Radulf, of the Order of Brothers Preacher, the aforesaid Master James of Poloniac, Master Bartholomew of Arlat, guardian of the prison of Toulouse, and Master William Raymond of Alayrac, canon of St-Afrodise of Béziers, notary public for the office of inquisition, who was present at the aforesaid things and, on the instruction of the aforesaid lieutenants <of the inquisitor>, accepted these <written depositions as formal records of what has been attested>.

Lawfully arraigned before the said lord Inquisitor and in the aforesaid place, I acknowledge and confess that each and every one of the aforesaid things, confessed by me and written by my own hand in the present book, is true and contains no falsity in whole or in part. And just as I deposed and confessed before the said lord Inquisitor's aforesaid lieutenant, I now depose and confess these things anew before the aforesaid lord inquisitor, as they are contained above and written below [*sic*], and I ratify them, I approve and confirm and assert that they are true thus <as they are written>; declaring and saying and asking for it to be allowed – if I omitted some of the things which I committed in the aforesaid crime or if things were to be found attested against me (through something else or through other people) – that I could confess anew before the said lord Inquisitor or his lieutenant. And since I have omitted nothing of what I can remember with certain knowledge, I also say and declare and confess that I confessed and said those things (which were written above by me and confessed and deposed before the said lieutenant) and that I now confess and say them, etc., in front of the said lord Inquisitor: not through the application of tortures, nor suborned, nor tricked or deceived by anyone, nor out of love or fear of anyone, nor through the entreaty or bribery or hatred of anyone; but rather freely, and from certain knowledge, and out of pure freedom of mind, with divine prompting and divine grace driving <me on>; not wanting to persist further or any longer in the aforesaid sin or error, but wanting to come to a good situation and to confession of the aforesaid things, and to persevere in this same thing – as is written above.

AD 1308, 10 days before the calends of November [23 October] [*Peter of Gaillac read out and confirmed his confession in front of Geoffrey of Ablis*]. …

And in clarification of his said confession, the said Peter of Gaillac, questioned by the said lord Inquisitor, said he heard the errors of the heretics (about which he deposed in his confession above), not on one day but on various days and times, not once only but many times, and from various heretics and their believers.

Item, he said that where there is mentioned in his said confession that he saw the heretic William Autier on another occasion, he saw him, so he said, at Tarascon in the house of William of Rodes of the said place. [*List of witnesses, and record of Peter's abjuration and reconciliation*]

And later, in the year as above, 9 days before the calends of November [24 October 1308] [*Peter Gaillac read his confession in the vernacular and confirmed it*] …

And he was asked by the said lord Inquisitor where the heretics could now be most easily found. And he said at Carol, in the house of en Berto, and beyond the said house in some hamlet in the house of the sister of William Morator; item, at Lavelanet in Mirepoix, in the house of the sister of William of Area of Quié, <and> in other places as is contained in his said confession.
[*List of witnesses*]

AD 1309, on the Friday that is 14 days before the calends of May [18 April], I, Peter of Gaillac, notary of Tarascon, lawfully arraigned in the city of Carcassonne in the House of the Inquisition, before the religious man, Lord Geoffrey of Ablis, of the Order of Preachers, deputed by the Apostolic See Inquisitor of heretical wickedness in the kingdom of France, swore on the holy gospels of God to say the truth as a witness about myself, as the principal person, and <also> about others living and dead, as a witness.

Questioned by the said lord Inquisitor, I said and deposed and confessed, adding to the confession made a long time beforehand in front of the said lord Inquisitor, having now recollected more things – since now I recollect more things and have memory from the time since the aforesaid confession that <such and such happened> and about things that I did not remember at the time of the said confession – that 4 years or thereabouts have passed since I saw in my father's house once, twice or three times (so it seems to me about the time) William Autier and James Autier and Peter Autier and Prades Tavernier, heretics, in a certain room, in various ways and at various times during the said year, staying there sometimes for two days, sometimes for five or more days; and that Galharda, my mother, used to prepare food for them both from her own goods and from those of others. Asked if I saw any man or woman seeing them at that time, I said yes, namely Guillelma, wife of Raymond Coc, Blancha, wife of William of Niaux, Emengardis, mother of Pons Cicred, William Carramat and his wife Guillelma, William of Rodes, Arnold Martin and his brother William, and many others whom at present I do not recall. Asked if I saw that any of those who saw them gave them anything, I said no.

Asked if I saw that any of the aforesaid adored the said heretics, there or elsewhere, I said no, except that in the said house, his father's, Otho of Bélesta of Tarascon adored Peter Autier, heretic. Asked if I saw any of the said heretics elsewhere, I said yes, namely in the house of Sebilia d'en Bayle of Ax: William and Peter Autier, heretics. Asked if I adored or made any reverence to the said heretics, then or at any time I said no; but that when I went to them, I would take off my headgear and kiss them on the mouth.

Asked if I ever saw any of the said heretics otherwise, I said not that I remember. However it seems to me, though I do not fully recall, that I saw some of the said heretics in the house of William of Area and in the house of Bernard Ceravel of Tarascon; however, when I have remembered, I shall come to <make> a full confession.

Asked if I ever had conversation or discussion with anyone on the matter of heresy, I said yes, namely with Thomasa, wife of Peter of Niaux, and with Peter of Niaux, who often said <something> to me, when he saw some brothers Preacher or brothers Minor or priests passing by in front of him. The same Peter of Niaux used to say to me and to bystanders (whom I do not recall), 'Look at them, their bad belief makes their souls such that we should hang them like lowly scum'.[228]

Item, I said I have often had discussion about the matter of heresy with the aforesaid Guillelma, wife of Raymond Coc, with Blancha, wife of William of Niaux, with Gaya, wife of Raymond Faure, with Sclarmunda, wife of Raymond Autier, with William of Area, with Arnold Autier, with Bernard of Niaux, with Raymond Sabatier of Lordat and with many others whom at present I cannot recall.

Item I said and confessed that next August it will be 3 or 4 years since Lady Galharda, my mother, was ill in her house in Tarascon. And that at the time of this illness William of Area of Quié escorted William Autier, heretic, to a certain house of my father's which is beside another house (but with the road between the two) next to another house half-way down the street – he stayed there for two or three days. One day – after these days had passed – my said mother drew towards her end. And in the room where she lay, there was I, and Alissendis the mother of my said mother, and Sclarmunda, wife of Raymond Autier, and many others, around 50 from the town of Tarascon, whom I do not remember. And then the said Sclarmunda said into my ear, 'Peter, do only this – get these people to leave the room, so that we can do that thing that you know'. And I immediately said to the women and men who were there, 'Gentlemen, let's go out, because it is getting very hot and we are tiring my mother'. And immediately I went out together with them into the hall where the fire was. And the said Alissendis and Sclarmunda, however, remained inside, and they closed the door to the room from the inside. Afterwards, as the same Sclarmunda told me, the same Sclarmunda got through to the other aforesaid house (where the said heretic William Autier was) via some beams and planks. And the same Sclarmunda took off her cape and sleeveless upper garment, and had them put on by the said heretic. And, clothed in this stuff, the said heretic went to the aforesaid room and there, as the said Alissendis told me, hereticated my said mother.

Item I said that after this was done, the said William Autier left the said house while it was dusk, and entered the house of William of Rodes. And I went to him together with the said Sclarmunda, and asked the said heretic what my mother – who was now dead – had done, and he

228 *malcreyre lor faria l'arma que per aull canilha pingariam*: our thanks to John Green, Catherine Léglu and Ruth Harvey for advice on the translation.

replied to me that <she had had> a good end, and that she had died in their sect.

Item, I was asked by the said lord Inquisitor if anyone ever encouraged me to depose falsely in the business of the inquisition, and I replied yes. Asked by whom, I said that Peter of Niaux of Tarascon came up to me in the square in Tarascon, at breakfast time on the first of last Lent. And he asked me if I wanted to play chess, and I told him yes. And when we were in the middle of the square or virtually there, the same Peter said to me, 'Master Peter, why you are not telling the Carcassonne Inquisitor what you had also said, by now a long time ago? And what would you confess about it?' And in reply I said to him,'What was this?', because I did not know. And he said to me, 'You are to say that the late Bernard Tornier of Tarascon escorted heretics to the house of William Bayard, at the time when one of his family, Jordan of Rabat, was ill'. And I replied to him, 'How would I say this, which was not true, because at the time of the said illness I was in Catalonia?' 'Yes, it's true', the same man said, 'you were there. Therefore', the same man said [*adjusting the story*], 'it was when Peter Raymond of Rabat, the son of the said Jordan, was ill!' 'Well', I said, 'that is absolutely not true, because at that time I was in Toulouse and listening to <lectures on> the *Decretals*. 'Good chap', he said, 'don't go overboard about this, just do your thing [*i.e. confession*] approximately'. 'By God', I said, 'In the business of the inquisition I will not say anything except what is true!' And we put these words aside and played chess.

Before these things I was asked by the said lord Inquisitor if I had ever said the aforesaid words to Peter of Niaux or if they were true. I said that I had not said the aforesaid words but if they were true, I said just as I deposed in my confession. I said also that the said Peter of Niaux said to me that if I were to do this, the same <Peter> and Andrew of Niaux and Bernard Peter of Lordat would do for me whatever I wanted: by which I understood that they would make provision for me for my expenses and necessities of travel going to and from Carcassonne.

Item, I said that on the same day, virtually at the hour of compline, William of Rodes asked me if Peter of Niaux had spoken to me, and I said yes. And the same William asked about the words he had spoken to me, and I replied that they <were> about such things that were not true, that I knew this, and that I would not say these words. And the same William said to me, 'If you can do what the same Peter wants you to do, do it!' And immediately the said William left me and said nothing more to me.

Item, in clarification of my confession, I said I heard it said by three (or about that number) believers in the sect of the heretics that there was some young heretic – he was not well known in the land and he was going about the land openly and during daytime – who hereticated Jordan of Rabat at Rabat; and that Arnold Martin of Junac organised the coming of the said heretic and the aforesaid reception <into the sect>.

Item, I said that while the said heretics[229] were in the house of my father, Peter of Gaillac, my father and my brother Bertrand saw the said heretics many times, and heard their preachings and sermons. Item, my sisters Ramunda and Alissendis saw the said heretics in the said house. However, they were girls and neither of them was <yet> of the age of nine. Item, I saw that the aforesaid who saw the said heretics in the said house – of which there is mention above – sometimes heard their preachings, and I saw this many times.

I also said that I heard it said by believers in the sect of the heretics (whom I do not remember) that Ramunda d'en Raymond Bernard, who lived in the suburbs of the *castrum* of Tarascon, was hereticated at her end – however I did not know by which heretic.
⌈*Confirmation of the confession*⌉

AD 1309, on the Friday named 14 days before the calends of May ⌈18 April 1309⌉, Peter of Gaillac … ⌈*appears, gives oath; reading out and confirmation of the confession; witnesses*⌉.

After these things, in the year as above, on Wednesday within the octave of the Ascension of the Lord ⌈14 May 1309⌉, the aforesaid Peter of Gaillac appeared before the religious man Brother John of Faugoux, of the Order of Preachers, lieutenant and acting in place of the said lord Inquisitor.

After swearing on the holy gospels of God and lawfully arraigned before the same <inquisitor>, he both said and confessed that during the most recent Lent, this year, on some day he said he could not remember, he who is speaking and William Tron, notary of Tarascon, were coming from the assizes of Alet-les-Bains. And when they were roughly halfway through their journey towards Tarascon and were talking about the business of the inquisition, the same William Tron said – to him who is speaking – that he who is speaking and the others

229 The questioning here switches to the Autiers and Tavernier.

who had been prisoners in the Wall had confessed easily and without great and lengthy detention,[230] and in this they did badly. Item, he who is speaking said that the same William Tron said that while the same William Tron was studying at Toulouse – 4 years ago back, or thereabouts – the same William was living in a room with a certain cleric whose name he does not remember, who was following a course in natural <philosophy> at Toulouse (<this is what> he who is speaking understood, so he said). And he [*William*] told him who is speaking that this cleric said to him many times that he and almost all the naturalists [*students of natural philosophy*] at Toulouse and Paris held that for bread to become the body of Christ and <for this to happen> through holy words was impossible and also against nature, and that the same William Tron more or less agreed with this argument.

Item, he who is speaking said that the said William Tron told him that at the time of the illness of Guillelma, wife of Bertrand Mercier of Tarascon, the wife of Bartholomew d'en Hugues of Tarascon, the same William Tron's sister, told the said William Tron that two men (who she believed were heretics) left Bertrand Mercier's house at night, and together with Philip of Larnat passed along in front of the hospice of the said woman (the said William Tron's sister), and entered the house of Bernard Ceravel, smith of Tarascon.

After these things, on the Saturday of the feast of saints Cosmas and Damian, 5 days before the calends of October [27 September 1309], the aforesaid Peter of Gaillac [*recitation and confirmation of confession*] …

Following this the said Peter added to the aforesaid confession and additions since, as he said, his memory is refreshed about the things written below. He said, confessed and deposed – about a certain sighting of the heretic William Autier, that happened in the house of William of Rodes of Tarascon, about which he had deposed above – that at the time of this sighting there were present there at the sighting Esclarmonda, wife of Raymond Autier of Ax, Ramunda, daughter of the late Raymond Lombard, wife now of the said Peter, Raymond Jotclar of Tarascon, Sebelia, wife of the late Raymond Sutran, and no others that he recalls. And he believes that sighting was that night during which the mother of same person who is speaking died. Asked how he knew that the said heretic was there, he said that William of *Curamato* of Tarascon told him <to go>, and that he who is speaking

230 This could also mean without holding back a lot from the confessions.

went with the intention of visiting the said heretic there. Asked if any preaching took place there, or adoration or reverence, he replied that he does not remember.

Asked what he understood and thought was about to happen to his aforesaid mother when his aunt Esclarmonda said to him who is speaking, 'Get these people to leave and we shall do that thing that you know', he said and replied that virtually a day or thereabouts earlier the said Esclarmonda had told him that she had prepared the coming of the said heretic for this: so that the said Gualharda, his mother, would be hereticated by him; and that he understood through the said hearing of her <saying this> that the said heretication would take place then. Asked what he understood when the said William Autier, heretic, said to him that his mother had made a good end, he said that he understood that she had died hereticated, because this was the meaning and mode of speech among the heretics and their believers: that when someone is received into their sect, they say that the dead person had made a good end, so he said. Asked if he believes or believed that the said heretic or aforesaid women spoke the truth to him regarding the aforesaid reception and end, namely that his mother was received and hereticated just as the aforesaid heretic and aforesaid women had told him (as he said), he said and replied that at the time when the aforesaid words were said to him he believed <them, but> now he does not; for at that time he believed the words of the heretics, <but> now he does not, so he says.[231] Asked why he made the people leave, as the aforesaid Esclarmonde told him, so that the aforesaid heretication could happen, and why he did not prevent happening what he understood from the words of the aforesaid Esclarmonde was about to happen, he said it was for this, because a long time [*sic*] beforehand, virtually a day, the said Esclarmonda had asked the said Peter who is speaking not to disturb or impede the said heretication, which she said had to be done: and which he now believes did not happen, except as he has deposed above. Asked if he wishes to persist with and stand by those things which he has confessed, now and otherwise [*i.e. earlier*], or elsewhere confessed, he wishes to stand by and persist, he replied yes, and <he promised> never to contravene.

[*list of witnesses and notary*]

231 If the inquisitor was asking whether Peter believed she had been hereticated, Peter may have been answering a different question, whether he believed this was 'a good end'.

55. GUILT OF THE SICRE FAMILY, 1308–12

These sentences and Doc. 56 below are from Bernard Gui's *Book of Sentences,* which details the punishments given to 633 people between 1308 and 1323; see Given, *Inquisition*, pp. 67–71. We have selected here the sentences given to four members of one family, which indicate Gui's active use of the records of a previous inquisitor (see D below) and include a rare mention of torture. Translated from A. Pales-Gobilliard, ed., *Le Livre des sentences de l'inquisiteur Bernard Gui* (Paris, 2002), I, pp. 730–8.

A. Guilt of William Sicre the younger, 1312

William Sicre the younger, son of the late Peter Sicre of Salliez, near Sègreville, just as is established by his judicial confession made lawfully before us 3 days before the ides of January, AD 1311 [11 January 1312], consented that Ayceline, his mother, should be hereticated at the end, in the illness from which she died, And he went to search for a heretic for the said ill woman, and the heretic was escorted at night to the house of the father of the same William, where the same William saw the same heretic; but the said ill woman was not hereticated because other people, whom he names, prevented it.

Item, he consented and arranged that Peter Sicre, his father, should be hereticated in that illness from which he died, and he went to search for a heretic at <the house of> Raymond of Maureville, who brought the heretic for the said ill man. And in the presence of the same William Sicre the said heretic received the said ill man to his sect and order. And after the heretication of the said ill man, the said heretic stayed in the same house for some days and nights, and he heard the words and preaching of the said heretic with other people, whom he names. And the same William sometimes served and looked after him.

Item, after the aforesaid things, he managed and arranged that the said heretic should return once again to stay there. And together with his brothers he prepared a secret place in which the heretic could stay hidden, where the same William, with his brothers, made a certain opening in the wall through which the said heretic could enter and exit more secretly. And they kept the said heretic there in hiding, until they heard that Raymond of Maureville, who had escorted the said heretic there, had been captured by the Inquisitor of Toulouse. They feared that he would reveal to the inquisitor that the said heretic was there, and it was decided that he [*i.e. the heretic*] should change location and leave there. And then the said heretic was moved from there at night. And the following day messengers came there, sent by the inquisitors for the said heretic, and they searched for him and did not find him. And the said William was asked by the said messengers to indicate and reveal <where> the said heretic was – on the inquisitor's behalf the inquisitor's notary was promising grace to the said William, if he would reveal and hand over the heretic. William refused to do this; and thus the heretic could not be found.

Item, he knew other people, whom he names in his confession, who were complicit in the business of the heretics.

Item, he believed the heretics to be good and true men, and that they had a good life and a good sect and a good faith in which a man could be saved, even though he knew that the heretics were persecuted by the Roman Church of Rome [*sic*] and by the inquisitors, and even though he had heard it said commonly that Peter Autier together with Peter William of Prunet had been burnt, not long ago, at Toulouse. And he was in the said belief from the time when he went for the said heretic to come to his ill mother, up until the time when the said heretic last left his house. He committed the aforesaid things within the half-year before he was arrested, nor was he willing to confess judicially about the aforesaid things until he was detained in prison, and was subjected to a certain amount of being pulled up by the cord,[232] and was denounced and accused by other people. At the beginning he perjured himself, concealing in court the truth about the aforesaid things.

B. Guilt of Raymond Sicre, 1308

Raymond Sicre, son of the late Peter Sicre of Salliez, near Sègreville, as is established by his judicial confession made lawfully before us 4 days before the nones of February, AD 1311 [2 February 1312], <said that> Raymond of Maureville spoke to him of the church of the heretics, trying to persuade him to be willing to do good to the said heretics.

232 That is, was tortured: for a contemporary description of suffering this method of torture (but inflicted by a secular power), see the opening chapter in J. H. Arnold, *What is Medieval History?* (Cambridge, 2008). This is the only occasion when Gui's sentences explicitly indicate that Gui instructed the use of torture.

Item, he consented that his father Peter Sicre should be hereticated in the illness from which he died, and he knew when the heretic was sent for, and he was present when his father was hereticated.

Item, he saw the said heretic many times in the house of his said father, where the heretic stayed at that time for 15 days, eating and drinking of the goods of the house of the same Raymond and his brothers. And over these days the same Raymond sometimes served and took care of the said heretic's needs. And he heard the words and preaching of the said heretic there, with other people whom he names; and the heretic was called Peter.

Item, he believed that the said heretic was a good man and had a good faith and a good sect, in which a man could be saved. And he was in that belief for five weeks.

He committed the aforesaid things over the three or four months before he judicially confessed them. Nor was he willing to confess until he was captured and detained and his brothers were captured – <the brothers> in whose house the said heretic was searched for <by the inquisitors' servants>; and <the heretic> had fled from it that same day.

C. Guilt of Peter Sicre, 1308

Peter Sicre, son of the late Peter Sicre of Salliez near Sègreville, as is established by his judicial confession made lawfully before us on the nones of February, AD 1311 [5 February 1312], agreed that Peter Sicre, his father, should be hereticated in that illness from which he died. And he saw and knew when a heretic was brought to hereticate his said father. And while the said heretic, who was called Peter Sans, was performing the said heretication for his father, the said Peter Sicre guarded the door of the house in which the ill man lay, to prevent anyone who came along then going in.

Item, the said heretic then stayed in the same house for 15 days, eating and drinking of the goods of the house. Over those days the said Peter Sicre served him often, and together with other people, whom he names in his confession, he heard the words and preaching and erroneous doctrine of the said heretic, <directed> against the faith of the Roman Church. And he saw the said heretic reading in a book those things that he taught and said.

Item, later on he consented to the said heretic's return to the aforesaid house, in which Peter Sicre with Arnold, his brother, had prepared a certain secret place in which the said heretic could stay hidden. And they made there an opening in the wall, through which the said heretic could enter and exit more secretly. And they kept the said heretic there, and the same Peter Sicre lay with the said heretic in the same bed.[233]

Item, on the news of the capture of Raymond of Maureville, who had brought him there, the said heretic was moved from there so that he could not be found if the said Raymond revealed him. And the same night that the said heretic left there, he had lain with the same heretic and he knew the reason he was leaving, because he feared being found and captured there. And the following day the messengers of the inquisitors came there, to search for and capture the said heretic. Neither was the same <Peter Sicre> willing in any way to indicate to them about the said heretic nor to direct them to have him <captured>, despite the fact that grace was promised him if he revealed the heretic.

Item, he gave the heretic a coat that had belonged to his father who had died hereticated.

Item, he believed the heretics were good men and had a good faith and good sect in which a man could be saved. And he was in that belief from the time when he first had knowledge of the said heretics – when <the heretic> hereticated his father – until his brothers were captured because of the business of the said heretic.

He committed the aforesaid things during the previous four months, persisting in this business <in the period> before he confessed judicially about the aforesaid things. Nor was he willing to confess until he was captured and detained.

D. Guilt of William Sicre the elder, 1308

William Sicre the elder of Salliez near Sègreville, son of the late Peter Sicre, as is lawfully manifest to us through the books and acts of inquisition, formerly confessed about those things he had committed in heresy, in front of Brother William Bernard of Dax, of the Order of Preachers, Inquisitor. <He said that> he saw two heretics, namely Gaucelm and his companion, and that he adored them, bending his knees according to the manner of the heretics, saying 'Bless me'.

Item, he said and admitted that he believed the heretics were good men and had good faith [*or* a good faith]. And he abjured heresy in front of

233 This has no sexual connotation; it was common practice to share a bed.

the aforesaid inquisitor in AD 1262, on the eve of the feast of St Vincent [23 March 1263]. See this in book 16, 33rd folio.[234] Item, afterwards he was sentenced to imprisonment for the things he committed in heresy.

The aforesaid William Sicre, as is lawfully established to us by his confession, made 12 day before the calends of March, AD 1311 [18 February 1312], after he had earlier confessed about the things he had committed in the business or crime of heresy in front of the inquisitors of heretical depravity, namely Brother William Bernard and Brother Renaud, of the Order of Brothers Preacher, was imprisoned by the same inquisitors, at a public sermon delivered at Toulouse in the church of St-Étienne.[235] Later he was let out of prison by the inquisitors and signed with the crosses and had pilgrimages <imposed> in penance. And then his crosses were removed from him by Brother Hugh Amiel, Inquisitor, of the Order of Preachers, in a sermon delivered at Limoux in the cemetery of the said place. And he judicially abjured heresy in front of the aforesaid inquisitors.

And now recently this year, around the time of the grape harvest, while Peter Sicre, brother of the same William, was ill with that illness from which he died, he visited the said ill man – as to the day, a certain Friday or Sunday, so it seems to him. And then when he left the house of the said ill man, William Sicre, son of the said ill man and nephew of the same aforesaid William Sicre, left with him. And then the said nephew asked him if he wanted to see <one> of the worthy or good men. And the same aforesaid William, as he said and admitted in court, understood that by this he wanted to talk to him about <one> of the heretics. And then he did not agree that he wanted to see one of those good men, by which he understood <one> of the heretics, so he said. And afterwards in the same place his said nephew said to him that during his illness the aforesaid ill man had been received by the heretics into the sect and order of those heretics and had been hereticated. And then the same William said to his aforesaid nephew that he had done badly, and that if he had one of the heretics in his house he should drive him out, because bad could happen to him; and thus he left his said nephew.

Item, the said ill man lived on – as to the day, until the following Thursday, so it seems to him. And during those days the said William

234 From forty-nine years earlier, preserved in the archive of the house of inquisition in Toulouse – where each book in a series was numbered – this is the oldest record cited by Gui in the sentences; the book is not now extant.

235 The cathedral.

visited the said ill man, his brother, at least once a day. And the said ill man understood and recognised him. And he heard it said by those who were around the said ill man, that during those days he did not eat anything, but he was drinking cold water. The same William neither reproached the said ill man for this, that he had been hereticated (as his said nephew, the son of the said ill man, had told him), nor did he urge him to repent and leave off the said heretication and abandon it. And he did this for this reason, so he said: because he did not want to know any more about the same ill man's business, nor get in any deeper – but he [*the ill man*] could go to his fate, so he said.

Item, after the aforesaid things, one evening 15 days or thereabouts after the death of the said ill man, the same William came to the house of his said brother, now dead, and there he found the said William, his nephew, and his other brothers, and they sat next to the fire. And there was there a certain man whom he did not know. And then that man took out a certain book and read out many words in the said book. And it seemed to him that he was speaking from the gospels [*or*: about the gospels]. And immediately when the same William heard this, he inferred and believed that this man was <one> of the heretics about whom his aforesaid nephew had spoken to him, and <that he was the one> who had received and hereticated the said ill man, his brother. And he was very frightened, and after a while he went away, leaving there his nephews next to the fire with the said man. Asked if the said man – whom he believed to be a heretic – was reading in the book with a light, and with what light, he replied, with the light of a crucible.[236] Asked who was holding the lamp, he replied that it was one of the aforesaid nephews, and it seems to him most likely to have been Peter. Asked about the book in which the said man was reading, whether it was small or large and with boards or without boards, he replied that it was little, and it seemed to him that there were no boards there.[237] Asked why he did not have the said heretic captured, or did not capture him <himself>, and why he did not come to reveal this to the inquisitors so that the heretic could be captured, he replied that it was because of his nephews: because he did not want his said nephews to come to harm on his account – although he believed, so he said, that the said man was a heretic.

236 Cross-shaped oil-lamp.

237 Gui may have been tracking a particular book 'without boards' (presumably the form of binding) referred to in an earlier interrogation conducted by Geoffroi d'Ablis, in May 1308.

[*The three Sicre brothers and their uncle were all sentenced to prison, and their house to be torn down; William Sicre the elder was perhaps lucky not to have been sentenced to death as having relapsed into heresy*].

56. A RENEGADE PRIEST AND WALDENSIANS IN GASCONY, 1319

The earlier confessions of the priest sentenced here may have been one of the sources of the tract about Waldensians translated in Doc. 53, and they provide us with a glimpse of heresy and inquisition in a part of France not usually visible to us.[238] Translated from Pales-Gobilliard, ed., *Le Livre des sentences*, pp. 1126–32.

[From 30 September 1319]
Guilt of a relapsed man
John Philibert, priest, originally from Chapelle-St-Sauveur near Mervans in Burgundy, son of the late Pons of Boibe, who [*John*] once lived at St-Laurent-la-Roche in Burgundy in the diocese of Besançon but now was living at Castelnau-Barbarens near Mazères in the county of Astarac in the diocese of Auch – as has been established lawfully by his confession, made in court 29 October AD 1311 – was sent 28 years ago, or thereabouts, from Burgundy into Gascon parts, together with someone else (whom he names), with letters from the inquisitor, in order to look for a certain Waldensian fugitive called Russ Jaubert. And they came to the diocese of Auch. And later he returned from Gascon parts into Burgundy, to those who had sent him. After some time, of his own volition he returned to Gascon parts, in which he lived for many years in the diocese of Auch. While living there he was led by some Burgundians (whom he names) into love of the Waldensians and familiarity and participation with them.

Item, in the said parts he often saw and visited many fully fledged Waldensians [Valdenses perfectos][239] in many places, houses and hospices and in various towns (which he names), knowing that they were such. And he often ate and drank with the same. And he sometimes

238 On Waldensians in Burgundy, see *Inquisitors and Heretics*, pp. 195–7; J. Duvernoy, 'L'unité du valdéisme en France à la fin du XIIIe siècle (Bourgogne, Sillon rhodanien, Gascogne)', *Valdo e il valdismo medievale, Bollettino della Società di Studi Valdesi* 136 (1974), 73–83; M. Schneider, *Europäisches Waldensertum im 13. und 14. Jahrhundert*, Arbeiten zur Kirchengeschichte 51 (Berlin and New York, 1981), pp. 31–3.

239 On 'perfectus' meaning 'fully-fledged', see Doc. 40.

prayed with them – four times on the same occasion – in various places and at various times, on bended knees, prostrate and bowed down in accord with the mode and rite that the Waldensians have for praying. And sometimes he accompanied Waldensians from place to place, and together with other persons who were their believers he heard the words, admonitions and exhortations and preachings of the said Waldensians. And he knew and saw that the said Waldensians – who were not and are not priests ordained by some bishop of the Roman Church, but were laymen – heard the confessions of sins of the men and women who believe in and consent to their matters.

Further, the names of the Waldensians whom he saw and with whom he participated are these: Christian, Humbert, Janquemin the Burgundian, Stephen the Burgundian, Perrin son of Wudri of Gaudoux, Mundin or Monidin who used to live at Mongausy, John Chapayro – not all of them together but sometimes two, sometimes three, sometimes four.

Item, on one occasion he was asked and entreated by the aforesaid Waldensians Christian and Humbert and by some others (whom he names) to aim to be one of these Waldensians and to be a fully fledged Waldensian like them. And he agreed with them that he wanted to follow them and to be of their sect and society, which he believed was good, although he knew that inquisitors persecuted the Waldensian sect. Item, the said Christian then said to him, 'It would be better for you to be looking after pigs than saying Mass, because you are in mortal sin'.

The aforesaid John Philibert, priest – as has been established lawfully by his confession, made in justice 30 July AD 1319 – was once (during the 2 years or thereabouts before the time of the great Indulgence at Rome [*i.e.* AD 1300], during the time of Pope Boniface VIII) arraigned before Brother Guy of Rheims, Inquisitor of heretical wickedness in Burgundy.[240] Asked by him three times to swear on the book of gospels to tell the truth, he refused entirely and would not swear. For he had heard from the Waldensians, whom he had seen earlier and with whom he had participated (as is more fully contained in his confession), that a man ought not to swear in any circumstance and that swearing is always a mortal sin, and at that time he believed it was thus. And on account of this he was arrested by the said inquisitor at the castle of St-Laurent-la-Roche in the diocese of Besançon. Summoned after this, he appeared in front of the said inquisitor at Besançon, where he was

240 Nothing else is known about this inquisitor.

under open arrest [in arresto largo] by the inquisitor. And lawfully arraigned in front of him in the Archbishop of Besançon's palace, in the presence of 10 or 12 witnesses and the said inquisitor's notary or scribe, he took an oath. And he confessed some things about the matter of the Waldensians, and he knowingly concealed <things> about the Waldensians whom he had seen earlier in Gascony and with whom he had participated (as is more fully contained in his confession). At that time he believed that the Waldensians were good men and that they had and held a good sect and that it was a sin that the inquisitors were persecuting them (as is more fully contained in the confession he made in front of the inquisitor at Toulouse), and after the confession he made then in front of the aforesaid Brother Guy, Inquisitor of Burgundy. On the demand of the said inquisitor he swore and promised to have Waldensians captured if and when he knew where they were. And then, required by the said inquisitor and lawfully arraigned, he abjured and repudiated every unlawful sect and especially the sect of Waldensian heretics.

After the aforesaid John Philibert left Burgundian parts – having taken an oath about capturing Waldensians in front of the aforesaid Inquisitor of Burgundy and having abjured the sect of the Waldensian heretics in court – he then often participated with the Waldensians. For from this time on – as has been established lawfully by his confession, made in court – and after he returned to Gascony, he saw and visited Waldensians often and in many places and towns, and he participated with them, eating and drinking and praying in their fashion and accompanying them from place to place.

Item, he knew and saw many persons of both sexes (whom he names in his confession) who consented to the matter of the Waldensians.

Item, he heard it taught or dogmatised by the Waldensians that they would not swear on the Book, but they would allow themselves to be killed before <doing this>, and that a man ought not to swear in any circumstance, for any reason, neither in court nor outside. Item, that swearing is always a mortal sin. Item, that God forbade all swearing. Item, he knew and saw and heard that[241] the Waldensians sometimes preach to their believers after supper at night-time, from the gospels and epistles in the vernacular. Item, that the Waldensians do not go to

241 That is, he did not rely on hearsay. 'He heard that … preach' rather than 'he heard them preaching' is the result of the notary's compression of separate items in the deposition into this *culpa*.

church, only perhaps out of pretence, through fear of being detected through this.

Item, that the Waldensians say they have the power of hearing confessions and imposing salutary penances, and he knew that they hear confessions and impose penances on those confessing to them. Item, when he used to make sacramental confession, he never confessed that he participated with the Waldensians and that he believed their sect was good – and despite this he used to celebrate masses and administer ecclesiastical sacraments. From the beginning he was unwilling to confess the aforesaid things, but when required in court he denied and hid the truth, against his own oath.

As has been established lawfully by his confession, made in court 4 April AD 1318, the aforesaid John Philibert, after he had confessed the aforesaid things and after it had been repeated – that for the second time he had abjured every heresy, and especially the Waldensian one, and all support for and belief in and participation with the Waldensians, in court, in front of Brother Bernard Gui, Toulouse Inquisitor, in AD 1311: after that, a certain believer in the Waldensians spoke with him at the gate of the Wall [*prison*], and told him that a certain fully fledged Waldensian (whom he names, that is to say, Hugh Pisaudi), was sending a mantle via him to a certain prisoner, that is to say, Stephen Porcheri, who was once a fully fledged Waldensian. Item, on two occasions and at various times this same believer carried and handed over to the aforesaid John Philibert a shirt and leggings, and he told him that Hugh Pisaidi, the aforesaid fully fledged Waldensian, was sending them to him, and he received them.

[*There follows the sentence for John Philibert to be degraded from the priesthood before being relinquished to the secular arm – i.e. put to death at the stake*].

57. OPPOSITION TO INQUISITION IN THE EARLY FOURTEENTH CENTURY

The Franciscan friar Bernard Délicieux positioned himself as a focal point for civic opposition to inquisition in the early fourteenth century, initially with some success. He was however eventually arrested (in relation to defending the Spiritual Franciscans) and charged with heresy, treason against the French throne and plotting the death of the pope, and was imprisoned. On his activities, see Friedlander, *Hammer*; very illuminating on inquisition problems in this period is J. Théry, 'Bernard de Castanet, une politique de la terreur', in *Les Inquisiteurs: Portraits de défenseurs de la foi en Languedoc (XIIIe–XIVe siècles)*, ed. L. Albaret (Toulouse, 2001), pp. 71–87. Bernard Gui's accounts of opposition to inquisition in these years are in Doc. 9 §9, 16. The trial records are lengthy, and detail a large number of heretical 'articles' alleged against Délicieux, arising from two different parts of the initial investigation; we present a selection from these first. Witnesses were also called against him; we translate an extract from one, giving a flavour of Bernard's preaching technique.

Translated from A. Friedlander, ed., *Processus Bernardi Delitiosi: The Trial of Fr. Bernard Délicieux, 3 September–8 December 1319* (Philadelphia, 1996), pp. 57–9, 65–72, 239–42, 244–7.

A. Charges against Bernard Délicieux, 1319

[Series I][242]

1. It has come to our hearing, brought by public rumour [fama], that Brother Bernard Délicieux arranged and gave counsel with William Fransa and certain others in a certain room in the house of the brothers Minor at Albi, that the same Brother Bernard and William Fransa should go and travel to Toulouse, to the Vidame of Amiens [*John of Picquigny*] and the Archdeacon of Auge [*Richard Leneveu*], royal officials [magistri];[243] and that the said Brother Bernard would declare in

242 These charges are presented in the trial as attached to a papal bull from John XXII, and comprise 44 articles in total; they may have been drawn up by Bishop Bernard of Castanet.

243 The two men had come to the south of France in May 1301, equipped with vice-regal authority as *enquêteurs-réformateurs*, to act on the king's behalf regarding the behaviour of all lesser royal officials in the region; Friedlander, *Hammer*, p. 69.

front of them – and he did declare – that many people of Albi and of other places who, because they supported royal right and honour, had been tricked by the Bishop of Albi and the inquisitors of heretical wickedness. And that they [*the inquisitors*] had induced and seduced them – and specially certain people of Albi – to confess; and they confessed before them that they had seen, adored and received heretics; which people, confessing this way because of false allegations and confessions, <the inquisitors> condemned to perpetual imprisonment; because of which the whole land was lost, unless the aforesaid agents took measures against the said bishop and inquisitors. Wherefor the said Brother Bernard petitioned the same officials governors to give security to all who wanted to make formal complaint about the aforesaid bishop and inquisitors, with the purpose of completely impeding and disrupting the office of inquisition into heretical wickedness, so that they could not make any proceedings (on heretical wickedness) against the men of Albi and Cordes and Carcassonne.

3. Item, another time in the said room <in the Franciscan convent>, the said Brother Bernard (together with many people from Albi) deliberated and gave counsel, consented, determined and arranged that the wives of those condemned for heresy from Albi – and all others they could get hold of – should go together with him to Toulouse to the said officials and governors, and raise an outcry in front of them and make a public complaint about the said bishop and inquisitors, that the said office would be impeded by the power of the said governors. <And> following the said counsel, they did this.

4. Item, urged on by the said wives and many others who were impeding the said office, the said Brother Bernard (together with certain other clerics and laymen), produced and dictated and had written down articles against the said bishop and inquisitors, containing among other things <the allegations> that the said bishop and inquisitors had by dint of heavy tortures forced people who had been condemned for heresy to confess that they had seen and adored and received heretics, and to name certain innocent people as being afflicted like them with a similar disease [*i.e. involvement with heretics*], in order to extort money from them; and that Brother Fulk was present there,[244] and, wearing a

244 Fulk of St-Georges OP, Inquisitor of Toulouse 1300–1, previously acted as lieutenant for the Inquisitor Nicholas of Abbeville. Délicieux's prevailing on Philip the Fair to bring about his removal from office was his most notable success. Bernard Gui's notices of him (Doc. 9 §16–17) are reticent.

dreadful <false> beard[245] so that he would not be recognised, he carried out the aforesaid tortures by his own hand; and that Brother Fulk had women arrested, so that he could have sex with them, and that he had sex with them when they were prisoners.

5. Item, that the said Brother Bernard, together with certain people from Albi, delivered to the said official the said articles – against the said bishop and inquisitors and the office <of inquisition> – in order to get the king, the whole country and the people roused up against the said bishop and inquisitors.

7. Item, that on some other occasion the said Brother Bernard plotted with the men of Albi, namely that he arranged and gave them counsel to go to Toulouse to petition the said officials, and to arrange with them for the wives of the aforesaid condemned men and a great multitude of the people of Albi to go to Carcassonne: and to make an outcry there, supplicating the officials to free from prison, by decree, those from Albi who had been immured. And following the said counsel, they went in this way to the said officials in Toulouse. And the said Brother Bernard and William Fransa worked enough on the said officials to make them promise to go to Carcassonne and to be <there> on a certain day and to expel the imprisoned from the Wall. And the said officials went on that day and to that place – and also the said wives and said multitude, making a great outcry and begging the said officials to free and take out of the Wall of the prison [*sic*] those from Albi who had been imprisoned for heresy. <As they went along>, the said Brother Bernard told those who were making the outcry, that the said officials had promised him that they would get the said imprisoned men out of the said Wall, and that they should not be frightened, because he would go with them to the said Wall, and ensure that before they returned, all who were imprisoned in the said Wall would be got out and permitted to go free: which is what happened.

[Series II][246]

1. Firstly, in AD 1300, the said Brother Bernard Délicieux together with Brother Bernard Raymond, then Guardian of the brothers Minor

245 portans unam barbadyram [i.e. barbam diram]: 'false' is our conjecture.

246 These are presented in the trial as being contained in a separate roll, with responses from Bernard (the responses appear then to follow the document, and are presented as occurring at a preliminary hearing in Avignon). They comprise 60 articles in

of Carcassonne, placed themselves in opposition to the Inquisitor of Carcassonne, Brother Nicholas of Abbeville, in his desire to proceed and in his proceeding against Castel Faure, who had died a heretic, as the inquisitor had found through unanimous witnesses; and he had it in commands (delivered with his own voice) from the lord pope, Boniface VIII, that he should proceed against him. And the said Brother Bernard presented himself in the defence of the said dead man, declaring that he was and had been Catholic.

3. Item, the said Brother Bernard Délicieux publicly and privately defamed the aforesaid inquisitors, and their processes and sentences given by them and also by the aforesaid lord Bishop of Albi against people guilty of heresy.

4. Item, the said Brother Bernard Délicieux often said and declared in front of the people – in many places (namely in Carcassonne, Albi, Cordes, and in Castres and elsewhere) and in public preaching and also in private – that the aforesaid lord bishop and inquisitors had condemned unjustly some people from Albi and the dioceses named above, and some people (in part named above) from Carcassonne and its diocese, claiming that the people condemned by them were and had been good and Catholic and free from the crime of heresy.

5. Item, the said Brother Bernard reported the aforesaid things against the aforesaid lord bishop and inquisitors, to Lord John of Picquigny, Vidame of Amiens, and Lord Richard Leneveu, Archdeacon of Auge in the church of Lisieux, who had been sent by Lord Philip, King of France, to the aforesaid parts. And because of the information and at the instigation of the aforesaid Brother Bernard, they made many difficulties and obstructions and brought them to bear upon the aforesaid lord bishop and the inquisitors and the office of inquisition and the ministers of the office of inquisition, and the members of the household and friends of the aforesaid bishops and inquisitors.

13. Item, constituted as a procurator and with the counsel of the Vidame and the Archdeacon, in AD 1302 the said Brother Bernard went to <the Île-de->France to the court of the king, with a certain Brother Minor called Hector as his companion. And they followed the king from Paris to Pierrefonds, Compiègne and Choisy-au-Bac, where the letter of support that had been granted by the lord king on behalf of the Inquisitor of Toulouse was blocked by the same Brother Bernard's procurations.

total. These, it has been argued, were drawn up by Bernard Gui; see Friedlander, *Processus*, p. 14 n.34.

And the same Brother Bernard said and suggested to the said king many things against the office of inquisition and against the aforesaid bishop and inquisitors, as he himself later recounted in a public sermon that he delivered at Castres.

14. Item, in AD 1303, around the Feast of the Ascension, when the people of Albi first came to Carcassonne from the Albigeois to ask the Inquisitor Brother Geoffrey <d'Ablis> to set free those who had been condemned and others who were detained in the inquisitors' prison for the crime of heresy, Brother Bernard Délicieux went there and was involved in all the counsels and dealings carried out by the Vidame against the business of inquisition, <acting> as the main adversary and impeder and disparager of the inquisitors.

19. Item, in the same year and month [July 1303] at Carcassonne, in order to get the people roused up against the inquisitor, the same Brother Bernard incited the aforesaid Vidame to get the consuls <of Carcassonne> who had brought about and arranged make peace and concord between the Inquisitor Nicholas of Abbeville and the town of Carcassonne, and to get hold of the instrument [*legal document*] that had been drawn up regarding the aforesaid peace. And that when the Vidame did this and got the document and wanted to return it to the consuls, the said Brother Bernard brought it about that the Vidame kept it, so that it could be published to the people.
[*Bernard was alleged to have then summoned the people of Carcassonne to a sermon in August, on the theme* 'Jesus, approaching the city, wept over it, saying "If you had known"' (Luke 19.41–2). *According to one report, having announced the theme of the sermon, Bernard paused, and wept grievously himself, before declaring 'I am Jesus!' – i.e. that he wept over their city of Carcassonne.*]

22. Item, there in the said sermon he read and explained in the vernacular the instrument that had been drawn up regarding the aforesaid peace and concord between the town and the inquisitors. And in order to stir up the people, he explained that there were many things contained in the document which were, according to his own understanding, not true, namely that the consuls and councillors who were then <in office> and the whole community of Carcassonne had made themselves *supporters* of heretics, because they had had dealings with seven people who had been falsely excommunicated and condemned by the inquisitors, whose names were William Garric, William Brunet, Raymond Maistre, etc. Item, that they had simply petitioned for themselves to be absolved by the inquisitor for that crime of support and

from the sentences <imposed on them>, and that the inquisitor had absolved them. Item, that they had abjured all heresy – <Bernard> very much exaggerating the word 'abjuration', saying that after this word, if they were to relapse [reinciderent] the fire would be the only outcome. Item, that the same instrument contained <a clause> that if anyone took up the cause of another or defended him against the course of inquisition, he would be deprived of all public office and dignity unto the third or fourth generation …

[*Further allegations of public preaching against inquisitors follow, in Albi and Castres; and then in Toulouse.*]

35. Item, the same year at Toulouse, in the presence of the lord king together with his counsellors and nobles and prelates, <Brother Bernard> said that he had laboured for many years to bring the business and deeds of the inquisition into the light, but he had not been able to: and he had shouted so much that his throat had become hoarse.

36. Item, he said there that he was certain that within the last 40 years no heretic or heretical people had been found in that land, namely in the Carcassès, Albigeois and Toulousain. And although he was criticised there for this statement, by the lord Archbishop of Narbonne and the Bishop of Béziers (now <Bishop of> Frascati) who were present and asserted the opposite, the same Brother Bernard nevertheless persisted obstinately in the aforesaid claim.

37. Item, he said there that if Saint Peter and Saint Paul were before the inquisitors, no matter how much they were and are good Christians, the inquisitors would maltreat them so badly that they would make them confess to heresy. And when he was reprimanded on this by the lord Bishop of Auxerre, saying what the apostle <Paul> said about himself 'For I am sure that neither death nor life shall be able to separate me from the love of Christ' [Rom. 8.38–9], the said Brother Bernard, unwilling to commit himself to argument, persisted obstinately in his claim.

B. A witness to events in Carcassonne, 1319

Gerald of *Meldis*, servant of the Bourg of Carcassonne, sworn as witness and interrogated on the articles relating to the treason carried out by the said Brother Bernard in the Bourg of Carcassonne, and on the public repute that the same Brother Bernard had gone to Perpignan to stir up treason … said that 15 years ago or thereabouts, on a certain Sunday which he said he cannot recall, he was present in the cloister of the brothers Minor in the Bourg of Carcassonne and he heard that the said Brother Bernard preached, and at the end of his sermon he indicated to the people with his hand that they should sit down for a while, for the same Bernard would narrate a good story [exemplum]. And then he began to speak: that once upon a time there was a certain good man in a certain town, who was never or hardly ever angry. And when that good man went one day into the square, those around said to each other that they would find out if there was any way in which they could make him angry. And then one of them said to the said good man, 'You have raped a good woman'. He replied, 'May God forgive you', and was not moved to anger. Again the man spoke to him, saying, 'You have robbed a merchant, you are a murderer'. And whatever aforesaid or similar words he said, the good man was not moved to anger, but always said, 'May God forgive you'. Then the one who had first come up to the said good man, seeing that he was not getting angry, said to him, 'You are a heretic'. And then the same good man, agitated and irate, struck him violently with his fist, saying he was lying in his throat. After which, the same Brother Bernard directed people's attention to the aforesaid words, saying to them, 'Good men, if anyone calls you heretics, you should defend yourselves if you want to, because you have good cause [bonum ius] to defend yourselves.' And when he had said these words in this way, the said Brother Bernard descended from the pulpit and left. And after the said sermon by the said Brother Bernard, all the people were stirred up and agitated and many men spoke about the aforesaid words.

Asked if he believed that it was because of the aforesaid words that people were roused up against the inquisitors and their followers, he said yes. Asked why he believed this, he said because of the words which he deposed earlier.

Item, asked about the article on treason, he said he did not know anything else, except that he had heard it said frequently and by many (by whom he said he could not remember) that the said Brother Bernard went to Perpignan, and carried a letter to Lord Ferrand, son of the King of Majorca, and had dealings with him regarding the said treason.[247]

And on the aforesaid words which the said Brother Bernard said in the aforesaid sermon, he said these were common and public knowledge in the Bourg of Carcassonne. And he said nothing else relevant.

247 On these allegations, see Friedlander, *Hammer*, pp. 178–211.

Asked if he had been induced or instructed to depose the aforesaid things in this present case through imprecation, bribery, love, hate or fear, he said no, but because it was the truth, as he said above.

INDEX

Acre 7, 259
Ad abolendam (1184) 149, 187
Ad extirpanda (1252) 149
adoration *see melioramentum*
Agen 17, 21, 71, 72, 75, 112, 132, 158, 311, 315, 329, 380
Aimery of Collet, Cathar deacon 354, 460, 461
Aix 236, 250
Alaman of Roaix 302, 400
Alan of Lille, OCist, *Quadripartite Work on Faith* 87
'Albanenses' 111, 112
Albi 17, 26, 51, 64, 72, 74, 77, 78, 79, 80, 81, 82, 92, 111, 112, 174, 182, 183, 184, 236, 266, 281, 298, 308, 315, 357, 359, 366, 403, 461, 501, 502, 503, 504, 505, 506
  rising against inquisition 64, 78–82
'Albigenses/Albigensians' 37, 40, 60, 63, 123, 124, 125, 126, 127, 128, 130, 131, 132, 133, 158
Albigensian crusade 2, 31, 33, 39, 116, 149, 151, 157, 187, 196, 198, 334, 336, 407, 436, 437–9
Albi *Summa of Authorities* 92–7
Alphonse of Poitiers, Count of Toulouse 420
  letters 172–3
Anselm of Alessandria, OP 34n
Antichrist 41, 46, 62, 135, 157
  see also Devil
apparellamentum ('Service') 247, 274, 308, 312, 314, 317, 341, 355, 399, 411
Aragon 9, 51, 159, 306
  village in Languedoc 9, 304, 343
Arles 5, 168, 215, 236, 250, 281
Arnold, John H. 188n, 215, 218, 236, 295
Arnold Catalan, OP, Inquisitor 308
Arnold of Villemur, co-lord of Saverdun 377, 413
Arnold Roger of Mirepoix, knight 360, 361, 363, 370
Arras 54, 90, 117
Aubri of Trois-Fontaines, OCist, *Chronicles* 53–6
Augustine of Hippo, St 56, 105, 109, 118, 122n, 137–8, 139, 234n, 235n
  On Heresies 131–3
Auriac 371, 381, 402, 403, 404, 412, 413, 430, 433, 434
Auxerre 33, 36, 62, 98, 102, 103, 104, 129, 138, 151, 152, 153, 154, 155, 159, 163, 165
Avignon 64, 209, 214, 215, 251, 262
  Consultation (1235) 214–17
Avignonet 18, 19, 61, 209, 300, 359, 360, 363, 364, 395, 403, 414, 415, 416, 417
  killing of inquisitors at 350n, 359–64, 403, 417–20
Ax 477, 481, 484, 488

'Bagnolenses' 111–12
Balaguier of Laurac, knight 360, 417
baptism, beliefs about 26, 41, 44, 52, 96–7, 108, 118, 119, 127, 287, 378, 382, 385, 387, 388, 397, 406, 411, 418, 421, 478, 479
Barcelona 218, 223, 228
Bartholomew of Carcassonne, heretic 158, 311
beguines 63
'believers' of heretics 42, 201, 202, 215–17, 219–28, 230–3, 239, 241, 242, 243, 247–9, 253, 255, 260, 275, 276, 289, 290, 298–508 *passim*
bells 43
Benedict of Termes, Cathar Bishop 305–6

Benedict XI, Pope 183
Benedictines 57, 117, 376n, 423n, 445n
Berengar, Bishop of Barcelona 218
Bergamo 102, 112
Bergerac 72, 73, 77, 84
Bernard Bonafos, Cathar deacon 296, 402
Bernard Délicieux, OFM 8, 74, 81–3, 182, 501–4
Bernard Gui, OP, Inquisitor 6, 8, 9, 55, 64–5, 69, 72, 76, 77, 133, 208, 213, 289, 310, 469, 476, 490, 500, 501, 502, 503
  Acts of the Provincial Chapters 208–10
  Book of Sentences 469, 490–6
  On the Foundations and Priors of the Preachers' Convents 32, 64–84, 310, 501, 502n
  Treatise on the Practice of Inquisition 213, 133n, 289–90, 469
Bernard Hugo of Festes, knight 304, 344
Bernard of Castanet, Bishop of Albi 77, 78, 501n
Bernard of Caux, OP, Inquisitor 6, 64, 70, 75–6, 312, 351, 357, 358, 379, 380, 382, 383, 393, 395, 412, 423, 433, 434, 440
Bernard of Clairvaux, OCist, St 109
Bernard of Lamothe, Cathar Bishop 298, 309, 376, 394, 401, 421
Bernard of Latour, knight 313, 450, 451
Bernard of Mayreville, Cathar deacon 347, 386, 412, 419, 428, 429
Bernard of Simorre, heretic 21, 49, 51, 52
Bernard of St-Martin, knight 360, 362, 370, 371, 398–400, 417
Bernard Prim, Waldensian (later Poor Catholic) 426
Bernard Raymond, Cathar Bishop 17–19
Bertrand Martin, Cathar Bishop 296, 305, 332, 345, 346, 366, 367, 368, 369, 370, 372, 373, 389, 398, 409, 410, 412, 429
Bertrand of Belcastel, OP, Inquisitor 75
Bertrand of Clermont, OP, Inquisitor 73, 77, 84
Bertrand of Quiriès 359, 385, 415, 419, 420
Besançon 159, 497, 498
Béziers 46, 47, 71, 82, 83, 84, 214, 236, 412, 442, 482
  Consultation (1246) 213–14, 250–61, 381n
  Council (1246) 202–7, 213–14, 250
Bible 13, 121, 127, 138, 362
  Cathars 13
  expounding and reading passages 20–8, 40, 100, 107, 140, 145, 315, 325, 327, 399, 478–9, 495
  Gospels as dead skins 130
  New Testament, vernacular 14, 312
  rejection of Old Testament 40, 93–6, 118
    variant text 23
  prohibition of lay possession of 195
  Waldensians 13, 216, 266, 269, 325, 471
Biget, Jean-Louis 4, 157
Bird, Jessalynn 1n, 31n, 33, 53n
bishops of Cathars 16–19, 21, 42, 49, 51, 55, 62, 108, 111, 158, 296, 298, 302, 305–6, 311, 334, 347, 366–73 *passim*, 394, 410, 428, 429, 454
  see also individually named people
Bohemia 293
Bologna 102
  University of 143, 151, 159, 218
Bonfils of Cassès, Cathar Deacon 305
Boniface VIII, Pope 498, 504
books and texts
  Cathars 2, 13–14, 20–8, 39, 40, 47, 62, 88, 92–7, 106, 107, 109–10, 128, 158, 206, 233, 247, 307–8, 312, 316, 317, 318, 321, 325, 327, 328, 330, 333, 349, 356–7, 373, 398, 399, 404, 419, 431–2, 434, 492, 495
    Contradiction 15, 20
    Perpendicular of Sciences 107
    Questions of John 14

Ritual 14, 422n; front cover illustration
Secret 40
Vision of Isaiah 20, 27
prohibitions of possession of 195, 260
Waldensians, 13–14, 264, 323, 326, 499
see also Bible; Inquisition, use of written records
Bordeaux 59, 61, 67, 68, 69, 70, 184, 190, 211, 380
Council (1214) 64n
Boulbonne (Cistercian abbey) 363, 412, 413, 439
Bourges 151, 155, 160, 163
Braida, heretic 335, 348, 349, 408
branding 140
bread, blessed by Cathars 248, 274, 300, 312, 314, 315, 317, 322, 323, 324, 325, 334, 340, 352, 369, 370, 371, 392, 416, 435, 478
see also Waldensians, holy supper
Bruschi, Caterina 111, 295, 463
Bulgaria 14, 18, 34, 54, 55, 56, 112, 132, 157
'Burgars' (or 'Bugars' or 'Bulgars') 34, 35, 59, 60, 117, 129, 132, 157
Burgundy 33, 107, 159, 263, 497, 498, 499

Cabaret 18, 371, 387, 388, 447
Cahors 3, 67, 70, 76, 84, 209, 267, 314, 315, 320, 351, 357, 358, 380, 442
Caldwell Ames, Christine 4, 64
Calmont 340, 363, 377
Cambiac 381, 430, 431, 432, 433
Camplong 340, 346, 350, 390, 409, 411
Caraman 303, 373, 413, 421
Carcassonne 14, 16, 17, 18, 19, 26, 46, 47, 49, 50, 51, 64, 66, 67, 71, 72, 73, 74, 78, 79, 81, 82, 83, 84, 111, 112, 149, 157, 158, 170, 174, 175, 177, 178, 179, 180, 182, 183, 184, 190, 236, 271, 281, 283, 298, 300, 306, 315, 332, 369, 411, 442, 443, 444, 445, 446, 447, 450, 451, 455, 457, 458, 459, 462, 463, 464, 465, 466, 467, 468, 476, 482, 483, 486, 502, 503, 504, 505, 506, 507
Carcassonne uprising 64, 72–5, 78, 505, 506–7
Castelnaudary 71, 302, 364, 391, 400, 405, 413, 436, 437, 438, 439, 440
Castelsarrasin 301, 302, 359
Castres 76, 81, 282, 412, 413, 435, 457, 462, 504, 505, 506
Catalonia 92, 298, 306, 486
Catbert of Barbaira, knight 363, 374, 439, 440
Cathars
'Cathars' as specific term 22–8, 90, 93, 111–12, 129, 132
diet 26, 42, 43, 119, 125, 132–3, 308, 315, 324, 325, 331, 332, 337, 345, 346, 349, 367–9, 372, 373, 391, 392, 399, 417, 420, 422, 423, 431, 434, 477–8
habit of heretics 42, 44, 130–1, 193, 200, 253, 254, 257, 260, 323, 330, 333, 337, 390, 423
hierarchy of sect 16–19, 42, 108, 158, 296, 298n, 305–6
'Churches' of 16–19, 111–12, 298n, 305n, 367, 368, 415n, 429n, 440, 491
women heretics 125–6, 130–1, 299, 313, 304, 305, 313, 316, 323, 324, 325, 328, 329, 330, 331, 333, 335, 336, 337, 338, 339, 340, 341, 342, 343, 344, 348, 349, 350, 351, 355, 356, 369, 371, 372, 373, 375, 376, 378, 383, 385, 386, 388, 390, 391, 392, 393, 397, 398, 400, 401, 404, 408, 409, 415, 421, 422, 426, 430, 431, 434, 440, 441, 456
see also 'Albanenses'; 'Albigenses'; *apparellamentum*; 'Bagnolenses'; bible, Cathars; bishops of heretics; books and texts, Cathars; bread blessed

Cathars (*cont.*)
by heretics; 'Burgars'; 'Concorezzo'; *consolamentum*; councils, held by Cathars; creation, beliefs about; 'Good men/women'; kiss of peace, in Cathar rites; 'Manicheans'; *melioramentum*; money, and Cathars; 'Patarenes'; 'Perfect'; *and other named heretics and other specific beliefs*

Caussade 321, 353, 354, 355, 356

Cavanac 443, 445, 446, 451, 452, 453, 454, 457

Chiffoleau, Jacques 5, 168, 215

Christ, beliefs about 40–1, 51, 105, 107, 126,

Cistercians 39, 45, 49, 53, 61, 82, 151, 157, 183

Cîteaux 45, 48, 49, 157

Clement V, Pope 68, 69, 74,
- Bull 182–4

Cluny 124, 151

'Concorezzo' 111–12

confession 118
- *see also* Waldensians

confirmation, beliefs about 41

Conques 429, 445, 447

Conrad of Porto, OCist, Cardinal, legate, letter 157–8

consolamentum (or 'heretication') 17, 42, 43, 44, 92, 96–7, 155, 176, 201, 247, 274, 298–507 *passim*

Constantinople 18, 95, 111, 112, 311, 312, 313, 314, 315, 317, 318, 319, 322, 325, 326, 327, 328, 329

Cordes 74, 78, 81, 182, 183, 351, 359, 502, 504

Cornèze 175, 446, 452, 454, 455, 456

councils,
- of the Church 187–8, 205n, 208, 213
- *see also* Béziers; Bordeaux; Dijon; L'Isle-sur-Sorgue; Montpellier; Narbonne; Paris; Sens; Tarragona; Toulouse; Vienne
- Fourth Lateran Council (1215) 54, 65, 104n, 140n, 151, 159, 194n, 202n, 207, 216n, 220, 224, 231n, 232, 242n
- held by Cathars 5, 16–19, 298, 305, 375, 428, 429
- held by Waldensians 470, 472–3

Count Hervé of Nevers 34

creation, beliefs about 2, 4, 21–7, 40–1, 51, 94–6, 98–9, 118, 145, 317, 319, 320, 326, 385, 387, 388, 394, 395, 397, 401, 406, 411, 418, 421, 439

Cremona 62, 99, 320, 327, 355
- bishop and Church of the heretics of 367, 372

Croatia 157

cross, beliefs about 20, 44, 50, 105–6, 139–41, 284, 479–82

crosses, assigned for heresy 137, 171, 193, 200–1, 204, 227, 228, 237, 256–7, 266–7, 272, 279–81, 310–31 *passim*, 389, 390, 422, 423, 443, 446, 447, 448, 449, 450, 451, 456, 494

Dalmatia 18, 157

deacons, of Cathars 42, 278, 296, 303, 304, 305, 306, 307, 309, 367, 369, 374, 376, 416, 428, 429, 431, 433, 460

debates, between heretics and others 5, 11, 13, 20, 46–52, 88, 92, 116, 126, 130, 131, 133, 140, 145, 188, 302n, 305n, 316, 317, 318, 320, 323, 325, 326, 351, 426, 463

Deeds of the Bishops of Auxerre 32, 36–8

Devil (*or* Satan) 21, 22, 41, 80, 108, 134–5, 158, 160

Diego, Bishop of Osma 44, 45, 46, 48, 49, 50, 123

Dijon, Council (1199) 152, 153

doctors, medicine 141
- Cathars 331
- practice prohibited 195, 206, 208, 257
- Waldensians 315, 322, 324

Dominic Guzman, St 50, 65, 66, 68, 69, 81, 124, 130, 143, 144, 145, 333, 381, 390, 422, 423

Dominicans 4, 5, 14, 32, 53, 57, 59, 60, 61, 64–84, 88, 102, 107, 111, 122, 134, 143, 159, 162, 163, 165, 168, 169, 170, 173, 174, 175, 179, 180, 183, 188, 208, 215, 218, 236, 243, 250, 262, 271, 275, 279, 281, 283, 285, 286, 298, 309, 310, 330, 359, 380, 383, 419, 458, 462, 466, 467, 468, 469, 476, 482, 484, 494 *see also individually named Dominicans*
Dondaine, Antoine, OP 214
Dossat, Yves 64, 157, 159, 165, 172, 173, 188, 198, 202, 230, 236, 250, 270, 279, 281, 295, 311, 359, 380
Dragovitsa/Drugunthia 18, 24, 26, 112
dualist beliefs *see* creation, beliefs about
Durand of Beaucaire, Bishop of Albi 308
Durand of Huesca, Waldensian (later Poor Catholic)
Anti-heresy Book 20
Book against the Manichees 15, 20–8, 88, 311n

Elias, OFM, Minister General 107
Esclarmonda [of] Bret 380, 394, 395, 440, 441
eucharist, beliefs about 41, 52, 89–90, 92–3, 96, 118, 222, 317, 319, 378, 382–421 *passim*, 426, 427, 440, 478, 488
Evans, Austin P. 1–2, 5, 9, 13, 15
Evrard of Châteauneuf 34–5, 45–6
excommunication 33, 47, 52, 66, 72, 83, 136, 140, 151–3, 155, 161, 166, 197, 203–5, 207, 216–17, 220–1, 225, 232, 237, 241, 248, 263–5, 267, 269, 275–6, 278, 358, 422, 441, 505
execution by burning 16, 34, 35, 138, 40, 50, 53, 54, 55, 57–8, 60, 95, 102–3, 107–9, 123, 125, 126, 128, 129–30, 131, 137, 141, 209, 219, 220, 225, 226, 227, 233, 240, 265, 267, 272, 310, 332, 335, 373, 393, 397, 409, 411, 422, 423, 428, 429, 433, 434, 456, 491, 500
extreme unction, beliefs about 41

Fanjeaux 18, 65, 304, 332–6, 337, 344–5, 349, 368, 407, 420–4, 440, 457
Federico Visconti, Archbishop of Pisa, *Sermon* 143–5
Ferrier, OP, Inquisitor 71, 84, 236, 266, 298, 309, 336, 350, 351, 374, 383, 385, 386, 387, 388, 423, 424, 428, 429, 440, 458
Feuchter, Jörg 5, 298, 299, 310, 322, 351
Flanders 33, 60, 90, 160
Florence 111, 162
Foix 8, 66, 378, 379, 476
France (i.e. northern France) 33–5, 36–8, 39, 45, 46, 48, 53–6, 57–8, 60, 81, 90, 105, 109, 111, 117–18, 126, 133, 149, 151–6, 159–64, 165–7, 205n, 270, 272, 283, 354, 365, 368
see also La Charité-sur-Loire; Paris, Tours, Troyes
Franciscans 57, 60, 74, 81, 107, 109, 168, 182, 271, 272, 285, 286, 298, 330, 469, 484, 501, 504, 507
fugitives ('faidits') 196, 204, 255–6, 286, 367, 397, 415, 416, 419, 497
Fulk of Neuilly 33
Fulk of St Georges, OP, Inquisitor 64, 78, 83, 182, 468, 502

Gaja-la-Selve 340, 341, 345, 346, 347, 348, 360, 361, 362, 371, 393, 397, 406, 408, 409, 410, 411, 412, 426
Gaucelin / Gaucelm, Cathar Bishop 21, 296
Geoffrey of Ablis, OP, Inquisitor 6, 8, 476, 483, 495, 505
Gerald (or Guiraud) of Gourdon, Cathar deacon 303, 308, 376

Gerald of Wales
Jewel of the Church 89–90
On the Instruction of a Prince 86, 90–1
Germany 1, 53, 63, 159, 471, 472, 473
'Good men/women' 23, 26, 42, 44, 93, 96–7, 216, 219, 226, 247, 249, 265, 269, 279, 311–507 *passim*
Gourdon 303, 310, 312, 314, 315
Gratian, *Decretum* x, 129, 132n, 231–5
Gregory I (Gregory the Great), Pope 89
Dialogues 122
Moralia 231n
Gregory VIII, Pope 151
Gregory IX, Pope 198, 216n, 219n, 223, 240
Bulls 149, 159–64
Five Books of the Decretals 218, 231–2
Grundmann, Herbert 2–3
Guilabert of Castres, Cathar Bishop 296, 302, 303, 304, 305, 306, 337, 341, 344, 345, 349, 376, 407
Guiraud Mercier, Cathar bishop 17–19
Guy Foulques (later Pope Clement IV), *Consultation* 214, 230–5, 295
Guy of Rheims, Inquisitor 498, 499

Hautpoul 18, 430, 461
Henry III, King of England 59
'hereticals' 71, 74, 78, 79
Hervé, Count of Nevers 34, 37
Holy Land 166, 169, 237, 443, 446, 447, 448, 479
see also Jerusalem
Hugh Amiel of Castelnaudary, OP 68, 71
Hugh of Bouniols, OP, Inquisitor 458, 462
Hugh of Noyers, Bishop of Auxerre 34–7, 151, 154
Humbert of Romans, OP, master-general *On the Instruction of Preachers* 120, 134–42

images, beliefs about 43, 80–1, 104–6
incarnation, beliefs about 41
Innocent III, Pope 20, 39, 45, 52, 89, 159, 232, 242n
Bulls 151–6
Innocent IV, Pope 143, 144
Inquisition
abjuration 52, 154, 220–1, 222–4, 226–7, 238, 253, 259, 261, 273, 275, 277, 279, 379, 383–440 *passim*, 457, 462
culpae 258, 272, 294, 310–31, 475, 490–5, 497–500
depositions 5, 6, 78–9, 176, 246, 252–3, 261, 271, 273–5, 294, 296, 298–309, 330, 332–57, 359–440, 449–69, 473, 476–89, 506–8
episcopal inquisition / participation in repression 6, 31, 34–8, 44–52, 54–5, 123–4, 126, 151–8, 159–67, 169, 182–4, 188, 190–4, 198–201, 202–3, 218–29, 236, 250–1, 271–2, 308, 323, 331, 335, 357, 366, 381, 383, 387–90, 435–53, 499–506
exhumation 225, 269, 277, 278
expenses 170–3, 208, 257
financial penalties 35, 140, 169, 171, 174, 193, 199–201, 203–4, 209, 243, 257, 260, 502
houses, demolition of 191, 192, 199–200, 260, 264, 496
interrogation 51–2, 57–8, 176–7, 253, 254, 298–309, 332–57, 432, 444, 445, 446–7, 448
killing of inquisitors 196
see also Avignonet
manuals and treatises 2, 5
inquisitors' handbook (1265) 262–9
see also Avignon Consultation; Bernard Gui; Béziers, Consultation; Narbonne, Council (1243); Tarragona, Council (1242); Guy Foulques; *Instruction in the way one should proceed against heretics*; *Narbonne Order of Procedure*; *On the Authority and Form of Inquisition*

opposition to 59–61 72–5, 78–82, 175–84, 209, 463–6, 467–8, 501–8
procedures 54, 57–8, 108–9, 133, 138, 152–6, 159–69, 175–84, 190–7, 202–7, 211–90
purgation 163–4, 219, 224, 226, 232, 241, 244, 447
sentences 5, 6, 126, 136–9, 154, 209, 213, 217, 220, 221, 254, 263–7, 269, 272, 275–80, 294, 357–8, 440, 441, 500
see also excommunication
sureties 154, 243, 254, 255, 442–4, 446–50
use of written records 2, 3, 5, 6, 57–8, 67, 70, 77, 78, 82, 161, 162, 169, 177, 184, 193, 194–5, 200, 209, 213–14, 225, 226, 229, 239, 241, 245, 252, 258–9, 261, 271, 275, 293–6, 330, 387, 419, 422, 445–7, 449–50, 458–62, 463–6, 469, 494
see also branding; crosses assigned for heresy; excommunication; execution by burning; parishes; pilgrimage, as penance; prison; time of grace; torture; *and listings for individual inquisitors*
Instruction in the way one should proceed against heretics 214, 270–88
Isarn of Castres, heretic 350, 426
Isidore of Seville, St 104
Etymologies 60n, 109, 129, 131, 132n
Islam 90–1, 108, 127, 237, 256
Italy 1, 4, 14, 17, 27n, 37, 59, 62, 89, 90n, 91, 102, 111–12, 116, 143–5, 149, 159, 166, 289, 296, 305n, 351, 355, 358, 367, 411, 417, 456, 472, 477
see also Bologna; Como; Cremona; Lombardy; Milan; Piacenza; Rome; Tuscany

Jacques Fournier, OCist, Bishop of Pamiers 3, 6, 476
James Autier, heretic 477, 481, 484
Jerusalem 20, 23, 40, 165, 259
see also Holy Land
Jews 34, 90, 93, 108, 207, 286–8
Joanna of Avignonet, heretic 299, 323
John Cambiaire, Cathar Bishop 296, 415
John Galand, OP, Inquisitor 180, 458, 465, 467, 468
Complaints of the City of Carcassonne 175–81
prison instructions, 174–5
John of Bernin, Archbishop of Vienne, legate 215
John of Collet, heretic 351, 354
John of Falgous/Faugoux, OP, Inquisitor 174, 462, 465, 468, 476, 482, 487
John of Picquigny, Vidame of Amiens 73, 79, 82, 501, 504
John of St-Benoît, OP, Inquisitor 279
John of St-Pierre of Bordeaux, OP, Inquisitor 70
John of St-Pierre, Inquisitor 6, 357, 358, 380–440
John Philibert, priest, Waldensian supporter 469, 497–500
John Vigouroux, OP, Inquisitor 83, 465
Jordan of Lanta 346, 408, 409, 410, 413
Jordan of Mas, knight 360, 361, 362, 369, 385, 389
Jordan of Saxony, OP, master-general 65
'Jovinians' 60, 63
Justinian
Codex 231
Digest 231, 234, 235

kiss of peace, in Cathar rites 44, 221, 248, 308, 312, 313, 314, 317, 323, 333, 341, 349, 355–6, 373, 412, 435, 472, 484
see also Waldensians, kiss of peace

Labécède 303, 399, 401, 406, 407, 426
La Charité-sur-Loire 31, 34, 36, 117, 151, 152, 153, 154, 159, 163, 165, 166, 232
Ladurie, Emmanuel Le Roy 6
Lantarais 303, 307, 408

Laurac 303, 304, 340, 350, 360, 370, 371, 388, 392, 393, 396, 398, 399, 406, 409, 410, 411, 413, 420, 426
Lavaur 51, 172, 173, 331, 406, 430, 435, 436, 440
Lavelanet 296, 333, 425, 481, 483
Lea, Henry Charles 4, 187, 463
Léon diocese 104
lepers, leperhouses, leprosy 39, 82, 128, 139, 396–7, 450
Le Puy 77, 230, 263, 266, 267, 281, 311, 313, 315, 316, 317, 318, 319, 320, 321, 322, 323, 324, 325, 326, 327, 328, 329, 330, 331, 446n
Lérida 18, 307, 309
Limoges 65, 66, 68, 69, 72, 74, 76, 77, 83
Limoux 74, 305, 332, 366, 387, 401, 407, 424, 494
L'Isle-sur-Sorgue, Council (1251) 442n
Lombardy 17, 62, 102, 107n, 111–12, 166, 355, 358, 367n, 411, 417, 456, 477
Lordat 371, 480, 481, 485, 486
Louis IX, King of France 61, 73, 172
  Cupientes 170, 190
  ecclesiastical office 68
  letters 71, 170–1
Lucas of Tuy
  Miracles of St Isidore 103
  On the other Life 103–10
Lyons 43, 105, 111, 128, 134, 143, 144, 165, 217, 222, 223, 224, 251, 267, 269, 289
  1st Council (1245) 9, 143, 165

Maisonneuve, Henri 151, 159, 170, 188, 190, 198, 202, 236, 250
Malviès 339, 443, 457, 466
'Manicheans' 20–8, 54, 56, 93–7, 98, 105, 118, 125–6, 129, 131–2, 144
Mark, Cathar bishop 17
marriage and sex, beliefs about 41, 43, 60n, 108, 118, 144–5, 194, 319, 378, 382, 385, 387, 388, 394, 395, 397, 401, 403, 406, 411, 415, 418, 421, 423, 429–31, 478–9
Marseille 144, 267
Mary, Blessed Virgin 51, 52, 55, 76, 77, 106, 109, 124, 195, 205, 227, 228, 263, 266–7, 281
Mas-Saintes-Puelles 270, 381, 382–90
Master Ralph, episcopal Inquisitor 335, 442, 451
Matthew Paris, OSB, *Greater Chronicles* 59–63
Maurens 405, 431, 433, 434
Mazerolles-du-Razès 294, 337, 338, 339, 340, 345, 346, 347, 393, 409, 413
melioramentum ('adoration') 230, 232, 247, 274–7, 279, 299–508 *passim*
Milan 54, 56, 62, 90, 112, 128, 215, 326
Mirepoix 306, 340, 341, 342, 343, 348, 359, 364, 366, 368, 370, 373, 375, 376, 377, 407, 409, 481, 483
Moissac 300, 302, 318, 327, 417
money
  and Cathars 24, 62, 91, 144, 162, 262, 274, 313, 314–15, 317, 320, 321, 327, 328, 331, 340, 353, 355, 357, 367, 368, 373, 377, 409, 414, 419, 422, 446, 452, 454–5, 464–5, 473, 475
    bequests 43, 206, 269, 313, 314, 316, 322, 323, 333, 378, 416
  and unspecified heretics 231, 274
  and Waldensians 13, 129, 216–17, 224, 226, 262, 266, 269, 317, 321, 322, 324, 470, 473, 475
    bequests 269, 323, 326, 327
  see also Inquisition, financial penalties; Inquisition, sureties
Mont-Aimé (Mont Wimer) 54, 56, 125
Montauban 5, 71, 76, 83, 298, 299, 300, 310, 321, 325, 326, 328, 329, 358, 427
Montcuq 105, 317, 318, 319, 321
Montgaillard 313, 367, 393, 425
Montgiscard 81, 377, 396
Montmaur 389, 413, 419, 430

Montolieu 304, 336, 341, 342, 343, 348, 349, 446, 449, 450, 455, 456
Montpellier 45, 67, 68, 71, 75, 81, 83, 84, 144, 208, 251, 267, 282, 357
  Council (pre-1246) 250–1
Montréal 18, 47, 48, 51, 65, 304, 305, 338, 339, 340, 348, 350, 407, 409, 410, 443, 448, 457, 459
Montségur 8, 105, 296, 298, 305, 340, 341, 359, 364–75, 392, 413, 428, 429
Moore, R. I. 2, 3

Najac 351, 352, 353, 355, 356
Narbonne 18, 39, 41, 46, 47, 48, 49, 61, 70, 71, 73, 77, 84, 132, 179, 180, 183, 190, 209, 214, 230, 250, 251, 254, 262, 266, 267, 270, 274, 281, 335, 370, 373, 387, 388, 439, 442, 448, 449
  Council (1243/4), replies to inquisitors 202, 236–49
Narbonne Order of Procedure (Ordo Processus Narbonnensis) 214, 270, 274–5
Nevers 34, 37, 45, 155, 232
Nice 16, 68, 71
Nicholas of Abbeville, OP, Inquisitor 73, 502, 504, 505
Niquinta (Nicetas), Bogomil bishop 17

oaths, beliefs about 118–19
  see also Waldensians
Octavian, papal legate 34, 37, 46
On the Authority and Form of Inquisition 289
orders, holy, beliefs about 118
Orléans 130, 152, 163, 283, 284

Palajac 367, 458, 459, 460, 461
Pamiers 7, 20, 48, 82, 375, 378, 379
Paolini, Lorenzo 4, 40, 87, 305
Paris 2, 33, 36, 49, 54, 59, 61, 65, 99n, 102, 155, 162, 179, 180, 187, 230, 270, 286n
  Council (1201) 34, 37–8, 46
  place in Languedoc 318
  Treaty of Paris (1229) 187n, 198–201
  University/schools of Paris 2, 46, 53, 55, 57, 62, 89, 98, 101, 117, 134, 151, 159, 165, 488
parishes 66, 205, 207, 221, 228, 237, 239, 248, 254, 282–5, 380–1, 398
  enquiry within 191, 194–5, 197, 202–3, 225, 259–60, 381, 433
'Patarenes' (*or* 'Paterines' *or* 'Patars') 59, 60, 61, 89, 90, 91, 127, 129, 132
Pauligne 332, 334, 454
Pegg, Mark Gregory 3, 297, 380
'perfect' (*or* 'perfected' *or* 'fully-fledged') 42, 43, 54, 99, 102, 118, 129, 201, 206, 213, 221, 227, 253n, 254, 263, 271, 289–90, 306, 313, 330, 469, 470, 472, 473, 475, 497, 498, 500
Perpignan 68, 71, 84, 506, 507
Peter, Archbishop of Tarragona 218, 223–4
Peter, King of Aragon 51, 58
Peter Amiel, Archbishop of Narbonne 236, 387, 388, 506
Peter Arsieu, OP, Inquisitor 71
Peter Autier, heretic, 296, 476, 477, 484, 491
Peter Bonet, Cathar deacon 367
Peter Capellan, heretic 351, 354, 460
Peter Durand, OP, Inquisitor 266
Peter Durant, Cathar deacon 304, 339, 357
Peter Fort, knight 345, 409
Peter Gallus, Cathar Bishop 62
Peter Isarn, Cathar Bishop 16, 19
Peter Martyr, OP, St 81
Peter of Alès, OP, Inquisitor 309
Peter of Castelnau, OCist 45, 46, 47, 51, 151
Peter of Corona, Cathar deacon 306, 307, 309
Peter of Les Vaux-de-Cernay, OCist, *Albigensian History* 5, 31, 32, 39–51

Peter of Mas, heretic 347, 348, 370, 397
Peter of Mazerolles, knight 338–9, 345–6, 347, 360, 406–13
Peter of Monceaux, OP, Inquisitor 83
Peter of Rouzégas, bailli 334, 434
Peter of Verona / Peter Martyr, OP, Inquisitor 8, 81, 359
Peter Paraire, Cathar deacon 372, 374, 456
Peter Pollan, Cathar Bishop 16, 19, 347, 410, 411, 413, 454, 459
Peter Rey of Fanjeaux, OP, Inquisitor 67, 71, 466
Peter Roger of Mirepoix, co-lord of Montségur 340–3, 359–74 *passim*, 378
Peter Seila, OP, Inquisitor 6, 65–6, 67, 68–9, 310–31, 357, 446
Peter the Chanter 58, 151
Peter William of Prunet, heretic 491
Philip III, King of France 283
Philip IV, King of France 73, 74, 79, 83n, 179, 504, 506
Philip the Chancellor 53
Piacenza 111, 355
Pieusse 16, 298, 305
pilgrimage 130, 201, 331,
as penance, 237, 258–9, 267, 272, 280, 282, 310–31, 443, 446, 494
Pons Garin, OP, Inquisitor 262, 263, 336, 350
Pons Guilabert, Cathar deacon 296, 307
Pons of Parnac, OP, Inquisitor 84, 270
Pons of Pouget, OP, Inquisitor 173, 281
Pons of Villeneuve, seneschal of Toulouse 341, 348, 349, 408
Poor Catholics 20
'Populicans' 34
Prades Tavernier, heretic 484
Praepositinus (Prévostin) of Cremona 99
Premonstratensians 33, 61
prison 58, 61, 72, 74, 79, 137, 150, 164, 169, 170, 171, 172–3, 174, 175, 176–8, 182–3, 193, 209, 220, 221, 222, 227, 235, 236, 238, 239–40, 241, 242, 243–4, 252, 255, 256, 257, 260, 263, 264–5, 269, 271, 272, 275, 279, 281, 282, 298, 310, 357, 358, 383, 393, 395, 418, 442, 444, 445, 448, 450, 451, 456, 457, 458, 465, 467, 477, 481, 482, 488, 491, 494, 496, 500, 502, 503, 505
Prouille 65, 67, 72, 332, 335
Provence 6, 39, 47, 64, 71, 83, 91, 125, 126, 132, 165, 168, 208, 250, 472
'publicans' 34, 153, 154
Puylaurens 7, 8, 190, 197, 305, 358, 367, 372, 435, 449, 450, 458, 459, 461, 462

Quercy 3, 8, 310, 324, 327, 351
Quié 306, 480, 481, 483, 485

Rabat 363, 407, 480, 487
Raimunda of Cuq, heretic 345, 369, 371
Rainerio Sacconi, OP, Inquisitor, *Summa about the Cathars and Poor of Lyons* 111–12
Ralph, OCist, papal legate 45, 46, 49, 51, 83
Raymond V, Count of Toulouse 35
Raymond VI, Count of Toulouse 47, 61, 331
Raymond VII, Count of Toulouse 61, 66, 172, 190, 193, 197, 214, 300, 307, 334, 359, 364–6, 399, 410n
Edict of (1233), 187, 189, 198–201, 214
Raymond Agulher, Cathar Bishop 305, 306, 373, 376
Raymond Bernard, Cathar deacon 303
Raymond Fort, Cathar deacon 431, 432, 433
Raymond of Casals, Cathar Bishop 17
Raymond of Le Fauga, OP, Bishop of Toulouse 383
Raymond of Mas-Saintes-Puelles, Cathar deacon 270, 278, 370, 371, 385

Raymond of Montouty (Raymond Donat), Cathar deacon 296, 347
Raymond of Niort, heretic 197, 372, 373, 407
Raymond of Peñafort, OP, Master General 162, 218
Raymond of Péreille, co-lord of Montségur 296, 340, 359, 375
Raymond of St Martin, Cathar deacon 368, 369
Raymond Rigaud/Rigaut, heretic 334, 421
Raymond Roger, Count of Foix 49, 376n, 378, 429
Raymond Sabatier 367, 450, 451, 480, 481, 485
Raymond Sans, Cathar deacon 407, 416
Razès 18, 305, 464
reincarnation 41, 99, 411
Renaud, OP, Inquisitor 494
Renous of Plassac, OP, Inquisitor 270
resurrection, beliefs about 41, 52, 100–1, 118, 378, 387, 388, 397, 406, 411, 419, 421
Richard Leneveu, Archdeacon of Auge 79, 501, 504
Richer of Senones, OSB, *Chronicle* 57–8
Robert IV, Count of Auvergne 127–8
Robert Lepetit/Robert le Bougre, OP, Inquisitor 6, 31, 53, 57, 149, 159, 165, 295
Robert of Auxerre, OPraem, *Chronicle* 32–5, 53
Robert of Courson, legate 61
Rocamadour 281, 446, 457
Rodez 78, 83, 266, 281, 315
Roger of La Tour, Knight 340, 360, 426
Roland of Cremona, OP, *Summa* 102–3, 129
Romanus Bonaventura, papal legate 190, 239
Rome 23, 35, 37, 68, 71, 73, 89, 151, 156, 472
see also councils, Fourth Lateran
Roquefort 319, 333, 334
Sackville, Lucy J. 3n, 87n, 88n, 115n, 188n, 214, 218, 289, 295
Saint-Gilles 49, 66, 282
Saissac 18, 43, 304, 305, 386, 388, 422, 423, 440, 449, 450, 458
Salliez 490–3
San Salvador of Asturias 311, 315, 319, 320, 322, 323, 325, 327, 328, 329, 331
Sanche / Sans Morlana, archdeacon of Carcassonne 180, 446, 464, 465
Saverdun 377, 378, 413
Sclavonia 111–12
Sègreville 490, 491, 492, 493
Sens 160, 163
Councils
(1198) 34
(1223) 157–8
Sermon from Arras 117–19
Sicard Cellarer, Cathar Bishop 17, 21
Sicard Figuiers / Figueiras, heretic 351, 352, 353, 354
Sicard Lunel, Cathar deacon, later inquisitor's agent 351, 354, 356, 460, 462
Simon, Count of Montfort 407
Simon Duval, OP, Inquisitor 283, 284, 285, 286
Sneddon, Shelagh 295
'Speronists' 129
Spoleto 111, 112, 143, 168
St-Denis 57, 72, 78, 171, 280, 311–33 *passim*
St-Félix 5, 14–16, 305, 363
St-Gilles 267, 311–33 *passim*
St James of Santiago de Compostella 71, 280, 281, 311–33 *passim*
St-Léonard 311, 315
St-Martial de Limoges 69, 311, 315
St-Martin-de-Lalande 390, 413, 425, 436, 440
St Thomas of Canterbury 311–33 *passim*
Stephen of Bourbon, OP, Inquisitor 115, 120–1, 122, 124
Treatise on the Gifts, about Various Preachable Materials 120–33

Stephen of Gâtine, OP, Inquisitor 173, 281
Stephen of St Thibéry, OFM, Inquisitor 350

Tarabel 303, 305, 427
Tarascon 83, 305, 365, 476, 477, 481, 483, 484, 485, 486, 487, 488
Tarragona, Council (1242) 191n, 215, 218, 223, 224, 262, 270, 273
Tartars 61, 144
Tento, Cathar Bishop 296
Theodoric, earlier known as William of Châteauneuf, heretic 45–6, 49, 52
Three Measures (Peter William), knight 345, 346, 407, 408, 409, 411, 412
Time of Grace 251–5, 261, 273, 312, 318
torture 83n, 149, 176–9, 183, 268, 414, 466, 483, 490, 491, 502–3
Toulouse (and the Toulousain) 5, 17–19, 26, 35, 40, 47, 48, 61, 64, 65–8, 69, 70, 72, 73, 77, 78, 79, 82, 83, 84, 102, 108, 111–12, 132, 144, 158, 172, 173, 182, 187, 188, 190, 193, 194n, 198, 270, 271, 280, 281, 296, 300n, 302n, 303, 309n, 310, 315, 325, 358, 364, 367, 373, 380, 383, 393, 395, 396, 400, 401, 402, 403, 404, 407–8, 412, 414, 415, 419, 420, 434, 436, 440, 458, 465, 468n, 477, 482, 486, 488, 491, 494, 499, 500, 501, 503, 504, 506
  Council of (1229) 7, 187, 190–7, 202n, 203, 207, 214, 239, 256, 381n
  Diocese of 65, 71, 76, 190, 279, 281, 298, 340, 341, 346, 358, 440, 441
  University of 477, 486, 488
Tours 77, 160
Troyes 54, 154, 165
Tuscany 62, 112

Urban IV, Pope, bulls 165–9

Valdes 43, 131
Val-de-Daigne 452, 453, 481
Verdun 18, 54, 305
Vergentis in senium (1199) 149
vernacular Occitan 14, 195, 260, 282, 295, 298, 312, 320, 351, 362, 483, 485, 499, 502
Vienna 63, 151
Vienne 83, 215, 250
  Council (1311–12) 9, 181
Vigouroux of La Bouconne, Cathar bishop 21, 158, 296n, 311, 318, 346, 377, 408
Villemur 298, 299, 307, 328, 329, 378
Villeneuve 163, 304, 336, 341, 348, 349, 405, 406, 415, 420, 425, 439, 441

Wakefield, Walter L. 1–2, 5, 15, 298, 359, 381
Waldensians 2, 4, 8, 13, 14, 15, 20, 43–4, 48–9, 51, 87,127, 129, 131, 133, 168–9, 215–17, 218, 219–26, 247–9, 253, 262–9, 270, 271, 273, 274, 289, 296, 298, 311–30, 332, 337, 351, 359, 375, 381, 405, 406, 415, 423, 426, 428, 435, 436, 439, 469–75, 497–500
  cemetery 322
  confession 216, 230, 248, 274, 324, 471, 472, 475, 498, 500
  councils 472–3
  holy supper, blessed bread 168, 216, 230, 247, 248–9, 265, 269, 274, 322–5, 470, 471
  hospital 325
  killing 222, 265, 266, 268, 319, 435, 436, 471, 475
  kiss of peace 168, 219, 221, 265, 269, 323, 435, 472, 473, 474
  names 128–9, 131, 217, 222, 224, 267, 268, 272, 469, 470
    see also 'Sandalled'
  oaths 44, 219, 222–3, 265, 266, 268, 269, 319, 321, 405, 435, 471, 475, 499
  purgatory 265, 268, 471

'Sandalled', sandals 26, 44, 219–29, 264, 268, 317, 470–4
women Waldensians 49, 265, 266, 269, 313, 318, 319, 321, 326, 405, 426, 435, 436, 439, 470–1, 474
see also individually named Waldensians
William Arnold, OP, Inquisitor 66, 67, 69, 350, 361, 362, 363, 379, 391, 395, 398, 406, 411, 417, 421, 422, 423, 424, 426, 438, 439, 440
William Autier 477, 481, 483, 484, 485, 488, 489
William Bernard of Airoux, heretic 304, 305, 343, 349, 459
William Bernard of Dax, OP, Inquisitor 67, 70, 279, 493, 494
William Brunet 72, 464, 505
William Clergue, Cathar deacon 376
William de la Broue, Archbishop of Narbonne 202, 250
William Garric 72, 505
William of Auxerre, *Golden Summa* 98–101, 103
William of Caussade heretic 318, 320, 321, 353, 354, 355, 356
William of L'Île (or Lahille), knight 332, 360, 362, 370, 417
William of Montreveil, OP, Inquisitor 70
William of Plaigne 359, 361, 362, 363, 364, 369, 370, 418
William of Puylaurens, *Chronicle* 69, 190, 201
William of St-Seine, OP, Inquisitor 465, 467
William of Valence, OP, Inquisitor 215, 262, 263
William Pelhisson, OP 64, 66, 308, 383, 393, 398, 404, 412, 426, 433, 434
William Raymond Golairan 361, 403, 417
William Raymond of Peyrecouverte, OP, Inquisitor 70
William Vital, heretic 384, 389, 399

Zerner, Monique 3, 16, 157